Bordeaux

Bordeaux

David Peppercorn, MW

MITCHELL BEAZLEY

Bordeaux
by David Peppercorn

First published in Great Britain in 1982 by Faber and Faber Limited.

This edition published in 2003 by Mitchell Beazley, an
imprint of Octopus Publishing Group Limited, 2–4 Heron Quays, London E14 4JP.

A CIP catalogue record for this book is available from the British Library.

ISBN: 1 84000 927 6

The author and publishers will be grateful for any information
which will assist them in keeping future editions up-to-date.
Although all reasonable care has been taken in the preparation
of this book, neither the publishers nor the author can accept any
liability for any consequences arising from the use thereof, or the
information contained therein.

Phototypeset in Berkeley Book by Intype Libra Ltd

Printed and bound in the UK

Contents

List of Maps

To my father, with affection and gratitude for setting me on the right path, and to my wife Serena for all her help and encouragement.

Also to Jean-Pierre Moueix, 'Ambassadeur Extraordinaire de Pomerol', as well as connoisseur of wine, art and living, who has offered me insights and inspiration which no one else could have done – as well as his friendship.

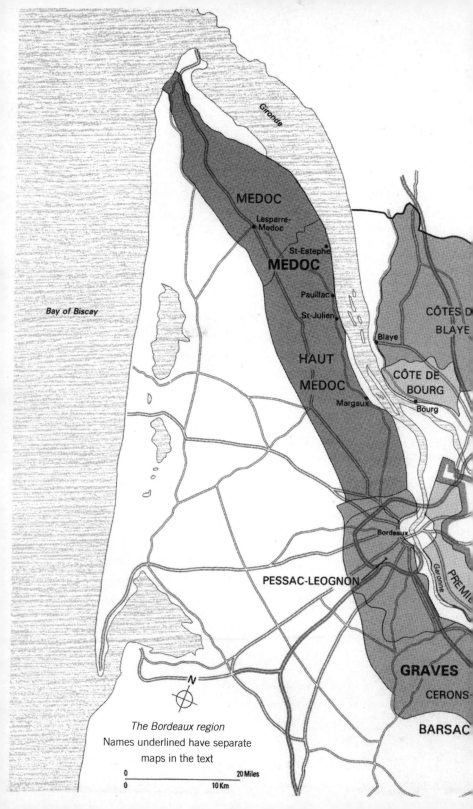

The Bordeaux region
Names underlined have separate
maps in the text

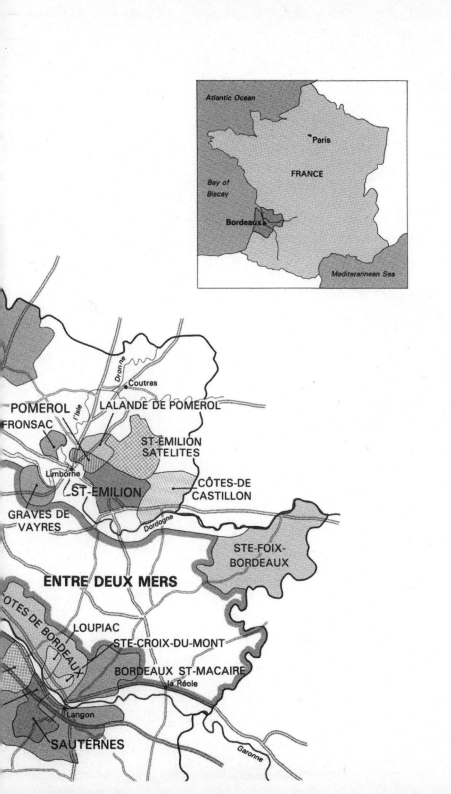

Preface

Writing a book on Bordeaux is rather like the proverbial painting of the Forth Bridge; it is always 'Work in Progress'. I have been particularly conscious of this when preparing this Second Edition which is, in effect, a new book.

The new material really comes under two headings. There is obviously a limit to the number of properties any one person can visit, or wines that can be tasted, so that, since writing the First Edition, I have made a point of visiting crus which I had not previously seen, and of extending the range of my tastings. There are many more tasting notes than hitherto, assisted by a new index of my notes! I have borne in mind that tasting notes need to be be reasonably recent to be useful, and so have concentrated on trying to convey the style and evolutionary cycle of each wine described.

The last decade has seen an acceleration in serious research into the history of Bordeaux's châteaux and the economic evolution of the region. The depositing of the archives of Château Latour with the University of Bordeaux in 1964 by the Château's new owners seems to have been a catalyst. Professor Enjalbert and his then pupil, René Pijassou, were both members of that team and contributed to the two-volume history of the Château, based on the archives. Now, Professor Pijassou has published his monumental treatise on the Médoc, while Professor Enjalbert has turned his attention to the much less explored field of the Libournais. The considerable expansion of the chapters on St Emilion and Pomerol and their terroirs is an attempt to bring to a wider audience the new perspective opened up by the late Professor. I have also considerably expanded the scope of the Graves chapter, to give recognition to the renaissance being experienced in this region. Both here and in other regions I have particularly tried to enlarge the space devoted to the less well-known crus which are constantly seeking a wider public, and are such a good barometer of the continuing vigour of the region.

I would like to single out a number of people to whom I owe a particular debt of gratitude over the period during which this Second Edition has been germinating. Christian Moueix found time to read the typescript of both the St Emilion and Pomerol chapters; Peter Vinding-Diers kindly read the Graves chapter; while Jean-Paul Valette (for St Emilion), Eric Fournier (for Sauternes-Barsac), André Lurton (for Pessac-Léognan-Graves), Jean Miailhe (for Cru Bourgeois Médocs), Patrick Danglade (for Canon Fronsac and Fronsac) and Michel Rolland (for Pomerol) all persuaded their fellow château-owners to lay on special tastings for me – which proved invaluable. Among *négociants* who either laid on special tastings, or allowed me to participate in their tastings, I must especially mention the generosity of Christian and Jean-Jacques Moueix at J.-P. Moueix, Yves Pardes at Moueix Export, Daniel Vergely at Domaines Cordier, Bill Blatch at Vintex, and Jacques Théo at Louis Eschenauer. I must also single out Bipin Desai of Los Angeles, who was the inspiration for the extraordinary Ausone tasting in 1988, and who staged the Haut-Brion Blanc/Laville-Haut-Brion Tasting Dinners in Los Angeles in 1989, as well as Bob Paul of Miami for his panoramic tastings of the 1978 and 1982 St Emilions and Pomerols. And finally to Andras Schiff, whose incomparable playing of Bach was my most treasured companion during many lonely hours of writing.

David Peppercorn, February 1991

1

Setting the Scene

The ancient ties of history and commerce between the British Isles and Bordeaux are sufficient reason in themselves for the interest and fondness which the English, not forgetting the Scottish, Irish and Welsh, have long shown for the wines of this region. At the same time these ties make it natural for an Englishman to write about and interpret the Bordeaux scene, particularly one working in the English wine trade, which is justly proud of being the oldest and most knowledgeable to be found outside the wine-producing countries. From the ranks of the English trade have stepped, over the last two hundred years, a number of men who have played prominent roles in its Bordeaux counterpart.

The Bordeaux trade has passed through a number of distinct phases, and while it is right to be mainly concerned with the present and the future, the contemporary scene should be set firmly in the context of what has gone before. The first distinct era of importance for Bordeaux was the period of its allegiance to the English Crown. I express it deliberately in this manner because it would be misleading to describe this relationship in modern terms by saying that Bordeaux belonged to or was part of England. In the feudal world before the existence of the nation state, a man thought of himself more as a citizen of London or of Bordeaux, owing allegiance to his lord, rather than as an Englishman or a Frenchman. This period of allegiance lasted almost exactly three hundred years from Henry II's marriage to Eleanor of Aquitaine in 1152 until the final defeat of Talbot, Earl of Shrewsbury, in 1453. During this time a large export trade was built up with England, and while much of the wine came from areas not today counted as Bordeaux, such as Bergerac and Cahors, the vineyards of the present Bordeaux region were also developed and expanded.

With the departure of the English, there followed a barren period as Bordeaux suffered from the ills afflicting the rest of France. Hardly had her period of probation as a somewhat reluctant newcomer to the realm of France been completed, when France herself was split by the Reformation. Bordeaux became one of the centres of Huguenot dissent. The Wars of Religion divided France as bitterly as the Civil War did England in the following century, and their effects were far more harmful and long-lived. Whereas English liberties were restored from Tudor and Stuart encroachments and given a modern direction, in France the Wars of Religion fatally eroded decaying medieval liberties and opened the way for Bourbon absolutism. France did not fully recover her strength or sense of purpose until Louis XIV established his personal rule over seventy years after the end of the Wars. It is from this time, in the second half of the seventeenth century, that one can discover the beginnings of the movement which during the eighteenth century saw the rise and development of the great estates or châteaux, as we now know them.

This new epoch began in circumstances that were far from propitious. The wars of Louis XIV, coupled with the protectionist measures of Colbert, were harmful to the interests of Bordeaux. At the same time, new beverages, such as chocolate, coffee and sweet mistelles, gained rapid popularity in both England and Holland from the middle of the seventeenth century. The first coffee house opened in London in 1652, and the period 1679–85 saw coffee houses become à la mode in London. One of the consequences of Louis XIV's succession of wars was that in 1697 discriminatory duties were levied against French wines imported into England, and these remained in force until 1786. Duties on French wines were now more than twice as high as those levied on wines from the Iberian peninsula.

Until this time, the large quantities of Bordeaux wine consumed in England had essentially been *vins de l'année* of ordinary quality. It was the new wine of the last vintage that was most sought after. But to surmount the formidable duty barriers now imposed, something better than *vin ordinaire* was needed. It was in these circumstances that "New French Claret" was born and the notion of growths or *crus* which commanded a premium in price terms is first encountered. René Pijassou has now documented for the first time the full story of this remarkable revolution in drinking habits. Of how the great Bordeaux landowners, like the

Pontacs of Haut-Brion and the Ségurs of Lafite, changed the face of the Médoc between 1680 and 1750, and how in the England of Queen Anne and the Hanoverians, an aristocratic and merchant upper class developed which demanded wines that were fine instead of ordinary. The copious records kept by men such as John Hervey, first Earl of Bristol, and Sir Robert Walpole, the first Prime Minister, show how the names of Haut-Brion, Lafite, Margaux and Latour first made their appearance at prices well above those of other Bordeaux wines. The name of Médoc first appeared in 1708 in the London Gazette, and by 1714 we find the first mention of "old" Margaux, to be shipped in bottle. Old, in this case, almost certainly means no more than older than the last vintage, since in this period the first growths were still exported as new wines, that is of the last vintage.

France experienced a period of considerable commercial prosperity in the years leading up to the Revolution, and Bordeaux, with its growing and energetic middle class, played a leading part in this expansion. Not only was this a time of renewed activity in the vineyards, but great prosperity also came to the city through the development of its port, and particularly through its trade with the West Indies. Although relatively few of the famous châteaux belong to this period – Beychevelle is an outstanding example – it has left us a glorious memorial in the fine public buildings constructed at that time in Bordeaux, notably the Opera House and the Place Louis XVIII.

The Revolution swept away many of the old proprietors, who had been members of the *noblesse de robe*. Under the *ancien régime* membership of this professional legal establishment was almost the only method of preferment open to those not of noble birth. Lafite, for example, came on the market when its proprietor, Pichard, president of the Bordeaux Parlement, had been guillotined – in fact, he was one of the very few in Bordeaux to suffer this fate. The estate passed to his daughter, who had fled the country, but was forfeit since all property belonging to *émigrés* was confiscated by the state. This was actually the largest single reason for changes of ownership in the Bordeaux region, where the Church was not a major owner of vineyards, as it was in Burgundy.

The places of the old proprietors after the Revolution and especially after the Restoration (the re-establishment of the Bourbon monarchy under Louis XVIII, brother of the guillotined Louis XVI, briefly in 1814 and then on a more permanent basis in 1815 after Napoleon's final defeat at Waterloo), went in many cases to a relatively new breed of men, the *négociants*, or merchants. In many cases their enterprises had begun during the eighteenth century as general import and export businesses, only gradually concentrating on wine. Often businesses had been launched by foreign merchants settling in Bordeaux to supply the needs of their home markets. Now that the protectionism of the *ancien régime* had gone and an era of freer trade was beginning throughout Europe, these men seized their opportunities. One such was Hugh Barton, who acquired a portion of Léoville from the family of the Marquis de Las Cases, as well as Langoa, while his partner, Pierre-François Guestier, not to be outdone, became his neighbour at Beychevelle. Although the Guestiers have now left the scene, their place has been taken by other partners of other firms, so that today a number of Bordeaux houses are also important château proprietors.

The Second Empire (1851–70) saw a new phase, the investment in Bordeaux properties by influential financiers from outside Bordeaux and the wine trade. The most notable of these were the two Rothschild purchases and that of the Péreires at Palmer.

However, viticulturally and economically the nineteenth century was equally a period dominated by the scourge of disease. The oidium of the 1850s proved a serious financial setback throughout Bordeaux, while the phylloxera and mildew period of the late 1870s and 1880s had a more profound effect still (see pp. 14–16).

While Bordeaux suffered far less from the French débâcle in 1870 (defeat in the Franco-Prussian War) than from the phylloxera, it was affected by general economic movements. That was certainly so in the depression at the turn of the century accompanied as it was by a lack of really top-class vintages. There is surely no period so barren of notable vintages than the two decades that separate the great wines of 1900 and 1920. But perhaps the most serious setback came between the wars when severe economic difficulties again coincided with a run of poor vintages in the 1930s.

As if to compensate for all this, the post-war era began with a sparkling array of splendid vintages: 1945, 1947 and 1949 have certainly now taken their rightful places among the famous vintages of the past. Yet it was only very gradually that prosperity returned. Prices after the war were still historically low and the vineyards were in a run-down condition after the bleak years of the thirties, followed by the difficulties of the war years. As a result of this the area under vine was at a very low ebb and the existing vineyards were often old and in need of attention. It takes a generation and a great deal of investment to reconstruct a vineyard, and that is certainly one reason why Bordeaux, with its resources at rock bottom after years of depression and war, took a long time to recover.

Unfortunately, just as the tide seemed to have turned decisively in favour of prosperity, with the highly successful 1953s succeeded by the large yield and higher prices of the 1955s, the uncertainties of nature again stepped in with the disastrous early frost of February 1956. Wine lovers are so used to hearing wine growers, like farmers, cry "wolf", that perhaps they may be forgiven for failing to appreciate just how significant that frost was to be. The repercussions were with us for over a decade and necessitated fresh investment on a large scale.

The great vintage of 1961 set a new level for prices which was not again to be reached until the 1970 vintage, except by the first growths. The sixties were a period of reconstruction and growth. Symbolic of the time for me was the replanting of Larose-Trintaudon. What had been a great wasteland on the drive from St Laurent to Pauillac, now became the largest vineyard in the Médoc. The vineyard, uprooted in the twenties, was replanted from 1964 to 1966 and now extends for some 172 hectares. The good vintages of 1962, 1964, 1966 and 1967 were tempered by the terrible vintages of 1963 and 1965, and the mediocre wines of 1968 and 1969.

It seemed at the time that the unusual vintage of 1970 had really ushered in a new era. The combination of yield and quality was something which had not been seen in the Gironde since 1934, and before that, one has to go back to 1900. It certainly marked the coming of age of the new plantings and was to be succeeded by a series of prolific years for red wines, with fresh records set in 1973, 1979, 1982, 1985 and 1986. 1970 was really the year when proprietors began to reap the profits from their investments. But the boom was to prove surprisingly shortlived.

The much smaller 1971 vintage showed a dramatic price rise, but the wines were good and in short supply for a market now avid for Bordeaux wines – or so it seemed. However, when the very mediocre 1972s appeared, and higher prices still were asked for them, the market hiccuped; and then, under the influence of the energy crisis and world recession, it collapsed in a manner unknown since 1927. Somehow the idea had taken root in Bordeaux that prices always rose and never fell, and that the world demand was such that the relatively small quantities of top wines produced in Bordeaux must always find their market. In particular the belief prevailed that the American market would always buy the first growths at any price. The combination of economic recession and poor wines at record prices proved an indigestible one, and administered a very salutary lesson in common sense to the market.

I so well remember my own first tastings of the 1972s in January 1973. My conclusion had been that with such an escalation of price for such modest wines, this was the moment to stop buying. Unfortunately, within weeks the whole wine trade allowed itself to be sucked into a vortex of buying at absurd prices. When the market collapsed, these stocks of 1972s proved a major obstacle to the recovery of the market, because few *négociants* could afford to halve their prices, and there was no money to buy the cheaper and much better 1973s. I do not say that there would have been no crisis if the price of the 1972s had more nearly corresponded with their quality, but it would have been less acute and less prolonged.

This is not the place to go into the crisis of 1973–4 in detail. But it is worth remarking that one special factor was the activity of speculators outside the trade. Of course, there have always been speculators in the Bordeaux trade itself. Sometimes they have made fortunes and sometimes they have gone bankrupt. But in the boom years of the early seventies, many people outside the trade were looking either for somewhere to place their money or even speculating with the help and often encouragement of the banks. I remember at least one instance of someone wishing to put £100,000 into wine, and this sort of thing was a very widespread experience at this time. In such a frantic atmosphere, prices easily escalated. But the writing was on the wall for those with eyes to see. One too often heard it said that so-and-so was selling his 1953 Mouton or 1949 Lafite because he could "no longer afford to drink it". The great Bordeaux had become something for buying and selling but not for drinking. The simple truth that a bottle of wine, unlike a painting or a piece of furniture, is not a joy for ever, but only has true worth once – when the cork is drawn – had been temporarily forgotten.

The recovery was slow and painful. It was not assisted by the sheer volume of the 1973 and 1974 vintages, the first light and charming, the second sound but uninviting. It needed the magnificent 1975s to rekindle true enthusiasm for Bordeaux. Since then, the market has progressed soundly and steadily, save for a minor hiccup with the 1984s, to keep abreast of inflation, without running ahead of what consumers are willing and able to pay.

One other important trend has also been apparent since the early seventies. As the yields of red Bordeaux have risen to record levels, so the yields of the less profitable whites have begun to decline. There has been a steady reduction in the area under vine, as vineyards, especially in the Entre-Deux-Mers, have been replanted to produce red wine. In the nineties, we shall probably see a shortage of white Bordeaux.

Looking to the present, one is struck by the great post-war boom in wine drinking. This has been a phenomenon not limited to any one country. The USA, West Germany, Holland and the Scandinavian countries, as well as the UK, have all experienced a greatly increased demand for good-quality wines as distinct from *vin ordinaire*. In France itself, the demand for staple *ordinaires* has stagnated and is now in decline, while the consumption of VDQS and AC wines grows steadily. Yet not until the seventies did Bordeaux take full advantage of this movement. The comparison with its ancient rival, Burgundy, was particularly striking. Burgundy, with its much smaller production (approximately two to three times as much Bordeaux as Burgundy), saw its sales go from strength to strength, while Bordeaux was depressingly undersold. This did not, of course, apply to the best-known classified growths, but to the thousands of small growths which form the backbone of Bordeaux.

Yet so much appears to favour Bordeaux. Its vineyards are arranged in relatively large and manageable units, while those of Burgundy are notoriously fragmented. There are a good number of large properties able to produce wine in quantities sufficient to be promoted, something unknown in Burgundy. For the Burgundians this has meant that, apart from Beaujolais, only the village names of the Côte d'Or could really be promoted, but in practice this has led to each *négociant* promoting his own name, since this is the sole outward mark to distinguish his wine from what is offered by his neighbour.

In contrast, the Bordeaux *négociant* has tended to fall between two stools. On the one hand, few *négociants* have succeeded in widely establishing their own brands of generic *appellations* such as Médoc, St Emilion and Sauternes; on the other, they have sold a wide variety of château wines, mostly on a non-exclusive basis. In the sixties a tendency developed for a few *négociants* to promote a number of châteaux on an exclusive basis, thus ensuring less cut-throat margins both for themselves and their customers, as well as a more effective and systematic distribution for the wines themselves. This system suffered a severe setback in the 1973 and 1974 depression, when many *négociants* were unable to honour their commitments. But the end result is that today the famous names of the past among the *négociants* have lost ground. There have been some important newcomers, but nobody has anything like a dominant position, and there are still too many very small firms. The Syndicat of Bordeaux *négociants* has 200 members.

It is this unique feature in the marketing of Bordeaux wines, that they are largely made and sold as individual properties, which has determined the shape of this book. Within each section, after dealing generally with the characteristics of the wines to be found in that particular region, I have listed the more important properties in alphabetical order with all the relevant information on each, the lesser growths being simply listed at the end with the latest production figures. I hope that in this way, information will prove easily accessible, and that the characteristics, production, and notes on past vintages of each particular property may all be conveniently found in one place.

Nothing stands still, and this is especially true of the reputation of individual châteaux. What I have tried to do here is to indicate both the general reputation in the Bordeaux trade and my own strictly personal view based on tastings over the years. I believe this is important because the opinions of experts so often differ, so that to give only a personal view could be misleading, while to present only the general view, though safe, could be monotonous. My aim has been to be informative and frank without being libellous, and at the same time I have tried to be fair and indicate my own preferences, so that the reader may discount them where appropriate.

On the technical side, I have tried to provide sufficient information for the serious student, while trying to make it interesting and easy to follow for the general reader. In describing the care of vineyards and the making of wine, I have been guided by what was clearly relevant to the end product rather than providing an exhaustive study.

2

Making the Wine

THE VINEYARDS

The making of wine starts, of course, in the vineyard, and here nothing is more important to the end product than the selection of the correct varieties of vine, or *cépages* as they are called in French. It is rightly said that four vital and interlocking elements are involved in the production of good wine: climate, soil, vine and the skill of man. But if the first two are right, the difference between a mediocre wine and a fine wine will ultimately depend on the correct *cépage* and human skill. This is especially so in a variable temperate climate such as that of Bordeaux, where the *encépagement* of a vineyard must be selected to counteract as far as possible the vagaries of the weather.

Bordeaux, like the Rhône but unlike Burgundy, uses several different *cépages* to make its best wines, both red and white. A few dry white wines are today made only with the Sauvignon grape, but this occurs mostly in lesser areas for the cheaper wines and is not typical of the region as a whole.

What is not always appreciated is that the selection of *cépages* did not begin before the second half of the eighteenth century. No fewer than thirty-four red varieties and twenty-nine white were recorded in the Libournais in 1784, in a report made by the Sub-Delegate of Libourne to his Intendant in that year. From this it is clear that selection in the Libournais was still in its early stages. In the Médoc, however, selection had already reduced the total to nine red and four white *cépages*.

Red

CABERNET SAUVIGNON is the classic *cépage* for the red wines of Médoc and Graves. This is a variety that does best on gravel. In St Emilion, where it is less widely planted, it is usually known as the "Gros Bouchet". It is generally less suitable for the colder soil of Pomerol. It produces wines which are fine, showing finesse and breed, a marked bouquet reminiscent of blackcurrants, and the small berries and thick skins provide plenty of tannin and a good colour. They ripen after the Merlot but are much more resistant both to *coulure* at the time of the flowering and to rot (*pourriture grise*) (see p. 16) before the vintage. They give a rather low yield.

CABERNET FRANC is known as the "Bouchet" in St Emilion and Pomerol, where it is widely planted. This *cépage* is a cousin of the Cabernet Sauvignon, with similar characteristics, but produces wines which are less coloured and fine, but very perfumed. It is sometimes said to be half-way between the Cabernet Sauvignon and the Merlot, but in terms of yield and character it is nearer the Cabernet Sauvignon.

MERLOT, with the Cabernet Sauvignon, is the most important and widely planted red grape variety in Bordeaux. Today, it is probably more numerous, particularly in the smaller estates, than any other. Merlot thrives when clay is present, just the conditions that Cabernet dislikes. The yield is more generous than for the Cabernet, but it is very susceptible to *coulure* and also to early rot in wet weather. The wine is highly coloured, lacks the tannin of the Cabernet, but produces a good acidity. The wines are also supple and full-flavoured, being higher in alcohol than the Cabernet. Although it is difficult to generalize about this factor, owing to the differing circumstances of age of vines and differences of soil, the difference is probably on average about 1 per cent alcohol by volume. On an average Médoc estate, when both varieties are properly ripe, the Cabernet Sauvignon will give about 11 per cent to 11.5 per cent, while the Merlot will give 12 per cent to 12.5 per cent. In great years, the final pickings will often produce alcohol levels as high as 14 per cent.

MALBEC is a variety which was never planted on a large scale, but most estates had 10 or 15 per cent. Nowadays, it is seldom replanted and few vineyards have more than 5 or 10 per cent, except in Bourg and Blaye where it still finds favour. It is early ripening, producing a high yield of soft, well-coloured wine – not unlike Merlot, but even more susceptible to *coulure*.

PETIT VERDOT, although not planted in quantity, is a very useful ingredient in the general make-up of a vineyard. Of medium yield, it produces wines high in alcohol, extract and acidity, which can be useful on light soils, or, where rather a lot of Merlot has been planted, as a corrective. It is a late ripener, and so seldom gives of its best except in the best years, when it makes a valuable contribution towards the completeness and complexity of a wine.

CARMENÈRE is included here for the sake of completeness. It is still found in some Médoc vineyards, but has ceased to have any importance. It is very prone to degeneracy.

White

SAUVIGNON. This is the same *cépage* that has become famous outside Bordeaux in recent years for producing dry, white wines which are distinctly aromatic in character. The best-known examples are Pouilly-Fumé and Sancerre, but the vine is to be found in many other areas as well. In Bordeaux it produces both dry and sweet wines. It is noticeable that further north the character of wines produced from this *cépage* is so strong that it becomes difficult to distinguish regional characteristics. However, in Bordeaux, where more ripeness is achieved, a combination of soil and climate gives Sauvignon wines more body and breed, while preserving their elegance. Even so, it has the disadvantage, when bottled as pure Sauvignon, of losing its distinctive character relatively quickly in bottle, after one to three years. This leaves a rather dull, characterless dry wine. For this reason, in the best vineyards of Sauternes-Barsac and Graves, wines are hardly ever made from the Sauvignon alone but are a partnership of Sauvignon and Sémillon. This is found to impart the distinctive style and breed of Bordeaux white wine at its best. But in the lesser areas, such as the Entre-Deux-Mers, some properties are now specializing in producing light, dry wines made only from the Sauvignon; such wines are often prone to excessive acidity and suffer from a certain coarseness. The yield is low.

SÉMILLON, the most widely planted and distinctive of white Bordeaux *cépages*, is more productive than the Sauvignon and less subject to disease. It is always blended with Sauvignon both in Sauternes-Barsac for sweet wines, and in Graves for dry wines, and is a much underrated variety. Its great advantage is that, in a blend with Sauvignon, it develops a distinctly fruity bouquet after two to three years in bottle, just at the time when the primal aromatic aromas of the Sauvignon are in decline. It is interesting to note that some leading Californian estates are now planting it to blend with their Sauvignon, and there are some fine dry Sémillon wines from Australia.

MUSCADELLE is a good yielder producing a distinctive, perfumed and aromatic wine. It is useful for producing sweet wines for early drinking in the Premières Côtes, but is also good in small doses in Sauternes-Barsac, and in the southern Graves where it imparts an attractive fruitiness, as an adjunct to Sémillon and Sauvignon.

It is part of the genius of Bordeaux wines that they reflect first and foremost their origins. That is to say that each district produces distinctive individual wines, and that within each district individual properties produce wines which can be readily distinguished from their neighbours. In other words, it is the soil and the wine maker who reign supreme here. The judicious mixture of *cépages*, creating the *encépagement* of a vineyard, is here the means of displaying the individuality of soil and place – it remains in the background. This is, of course, in marked contrast to Burgundy, where the Pinot Noir very much holds the foreground.

Recently work has been done which suggests that the natural yeasts to be found in each vineyard and *cuvier* may also play an important role in determining the individuality of each *cru*. Peter Vinding-Diers – the administrator of Château Rahoul in Portets, Graves, for over a decade – carried out experiments during the 1985 and 1986 vintages with yeasts from two Médoc properties. He inoculated a wine from the same vat drawn off into three casks with his own Rahoul yeasts, and those of a Margaux and a Pauillac. The result was three quite distinctive wines. When the results were demonstrated to the Académie de Bordeaux in 1986, quite a lot of interest was aroused, since this is a line of enquiry not previously pursued by the oenologists at the University of Bordeaux. It comes at a very pertinent time, just as some proprietors were beginning to think in terms of using commercially produced cultured yeasts. The suggestion must now be that the natural yeasts found in each vineyard are an integral part of that very individuality which is so vital to the great *crus* of Bordeaux.

I have often heard it said that a certain claret has strong Cabernet characteristics. I think it truer to say that in Pauillac, where a high proportion of Cabernet Sauvignon is general, the wines have a most distinctive character. But this is as much the character of Pauillac as of the Cabernet Sauvignon which, as with other *cépages* in Bordeaux, enhances the character of the place rather than imparting in a general way its own character. The best *crus* of Margaux, for instance, often have as high, or higher proportions of Cabernet Sauvignon than those of Pauillac, yet their characteristics are quite different: Durfort-Vivens and Le Tertre 80 per cent, Margaux, Giscours and d'Issan 75 per cent, contrasting with Lafite, Grand-Puy-Lacoste and Lynch-Bages with 75 per cent, Mouton-Baronne-Philippe and Haut-Batailley with 65 per cent. This distinction can be most clearly seen when Bordeaux reds are compared with the single-variety wines of other countries, notably California.

It is worth remarking at this point that perhaps the strongest single influence on the present selection of *cépages* in Bordeaux was the phylloxera. This great scourge of the European vineyards was first observed in the vineyards of the *palus* at Floriac in 1866, but its progress was slow, especially in the Médoc, Graves and Sauternes districts where the soil was less suitable for the spread of the disease. For this reason, the battle against the phylloxera was a long drawn-out affair. At first, every sort of chemical treatment was tried and vineyards were even subjected to flooding where this was possible. But eventually it became clear that the only sure and permanent remedy was to replant on resistant American root-stocks. Whereas the European vines are of the type *vitis vinifera*, the American vines are of quite different species – *vitis riparia* and *vitis rupestris* – which are resistant to phylloxera.

The major replanting of the Bordeaux vineyards took place over a much longer period than is generally supposed. The full effects of the phylloxera were felt from 1879 onwards. But both Professor Enjalbert and his pupil, Professor Pijassou, have shown conclusively how – in both the Libournais and in Médoc – the leading *crus*, realizing that their quality and reputation depended on conserving old vines, successfully did just that, using carbon disulphide. The result was that, unlike the vineyards of the Midi, those of Bordeaux were not destroyed. Indeed, production actually rose at most leading châteaux, owing to the much increased use of manure, and owners were able to take their time and gradually transform their vineyards to grafted vines while maintaining a good average age. It now seems that this process was hardly completed before the outbreak of the First World War in 1914 – over thirty-five years after the beginning of the crisis.

It took some time to discover which root-stocks were best suited to the different soils and types of *cépage*. A list of American root-stocks now used in Bordeaux can be found in Cocks & Féret, 13th edition, 1982, pp. 70–3 (see Bibliography). But ultimately, it gave every vineyard owner the opportunity of reselecting his *encépagement*, and led to a considerable reduction in the number of varieties planted – as a glance at any pre-phylloxera edition of Cocks & Féret will testify. It also meant that work in the vineyards could be mechanized. The old European vines were often propagated by taking a shoot from an existing vine and stapling it into the soil. As soon as it had rooted, it was detached from the scion. This method was particularly used to replace damaged or diseased vines in a vineyard. With the necessity for using only American root-stocks, this form of propagation became impossible.

The grafting itself is naturally a most important process. These days it usually takes place in a nursery rather than *sur place*. This ensures that only successful grafts are used, which is important in times of high labour costs. Matching incisions are made in both the American root-stock and the European cutting; these are then joined together and bound up. The grafts are then usually placed in sand-filled trays for some days to ensure that the European graft is above the soil, so that it cannot root itself and thus run the risk of becoming infected with phylloxera.

While the unique phenomenon of the phylloxera did bring some benefits as well as tragedy, the same cannot be said for other diseases of the vine. These are usually divided into three categories: fungi, animal parasites, and afflictions caused by weather conditions.

After the phylloxera, fungi have actually proved the most serious menace to the Bordeaux vineyards historically. The first to attack Bordeaux was the oidium. This fungus attacks all the green parts of the vine: the young wood, leaves and young, unripe grapes. Small whitish spots appear and rapidly spread. The effect is that leaves curl up and drop off, and grapes darken in colour, split and so dry up. It first appeared in Bordeaux in 1852 and made rapid progress, drastically reducing yields. But by 1858 it had been successfully mastered with the aid of sulphur preparations. Since that time there has never been any difficulty in controlling the disease, provided the weather is not so wet as to make spraying ineffectual. Nowadays, various chemical preparations are available which are more effective than sulphur, although some growers still prefer to use sulphur as certain chemical sprays appear to make grapes less resistant to rot in wet weather.

The mildew arrived in Bordeaux when phylloxera was at its height, appearing first in 1883. As with the oidium, this fungus attacks the young green parts of the vine, appearing in white spots on the underside of the leaves and yellow-brown patches on top. But unlike oidium, mildew does not cause the grapes to be spoiled so that the yield is affected – rather, it ruins the flavour of the wine. As with oidium, the cure proved to be quickly at hand in the form of a copper sulphate spray, known as Bordeaux mixture. This distinctive bluish spray is now a familiar sight in every vineyard in France and elsewhere, and is still largely preferred to more modern chemical preparations because it is known to be harmless and deals with other pests at the same time.

Black rot is another fungoid pest which originated in the USA. It appears in the form of stems speckled with black on the green parts of the vine, and the grapes shrivel and turn brown. The vines are most susceptible to it in warm, humid conditions. In Bordeaux it has been chiefly noticeable since the Second World War and especially since 1952. The best treatment is again the copper sulphate spray.

Pourriture grise or grey rot is actually caused by the same fungus that is responsible for *pourriture noble*, that noble rot which produces the fine sweet wines, especially Sauternes. In conditions of alternating rain and sunshine, such as often occur in Bordeaux in September, this rot thrives. It was very prevalent in the sixties and was especially bad in 1963, imparting a sickly flavour to the wine, which was also noticeable on the nose. The high incidence of this disease since 1958 has led many growers to believe that some of the chemically based sprays used in recent years have lowered resistance to this particular disease by making the skins less hardy and so more liable to split. In consequence, many have returned to copper sulphate spraying, and new preparations have also been applied in wet weather specifically to allay the spread of this rot, with notable success. In consequence no vintage has been seriously affected by rot since 1968. It is noticeable that the use of anti-rot sprays has been dramatically more successful in Bordeaux than elsewhere in France. Various explanations have been given. The large units make systematic treatment much easier than in Burgundy. Skins are thicker and less fragile than those of the Pinot Noir; this seems to be true even of the Merlot. And growers have been careful to vary the sprays, not using one sort for more than three successive seasons.

Eutypiose is the cause of the most recent fungus alarm, although it has long been present in the Bordeaux vineyards. It infects a vine through a cut in the wood and is therefore easy to spread when pruning. Curiously, it attacks mature vines between ten and fifteen years of age, not young ones, and the Cabernet Sauvignon seems more suceptible to it than the Merlot. The disease now seems to spread more easily than in the past and is being taken very seriously by INRA; but to suggest, as some have done, that it poses the gravest threat since the phylloxera seems premature and alarmist.

The last disease in this section is a virus rather than a fungus. Infectious degeneration or *court-noué* was until recently the most serious menace in the vineyards of Bordeaux. It is spread in the soil by the vector *xiphema index*. The symptoms are that the leaf turns yellow along its veins and in patches between them; the leaves then become misshapen, shoots bifurcate and multiply laterally and the flowers form double clusters. The disease will form in a small piece of vineyard and then spread slowly through it. The seriousness of the disease lies in the fact that it progressively shortens the life of the vine, which gradually becomes sterile; it lives in the soil and so will attack a new vine as soon as an infected one is pulled up. During the last decade, the work of the Institut National de la Recherche Agronomique (INRA) has, however, been crowned with success. The problem was that not only was it necessary to have virus-free root-stocks, but also virus-free grafts as well. This has now been achieved through a process called "thermo-therapy". The soil of the old vineyards is then disinfected and should be left fallow for two to three years. Previously, a period of eight to nine years had been recommended and even this, of course, would not have been effective if the new vines were not virus-free. So, perhaps, the greatest menace of the Bordeaux vineyards has been finally overcome through the wonders of modern technology.

The list of animal parasites, is, of course, headed by the phylloxera, the historical effects of which have already been discussed. The disease is caused by a louse or aphid which has a remarkable reproductive system. (See *Sherry* by Julian Jeffs, 3rd edition, Faber, 1982, pp. 169–73, for an excellent description.) It first of all attacks the roots of the vine and then the leaves. The vine withers and eventually dies. This louse is endemic in the North American vineyards where the *vitis riparia* and *vitis rupestris* are resistant to it, but when it was carried into the European vineyards during the 1860s, it rapidly spread, leaving a fearful trail of destruction behind it. As has already been mentioned, the grafting of European vines on to American root-stocks is the only sure remedy. It is usually claimed that this has shortened the life of the vine. One should say, however, that there are still some healthy vines growing in Bordeaux and elsewhere in France, which are first grafts after the phylloxera, planted in the last decade of the nineteenth century. Added to this, a great deal less was known then than now about the selection of the most suitable root-stocks. But the notion that grafted vines have a shorter lifespan than ungrafted ones probably rests mainly on the fact that it is only since the phylloxera that infectious degeneration has appeared – and has until recently been the major menace to European vineyards.

Next comes a group of three types of moth which produce larvae which feed on the grape branches or the leaves – *cochylis* and *eudemis*, which attack the grapes themselves, and *pyrpalis*, which attacks both grapes and leaves. It was the *cochylis* which was principally responsible for the very small yield in 1926. I recall Baron Philippe de Rothschild telling me that at Mouton, where they sent out workers prior to the vintage to remove infected berries, several barrels were filled with this destructive grub. The cure today is really good husbandry, that is, spotting the trouble as soon as it starts and spraying immediately with one of the very effective insecticides now available.

Of increasing importance during the last twenty years is the red spider, which causes considerable damage by attacking young shoots and leaves. Its causes are, as yet, little understood. Unfortunately, although there are efficient products available to combat this pest, it has proved hard to halt in practice because the treatment must be carried out in the early spring, before any sign of the spider has appeared.

The last group of hazards for the *vigneron* are those attributable to nature – that is, weather and soil.

Chlorosis is a yellowing of the leaves due to an excess of calcium in the soil associated with an iron deficiency. This occurs in Bordeaux on the calcareous soils, and the best remedy seems to be the selection of resistant root-stocks (*vitis berlandieri*).

Coulure is one of the most common problems to be found in the Bordeaux vineyards. It is the dropping of the blossom during the flowering or of the tiny berries just after the flowering, and is caused by weather conditions. Wet and cold are the main causes and *coulure* is the chief reason these days for small vintages. 1945 and 1961 are classic examples. The widespread *coulure* experienced in 1984 showed that the causes of this problem were not as well understood as had been thought. On this occasion, the weather during the period of flowering itself was good but there were cold conditions immediately beforehand, leading to an abrupt change of conditions. The comparison with 1985 is most instructive.

Climatic conditions during seventeen days during the flowering

	1984	1985
Sum of temperatures (degrees C)	345	271
Number of days above 25°C	9	0
Precipitation in millimetres	21	29
Number of days of rain	6	8

(Figures published by P. Ribereau-Guyon and G. Guimberteau of the Institut d'Oenologie, Université de Bordeaux II.)

It will be seen from the above figures that 1985 was actually cooler and wetter during the flowering than 1984. Yet 1984 saw one of the most severe attacks of *coulure* for Merlot in living memory; 1985 experienced a very successful setting and a record crop, thus turning conventional wisdom on its head.

Closely associated with *coulure*, and sometimes confused with it, is *millerandage*. This is when one finds a bunch containing a number of stunted green berries about the size of a green pea. They are hard and never develop any further. This is usually an aftermath of *coulure* and is also caused by unsatisfactory fertilizing conditions during flowering. Like *coulure, millerandage*, of course, reduces the size of the crop, but poses an additional problem. Unless the stunted berries are removed when the bunch is cut, they will much increase the acidity of the wine.

Frost is not as dangerous in Bordeaux as in some other regions, but occasionally does very great damage. In more northerly areas, the great danger is spring frost, which just catches the first shoots. As so many of the Bordeaux vineyards lie near one of the great rivers which characterize the region, most of the important areas are generally immune. But areas like the plateaux of St Laurent and Pomerol, as well as parts of the Graves, do occasionally experience very severe frosts, which do great damage. These are usually the black frosts, when the temperature falls well below the normal winter level and freezes the rising sap, killing the vines. This is what happened in February 1956 and to a lesser extent in March 1977 – but the rarity of such occurrences may be judged from the fact that 1956 was the second severest winter in the Gironde since 1709, which was the year that the vineyards of Muscadet were destroyed and the wine froze on the tables at Versailles. In 1985 temperatures of − 10°C were recorded during five consecutive days of January, dropping to − 15° on two days, and − 22° was registered in some inland places in the Gironde. These were the lowest temperatures since 1956, but did much less damage because they came in January and not February, and conditions were dry beforehand and not damp. Because of the infrequency of frosts, no general frost precautions are taken in Bordeaux.

Hail is not as serious a problem in Bordeaux as it is in the Beaujolais, for example. It is always extremely localized, and often one part of a vineyard will be affected and not another. The most usual time for hail is June and July. The damage is quite dramatic – vines stripped bare of leaves and the wood of the vine itself lacerated with smaller shoots often broken off. Severe hail damage not only greatly reduces the yield in the year it occurs, but, by damaging the wood, it can affect the following year's crop as well. A certain amount of success has been achieved by letting off rockets to disperse the hail clouds, provided that the local weather station is able to give sufficient warning.

The last major vineyard topic to be discussed in this section is pruning. Pruning itself is a highly technical matter which can only be made intelligible with pictorial aids. Fig. 1 illustrates the methods in use in Bordeaux. The actual work takes up most of the winter months. Although one often reads in textbooks that late pruning is advisable to counter the danger of spring frosts, in practice there is too much to be done to leave the job until the new year. No doubt, on particular estates, any parts of the vineyard known by experience to be prone to late frost damage would be left until last. What is interesting about pruning, however, is not the technical details, but the influence it can have on the quality of the wine to be produced. The laws of *Appellation Contrôlée* lay down general rules about pruning for each region, and the *rendement* states how much may be produced in any particular vineyard which can bear the *appellation* and name of the growth. But, in practice, pruning allows the *vigneron* a fairly wide discretion in controlling the yield of his vineyard.

Of course, in a region such as Bordeaux, where nature so often takes a hand in limiting the yield with poor weather during the flowering (*coulure and millerandage*) and wet autumns (*pourriture grise*), to say nothing of other diseases, there is a strong temptation not to prune too severely to allow for natural hazards. Years when everything goes right, from the beginning to the end of the season, as in 1970, 1982 and 1985, are the exceptions, not the rule. What is undeniable, though, is that

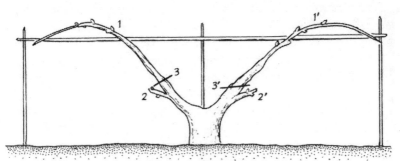

Figure 1   Pruning methods

1 and 1′ are the branches of the year kept after pruning which will bear grapes during the following Summer and Autumn. 2 and 2′ are shoots left on old wood which will produce non-fruiting branches. After vintaging, instead of keeping one of the branches growing on 1 and 1′, one branch will be selected on 2 and 2′ for the following year's crop and the pruning will be done at points marked 3 and 3′.

husbandry – the effective control of pests and diseases and general care of vineyards – has markedly improved since before the Second World War, and that, as a result, yields are generally higher. The figures show this unmistakably. My guess would be that most *vignerons* are pruning in much the same way they were thirty or forty years ago. It is not this aspect that has changed, but rather the other factors already mentioned. In other words, if all improvements are taken into account, pruning can now afford to be more severe than it was. But if there is a tendency to be discerned, it is probably in the other direction.

So what effect does yield have on quality? This is not a simple question to answer in the Bordeaux context. It is much easier to see that over-production of the Pinot Noir debases quality, not so easy to determine its effect on the more complex *encépagement* of the Bordeaux vineyards. It is evident, for example, that the Cabernet Sauvignon yields less than the Merlot, so presumably there must be an ideal yield which will produce a good quality under the best conditions. This is precisely where the permutations become complicated. It is clear that many vineyards in 1961 produced exceptional wines notable for their richness in extract, this with yields perhaps of between 20 and 30 hectolitres to the hectare – depending on the type and age of the wines. It is equally clear that some very disappointing wines were made in 1969 when many yields were also very low. On the other hand, in 1970 some vineyards made over 100 hectolitres per hectare and the wine was acceptable, if usually of very average quality, while some top growths made very fine wines with yields around 60 hectolitres per hectare. This experience of high yields and exceptional quality has since been repeated in 1982 and 1985, 1986 and 1989.

I would suggest that this means that the ideal yield varies according to the conditions of the year. There is certainly some figure above which good wine could not be made in the most perfect conditions. On the other hand, in some years even an average yield will be too much to bring to a satisfactory maturity – given the particular weather conditions. So it looks as if this is likely to remain an inexact science, with the *vigneron* who prunes hard producing the most consistent results, even if the high yielders will sometimes do well.

Another reason for increased yields is the use of fertilizers. I remember being told by old Monsieur Dubos of Cantemerle in the early fifties that

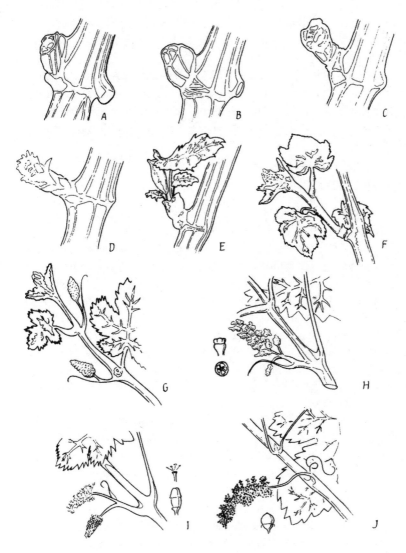

Figure 2   Principal stages in the evolution of the vine

A. Winter bud   B. Bud coming through   C. Bud turns green   D. Leaves visible   E. Leaves fully visible   F. Bunches on which grapes will appear are visible   G. Bunches clearly separated from leaves   H. Flower buds already visible   I. Flowering   J. Setting of the fruit it was his custom to manure his vines only every other year. Today organic manures are hard to come by and the use of artificial fertilizers widespread.

On the other hand, the revision of the *Appellation Contrôlée* regulations on *rendement* in 1974 has introduced both more flexibility and more certainty into this vexed subject, so that the worst excesses of over-cropping are now effectively discouraged, while the variations from year to year are reasonably allowed for.

THE VINTAGE AND THE VINIFICATION

The first and most important decision that has to be taken is when the picking is to begin. An examination of vintaging dates over the last one hundred years shows that, even allowing for inevitable variations, vintaging now begins later than it used to. This is because it is now possible to obtain a fairly accurate idea of the degree of ripeness attained at any particular time in various parts of the vineyard. But it should also be noted that, whereas today the time of 110 days from the time of flowering to the picking is taken as a reliable guide, nineteenth-century works usually quote ninety days as being the time then allowed.

That grapes were picked before they had achieved full ripeness can also be gauged from the alcohol levels obtained. Thus, first growths of the Médoc in the 1840 vintage showed levels of between 8 per cent and 9 per cent only (see Franck, *Vins du Médoc*, 4th edition, 1860), while some Ausones of the 1880s were still around or below only 10 per cent alcohol per volume. At a lunch in Ausone in April 1985, when Madame Dubois-Challon most generously produced Ausone 1949, Belair 1920 and Ausone 1849, we fell to discussing this topic, whereupon Pascal Delbeck, the Administrator, tested the three wines in his own glasses. The Ausone 1949 was 11 degrees, Belair 1920 was 9.5 degrees and Ausone 1849 only 9 degrees. It now seems clear that the *vignerons* of the past picked early, precisely to avoid high sugar levels, because they were nervous of stuck fermentations since little was done, or known about, controlling the temperatures of fermentations. It also explodes the notion that high alcohol levels alone promote longevity in wine. Conversely, these levels meant that the acidity in these wines was much higher than we would find tolerable today. This would also account for the need to keep these wines four or five years in cask before bottling.

Once the use of accurate hydrometers enabled growers to measure the progress of maturation over the weeks leading up to the vintage, there was a natural tendency for some to wait just that little bit longer in the hope of obtaining a better alcohol level. Most growers, however, have been happy to see a good average level and then begin picking while the weather held.

The result of this has been a tendency to forget that sugar content is only one half of the picture. There comes a point where these twin factors achieve an ideal harmony. If the picking is then further delayed, a degree of over-ripeness is reached which is likely to affect the balance and the development of the wine. This, in my view, is why some châteaux today – Lafite immediately springs to mind – are producing much softer but richer wines than they used to. This has much more to do with the degree of ripeness at the picking than with any of the changes in vinification methods which are usually cited as the reason for wines maturing more rapidly. Again, I must stress that this is very much a personal view.

One of the most interesting aspects of vintaging in Bordeaux is the variation in starting dates through the region. St Emilion and Pomerol are always the first to begin, the Graves and Margaux follow, and points in the Médoc further north begin a little later still. It should be emphasized that this is, of course, a generalization; the gaps can be greater or less depending on the conditions of the year. But in the Médoc, for instance, I have known ten days to elapse between the first picking in Margaux and that at Château Loudenne, the IDV property which lies on the boundary of the Haut-Médoc and the Bas-Médoc. 1978 was the first vintage of my experience when vintaging in the Médoc began at the same time as that in St Emilion and Pomerol.

All this is for red wines. The picking of the white grapes usually begins at about the same time as in St Emilion for the red wines, or even earlier. For the great Sauternes it does not usually begin until after the red grape harvest is finished. The most general time for the beginning of the vintage in recent years has been the last week in September. Anything before this is considered early. A start at the beginning of October is late. The Sauternes-Barsac vintage usually begins in early October, and in good years can continue until mid-November.

What is interesting about all this is the light it throws on the micro-climates of the region. Even a cursory glance at the map will show how diverse it is geographically. The most striking feature is the river system, with the Garonne and the Dordogne converging to produce the Gironde. Then the districts themselves are strongly contrasting, with the flat, gravelly areas of the Graves often heavily wooded, while the Médoc is open and almost bare, with its low-lying slopes descending easily to the river. On the other side of the Gironde and Dordogne, the vineyards lie among much more hilly country, where limestone, clay, sand and gravel predominate, and hilly, attractively wooded country is also to be found in the Premières Côtes, across the Garonne from the Graves. It is therefore hardly surprising to find that vineyards on different sides of large rivers, on differing soils and with differing expositions, contrive to experience small climatic differences. These small differences of rainfall, sunshine and temperature can add up over a season to produce measurably different results, so that not only can a year which is outstanding in St Emilion and Pomerol be only average in Médoc – as was the case in 1964 – but results in, say, Margaux can be different from those in St Estèphe, as in 1977. A further insight into the differences within even a small area can be gauged from the experience of Chardon père, the famous *régisseur* of Palmer, who used to supervise two other properties in the Margaux *appellation* – Siran at Labarde and Angludet at Cantenac. Over a period of some years, he found that the flowering in each vineyard always began at intervals of a few days from the others, and always in the same order.

The actual process of vintaging is straightforward enough. The pickers these days are drawn from a wide spectrum. Many Spaniards are brought in under contract in much the same way as hop-pickers from London were in England. But on many of the smaller estates, local labour pre-dominates, interspersed with the inevitable students. With the growth of the University of Bordeaux, the use of these students has much increased. Most of the larger estates both house and feed their vintagers, but those near to Bordeaux often return them there by bus every evening.

The most important development in harvesting, during the last decade, has been the remarkable spread in the use of harvesting machines. Their use began in the Entre-Deux-Mers in the mid-seventies. In 1979 a demonstration was given at Château Loudenne to show how machines could function in a Médoc vineyard without altering the methods of pruning. By 1983, 1,050 machines were in use in the Gironde, more than in any other department of France. By 1986 there were estimated to be over 1,500 machines in use, harvesting more than 50 per cent of the area under vine in the Gironde. Even more startling perhaps, more than 70 per cent of all vineyards of over 20 hectares were now being mechanically harvested. The large properties and the generally flat, undulating landscape of the Gironde are ideally suited to this practice.

Everyone who has seen the results of mechanically harvested wines has, I think, been agreeably surprised by the quality that can be produced. Several points are worth making. Mechanical harvesting can enable the vintage to be brought in much more speedily. On a large estate, this can be very important and could result in a far higher proportion of the vintage being collected at optimum ripeness, as well as avoiding disappointments when the weather changes. It should not be forgotten that on a large property with a big vintage, such as 1982 or 1986, it can easily take two to three weeks to bring in the harvest. Another point is that mechanical harvesting will remove only ripe grapes. Unripe ones are left behind, thus ensuring a more effective selection than is often possible from unskilled hand-picking. One of the early problems of mechanical harvesting was oxidation, particularly serious, of course, for white grapes. But now that it is possible to hold the grapes in a container on the machine under inert gas, this problem has been overcome and, indeed, the quality of those white wines which I have tasted from mechanical harvesting has been exceptionally good.

The pickers work their way methodically down the rows of vines, cutting the bunches of grapes and placing them in light wooden baskets called *paniers*. These are then emptied into larger containers called *bennes* carried on the backs of the workers, who walk up and down the rows of vines so that baskets may be emptied as required. When these large *bennes* are full, they are emptied in their turn into a container drawn these days by a tractor, which is waiting nearby. At some properties – Pavie is a case in point – the grapes are collected in plastic boxes which can be loaded two or three high on an open-sided trailer. This safeguards the quality of the grapes by preventing any premature pressing caused by the accumulated weight of grapes. In some places one still sees the traditional round wooden tubs used for this final collection, but they are generally being replaced by a single large steel container. The exception is Sauternes-Barsac, where the smaller wooden tubs are more suitable for the reception of the over-ripe berries. When the container or the wooden tubs are full, the tractor proceeds with them to the vat-house, or *cuvier*.

In difficult years, when rot is prevalent in the vineyards, a system of selection, or *triage*, is carried out. To begin with, the pickers are instructed to remove obviously rotten berries from the bunches as they are picked. But, as many of the pickers are far from skilled, this alone is insufficient. A trellis is therefore set up at one end of the container and the carriers empty their *paniers* on to these trellises. Several experienced pickers then sort the bunches by hand, discarding all rotten berries. This process can also be carried out when the tractor arrives with its load at the *cuvier*, but it is easier and probably more effective when done as described in the vineyard, before too many rotten grapes have become squashed. The dire results experienced in 1963 led to this type of *triage* being used in 1965, and even more extensively in 1968. It is interesting to note that, although conditions in 1968 were similar to the other two years, far better results were obtained, and some wines even resembled the more successful 1960s.

The system for gathering white grapes differs only in the areas producing sweet wines. Here, on the best estates, the pickers go through the vineyard three or four times, selecting only the individual berries or parts of bunches which have been affected by *botrytis cinerea* or *pourriture noble*. This fungus attacks the over-ripe grapes, forming a furry coating on the skins, and has the effect of sucking the water content out of the berry, thus dehydrating it and leaving a far higher concentration of sugar.

When the grapes arrive at the *cuvier*, the procedure for red and white grapes diverges. The red grapes are emptied into a V-shaped receptacle with a large stainless steel screw running along the bottom of it. This draws the bunches into the *fouloir-égrappoir*, which de-stalks the grapes and gently breaks the skins. This is often referred to in English as a de-stalker and crusher, but this is rather misleading. The grapes are not really crushed so much as broken, just sufficiently to allow the fermentation to begin. In the past few years considerable refinements have been made in this important piece of equipment. It has been realized that, if well executed, this operation can significantly improve the resulting quality of the wine; or, conversely, diminish it if crudely done. For this reason, many new *fouloirs-égrappoirs* have appeared in Bordeaux *chais* in the last five years. A new model made by Amos in Germany is much favoured now by oenologists. Vaslin have now produced a model which uses similar principles. The bunches of grapes are de-stalked in a perforated horizontal drum. Inside the drum there is a shaft to which paddles are affixed. Both rotate at speeds which can be controlled. The resulting pulp is then pumped into the fermentation vat or *cuve*.

The traditional Bordeaux *cuve* is wooden and cylindrical in shape (Fig. 3). The top is covered by wooden sections which can easily be removed. In the twenties, the first concrete vats lined with tiles were installed. One of the first was built at Loudenne in 1920. The latest innovation is the stainless steel *cuve*, first installed at Haut-Brion and then at Latour.

In most traditional *cuviers*, the wooden *cuves* are free-standing. This arrangement can still be seen at Lafite and Calon-Ségur, although the *cuves* at Calon have not in fact been used for some years. But in the 1860s and 1870s, a series of *cuviers* was built where a wooden floor was inserted, level with the top of the vats. The grapes were then unloaded at this first-floor level, which made the filling of the vats easier in the days before electrical pumping. This arrangement may still be seen at Mouton and Pontet-Canet, amongst others.

Originally, the de-stalking was done by hand on a table with a sort of griddle top, the stalk of the bunch being held and the bunch rubbed on the griddle until all the grapes had been rubbed off. This practice survives now only as an occasional practice at Palmer and Pichon-Lalande,

Figure 3   The traditional Bordeaux cuve

principally as a method of *triage* in poor years. It is interesting to note, however, that Professor Amerine believes that hand *égrappage* is actually less efficient than with the present mechanical *égrappoir*, because it separates the berries from the stalk less cleanly, allowing a certain amount of oil and tannin from the stalk into the must ("The Golden Ages of Wine", lecture given in July 1969 to the Institute of Masters of Wine).

Once the grapes are in the vats, the fermentation begins. The natural yeasts which come from the skins of the grapes rapidly get to work, changing the sugar in the grapes into alcohol and at the same time extracting colour and tannin from the skins. For red wines, cultured yeasts are seldom used in Bordeaux. (See p. 13 for recent work on yeasts.)

When the fermentation is under way, the solid matter in the grapes, mostly skins and pips, rises to the top of the vat to form what is known as the *chapeau*, or cap. Great vigilance is now required on the part of the wine-maker. He must watch the temperature carefully and he must not allow the *chapeau* to become dry and hard. The very act of fermentation releases energy in the form of heat, but if this is allowed to rise too much, the fermentation itself is endangered. Just as, if the temperature is too low, the yeasts are inhibited from beginning their work, so if it rises too high, an environment is created where aceto-bacteria flourish, and vinegar will result. A temperature of 35°C is regarded as the upper safety limit, and most wine-makers prefer a fermentation at around 28°–30°C. The other associated problem is that the *chapeau* gets a good deal hotter than the must below it, and if it is allowed to get dry and its temperature goes unchecked, bacteria rapidly breed and these can again produce vinegar. So the system called *remontage* is employed. This consists simply of drawing off the must from the bottom of the vat and pumping it to the top, where it is poured on top of the *chapeau* and so permeates it. If the general temperature is considered to be getting too high, the must will be passed through a simple device like a milk-cooler, where cold water flows over the pipes through which the wine is pumped. More sophisticated devices are also now in operation. Where stainless steel vats are in use, a thermostat can turn on cold water which runs down the sides of the vats to reduce the temperature. But one of the most ingenious solutions is that pioneered by Monsieur Henri Woltner at La Mission-Haut-Brion. Here, after experimenting for several years with one or two trial vats, Monsieur

Woltner installed a complete system of vitrified steel vats in 1950. Their size and construction kept the fermenting must at a steady temperature by losing heat, and the *maître de chai* said that since their installation in 1950, the temperature had never risen above 30°C. This very successful system was never copied elsewhere, although it is cheaper than the stainless steel favoured by Haut-Brion and Latour and was replaced by stainless steel by the new owners in 1987. The submerged cap method, generally favoured in hot countries, is another solution. Here, the cap is held down by a wooden grille, and the carbon dioxide released by the fermentation forces the must up through a pipe and so on to the top of the cap. This has the advantage of controlling the temperature and moisture of the cap automatically, and of extracting colour more rapidly. The disadvantage is that there is some danger of oxidation. This method is now used at Branaire.

Some of the most recent stainless steel fermentation vats embody built-in cooling jackets which circle the vats at intervals. Another variation is a cooling serpent which is actually inside the vat. There are also heat exchangers, for use in older *cuviers*, which can in quite a short time lower the temperature of a vat by several degrees or, conversely, increase it to warm the must in cold conditions. The most advanced *cuvier* is the new one installed at Rausan-Ségla in 1986, which is completely automated and computerized.

All this serves to emphasize the importance now attached to controlling the fermentation. It should be remarked, however, that although most oenologists and producers now aim to ferment their red wines at between 28° and 30°C, there is a view that there are occasions when extra dimensions and extract can be gained by allowing it to rise briefly to around 33°C. Genius sometimes requires one to live dangerously!

During the fermentation, a chart is kept on each vat, showing both the temperature and the progress being made in converting the sugar into alcohol. It is watched just as carefully as any patient's chart on a hospital bed. The time required to complete the fermentation varies considerably, both from year to year and from district to district. I have observed, for instance, that generally fermentation seems to be completed more rapidly in St Emilion and Pomerol than in Médoc. One year, when it was taking eight or nine days in the Médoc, it was generally being completed in four or five days the other side of the river.

Once the alcoholic fermentation has actually finished, the new wine is drawn off into the traditional Bordeaux barrels of 225 litres. Some châteaux do this almost immediately, others follow the more traditional practice and keep the wine in vat in the hope of extracting more colour and tannin from the skins. But whereas vatting for upwards of a month was once usual, now ten days to a fortnight is the maximum. Some châteaux now prefer to keep the wine in vat, at least until the malolactic fermentation (see p. 40) is complete. In difficult years, or when colour but not too much tannin is required, some châteaux heat the must. The results are inconclusive. I myself feel that such wines tend to flatter at first but disappoint later on, just when one would expect them to be reaching their best.

The process for white wines differs in a number of important respects, and there are differences between the production of dry and sweet wines as well. To begin with, the stalks are not removed. This is because the juice must be quickly separated, so that no colouring is picked up, and retaining the stalks makes the pressing easier. To illustrate the point, I shall always remember Monsieur Jean Quancard telling a Study Course session for the Master of Wine Examination that, as a young man in the trade, he had wondered why the stalks were retained for white grapes. When first he was put in charge of overseeing the reception of a vintage, he thought he would experiment and de-stalk some white grapes to see what happened. When the grapes were put in the press, the must shot out all over him! This, of course, was the old type of hydraulic press now used only in some of the most traditional Sauternes estates such as Yquem (Fig. 4).

Most white wines are today made with the aid of the cylindrical presses (Fig. 5) which are so familiar in Germany, on the Loire, and indeed for the production of most white wines. They are of two basic types. That most widely found in Bordeaux uses two plates on a central screw, which move gradually towards each other, slowly pressing the grapes. When they then move apart, the pulp is broken up by chains which run the length of the cylinders. All the time the cylinder rotates, thus facilitating the running of the juice. In this type of process it is very important to control the speed and strength of the initial pressings. The other type employs a central rubber bladder which is gradually inflated, pushing the grapes against the sides of the press as it rotates. Advocates

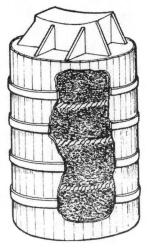

Figure 4   The traditional hydraulic press

of this system claim that it is more gentle than the other, and it has certainly gained some ground recently. As the juice is run off, it is either pumped straight into casks or vats to begin the fermentation, or goes into a *cuve* for the process known as *débourbage*. This simply means that the juice is sulphured just sufficiently to arrest the onset of the fermentation, and then rests in a *cuve* for about twenty-four hours, during which time any solid matter can fall to the bottom. When the fermentation begins, it is likely to proceed more satisfactorily with a relatively clean must; also,

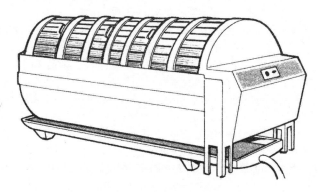

Figure 5   Cylindrical press

the wine will not have to be racked so often, which is always an important consideration with white wines where handling must be kept to a minimum to guard against oxidation.

In Bordeaux, it is traditional for the fine Graves and Sauternes to have their fermentation in cask. But, with the increasing demand for white wines which are light, fresh and fruity, many properties now ferment in *cuve*. Loudenne, which makes one of the few white wines in the Médoc, has a model installation of this type, installed in the sixties but now widely found throughout the region. The *cuves* are of stainless steel and small in size (containing only 20 hectolitres each). By running cold water down the sides, the temperature of the fermentation can be controlled and kept down to a maximum of 18°C, far cooler than would otherwise be possible. This much enhances the delicacy and flavour of the wine.

For sweet wines, the process is slightly different. Again, the stalks are not removed. Since the grapes are already over-ripe, the pressure of the bunches tends to break the skins and cause the juice to begin to flow. The traditional process in Sauternes is for the bunches to be emptied straight into the presses on arrival at the *cuvier*, where the weight of the grapes causes a certain amount of the juice to run off. The grapes are then pressed in the normal manner. Many properties today, of course, use the modern type of press already described.

One important topic has not so far been mentioned: chaptalization. This is the adding of sugar to the must (i.e. the grape juice before it has begun fermenting) in order to raise the alcoholic strength of a wine. This process takes its name from Jean-André Chaptal, a noted French chemist, who suggested the idea at the beginning of the nineteenth century, although it was a very long time before his ideas were adopted.

It is only since 1938 that chaptalization has been permitted in Bordeaux, and then not generally. In practice, it has been widely employed only since 1962. The authorities (l'Institut National des Appellations d'Origine, or INAO) take a decision each year, when growers make an application just before the vintage; this is in contrast to Burgundy, where there is general permission every year. There has been a definite tendency in recent years for permission to be given more frequently.

There is still a feeling in some quarters that there is something faintly indecent in sugaring the must. Nothing could be further from the truth, provided that it is not overdone. Chaptalization is desirable and necessary when the sugar content of the grapes falls short of what is normal for a good year – in other words, when the grapes do not reach perfect maturity. This can sometimes happen because there is a larger crop than usual and only an average amount of sunshine, or weather conditions may compel growers to pick earlier than they would wish, to save the crop. Whatever the reason, there can be no doubt that in recent years many wines have been much improved in this way. Most authorities in Bordeaux agree that the alcoholic content should not be raised by more than 1–1.5 per cent by volume by this method, an example which unfortunately few Burgundians follow. Happily, there is as yet no fetish in Bordeaux about alcohol – certainly as far as red wines are concerned – and this limit is generally respected.

In the last decade a practice has grown up – especially among the leading *crus* – to "top up" the fermentation with some chaptalization almost every year. In Médoc, for example, where the great wines of the forties usually had 11 to 11.5 degrees, 12.5 degrees is now regarded as the norm to be aimed at. Part of the problem is that oenologists have realized that the extra alcohol makes wines more flattering when very young, something they have learnt from observing Californian wines which, of course, achieve their higher alcoholic levels naturally. Personally, it is a trend I regret and, clearly, it has nothing to do with ensuring the longevity of wines.

I have sometimes heard it suggested that in some mysterious way chaptalized wines have a "sweet" taste which is discernible, in spite of the fact that all the sugar is, of course, turned into alcohol. The real cause of this impression is that chaptalization, by increasing the alcohol in a wine, changes its balance slightly and incidentally helps to precipitate cream of tartar. This makes the wine seem softer and less acid than it might otherwise be, and, incidentally, more agreeable to drink, as already pointed out.

The system of vinification I have described is, in essence, the same as that used over very many years. What is meant therefore when wine lovers speak darkly of changed methods of vinification? This is, of course, all part of that age-old belief that things are not what they were; and indeed, it is fortunate for the average wine drinker that they are not. It is very unusual nowadays for wines to be spoiled by volatile acidity, for example. In other words, wines are much more consistent than they used to be because the fermentation is better controlled. It is this ability to control more precisely that differentiates today's wine-maker from his predecessors, and so serious mistakes are far rarer – the result, usually, of pure negligence.

The main differences, then, in the vinification of red wines in Bordeaux are the vatting of wines after the alcoholic fermentation has finished, and the control of temperature during the actual process of fermentation. Of the two, I would have no hesitation in saying that the control of temperature is by far the more important. This is not simply a matter of preventing the wine from spoiling by becoming too warm, although this is important enough when one remembers that as recently as 1945 half the crop at Cheval Blanc had to be pasteurized. Just as important are the positive benefits to be obtained by a cooler, and therefore longer, fermentation. Monsieur Henri Woltner at La Mission Haut-Brion was certainly one of the pioneers of what he called the *fermentation froide*. What this really means is a long, cooler fermentation with the temperatures held at below 30°C. This seems to produce very well-balanced wines with plenty of colour, and sufficient but not excessive tannin, so that the wine can be drunk with pleasure when relatively young, but will have the potential for ageing as well.

Balance is really the key word. The idea that wines will not last unless they have a lot of tannin, or that if wines are drinkable early they cannot last, is certainly erroneous. Very tannic wines may not be drinkable for many years, but will not be any the better for their long period of gestation unless they also have plenty of fruit and good acidity. Some 1928s have ultimately proved disappointing after a very long wait, and the same can be said of some 1937s and 1945s. To go back even further, contemporary writers reported that the 1900s were delicious at a very early stage, and for this reason it was thought that they would not last so well as the harder 1899s. My own experience of the two vintages in the sixties, when I was fortunate enough to taste a number of bottles, is that the 1900s were still superb – I have never had a poor bottle – while the 1899s were fading and are now less consistent. Indeed, so-called light vintages nearly always seem to last well.

The part played by long vatting is doubtful, if the fermentation has been controlled in the manner described. I would suspect that with the longer, cooler fermentation, not much is likely to be gained by vatting for more than ten days or so.

Ultimately, this argument calls in question the basis on which we judge our wines. Is there any merit in longevity in itself? It is very fascinating to drink a bottle of claret which is 100 years old, but one must recognize that this is a curiosity and that it is not the object of the wine-maker to produce a wine which will live indefinitely, since very few bottles indeed will have the opportunity to be tasted in this way. Rather, I would suggest that our judgement would be better based on some sort of hedonic scale, by which the prize went to the wine that could be drunk with pleasure for the longest time in the first twenty to thirty years of its life. On such a reckoning, the 1953s would clearly come out above the 1945s, as would the 1961s – the first vintage of this type to benefit from something approaching control.

Special mention must be made of Dr Emile Peynaud of the Station Agronomique et Oenologique of Bordeaux. His forty years of service to Bordeaux has done more than anything else to update this innately con-servative region. It has been in the last twenty-five years that his labours have really borne fruit, and the culmination came when he was called in in the mid-seventies by Lafite and Margaux to advise them. It has become something of a standard joke in the Médoc for a proprietor to announce that Professor Peynaud is in charge. In fact, of course, it is more a question of establishing the right systems, seeing there is a competent manager, or *maître de chai*, to carry them out, and then just keeping an eye on things. The sixties and seventies have certainly been the Peynaud era in Bordeaux.

Another legacy of Peynaud has been no less important – and that is selection. Although it had begun well before, it has been most noticeable during the increasingly large vintages of the eighties, as more and more of the leading *crus* began to commercialize second wines on a regular basis. Certainly, nothing has done more to raise the quality at châteaux such as Margaux, Léoville-Las Cases and Pichon-Lalande. As Emile Peynaud begins to take life a little more easily – although his so-called retirement still looks like most people's normal working life – so the work of Professor Ribereau-Gayon assumes an increasingly important place. But nothing can detract from the unique contribution which must serve as a permanent monument to Professor Emile Peynaud, the premier position now occupied worldwide by the great Bordeaux wines.

HANDLING THE WINES FROM VINIFICATION TO BOTTLING

The French term for this process has always seemed to me very apt. *Elevage* carries the suggestion of rearing a delicate or perhaps difficult child. Applied to wine, it rightly implies the continued care and vigilance necessary.

We left the red wines with their alcoholic fermentation complete, racked off their fermentation vats. Although the tradition is to put them straight in cask, some properties keep the wines in *cuve* through the first winter, which tends to hold back the wines somewhat. When the wine is kept in cask, the loss through evaporation is, of course, more serious, and the wines are usually topped up every few days to keep them full to the bung, which at this stage is placed only lightly in the bung-hole and is not driven home. For, although the alcoholic fermentation is finished, the malolactic fermentation now follows, during which a certain amount of carbon dioxide is given off, and the presence of some air is in any case desirable for this.

The malolactic fermentation is the changing of the malic acid in the wine into lactic acid. This greatly reduces the tartness, or apparent acidity of the wine, and is an essential process in its development. The actual process is chemically very complex and, until recently, was surrounded more by folklore than by science. What had been observed was that the timing and duration of the malolactic fermentation varied greatly from vintage to vintage, and even from property to property within the same vintage. As it now appears that no fewer than eighteen different amino-acids must be present for the fermentation to function normally, the complexity of the process may be more readily imagined. In a wine such as Beaujolais, the malolactic fermentation often occurs concurrently with the alcoholic fermentation. In Bordeaux, the process usually begins soon after the completion of the alcoholic fermentation and continues through the winter, finishing around March. Sometimes it is much slower to start, particularly if the weather in November and December is very cold. In such cases, it may not begin before the spring, and can continue into the summer months.

It is usual for the best growths to use new casks to receive each new vintage. These casks are made of oak. Before the war, the best oak was said to come from Memel in Lithuania; today, French Limousin oak as well as American oak is used. The use of new wood imparts a certain amount of additional tannin to the wine, as well as incurring a greater loss through evaporation. This loss of wine is an important factor in the cost of *élevage*, and is reckoned to amount to between 7 per cent and 8 per cent in the first year, decreasing to 4 per cent and 5 per cent in subsequent years. While it is normal practice for those who can afford it to put new wine into new wood, there are different opinions as to whether this is invariably the best procedure. That gifted and thoughtful wine-maker, Monsieur Henri Woltner, believed that, in light vintages, new oak tended to mask the characteristics of the wine with its own. I have certainly seen cases where this has happened, while La Mission's remarkable run of good off-years is eloquent testimony to the success of Henri Woltner's approach. For purely economic reasons, many leading growers today put only between a third and a half of the new vintage in new oak.

One important development over the last twenty years has been the realization that only relatively new casks actually contribute quality to the maturation of a wine. Since the cost of a new cask now approximates to the market price of 225 litres of Bordeaux *rouge*, the use of anything other than third- or fourth-hand casks is out of the question for such wines. Unfortunately, old casks are more likely to impart off-flavours to wines than quality, so the standards of lesser or *petits* châteaux have actually been enhanced by keeping them in vat rather than cask. Another bonus is that such wines can be bottled and drunk earlier, because the vat ageing preserves their clean fruitiness better and they recover from bottling more rapidly. So the advantages for both producer and consumer are obvious.

Another important part of the maturation process is the racking of the wine. This is simply the drawing-off of the wine from one cask, or *cuve*, to another, so as to leave the lees, or deposit, which have accumulated at the bottom, intact. In the process the wine is, of course, aerated to some extent. The amount of racking depends very much on the constitution of the wine. A robust, full-bodied wine will be racked more frequently than a delicate, light one. Traditionally, the first racking occurs in March, the second at the end of June – coinciding with the flowering – the third in

October, after which the wine is placed on three-quarter bung, so that the bung is covered by the wine. A recent development is that some châteaux now put their wines on three-quarter bung in the spring, after the second racking; this has the advantage of reducing evaporation and thus costs. If things go according to plan, the malolactic fermentation will have finished just before the March racking, and the new wines may be properly judged for the first time when they have settled down after the racking.

The wine also has to be fined, a process which helps to remove unstable elements, so bringing it forward to the time when it may be bottled. The traditional fining is with white of eggs, and this is still done in many châteaux. But in *négociants'* cellars, where several thousand casks may have to be fined at any one time, this is hardly practical, and gelatine is used instead. Again, the number of finings depends on the constitution of the wine – two finings are usual, but three may be needed on occasion.

The decision when to bottle is clearly most important. These days, there is a tendency to bottle rather earlier than used to be the case; this helps preserve the fruit and can make the wine agreeable to drink at an earlier stage without in any way affecting its keeping properties. The correct fining prior to bottling will ensure that the deposit which will eventually form in bottle in most years will not be any heavier than would have been the case had the wine been bottled later. It has thus become common for even classified growths to bottle in the summer or even late spring of the second year, instead of during the third winter, perhaps on average six months earlier. Even the first growths have now abandoned their tradition of bottling in the March of the third year.

My personal experience has certainly been in favour of earlier bottling. When, on occasion, I have seen wines which for one reason or another were bottled late, they invariably seem to dry up after several years in bottle. This would appear to confirm the belief that if wines are kept too long in cask, they may lose fruit and become tough in bottle. It is also important to maintain a flexible approach to the bottling time – vintages like 1975 required longer in wood to develop their characteristics than a lighter vintage like 1976.

Much has been written on the subject of English bottling versus château bottling. It should be remembered that if an English merchant announces his intentions to bottle in England at the time when the wine is purchased, the Bordeaux *négociant* will invariably bring the wine into his own cellars for the *élevage* – so that this will not be identical with the wine to be château-bottled. The process of shipping in bulk ages the wine to some extent and unsettles it. Certainly, the English bottling of robust wines is invariably more successful than that of light off-vintage years. But, finally, it means that there will be a number of different versions of the same wine, however carefully it is handled. This is why the leading properties now prefer to keep the bottling under their own control. When I have had the opportunity of comparing English- against château-bottled wines from the same vintage, I have found the château-bottled ones to be almost invariably superior. The most noticeable difference is that the château-bottled wines have more bouquet, and more roundness and fruit on the palate.

The *élevage* of white wines has changed far more than that of red wines – as has their vinification – and for the same reason. White wines vinified to emphasize their freshness and fruit are usually not kept in cask at all now, but are bottled in the spring or early summer after only a single fining and racking. Some of the finest Graves, however, are still matured in cask, and are not normally bottled until the second winter or the following spring. Such wines, of course, develop more character in bottle and last longer. These very early bottlings, however, do provide fresh attractive wines which are very enjoyable and a welcome change from the general run of over-sulphured wines which for too long were synonymous with the cheaper white Bordeaux.

The great Sauternes, and indeed all the sweet wines to some degree, take much longer to clarify than either dry white wines or red wines. Because of the concentration of sugar in the must, and the inevitably dirty state of a must obtained by pressing grapes infected by *pourriture noble*, the actual alcoholic fermentation takes far longer than for other wines. In a successful year, a Sauternes must will obtain a Baumé reading of 20 degrees, and up to 24 degrees in exceptional years. The fermentation in cask progresses very slowly, sometimes for nearly a year, until the alcoholic level inhibits any further work by the yeasts. Even so, the top Sauternes growths can achieve 15 per cent or 16 per cent alcohol by volume, with anything between 4 degrees and 7 degrees Baumé of unfermented sugar left. But, if the grapes are uniformly botrytized, this inhibits the fermentation so that it can be successfully finished with only

13.5 per cent to 14 per cent alcohol. This produces a fruitier, better-balanced wine than one with over 15 per cent. Failure to pick at the right moment can thus produce wines with an alcoholic "burn" and a lack of finesse – as happened in 1975.

Traditionally, these wines remain in cask for three years, and the practice is still observed at Yquem. But, increasingly, growers believe that it is better to bottle after two years, preventing oxidation and preserving freshness. Many experts believe that the extra year in cask does not achieve anything useful now that better fining agents, such as bentonite, are available to correct any faults in the wine, and that it is better not to expose the wine to the danger of oxidation.

BOTTLING AND MATURATION IN BOTTLE

The traditional Bordeaux bottle has become so synonymous with the region, that bottles of this shape are referred to as Bordeaux bottles, even in other countries such as Italy. Its distinct and classic outlines are common to both red and white wines. The bottle holds 0.75 litres. The long, straight neck is ideal for holding the long, hard, straight corks for which Bordeaux is justly famous. Certainly, no finer corks are used anywhere, and their lasting powers are ample testimony to this quality. When wines are kept for very long periods, as in the magnificent private cellars at Lafite and Mouton, which certainly contain the finest libraries of Bordeaux wines in the region, the practice is to recork every twenty-five years. This is not to say that the corks will not last longer, but at this age all corks should be able to be drawn without problems – at a later stage there will be some which will have deteriorated. The oldest cork I have drawn intact from an old claret was a Latour 1909, which would then have been over fifty years old. Even more remarkable was the perfectly preserved cork in a bottle of Guiraud 1893. Something in the constitution of this great Sauternes seemed to have preserved its cork – perhaps the sugar and lower acidity than would be found in a red wine. All those concerned in the selection of corks are agreed that their quality is not what it was. One disturbing result of this trend will be that the corks used for the great vintages of the seventies and eighties seem unlikely to last as well as those found in bottles of 1945, 1947 or 1949.

The actual bottling was until recently still carried out at many properties directly from the cask without any sort of filtration. This is, of course, a slow business, and now that compulsory château-bottling is becoming more general, more châteaux assemble their wines into bottling tanks and then gravity-feed through a light polishing filter. This is perhaps even more essential for white wines, which must be star-bright on bottling and remain so.

The practice of bottling from cask to cask is the principal reason for the considerable variations often reported between different bottles of the same wine. The practice of assembling the wine in vat prior to bottling to ensure homogeneity is very recent, and was generally adopted only during the sixties and early seventies.

The maturation in cask is a relatively rapid business during which the wines find their equilibrium and dispose of unwanted impurities and unstable elements. Once the wine has been bottled, a much slower form of maturation begins. For the first few months after bottling, red wines often suffer from bottle sickness during which time it is impossible to judge them or indeed drink them. After this the steady, even tenure of maturation continues, its timing and shape determined by the constitution of the wine.

The simplest way of explaining the life of a bottle of fine claret or Sauternes is in graph form (Fig. 6). The initial stage of maturation is

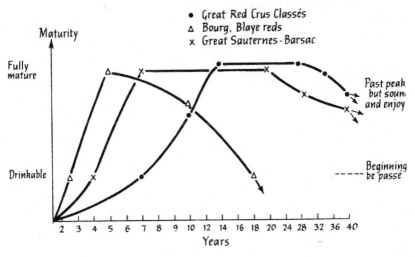

Figure 6   Graph illustrating the life of a bottle of claret or Sauternes

highly flexible. For some 1967s, 1971s or 1973s, it has amounted to as little as two years in bottle. On the other hand, in years like 1945 or 1937, and even in some 1961s and 1970s, this stage may have lasted for ten years. Two years in bottle for Bourg, Blaye, Fronsac and the lesser St Emilions and Pomerols is about average; three to five years for the better St Emilions, Pomerols, most Graves and Médocs is probably about right. At the end of this stage, the wine is enjoyable to drink, but its full potential has not yet been reached. This second stage may be longer than the first; on average it is usually rather similar. Then one can say that the wine is truly mature. The line on our graph here levels out, and most of the finest wines will continue steadily at about this level for twenty, thirty, fifty years, before beginning on a downward path. Of course, lesser wines, such as those of Bourg and Blaye, will seldom remain at their peak for more than about five years. The finest white Graves are usually at their best in about five years, and will keep for between ten and twenty years. The great Sauternes take longer to reach their peak, as the alcohol and sugar have to mellow and achieve harmony. This usually takes seven to ten years in the best vintages. But these wines may stay at their best, before beginning to lose fruit and sugar, for a further ten to twenty years, and in exceptional cases for longer still. Very luscious wines like Yquem sometimes mature more rapidly, and pass their peak more quickly.

Finally, it should be emphasized that storage conditions during this maturation in bottle are of supreme importance, and this is the principal reason why some bottles keep better than others. Dryness or dampness do not matter so much as a reasonable steady temperature, which in turn means that an even temperature from night to day is more important than some seasonal variations. Equally important is that wine should not be moved too much. Whether a bottle has been kept in a Bordeaux château or a Scottish castle does not matter so much as does the fact that it has remained in the same place untouched. In the end, if all these points have been observed, it is probably true to say that a Bordeaux wine will keep as long as its cork. At the first sign of trouble from this quarter, it is best to open and drink, unless you are able to re-cork.

3

Classifications Old and New

We are told that the desire to categorize is very French, but I suspect that to argue on the respective merits of well-tried favourites is a universal pastime. Horse racing has its form book, and cricket lovers spend the winter months selecting their World XI or England pre-1900 v. England post-1920 XIs. The French being an essentially practical people, their classifications of wines have usually had a strictly commercial rather than a mainly esoteric purpose.

Classifications are first recorded in the eighteenth century in the Médoc, and also in Bourg, a district then more favoured than the Médoc. It seems clear that they were essentially the grouping together by price of the best-known wines. In the Médoc there were normally four categories: the first always extremely small, the second only slightly larger, then the third and fourth often merging into one another. Such lists were compiled by brokers (*courtiers*), merchants and by wine enthusiasts. What is noticeable, when comparing various lists compiled in the thirty years prior to 1855, is that while a fair degree of unanimity existed about the first and second categories, there were wide divergencies lower down the scale. There were also frequent comings and goings. Because nothing was official, nothing was fixed and this helped to keep interest and ambition alive.

When, almost by accident, one particular list received official status in 1855, the process of change and renewal received a setback, and a living tradition became ossified. This all happened when the organizers of the great Exposition Universelle of Paris invited the Bordeaux Chamber of Commerce to produce a representative selection of the wines of Bordeaux. This Exhibition was the first great *manifestation* organized to display the splendour of Napoleon III's new Empire. The Chamber of

Commerce decided that each commune should be represented by an example under a neutral label, but that the great estates of Bordeaux should also be represented. So as to decide in the most impartial way possible on such a selection, the brokers attached to the Bordeaux Bourse were invited to prepare a list. This they duly did, basing it on the state of the market at that moment. Certainly, it bears a strong resemblance to previous unofficial lists, but with many understandable variations in the lower echelons. Had this list not then become enshrined like some law of the Medes and Persians, it most surely would have continued to evolve and change, not in its essentials but in details, as is healthy and normal in any living body.

It is often said by supporters of the status quo that there is no need to revise the old classification, since it was essentially a classification of the soil, and this is something which does not change. Unfortunately this is only a half-truth. The actual composition of many of the classified-growth vineyards has changed, often radically. This is because there is nothing to prevent one proprietor from buying new pieces of vineyard in times of prosperity, and another from selling up pieces in difficult times. After a hundred years, the name of a property may be the same, but the actual vineyard may be quite different from what it was at the beginning. In effect, it is the chateau name that is classified and not the vineyard. Another problem is that since every château wine is an *assemblage* from all parts of the vineyard, it is not easy to know what differing qualities each part of the vineyard produces. This is something probably only learnt with much experience by a *maître de chai* or a really knowledgeable and interested owner. In the end, therefore, we can judge a château only by the wine it actually produces. Even the price fetched over a period of years is not quite such a reliable guide as it once was, owing to differing marketing methods employed by various proprietors. Price is a factor, however, which must play an important part in classifying a wine, and certainly cannot be ignored in any realistic assessment.

Let us now look in more detail at the Médoc classifications. The pre-1855 classifications were unanimous about the first growths – Lafite, Margaux, Latour and Haut-Brion. The second growths of two early classifications, in the possession of Anthony Barton, and that of Charles Cocks compare as shown on p. 47.

As can be seen, the lists are remarkably consistent, the unfamiliar name of Gorse being the present Brane-Cantenac, and all seven names appeared as second growths in the 1855 list. But by then, the qualities of Pichon, Ducru-Beaucaillou, Cos d'Estournel and the newcomer, Montrose, were recognized as entitling them to a place in this elevated company.

1824	1827	1846		
Brane Mouton	Brane Mouton	Mouton		
Rauzan	Rauzan		⎧	Poyferré
		Léoville	⎨	Barton
			⎩	Marquis de Las Cases
Lascombes	Léoville			
Durefort (de Vivens)	Gruau-La-Rose	Rauzan		
Gorse		Durefort		
Léoville		Gruaud-Larose		
Gruau-La-Rose		Lascombes		
		Gorse		

Efforts to reform or renew the 1855 classification have, in the end, all come to nothing. The INAO did get as far as making a proposal in 1960 for an entirely new classification divided into three categories instead of five. But the storm of protest which this aroused soon persuaded the powers that be that this particular hornets' nest was best left alone. The only concrete achievement was the official acceptance in 1973 of the *de facto* position of Mouton-Rothschild as a *premier cru*.

In the absence of the likelihood of any official action in the foreseeable future, the way has been left open for plenty of unofficial speculation. The doyen of unofficial classification compilers was Alexis Lichine, who first published his in 1962. It has been revised and significantly altered on a number of occasions since, most recently in 1985, by which time it had grown to a rather unwieldy 195 *crus*, divided among *Crus Hors Classe* (8), *Crus Exceptionnels* (23) *Grands Crus* (27), *Crus Supérieurs* (45), and *Bons Crus* (92). The unique feature of the Lichine classification was its attempt to compare the wines of all the major districts of Médoc, Graves, St Emilion and Pomerol. The most recent effort is that by Robert Parker in 1985, whose approach has been to compile a classification of the top 100 wines from Bordeaux's same four leading districts. These are divided into First Growths (15), Second Growths (15), Third Growths (11), Fourth Growths (11) and Fifth Growths (48).

A careful look at these two personal selections highlights several interesting points. In his introduction to his own classification in the 1986 edition of his *Guide to the Wines and Vineyards of France*, Alexis Lichine says: "In assimilating wines with varying characteristics it becomes increasingly difficult to identify peers as one moves towards the lesser growths. It is easy, for example, to compare the very best wines of St Emilion and . . . of the Médoc . . . but the more common and undifferentiated the wine, the narrower the base for comparison."

These two classifications bear witness to the truth of this observation. No less than 48 per cent of the wines in Parker's classification are to be found in his fifth category, as are 47 per cent of Lichine's in his. In other words, while it is not too difficult to agree about the leading wines, if one has to classify too far down the line it is hard to find a cut-off point, and one lands up with a large and rather amorphous collection of doubtful value to the consumer or the proprietor.

As one reads through the list of Lichine's *Bons Crus* (the fifth category) one cannot help feeling the net has been cast far too wide while, with Parker, the insistence on squeezing his list into the strait-jacket of 100 seems unnecessarily arbitrary. Can the object of producing the best 100 wines – like the best 100 tunes – be reconciled with a serious attempt to classify the best?

So what are, or should be, the criteria for deciding such thorny points? Part of the problem lies in trying to separate the intrinsic merits of the *"terroir"* from the excellence, or otherwise, with which the proprietor makes and bottles his wine. Clearly the changeable factor is indeed the skill of the wine-maker and *vigneron*. They can in fact change one's perception of what is the actual potential of the *"terroir"*. A good current example is Lagrange in St Julien. It was classified as a third growth in 1855 but for many years had made wines which were often coarse and seldom as good as the best fifth growth. Yet although some outlying parts of its large vineyard had been sold off, the main core of the property surrounding the château remained. Today, under the most skilled management, it is again producing top-flight wines worthy of its original classification.

On the other hand, you can have a property such as Meyney in St

Estèphe which has been well run for years, where standards have kept up with the best trends, where the wines are consistent and enjoyable. But are they truly the stuff of which *crus classés* are made? To me they are marked by a strong "*goût de terroir*", a certain coarseness, which will not be found in its neighbour Montrose. I do believe that a *cru classé* must have a quality of complexity and that certain stylishness and power, often identified as finesse, which is often most noticeable in the bouquet, if the term *cru classé* is to retain its *réclame*.

Certain soils consistently produce wines of distinction. The proportion of the *vignoble* of St Julien producing *cru classé* wines is higher than in any other commune, that of St Estèphe lower than any other. And this has been true over a very long period of time, through times of differing degrees of wine-making procedures and skills. On the other hand, the wines of St Laurent are today much less admired than those of Moulis. So we have to be on our guard against claiming *cru classé* status for a very well-made, attractive wine which, however, lacks that essential flair which makes it somehow special and enables it to stand apart from many other good honest wines. Nor must we simply write off a well-placed property which has done well in the past but which is currently going through a bad patch.

Bearing all this in mind, I feel that the most useful contribution I can make towards this debate is to indicate those wines which are on the move in 1988, rather than to propose yet another quasi-classification. In trying to assess the merits of any particular *cru*, it is important, I believe, not only to have tasted a range of vintages, but also to have compared a number of different wines side by side in blind tastings. While such anonymity is not the answer to every problem and clearly cannot be used on every occasion, it is nevertheless a discipline to which every serious taster must be prepared to submit himself, and it is the only sure antidote to the prejudices which lurk in every one of us.

The status of first growth has a very special place in the annals of Bordeaux, and is not lightly or easily to be extended. Its accolade should belong only to those châteaux which have carved a special place for themselves over a period of time, in terms of the ultimate in quality and excellence. Price must also come into the reckoning, although for many years the prices of Ausone and Cheval Blanc, for instance, fell well short of what was achieved by the firsts of the Médoc.

Taking these criteria into account, there is really only one property that looks like joining the august company of Lafite, Latour, Margaux, Mouton-Rothschild, Haut-Brion, Ausone, Cheval Blanc, and Pétrus, and that is La Mission Haut-Brion. Having produced consistently superb wines for many years during the Woltner ownership, it is now under the same dedicated stewardship as its neighbour, Haut-Brion. The wines seem to be even more brilliant than before, while the individuality is as marked as ever. The contrast is an analogy of Lafite and Mouton, and La Mission deserves its promotion just as much as Mouton did earlier. Its price is now also very close to the firsts, and well above all the super-seconds.

I find the concept of the super-second, as applied to the wines of the Médoc, a useful one. I am also including Graves in the exercise because this district fits in naturally with Médoc. It has, in practice, been accorded to a handful of wines which have over the past few years clearly moved out ahead of their peers in terms of quality and consistency, and eventually price. At the present time, I would accord this accolade to the following wines – listed in alphabetical order:

Domaine de Chevalier (Graves-Léognan)
Cos d'Estournel (St Estèphe)
Ducru-Beaucaillou (St Julien)
Gruaud-Larose (St Julien)
Léoville-Las Cases (St Julien)
Palmer (Margaux)
Pichon-Lalande (Pauillac)

The following very good wines of the seventies have become even better during the eighties.

Duhart-Milon (Pauillac)
Fieuzal (Léognan-Graves)
Grand-Puy-Lacoste (Pauillac)
Léoville-Barton (St Julien)
Lynch-Bages (Pauillac)
Montrose (St Estèphe)
Talbot (St Julien)
La Tour-Haut-Brion (Graves-Pessac)

The following wines which, for differing reasons, under-performed in the seventies have made new beginnings in the eighties.

Beychevelle (St Julien) since 1981
Cantemerle (Haut-Médoc) since 1982
Clerc-Milon (Pauillac) since 1981
Durfort-Vivens (Margaux) since 1982
Haut-Bages-Libéral (Pauillac) since 1982
Haut-Bailly (Graves-Léognan) since 1979
d'Issan (Margaux) since 1979
Lagrange (St Julien) since 1985
Léoville-Poyferré (St Julien) since 1981
Pape-Clément (Graves-Pessac) since 1985
Pichon-Longueville-Baron (Pauillac) new owners 1987
Rausan-Ségla (Margaux) since 1982
St Pierre (St Julien) since 1982
Smith-Haut-Lafitte (Graves-Léognan) since 1983

The following *crus* are performing very consistently at their level and some are perhaps underrated.

Batailley (Pauillac)
Branaire-Ducru (St Julien)
Brane-Cantenac (Margaux)
Calon-Ségur (St Estèphe)
Giscours (Margaux)
Haut-Batailley (Pauillac)
La Lagune (Haut-Médoc)
Langoa-Barton (St Julien)
Prieuré-Lichine (Margaux)
du Tertre (Margaux)

Wines not mentioned above, where there are nevertheless signs of improvement, and are therefore worth watching are:

Belgrave (Haut-Médoc)
Dauzac (Margaux)
Grand-Puy-Ducasse (Pauillac)
Kirwan (Margaux)

Lascombes (Margaux)

Lynch-Moussas (Pauillac)

Marquis-de-Terme (Margaux)

Mouton-Baronne-Philippe (Pauillac)

Pontet-Canet (Pauillac)

The following unclassified wines have the necessary style and consistency to deserve classification.

d'Angludet (Margaux)

Chasse-Spleen (Moulis)

Fourcas-Hosten (Listrac)

Gloria (St Julien)

Haut-Marbuzet (St Estèphe)

Lanessan (Haut-Médoc)

La Louvière (Graves-Léognan)

de Pez (St Estèphe)

Poujeaux (Theil) (Moulis)

In 1985 the second revision of the 1955 St Emilion classification (the first was in 1969) unexpectedly breathed new life into it, and at the same time caused a good deal of controversy, probably creating more publicity for the St Emilion classification than it has ever known. The Commission cleverly kept well away from tasting evaluations, which are so easy to challenge as subjective, and concentrated instead on cases where the conditions laid down by the Syndicat of St Emilion itself had not been observed.

The most celebrated case was the demotion of Beau-Séjour-Bécot from *Premier Grand Cru Classé* to *Grand Cru Classé* because, in 1979, without prior application or consultation, the proprietor had incorporated his two adjoining vineyards of La Carte and Trois Moulins, classified only as *Grands Crus Classés*, into Beau-Séjour, thus greatly increasing its size from 10 to 18.6 hectares. In another case, the wine was not bottled at the property, or indeed within the district, while in a third case, the wines of three properties, all classified, were vinified together in the same *chai* without any attempt to differentiate between them.

On the other hand, there was general agreement that Berliquet deserved its promotion to *cru classé* status. The vineyard is superbly placed on the plateau and *côte* adjoining Magdelaine and Canon but had been vinified and bottled at the château only since 1978.

This revision proved a rude awakening for those who thought that the sole purpose of such an exercise was to promote, comfortably banishing any thoughts that promotion should be linked with the possibility of relegation. Personally I believe that in the long run the example of the 1985 revision will do good, and give a new credibility to the whole classification.

The 1985 St Emilion classification

Premiers Grands Crus Classés
(A) Ausone
Cheval Blanc
(B) Beauséjour (Duffau-Lagarrosse)
Belair
Canon
Clos Fourtet
Figeac
la Gaffelière
Magdelaine
Pavie
Trottevieille

Grands Crus Classés
l'Angélus
l'Arrosée
Balestard la Tonnelle
Beau-Séjour-Bécot
Bellevue
Bergat
Berliquet
Cadet-Piola
Canon-la-Gaffelière
Cap de Mourlin
Chauvin
Clos de l'Oratoire
Clos des Jacobins
Clos la Madeleine

Clos St Martin
la Clotte
la Clusière
Corbin
Corbin-Michotte
Couvent des Jacobins
Croque-Michotte
Curé-Bon la Madeleine
Dassault
la Dominique
Faurie de Souchard
Fonplégade
Fonroque
Franc-Mayne
Grand-Barrail-Lamarzelle-Figeac
Grand-Corbin
Grand-Corbin-Despagne
Grand-Mayne
Grand-Pontet
Guadet-St Julien
Haut Corbin
Haut Sarpe
Lamarzelle
Laniote
Larcis-Ducasse
Larmande
Laroze
Matras
Mauvezin
Moulin-du-Cadet
Pavie-Decesse
Pavie-Macquin
Pavillon-Cadet
Petit-Faurie-de-Soutard
le Prieuré
Ripeau
St Georges-Côte-Pavie

Sansonnet
la Serre
Soutard
Tertre-Daugay
la Tour-du-Pin-Figeac (Giraud-Bélivier)
la Tour-du-Pin-Figeac (Moueix)
la Tour-Figeac
Trimoulet
Troplong-Mondot
Villemaurine
Yon-Figeac

The *Premiers Grands Crus* are now much more uniform in their standards than was the case in the seventies. Pavie and Canon especially have made great strides, and there has also been a marked improvement at Clos Fourtet. The two weakest *crus*, Beauséjour (Duffau-Lagarrosse) and Trottevieille, also showed promising signs in the 1985 and 1986 vintages.

The sixty-three *Grands Crus Classés* are a much more disparate group, covering a wide range of qualities and styles, due both to varying standards of vinification and the many combinations of soil types to be found in St Emilion. (See the chapter on St Emilion for a fuller treatment.) In recent years I have been able to taste the 1978 to 1986 vintages of a wide range of these wines, and from this experience would pinpoint the following *crus* as consistently successful and achieving high standards in varying styles.

Angélus (especially since 1983)
Balestard-la-Tonnelle
Cap-de-Mourlin
Croque-Michotte
La Dominique
Haut-Sarpe
Clos des Jacobins
Larcis-Ducasse
Larmande
La Serre
Tertre-Daugay
La Tour-du-Pin-Figeac (Moueix)

La Tour-Figeac
Troplong-Mondot (since 1983)

In addition, there has been a notable improvement at Fonplégade (1983, 1985 and 1986) and Petit-Faurie-de-Soutard.

To the above list should now be added Beau-Séjour Bécot.

Apart from the above the following wines have also much impressed me, but I have not seen more than one or two recent vintages.

L'Arrosée
Corbin-Michotte
Couvent des Jacobins
Grand-Corbin-Despagne
Laniote
St-Georges-Côte-Pavie
Soutard

The only great wines of Bordeaux not to be classified are those of Pomerol, for the simple reason that the growers there have never wanted a classification, and indeed seem to have got on very well without one. They do, of course, recognize Pétrus as their peer, a wine *hors classe* which is now one of the great *premiers crus* of Bordeaux. After this, the following are now generally recognized as the greatest wines, and obtain the highest prices.

Certan-de-May
La Conseillante
L'Evangile
La Fleur-Pétrus
Gazin (underperforming until the late 1980s)
Lafleur
Latour à Pomerol
Petit-Village
Trotanoy
Vieux-Château-Certan

So far, I have concentrated almost exclusively on the leading growths. This is because these are the wines which create the most interest and at the same time are the simplest to categorize. As has already been pointed out, the lines have always been much more blurred in the lower echelons, which is precisely why regular scrutiny and revision are necessary. I feel that such a review of the state of play in the classification controversy would be incomplete without looking at some of the unclassified growths in the Médoc, apart from those already mentioned as meriting classified status.

It should first be noticed that there now exists a gap in the classification system, in that a number of leading unclassified growths are not members of the Syndicat des Crus Grands Bourgeois et Crus Bourgeois du Médoc, with the result that they did not feature in that Syndicat's new classification of 1966 (revised in 1978) which was not unreasonably limited to its own adherents. These include four of the six wines classified as *Crus Exceptionnels* in 1932: d'Angludet, Bel-Air-Marquis d'Aligre, La Couronne, and Villegeorge. It is interesting to note in passing that Villegeorge is the only growth classified as *Cru Exceptionnel* both in 1932 and in 1966. In addition, the following leading growths are also in the same limbo: in Labarde – Siran; in Soussans – La Tour de Mons; in Moulis – Gressier Grand Poujeaux; in St Julien – Gloria; in St Estèphe – de Pez. This is not to say, of course, that all these wines or only these wines should be accorded the accolade of a superior classification.

I have already mentioned the classifications of the *Bourgeois* growths of the Médoc, and I want to conclude this chapter by looking at the classifications of 1932 and 1966. Although they are two very different beasts, a comparison does throw up some interesting facts about the position of the lesser growths in the Médoc today.

The 1932 list was drawn up by five *courtiers*, or brokers, with the backing of the Bordeaux Chamber of Commerce and the Gironde Chamber of Agriculture. It consists of six *Crus Bourgeois Supérieurs Exceptionnels*, ninety-seven *Bourgeois Supérieurs* – all from the Haut-Médoc – and no fewer than 387 *Crus Bourgeois*, embracing both Haut-Médoc and Bas-Médoc. In 1962 the *Bourgeois* growths of the region formed themselves into a Syndicat, and this Syndicat then decided to establish a classification of its members to provide a guide to the current standing of these growths. The result was the 1966 classification, revised in 1978, with eighteen *Grands Bourgeois Exceptionnels*, forty-one *Grands Bourgeois* (including nine from the Bas-Médoc) and fifty-eight *Bourgeois*.

In addition, there are six properties listed as being reconstructed. Since 1978 a further sixty-one properties have joined the Syndicat, but have not been classified owing to problems with EEC regulations. At present the terms *Grand Bourgeois Exceptionnel* and *Grand Bourgeois* may not be used on labels.

As has already been pointed out, a number of leading unclassified growths who believed that they would or should be classified, did not join the Syndicat in 1962. It is also true that quite a number of smaller growths are not members. Nevertheless, the discrepancy between the number of growths in the 1932 list and that in the 1978 list does, to a large extent, reflect the contraction of the lesser vineyards.

The reconstruction that has occurred in the Médoc vineyards in the last decade is vividly illustrated by the fact that in the area as a whole, the area of AC vineyards in production rose by 42.7 per cent between 1975 and 1986. The largest increases were in the two largest *appellations* of Médoc and Haut-Médoc, up by 60 and 67 per cent respectively. Moulin was not far behind with 57 per cent, while the largest increase among the best *appellations* was 37 per cent in Margaux. On the other hand, St Julien and St Estèphe both show increases of under 12 per cent. But a study of the Médoc *appellations* taken from the 1978 declarations when considered in conjunction with figures which show the number of proprietors, shows how vineyards are increasingly in fewer hands. They also show the predominance of the leading growths in the Médoc context. Thus, in Pauillac, 753 hectares are classified growths against 88 for *Bourgeois* growths, 13 for *Artisan* growths, and 185 for the *Coopérative*. In Margaux, the picture is 721 hectares of classified growths, 256 *Bourgeois* growths and only 87 for *Artisan* growths.

Will there be a new classification of the Médoc? The INAO has been very busy in Graves and St Emilion, but the Médoc has proved a stumbling block. Their carefully leaked proposals in 1960 met with a storm of protest, and have not been heard of since, despite numerous rumours that something was about to happen. The only event has been the decree of 1973, placing Mouton among the first growths – hardly a controversial topic. Perhaps one day, sooner or later, something will happen. Meanwhile you and I can continue to enjoy ourselves by following in Alex Lichine's footsteps, and making our own personal classifications.

4

The Médoc: Margaux and St Julien

The Médoc as we know it today covers an enormous area stretching from Le Taillan and Blanquefort in the south to Soulac in the north, a distance of 80 km (50 miles). The best vineyards extend along a fairly narrow ridge with a wider plateau of good but lesser vineyards behind and parallel to them. The area is divided into eight by the laws of *Appellation Contrôlée*. These divisions comprise the Haut-Médoc, within which are the separate *appellations* of Margaux, St Julien, Pauillac, St Estèphe, Moulis and Listrac, and Médoc, traditionally known as the Bas-Médoc. Until well into the second half of the nineteenth century, it was usual to find a rather different division applied, that of the *arrondissements* of Bordeaux and Lesparre. The boundary between these two administrative regions was drawn along the southern boundary of the communes of St Julien and St Laurent.

This is both the largest and most important red wine district of Bordeaux. Indeed, for many Englishmen, Médoc is almost synonymous with claret, an attitude which reflects both the ascendancy enjoyed by the region during the nineteenth century and our own traditional conservatism. It was the building up of large estates by wealthy Bordeaux families in the eighteenth century, and proximity to the city and port of Bordeaux, that gave the Médoc such an advantage over its rivals when the claret boom of the mid-nineteenth century came. This flying start is something the region has never wholly lost, through all its vicissitudes.

HAUT-MÉDOC

I do not intend to go through this area in strict geographical order as in a travelogue, but will deal first with the six most important communal *appellations*. Although all the wines of the Médoc possess a certain family resemblance, it is possible nevertheless to find within its boundaries variations of style as great as any among the red wines of Bordeaux. The common denominator is a certain crispness of definition on nose and palate. The wines have rather less alcohol and less body than their cousins across the river, but they develop and sustain with age a bouquet of exceptional purity and subtlety. They are slow to develop at first, and even small growths in good years may require two years in cask and three years in bottle before shaking off the brusqueness of youth to reveal some charm and finish. Many wine novices have been put off Médoc wines by attempting to consume them too young, and it is often surprisingly difficult for the unpractised palate to perceive the delicacy and character which is to come when youth has mellowed into maturity.

As a general rule, it may be said that the first line of vineyards towards the river produces wines with the most finesse and breed, while those from the plateau behind have most body and vigour but are less fine. Similarly, the wines in the south of the area have less tannin and more delicacy than those further north.

MARGAUX

This is one of the few examples of the name of a famous commune being extended to neighbours producing wines of a similar style, a practice common in Germany and much approved by all who seek simplification and a degree of logic in wine laws. Unfortunately, such common sense is rare, local interests tending to favour subdivisions rather than amalgamations. Vineyards from the communes of Labarde, Arsac and Cantenac to the south and from Soussans to the north are included now in the Margaux *appellation*.

The name of Margaux itself conjures up so many feelings and evokes such memories for any lover of claret. It is the only example in the region of a district whose name is taken from its most renowned growth. In the nineteenth century, the wines of Margaux were especially loved in England, and even today, with a new generation of wine drinkers, these wines have retained a special place of affection.

To capture the quintessence of the Margaux character in mere words is particularly hard. Its wines are delicately perfumed in youth and this

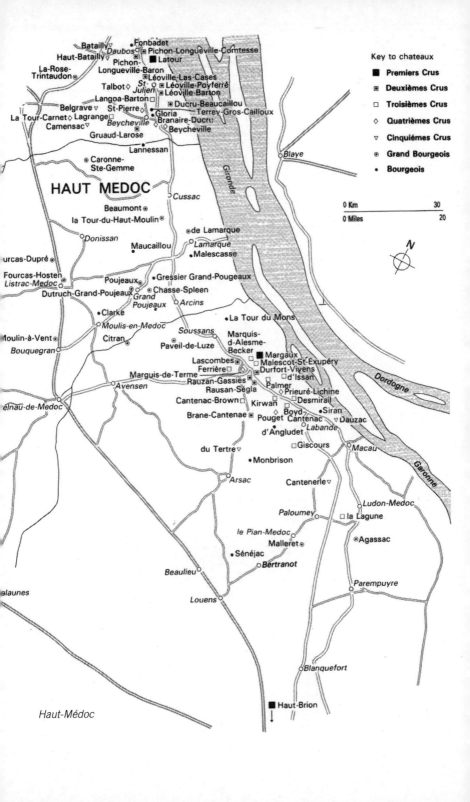

Batailly ▽
Fonbadet •
Haut-Batailly ▽
Daubos ○◇
Pichon-Longueville-Comtesse ⊡
Pichon-
Longueville-Baron ⊡
La-Rose-
Trintaudon •
Latour ■
Léoville-Las-Cases ⊡
Talbot ◇
St-
Julien ○
Léoville-Poyferré ⊡
Léoville-Barton ⊡
Langoa-Barton □
Belgrave ▽
St-Pierre ◇
Ducru-Beaucaillou ⊡
La-Tour-Carnet ◇ Lagrange □
Terrey-Gros-Cailloux
Camensac ▽
Gloria •
Beychevelle ◇
Branaire-Ducru ◇
Beychevelle •
Gruaud-Larose •
Lannessan •
Caronne-
Ste-Gemme ◉

HAUT MEDOC

Cussac •
Beaumont ◉
la Tour-du-Haut-Moulin ◉
Donissan ○
de Lamarque •
Maucaillou •
Lamarque •
Malescasse •

Gironde

urcas-Dupré ◉
Fourcas-Hosten ○
Listrac-Medoc ○
Poujeaux ◉
Gressier Grand-Pougeaux •
Dutruch-Grand-Poujeaux ○
Chasse-Spleen ◉
Grand
Poujeaux
Arcins •
Clarke •
La Tour du Mons •
Moulis-en-Medoc ○
Moulin-à-Vent ◉
Citran •
Soussans •
Bouquegran
Marquis-
d-Alesme-
Becker ◇
Paveil-de-Luze •
Margaux ■
Lascombes ⊡
Malescot-St-Exupéry ⊡
Ferrière □
Durfort-Vivens ⊡
Marquis-de-Terme ◇
d'Issan ◇
Rauzan-Gassies ⊡
Palmer ◇
Avensen ○
Rausan-Ségla ⊡
Prieuré-Lichine ◇
Cantenac-Brown □
Kirwan □
Desmirail □
élnau-de-Medoc ○
Brane-Cantenae ⊡
Boyd ◇
Siran •
Pouget Cantenac ◇
Dauzac ▽
d'Angludet •
Labande
du Tertre ▽
Giscours □
Macau ○
Monbrison •
Arsac ○
Cantenerle ▽
Ludon-Medoc •
Paloumey •
la Lagune □
le Pian-Medoc •
Malleret ◉
Agassac ◉
Sénéjac •
Bertranot •
Beaulieu ○
Parempuyre •
alaunes
Louens •

Dordogne

Garonne

Blaye •

Blanquefort •

Haut-Brion ■
↓

Haut-Médoc

Key to chateaux

■ Premiers Crus
⊡ Deuxièmes Crus
□ Troisièmes Crus
◇ Quatrièmes Crus
▽ Cinquièmes Crus
◉ Grand Bourgeois
• Bourgeois

0 Km   30
0 Miles   20

N

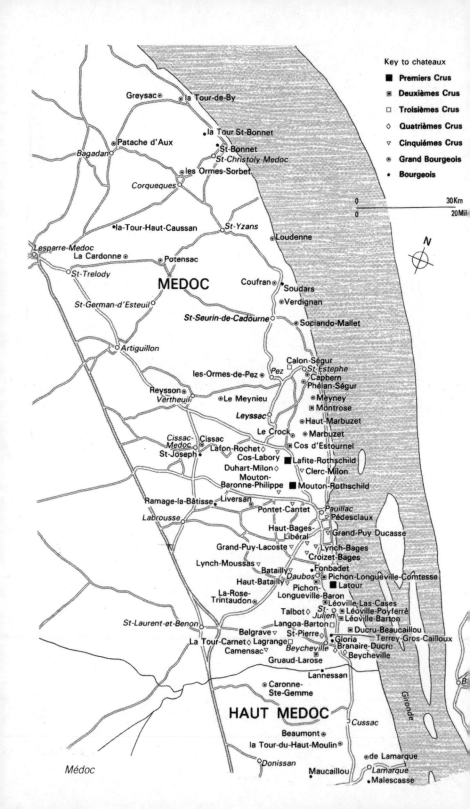

perfume fills out and deepens in the years of maturity. On the palate, although lacking somewhat in body, they fill the mouth with flavour at once delicate, refined and subtle, full of nuances and finesse. Often in youth their charm seems too insubstantial to survive into age, but this impression is wholly misleading. As the years pass they broaden out a little and take on fresh colours and textures. It is a change of key, as in some exquisite musical development when the theme is subtly transformed during the exposition, the colours become richer, the tone more authoritative, but the quintessence of the originally simple theme remains.

The vineyards of Margaux immediately strike the visitor by their almost white appearance. This is due to a light, fine, pebbly gravel which is responsible in part for the finesse and delicacy of these wines. There is, of course, considerable variety among the wines themselves. Generally speaking, the wines of Labarde, Cantenac and Arsac are rather fuller-flavoured, without quite the finesse of the wines from the exceptionally light, stony soil of Margaux itself. These wines might be described as the St Emilions of Médoc and it is often quite easy to confuse them with their cousins across the water, especially in youth. There is something of the same richness and softness of flavour – only their actual flavour when compared side by side invokes their true origin. Some growths in Margaux itself are even quite firm and powerful at first, but such individual differences will best be dealt with under the appropriate châteaux.

Château d'Angludet

Cru Bourgeois Supérieur Exceptionnel 1932. Owner: Monsieur and Madame Peter A. Sichel. 30 hectares. 12,000 cases. CS 45%, Mer 35%, CF 15%, PV 5%

This is an example of a growth which was once regarded as a classified growth, failed to be classified in 1855, and is now once more making a come-back to classified-growth status. In 1874, Féret records a melancholy state of affairs. The property, formerly one large and important growth, was divided among three different proprietors. Before the Revolution, it had been in the Legras family and was regarded as a fourth growth, but when the head of the family died in 1791 it was divided among four sons. It is significant that it was not mentioned in the best classifications of the 1820s or in Cocks's list of 1846. A revival began

THE OFFICIAL CLASSIFICATION OF THE GREAT GROWTHS OF THE GIRONDE:
CLASSIFICATION OF 1855

	COMMUNE	HECTARES	CASES
Premiers Crus (First Growths)			
Château Lafite	Pauillac	90	25,000
Château Latour	Pauillac	60	16,000
Château Mouton-Rothschild*	Pauillac	72	20,000
Château Margaux	Margaux	85	21,000
Château Haut-Brion	Pessac-Graves	41	12,000
*Decreed a first growth in 1973			
Deuxièmes Crus (Second Growths)			
Château Rausan-Ségla	Margaux	42	10,000
Château Rauzan-Gassies	Margaux	30	8,300
Château Léoville-Las Cases	St Julien	85	30,000
Château Léoville-Poyferré	St Julien	63	18,500
Château Léoville-Barton	St Julien	39	16,000
Château Durfort-Vivens	Margaux	20	5,500
Château Lascombes	Margaux	94	35,000
Château Gruaud-Larose	St Julien	82	35,000
Château Brane-Cantenac	Cantenac-Margaux	85	29,000
Château Pichon-Longueville-Baron	Pauillac	30	14,000
Château Pichon-Lalande	Pauillac	60	25,000
Château Ducru-Beaucaillou	St Julien	49	17,000
Château Cos d'Estournel	St Estèphe	54	18,000
Château Montrose	St Estèphe	67	23,000
Troisièmes Crus (Third Growths)			
Château Giscours	Labarde-Margaux	81	29,500
Château Kirwan	Cantenac-Margaux	31	11,300
Château d'Issan	Cantenac-Margaux	32	12,000
Château Lagrange	St Julien	49	19,000
Château Langoa-Barton	St Julien	20	8,000
Château Malescot-St-Exupéry	Margaux	34	15,000
Château Cantenac-Brown	Cantenac-Margaux	32	15,000
Château Palmer	Cantenac-Margaux	45	12,000
Château La Lagune	Ludon	55	25,000
Château Desmirail	Margaux	18	4,000
Château Calon-Ségur	St Estèphe	48	15,000
Château Ferrière	Margaux	5	4,500

	COMMUNE	HECTARES	CASES
Château Marquis-d'Alesme	*Margaux*	9	4,150
Château Boyd-Cantenac	*Margaux*	18	7,500

Quatrièmes Crus (Fourth Growths)

	COMMUNE	HECTARES	CASES
Château St-Pierre-Sevaistre	*St Julien*	20	5,000
Château Branaire-Ducru	*St Julien*	48	20,000
Château Talbot	*St Julien*	101	40,000
Château Duhart-Milon-Rothschild	*Pauillac*	50	12,500
Château Pouget	*Cantenac-Margaux*	10	3,500
Château La Tour-Carnet	*St Laurent*	30	
Château Lafon-Rochet	*St Estèphe*	45	12,000
Château Beychevelle	*St Julien*	72	25,000
Château Prieuré-Lichine	*Cantenac-Margaux*	60	25,000
Château Marquis-de-Terme	*Margaux*	35	12,000

Cinquièmes Crus (Fifth Growths)

	COMMUNE	HECTARES	CASES
Château Pontet-Canet	*Pauillac*	75	30,000
Château Batailley	*Pauillac*	50	22,000
Château Grand-Puy-Lacoste	*Pauillac*	45	12,000
Château Grand-Puy-Ducasse	*Pauillac*	36	17,500
Château Haut-Batailley	*Pauillac*	20	7,500
Château Lynch-Bages	*Pauillac*	80	28,000
Château Lynch-Moussas	*Pauillac*	25	12,500
Château Dauzac-Lynch	*Labarde-Margaux*	50	15,000
Château Mouton-Baronne-Philippe (formerly known as Mouton Baron Philippe)	*Pauillac*	50	15,000
Château du Tertre	*Arsac-Margaux*	48	14,000
Château Haut-Bages-Libéral	*Pauillac*	26	10,000
Château Pédesclaux	*Pauillac*	18	8,300
Château Belgrave	*St Laurent*	55	18,000
Château Camensac	*St Laurent*	60	20,000
Château Cos Labory	*St Estèphe*	12	6,700
Château Clerc-Milon	*Pauillac*	30	8,700
Château Croizet-Bages	*Pauillac*	22	8,500
Château Cantemerle	*Macau*	53	20,000

when two of the four portions came into the hands of Paul Promis, grandson of a former proprietor of Giscours, and by 1880 he had raised the production of his share from 25 to 45 tonneaux. At this time one part was called Domaine d'Angludet and the other part, now reunited under Jules Jadouin, was again known as Château d'Angludet. In 1891 Jadouin had the satisfaction of reuniting the property exactly a century after it was first divided.

By this time, the excellence of the wines of Angludet was firmly established again, and the growth fetched prices equal to those of classified wines. It was recognized that, with such excellent soil, the property had missed classification only through its unhappy division. During the period of this renaissance, England is frequently mentioned as one of the best markets for Angludet. At this time the production amounted to 150 tonneaux from the excellent vineyard which lies at the back of Cantenac and is partly framed by trees, offering prospects towards Giscours, Brane-Cantenac, Kirwan and Le Tertre.

After the Second World War, Angludet fell into a sad state of neglect, so that production declined to a few tonneaux. Happily, in 1961 the Sichel family acquired it and it became the home of Mr Peter Sichel. The château itself is a single-storey building dating from the eighteenth century, with some very interesting equestrian tapestries in the salon which have been fully restored.

As the completely reconstructed vineyard has matured, the wines have become more and more impressive. They always showed the finesse and breed one would have expected from such soil allied to meticulous winemaking. Now there is an additional dimension to the wines, a complexity and depth of flavour which was missing before. I find this consistently present, at least since 1978; this is a wine of great class, complex, full and stylish and, as usual, preferable to a good 1979 which is firmer, more powerful but less stylish. The 1980 is delicious, exceptionally good for the year, 1981 promises a fine future, with length, breed and middle fruit, and there is an exotic and complex 1982. The 1983, 1985, 1986, and 1989 are all superb, with marvellously long flavours and great "race", classic Margaux with exciting futures. The 1984 is very honourable in the context of the year, if a shade lean. I believe that d'Angludet has now come of age and is of clear cru classé standard.

CHÂTEAU BEL-AIR-MARQUIS-D'ALIGRE

Cru Bourgeois Supérieur Exceptionnel 1932. Owner: Pierre Boyer. 17 hectares. 4,500 cases. Mer 35%, CS 30%, CF 20%, PV 15%. Second label: Château Bel-Air-Marquis-de-Pomereu

This is the second of the Soussans growths which was proposed both by the INAO and Alexis Lichine for classified-growth status. Earlier, it had been named as one of the six *Crus Exceptionnels* of the *Crus Bourgeois*. By the end of the nineteenth century, wines of Bel-Air were highly esteemed and fetched prices on a par with third and fourth growths. The vineyard is beautifully situated on a plateau of light, pebbly soil, and has been reconstructed by the present proprietor, a perfectionist who makes his wines with great care and low yields. Only organic fertilizers are used in the vineyards. The wine has real Margaux breed and often a certain unctuousness combined with delicacy and finesse. The wines command high prices.

CHÂTEAU BOYD-CANTENAC

Troisième Cru Classé. Owner: Pierre Guillemet. 18 hectares. 7,500 cases. CS 67%, Mer 20%, CF 7%, PV 6%

This growth has had a strange and chequered history. It was classified as a third growth in 1855 and had appeared as a fourth growth in earlier unofficial classifications of the 1820s. In 1860 it lost the major part of its vineyards, which then became Brown-Cantenac. Soon after 1874, Château Boyd, now classified as a Margaux rather than a Cantenac, was bought by Monsieur Abel Laurent, owner of the château of the same name. He proceeded to sell its wines under the name of his own property, which then enjoyed a good reputation. But in 1910 the then proprietor, Monsieur Marcel Laurent, again claimed and won the right to sell Boyd-Cantenac separately as a third growth after a gap of some forty-five years. So it reappeared as a separate entity again in the 1922 edition of Cocks & Feret with a production of 25 tonneaux. Subsequently it was acquired by Monsieur Ginestet who, having sold the building to Château Margaux, made the Boyd wines at Lascombes. It now belongs to Monsieur Guillemet, proprietor of Château Pouget, and the *chai* and *cuvier* are on the opposite side of the road to Pouget. Until 1982 the two wines were vinified and matured in the same buildings but since the 1983 vintage Pouget has been moved out of the Boyd buildings and the two are now completely separated. The wines produced in the seventies were rich and supple in style, with the most successful being 1970, 1971, 1975, 1978 and 1979. But I have found more recent vintages tougher and more tannic. They will certainly take longer to mature, but will they actually be better, more enjoyable wines? This is a *cru* which is no longer of third-growth standing and must be marginal as a *cru classé*.

CHÂTEAU BRANE-CANTENAC

Deuxième Cru Classé. Owner: Lucien Lurton. 85 hectares. 29,000 cases. CS 70%, Mer 15%, CF 13%, PV 2%. Second label: Château Notton

This has long been a very large and important growth. It was the only property in Cantenac classified as a second growth in 1855. It owed its fame and importance to the work of the great viticulturist, Baron de Brane, who was also responsible for the rise of Mouton. After the sale of Mouton in 1830, the Baron devoted himself entirely to the improvement of Brane-Cantenac and its wines. Before its acquisition by Baron de Brane, it was known as de Gorce.

It does not today quite maintain its former position as the best wine in Cantenac, a position yielded almost without dispute to Palmer, but under its present proprietor, Monsieur Lurton, great progress has been made. The property, always large, is now one of the most productive in the whole of the Médoc. It occupies a magnificent plateau behind Cantenac and Margaux, and adjoining Angludet and Le Tertre, while the stark whiteness of the gravelly soil typifies the best of Margaux. The wine is very supple and elegant in style with considerable finesse, a quintessential Cantenac in contrast to the tannin and power of a Margaux such as Durfort. Thus, in spite of its high proportion of Cabernet Sauvignon, a good example of how soil influences the characteristics of grape varieties. The 1957 was one of the more agreeable and drinkable wines of that vintage, and the 1961 and 1962 were especially successful. They were followed by 1964, 1966 and 1967. The best vintages of the seventies were 1970 – more forward and charming than many – 1971, 1975 – one of the most attractive wines of the vintage for drinking by the time it was ten years old – a charming 1978 and a stylish, fleshy 1979. In the eighties, the 1981 is noticeably firmer in style than most Brane-Cantenacs of the previous decade, but retains the customary delicacy and grace. The 1982 is a great success, with richness and more concentration than usual.

I thought it better than Palmer in cask. The 1983 is rather light in style again, and is certainly outshone by Durfort. The 1984 was a success here and is worth watching for early drinking – very elegant and charming but with good compact fruit. The 1985 has the breed and charm of the year and the *cru*, while 1986 in its early stages was rather dominated by tannin. Fine classics, with great concentration, were produced in 1988 and 1989. The overall picture, then, is one of consistency, with rather more concentration added to the traditional charm and breed in recent vintages.

CHÂTEAU CANTENAC-BROWN

Troisième Cru Classé. Owner: Société Civile du Château Cantenac-Brown. Administrator: Jean-Michel Capes, 32 hectares. 15,000 cases. CS 75%, Mer 15%, CF 8%, PV 2%. Secondary labels: Château Canuet (Margaux), Château Lamartine (Bordeaux Supérieur)

In the 1855 classification, no mention is made of Cantenac-Brown, but only of Château Boyd in the commune of Cantenac, with "*plusieurs propriétaires*". The Brown name comes from John Lewis Brown, son of a well-known Bordeaux *négociant* of the day, of English origin. He was also an artist famous for his animal pictures, and was responsible for building the château, dubiously described as being in the *Renaissance anglaise* style – a Victorian pile would be a more apt description! In 1860, the vineyard was sold to Monsieur Armand Lalande, and from thenceforth the property has been known as Cantenac-Brown. It was Armand Lalande, who was really responsible for establishing the reputation of this *cru*. The Lalande family have an ancient and continuous history in the Bordeaux wine trade and were *courtiers* before and after the Revolution; Armand Lalande then founded the firm of *négociants* which still bears his name. In 1968 the château was sold to the firm of de Luze, which soon afterwards was bought by the British paper firm of Bowater. When the firm was sold, the property remained with the du Vivier family, who sold it in January 1987 to La Compagnie du Midi, an insurance firm. New installations were speedily prepared in time for the 1987 vintage.

Although the production of Château Boyd was given as only 35 tonneaux in 1860, by 1881 the separated Cantenac-Brown was making 130 tonneaux, and in 1893 achieved 250 tonneaux. The Château has lost some of the considerable importance it formerly enjoyed. The wines today lack the elegance and finish of the best wines of Cantenac, and I find a rather coarse streak in them. It will be interesting to see what the new owners can achieve here, and whether the defects of this *cru* are due to shortcomings in the soil, as some allege, or in the wine-making. In 1985 the du Vivier family bought the *cru bourgeois* property of Canuet from the Rooryck family. This was sold to the Compagnie du Midi along with Cantenac-Brown, and they have decided to use this as the second wine, in place of La Fontanelle.

CHÂTEAU DAUZAC (FORMERLY SPELT DAUZATS)
Cinquième Cru Classé. Owner: MAIF. 50 hectares. 15,000 cases. CS 60%, Mer 30%, CF 5%, PV 5%

The name came from the first recorded owner, Pétrus d'Auzac, who was granted the land by Richard Comte de Poitiers, better known in later life as Richard Coeur de Lion. The original deed is preserved in the archives of the Tower of London. There are records of the vine being cultivated here in the thirteenth century, one of the earliest to be recorded in the Médoc. By this time it belonged to the Abbaye de Ste Croix in Bordeaux, which also owned Carbonnieux in Graves. In the Middle Ages, the property was also known as Château Labarde, a name now used for the second wine. The foundations of the original château, pulled down at the end of the seventeenth century, were uncovered when the new *cuvier* was being built in 1980. This is a growth which did not assume importance until the middle of the nineteenth century. It is not mentioned in Cocks's classification as late as 1846, but was classified a fifth growth in 1855, when it belonged to a Monsieur Wiebrock and produced between 50 and 60 tonneaux. At an earlier date, the château, an eighteenth-century building of pleasing proportions, had been the home of Jean-Baptiste Lynch, although the vineyard does not seem to have excited much attention at this time. The great age of Dauzac came in 1863 when it passed into the hands of Nathaniel Johnston, a member of the famous family of that name of Irish-Scottish ancestry. In this period, the firm of *négociants* was actually run firstly by his father and then by his brother, Harry Scott Johnston. Nathaniel Johnston was a notable figure in the Médoc of his day. He had qualified as a civil engineer and was very active in the Société d'Agriculture de la Gironde, whose gold medal he was awarded. He was also the proprietor of Ducru-Beaucaillou and ran this property and

Dauzac in harness. It was here that Bordeaux mixture was first successfully tried to combat mildew, the scourge of the 1880s. In spite of his great interest in these properties and in all matters connected with viticulture, Nathaniel Johnston also found time to stand for the National Assembly in 1871, to which he was duly elected. During his proprietorship, wines from the *palus* of this estate were used to make a well-known sparkling wine known as Royal Médoc Mousseux.

From the description of the wines of Dauzac at this period they seem to have resembled those of other wines of the commune such as Giscours. In recent years, however, the wine has been rather atypical of Labarde or Margaux, a little firm and austere, lacking the mellowness and fruit usually associated with this region.

In 1965 the property was acquired by Monsieur William Alain Burke Miailhe, the proprietor of the neighbouring Château Siran, whose wines now have a better reputation than those of Dauzac. Monsieur Miailhe is also part-proprietor of Pichon-Lalande and a partner in Palmer. At this time he managed his family's interest in all these properties. As the vineyards of Siran and Dauzac are contiguous, the advantages of running the two estates as one seemed obvious. But then in 1978, as part of the settlement of a family dispute, Dauzac, together with the Miailhe champagne house St Marceaux, was sold to the Chatellier family, owners of Les Grands Champagnes de Reims, which also includes the firms of Abel Lepitre and Georges Goulet. They built a new *cuvier* and *chai*, which also has an underground, air-conditioned maturing cellar. Then in 1989 they sold to an insurance group, MAIF.

With more money now available for investment and Professor Peynaud to advise (as he did during the Miailhe regime), progress has clearly been made, but, personally I still find the wines have a certain coarseness and lack the finesse of good Margaux – and a tendency to over-oak makes matters worse. I tasted the 1980, 1979 and 1978 in November 1983 and again in August 1987. Time has not improved them. I still found the 1978 the best of a disappointing bunch. With the help of a lot of new oak, 1988 and 1989 do look more promising.

CHÂTEAU DESMIRAIL
Troisème Cru Classé. Owner: Lucien Lurton. 18 hectares. 4,000 cases. CS 80%, Mer 10%, CF 9%, PV 1%

This is a property which was literally dismembered during the Depression but happily has just been reborn under the devoted care of Lucien Lurton, the largest vineyard owner of Margaux, and indeed of the Médoc. Originally Desmirail formed part of the great estate of the Marquis de Rausan, but was part of the dowry of a Mademoiselle Rausan de Ribail to Jean Desmirail. By the second half of the eighteenth century, Desmirail was fetching the price of a *troisième cru*, and this standing was confirmed in 1855. At this time it belonged to Monsieur Sipère, the *régisseur* of Château Margaux, and he it was who built the château in 1860, a flamboyant affair in what was called "*style Louis XIII*", the French equivalent of Victorian Jacobean. In 1903 it was bought by Robert Mendelssohn, a Berlin banker, who was not only related to the composer, but also had Bordeaux connections, his maternal grandfather having been the poet Biarnez, celebrated as the laureate of the *grands crus* of Bordeaux. The estate was sequestrated as enemy property in 1914 and eventually sold to a Monsieur Michel. He it was who, in 1938, sold the château to Paul Zuger (since when it has been the château for Marquis d'Alesme), and the brand and the vines in Cantenac to Palmer, and the vines in Arsac to Lucien Lurton's father.

Lucien Lurton gradually reassembled the vineyards of Desmirail as they had existed prior to 1820 and at last, in 1980, made an exchange with Palmer, acquiring a final two hectares and the right to the name. He bought some attractive eighteenth-century buildings in the village of Cantenac and these are now the château and *chai* of the reborn Desmirail. The first wine was the 1981. In style, the wines have the Margaux "*race*", and are perfumed, soft and elegant, in spite of the high proportion of Cabernet Sauvignon. They have less concentration and depth than Brane-Cantenac but are undeniably of *cru classé* status. I have been particularly struck by the charm and style of every vintage so far made, even the 1984. The outstanding vintages so far are 1983 and 1985, while I detected a lovely aroma of damsons in the 1986. Certainly a wine to watch.

CHÂTEAU DEYREM-VALENTIN
Cru Bourgeois 1932. Owner: Jean Sorge. 10 hectares. 5,000 cases. CS 45%, Mer 45%, CF 5%, PV 5%

This vineyard is situated in the best part of Soussans, and neighbours include Lascombes, Malescot and the two Labégorces. The Sorge family has owned the *cru* since 1928, and Jean Sorge is a working resident proprietor. The wines are rather light in body, but have the bouquet and finesse associated with Margaux.

CHÂTEAU DURFORT-VIVENS
Deuxième Cru Classé. Owner: Gonzague Lurton. 20 hectares. 5,500 cases. CS 80%, CF 12%, Mer 8%. Second label: Domaine de Cure-Bourse

This famous growth has also had a rather chequered history. It originally belonged to the family of Durfort de Duras, illustrious as a military family during the seventeenth and eighteenth centuries. Apart from Durfort, they also owned the fortified château at Blanquefort. The last member of the family was the Duc de Duras and the last Seigneur of Blanquefort. As general in command of the National Guard in the Gironde at the time of the Revolution of 1789, he made great efforts to keep this body loyal to the Royalist cause before being forced to emigrate. He finally died in England in 1800. In 1824 a new proprietor, Monsieur Vivens, added his name to that of Durfort and this has remained unchanged ever since. In 1895 the vineyard was acquired by Monsieur Delor, head of the Bordeaux shipping house of the same name. More recently it belonged to the Ginestets who sold it in 1961 to Monsieur Lurton, the proprietor of Brane-Cantenac

In the past, this growth has produced rather powerful wines, maturing fairly slowly, of the Rauzan type rather than the Lascombes type. Now, under the new proprietor, the vineyard has been reconstituted and the fruits of this are beginning to show. During the sixties and much of the seventies Durfort was more powerful and denser than its stablemate Brane-Cantenac, but lacked its finesse and breed. It also needs longer to show its real qualities. The most successful vintages during this interim period for Durfort were 1966, 1971 and 1975, all vintages where the concentration of the year produced fine wines of real style in the end. More recently the great successes have been 1978, 1981, 1982 and 1983 (which really outshines Brane-Cantenac), while 1985, 1986, 1988 and 1989 show very great promise. The comparison with Brane is inevitable since they are under the same management, and whereas Brane was usually a clear winner, now that Durfort has found the fruit and richness to match its tannin the competition is far keener, and the difference has become one of a contrast of styles rather than simply one of quality.

CHÂTEAU FERRIÈRE

Troisième Cru Classé. Owners: Madame André Durand-Feuillerat (héritiers). 5 hectares. 4,500 cases, CS 47%, Mer 33%, PV 12%, CF 8%

This old vineyard in the heart of Margaux now has the distinction of being the smallest surviving growth of the 1855 classification. Others have been smaller but are now larger, like Marquis d'Alesme, or were small and have been absorbed, like Dubignon, but Ferrière has always been small and remains unaltered. In 1860 an average of 10 to 15 tonneaux was recorded. After the phylloxera, 20, and then 25, tonneaux were made.

One remarkable feature of the growth is that it has been in the possession of only two families for over 200 years. The Ferrière family owned the estate to which they gave their name from the middle of the eighteenth century until 1914. Dutch in origin, they were an important and wealthy family of Bordeaux merchants. Gabriel Ferrière, who was a *courtier royal* and *officier des chasses du Roi*, left the property in 1777 to his cousin of the same name. He and his brother Jean were bourgeois of Bordeaux but also held a number of official positions; they were imprisoned under the Terror, but in 1795 Jean became Mayor of Bordeaux. Henri Ferrière was the last member of the family to own the property.

The purchaser in 1914 was Monsieur Armand Feuillerat, the proprietor of Marquis de Terme, and he gave it to his daughter in 1921, who is now Madame André Durand, the present proprietor. In recent years the vineyard has been leased to Château Lascombes where the wine is now made, but it is quite separate from Lascombes, and the wine is distinctly different. It is characterized by a most distinctive and powerful bouquet, being full-flavoured and yet elegant. The 1961 and 1962 were particularly successful and were made available in England for the first time in many years. But the wine these days is mostly sold in France to the restaurant trade. The 1847 has long been one of the legendary wines of Bordeaux.

CHÂTEAU GISCOURS

Troisième Cru Classé. Owner: GFA du Château Giscours. Administrator: Pierre Tari.
81 hectares. 20,000 cases. CS 53%, Mer 42%, PV 5%

This important property lies in the commune of Labarde. The records go back to 1552 when Seigneur de la Bastide sold it to Pierre de l'Horme. Before the Revolution, it belonged to the Saint-Simon family but was confiscated by the state during the Revolution. In 1793, it was acquired for two Americans, John Gray and Jonathan Davis of Boston.

The great era of Giscours as a vineyard began when it was purchased in 1845 by J.-P. Pescatore, a banker, for the sum of 500,000 frs (approx. £100,000). In 1847 he secured the services of Pierre Skawinski to manage the estate. This remarkable man was one of the great agriculturalists of the Médoc in the nineteenth century, and it was largely due to men like him that such strides were made in the region during this period. Skawinski himself was a Pole born in Lublin in 1812. He studied at the Ecole Agricole under Grignon, and then managed a property on the Loire near Montrichard. For fifty years, first under Pescatore and then under the Cruses, he managed Giscours, and it was under his management that Giscours became one of the finest and most sought-after of the third growths. He invented, in 1860, a special plough for the vineyards, which bore his name, and in 1882 he began the first experiments in combating mildew. The extent of his influence may be gauged by the fact that his three sons managed at various times Pontet-Canet, Léoville-Poyferré, Cantenac-Brown, Léoville-Las Cases, La Couronne (Pauillac), Lamartine (Cantenac), Sénilhac (St Seurin de Cadourne) and Laujac (Bégadan).

The château itself was built by Monsieur Promis in 1837 and replaced an ancient and important château of historic interest. Later, under the Cruses, a large range of farm buildings and a new *cuvier* were constructed. During this great period Giscours consistently made about 100 tonneaux. The Cruses having sold the property in 1913, Giscours, like so many others, went through a bad period between the wars and by the post-war period production had fallen to 20 tonneaux. In 1954 the present proprietor, Monsieur Nicolas Tari, acquired Giscours, having formerly been a wine-maker on a considerable scale in the Oran district of Algeria. Under the new regime, the vineyard has been reconstructed and enlarged so that this is now one of the most productive estates in the

Médoc. In 1974, an agreement was made with Gilbey-Loudenne for the exclusive worldwide distribution of the wine, a great act of faith in the future, given the situation at that time. An interesting feature of the agreement is that one-third of the crop is sold in instalments over two years. This protects both buyer and seller from speculative movements of the markets.

At its best, Giscours is a most attractive wine distinguished by a delicately perfumed bouquet of elegance and finesse. In January 1987 Pierre Tari, who has now taken over responsibility for Giscours from his father, brought a bottle of the 1865 vintage to Houston, Texas, for a special lunch. It had come from the Lafite cellar and had been re-corked in 1985. It was only pale tawny in colour and the nose was mushroomy and sweet, yet the flavour was still long and delicate with a lacy texture but, more amazingly perhaps, it actually filled out after half an hour in the decanter, instead of dying as one could have expected; a rare testimony to the longevity of Bordeaux wines. The 1899 and the 1929 were both fine examples of these great years. In more recent years, the 1953 was delightful and the 1955 more attractive than many wines of this vintage, with considerable finesse. There followed a period when, with the greatly increased production and rather young vines, the wine was not always consistent and sometimes lacked the distinction of past vintages, but as the vineyard acquired maturity so the wine improved, and the growth once again occupied an important place in the Médoc. The excellent 1966 was followed by a good 1970, an especially fine 1971 and an above-average 1973. The recent form has been very consistent. The 1976 has a roasted character and tannic finish to remind us of the exceptional heat of this vintage. The 1978 has well-balanced richness and tannin while the 1979 has been slow to develop and was still rather tannic and tough in October 1986. The 1980 is a delicious example of the year with finesse and breed. The 1981 has a lovely flavour with great charm and good structure. The 1982 is very powerful with considerable tannin and fruit, a fine *vin de garde*; in contrast, 1983 is developing more quickly, with attractive, fleshy fruit. The 1984 is frankly disappointingly lean and needs early drinking. The 1985 has lots of ripe fruit and charm and should make a delicious bottle. I sometimes feel that these recent vintages have less finesse and breed than in the past, and their power can sometimes seem coarse-grained.

Pierre Tari, as well as running Giscours, is also a tireless publicist for Bordeaux, and for his own wine. He was founder and first President of the Union des Grands Crus de Bordeaux, founder and Vice-President of the Groupement d'Intérêt Economique des Vins du Médoc, as well as Secretary-General of the Association of the Crus Classés of 1855.

CHÂTEAU LA GURGUE

Cru Bourgeois Supérieur 1932. Owner: Société Civile du Château La Gurgue. Administrator: Madame Bernadette Villars. 12 hectares. 5,000 cases. CS 70%, Mer 25%, PV 5%

This well-placed vineyard shares with Desmirail the distinction of being the closest neighbour to Château Margaux on its western boundary. In 1978 it was acquired by Monsieur Jacques Merland, the dynamic owner of Chasse-Spleen and therefore benefits from the talents of his daughter, Madame Bernadette Villars, a qualified oenologist of rare talent and enthusiasm. Things were so bad when she took over that the 1975 had been refused the Margaux *appellation*. Altogether nearly a million francs have been spent in recent years in totally renovating the property.

Under this new regime, the wines are rather tough and massive at first, but develop a commendable degree of breed, character and balance. This came through well in an excellent 1980, which was lovely and full of flavour but also light and elegant. Even more successful is the 1981, combining richness with breed and a fine character. The 1982 is rich and opulent but still far from ready when four years old. The 1983 has the power and firmness found in many of the best Margaux in this year, but needs time. The 1984 showed rather tough and austere, and a shade lean when two years old, and the 1985 has lots of extract and power, a promising wine. The 1986 was very scented in cask, with considerable richness and fat, yet very firm and tannic behind. The character is forthright, but there is charm as well, promising an impressive future. So this is very much a *cru* to watch. There is clearly the potential to do something impressive here.

CHÂTEAU D'ISSAN

Troisième Cru Classé. Owner: Madame Emmanuel Cruse. 32 hectares. 12,000 cases. CS 75%, Mer 25%

This ancient property can be traced back to the period of the English occupation. In the thirteenth century, a fortress called Château Lamothe de Cantenac was erected which was replaced in the seventeenth century by the present château. Before the Revolution, the property belonged to the ancient and noble family of Foix-Candale. It is interesting to note that in a classification of 1824 the château is referred to as Château de Candale. The rise in the value of vineyards is well illustrated by the various sales of Issan during the nineteenth century. Monsieur Duluc bought it from the Foix-Candale family in 1825 for 255,000 frs. It passed to his heirs in 1859 for 470,000 frs and was sold by them to Monsieur Gustave Roy in 1866 for 790,000 frs. After it became a Société Vinicole, the château continued to be administered by the Roy family until it was purchased by the Cruse family in 1945, and is now the home of Madame Emmanuel Cruse whose husband had to undertake the complete restoration of the château in 1952–3 when the ancient fabric threatened to collapse.

The vineyard and château are situated just below the *route du Médoc* as one leaves Cantenac for Margaux, and part of the vineyard is surrounded by a fine old stone wall. The château itself is certainly one of the oldest and most interesting in the Médoc, and above the gateway of the château is carved the proud motto *Regum Mensis Arisque Deorum* – "For the tables of kings and the altars of the gods". The original chai with its fine timbered roof has now been restored and is used each year for concerts during the "Mai Musical".

The wine of Issan has always been considered rather untypical of Margaux, owing to the particularity of the soil. Edouard Féret described it as having the power, fleshiness and colour of a St Julien, and the same is true today. This growth, the favourite wine of the Emperor Franz Josef, was also very popular in England, but for many years was seldom seen in this country. Now, with a welcome revival in the fortunes of the château, this excellent wine has become much more widely known and appreciated. Madame Cruse's son Lionel, until the crisis of 1974 the managing director of the Cruse *négociant* business, then began devoting his attentions towards improving the wine and seeing that it was better distributed. In 1983 he arranged a tasting of the wines of d'Issan for me, going back to 1970. This showed that in spite of a worthy 1970 and a surprisingly delicious 1973, the turning point had come in 1979, which achieved body, fruit and power with real "*race*" – discernibly better than the 1978. Since then, the 1980 has been exceptionally successful for the year, developing charming fruit while having more firmness and structure than most 1980s. The 1981 is fine but slow-developing, a good example from an underestimated year. There is a splendid 1982 of great finesse and power, a real *vin de garde*, and an almost equally powerful 1983 of great promise. The 1984 is much lighter and is developing more quickly than the 1980. The 1985 and 1986 here should prove a fascinating pair in a few years; both look like making superb bottles for long maturing.

This is certainly one of the most improved wines in Médoc and thoroughly deserves its fast-growing reputation. Older vintages which were outstanding were 1945, Emmanuel Cruse's first vintage – only 100 cases were produced! A magnum of 1959 at the château was superb in October 1985, but a Harvey's-bottled example tasted in 1987 was dry and tough. The 1961 has real depth of flavour and breed.

CHÂTEAU KIRWAN

Troisième Cru Classé. Owner: Schröder and Schÿler. 31 hectares. 11,300 cases.
CS 40%, Mer 30%, CF 20%, PV 10%

This is another property in Cantenac; it takes its name from an Irish family who, like the Lynchs, hailed from Galway. It had belonged to the Seigneur de la Salles until a Kirwan married his daughter in 1750, giving his name to the property. He was the first proprietor to take a personal interest in the running of it. Unhappily, Kirwan was a victim of the Terror, being guillotined in 1792. The château acquired a great reputation in the nineteenth century, being placed at the head of the third growths in 1855 and subsequently achieving prices comparable to a second growth. In 1881 the proprietor, Camille Godard, died leaving the property to the city of Bordeaux. In 1901, the firm of Schröder and Schÿler acquired the monopoly of the crop, and purchased the vineyard in 1925. It was here that the first of the many artesian wells was successfully drilled in the Médoc, where there had always been a great shortage of water. Its depth is 85 m (approx. 225 ft).

Kirwan was one of the last classified growths never to be château-bottled, the wine being kept and bottled in Schröder and Schÿler's Bordeaux cellars. This practice ended with the 1966 vintage, 1967 being the first to be château-bottled. The reputation of this growth has suffered in the last forty years, and the wine no longer occupies the exalted place it held in the nineteenth century; it is seldom seen in England nowadays. Since 1972 Schröder and Schÿler have carried out extensive replantings and improvements. New wood was used as part of the cask maturation for the first time for the 1978 vintage. There has certainly been a major effort to upgrade Kirwan. The wines tend to be deep-coloured and powerful but I find them rather over-oaked now, which gives some of the wines a rather dry finish and hides the Margaux charm, making them seem rather coarse. But good wines are being made, especially in 1979, 1982, 1983 and 1985. The 1978 is lighter, less intense in style. Certainly a *cru* to watch.

CHÂTEAU LABÉGORCE (MARGAUX)

Cru Bourgeois Supérieur 1932. Owner: Hubert Perrodo. 29 hectares. 11,000 cases. CS 55%, Mer 40%, CF 5%

CHÂTEAU LABÉGORCE-ZÉDÉ

Cru Bourgeois Supérieur 1932. GFA Labégorce Zédé. Administrator: Luc Thienpont. 26 hectares. 9,500 cases. CS 50%, Mer 35%, CF 10%, PV 5%. Second label: Château de l'Amiral

Because of the confusion which these two similar names are bound to cause, it seems sensible to deal with them together. There can be no doubt that at one time they formed a single property, the origins of which have been traced back to the fourteenth century. Deeds show that it belonged to the noble family of La Bégorce in 1332. It passed through a number of noble hands before the Revolution, including the de Mons who took the title of Seigneur de Labégorce in 1728. By the middle of the nineteenth century we find Capelle, formerly Abbé Gorsse and de Gorsse, the property of the widow de Gorsse, and Zédé, the property of Emile Zédé, all at Soussans, while in Margaux, l'Abbé Gorsse was also the property of widow Gorsse. The mixture of Soussans and Margaux seems to have been more a question of the position of the houses rather than the vineyards. There are vineyards in both communes, and even in the case of Zédé, much of the vineyard is in fact in Margaux.

The present Labégorce is descended from the Capelle formerly Abbé Gorsse, and its prosperity principally dates from its acquisition in 1865 by a Monsieur Fortune Beaucourt who greatly improved the vineyards and the buildings so that the production rose from 50 to 60 tonneaux in the 1860s, and to 80 to 90 tonneaux at the end of the century. After Monsieur Beaucourt's death, production gradually declined, although the château maintained its excellent reputation.

The Condoms took over in 1965, and Jean-Robert Condom in turn took over the management from his parents in 1978. There have been improvements and modernization of the vinification, as well as an increase in the use of new oak in the cask maturation. The wines are fruity and attractive, maturing fairly quickly. The 1981 was very enjoyable by 1985. The standard is of a good *cru bourgeois*, but is not outstanding. Distribution is undertaken by Dourthe Frères, but there is also *vente directe*. In 1989 the property again changed hands. The newcomer is a French oil tycoon who loves wine. The château, built in the 1830s in the style of Louis XVI, is attractive and has nothing *bourgeois* about it. The vineyards are in the communes of Margaux and Soussans.

L'Abbé Gorsse de Gorsse remained in the possession of the widow de Gorsse and then of her daughter until nearly the end of the nineteenth century, when it was bought by Edouard Peres who remained the proprietor until the Second World War. The vineyard is at present being reconstituted.

Labégorce-Zédé belonged to Admiral Zédé and his heirs until the inter-war period, and the production has now been restored to a figure approaching what was achieved in its heyday at the turn of the century. Recent tastings of these wines suggest that Labégorce-Zédé is now the best of the three. It has the finesse and distinction of a fine Margaux, rather in the style of d'Angludet, but with a little less depth of flavour at present. The difference has been most marked since Luc Thienpont took over in 1979. About one-third new wood is now being used, and the wine supports it without dryness. This is very much a *cru* on the upward path. The largest part of the vineyards is in Soussans.

CHÂTEAU LASCOMBES

Deuxième Cru Classé. Owner: Bass-Charrington. Administrator: Dominique Befve. 94 hectares. 35,000 cases. CS 65%, Mer 30%, CF 3%, PV 2%. Second label: Château Segonnes

This property was once part of Durfort and takes its name from the Chevalier Lascombes, an eighteenth-century *Procureur du Roi* at the admiralty. As late as 1860 it was still described as Domaine de Lascombes. At the time of the classification it comprised a small vineyard producing only some 10 to 15 tonneaux. This rose to 30 to 35 tonneaux under the direction of the Chaix-d'Est-Ange family who enlarged the vineyard. During the last thirty years of the nineteenth century the reputation and quality of Lascombes prospered. The period after the First World War was an unhappy one, seeing many changes of ownership. In 1951 Alexis Lichine persuaded a syndicate of largely American friends to buy the property, and after Lichine's departure from the company, Bass-Charrington purchased control in 1971. By 1951 the château was in a poor state. The quality and reputation of the wines were at a low ebb, the vineyard neglected. The vineyard has now been both restored and much enlarged. There was a big initial improvement in the quality of the wines, but the combination of a great increase in production and the departure of Lichine depressed the quality for years. Now there are signs of improvement.

The main part of the vineyard is situated in the best part of Margaux, the soil being light and stony. The wines at their best have real delicacy and finesse; those of recent vintages tend to be on the light side, probably owing to the reconstruction of the vineyard. The château, a late nineteenth-century edifice with towers and turrets, has been restored and decorated in a startlingly modern manner. Lichine started, during the summer, an exhibition of modern paintings under the general heading of La Vigne et le Vin, which is one of the features of the Médoc and has been continued now at Maucaillou.

Some old vintages of Lascombes are charming and show the breed and style which the growth traditionally had. Of those I have tasted, the 1892 was particularly remarkable, with the depth of colour of 1982, but much browner. It had a superbly powerful and rich bouquet, and was a wine of amazing completeness and majesty, unbowed in its seventy-third year, comparable certainly to some of the 1899s and 1900s I have had. I shall always remember drinking it with Alexis Lichine in his charming dining-room at the Prieuré. He has always been the most generous of men with his great bottles. In later years, the 1926 and 1929 were both particularly fine.

Under Lichine, the 1953 and 1961 were the great successes. Both the 1964 and the 1962 promised much in cask but have been rather disappointing since they were bottled. After this Lascombes went through a lean period. The wines seemed diluted and lacking in breed. More recently there has been an improvement. The 1979 produced a good example of the year, ripe and quite luscious if a little simplistic. There was a good 1980, quite full-bodied and attractive for early drinking, if short. The 1981 is powerful and concentrated with definite promise. The 1982 is deep-coloured, perfumed, tannic and rich, a wine of character and some promise, and 1983 has the power and tannin found in Margaux in this year, but seems short on middle richness. The 1985 is, again, tough but has lots of body and is promising. With 1986 I found more finesse and breed than for a long time, allied to great richness in fruit and ripe tannins, while 1989 looks even better – perhaps a pointer to a brighter future.

CHATEAU MALESCOT-ST-EXUPERY

Troisième Cru. Classé. Owner: Roger Zuger. 34 hectares. 15,000 cases. CS 50%, Mer 35%, CF 10%, PV 5%. Secondary labels: Château de Loyac, Domaine du Balardin

At the time of the 1855 classification, Malescot was an ancient but very small domain, producing 20 tonneaux on average. It had long been the property of the Comtes de St-Exupery from 1827 until sold by them in 1853 to Monsieur Fourcade for 280,000 frs (approx. £56,000). The new proprietor proceeded to reconstruct the domain so that the production by 1874 had risen to 150 tonneaux. The vineyard of Philippe Dubignon, which had also been classified as a third growth in 1855, was added to Malescot at this time and then disappeared from the list of classified growths. An attractive château was also constructed in the village of Margaux, which has been completely renovated and restored.

Between 1912 and 1955, the château belonged to the English company of W. H. Chaplin (subsequently Seager Evans), who then sold it to their manager, Mr Paul Zuger. His grandson Jean-Luc now manages it. The wine today again enjoys an excellent reputation, and is noted for a bouquet of exquisite fragrance and delicacy. It is a wine of real breed and finesse, with sufficient body.

CHÂTEAU MARGAUX

Premier Cru Classe. Owner: Société Civile du Château Margaux (Mentzelopoulos family). Administrators: Paul Pontallier and Philippe Barre. 87 hectares. Red: 29,000 cases; CS 75%, Mer 20%, PV and CF 5%. White: 3,300 cases; SB 100%. Secondary labels: Pavillon Blanc and Pavillon Rouge du Château Margaux

Château Margaux has always been accounted a first growth since classifications began. Its wines are particularly mentioned as being in all the best English cellars by the first half of the eighteenth century.

The origins of this growth can be traced back to the fifteenth century when it was known as La Motte de Margaux. The word *"la motte"* means a hill or mount. Further north the same word later became corrupted to *"mouton"*. There is also the attractive theory, put forward by Bernard Ginestet, son of the former owner, that the name "Margaux" conies from a villa of the Roman poet Ausonius, called Thermae Mariolicae, and that this was situated at La Fontanelle, which is at the north-eastern corner of the estate near the river.

The estate as we know it today was formed by the Lestonnac family who arrived in the last quarter of the sixteenth century and began to build up the property by purchase and exchange from numerous peasant proprietors, a pattern to be followed by many Bordeaux families during the seventeenth and eighteenth centuries. Effectively the ownership of Margaux was to remain undisturbed until the beginning of the nineteenth century, although the names changed, to d'Aulède, then Fumel and d'Hargicourt or d'Argicourt, each time passing through the female side. But the most crucial alliance was with the Pontacs of Haut-Brion through a marriage made in 1654. This led directly to Margaux's inclusion among the four firsts with Lafite, Latour and Haut-Brion, as they emerged as the first great named wines at the beginning of the eighteenth century. The great expansion of the vineyard occurred between the 1740s and the 1780s, when Thomas Jefferson put it at 150 tonneaux, well over double what it had been forty years earlier. In 1802, it was bought by the Marquis de la Colonilla for 654,000 frs (approx. £131,000). He pulled down the old château and built the elegant neo-classical mansion which is so familiar today, a building unique in style and importance in the Médoc. It was ready for the Marquis to move into by 1812. In 1836 it was purchased by a Spanish nobleman, Alexandre Aguada, Marqués de la Marismas, for 1,350,000 frs (approx. £260,000). The decoration and furnishing of the interior of the château dated from the Aguada period, roughly corresponding with the period of the Second Empire, in a much more elaborate and less classical mould than that favoured at the beginning of the century, and reflected in the austere simplicity of the building itself. When the present proprietors took over, they decided to restore and refurnish the interior as it might have been when the château was first built, and the result dazzlingly complements the beauty of the architecture. In 1879 it changed hands once more when the son of the original Marqués de las Marismas sold it to Vicomte Pillet-Will. The Pillet-Will era ended in 1920, when it was sold to a syndicate headed by Pierre Moreau, a broker associated with Margaux for many years. They in turn sold in 1934 to a group headed by Fernand Ginestet. Monsieur Pierre Ginestet, his son, gradually bought out the other shareholders until he became sole proprietor in 1940. It was to remain Pierre Ginestet's home for the next thirty years.

In the aftermath of the Bordeaux slump, the Ginestet *négociant* business experienced acute financial problems which necessitated the sale of Château Margaux. At first it seemed likely that the new owners would be the American company, National Distillers. But this was vetoed by the French government, and in 1976 it was acquired by Monsieur André Mentzelopoulos, through the grocery chain Felix Potin, for 72 million francs. From the outset, Monsieur Mentzelopoulos took a keen personal interest in this new venture, and a very considerable investment has been made in restoring the buildings and vineyards, where the hand of neglect had become increasingly evident in recent years. Unhappily, after only four years as proprietor, André Mentzelopoulos died in December 1980. But already his impact on Margaux, and on Bordeaux as a whole, had been substantial, and he had at least had the consolation of seeing the 1978 and 1979 vintages acclaimed as exceptional. Madame Laura Mentzelopoulos, his widow, and her daughters are now the proprietors, with Corinne Mentzelopoulos supervising the management.

In the 1850s the production of the first wine amounted to only 80 tonneaux, but this increased steadily as the century progressed and the prestige of and demand for the great wines of the Médoc mounted. Thus figures of 125 tonneaux in 1874, 150 tonneaux in 1881, and 225 tonneaux in 1898 are recorded in the works of Edouard Féret and his edition of Cocks. Today the production averages around 29,000 cases of red wines, of which between a quarter and a third are sold under the second label, Pavillon Rouge du Château Margaux, and 3,300 cases of the white Pavillon Blanc.

The wines of Château Margaux have all those qualities described as being particular to Margaux, and in the most exalted degree and perfect balance. The *courtiers* who compiled the 1855 classification placed Margaux in the first growths, second only to Lafite. It is not hard to see why. If we acclaim Lafite as the king of Médoc wines, then Margaux is surely the queen. Lafite may be the most complete Médoc, with its fascinating combination of delicacy and power: Margaux is a more feline and feminine wine, but it comes closest to Lafite in its finesse and breed, in its sheer beauty of flavour. The delicacy of the early years belies the longevity of the great years. I had a bottle of the 1875 on its ninetieth birthday and it was still beautifully preserved, one of the best bottles of old wine I have ever drunk, full-flavoured but light, sweet as only old claret can be, and still beautifully fresh. Undoubtedly one of the greatest vintages which still lives is the 1900. When sixty-three years old, its lovely colour was still unfaded, its bouquet was gloriously undimmed, a marvel of delicacy and penetration. The wine still had all those wonderful characteristics which words can sketch only feebly – great finesse, charm and a serene and perfect balance. This was, and no doubt still is, an ageless beauty and a fitting monument to the golden age of Margaux.

Although there were no great vintages between 1900 and 1920, some charming wines were made during this era, and I have had good bottles of the 1907 and the 1909. The period between the wars was a disappointing one in the history of this great wine. Neither in 1928 and 1929, nor again in 1934 and 1937, did Margaux rank with the best wines of the vintage. The outstanding wine of the period in my experience is the 1924. Ever since I first saw the wine at Lebègue's famous survey of wines of the château in 1952 and was struck by its superiority to more famous years, I have never been disappointed by this lovely wine. Although now beginning to show its age, it was still graceful, charming and vigorous when last tasted in 1977. During the Ginestet years the great vintages were 1945, 1947, 1949, 1950, 1953, 1961 and 1966. In lesser years, Margaux is inclined to produce a rather small wine with a rather limited future; the 1957 and 1958 were typical. But 1950, and to a much lesser degree 1960, produced wines of great charm with the breed and style of true Margaux, if not on the grand scale.

The 1962 is successful but rather dry; the 1961 is a great Margaux with a long life ahead of it and great depth and fruit. The 1960 is one of the successes of the vintage, a follower to the Margaux 1950. The 1959 is good but not outstanding, better than 1957 and 1955, but not in the 1947, 1953, 1961 category. The 1957 is sound and decent but unexciting, while the 1955 does not quite come off in spite of some promise – like many wines of this vintage. But after the great 1961 vintage, Margaux fell well behind the other first growths and indeed was often outshone by its neighbour Château Palmer. Respectable wines were made in 1970 and 1971, but they lacked the flair of the best that Margaux can do. On balance, the 1966 is probably the finest of these wines, combining finesse with lasting qualities. The 1975 has promise but is not among the front runners of this year. But with the new regime, a renaissance is well and truly under way, and a new Golden Age has dawned. The 1978 seems to set the stamp on it, easily the best wine made since 1961, I thought, when first tasted in the spring after the *soutirage*. Subsequent tastings have shown it to be amongst the best wines of this vintage. Even in the modest 1977 vintage, an exceptionally attractive and stylish wine was made. The 1979 has opulence and a marvellous bouquet, which reminds me of the 1949 vintage here. The 1980 has soft, elegant fruit, yet is also well structured – one of the very best wines of the vintage. The 1981 has great persistence of flavour combined with an intensity unusual for the year. It promises a long development. The 1982 is one of the giants of this great year with truffles and spice on the nose and a balance of richness, concentration, complex tannins, and finesse which is extraordinary – perhaps a wine with which to see in the twenty-first century! The 1983 here is one of the successes of the vintage, extremely rich in fruit and tannins, more massive than the 1981 and with a long future ahead of it. The 1984 has a higher proportion of Cabernet Sauvignon than usual, and has a very frank Cabernet character with all the "*race*" we expect of Margaux. The 1985 is yet another classic of the reborn Margaux with great beauty of flavour and breed but also concentrated fruit and tannins, while 1986 promises to provide a fascinating contrast and is full of complex tannins with massive fruit slowly coming through. 1988 and 1989 are another great pair of vintages. So future years should hold many delights in store for Margaux lovers.

Some wines are immensely impressive almost as soon as they are made. Others hide their great qualities until their second year in cask or until they have had bottle age. Margaux was such a wine. When I first tasted Margaux in cask, I was quite unimpressed and indeed disappointed. The wine was usually more easily judged in its second year in cask, became disappointing again during the months preceding bottling, and showed well in bottle only after at least two or three years. But with improved wine-making and earlier bottling this is changing. It was customary at Margaux to bottle the wine only after the third winter, and I often wondered at the wisdom of this practice in any but the greatest years. The wines of light years seemed to take a long time to recover after bottling and in the interim period looked rather tired. Under the new regime, Professor Peynaud has encouraged a more flexible approach, and the 1977 benefited from early bottling.

The secret of the remarkable string of successes at Margaux since 1978 is to be found in the management team they have built up. First they inherited the skills and devotion of Jean Grangerou as *maître de chai* – the third generation of his family to hold this position. Then André Mentzelopoulos brought in Philippe Barré as estate manager – he had been responsible for a large estate in Provence and is strong on the viticultural side. Finally Corinne Mentzelopoulos recruited Paul Pontallier, a brilliant young oenologist with wide horizons, whose skills perfectly complement those of Philippe Barré. They now work in tandem as estate directors or *régisseurs*.

CHÂTEAU MARQUIS D'ALESME-BECKER

Troisième Cru Classé. Owner: Jean-Claude Zuger. 9 hectares. 4,150 cases. CS 40%, Mer 30%, CF 20%, PV 10%

A very small but very ancient property in the heart of Margaux. Its history has been traced back as far as 1616 when vines were first planted here by a nobleman called d'Alesme, and remained in this family until 1809. The family were cavalrymen and it was from this that the horseshoe on the label originates. The Becker who bought the property in 1809 was Dutch, and for simplicity's sake it was usually referred to as Becker in the nineteenth century. At the time of the classification, the production was only 5 tonneaux; by the end of the century, 25 to 30 tonneaux were achieved. In 1919, it was bought by the then proprietor of Lascombes for incorporation into this growth whose vineyard it adjoins, but the plan was not carried out, and the property was sold again to W. H. Chaplin who ran it in conjunction with Malescot, and sold it to Paul Zuger at the same time as Malescot. The property is now run by Jean-Claude Zuger, Paul's son, and brother of Roger Zuger at Malescot. The château was originally that of Desmirail, the original Marquis d'Alesme château now serving as the offices for Château Lascombes. Until 1979 the property was run in tandem with Malescot, but is now quite separate. The wine is not well known today, but it is a good and typical Margaux with style and breed.

CHÂTEAU MARQUIS-DE-TERME

Quatrième Cru Classé. Owner: Sénéclauze family. 35 hectares. 12,000 cases. CS 45%, Mer 35%, CF 15%, PV 5%. Second Label: Châteaux des Gondats

This property lies at the back of Margaux and is extremely well kept. It is of ancient origin and appeared in all the old classifications. Its vineyards are very fragmented and are scattered over the communes of Margaux, Cantenac, Soussans and Arsac. The name comes from an eighteenth-century proprietor who acquired it through marrying a niece of the celebrated Marquis de Rausan in 1762. From the era of the classification, Oscar Sollberg owned and improved it for many years until it passed into the hands of Frédéric Eschenauer under whose care it continued to prosper. It was bought by Monsieur Pierre Sénéclauze, a *négociant* from Marseilles, in 1936. His three sons, Pierre-Louis, Philippe and Jean, are the present owners.

Production, which at the time of classification amounted to 45 tonneaux, averaged 100 tonneaux by the end of the century. In recent years, considerable efforts have been made to improve the quality of the wines. The present *régisseur*, Monsieur Jean-Pierre Hugon, took over in 1972, and was joined in 1980 by Monsieur Alain Gouinaud as *maître de chai*. A policy of using 30 per cent new wood for the cask maturation was begun in 1977, and a fine new insulated *chai* for both cask and bottle ageing was completed in 1981. Included in this is a reception room for functions and tastings, commanding a view of the cask storage through a plate-glass wall.

In the autumn of 1985 I was able to taste a wide range of vintages from Marquis-de-Terme which helped to put these improvements in perspective. Thus, although the 1961 was delicious and the class of the vintage had completely triumphed over any other shortcomings, 1966 has drying-out tannins and some oxidation, while 1970 showed a dense, coarse character and lack of style and was of no more than decent *bourgeois* standard. There is a real improvement with the 1975, which has lots of fruit and richness to balance the tannin, but the 1976 is not so well balanced with a dry, tannic finish. The 1977 is surprisingly attractive for the vintage. The 1978 is more advanced and complex than the 1979, which at this stage was rather solid and tannic, less advanced indeed than the stylish, if slightly lean, 1981. In between, 1980 is a most attractive example of the year, with elegant, well-balanced fruit. The 1982 has all the rich opulent fruit of the year, but with plenty of ripe tannin behind, and is better than the well-structured and moderately rich 1983. The 1984 looked a little lean at this stage and still marked by new wood, but developed well enough in the glass to suggest it could prove a worthy fellow to the 1980. The 1985 has a most attractive flavour, good concentration and balance, and the charm of the year.

The style which emerges from the recent vintages is of solid, well-balanced wines in place of the rather tough, rustic efforts of earlier vintages. But there is still something a little coarse-grained which separates them from the top Margaux.

It should be noted that the second wine, Château des Gondats, has only the Bordeaux Supérieur *appellation* and not the Margaux one. This is because the vineyards of Château Gondat lie on the *palus* to the east of the village of Margaux. You pass them when you drive to the Relais de Margaux. The wines of this property are blended with vats of Marquis-de-Terme which have been eliminated from the *grand vin*. I find these wines have a robust but decidedly coarse character which I personally think unattractive but which undeniably has its followers.

CHÂTEAU MARSAC-SÉGUINEAU

Cru Bourgeois 1932. Owner: Société Civile du Château Marsac-Séguineau.
Administrator: Jean-Pierre Angliviel de la Beaudelle. 10 hectares. 3,350 cases.
Mer 60%, CS 28%, CF 12%. Second label: Château Gravières-de-Marsac
Since this property joined the Mestrezat stable – they distribute the wine

– much has been done to reorganize the vineyards, and one can expect to see progress, as has been the case in their other properties. The wines are full-flavoured and supple in style, and last well.

CHÂTEAU MARTINENS
Cru Bourgeois Superieur 1932. Owners: Simone Dulos and Jean-Pierre Seynat-Dulos. 30 hectares. 7,000 cases. Mer 40%, CS 30%, PV 20%, CF 10%
There is an interesting English connection here. The charming château – a classically simple *maison bourgeoise* – was built in 1767 by three English sisters from London, Ann, Jane and Mary White. But they sold out in 1776. The present owners have been here since 1945. The vineyard, in the commune of Cantenac, is in a single piece surrounding the château. Since 1979, a proportion of new oak has been used in the cask maturation. The wines enjoy a good reputation as stylish, charming and well made.

CHÂTEAU MONBRISON
Cru Bourgeois. Owners: Elizabeth Davis and Sons. 14 hectares, 5,500 cases. CS 45%, Mer 35%, CF 15%, PV 5%. Second label: Château Cordet
Elizabeth Davis is the daughter of an American who was Commissioner in the Red Cross in Europe during the First World War, and bought the property in 1921. It is now run by her sons, Bruno, Jean-Luc and Laurent Vonderheyden. Recent vintages show considerable breed and finesse, highlighted fruit and good structure. Excellent wines were made in 1979, 1981, 1982, then 1985, 1986, 1988 and 1989 are especially outstanding. The second wine, Château Cordet, is the product of young vines and is a pretty light wine for early drinking, but here too the breed comes through. This is now one of the best unclassified wines in the *appellation*.

CHÂTEAU MONTBRUN
Cru Bourgeois 1932. Owner: J. Lebègue and Company. Administrators: Jacques and Alain de Coninck. 8 hectares. 3,500 cases. Mer 75%, CS and CF 25%
This small, well-placed vineyard in Cantenac was once part of Château Palmer. The de Conincks, who run it for proprietors Lebègue, are themselves owners in St Emilion and Fronsac, so should know how to handle the unusually high proportion of Merlot in the vineyard. The wines are

predictably rich and full-bodied. J. Lebègue and Co. are now quite unconnected with the English firm of the same name.

CHÂTEAU PALMER

Troisième Cru Classé. Owner: Société Civile du Château Palmer. Administrator: B. Bouteiller. 45 hectares. 12,500 cases. CS 55%, Mer 40%, CF 3%, PV 2%

This is today not only the outstanding growth in Cantenac, but the best growth in the Margaux *appellation* after Château Margaux itself. It is now ranked among the best of the second growths, and regularly commands a higher price than any other.

The property has an interesting history, in which are mirrored many of the salient features of the history of the region. We are fortunate in having an excellent monograph on the history of Palmer by Monsieur R. Pijassou published by the Fédération Historique du Sud-Ouest in 1964 and embodying all the latest research, and the following is a summary of the most interesting parts of that history.

The property appears to have originated from a division of the ancient domain of Château d'Issan among the heirs of the Foix-Candale family in 1748, when a portion seems to have passed into the hands of the de Gascq family. The members of this ancient and important family belonged, like all leading proprietors of the eighteenth century, to the *noblesse de robe as conseillers* of the Bordeaux Parlement, and several held important posts in it, as well as being noted patrons of literature and the fine arts. The wine from their property, known as Château de Gascq, became popular at the court of Louis XV. At that time the entire domain amounted to only 50 hectares.

The end of the revolutionary period and the Napoleonic wars found Madame Marie Bumet de Ferrière, the widow of Blaise-Jean-Charles-Alexandre de Gascq, as sole proprietor. In 1814 Major-General Charles Palmer, having arrived with Wellington's army, decided to settle in Bordeaux and invest his money in property. It seems probable that he had some introduction to one of the *courtiers* of the city, and his attention was directed to Château de Gascq, consisting then of a fine vineyard but no noble château. For this he turned to another property at Cenon. The price paid amounted to 100,000 frs (approx. £20,000). But for the next seventeen years, the General steadily augmented his original purchase and by 1831 he had invested 370,906 frs (approx. £74,200) in a domain of 162 hectares, and Palmer could vie with her great neighbours Margaux and Beychevelle in size and importance. One of the most important of these acquisitions was the vineyard called Boston of over 30 hectares, situated between the communes of Cantenac and Soussans. In this first great age of Palmer, the estate was organized on the grand scale. Jean Lagunegrand, the *régisseur*, was one of the most highly paid in the Médoc, the equal of Joubert at the Bartons' domain of Langoa-Léoville. At this period in the 1830s and 1840s, around 100 tonneaux a year were made.

Between 1841 and 1843, the General ran into financial trouble, and this in its turn was to affect Palmer's position when the 1855 classification was made. The high cost of running the estate was aggravated by economic difficulties in France and high duties detrimental to trade. After several poor vintages, in 1843 the General was forced to sell to Madame Françoise-Marie Bergerac for only 274,000 frs (approx. £54,800), substantially less than his original investment. After the inauguration of the Second Empire in 1851, a more prosperous period began, and in this era the power and influence of the great bankers reached its zenith. In 1853, Baron Nathaniel de Rothschild bought Mouton, and his rival Isaac-Rodrigue Péreire bought Palmer.

The Péreires were a Jewish-Portuguese family who became financiers and were principally concerned in the development and exploitation of the French railways. They were also responsible for the development of Arcachon as a resort. The sum paid for Palmer was 410,000 frs (approx. £82,000) but Péreire had bought at a difficult time, for the Palmer vineyard was already wasting under the scourge of oidium, and by 1858 the entire vineyard had to be completely replanted. Soon the production rose again to 125 tonneaux, and as the vineyard was again increased between 1857 and 1887, so production rose still further. During the 1870s, it could average 170 tonneaux. This figure was halved during the phylloxera period of the 1880s, to emerge in the plentiful vintages at the end of the century at over 200 tonneaux. The charming château, which is such a familiar landmark on the *route de Médoc*, was built by Isaac Péreire between 1857 and 1860 on land known as the Palu d'Issan specially purchased for the purpose from Madame Lowick of Château d'Issan.

The Société Civile Péreire, which was formed in 1889, continued as proprietors until 1937–8. In the final period of the Péreire regime, Palmer, like many other Médoc growths between the wars, fell on bad times, and the vineyard at Boston was disposed of. Palmer was sold to a Société Civile in which there were originally three partners, Mahler-Besse – the *négociants* of Dutch origin, Sichel, the English *négociants*, and the Miailhe family, formerly *courtiers* and now important proprietors. Owing to French inheritance laws, the Sichels, with 34 per cent, are now the largest single shareholders, the Mahler-Besse holding now being held individually between fourteen members of the family instead of as a single family holding as before, while the Miailhes have sold out to the other shareholders.

For over 100 years now Palmer has been fortunate in having the Chardon family as *régisseurs*, and under the devoted attention of Pierre and his sons Claude and Yves the position of Palmer has been restored until its reputation is now as high as at any time in its history. In recent years, the 1949, 1953, 1955, 1957, 1959, 1960, 1961, 1962, 1966, 1970, 1971, 1973, 1975, 1976, 1978 and 1979 were all successful examples of the vintage. The 1953, 1960, 1961 and 1971 were accounted amongst the finest examples of their respective vintages. At a blind tasting of 1961s, made possible through the generosity of Dr Taams at his home in Holland in May 1978, the 1961 was clearly placed first, ahead of all the first growths of the Médoc. More recently, in spite of some variation between bottles, the best examples were still superb in 1986. The 1959 is also a great year here, overshadowed only by the 1961. The 1970 is a classically luscious and long-lived Palmer, but 1971 is untypical in being more Cabernet Sauvignon than usual, and it is quite one of the best wines made in Médoc that year. More recently, the 1976 is powerful and well balanced, the 1978 is rather underpowered but charming, while 1979 seems more of a stayer and more typically Palmer. The 1982 is just a shade understated for Palmer in a great year. Here, the success was 1983. There is a very good 1984, without the dryness often found in this year. The 1985 could be even better than 1983, with delightful concentration, length and finesse, a great Palmer in the making; 1986, and even more 1988 and 1989, show great promise.

In the most successful years, Palmer is a very fat and generous wine to begin with, and has an almost Burgundian opulence which is very noticeable on the nose. This is due in part to the proportion of Merlot in the vineyard, and such wines can easily be mistaken for St Emilions. When tasting the famous 1953 with Allan Sichel, I recall his opinion that the proportion of Merlot at that time was excessive, and that more Cabernet Sauvignon was needed. While there has been some correction of the imbalance in the vineyard, the impression remains that Palmer is more Merlot than is usual for Margaux or the Médoc. But with maturity, the wines develop a bouquet of rare penetration and show all the finesse of a fine Margaux with rather more body and richness.

CHÂTEAU PAVEIL-DE-LUZE

Cru Bourgeois. Owner: GFA du Château Paveil. Administrator: Baron Geoffroy de Luze. 24 hectares. 7,000 cases. CS and CF 70%, Mer 30%. Second label: Château de la Coste

Before the Revolution, the property belonged to the Bretonneaux family. In 1862 it was bought by Baron Alfred de Luze, who in 1820 had founded the Bordeaux *négociants* of that name. It has belonged to the family and firm of de Luze ever since. Production, which was 125 tonneaux in the 1870s when the domain spread over the communes of Soussans, Arcins, Avensan and Moulis, fell over the First World War to 25 tonneaux and has only of late revived. In the days when the de Luze family also owned the *négociant* house, the wines of Paveil were bottled in their Bordeaux cellars and were sound but lacking character. Now the family has parted company with their old firm, which belongs to Rémy Martin, more time and effort seems to be going into this property. The wines are château-bottled and have some breed and charm, but tend to be light in body. This was certainly true of the 1981, but 1983 promised to be richer and more powerful. The 1985, after three months in bottle, looked opulent if a little soft, with lots of charm and richness. The 1986, still in vat at vintage time, prior to having six months in cask, again showed the elegance and breed achieved here, but with a lot of richness and some concentration. Certainly a *cru* to watch.

The seventeenth-century château deserves a word. It is long and low with two towers, typical of the *chartreuse* style, looking out from its open courtyard to the main expanse of the vineyard. The interior has been restored and redecorated with great taste to underline the spacious and relaxed elegance of its period.

CHÂTEAU PONTAC-LYNCH

Cru Bourgeois Supérieur 1932. Owner: GFA du Château Pontac-Lynch.
Administrator: Serge Bondon. 9 hectares. 3,000 cases. Mer 47%, CS and CF
45%, PV 8%. Second label: Château Puy Lesplanques

The fame of two great wine dynasties of the eighteenth century unfortunately far outshines that of this modest *cru* today. Apparently, in the middle of the eighteenth century its wines sold for higher prices than those of its neighbours which are today classified growths. Recently, the wines have been winning medals, and so could be worth looking for.

CHÂTEAU POUGET

Quatrième Cru Classé. Owner: GFA des Châteaux Boyd-Cantenac et Pouget.
Administrator: Pierre Guillemet. 10 hectares. 3,500 cases. CS 66%, Mer 30%, CF
4%

This property in Cantenac has ancient origins, the vineyard having originally been the property of the abbey of Cantenac. The growth is mentioned in all the old classifications during the first half of the nineteenth century.

The property has belonged to the Guillemet family since 1906, and the present member of the family in charge is Pierre Guillemet. Until the 1982 vintage Pouget and Boyd-Cantenac were made in the same *chai* and *cuvier* and Pouget was regarded as the second wine of Boyd-Cantenac. But from the 1983 vintage there have been separate facilities. Rich, supple wines were made in 1970, 1971, 1975, 1978 and 1979. In the eighties the wines seem to have become more tannic, but coarser in style.

CHÂTEAU PRIEURÉ LICHINE

Quatrième Cru Classé. Owner: Sacha Lichine. 60 hectares. 25,000 cases. CS
55%, Mer 33%, CF 6%, PV 6%. Second label: Château de Clairefort

The charming old château was once the priory for the monks of Cantenac, and backs on to the parish church of Cantenac. After the property was bought by Alexis Lichine in 1952, he completely restored the château in the most original and decorative fashion.

The reputation of the vineyard goes back some 300 years, although it did not appear in classifications prior to 1855. Since the change of ownership in 1952, the vineyard has been enlarged and reconstructed, so that the château now has vineyards scattered all over the commune, some of them on long leases. This was very much Alexis Lichine's European home and he devoted a large part of his time to the Prieuré since severing his connections with the Alexis Lichine *négociant* company and Lascombes. Following his death in 1989 his son Sacha has ably taken up the reins.

The style at Prieuré is now for full-bodied, rich wines of great consistency. While they may ultimately lack the finesse of the top Margaux these are well made and highly dependable, enjoyable wines. The most impressive recent vintages have been 1967 – exceptional for the year and it has lasted – 1970, 1973, 1975, 1976, 1978, 1981, 1982 – good but not outstanding in the context of the year, while 1983 has more power. The 1985, 1986, and 1988 all looked impressive and should make fine bottles.

CHÂTEAU RAUSAN-SÉGLA

Deuxième Cru Classé. Owner: Walker family trust. 45 hectares. 10,000 cases. CS 66%, Mer 28%, CF 4%, PV 2%

This was one of the important vineyards owned by the Marquis de Rauzan in the eighteenth century. It became separated from his other property of Gassies in the nineteenth century. For a long period it belonged to the family of Durand-Dasier, and then for many years to the Cruse family, until its sale by them in 1957. Until 1989 it belonged to the Liverpool shipping firm of John Holt (themselves part of the international trading giant, Lonrho), when it was sold to the present owners.

There is a small but charming château dating from the beginning of this century, though the style is rather reminiscent of Haut-Brion, with its little towers and gabled windows. When John Holt acquired the property in 1960, the vineyard consisted of 37 hectares. Since that time, there has been a steady programme of replanting amounting to 19.65 hectares between 1960 and 1986. In 1986 the vineyard had reached 45.4 hectares and the final target is for a vineyard area of 46.6 hectares.

The reputation of Rausan-Ségla has long lagged behind its exalted position in the classification. The last years of the Cruse regime after the war were undistinguished, and although there were some welcome reinvestment by Holt, principally in the vineyards, the wines still lacked the breed and distinction one looked for. However, there are, at long last, signs of real improvements. The arrival at Eschenauer of Jacques Théo led immediately to a fresh impetus for quality at the properties it manages. In 1982 Professor Emile Peynaud had already become consultant oenologist here. The result, apart from more careful wine-making, has been a much greater emphasis on selection and the first results are already plain. The 1982 itself is really rich and ripe with all the harmony of that year, while the 1983 is lighter and more forward, but elegant and fine. The real potential is seen in the 1985, where the style and breed shine through and there is really concentrated fruit, length and ripeness. In 1986 a new *cuvier* was installed in time for the vintage. It is completely automated and must be the last word in modern functionalism, and certainly a new showplace for the Médoc.

One has to remember that, at present, owing to the work of replanting already mentioned, the average age of the vineyard is only twenty years, so one can expect even more interesting results in the future. During the seventies good wines were made in 1970 and 1975.

CHÂTEAU RAUZAN-GASSIES

Deuxième Cru Classé. Owners: Madame Paul Quié and J.-M. Quié. 30 hectares. 8,300 cases. CS 40%, Mer 39%, CF 20%, PV 1%. Second label: Enclos de Moncabon

This ancient domain belonged to Gaillard de Tardes in the sixteenth century and to Bernard de Baverolles in the seventeenth century, before passing into the hands of Monsieur de Rauzan, the *conseiller au Parlement*, in the eighteenth century, who gave it his name. There have been many owners, but Monsieur Paul Quié and his heirs have been the proprietors since the last war.

More powerful than many Margaux and with nearly as much body as a Cantenac wine, at its best it possesses the delicacy and charm of the finest Margaux wines. Like Ségla, it usually takes rather longer to come round than most Margaux wines these days.

The 1875 was a very great wine which was still remarkably fine and well preserved when I drank it in 1962 and 1963. Of more recent vintages, the 1920 and 1926 were both very fine, very much in their prime still when I last had the pleasure of drinking them. In recent years Rauzan-Gassies has been an inconsistent performer, as was underlined by a wide-ranging tasting of its wines I did in 1986. The 1961 was still most enjoyable but without the real concentration of the best 1961s and with a slightly dry, rustic note at the finish. The 1962 showed the best breed, harmonious fruit and length of any of the wines of this decade. The 1964 was awkward and ungainly, raw and tannic, without style. The 1966 was second only to 1962, with well-combined fruit and tannin, good stamina, but a touch of coarseness on the finish. The 1970 lacked life or charm and seemed to be falling apart. The 1971 also disappointed, its light fruit fading and with a sour finish. The 1973 lacks the charm of the year or any Margaux breed. The 1975 has depth of flavour and was clearly the most sucessful wine since 1966, but is forward for 1975 and not really top class. The 1976, in spite of a promising bouquet, had a diluted and rather soapy flavour. The 1978 showed much more breed and style with some depth and complexity. The 1979 was less developed than the 1978, with charming, elegant fruit, an attractive flavour and finesse. The 1982 is very rich and powerful but dominated by its tannins at present and showing a shade coarse, but 1983 had much more breed and style with lovely ripe, rich fruit. All in all, this is a very mixed picture with a really bad patch in the late sixties and early seventies, and overall a certain coarseness which places it well below the standard one would expect from a prime position in Margaux. There are signs that the pro-prietor understands that there is much to do and some improvements are in the pipeline.

CHÂTEAU SIRAN
Cru Bourgeois Supérieur 1932. Owner: William-Alain B. Miailhe. 35 hectares. 12,500 cases. CS 50%, Mer 25%, PV 15%, CF 10%. Secondary labels: Château Bellegarde, St-Jacques (Bordeaux Supérieur)

This growth is officially classified as a *bourgeois supérieur* but was included in the INAO's proposal for a new classification published in 1961 as a *grand cru classé*, an opinion underlined by its inclusion in the Alexis Lichine Classification (see Chapter 3).

For many years, this property belonged to the Comtes de Lautrec, but was sold by them in 1848 to Monsieur Léo Barbier who greatly improved the vineyard, so that by 1874, Féret could write that Siran was by then one of the best *crus bourgeois* in the Médoc. The present proprietor, Monsieur W.-A. B. Miailhe, is descended from Léo Barbier, and the pro-perty has greatly benefited from continuity of management.

The vineyard is very well tended and the wine is consistent. During the fifties and much of the sixties, I noted that the wines here were gently perfumed, delicate, and on the light side, with a delicious flavour which filled the mouth. Typical of such wines were the lovely 1953, a light but charming 1960, and a gorgeous 1961. Good examples were also made in 1962, 1964 and 1966. But when I did a panoramic tasting in September 1986 of all the vintages since 1970, I thought I detected a change of emphasis. The wines generally are fuller-bodied and often more tannic, but seem to me to have less finesse and flair. The outstanding vintages were 1970, with its rich concentrated fruit, classic flavour and balance, 1975 with considerable tannin and extract but well balanced with a fine flavour, 1978 with more finesse and delicious now although still improving, and 1981 which seemed more classic in its balance of fruit and tannin than 1982 at this stage. The 1982 itself had the great ripeness of the year and the fruit still hid the tannin to an extent, and 1985, still in cask, had considerable richness and fruit, but showed a touch of coarseness at the finish. Of the other years, I enjoyed the delicious 1980, the 1979 was still very tannic and closed in full evolution. The 1973 was light and delicious but beginning to fade, 1974 had a charm seldom found in the year and was holding up well. The 1976 was attractive for current drinking, but had that quality of richness slightly diluted, often found in this vintage. A recent innovation is labels decorated by well-known artists – à la Mouton-Rothschild. This began with the 1980 vintage. Each artist is asked to design something topical for each particular year. Since Alain Miailhe severed his connections with Pichon-Lalande in 1978, as part of a realignment of family interests, he has devoted all his considerable energies and talents into improving Siran, of which he is now sole owner. One innovation has been the construction of a nuclear fall-out shelter, in which an extensive library of Siran and the best wines of the Médoc are stored, mostly in large sizes (magnums, double-magnums and jeroboams). More conventionally, there is also a fine display of rare porcelain.

The château is small but charming, and the small park is noted for its sea of cyclamens at vintage time. It lies just to the west of the *route des châteaux* (D2) where it is joined by the D108.

CHÂTEAU TAYAC
Cru Bourgeois. Owner: André Favin. 34 hectares. 15,000 cases. CS 65%, Mer 25%, CF 5%, PV 5%

This is the largest of the *crus bourgeois* of Margaux, and the vineyard is in Soussans. Its present excellent reputation is due to the hard work of its present owner, who inherited it in 1960. The wines are perfumed and robust, with a certain rustic touch in their make-up which is nevertheless rather agreeable. Of recent vintages, I have particularly liked the 1981 and 1983. On this form the 1982 must also be worth searching out.

CHÂTEAU DU TERTRE (OR LE TERTRE)

Cinquième Cru Classé. Owner: Philippe Capbern Gasqueton. 48 hectares. 15,000 cases. CS 40%, CF & PV 25%, Mer 35%

This vineyard occupies a very fine position in the commune of Arsac, of which it is the only classified growth. The château stands in an elevated position commanding a fine view of the plateau on which the vineyard is planted. This is fine, pebbly soil with views towards the vineyards of Giscours and of Cantenac, and exceptionally the vineyard is in a single piece. "*Tertre*" means a hillock or rising ground.

With one of those cross-references with which the Médoc abounds, this was once one of the numerous properties of the Marquis de Ségur, who also owned Calon-Ségur, now the property of the Gasquetons, who in turn are now the owners here. By the 1840s, under the ownership of Charles Henri, it had a good reputation and was in demand in Holland. This reputation was greatly increased after its acquisition by Henri Koenigswarter in 1870. The production now rose from 60 or 70 tonneaux, to 100 and up to 160 tonneaux. The reputation and production fell away considerably after the Second World War, but happily it was bought by Monsieur Philippe Gasqueton, one of the partners in Calon-Ségur, in 1961. He, together with his Belgian partners, have steadily restored both vineyard and château. The production has been restored from about 25 tonneaux to 200 tonneaux. The wine now being made resembles a Cantenac, but has a particularly brilliant colour and a beautifully perfumed bouquet with a very fine and elegant flavour. The 1964 and 1966 were the beginning of a line of attractive vintages. Since then the wines have proved consistent and are improving. Of recent vintages, the 1978 is more stylish than the 1979, as is often the case. The 1980 is exceptionally attractive. The 1981 is developing rather slowly. It has a fine flavour and a medium weight. The 1982 is very rich and supple, and will well repay keeping. The 1983 promised very well in cask, with that especially vivid fruitiness I always associate with good vintages at du Tertre. The 1984 has the fruit, finesse and balance to make an attractive bottle for early drinking, and the 1985 in cask had those lovely highlights, balance and beauty of flavour which promise another outstanding vintage. This excellent *cru* deserves to be better known and appreciated. It has the finesse and breed of a fine Margaux, if not the weight of the very top *crus*.

CHÂTEAU LA TOUR-DE-BESSAN

Owner: Lucien Lurton. 21 hectares. 8,000 cases. CS 90%, Mer 10%

Lucien Lurton is the largest vineyard owner in Margaux (Brane-Cantenac, Durfort-Vivens and Desmirail) and also owns Villegeorge nearby, to say nothing of Bouscaut in Graves and Climens in Barsac. This is his most modest Margaux, a wine with the breed, scented and supple, if light, and for early drinking, although the 1979 was still excellent after eight years. The "Tour" in question is a ruined watch-tower of the fifteenth century dating from the last eight years of English rule.

CHÂTEAU LA TOUR-DE-MONS

Cru Bourgeois Supérieur 1932. Owners: Clauzel-Binaud-Cruchet. Administrator: Bertrand Clauzel. 30 hectares. 10,000 cases. CS 45%, Mer 40%, CF 10%, PV 5%

This is another excellent property which was ranked as a classified growth, both in the INAO proposal and by Lichine. It is an estate of very ancient origins; the château can be traced back to the fifteenth century and was much restored around 1615, at which time it passed into the family of de Mons through the marriage of Pierre de Mons with the only daughter of Baron de Soussans. Catherine de Mons took the property as her portion in 1740 when she married J.-B. de Secondat de Montesquieu of La Brède, the son of the famous author of *L'Esprit des lois* and *Lettres persanes*. The son was himself a distinguished naturalist, becoming the director of the Académie de Bordeaux in 1736 and a Fellow of our own Royal Society. He had no children and bequeathed the property back to the Mons des Dunes family. Since this time, the names of the proprietors have changed from time to time, but the property has remained in connecting families, passing through the female line on several occasions. It now belongs to the Clauzel, Binaud and Cruchet families, heirs of

Pierre Dubos, for over forty years the proprietors of Cantemerle as well as La Tour-de-Mons.

For over ninety years it has been regarded as one of the leading growths in Soussans. Unfortunately, under-investment, as at Cantemerle, has had its effect here, and the reputation of this famous old *cru* has suffered accordingly. At a blind tasting of 1981s in 1986 for instance, I found I preferred Paveil-de-Luze and Tayac to La Tour-de-Mons, which was coarse-grained and strong-flavoured but lacked breed, a quality which one always expected to find here. It is a wine of race and breed, a little firm at first but developing finesse and delicacy with ageing. It is the monopoly of the *négociants* H. & O. Beyermann, who are now owned by Atkinson Baldwin, the wine side of Drambuie. However, the sale of Cantemerle released much-needed funds which have now been reinvested here. There are a new *chai* and *cuvier*, and the improvement in the wines is clear. The 1982 has the opulence expected of the vintage, but with the tannins and marked character typical of La Tour-de-Mons. The 1983 follows the pattern of impressive wines made in Margaux in this vintage and is rich-textured and tannic for long-term development. In cask, 1985 and 1986 both had a wonderful scent of violets but the contrast was not as marked as at many properties since the 1985 was vigorous and tannic as well as charming, but the 1986 looked as if it could be even better, with great richness and fruit coming through the massive tannins. The assertive character of this *cru* comes from the presence of more clay in the soil than is usual in the Margaux *appellation*, and this calls for careful handling to bring out the finesse that is certainly there. The longevity of the wines is undoubted.

The charming label shows the fortified château as it was before being burnt down in 1895. Today the old schoolhouse serves as home for Bernard Clauzel and his family.

CLASSIFICATION OF *BOURGEOIS* WINES OF THE MÉDOC AND HAUT-MÉDOC: 1978

Grand Bourgeois

Château d'Agassac	Ludon	*Exceptionnel*
Château Andron Blanquet	St Estèphe	*Exceptionnel*
Château Beaumont	Cussac	
Château Beausite	St Estèphe	*Exceptionnel*
Château Bel-Orme	St Seurin-de-Cadourne	

Château Brillette	Moulis	
Château Capbern	St Estèphe	*Exceptionnel*
Château La Cardonne	Blaignan	
Château Caronne Ste-Gemme	St Laurent	*Exceptionnel*
Château Chasse-Spleen	Moulis	*Exceptionnel*
Château Cissac	Cissac	*Exceptionnel*
Château Citran	Avensan	*Exceptionnel*
Château Colombier Monpelou	Pauillac	
Château Coufran	St Seurin-de-Cadourne	
Château Coutelin-Merville	St Estèphe	
Château Le Crock	St Estèphe	*Exceptionnel*
Château Duplessis-Hauchecorne	Moulis	
Château Dutruch-Grand-Poujeau	Moulis	*Exceptionnel*
Château La Fleur-Milon	Pauillac	
Château Fontesteau	St Sauveur	
Château Fourcas-Dupré	Listrac	*Exceptionnel*
Château Fourcas-Hosten	Listrac	*Exceptionnel*
Château du Glana	St Julien	*Exceptionnel*
Château Greysac	Bégadan	
Château Hanteillan	Cissac	
Château Haut-Marbuzet	St Estèphe	*Exceptionnel*
Château Lafon	Listrac	
Château Lamarque	Lamarque	
Château Lamothe	Cissac	
Château Larose-Trintaudon	St Laurent	
Château Laujac	Bégadan	
Château Liversan	St Sauveur	
Château Loudenne	St Yzans	
Château MacCarthy	St Estèphe	
Château Malleret	Le Pian	
Château Marbuzet	St Estèphe	*Exceptionnel*
Château Martinens	Margaux	
Château Meyney	St Estèphe	*Exceptionnel*
Château Le Meynieu	Vertheuil	
Château Morin	St Estèphe	
Château Moulin à Vent	Moulis	
Château Les Ormes-de-Pez	St Estèphe	
Château Les Ormes-Sorbet	Couquèques	
Château Patache d'Aux	Bégadan	
Château Paveil-de-Luze	Soussans	

Château Peyrabon	St Sauveur	
Château Phélan-Ségur	St Estèphe	*Exceptionnel*
Château Pontoise-Cabarrus	St Seurin-de-Cadourne	
Château Potensac	Potensac	
Château Poujeaux	Moulis	*Exceptionnel*
Château Reysson	Vertheuil	
Château Ségur	Parempuyre	
Château Sigognac	St Yzans	
Château Sociando-Mallet	St Seurin-de-Cadourne	
Château du Taillan	Le Taillan	
Château La Tour-de-By	Bégadan	
Château La Tour-du-Haut-Moulin	Cussac	
Château Tronquoy-Lalande	St Estèphe	
Château Verdignan	St Seurin-de-Cadourne	

Bourgeois

Château Aney	Cussac
Château Balac	St Laurent
Château La Bécade	Listrac
Château Bellerive	Valeyrac
Château Bellerose	Pauillac
Château Bonneau	St Seurin-de-Cadourne
Château Le Boscq	St Estèphe
Château Le Breuil	Cissac
Château La Bridane	St Julien
Château de By	Bégadan
Château Cap-Léon-Veyrin	Listrac
Château Carcannieux	Queyrac
Château Castéra	St Germain-d'Esteuil
Château Chambert	St Estèphe
Château La Clare	Bégadan
Château La Closerie	Moulis
Château Duplessis-Fabre	Moulis
Château Fonpiqueyre	St Sauveur
Château Fonréaud	Listrac
Château Fort Vauban	Cussac
Château La France	Blaignan
Château Gallais Bellevue	Potensac
Château Grand-Duroc-Milon	Pauillac
Château Grand Moulin	St Seurin-de-Cadourne

Château Haut-Bages-Monpelou	Pauillac
Château Haut-Canteloup	Couquèques
Château Haut-Garin	Bégadan
Château Haut-Padarnac	Pauillac
Château Houbanon	Prignac
Château Hourtin-Ducasse	St Sauveur
Château de Labat	St Laurent
Château Lamothe-Bergeron	Cussac
Château Le Landat	Cissac
Château Landon	Bégadan
Château Lartigue-de-Brochon	St Seurin-de-Cadourne
Crû Lassalle	Potensac
Château Lestage	Listrac
Château MacCarthy-Moula	St Estèphe
Château Monthil	Bégadan
Château Moulin Rouge	Cussac
Château Panigon	Civrac
Château Pibran	Pauillac
Château Plantey-de-la-Croix	St Seurin-de-Cadourne
Château Pontet	Blaignan
Château Ramage-la-Batisse	St Sauveur
Château La Roque-de-By	Bégadan
Château de La Rose-Maréchale	St Seurin-de-Cadourne
Château Saint-Bonnet	St Christoly
Château Saransot	Listrac
Château Soudars	Avensan
Château Tayac	Soussans
Château La Tour-Blanche	St Christoly
Château La Tour-du-Mirail	Cissac
Château La Tour-Haut-Caussan	Blaignan
Château La Tour-St Bonnet	St Christoly
Château La Tour-St Joseph	Cissac
Château des Tourelles	Blaignan
Château Vieux-Robin	Bégadan

The following vineyards were not classified because they were being reconstituted in 1978

Château Les Bertins	Valeyrac
Château Clarke	Listrac
Château Larivière	Blaignan

Château Romefort	Cussac
Château La Valière	St Christoly
Château Vernous	Lesparre

The following properties have joined the Syndicate of Bourgeois Growths of the Médoc since 1978 but are at present not classified because of EEC regulations

Château Anthonic	Moulis
Château Beausite	St Estèphe
Château Bellevue	Valeyrac
Château Blaignan	Blaignan
Château Bonneau	Avensan
Château Bourdieu	Vertheuil
Château Bournac	Civrac
Château Cailloux-de-By	Bégadan
Château Canuet	Margaux
Château Charmail	St Seurin-de-Cadourne
Château la Commanderie	St Estèphe
Château de Conques	Couqueques
Domaine de la Croix	Ordonnac
Château L'Estruelle	St Yzans
Château Goudy-la-Cardonne	Ordonnac
Château Grivière	Blaignan
Château-Haut Logat	Cissac
Château Hauterive	St Germain-d'Esteuil
Château Lacombe-de-Noaillac	Jau
Château Lagorce	Blaignan
Château Lagrave	St Sauveur
Château Lalande	Listrac
Château Lestage-Simon	St Seurin-de-Cadourne
Château Lieujan	St Sauveur
Château Liouner	Listrac
Château Magnol-Dehez	Blanquefort
Château Malmaison	Listrac
Château Martinens	Cantenac
Château Malescasse	Lamarque
Château Marsac-Seguineau	Soussans
Château Maucaillou	Moulis
Château Maucamps	Macau
Château Monbrison	Arsac
Château Moulin-de-Castillon	St Christoly

Château Moulin-de-Laborde	Listrac
Château Moulin-de-la-Roque	Bégadan
Château Moulin-Riche	St Julien
Château Moulin-de-St Vincent	Moulis
Château Moulis	Moulis
Château le Plantey	St Yzans
Château Pey-Martin	Ordonnac
Château Peyredon-Lagravette	Medrac-Listrac
Château Pomys	St Estèphe
Château Preuilhac	Lesparre
Château Puy-Castera	Cissac
Domaine de La Ronceray	St Estèphe
Château St Ahon	Caychac
Château Saint Aubin	Jau
Château St Estèphe	St Estèphe
Château St Paul	St Seurin-de-Cadourne
Château St Roch	St Estèphe
Château Sénéjac	Le Pian
Château Senillac	St Seurin-de-Cadourne
Château Sestignan	Jau-Dignac-Loirac
Château Terrey-Gros-Cailloux	St Julien
Château La Tour-de-Mons	Margaux
Château Tour-du-Roc	Arcins
Château Tourteran	St Sauveur
Château Troupian	St Seurin-de-Cadourne
Château Les Tuileries	St Yzans
Château Vieux-Robin	Bégadan

ST JULIEN

This is the smallest of the four great communes of the Haut-Médoc, and the *appellation* limits the name to wines produced within the commune. The gravelly soil of St Julien resembles that of Margaux but contains more clay. This results in a wine with something of the finesse and breed of Margaux but with some of the vinosity and body of Pauillac. The bouquet of these wines is especially fine and develops early, and while they are in a sense somewhere between a Margaux and a Pauillac, this is a very inadequate description because it takes no account of their exceptional individuality. One cannot do better than to quote what Franck wrote of them long ago when speaking of their incomparable flavour which, he said, "cannot be well compared to that of any other claret. They combine all the qualities which constitute the very best wines." (*Traité sur les Vins du Médoc*, 4th edition, 1860.)

Within St Julien itself one can discern a distinct progression in the style of the wines. Those vineyards situated on the slopes along the river-front produce the wines with the most pronounced bouquet and finesse. Here are to be found the best parts of vineyards such as Léoville-Las Cases, Ducru-Beaucaillou and Beychevelle. As one moves inland towards the plateau of St Laurent, the wines become more full-bodied, more highly coloured and richer. Gruaud-Larose is an example of the best type of wines in this category. There are, of course, many variants between the two extremes because, apart from other factors, many vineyards are to be found in different parts of the commune and on differing soils.

St Julien used to be the most popular generic or district name for claret. Unhappily, wines sold under this name alone had to be viewed, especially in England, with a certain degree of suspicion. This was because a high proportion of the wines of St Julien was already sold under the names of individual châteaux and, apart from poor years, the quantity of genuine St Julien available for sale under the generic *appellation* was not large, and was certainly never cheap. Of a total of 820 hectares under vine, around 95 per cent are *crus classés*, the highest percentage in any *appellation* of the Médoc, and eloquent testimony to the qualities of its soil. Now, generic St Julien is essentially a thing of the past, except when the production of young vines is sold off without the name of the property, just under the AC St Julien.

It is one of the curiosities of St Julien that, while the percentage of fine wines produced is exceptional, and the quality of its wines represents much that is best in claret, no first growth is to be found here. But it must be said that in some years its best growths produce wines which equal, or can indeed surpass, the first growths.

CHÂTEAU BEYCHEVELLE

Quatrième Cru Classé. Owner: Société Civile du Château Beychevelle.
Administrator: Maurice Ruelle. 72 hectares. CS 60%, Mer 28%, CF 8%, PV 4%.
Second wine: L'Amiral de Beychevelle

This beautiful property has a long and interesting history. It can be traced back to the fourteenth century when it was a feudal castle and one of several important properties belonging to the de Foix family. This family became known as Foix de Candale after one of them, Jean de Foix, had refused to sign the surrender of Bordeaux in 1451 and had fled to England, where he was rewarded for his loyalty by being given the title of Kendal. This he mysteriously kept after his return to France and submission to Louis XI in 1463, when Kendal became Candale.

The property passed to the Duc d'Epernon when Marguerite de Foix-Candale, one of the greatest heiresses in France, became his third wife in 1587. Jean-Louis de Nogaret de la Valette, first Duc d'Epernon, was one of the great men of his age, deeply involved in the politics of the turbulent period in which he lived. He was the confidant and favourite of Henri III under whom he became an Admiral of France as well as a Duc, and was in the coach with Henry IV when the king was assassinated. He has been described as ambitious, vindictive, haughty, insolent but brave to the point of recklessness, and recognizing no bounds to his power – the last personification of the old nobility before the age of Versailles destroyed their virility. It was through the Duc d'Epernon's position as Admiral of France that Beychevelle acquired its name. Ships passing by on the Gironde were required to lower their sails as a salute when passing the residence of an Admiral of France. Beychevelle is a corruption of *Baisse-Voile, baisse* meaning lower and *voile* sail.

After the death of the second Duc d'Epernon without heirs, Beychevelle reverted to the Crown, who sold it to pay off the debts left by the Duc. In the eighteenth century, Beychevelle was still very much a feudal property, probably with a good deal of mixed farming as well as vines. It was under the ownership of the Marquis de Brassier (1740–1755), a *conseiller* of the Parlement de Bordeaux, that the viticultural reputation of Beychevelle was established. There were then 32 hectares of vines producing 80 tonneaux of *grand vin*, and the Marquis had a very considerable estate extending over six parishes and including Château Lamarque and Château Poujeaux in Moulis, where the seigneurial rights and jurisdiction of the Marquis held sway. The income from this property was as much as 400,000 *livres* in rent, dues and feudal rights.

At the time of the Revolution the Marquis's son was proprietor, and as he became an *émigré* the State seized the property and put it up for sale.

It was purchased by the Marquis's sister, Madame de Saint-Herem, who soon resold to Jacques Conte, a prominent Bordeaux shipowner. But the fame of Beychevelle as a great vineyard must be traced from the time of its purchase by Pierre-François Guestier in 1825 for 650,000 frs (approx. £130,000). It is interesting to note that while Beychevelle does not feature in classifications of the 1820s, it does appear on Charles Cocks's list of 1846, and was classified as a fourth growth in 1855, as was its neighbour, Branaire.

Pierre-François Guestier was an important figure in the Bordeaux of his day. Because of the Revolution and his father's friendship with the Bartons, he was largely educated in England. Apart from his activities as a partner in Barton & Guestier, of which he was one of the founders, he was keenly interested in all agricultural matters. Thus he established a plantation of cork trees at Beychevelle, which excited considerable interest and was responsible for his being presented with the Gold Medal of the Société d'Agriculture de la Gironde in 1845. It was not until 1866 that the same Société awarded him a Gold Medal for the cultivation of the vine at Beychevelle. No doubt because of liberal sentiments acquired in England, Monsieur Guestier was much in sympathy with the regime of Louis-Philippe and was active in politics during this period. He was first Deputy Mayor of Bordeaux, then Conseilleur-Général, and finally representative for Lesparre in the Chamber of Deputies. In 1847 he was made a peer of France, but took no further part in public life after the 1848 Revolution.

On Monsieur Guestier's death in 1874, the property was sold to Armand Heine, and on the death of his widow, it passed to her son-in-law, Monsieur Achille-Fould. The Achille-Foulds maintained the interest in public affairs which has marked former proprietors, the father of the last Achille-Fould proprietor having been Minister of Agriculture in one of the inter-war governments of the Third Republic, while his son was for many years a deputy representing the Médoc, and held ministerial office. In 1984 the family sold a minority interest to the important insurance company Crédit Foncier, who have since acquired control, and sold a minority interest to Axa (see Pichon-Longueville-Baron). They have been making some much-needed investment in the property, including the building of a new *chai*. For some years there had been a lack of direction at Beychevelle, and while it is sad to see this jewel of the Médoc no longer a family property, there is some compensation in the improvements that are now showing through in the wines themselves.

The château itself, which commands a prominent position on the *route des châteaux*, has a fair claim to being the most beautiful in the *Médoc*. The present building dates from 1757 and the era of the Marquis de Brassier. It follows a classic Bordeaux formula which was often repeated, though never with such effect, in the nineteenth century. This provides a central single-storey building in which is the principal salon, and twin-storey towers at each end. The perfect proportions of the building are beautifully set off by delightful wrought-iron railings and sumptuous flower-beds, which invariably attract the attention of the passing motorist. On its river side is a beautifully laid-out garden and lawns running down to and commanding an unrivalled view of the Gironde.

Beychevelle has long enjoyed a great reputation in England, and today its quality and prices place it among the second growths. It is one of the largest estates in the Médoc and has always had a considerable production. This averaged between 160 and 180 tonneaux by the end of the last century, although in years such as 1889, 1893 and 1900, well over 200 tonneaux were made. A small piece of the vineyard lies in the neighbouring commune of Cussac. The wine from this vineyard is now sold separately under the name Les Brulières de Beychevelle, and has the Haut-Médoc *appellation*, not that of St Julien.

There is a saying that a good year for Beychevelle is a good one for Bordeaux. It is true that this wine usually succeeds very well in the best vintages but is seldom very distinguished in small years. This slight inconsistency, however, is really the only reservation to be made about a wine which is, at its best, a very beautiful and charming St Julien. It has a bouquet of great elegance, and its ripe, fresh flavour is usually evident very early on, so that it often makes delicious early drinking.

Among old vintages, the 1928 was a rather typical wine of the year in taking a long time to come round, but then made one of the most enjoyable and sublime bottles of the vintage. The 1933, on the other hand, was a delightful wine, one that in the old days would have been called ideal luncheon claret – soft, delicate, fruity and quite charming. The 1945 was a fine wine, slow to mature, the 1953 was a beauty, all charm and almost too pretty in its first youth – it then filled out and deepened like an enchanting treble who to everyone's surprise turns into a first-rate tenor as well. The 1954 was a pleasing wine for the year, but the 1955 was a disappointment. The 1957, on the other hand, was one of the best wines in the Médoc. Neither the 1958 nor 1960 was very good, but Beychevelle has continued to do well in good years and was particularly outstanding in 1961, followed by a 1962 which was somewhat reminiscent of the 1953 and just as full of charm. A magnum was still delicious, with great breed, in 1987. Then came 1964 (above average), 1966 (a fine classic), 1970 (one of the earlier developers in this slow year), 1971 (really magnificent) and 1975 and 1976 both classics of these two very different years. There is a feeling that 1978 and 1979 are not quite as good as they could have been. The 1978 has a lovely flavour, complexity and breed, but was very well advanced when nine years old, and may not make old bones, while 1979, although looking younger, has a rather diluted finish. The 1980 is really delicious, harmonious and with good fruit, an excellent example of the year, to drink young. The 1981 is also advanced but elegant, fine and delicious. From this point onwards the wines seem to grow in power. The 1982 has real concentration behind its gorgeous flavour, and blackcurrants on the nose, promising an exceptional bottle. The 1983 was in an intermediate stage when tasted in late 1987, showing just a little tannic and dry but with enough attractive fruit to hold out the hope of a good evolution. The 1984 is honourable with a pleasant frank flavour, short but not dry, now ready to drink. The 1985 and 1986 are a great pair of Beychevelles. The 1985 is marvellously opulent and perfumed, with lovely highlights and great "*race*" and length, even after only three months in bottle. The 1986, with 55 per cent new oak against 50 per cent for the 1985, is marvellously balanced with very ripe, powerful tannins matching great fruit and richness. A classic *vin de garde*, with the breed shining through. On this form a new era seems assured for this archetypal St Julien.

CHÂTEAU BRANAIRE
Quatrième Cru Classé. Owner: Société Anonyme du Château Branai-re-Ducru. Administrator: Pierre Tari. 48 hectares. 20,000 cases. CS 60%, Mer 20%, CF 15%, PV 5%

This charming property faces Beychevelle across the road and looks out over vineyards and the S curve of the *route des châteaux* towards Ducru-Beaucaillou. The château itself is well worthy of mention. Its beautiful classical bearing is unusual in the Médoc for its elegance and simplicity. Built in 1780, it is a monument to that renaissance of prosperity and good taste which beautified Bordeaux in the decades just before the Revolution. The fine *chais* include magnificently cool, sunken cellars for the maturation of cask wines in their second and third years. This plays an important part in the fine development these wines always show in cask. There is also a charming orangery, restored for the entertainment of visitors.

There is a notable history of continuity at Branaire, for although its name and those of its proprietors have changed, it remained in the possession of connected families, so that there is an unbroken link from the 1740s until the time of the First World War. During this time, the property was known successively as Duluc, Branaire-du-Luc, and finally Branaire-Ducru. It is mentioned in classifications of the 1820s as a fourth growth, but its eminence really dates from the stewardship of Louis du Luc from 1825 onwards.

In the 1855 classification, it was placed among the fourth growths, but already by the 1860s its wines were fetching the prices of a third, and sometimes of a second growth. It was at this period that Branaire passed, after the death of Louis du Luc's widow, into the hands of a relative, Monsieur G. Ducru, whose family had just sold the neighbouring Beaucaillou, to which they had also given their name, to Nathaniel Johnston. It was under Ducru that the property reached the zenith of its reputation in the nineteenth century, although for a time this was well maintained by Ducru's nephew and heir, the Marquis de Carbonnier-Margac. After the death of the Marquis, the ownership was in the hands of a number of heirs, and it was from these that Monsieur Mitel bought Branaire after the Second World War.

As with many other properties, the affairs of Branaire languished just before and just after the Second World War, until Monsieur Jean Tapie acquired it in 1952. Since then, he and his son Jean-Michel have gradually reconstituted the vineyard, always being careful to preserve a good proportion of old vines, but ensuring that new plantations were maturing to take their place, so that a correct rotation was reintroduced. In the *cuvier* Monsieur Tapie introduced the submerged cap method of vinification, familiar in North Africa. This seems to give colour and generosity to the wines while keeping them supple, and there is some evidence that the results that have been achieved here are more encouraging than the practice of heating the must, which is employed at some other properties. The combination of a good Médocain *maître de chai* and a proprietor with Algerian experience, who is neither afraid of new ideas or unmindful of what tradition has to impart, has proved remarkably successful. On his father's death, Jean-Michel Tapie inherited with his sister, who is the wife of Nicolas Tari of Giscours, another "*pied-noir*" who bought his château in the same year as the Tapies bought Branaire. In 1987 Jean-Michel Tapie sold his 50 per cent share to Sucrière de Toury, a leading French sugar refiner, leaving the Tari family with the other 50 per cent. The production, which throughout the history of the property has been very consistent, has now been restored to the high level it enjoyed at the end of the last century.

The reputation of this growth has also revived considerably after its acquisition by the Tapie family. Fine wines were made in 1953, 1959, 1961 and 1962. The 1960 was exceptional for the year, while the 1964 and 1966 were very good examples of their respective years. In 1966 Monsieur Jean-Michel Tapie decided to launch a non-vintage wine, the object being to improve the quality of the off-vintage wines by blending them with some wine from the best years. As a corollary to this, only the best years were to appear as such under the Branaire label. This was a bold move at the time, designed to arrest the debasement of the "vintage" wine which had been an unhappy feature of Bordeaux in the early sixties. As a result, 1963, 1965 and 1968 were not sold under the vintage label. But with the changed circumstances of the seventies, the experiment came to an end. In more recent years, a very fine and characteristic 1970 was made, a charming 1971, and an outstanding 1975. The 1976 is attractive and balanced, 1977 is one of the successes of the year, and 1978 is again top-flight. The 1979, like many wines of this year, was slower to open out, and seems tighter-knit and younger. There was a decent 1980, which took longer than usual to shake off the effects of new oak. The 1981 is elegant and firmer than usual, 1982 is a lovely example of the year with lots of concentration combined with complexity and style, 1983 has a rather diluted character and is for early drinking. In contrast, the modest 1984 vintage produced a delicious wine, light but with length of flavour, all fruit and finesse. The 1985 was promising in cask, tannic, powerful and rich. So the wines of Branaire have shown great consistency and a steady improvement for some years. Although not yet a really fashionable *cru*, it is another example of the remarkable strength in depth that is the Médoc today.

The wines of Branaire have a marked individuality. The bouquet is very powerful, with an almost Pauillac assertiveness. The wine is rich, generous and supple with a most distinctive flavour. It has rather more body than most St Juliens. This particular personality is probably due to the fact that a part of the vineyard is on the plateau of St Laurent and, though not large, lends its personality to the whole. Amongst his other gifts, Jean-Michel Tapie had a special touch when it came to the *assemblage*. I have, on a number of occasions, tasted the constituent parts of a new vintage with him before the final *assemblage*, and it has been fascinating to see how the various elements have been fitted together to achieve a whole more satisfying than any of the individual constituents – the true test of any blending of wines of different *cépages*, and from wines of varying ages and soils.

This is one of a number of examples in the Médoc of classified growths with a part of their vineyard in a commune other than that of their *appellation*. As these anomalies are nearly always of long standing, the *appellation* authorities do, in fact, give special permission for such wines to be incorporated in the final blend without in any way affecting the right of this blend to its traditional *appellation*.

CHÂTEAU LA BRIDANE

Cru Bourgeois. Owner: Pierre Saintout. 15 hectares. 8,000 cases. CS 55%, Mer 45%

This is a decent middle-of-the-road *cru bourgeois* of good repute. In the eighties, the Cabernet Franc had been eliminated and the Merlot increased. I have found recent vintages to be attractively fruity, with medium weight, and drinkable young.

CHÂTEAU DUCRU-BEAUCAILLOU

Deuxième Cru Classé. Owner: Jean-Eugène Borie. 49 hectares. 17,000 cases. CS 65%, Mer 25%, CF 5%, PV 5%. Second label: Château la Croix

This charming property adjoins that of Beychevelle, and indeed both châteaux are rather similarly placed, commanding a fine view across low-lying meadows to the river. As a building, Beaucaillou cannot, it is true,

equal its neighbour, but with its elegant terrace and its pleasing proportions, this rather distinctive Victorian mansion has an attraction all its
own. The château is unusual for Bordeaux in having its *chais* situated
beneath it and its *dépendances* in large underground cellars.

In the early part of the nineteenth century this growth was known as
Bergeron, but when it came into the possession of the Ducru family their
name was adopted, together with that of Beaucaillou, the name given by
them to the place itself. The fame of Beaucaillou dates from the care and
improvements effected by Monsieur Ducru, and subsequently by
Nathaniel Johnston who acquired the property in 1866. Under him, it
was usually known simply as Beaucaillou.

The reputation of Beaucaillou declined between the wars, but since the
property has come under the management of Monsieur Jean-Eugène
Borie, whose father had bought Beaucaillou during the Second World
War, a renaissance has occurred in its quality and reputation. Monsieur
Borie is a devoted enthusiast, and one of the relatively few resident proprietors among the top-growth Médocs, so that visitors to the château are
frequently welcomed by the proprietor in person; he is also one of the
best-liked and most respected proprietors, a man of engaging modesty
about his own wines, and always a generous judge of his neighbours'. He
is also a much-travelled ambassador for Bordeaux wines abroad.

The vineyard itself, lying beside that of Beychevelle and south of
Léoville-Las Cases, produces a wine typical of the best of St Julien.
Beaucaillou has the elegance, lightness and breed of a wine from a vineyard near the river, a superb bouquet and a flavour which fills the mouth.
Compared with Las Cases, it is a little softer and lighter and lacks the
richness of growths like Gruaud-Larose which lie further inland. There is,
interestingly enough, a small parcel of vines in the neighbouring
commune of Cussac.

I have seen few examples of pre-war vintages, and of these two were
worthy of note: the 1910, which was still very fruity and generous, typical of its year, sound in wind and limb when drunk in 1963. The 1928
was curious for being already faded and light in 1958. The first Borie
vintage I tasted was the 1945. By 1987 the tannins were ripe and soft and
the wine was delicious, without perhaps the depth of some of the great
1945s, but then it was very drinkable! The vintage which did more than
anything else to reestablish the reputation and standing of Beaucaillou

was 1953. This has developed into a really delicious wine with an outstanding bouquet and an almost silky texture on the palate – one of the top 1953s. The 1955 is more attractive than most, the 1957 one of the most approachable wines of this vintage, and still delicious in 1985. The 1958 and 1960 were both charming wines, light, elegant and flavoury, at their best when about five years old but holding up well afterwards for several years. The 1959 has been a great success, with more length in middle life than many wines of this vintage; it has consistently lived up to its early promise, one of the few 1959s that can stand beside the 1961. The 1961 is one of the great examples of the extraordinary qualities of this vintage with its phenomenal power and depth. In a blind tasting in Holland in 1978, this wine was placed first among ten leading growths of the year, and was then placed on a par with some of the first growths in the second half of the tasting. The 1962 is outstanding for its attractive ripeness, while the 1964 was one of the best Médocs in a disappointing year. Since then, a string of successes has followed: 1966 and 1967, 1970 (exceptional) and 1971 (an outstanding example of the vintage), 1973 and a 1974 with more charm than most, a great 1975, a 1977 of charm and a classic 1978 with depth and complex dimensions. Unusually, 1979 is more advanced than the 1978 and lacks Beaucaillou's usual complexity. The 1980 is a soft, full-flavoured wine for early drinking. The 1981 has power matched by breed. The 1982 has all the qualities one looks for in this remarkable year, while 1983 is most successful with lots of power. The 1984 has style and fruit, so should make a charming bottle for early drinking. In cask, 1985 combined concentration with considerable style while 1986 is exceptional for the year with rich, ripe fruit balancing the strong tannins. All this goes to show that since 1953 Beaucaillou had consistently produced fine wine and is today undoubtedly one of the jewels of St Julien.

CHÂTEAU DU GLANA

Cru Grand Bourgeois Exceptionnel. Owner: Gabriel Meffre. 45 hectares. 17,000 cases. CS 68%, Mer 30%, CF 2%

This property is of relatively recent importance, although its origins go back a little further than Gloria's (see below). It was the creation of the Kaelin family who built it up in the early years of the century from an obscure *artisan* growth making only a few tonneaux to an important property. It is, with Gloria, the largest growth after the classified ones in St Julien.

The massive and strictly functional *chai* and *cuvier* are opposite the turning to Ducru-Beaucaillou, and next to Gloria. The ugly little red-brick villa that appears on the label is not now part of the property. The reputation of du Glana is rather mixed. I have found the wines well made, easy, fruity and delicious, designed for early drinking, but typical of their *appellation*, commercial in the best sense of that word.

CHÂTEAU GLORIA
Cru Bourgeois. Owner: Henri Martin. 45 hectares. 16,000 cases. CS 65%, Mer 25%, CF 5%, PV 5%. Secondary labels: Châteaux Haut-Beychevelle-Gloria, Peymartin

Gloria is not a name which will be found in any old book of reference, for it has been created in the space of a generation by Monsieur Henri Martin. The project began from small beginnings just before the war. Monsieur Martin purchased the *chai* of St Pierre, but did not have the money then to buy the brand, hence Gloria is not a classified growth. Instead, he set out to build up a vineyard which would be acclaimed for what it was and judged solely on its own merits.

The vineyard is, in fact, in the best part of St Julien near the village of Beychevelle and contains parcels of land bought at various times from Léoville-Poyferré, Gruaud-Larose, St Pierre and Duhart-Milon. The proprietor, Monsieur Henri Martin, is one of the leading personalities in the Médoc today. Mayor of St Julien, he was for many years President of the Comité Interprofessionel and is still one of the leading figures in the Bontemps du Médoc. More recently he has played an important role in the new management of Château Latour.

The wine itself is a fine and typical St Julien of the more generous kind, combining true finesse and breed with a fullness of flavour and richness of body – the Gruaud-Larose type rather than the Léoville-Las Cases or Beychevelle style. It is very consistent and was included in the INAO's proposal for a new classification in 1961, an opinion also endorsed by Alexis Lichine. The 1953 was worthy of the vintage, the 1961 was fine if not so relatively outstanding, and very successful wines were made in 1962, 1964, 1966, 1970, 1971, 1973, 1975, 1976, 1978 and 1979. In the most recent years 1980 produced a delicious wine for early drinking, with real St Julien "*race*". 1981 is on the light side for the year, there is a fine 1982 and the 1983 has plenty of richness and attraction. The very attractive 1985, with lots of fat and ripeness, is closer in quality to St Pierre than it was in 1982 or 1983. The dense, tannic 1986 has the breed shining through, and promised an exceptional bottle when in cask. In recent vintages, the price of Gloria has edged up to that of that classified growths, and indeed this is well warranted by its own intrinsic merits. The names of Haut-Beychevelle-Gloria and Peymartin are used as subsidiary *marques*; the former is now to be found in England, and the latter, the product of younger vines, in America. With Henri Martin now one of the grand old men of the Médoc, it is reassuring to see him so ably and keenly assisted by his son-in-law, Jean-Louis Triaud.

CHÂTEAU GRUAUD-LAROSE

Deuxième Cru Classé. Owner: Cordier family. 82 hectares. 35,000 cases. CS 62%, Mer 25%, CF 9%, PV 4%. Second label: Sarget de Gruaud-Larose

This is another example of a large estate which was created during the eighteenth century by a wealthy and enthusiastic proprietor, Monsieur Gruaud. It was in 1757 that he combined three properties, Tenac, Sartaignac and Dumarle, to form this important growth which was at first known as Fonbedeau before assuming that of Gruaud, or Gruau as it was sometimes spelt. Gruaud made a name for himself both as an enthusiastic viticulturalist and as something of an eccentric, for to live on one's estate and personally supervise its management in every aspect was hardly the norm in the France of the *ancien régime*. He even built a tower especially, so that he could observe work on all parts of his large estate, and from the top of which he would fly a flag whenever a vintage had been successfully gathered in.

On his death in 1778, he left the estate to Monsieur de Larose, a member of the *noblesse de robe* which played so important a part in the development of the Médoc in the years before the Revolution. He was Lieutenant-General of the Sénéchaussée of Guyenne as well as being president of one of the law courts. The château now became known as Gruaud-Larose and the fame of its wine became more widespread, so that it found its way on to the greatest tables in the land. It was during this period that it boasted the proud device which has for long appeared on its labels, "Le Roy des Vins, le Vin des Rois". When the heirs of Monsieur

Larose disposed of the estate in 1812 for the sum of 350,000 frs (approx. £70,000) it was bought by the house of Balguerie, Sarget, Verdornet & Cie. The driving force in this enterprise was the remarkable Pierre Balguerie-Stuttenberg, one of the most successful and colourful figures of Bordeaux. His history is typical of the vigour and enterprise which characterized Bordeaux commerce at this time. His family having been ruined by the revolution on St Dominique, he began by working for the drapery business of Diré and Verdornet. His aptitude for business, combined with his industry, intelligence and loyalty, so impressed his employers that he was taken into partnership in 1805, at the age of twenty-nine. Two years later he married a Mademoiselle Stuttenberg, the daughter of a Hamburg merchant who had offices on the Chartrons; when his father-in-law died soon afterwards, Balguerie-Stuttenberg took over the running of the business, and thus his connection with wine began and he became associated with the future Baron Sarget. For Balguerie-Stuttenberg, wine and Gruaud-Larose were very much a sideline left in the capable hands of Sarget, while he occupied himself with the affairs of a rapidly growing shipping and trading business which was to extend as far as China and South America. He and Sarget were both concerned with the project for building the bridge across the Gironde at Bordeaux. He was also instrumental in improving the port of Bordeaux, established a telegraph between Royan and Bordeaux and became noted for his charitable works as well.

After Balguerie-Stuttenberg died in 1825, worn out by his remarkable industry, Sarget became solely concerned with the management of Gruaud-Larose and acquired a considerable reputation as a viticulturist. All the early classifications of the nineteenth century are unanimous in placing Gruaud-Larose among the then rather small group of second growths, and this was confirmed in 1855. Although the Sarget family maintained a very long connection with Gruaud-Larose, unfortunately they divided the estate in two, selling the other portion of it in 1867 to Edouard and Charles de Bethmann and Adrien Faure. The two Bethmanns came of a German family in Frankfurt who had settled in Bordeaux in the eighteenth century. Their father, as noted for his philanthropic work as for his banking, was in fact Mayor of Bordeaux at the time of the purchase. In this era many gold medals and diplomas were awarded to both growths, and in 1879 Sarget was awarded the Gold

Medal by the Ministry of Agriculture for the best-kept vineyard in the Gironde. New *chais*, cellars and *cuviers* had been constructed in the 1870s.

After the First World War the Sarget family sold their property to Désiré Cordier after a connection of over a century with the growth, and in 1934 Monsieur Cordier had the satisfaction of reuniting the property when he purchased the Faure portion. The house of Cordier is now one of the most important in Bordeaux; Gruaud-Larose is meticulously run and is something of a showplace. The garden is one of the finest to be seen in any Bordeaux château although, unlike some other châteaux, it does not encourage visitors without specific trade introductions. Monsieur Cordier believes that too many visitors can interfere with the work of a château. One unusual feature of the *chais* are the large wooden *cuves* of around 60 hectolitres each, where the wine undergoes a part of its maturation. Wine is also kept in the traditional 225-litre *barrique bordelaise*, but this is carefully monitored according to the constitution of each individual wine. It is felt that these large *cuves* enable a slower maturation to be achieved, enhancing the fruit of the wine, which is such a feature of modern vintages of Gruaud-Larose. The production has always been one of the most consistently large in Médoc. In 1985 the Cordier family entered into an agreement with the Compagnie La Hénin, a large banking and investment group, to sell their control of the company by stages, over a period of years. The management has, to date, remained essentially unchanged.

A tasting organized in 1990 by Dr Marvin Overton in Fort Worth, Texas – in collaboration with Cordier – provided a unique opportunity to assess Gruaud Larose between 1819 and 1989. The 1819 was a most remarkable wine, amazingly preserved, with remarkable vigour, freshness and harmony – it had never left the château. Then came 1834 (a *rôti* nose with just so much fruit and richness), 1870 (clean, fresh vinosity, fullness and elegance), 1893 (more body than the 1899, with richness, vinosity and breed but some acidity), and 1899 (a wonderful perfume, complex and gorgeous still on the nose, but delicate, faded and ethereal in flavour – an old beauty).

Sadly, there was no bottle of the fabled 1900, but 1906, almost black in colour, was very impressive with great concentration, full of power and attack. From the twenties, the most interesting wines were 1921 (tough, dry tannins but lots of richness and flavour), 1924 (drier than the 1926, but still rich in fruit and very stylish), 1926 (high-toned but powerful, with more fruit and life than the 1928). The 1928 was better on the nose than the palate, having gone dry and tannic, and the 1929 was a disappointment, nearly gone. Then there was a deliciously rich and fruity 1934, and an impressive, austerely masculine 1937. The 1943 had real class, fine flavour, rich and dry. Then came the great post-war years: a great 1945, very concentrated with a wonderful flavour, still very tannic and full of life; 1947, exceptional for a Médoc, where volatile acidity undermined so many great wines. This was wonderfully opulent, with perfect harmony of rich fruit and ripe mellow tannins. After a disappointing 1949, 1950 was remarkable for the year, rich and coffee-like. Following a dull 1952, 1953 was wonderfully perfumed and spicy. A double magnum still had sumptuous fruit which filled the mouth, a wine at its apogee, but the bottles were noticeably less sumptuous, a real advertisement for big bottles! With its liquorice scent, great extract and powerful tannins, 1955 was still impressive. While very rich, powerful and tannic, 1959 lacked the class of the marvellous 1961 which, having been one of the first wines of the vintage to become drinkable in the late sixties, is still vigorous, with a wonderful rich sweetness and complexity, a gorgeous wine. The lovely 1962, with its complex flavours, great finesse, length and elegance, is also an exceptional example of the vintage, as is the 1964, with its incredible scent, great finesse and succulent luscious fruit in double magnums. The bottles were less rich, but still among the best wines of this vintage (and all this in spite of the fire of 1965 which destroyed a part of the crop). The 1966 is a classic, with its spicy rich tannins and fruit, and what a lovely assertive flavour! The 1967 was harmonious and fruity, the 1968 still alive and fruity. The 1970 in bottle was probably at its best, elegant and delicious, but a magnum had more dimensions, richness and power. The 1971 was drying out; the 1973 was big and coarse, perhaps over-adjusted with *vin de presse*; the 1974 as so often was the poorest wine of the decade; while the 1975 was the best, very rich and concentrated, tannic without being too dry, with a dimension lacking in the 1978. The 1976 had the roasted character of the year with powerful tannins but dusty at the finish. The 1978 is a lovely wine, scented, elegantly fruity and stylish, perfect drinking, while the 1979 had that touch of coarseness of the year but was harmonious and still not quite mature. The 1980 was absolutely delicious, with lovely fruit and great charm, in contrast to the unready 1981, which was firm and a little dry. The 1982 had a splendid flavour, real concentration of ripe tannins and depth of fruit, a great '82. At present, the 1983 tastes rather hollow, with dominant dryish tannins, but one should wait for it. The 1984 is a decent small wine, without much personality. Which will be the best, the 1985 or the 1986? Both promise to be great wines. Beauty of flavour, great charm and elegance of fruit, combined with impressive structure in the 1985 contrast with the less evolved 1986 with its massive flavour and lovely fruit encompassing powerful tannins. The attractive, yet solid and compact 1987 should prove a good follow for the 1980 as an early drinker with breed. And, finally, another great pair, 1988 and 1989. The first is a classic *vin de garde* with great richness and concentration, the second, at this early stage, was impressive for its intensity of fruit and rich tannins, but it will be several years before a clear pattern appears.

This remarkable tasting wonderfully demonstrated the consistent style and great quality of Gruaud-Larose. In the eighties, it has impressively risen to the challenge of some exceptional vintages by producing wines of unusual concentration, without any loss of its inimitable breed and style.

In 1979 a second wine, Sarget de Gruaud-Larose, was introduced. While it retains the depth of colour and richness of the *grand vin*, it is much softer and so is ready to drink when three to four years of age. A very consistent standard has been maintained.

CHÂTEAU HORTEVIE

Cru Bourgeois. Owner: Henri Pradère. 3.5 hectares. 1,500 cases. CS and CF 70%, Mer 25%, PV 5%

This is a wine I first saw under the Wine Society label. It is a very small vineyard lying just behind the village of St Julien-Beychevelle, and is run in conjunction with the larger and better-known Terrey-Gros-Caillou, by the same proprietor. A good example of the marvellous "*terroir*" of St Julien, this is a wine of real breed and quality.

CHÂTEAU LAGRANGE

Troisième Cru Classé. Owner: Château Lagrange SARL. Administrator: Marcel Ducasse. 113 hectares. 19,000 cases. CS 66%, Mer 27%, PV 7%. Second label: Les Fiefs-de-Lagrange

If many Bordeaux châteaux have had their ups and downs, few have been as spectacular as at Lagrange. In the nineteenth century it rose to fame dramatically after its purchase by a powerful political figure. Then, in the eighties, after many years of neglect and obscurity, it was once more catapulted to fortune by becoming the first *cru classé* to be bought by Japanese.

The property is of ancient origin. In 1287 it formed part of the Manor of the Templars at St Julien. In 1669 it was called Pellecahus. On the dissolution of the Templars at the beginning of the fourteenth century, it had passed into the hands of the de Cours, *seigneurs* of Pauillac and Lagrange. In 1787, for the first time, its viticultural importance becomes clear. Under the name of d'Arbouet it appears in a classification (as reported by Thomas Jefferson) as a third growth. At about the same period, it also appeared on Belleyme's map, which for the first time enabled one to see precisely what areas of the Gironde were then planted with vines. By 1815, it appears under the name of Cabarrus and is classified by Lawton as a "troisième" once more. This change of name had occurred through the purchase of the estate by Jean Valère Cabarrus in 1796. He became a Count of the Empire, and Napoleon I's Finance Minister in Spain. In 1832 it was purchased for 650,000 frs (£162,500) by a John Lewis Brown (see also Cantenac-Brown), and then sold by him in 1842 to Comte Duchatel for 940,000 frs. Comte Duchatel, whose father had been a prominent administrator in the Gironde, under the Consulate and Empire from which the title derived, was then Minister of the Interior in the government of Louis-Philippe. To emphasize the wealth and importance of the new proprietor, a massive tower was constructed at the château. The edifice dwarfed a decent, sober, classical portico and mansion of modest but comfortable proportions, built in 1771. This monument of wealth and ostentation is constructed in a parody of the Italian style, much in vogue during that period.

As we have already noted, the standing of Lagrange had been high for over fifty years prior to the Duchatel purchase, but in this period, from 1842 to 1875, it reached its zenith. It was the largest estate in the Médoc with 300 hectares, of which 100 were planted, and lay in a single piece surrounding the château. In 1852 a scheme of drainage in the vineyards, using earthenware pipes buried more than a metre deep, was undertaken, the first of its sort in the Gironde. In 1855 its position in the hierarchy of the Médoc was confirmed when it was placed among the third growths. In 1875 it was sold to Monsieur Louis Mouicy, and then in 1925 it was bought by Señor Manuel Cendoya, a Spanish wine-grower. This was the beginning of a bad period for Lagrange. With the years of the Depression beginning in the late twenties, and carrying on through and after the war years, the Cendoyas had financial problems, which they attempted to solve by selling off parcels of their extensive vineyards. By the time of the sale to Suntory in 1983, the 300 hectares of the original estate had shrunk to 160, with less than fifty actually planted, but still in a single block.

It was on 15 December 1983 that the great Japanese drinks group Suntory actually bought Lagrange, having succeeded in overcoming French government apprehension by undertaking to provide the massive investment required to place Lagrange back among the leading *crus* of the Médoc. They invited an enthusiastic Professor Emile Peynaud to act as adviser, and appointed Marcel Ducasse, a former Peynaud pupil, as *régisseur*. Later, Michel Delon of Léoville-Las Cases joined the team to bring his immense practical skills to the assistance of Lagrange. To provide vital liaison, Marcel Ducasse has been joined by Kenji Suzuta, who had earlier been sent by Suntory to study oenology in Bordeaux.

They have renovated the vineyards (there was too much Merlot) and gradually doubled their area, restored the splendid nineteenth-century *cuvier* and *chai*, and then built a massive new maturation *chai* for the first-year wines. The first stage of the new building programme was complete by the spring of 1987, together with the complete renovation of the château and the park. The new *chai* is in traditional stone and blends in excellently with the existing buildings. This programme represents an initial investment of around 100 million francs (£10 million). The remarkable new *chai* can be entered by a tunnel from the restored *cuvier*, now resplendent with stainless steel vats with their built-in cooling systems. It is a breathtaking sight, some 100 metres long with six lines of casks, the whole normally air-conditioned to achieve about 16 °C. This was operational in 1987. Another *chai*, of identical size, was then built on the far side and parallel, and the whole programme was finished in 1989. In the initial three-year planting programme, begun in 1984, new plantations of Cabernet Sauvignon have increased the proportion of this prime Médoc variety to 66 per cent, and reduced the Merlot to a more normal 27 per cent, instead of the 50 per cent to be found when Suntory took over.

In 1987 I was able to gauge the progress which had so far been made by tasting, in the beautifully appointed new sample room, the vintages from 1981 to 1986 with Marcel Ducasse. A charming wine was produced in 1981, with elegance and finesse but just a little fluid at the finish. The 1982 has delicious ripe, rich fruit, is quite advanced for the year, and lacks real concentration. The 1983 was vinified by the Cendoyas, but the *élevage* was done by Marcel Ducasse and his team. The use of new oak immediately brings out extra breed on the nose and the stricter selection of vats adds more weight and length to the finesse and undoubted breed. The 1984, the first wine made entirely under the new owners' control, but with the existing *cuvier*, already shows a better colour than the 1983. It is a good wine for the year, but too dry and marked by new oak when three years old. Perhaps it will adjust in time. The 1985 crop was split 40 per cent Les Fiefs-de-Lagrange, the second wine first introduced in the 1983 vintage, and 60 per cent *grand vin*. The Les Fiefs 1985 was actually better than Lagrange 1984, and had delicious, easy, ripe fruit, well balanced and ideal for early drinking, while the Lagrange itself was much more rich and concentrated, without sacrificing any of the charm. It was really much better than the 1982, a fair measure of what has already been achieved. The cask sample of 1986 Les Fiefs was very tannic and concentrated, an impressive wine that will take longer to mature than the excellent 1985, while Lagrange, after three months in cask, had more fruit and great richness and concentration which should ensure a remarkable wine.

A brief postscript on Lagrange pre-Suntory may also be useful. In the fifties the wines were mostly tough, stalky and coarse in style. There was an improvement in the sixties, and respectable wines were made in 1961, 1962 and 1964. Then the château was put under contract to Alexis Lichine & Cie, and Professor Peynaud was called in to safeguard their interest, in an attempt to produce better results. After the end of the contract, good wines were also made in 1978 and 1979.

CHÂTEAU LALANDE-BORIE

Cru Bourgeois Supérieur. Owner: Jean-Eugène Borie. 18 hectares. CS 65%, Mer 25%, CF 10%

This excellent *cru* is a creation of Jean-Eugène Borie of Ducru-Beaucaillou. The vineyard was formerly part of Lagrange, and was planted only in 1970. It has its own separate *cuvier* and *chai*. The 1978 was the first significant vintage, but this *cru* has really come into its own during the eighties, with excellent wines, showing typical St Julien finesse, made in 1982, 1983, 1985, and 1986. Up until now, they have been best drunk young, but as they gain weight and power – as in the 1986 – they should certainly repay keeping as well. The wines are impeccably made, as one would expect from Jean-Eugène Borie.

CHÂTEAU LANGOA-BARTON

Troisième Cru Classé. Owner: Société Fermière du Château Langoa-Barton. 20 hectares. 8,000 cases. CS 70%, Mer 15%, PV 8%, CF 7%

Nowhere perhaps does one see such a handsome collection of châteaux in so short a distance as around the tiny village of Beychevelle-St Julien. Beychevelle and Branaire face each other across the road, then Beaucaillou is to be seen away on the right across the vineyards, and finally, as one leaves the village for St Julien itself, there is the more massive but distinctly fine château of Langoa. It is in the best eighteenth-century style, built by Bernard de Pontet in 1758, so is an almost exact contemporary of its neighbour, Beychevelle. These are the two most impressive Médocain châteaux of the eighteenth century, with Beychevelle perhaps the more elegant, with its unbroken central roof-line, but Langoa is weightier and more imposing. It has the distinction of having been in the Barton family continuously since 1821, longer than any other classified growth; at that time the property was known as Pontet-Langlois. Perhaps English mispronunciation soon turned Langlois into Langoa. The advantages of continuity are evident as soon as one steps over the threshold, for this is a château that has been continuously occupied by the same family apart from the interruption of war, and indeed some of the hangings and decorations go back to Hugh Barton's time. At the entrance there is a most pleasing staircase, leading up to the ground floor which is at first-floor level and is built over the private cellar – a charming arrangement.

The extensive *chai* houses the wines of both Langoa and the Bartons' portion of Léoville. It is one of the curiosities that the wines of Langoa were never château-bottled until 1969, but were removed to Barton & Guestier's cellars in Bordeaux and bottled there. The wines of Langoa maintain a good standard; they somewhat resemble those of Léoville-Barton in style, but are rather lighter and seldom quite match up to it in quality. It is interesting to note that in two vineyards under the same ownership, as in 1855, and with the composition of the vineyards virtually unchanged, the classification is nearly always right in placing Langoa in a lower category to Léoville-Barton. It is nevertheless a thoroughly reliable wine, a true St Julien and deserving its present reputation. The only old vintage I have tasted recently is 1929, and that was a great bottle, opulent and very rich still, its freshness suggesting a much younger wine. Among the recent vintages, the 1970 produced a classic St Julien, 1971 is outstanding, better in my view than the Léoville, 1973 is already showing age, but the 1974 is unusually attractive for the year, better than the 1973 and better than the Léoville. The 1975 is typically rich and tannic but with plenty of fruit and fat; it should mature more quickly than the Léoville. The 1976 is now soft and ripe but lacks finish. The 1977 is a success for the vintage. The 1978 is a classic of the vintage, marvellously scented, with depth, power and style, while 1979 is something of a lightweight but elegant and fine. There is a well-structured and attractive 1980. The great vintages of the eighties are ushered in by a fine-boned 1981, an exotically spicy 1982, and a stylish, well-balanced 1983. The 1984 looks a little lean, but has some length and finesse. In cask, 1985 had a lot of St Julien charm, a compact wine of medium weight, while 1986 was of quite another dimension and style, rich, very powerful and tannic.

Now that Anthony Barton has taken over from his uncle Ronald (see under Léoville-Barton), a new generation is breathing fresh life into both the château and its wine, and the future looks bright for Langoa, which has the capacity to improve on its rather understated reputation – at least outside Ireland, and England!

CHÂTEAU LÉOVILLE-BARTON

Deuxième Cru Classé. Owner: Société Fermière du Château Léoville-Barton. 39 hectares. 16,000 cases. CS 70%, Mer 15%, PV 8%, CF 7%

Like Poyferré, Léoville-Barton is a quarter portion of the original Léoville domain. The circumstances of the Barton purchase were rather unusual. During the Revolution, Léoville was sequestrated because the Marquis de Las Cases was an émigré. But other members of the family who had not emigrated successfully petitioned for the return of all but one part of the domain. That part was auctioned and eventually bought by Hugh Barton with the intention of returning it to the Marquis on his return. Unfortunately the Marquis was unable in the end to recompense Hugh Barton for his outlay, so eventually in 1826 the latter became proprietor of this estate. Hugh Barton was an Irishman whose grandfather had first come to Bordeaux in 1725. In spite of this, the Barton family then and now remains an Irish family with close ties with their homeland. Having acquired the neighbouring property of Langoa in 1821, Hugh Barton was able to use the *chai* of Langoa for housing the wines of his portion of Léoville, so that there has never been a separate *chai*, or château, for this property. These two properties have been in the ownership of a single family for longer than any other classified growth in the Médoc, for Hugh Barton's descendant, Mr Anthony Barton, today owns and runs Langoa.

The production of this portion of Léoville has increased in recent years: it is recorded at 50 to 60 tonneaux in 1860 and is around 125 today although in the prolific vintage of 1893 it reached 164. The reputation of Léoville-Barton has remained very consistent over a long period and, as might be expected, it has long enjoyed a considerable following in the UK. For sixty years the story of Léoville and Langoa centred around one man, Ronald Barton, who succeeded to the family inheritance as a very young man in 1927, after his father, Bertram Hugh Barton, was killed hunting in Ireland; he had joined the family firm of Barton & Guestier only three years before his father's death. He was very much the resident proprietor, closely supervising his wines and setting the highest standards for them. He was a greatly loved figure in Bordeaux and the Médoc, a traditionalist who disliked most of the changes he saw around him in his last years. Although he was childless, the family had wisely provided him with an heir from among its Irish resident members. Anthony Barton, Ronald's nephew, went to Bordeaux in the fifties, so had a prolonged apprenticeship before his uncle died in 1986. Fortunately everything had been formally handed over several years before, so the transition was a smooth one. With an ear for languages, Anthony Barton is as witty and inimitable in French as in English, and he has already made important strides in modernizing the wine-making facilities, especially by improving temperature controls. Although very fine wines were made throughout Ronald Barton's stewardship, it had become clear in his last years that there were some inconsistencies and occasional disappointments and the improvements seen in other properties in the seventies, through stricter selection, were not happening here.

I have not seen any very old examples of this château in fine years, but the 1929 was a fine wine, if not quite the equal of the Poyferré of that year. This is a wonderfully consistent growth; very attractive wines were made in rather mixed vintages such as 1934 and 1948, while the 1945, 1949 and 1959 were particularly successful. More recently, classic wines were made in 1961, 1962, 1964, 1966, 1970, 1971, 1975 and 1978. Unusually, the 1974 is to be preferred to the 1973, but 1979 was a little disappointing. Since then, stricter selection and improvements in vinification have been evident. The 1980 is excellent. There is a rich and elegant 1981, a beautiful 1982, and a 1983 that combines charm and breed with considerable power. The 1984 is a success for the year. In cask the 1985 had great beauty and charm, the 1986 had tremendous power and tannin, a fascinating pair for the future. It is clear that, as at Poyferré, things are on the move here and that sights have been raised. Future comparisons between the three Léovilles are likely to be closer and more interesting, placing Léoville-Barton among the leading *crus* of St Julien.

CHÂTEAU LÉOVILLE-LAS CASES
Deuxième Cru Classé. Owner: Société Civile du Château Léoville-Las Cases. Administrator: Michel Delon. 85 hectares. 30,000 cases. CS 65%, Mer 18%, CF 14%, PV 3%. Second label: Clos-du-Marquis. Third label: Domaine de Bigarnon

This great growth must take pride of place among the wines of St Julien. It represents the major portion of the pre-Revolution estate of the Marquis de Las Cases, and its label still proudly, if rather confusingly, proclaims its lineage "Grand Vin de Léoville de Marquis de Las Cases".

Before the Revolution, this was one of the greatest estates in the Médoc of the eighteenth century, extending from Château Latour to Château Beychevelle, its vineyards broken only by the village of St Julien, and situated on the unrivalled slopes above the *palus* (the alluvial, low-lying land by the river) commanding a fine prospect of the river. The present estate comprises half the original domain, a quarter having been sold to Hugh Barton and a quarter to Baron de Poyferré in 1840. It has remained unchanged since that time, and the jewel of the vineyard is its famous 50-hectare *grand clos*, surviving in a single piece from Latour to the village of St Julien. The whole is enclosed by a fine wall, and the main entrance is marked by an arch, recently repaired, which is a notable landmark on the *route des châteaux*, and has long adorned the château label. It is one of the largest vineyards in a single piece in the Médoc.

Until 1900, it remained in the hands of the Las Cases family. Then, all but one of the Las Cases heirs having sold out, a Société Civile was formed, with Madame d'Alauzier, granddaughter of the colourful Marquis de Las Cases who had followed Napoleon to St Helena, holding eight of the twenty-one shares. One solitary share was acquired by the *régisseur*, Monsieur Théophile Skawinski, son of the famous agriculturalist whose career has already been touched upon under Giscours. It is now under the direction of Monsieur Michel Delon whose grandfather André Delon was Théophile Skawinski's son-in-law; thus he is the fourth generation of his family to supervise the property, so that a remarkable degree of continuity has been achieved from the eighteenth century through to the present day. Although, like his famous father, Paul Delon, before him, Michel Delon is a rather controversial figure in the Médoc, there can be no doubt that he is one of the most capable proprietors in the region today. With a passion for quality, he controls all with a precision that commands admiration. This is nowhere better illustrated than in his preparation for the *assemblage* each year. Once the fermentation is finished, he tastes and charts the progress of each vat until the *assemblage* takes place several months later. So this crucial operation is not just a matter of a single tasting, as is usual, but the culmination of an organic process spread over months.

Over the years, with certain exceptions, Las Cases has maintained its position as the finest wine in St Julien. There was certainly a period before the war when Poyferré was often its equal and sometimes its superior. Again, there was a period in the fifties, when, owing to a preponderance of young vines following extensive replanting, the wines failed to achieve their usual excellence. But from 1959 onwards, even in off-vintages, Las Cases has consistently been one of the best second growths in the Médoc. The essence of Las Cases is a bouquet of great elegance and suavity and an incomparable flavour which is almost silky in texture when mature, very long but at the same time firm and well balanced. A good Las Cases is a very complete wine in the fullest sense of that word.

A word about the historic vintages may be of interest. The 1899 was still well preserved when I was last privileged to drink it in 1963. But much more remarkable was the 1900. On both occasions when I drank this wine in 1962, I thought it one of the greatest clarets I have ever drunk, the equal of any first growths. The bouquet was still wonderful and continued to expand in the glass, while the flavour was delicious, a perfection of breed and finesse and perfect harmony, without a trace of decay. In 1971 I tasted a bottle from the cellar of Glamis Castle which was every bit as fine and vigorous. This is truly one of the immortals. Next, one must mention the 1928. The Las Cases of this vintage was the best wine of the year, superior to any of the first growths. When last drunk in 1979, it was in a state of complete perfection, a wine stunning in its sheer beauty. Its fascination is that it combines the bouquet and finesse of a great 1929 with the power and solidity of a 1928, and in so doing, it far outstrips its contemporaries which seem dry and harsh in comparison.

I have mentioned the lean years in the fifties. Before this, good wines were made in 1945, 1947 and 1948. The 1959 was a very fine comeback and has fully lived up to its early promise. The 1960 was a most attractive wine and was one of the best Médocs of the vintage, while the 1961 was one of the best wines of this great year. Along with Palmer, Ducru-Beaucaillou and Gruaud-Larose, it is one of those on a similar plane to the first growths, as has been clearly shown in recent blind tastings. The 1962 was also one of the best wines of the year, which has continued to develop in complexity and interest over the years, and the 1964 was one of the most successful Médocs in a year when the region generally failed to live up to its early reputation. The 1966 was excellent, and was only just approaching full maturity in 1987, a true coming-of-age. The 1967 is one of the best wines of a mixed vintage, and unlike most Médocs, has not dried up. The seventies have produced another string of classics: a great 1970, an aristocratic 1971, with the power and compactness of a 1970, an above-average 1973, great 1975s and 1976s, and an exceptional 1977 in the context of the year. The 1978 is a classic of this vintage with great complexity and finesse, 1979 is developing more slowly and has concentration and breed. The 1980 has been slower to develop than most wines of the vintage, and is more solid. The 1981 has a gorgeous flavour and great breed but is tannic and powerful, a wine for the nineties. The 1982 is a regal wine of exceptional concentration and character, while 1983 has remarkable depth and power, a real *vin de garde*. These two should make a fascinating pair in years to come. Severe selection has produced an out-of-the-ordinary 1984. In cask the 1985 gave every indication of being a great wine in the making, with remarkable completeness, opulence and power, while 1986, a selection representing only 45 per cent of the whole production, has the almost opaque depth and concentration to promise great things.

The second wine, Clos-du-Marquis, has been in continuous existence for longer than most second *marques* – since 1902. It has always been a good wine offering good value, but in recent vintages has become even more impressive. Since 1980 a third *marque*, Domaine de Bigarnon, has skimmed off the production of young vines and the Clos-du-Marquis has gained in richness and depth of flavour.

In conclusion, it should be said that today Léoville-Las Cases, because of its quality and consistency, is one of those top Médocs which are separated from the first growths only through the rigid traditions of Bordeaux's ossified classification system, and their price. As such, it represents wonderful value – a wine enabling connoisseurs to enjoy claret of first-growth quality at half the price.

CHÂTEAU LÉOVILLE-POYFERRÉ

Deuxième Cru Classé. Owner: Cuvelier family. Administrator: Didier Cuvelier. 63 hectares. 18,500 cases. CS 65%, Mer 35%. Second label: Château Moulin-Riche
The growth began its separate existence when one of the Las Cases heirs sold her portion to her sister, who was the wife of Baron de Poyferré-Céres. In 1866 it was bought for one million frs (approx. £200,000) by Monsieur Armand Lalande and the Baron d'Erlanger. The property then passed in the 1890s to Edouard Lawton and, after the First World War, to the Bordeaux *négociants* H. Cuvelier & Fils. During the second half of the nineteenth century this growth enjoyed an exceptional reputation as one of the very finest of all the second growths, and Biarnez's poem was often quoted, where he proclaimed: "Et je ne comprends pas quel expert

inhabile a pu dans les seconds classer le Léoville", the implication being that Poyferré should have been a first growth.

At its best, the style of Poyferré was essentially similar to Las Cases, as might be expected, and indeed during this period the very same Skawinski who managed Las Cases also ran Poyferré. The greatest Poyferrés I have seen were the 1928, which was second only to the Las Cases in that vintage, and the magnificent 1929. It is interesting to find Morton Shand, always a lover of old wines, still echoing the nineteenth-century view of Poyferré in 1920 in finding Poyferré the best of the Léovilles. I have not seen enough examples of the wines from the inter-war years to express an opinion as to whether this was generally true in this period, but in recent years, Poyferré has in general been well behind Las Cases in quality. While there were some attractive, stylish wines, such as the 1959 and 1966, 1970 is a grave disappointment, but 1973 was a delicious early-drinking wine. There is a good 1975, already drinking well by 1985, and 1978 is attractive enough but 1979 is disappointing. However, an important change occurred in 1979 when Didier Cuvelier took over the administration and began a programme of much-needed reinvestment. The old *fouloir-égrappoir* was changed, the *chai* had a face-lift and more new casks were introduced. Finally, an enthusiastic young *maître de chai*, Francis Dourthe, as committed to quality as Didier Cuvelier, arrived in 1982. The improvement has been dramatic. A much better 1980 has been followed by outstanding wines in 1981, 1982 and 1983. They have all the breed, length and beauty of flavour one expects, or could hope for. The 1984 is elegant and harmonious. The 1985 had great promise in cask, as had the more tannic 1986.

So a new era has dawned for Poyferré. The wines lack the weight and concentration of Las Cases but have real "*race*" and distinction. With recent improvements at Barton as well, it will soon be possible to com-pare the three Léovilles without the old handicaps of slipshod wine-making or poor equipment.

CHÂTEAU ST PIERRE
Quatrième Cru Classé. Owner: Henri Martin. 20 hectares. 5,000 cases. CS 70%, Mer 20%, CF 10%

This property is one of ancient origins. Its archives go back to 1693 when it was known as Serançon and belonged to the Cheverry family. In 1767 it was acquired by a Monsieur St Pierre who gave the estate his name. His family's connection continued until after the Second World War.

The division of the estate, and the confusing nomenclature which resulted, took place in 1832 after it was divided among different members of the family. About half the estate remained in the hands of Lieutenant-Colonel Bontemps-Dubarry, a grandson of Monsieur St Pierre, so that the name of Bontemps-Dubarry was then added to St Pierre to distinguish his portion from the rest. Some time later the largest part of the remainder came into the hands of Bontemps-Dubarry's daughter, from whose estate it was purchased by Monsieur Leon Sevaistre. This was how the second portion of the St Pierre estate came to be known as St Pierre-Sevaistre. The other part of the estate continued in the hands of Lieutenant-Colonel Bontemps-Dubarry, then of his son and his son's brother-in-law, Monsieur Kappelhoff of the Bordeaux house of Journu Frères and Kappelhoff. Monsieur Kappelhoff's son then became proprietor and was known as Bontemps-Kappelhoff. The Sevaistre part was sold to the Antwerp firm of Van den Bussche just after the First World War, and they acquired Bontemps-Kappelhoff's part just after the Second World War, thus reuniting the property after over a hundred years of division. In 1982, Henri Martin and his son-in-law, Jean-Louis Triaud, bought St Pierre, thus fulfilling a long-held ambition of Henri Martin, who already had 10 hectares of the original St Pierre vineyard in Gloria. The château and park have now been restored and the Martins and Triauds have made it their home. It stands just past Branaire on the same side of the road, right on the corner of the sharp bend as the road turns towards St Julien itself.

There were a number of small properties owing their origins to St Pierre; these, with one exception, have been absorbed into other growths. On the other hand, other properties, notably Gloria and du Glana, contain important portions of the original St Pierre vineyard. In the classification of the 1820s, St Pierre appeared among the fourth growths. The divided property was placed among the fourth growths in 1855.

In the last years of the Van den Bussche era, some elegant, rather light wines were made. They had a definite finesse but were often surpassed by the neighbouring Gloria. However, I tasted an impressive 1945, and in 1972 they made one of the better wines in this poor vintage. The difference once Henri Martin took over was immediately noticeable: 1982 had simply more of everything than the very good Gloria. The class of the wine shone out, and there was concentration and richness. But after all, this was 1982. In the more variable vintage of 1983, there was again richness and tannin to set off the great "*race*" and finesse. The 1985 is also beautifully perfumed, supple and rich. The 1986 in cask was exceptionally tannic and powerful, with great finesse. So the stage looks set for a new era at St Pierre, and this will be one of the *crus* to watch in the nineties. Once more it has been shown that if the right soil is there, it needs only a skilful hand to bring a forgotten *cru* back into favour.

CHÂTEAU TALBOT

Quatrième Cru Classé. Owner: Jean Cordier. 101 hectares. Red: 40,000 cases. CS 71%, Mer 20%, CF 5%, PV 4%. White: 2,500 cases. Secondary labels: Connétable Talbot, Caillou Blanc du Château Talbot (Bordeaux Blanc AC)

This well-known growth has long been popular in England, not least because of its English name derived from that Earl of Shrewsbury who was killed in the last important action of English arms before the loss of Gascony to the English crown. Curiously enough, there seems to be some doubt as to whether the property ever actually belonged to him. Two families have dominated the history of Talbot: those of the Marquis d'Aux, and of Cordier. The wines of Talbot first became well known when the d'Aux family were proprietors. Surprisingly, it did not feature in unofficial classifications of the 1820s, but appears in Cocks's list of 1846, and in 1855 Talbot, Branaire and Beychevelle were all placed among the fourth growths. The vineyards of Talbot lie further inland than those of the other two, on that rising gravelly plateau which reaches back towards St Laurent, and its neighbours are Gruaud-Larose and Lagrange. During this period of its history, the property was usually known as Talbot d'Aux or as d'Aux Talbot, or Château Marquis d'Aux. Throughout the nineteenth century, production remained fairly constant between 100 and 120 tonneaux.

The property left the d'Aux family at the end of the nineteenth century, and was acquired by George Cordier after the First World War from Monsieur A. Claverie. The Cordiers have in recent years done much to improve and modernize, especially in the *chai*. The wine itself is a true St Julien – elegant, soft and distinctive. It is always interesting to compare its wines with those of Gruaud-Larose, its neighbour and now under the same ownership. The style of the two wines is remarkably similar, but the Gruaud is nearly always the better of the two, with more body, more bouquet and concentration of flavour. The comparison between the two is rather similar to the Léoville-Langoa relationship on the Barton estate not far away, although of course the marriage is far more recent.

Lovers of Talbot will have happy memories of the 1929 and 1934, both delightful and typical wines, the 1934 being more attractive and enjoyable than many wines of this vintage. In recent years, the wines, as at Gruaud, have been noticeably quicker to mature.

A magnum of 1945 drunk in 1982 not only had the concentration and great depth expected, but plenty of fruit and fat as well. The 1959 and 1962 were both successful years which made pleasant drinking early but have stayed the course well. Since then, the most successful years have been 1966, 1970, 1971, 1973, 1975 and 1976. The 1978 has been a slow developer, elegant and long-flavoured but still a shade tough at the finish in 1987. In contrast, 1979 is seductive and delicious, more forward and typically Talbot. The equally delicious 1980 developed more quickly than the Gruaud-Larose. The 1981 has a lovely bouquet of ripe blackcurrants, a lovely wine already drinkable by 1987. The 1982 is a marvellous wine, a real *vin de garde*, with great concentration of fruit and ripe tannins. Conversely, 1983 is a little soft-centred and diffuse at the finish, an early developer. The 1984 has lovely mellow fruit and was already delicious to drink when three years old. Again, there was a strong contrast in styles between 1985 and 1986 in cask, with 1985 all opulent, rich fruit compared to the dense, tannic 1986, a wine of real concentration promising a great future. It is interesting to note that here, as at Gruaud-Larose, large wooden *cuves* of around 60 hectolitres are used for part of the maturation. I used to feel that these Cordier properties flattered early but then disappointed in the middle life. However, the development of the vintages since 1959 has, I think, shown this fear to be unfounded. (For the change in control of the Cordier company, see under Château Gruaud-Larose on p. 124.)

Recent developments at Talbot have been the expansion of its white wine, Caillou Blanc, and the introduction of a second wine, Connétable de Talbot. There are now 6 hectares of Sauvignon producing Caillou Blanc, which is kept in vat and bottled early. It is a very scented wine, with a lively, fruity acidity, best drunk when one to two years old. The

Connétable was introduced with the 1979 vintage. It has the vivid fruit of Talbot, but develops more quickly, so is ideal for early drinking, normally when three to four years of age. A high standard has been maintained.

CHÂTEAU TERREY-GROS-CAILLOU

Cru Bourgeois. Owners: André Fort and Henri Pradère. 15 hectares. 8,000 cases. CS and CF 65%, Mer 30%, PV 5%

This is probably the best non-classified *cru* in St Julien today, after Gloria. The vineyard is in several parcels, the most important of which is behind the village of Beychevelle, adjoining Talbot and Léoville-Barton. The *chai* is situated here. Another parcel adjoins Gruaud-Larose, and another Beychevelle and Ducru-Beaucaillou.

My interest in this *cru* was first aroused when I came across the 1966 in cask. Not only does it have the breed and style of a true St Julien, it also has body and power in the good vintages. The high standards now being attained may be gauged by the fact that, even in high-yielding years such as 1979 and 1983, when some wines were a little diffuse, Terrey-Gros-Caillou had concentration and balance. More recently the 1986 in cask promised to be a fine *vin de garde*. This really is the wine for those who love St Julien but do not always want to pay *cru classé* prices.

5

Pauillac and St Estèphe

PAUILLAC

This is the most important commune in the Médoc, both in terms of size and the sheer volume of fine wines it produces. While the signboard at Margaux proudly proclaims "Vins rouges les plus célébrés du monde", Pauillac's boast is simpler and more complete, "Les premiers vins du monde". Yet the curious thing is that the name of Pauillac itself is not so well known. One hardly ever sees generic wines simply sold as Pauillac; Margaux and St Julien are much better known and more sought-after.

The fame of Pauillac lies in its great growths, which stand as sentinels at either end of the commune; Latour at the southern end adjoining St Julien, Lafite to the north, looking across a marshy brook to Cos d'Estournel and St Estèphe on its neighbouring hilltop. The variety and individuality of these wines are such that any generalizations about Pauillac wines are extremely difficult. On the whole they are more powerful than other Médocs, with slightly more body and firmness than the bigger St Juliens. The lesser wines lack the finesse and breed of St Julien or Margaux, or the bouquet of St Estèphe, and are sometimes a little mean at first. But the best wines have a regal quality which is unsurpassed among Bordeaux wines for its combination of power, elegance and individuality. They age superbly and are amongst the most long-lived of natural red wines.

The town of Pauillac, known to Ausonius as *Pauliacus*, is the most sizeable in the Haut-Médoc, but its river-front had, until recently, a curiously desolate and run-down quality, like a seaside resort perpetually out of season. Now a small marina has been built, and life, albeit of a different kind, has returned to Pauillac's waterfront. In the days of sail, when the journey on to Bordeaux took valuable time, this was an important port, and it was from here that Lafayette, once a magnet of Francophile feelings on the other side of the Atlantic, set sail in 1777 to champion the cause of the rebellious colonies and hasten England's discomfort. The headquarters of the Commanderie du Bontemps du Médoc is housed in the new ultra-modern Maison du Vin, which has taken the place of Château Grand-Puy-Ducasse, now repossessed by its present owners. Except for special investitures during the three *fêtes* which punctuate the Commanderie's year, new members are usually invested here. The pastoral tranquillity of Pauillac has now been somewhat shattered by a Shell refinery, small by the standard of such things, but looming large in this low, undulating landscape. Nevertheless, it has found a new use for the port.

Pauillac itself incorporates a number of very small communes which once had a separate existence, sometimes of some importance. St Lambert was at one time a separate parish before it was united with Pauillac – Latour and the Pichons lie within its boundaries. Other villages are Artigues, Bages, Milon, Mousset and Le Pouzalet.

CHÂTEAU BATAILLEY

Cinquième Cru Classé. Owner: Emile Castéja. 50 hectares. 22,000 cases. CS 73%, Mer 20%, CF 5%, PV 2%

I have always had an affection for this growth, since it was one of the earliest I came to know well during my early visits to Bordeaux. The property lies a little way out of Pauillac on the road to St Laurent. The château is a pleasing example of the classic mid-nineteenth-century type, similar in scale and layout to Palmer but without the towers. The vineyard is well placed on the high plateau at the back of Pauillac, adjoining St Laurent.

The present management dates from 1942, when Monsieur Marcel Borie of Borie-Manoux, Bordeaux *négociants*, purchased it. The early reputation goes back to the period of Daniel Guestier of Barton & Guestier who bought it in 1818, his heirs selling it to Monsieur Constant Halphen, a Parisian banker, in 1864. The château was first mentioned in a classification when it featured among the fifth growths of Lawton's 1815 list, under the name of Bedou, and in 1846 Charles Cocks lists it together with the name of the proprietor. Since Monsieur Marcel Borie's death in

1961, the estate has been managed by his son-in-law, Monsieur Emile Castéja, himself from an old proprietorial family (see Lynch-Moussas).

The wines of Batailley are typical of the best sort of Pauillacs in the second rung of quality – solid and dependable, very consistent, but only occasionally really memorable. In its less successful moments such as 1955, for example, there is a tendency to be rather tough and mean, lacking flesh and fruit. Through the generosity of the proprietors, I have had the opportunity to drink several old vintages: the 1911, 1928 and 1934 were all successful wines of their years, and the 1911 even held up well when over fifty years old.

Since the war, the 1945 was fine but austere, the 1953 outstanding, the 1955 a trifle lean and austere, the 1959 generous, ripe and full-bodied, the 1961 a very good example of the year, the 1964 outstanding – certainly one of the best Pauillacs of this year of mixed fortunes – and the 1966 good without repeating the magic of the 1964. During the seventies, powerful and typical wines were made in 1970, 1975 and 1976. The 1978 is delicious, with the finesse and style of the year, but a policy of stricter selection produced an even better 1979, with more richness and depth, yet without sacrificing any charm. After a pleasant, light 1980 for early drinking, 1981 has a fine flavour backed by ample fruit and structure, 1982 is a classic with great ripeness and depth, 1983 is one of the better Pauillacs in this vintage, with tannin and body, 1984 is very honourable for the year, without dryness, and 1985 has the balance and seductive depth of fruit looked for in this vintage. So the overall picture is one of consistency, with sights raised – as at so many properties in recent years, and especially since 1979. Because this wine is sold exclusively through the *négociants* Borie-Manoux, it does not appear on the Bordeaux market, so does not feature in other merchants' comparative tastings. On top of this it is sold at very modest prices, which can give the impression that it is less good than is, in fact, the case. The obvious point of comparison is with the wine from the other portion of the original property, Haut-Batailley. While it is true that Haut-Batailley can have an advantage in finesse, Batailley is more full-bodied and richer in texture and in recent years has improved in terms of stylishness. In my opinion a comparison between the two would often give the advantage to the less fashionable Batailley.

CHÂTEAU CLERC-MILON

Cinquième Cru Classé. Owner: Baron Philippe de Rothschild SA. 30 hectares.
8,700 cases. CS 70%, Mer 20%, CF 10%

This property is situated in the small village of Milon. When driving from the village of Pouyalet north towards Lafite, one comes across it on a slope between the road and the river. Some of the vineyard lies on this side facing the road, some on the other side facing the river.

Monsieur Clerc was the proprietor at the time of the 1855 classification. Monsieur Mondon, whose name used to be joined to those of the château, was a notary in Pauillac, and until recently the proprietors were his two granddaughters, themselves the sisters of Monsieur Jacques Vialard, the leading notary of Pauillac. In 1970 they sold to Baron Philippe de Rothschild. From 1947 until the sale, the exclusivity for the distribution of the wine was in the hands of Dourthe, *négociants* in Moulis and Bordeaux.

At the time of the sale, the excellence of the soil was held out as the main reason to expect a dramatic improvement in the wines here. Had it merely been a question of improved wine-making, we should have seen rapid results, but extensive work had to be done in the vineyard, and a programme of replanting takes time to show through in terms of better wines. For this reason the climb in quality has been a slow one. In September 1986 I was able to have an up-to-date view of what was happening at a tasting held at Mouton-Rothschild. The 1978 was a supple, attractive and very drinkable wine, but without the breed of its rival, Mouton-Baronne-Philippe, whose wines were tasted alongside, providing a useful benchmark for the progress of Clerc-Milon. The 1979 was a less attractive wine, more powerful and assertive in character. The 1980 was a pleasant, soft, fruity wine for immediate drinking, and no more. But with 1981 the tide began to turn. The colour was deeper and younger than the Mouton-Baronne-Philippe, the nose fuller and richer, the flavour fruitier and more stylish and harmonious – Clerc-Milon had suddenly changed gear and gone into the lead. The 1982, on the other hand, had less depth of colour than Mouton-Baronne-Philippe, but the tannins seemed riper and softer; and this is a fine wine with a good future. The 1983 is frankly a disappointment. The wine had a rather diffuse flavour, lacking a solid middle, and finishing short. The 1984 was honourable for the year, with medium weight and harmonious fruit and tannins. The 1985 was the most impressive wine in the tasting: still in cask, it had more charm and breed than Mouton-Baronne-Philippe. The lovely fruit flavours were well supported by richness of texture and powerful tannins, a wine with a fine future, and the best wine made here to date. Subsequently, the 1986 was every bit as impressive: its lovely flavour, great richness and supple tannins again surpassing the Mouton-Baronne-Philippe tasted alongside.

It is clear then that 1981 marked an important step forward in terms of quality and style, while in 1985 the wine achieved a new dimension rather as Grand-Puy-Lacoste has since 1981. So the future looks exciting at Clerc-Milon, as it rises to new heights among its fellow Pauillacs. It is marked out as one of the stars of the eighties.

CHÂTEAU COLOMBIER-MONPELOU

Cru Grand Bourgeois. Owner: Bernard Jugla. 15 hectares. 7,000 cases. CS 68%, Mer 18%, CF 6%, PV 5%, Mal 3%. Second label: Grand Canyon

For many years this was probably the best wine made at the *cave coopéra-tive*, although always sold under its own name. Then it was bought by Bernard Jugla, proprietor of the adjoining Pédesclaux, in 1970. Since Colombier had lost its château and *chai* in 1939 – they now serve as the headquarters for Baron Philippe de Rothschild SA – a completely new installation had to be built. The wines are fermented in vat and then aged in casks, of which one-third are renewed each year. The reputation for good honest Pauillacs, with a certain suppleness and pleasing fruit, has been growing in recent years.

CHÂTEAU LA COURONNE

Cru Bourgeois Supérieur Exceptionnel 1932. Owner: Madame des Brest-Borie. 4 hectares. 1,750 cases. CS 70%, Mer 30%

This growth was classified in 1932 as a *cru exceptionnel*. It was only created in 1874 by Monsieur Armand Lalande, the founder of the *négociant* A. Lalande & Cie, and owner of Léoville-Poyferré and Brane-Cantenac. Hence it was not classified in 1855, but has been granted the special status of a *cru exceptionnel*. The vineyards are very well sited in the southern part of Pauillac on the inland plateau. Today the vineyard belongs to the Borie family and has been administered since 1952 by

Monsieur Jean-Eugène Borie on behalf of his sister. Since the construction of a new *chai* and *cuvier* for 1974, the wine is made in Pauillac, and like all Monsieur Borie's wines, is most meticulously made. The style is very true Pauillac, sometimes a shade aggressive to start with, but developing good fruit and always harmonious and well balanced. A very good standard is being maintained, and the wine is as good as many fifth-growth Pauillacs.

CHÂTEAU CROIZET-BAGES

Cinquième Cru Classé. Owner: Madame L. Quié. Administrator: Jean-Michel Quié.
22 hectares. 8,500 cases. CS 37%, CF 30%, Mer 30%, PV and Mal 3%

When I first visited the *chai* of Croizet-Bages (there is no château) in the early sixties, it had a distinctly rustic appearance, and I remember thinking that this was how most *chais* must have appeared in the nineteenth century – with an earthen floor, a low, cobwebby roof and grimy casks in disorderly profusion. Now things are as spick and span as everywhere else.

The property lies on high ground behind Lynch-Bages, and was created out of the old domain of Bages during the eighteenth century, by the brothers Croizet. By the time of Lawton's classification of 1815, its reputation was sufficient to place it in his lowest category of *crus*, alongside d'Armailhacq (Mouton-Baronne-Philippe). Its best-known proprietor was Monsieur Julian Calvé, who bought the property in 1853 and whose name was sometimes found appended to the château title. It remained in the Calvé family until 1930, and was purchased by Paul Quié in 1945. Since his death it has been administered by his widow, and now by his son Jean-Michel Quié.

Croizet-Bages produces good, robust, full-flavoured Pauillacs which mellow fairly early, assisted, no doubt, by the lower than usual proportion of Cabernet Sauvignon, and the generous amount of Merlot and Cabernet Franc, compared to neighbouring Lynch-Bages. After the 1945 which, while fruity, remained hard and tough for many years, came a number of most attractive and successful wines. The 1953 had all the ripeness and charm of the year and was at its peak when ten to fifteen years old; the 1955 was rather firm for some time but was more attractive than many wines of the vintage; the 1957 was a success, developing fruit and mellowness; the 1959 was attractive if not outstanding; the 1960 has been one of the most long-lived wines of the year and was still at its best after eleven years, when many others were fading; the 1961 is worthy of the year – an outstanding wine. In 1986 I did a vertical tasting of Croizet-Bages, going back to 1962. This wine, which some years ago I characterized as easy and agreeable with a lot of fruit, had stood the test of time well, still having a lovely flavour, even if a touch of acidity had crept in. The 1964 was actually better; it had breadth and style, and a richness and depth of flavour that was impressive in this vintage of mixed fortunes. The 1966 reached a similar level of quality, with elegant, lacy fruit on the nose, while the fine flavour showed finesse and richness. The 1970 has been a slow developer. The richness and charm on the nose were not, at first, matched on the palate. But the rather tough, dry flavour expanded and filled out well in the glass. In contrast 1971 had instant charm and drinkability, a really lovely flavour with a depth and richness that had matured into elegance – a wine at its best. The 1973 was a curious wine: it had lovely initial mellow fruit, but then descended into a coarse, harsh finish suggesting over-correction with *vin de presse*. The 1976 had the roasted nose often found in 1976s, and concentrated fruit and extract in the flavour, quite harmonious and without any trace of dilution – a very good 1976. But the 1978 was a disappointment, its solid, meaty character becoming tough and coarse. In contrast 1979 had more refinement, with an attractive ripe fruitiness and balance, yet without real depth. The 1982 was a good example of the vintage with that taste of prunes, high extract and dense-textured. A wine to follow the 1961. In contrast 1983 was almost ready to drink, like a number of northern Médocs. There is a lovely plummy flavour and a touch of breed, but the undoubted dilution makes this a wine to drink early.

To sum up, the older vintages have aged well, the more recent ones are a mixed lot, sometimes doing very well in the challenging years like 1976, yet disappointing in some respects in 1978 and 1983. They are good middle-of-the-road wines, not undeserving of their classification, and offering the consumer good value for money.

CHÂTEAU DUHART-MILON-ROTHSCHILD
Quatrième Cru Classé. Owner: Domaines Barons de Rothschild. 50 hectares. 12,500 cases, CS 57%, Mer 21%, CF 20%, PV 2%. Second label: Moulin de Duhart

It is remarkable that in the commune of Pauillac, after the heights of Lafite, Latour, Mouton and the two Pichons, there should be no third growths in the 1855 classification and but one fourth growth. Is it really true that such a gap exists? I believe that, although certain growths do today deserve a higher rating, there is in reality a significant difference in style and quality between the great first and second growths of the region and the rest.

Duhart-Milon, called simply Duhart in the 1855 classification, was a much more important growth in the nineteenth century than it has been in recent years. For most of this time it belonged to the Castéja family, who at one time were the hereditary notaries of Pauillac. Indeed, in Charles Cocks's list of 1846, the property is mentioned as Castéja, formerly Duhart. The family fortune was the work of Pierre Castéja, who was born in Pauillac in 1799, his father of the same name being mayor of Pauillac, and mentioned as being the proprietor of Duhart-Milon. Pierre Castéja had a very successful legal career, taking him from local councils in Lesparre and Pauillac on to that of Bordeaux and finally, in 1859, to be mayor of the city. In this role he was responsible for carrying out numerous improvements during a period of progress and prosperity in the city's history.

It is difficult to determine quite when Duhart-Milon's decline really set in. Certainly the 1929 was a very fine wine, but the 1949 was no more than passable, while wines of the fifties were hard and tannic, with little grace, charm or breed. Part of the vineyard seems to have been sold off, and in the 16 hectares that remained in production there was an excessive proportion of Petit Verdot. Originally the vineyard had been in two parts, on the plateau of Carruades by Lafite and around the village of Milon.

In 1962 the Lafite-Rothschilds bought the property and reconstituted the vineyard, which obviously fits in very neatly with Lafite. Improving a really run-down property takes time, and it was hardly surprising that for some years after the Rothschild purchase, the wines, while certainly more attractive than hitherto, were hardly distinguished. But the new vineyard probably finally came of age with the 1978 vintage, an elegant wine, rather similar in style to Haut-Batailley. The 1979 is ripe and concentrated, more four-square. The 1980 is a delicious wine for early drinking. Then in the great years of the eighties more long-flavoured, stylish wines were made in 1981, 1983 and 1985. The 1982 is much more massive, powerful and complex, while the 1986 has extra concentration and opulence. The second label, Moulin de Duhart, is a recent and logical development.

There is no château, and the *chai* and *cuvier* are in the town of Pauillac.

CHÂTEAU LA FLEUR-MILON

Cru Grand Bourgeois. Owner: André Gimenez. 13 hectares. 5,000 cases. CS 45%, Mer 35%, CF 20%

To make fine wine, you need both well-placed vineyards and good wine-making. Here the various small plots adjoin such illustrious neighbours as Mouton-Rothschild, Lafite-Rothschild, Duhart-Milon, and Pontet-Canet. But you would never know this from tasting the wine. The present owner has been in charge since 1955, and is a real working proprietor. The *chai* is in the village of Le Pouyalet (there is no château). The wines are still bottled in the old way, from cask to cask. In style the wines are very "*artisanal*", that is to say coarse and tough, with that sort of stalky taste that suggests too much *vin de presse*.

CHÂTEAU FONBADET

Cru Bourgeois Supérieur 1932. Owner: Pierre Peyronie. 15 hectares. 6,500 cases. CS 60%, Mer 19%, CF 15%, Mal 4%, PV 2%. Secondary labels: Châteaux Haut-Pauillac, Padarnac, Tour-du-Roc-Milon, Montgrand-Milon

No Pauillac *cru bourgeois* enjoys a better reputation today than Fonbadet. The charming eighteenth-century château is in the village of St Lambert, just past the two Pichons, as you drive north from Bordeaux. Its small park is an oasis of green in this sea of vines. The present owner is a resident, working proprietor, who uses 25 per cent new casks each year to produce solid, classic Pauillacs. In recent years these wines have consistently done well in blind tastings, always a good sign. One factor apart from good wine-making is old vines. I noted that the 1985 in cask was very deep in colour, beautifully scented, had plenty of middle fat, and a lovely flavour, lifted with a touch of new oak. Certainly this is a wine to watch.

CHÂTEAU GRAND-PUY-DUCASSE

Cinquième Cru Classé. Owner: Societé Civile de Château Grand-Puy-Ducasse. 37 hectares. 11,660 cases. CS 62%, Mer 38%. Second label: Artigues-Arnaud. 5,000 cases

This was a small vineyard of 10 hectares, rather fragmented for a classified growth, consisting of three separate parcels. The château and *chai* are actually in the town of Pauillac, and the château – a pleasing, neo-classical building on the quayside – for some years acted as the Maison du Vin and headquarters of the Bontemps du Médoc. Now the present owners have installed a modern *cuvier*, with stainless steel vats, and are restoring the château for their own use. Like the other Grand-Puy, Ducasse owes its name to an eighteenth-century member of the *noblesse de robe*, who pieced the property together in the 1740s from a number of smallholdings. It featured in the classifications of Lawton in 1815 and of Franck in 1824, and in the 1855 classification in which it appeared under the name of Artigues-Arnaud. For a number of years it was the property of the Bouteiller family, proprietors of Pichon-Baron and Lanessan, but was sold to a *syndicat* associated with the well-known *négociants* Mestrezat in 1971. The new owners bought a further 10 hectares of old vines, and 10 hectares of fifteen-year-old vines, thus trebling the size of the vineyard.

The wine is not very well known in England, but whenever I have come across it, I have found it a very classic Pauillac in bouquet and flavour, with vigour and breed. The 1945 was still rather tough after twenty-two years, but the 1947 and 1949 were both outstandingly fine, as were the 1953 – more vigorous than most – and 1955. The new regime took a little time to establish the same quality with the larger vineyard. However, the 1975 is very rich and attractive with more fat and suppleness than many wines of this year, the 1976 has plenty of depth and the 1977 is fuller than most 1977s, but the 1978 is rather lightweight, with a suspicion of coarseness. There is a definite improvement with the 1979, which is really rich and opulent, while the soft, attractive fruit of the 1980 provided perfect drinking by 1987. The 1981 has that marked Cabernet Sauvignon character one always associated with the old vintages, the 1982 is all concentrated richness, powerful and tannic, a classic *vin de garde*, and 1983 seems rather tough and coarse, lacking in richness to match the evident tannin. On the other hand, 1984 seems surprisingly promising with some concentration and enough fruit. The 1985 has the gloriously opulent fruit reminiscent of 1953, while the 1986 has that combination of richness, tannin and beauty of flavour to promise something excellent in bottle. So the improvement since 1979 is clear, and this is now a wine to watch, especially at the extremely reasonable prices at which it is at present being sold.

CHÂTEAU GRAND-PUY-LACOSTE

Cinquième Cru Classé. Owner: Borie family. Administrators: Jean-Eugène Borie and Xavier Borie. 45 hectares. 12,000 cases. CS 70%, Mer 25%, CF 5%. Second label: Lacoste-Borie

The recorded history of this property goes back to the fifteenth century, when it belonged to a Monsieur de Guiraud, one of whose daughters married Monsieur de Jehan, a *conseiller* of the Bordeaux Parlement. It was a great-granddaughter of Jehan who married a Monsieur Saint-Guirons, whose name still appears on the label. He was a member of the *noblesse de robe*, and one of his daughters received a portion of the Grand Puy estate on marrying Monsieur Lacoste – hence Grand-Puy-Lacoste. The vineyard itself was a creation of the first half of the eighteenth century, and in 1824 William Franck placed it among the fourth growths.

However, the present high reputation of this wine rightly reflects the efforts of Monsieur Raymond Dupin, the proprietor from 1932 to 1978. This energetic and delightful man was certainly one of the most universally loved in Bordeaux – one of the few men in this competitive business with no enemies. Although Monsieur Dupin did not restore his château, as many of his neighbours did, he maintained essentials. His hospitality was proverbial, and the legendary Antoinette presided in the kitchen to the satisfaction of his many guests. In 1978, perhaps feeling the need to share his burden in advanced years, Monsieur Dupin sold a controlling interest to Jean-Eugène Borie of Ducru-Beaucaillou. The Borie family bought the rest of the shares before his death in 1980. In this new venture, it is Xavier Borie, under his father's watchful eye, who has responsibility for managing the property, and he and his wife are now installed in a wing of the château which has been tastefully restored. He was fortunate in his first vintage – 1978 – and made the most of it. After the 1980 vintage had been vinified, Jean-Eugène Borie decided that the *cuvier* with its old, traditional wooden vats drastically needed renovation.

After much soul-searching, it was eventually decided to make a clean sweep and install glass-lined steel tanks. They are not as attractive as the old ones but certainly make for easier maintenance and control of vinification. The whole installation was ready for the 1981 vintage.

In style and quality Grand-Puy-Lacoste belongs to the same category as Batailley; it is full-bodied and typically Pauillac, perhaps a shade tough at first, but once the initial brusqueness has worn off, an attractive and rewarding wine. The big, immediate post-war vintages – 1945, 1947 and 1949 – are still full of life and interest; the 1953 at its best but not quite up to Ducasse by 1978; the 1955 was an attractive wine which came on early for a Pauillac; the 1960 was one of the successful wines of the vintage; 1961 and 1962 are typical of the years; 1964 was one of the wines picked before the rain, but was slow to develop and rather tough, while both 1966 and 1967 are very good examples of these two very different years, but the 1967 is now beginning to dry up. This consistency was maintained in the seventies, with big wines being made in 1970, 1975, 1978 and 1979, while 1977 was unusually full for the year. The 1980 I felt rather overdid the tannin and lost the fruit and charm one looks for from this vintage. But then the new regime really got into its stride with three splendid wines in a row. The 1981 is exceptional for the year, with lovely middle richness and a fine finish, power perfectly mingled with breed. The 1982 has great opulence and is concentrated and dense-textured, a great vin de garde and a top specimen of its year. The 1983 is full of beautifully highlighted Pauillac power, has great breed and style and a lovely balance – a wine with a fine future. The 1984 promises to be more balanced than the 1980. The 1985 and 1986 are very finely matched wines, the 1985 having more concentration and sheer richness than many wines of this vintage – I found it at a similar level of quality as the Lynch-Bages – while the 1986 seems to achieve the harmony between concentrated tannins and rich fruit which is so essential in this year. There can be no doubt that the new management has succeeded in adding an extra dimension to what was already a very good wine, especially since 1981. It has moved up from a quality comparison with Batailley, to one with Lynch-Bages, and at a time when Lynch-Bages itself has been improving.

CHÂTEAU HAUT-BAGES-LIBÉRAL

Cinquième Cru Classé. Owner: Société Civile du Château Haut-Bages-Libéral. 26 hectares. 10,000 cases. CS 70%, Mer 25%, PV 5%

This *cru* is just emerging from a long period of obscurity and mediocrity. That it should have spent so long in the wilderness becomes all the more surprising when one sees where its vineyards lie. The larger of the two portions, together with the *chai* and *cuvier*, adjoins Latour immediately to the north, but is some three metres lower (Latour is 15 metres above the river, and Haut-Bages-Libéral 12). This part of the vineyard lacks a good drainage system, which is gradually being installed but will take twenty years to complete, since it can be done only when vines are to be replanted. The other part of the vineyard is on the plateau of Bages, from which the property takes its name.

The history of this *cru* is uneventful. It is mentioned in none of the pre-1855 classifications. It seems to have been created by the Libérals, a family of *courtiers*, in the mid-eighteenth century, and they continued to own it until the beginning of this century. In 1960 it was bought by the Cruse family, who incorporated a vineyard adjoining Pontet-Canet into that property, and bottled Haut-Bages-Libéral in their Bordeaux cellars. In 1972 they had to restore the installations at Haut-Bages-Libéral to accommodate compulsory château bottling. In 1983 the Merlaut family consortium, who also own Chasse-Spleen, bought the property, and the dedicated and talented Madame Bernadette Villars, daughter of Monsieur Jacques Merlaut, head of the company, took matters in hand. Her first discovery was that half the 1982 crop was still in vat, so she immediately bought 500 new casks, determined to make the best of this great year.

Of the pre-Merlaut, or perhaps I should say Villars, wines, I have tasted a respectable 1976, but the 1979 looks over-produced and one-dimensional. The 1981 is rather austere and tough, but may have potential. The rescued 1982 is impressive, superbly opulent, with the sweetness of a great year. Although Madame Villars did not vinify the 1983, she was able to make the *assemblage*, vital in a year where selection was all-important. The wine is tannic and powerful, with no sign of dilution, and should have a fine future. The 1984 seems to me too tannic and tough for its weight, and could prove a disappointment. The 1985 in cask had a strong assertive character, with plenty of fruit and length, and an intensity suggesting a long development in bottle. But 1986 looked even finer, with an impressive balance of ripe fruit and tannins, without a hint of astringency, a fine *vin de garde*.

The future then looks bright indeed. These are powerful, assertive Pauillacs, to which Madame Villars is adding complexity and polish, certainly one of the rising stars of the eighties.

CHÂTEAU HAUT-BAGES-MONPELOU

Cru Bourgeois. Owner: Emile Castéja. 10 hectares. 3,000 cases. CS and CF 70%, Mer 30%

This is one of the faithful regulars among the lesser lights of the Borie-Manoux stable. The small vineyard was once part of Duhart-Milon. The wines are quite full-flavoured but on the soft side, made for drinking young. These are dependable, pleasant wines sold at very reasonable prices.

CHÂTEAU HAUT-BATAILLEY

Cinquième Cru Classé. Owner: Madame des Brest-Borie. Administrator: Jean-Eugène Borie. 20 hectares. 7,500 cases. CS 65%, Mer 25%, CF 10%. Second label: Château la Tour-d'Aspic

At the time that Batailley was acquired by the Borie family, the property was divided, this smaller portion going to the brother of Monsieur Marcel Borie, who at the same time bought Ducru-Beaucaillou. The property then passed to his daughter and is administered by Monsieur Jean-Eugène Borie, the dedicated administrator of Ducru-Beaucaillou.

The château and *chai* having gone with the larger portion of the property, the wine of Haut-Batailley was for years vinified and kept in the *chai* at Beaucaillou, but since 1974 this has been moved to the new La Couronne *chai* in Pauillac. Because this part of the vineyard was completely reconstituted, the wines were for a long time lighter and not as powerful as those of Batailley; but as they achieved maturity, so the quality of the wine showed a marked improvement. The 1961 showed the full potential of the vineyard, and since then there has been a steady improvement, so that today its wines are a worthy rival of those of Batailley, although the style and emphasis are somewhat different. As now vinified by Jean-Eugène Borie, the wine has more elegance and less weight than most Pauillacs, and in this respect resembles recent vintages of Duhart-Milon. The 1962 was still delicious and charming when twenty-five years old, and 1966 was charming but at its peak by 1981. In the seventies, 1970, 1971, 1975, 1976 and 1978 have all been marked successes. The eighties began with an elegant, attractive 1980, 1981 has more tannin than usual, 1982 has real weight and richness, in line with the style of the year, while 1983 is particularly successful, with great length of flavour and well-matched fruit and tannin. The 1985 and 1986 will be an interesting pair, with the 1985 quintessential Haut-Batailley, all charm and elegance, but looking just a little light in cask; the 1986 has more tannin yet was completely harmonious and beautifully ripe in flavour, again at the cask stage. These beautifully made wines are wonderfully consistent and can be relied upon to give very enjoyable drinking without waiting too long.

CHÂTEAU LAFITE-ROTHSCHILD

Premier Cru Classé. Owner: Domaines Rothschild. 90 hectares. 17,000 cases. CS 70%, Mer 15%, CF 13%, PV 2%. Second label: Les Carruades. 17,000 cases

At the northern extremity of Pauillac stands the most renowned of its *crus*, and indeed of all clarets, Lafite. The history of Lafite is almost as interesting as the wine.

As with most Médocs, although mention of the property first occurs in 1355 and the wine itself is first mentioned in 1641 (only among the *vins de Graves et du Médoc*), the fame of Lafite first dates from the eighteenth century, when it was the property of Nicolas-Alexandre, Marquis de Ségur. In 1707 it is mentioned in an advertisement in the *London Gazette* along with Latour and Margaux, and we know that Sir Robert Walpole regularly shipped Lafite in the 1730s. After the death of the Marquis de Ségur in 1755, it took some years to settle the estate owing to its considerable extent and complexity, as well as to the competing claims of the heirs. Eventually it passed into the hands of Nicolas-Pierre de Pichard, President of the Bordeaux Parlement, who retained it until the Revolution.

The ownership of Lafite in the eighteenth century mirrors very faithfully the economic and social pattern of the period. Ségur was an immensely wealthy man who owned Latour, Mouton and Calon-Ségur, as well as Lafite; he was a provost of Paris as well as being President of the Bordeaux Parlement, and a man of letters who was a member of the Bordeaux Academy. In spite of his great interest in the region, he spent more time in Paris than in Bordeaux, and it is interesting to note from the inventory of his property made eight years after his death that Lafite is referred to simply as a *maison noble* and not as a château. Pichard's family was old and noble but not as aristocratic as that of Ségur. His interests were more completely centred in Guyenne. Born in Bordeaux in 1734, he became Avocat-Général of the Parlement in 1755, and its President in 1760. He was one of the relatively few proprietors guillotined in the Revolution, being executed in Paris in 1794.

It is often said that the Duc de Richelieu was responsible for popular-izing Bordeaux wines, and especially Lafite, at the court of Versailles. He was appointed governor of Guyenne in 1755 and is said to have recommended and served Lafite at Versailles on his return. The story is universally reported and seems reasonable enough, so that I can see no good reason to doubt it. Certainly from this time onwards, Bordeaux wines were in fashion at the court of Louis XV, and both Madame de Pompadour and Madame du Barry are reputed to have regularly served Lafite at their tables.

Before the execution of Nicolas-Pierre de Pichard, his sole heir, Anne-Marguerite-Marie-Adelaïde had fled the country with her husband, the Comte de Puységur. This meant that as an *émigrée* she was proscribed and unable to inherit, so Lafite became the property of the state and was put up for auction on 15 Fructidor of the year V of the Republic, better known as 2 September 1797. The buyers were a Dutch syndicate, who sold again in 1803 to one Ignace Joseph Vanderberghe for 1,200,000 frs (£240,000).

It is at this stage that the history of Lafite's ownership becomes extremely complicated. Fortunately the puzzle has now been unravelled by Cyril Ray in his excellent history of the property (see Bibliography). Vanderberghe was a grain merchant, financier, army contractor and at this time Napoleon's Head of General Supplies. He was an associate of Ouvard, a notorious speculator, and the two of them went into bankruptcy in 1808. Vanderberghe's battle with his creditors was still dragging on at the time of his death in 1819. The year before, he had taken the precaution of transferring Lafite to his former wife, Barbe-Rosalie Lemarie, for 1,000,000 frs, in spite of the fact they had been divorced as long ago as 1800. It has always been said that Vanderberghe was Dutch, but Cyril Ray has shown that he was in fact a Frenchman of presumably Flemish origins, born in Douai in 1758, the father-in-law of Napoleon's General Rapp.

In 1821 Barbe-Rosalie Lemarie apparently sold Lafite for the same sum she had paid for it to Mr Samuel Scott, an English banker. From this date until 1868, it was generally supposed that Mr Scott (who succeeded to his father's baronetcy in 1830), and after his death in 1849 his son, also named Samuel, were the owners of Lafite. But in fact they were simply administrators, having bought the property on the account of and with the money of Vanderberghe's son. This transaction was kept secret lest it should fall into the hands of his father's creditors, for it was not until 1856 that the Tribunal Civil de la Seine formally declared the Vanderberghe inheritance free from further claims. The real situation was finally revealed on the death of the younger Vanderberghe in 1866, when the bank registered a formal declaration that it had bought and administered Lafite on his behalf, and Lafite was now put up for auction for the benefit of Vanderberghe's heirs.

It was thus that on 8 August 1868 Lafite was knocked down to the agents of Baron James de Rothschild for 4,440,000 frs (£880,000). But the sale was not without incident. A syndicate of Bordeaux merchants had been formed in an attempt to save Bordeaux's most precious jewel, following Margaux and Mouton, from falling into the hands of Parisian bankers. For some unexplained reason the first auction on 20 July failed to produce a result, the reserve price of 4,500,000 frs not being reached, although both sides claimed to have resources in excess of this figure available.

The unique value set on Lafite may be gauged from the fact that Nathaniel de Rothschild had paid 1,125,000 frs for Mouton in 1853, and the neighbouring Cos d'Estournel had changed hands in 1852 for 1,150,000; while exactly a year later the pride of Burgundy, the Clos de Vougeot, was bought by Baron Thénard for 1,600,000 frs.

Following the sale of the property, a remarkable sale took place in the *chai* at Lafite of a wonderful collection of old vintages of the château. It is interesting to note that Cyril Ray, relying on Bertall, described this as a sale of the wines belonging to the château itself, whereas Maurice Dubois in *Mon Livre de cave* states categorically that this was the sale of old wines in bottle which had formed the collection of Monsieur Goudal, the father of the then *régisseur*, Emile Goudal. This sounds reasonable, as the elder

Goudal had been *régisseur* from 1798 until 1834. In all, according to Dubois, 5,252 bottles were put up for sale and realized more than 110,000 francs, while six barrels of the 1865 vintage were sold for 3,000 francs each. At today's value, this means an average price per bottle of around £19, an unheard-of price in those days. The record price was fetched by the 1811, the famous wine of the Comet. The twenty-one bottles available were auctioned in two lots, the first of eleven bottles fetching 976 francs, while the remaining ten bottles went for 121 francs each, or around £109 each in today's terms. No wonder this was spoken of as the greatest wine auction that had, up to that time, ever been seen.

Within three months of the purchase, Baron James de Rothschild was dead, and the new jewel in the Rothschild treasure went in equal parts to his three sons, Alphonse, Gustave and Edmond. Today the property is divided into six shares, of which Baron Guy de Rothschild as head of the family has two; the remaining three great-grandsons, together with the widow of a grandson, have one each. After the Second World War, it was Baron Elie who was entrusted with the running of the property. During this period, one has the impression that the Lafite-Rothschilds were never really close to Lafite and its wine. It remained one amongst many interests and concerns to be visited and supervised as necessary, enjoyed but not perhaps loved in the way that Baron Philippe loved Mouton and its wines. However, a new and promising era opened in the seventies with the appointment, in 1974, of a member of the next generation of Rothschilds, Eric, the son of Baron Alain. One of his first acts was the appointment, in 1975, of Professor Emile Peynaud as consultant, while Monsieur Jean Crété was appointed *régisseur*. The arrival of Monsieur Crété was in its way even more important than Professor Peynaud's advice. With his experience of Léoville-Las Cases under Monsieur Paul Delon, he could have received no better preparation for the great responsibility now vested in him. Already all the signs are that a new golden age for Lafite has begun.

With 90 hectares under vine, Lafite is the largest of the first growths in terms of area and production. The fluctuations in its production, however, have been very marked. In the heyday before the phylloxera, for instance, 195 tonneaux were made in 1865, 189 in 1870 and 246 in 1875. After the phylloxera, 224 were made in 1888, 210 in 1893, 145 in 1899 and 213 in 1900. Then came a period of much lower yields: only 63 tonneaux in 1920, 160 in 1924 and a meagre 40 in 1926, when the wine was superb but greatly reduced by disease. Both 1928 and 1929 yielded 150 tonneaux, but 1934 was the best inter-war year for yield (apart from the disastrous 1925), with 190 tonneaux. The great 1945 only made 90 tonneaux; 1947, 107. The first decent, if not great, year since 1900 to exceed 200 tonneaux was 1950 with its 247, and this was the beginning of much higher yields: 202 in 1953, 236 in 1955, 158 in 1959, 218 in 1962, 318 in 1964, 323 in 1966 and 335 in 1967. This gives a good example of how difficult it is in Bordeaux to speak of an average. In the decade 1957 to 1967, the production at Lafite varied from 116 to 335 tonneaux. On five occasions it was under 200 tonneaux, on three occasions over 300. There are now signs of lower, more controlled yields. Thus the prolific vintages of 1979 and 1982 here yielded 282 and 314 tonneaux respectively.

And what is one to say of the wines of Lafite that has not already been expressed with all the gloriously extravagant rhetorical fantasies of bygone days? André Simon, Maurice Healey, Warner Allen, Morton Shand have all sung its praises, vying with one another to convey its ethereal qualities. I will say only that factually Lafite, together with Margaux, is lighter in body than Latour or Mouton, and is a softer, more feminine wine than any other Pauillac. Its successful and great years were not so frequent until after 1975 as were those of Latour, and its lesser years tended to be exquisitely pretty but decidedly small wines. But a great vintage of Lafite is the quintessence of all that claret aspires to; a bouquet at once perfumed, delicate and powerful, in texture rich but elegant, in flavour subtle, silky and long. Because of its higher proportion of Merlot, Lafite is always a softer wine than its neighbours, but this is deceptive because its great vinosity and power enable it to last and improve much longer than seems likely early on. The 1953 is proving to be a case in point, provided one is fortunate enough to get the right bottling.

The longevity of Lafite is proverbial. A magnum of 1848 from the Rosebery cellar was still very much alive in 1989. The greatest bottle of old Lafite, though, was the legendary 1865, drunk at the château in 1988, with its extraordinary richness and concentrated exotic taste of prunes. This was one of a trio of outstanding vintages in the sixties, the others being 1864 and 1869. These were followed by the famous 1870 – giant of a wine even now, crude beside other Lafites and still the most commonly found old Lafite – 1871, 1874, 1875 and finally 1878, the last fine pre-phylloxera wine. From then onwards, the mildew combined with the phylloxera to give Bordeaux the most disastrous sequence of vintages in its history. Although there were decent wines made again in 1888 and 1889, it was the 1893 that really set the seal of success on the vineyard's fight back to prosperity. The 1893 Lafite was a very fine wine which was still at its best when I first drank it in 1957, although the last bottle I saw in 1962 was fading.

My own introduction to old Lafites was a most fortunate one. That great wine lover and master organizer, Mr Tony Hepworth, managed in 1954 to stage in Yorkshire a remarkable dinner for which Baron Elie sent six vintages of pre-First World War Lafite, having been persuaded to this most generous gesture by Dr Otto Loeb. After six months' rest, the members of the West Riding Wine and Food Society and their guests, among whom I was fortunate to be numbered, sat down to the most memorable of memorable meals. The 1914 which came first was a pleasant light wine, the least remarkable of the six, and the only one to fade in the glass. The 1906 was in wonderful condition but lacked the graciousness and finesse of the older wines. The 1900 was an enormous, mellow, ripe wine of great quality which took some time to come out and show its paces. Of the 1899 I wrote, "the finest claret I have ever tasted". Although I have drunk many superb wines since, this must remain one of the giants. The bouquet was still superb, the wine perfectly balanced, the flavour wonderful, and there was no sign of decay at all. Finally, the 1896 was a really lovely wine still in perfect condition and only just beaten by the 1899. It is seldom that one gets an opportunity to compare old wines in this way, which is why it seemed worth while recording this occasion.

The 1920 is a giant among Lafites but, after this, the inter-war era was not a great one for Lafite. The 1928 had to be pasteurized, and I have always found the 1934 singularly lacking the usual Lafite charm and finesse. The 1924 was perhaps the most charming and typical wine of this era, the 1919 was unfortunately overshadowed by the fate of the 1928. The 1937, however, I would rate a very good wine for the year; although uncharacteristically firm, it has more charm than most. Of the wartime years, I found the 1944 the most enjoyable: although lighter than the 1943, it had more breed and charm.

Since the war, the 1945 is a very great wine, the best produced at Lafite for many a long year. This proved a good omen, for it was to be followed by the 1947, 1948 (an exceptionally elegant and fine wine for the year), 1949 (a very great wine), 1950 (one of the most successful Lafites in a light year), 1952 (elegant but now drying up), and 1953 (a great and classic Lafite). The 1955 is more attractive than many wines of this vintage; 1959 has now fulfilled its early promise, and is complex with a superb flavour, at once concentrated and rich, but with a firm finish; 1960 is a light wine of great charm but too light, not the equal of the 1950; 1961 is a very great wine but, while among the best of the year, has shown a distressing irregularity from bottle to bottle; 1962 is a very classic and elegant Lafite. For me, this was the last outstanding Lafite until 1970 and 1975. The 1963 should never have been given the Château label and the 1964 I find disappointing – it is light and has a touch of coarseness, which suggests too much *vin de presse*, to me – while the 1966, although a good wine and certainly superior to the 1964, lacks the richness and great breed of the 1962.

After a light, supple 1967 and a poor 1969 (the 1968 is best forgotten), the 1970 has not maintained its early promise and seems to be drying out. In spite of its fruit and some flavour, it lacks the *gravitas* of a fine Lafite. The 1971 I find disappointing and already old. The 1973 is something of a curiosity. Previously I wrote that it was a victim of the old policy of bottling only after three years, and when tasted in the summer of 1974 it already looked too light and insubstantial. Yet the last bottle I drank in 1987 had depth of flavour, breed and length, without a hint of the dryness I had seen earlier. Was this a further example of the vagaries of bottling from cask to cask, or just another Lafite miracle? The 1975, while not made by Jean Crété, was raised under his new regime. I was disappointed in the 1975 when I first saw the wine just prior to bottling in 1977, but after settling down in bottle it gives the impression of being a great wine in the making. The 1976 is the first wine made by Jean Crété, in an admittedly difficult vintage. The wine has steadily grown in stature. When last tasted in 1987 it immediately impressed me by the elegant complexity of the bouquet and the long supple flavour, with its lovely balance and freshness, but the wine seemed relatively light-textured. An hour later it had filled out considerably and developed in complexity, thus demonstrating that this wine is still evolving and improving. The

1977 benefited from the scrapping of the old three-year bottling rule. The 1978 and 1979 are a particularly interesting pair here because the 1979 is so good and, for once, not inferior to the 1978. From the beginning I have found the 1979 a more exciting wine, impressive as the 1978 undoubtedly is, but there is still development to come, for both wines. The 1980 seems a little light and lean, but has developed more slowly than most 1980s. The great vintages of the eighties were ushered in by a classic 1981 which is also the quintessence of Lafite. Rather low-keyed to start with, perhaps, but the sheer beauty of perfume and flavour, combined with elegance, harmony and firmness of tone, promise a long and interesting future. Both 1982 and 1983 produced great Lafites which should become classic examples of these two very different years, with the 1983 a true *vin de garde*, unlike many Pauillacs of this year. The 1984 vintage produced an elegant, attractive wine, without hardness or dryness, which should be useful for earlyish drinking. Then another great pair of wines, 1985 and 1986, will provide yet another marvellous contrast. Here 1985 is the classic Lafite, very perfumed, very ripe, with great beauty of flavour and texture, while 1986 is very tannic, with exceptional weight and power for Lafite, similar in style to the 1986 Margaux, and clearly a great wine in the making. The 1988 and 1989 in their different styles look like great wines.

In the midst of these great vintages, Jean Crété retired in 1983, and handed over to his friend Gilbert Rokvam. The latter's progress to this exalted and prized position came by a rather unusual route, for he is the son of a Norwegian diplomat and a French mother, who in retirement had settled in the Dordogne. After studying agronomy in that region, he trained on the Crété family estates in Tunisia before working for Swiss proprietors in Spain. It was thus that his friendship with Jean Crété and their mutual respect began, which finally led to Lafite.

As a postscript to this survey of vintages, it must be said that there have in past years been far too many variations between bottlings of the same vintage. The 1953 and 1961 have been particularly instanced. While the 1953 was a large vintage and was apparently bottled over a long period, the same cannot be said of the 1961. It should be an axiom of château bottling that the wine can be relied upon to be consistent. Now that so many tastings are written up, owners of fine vintages of Lafite have often found themselves disappointed by wines reported as being magnificent elsewhere. Fortunately these mishaps are now past history, but unfortunately past history lingers on in many cellars, on both sides of the Atlantic. When such high prices are asked and paid today, the consumer has a right to expect that what he receives will be as good as that which goes into the private cellar at the château.

Something should be said here of the Carruades. The name comes from perhaps the finest stretch of vineyard on the property, but the wine came from young vines wherever they happened to be on the property. The general rule at Lafite is that only wine from vines of twelve years or older goes into Lafite, and that from seven to twelve years goes into the Carruades; any younger wines are simply sold off with the generic *appellation* only. Thus the quantity of Carruades was always much smaller than that of Lafite, and it was a more quickly maturing wine, bottled before the Lafite itself. It was nevertheless true Lafite, was always château-bottled and was sometimes not far behind Lafite in excellence. There has been some chopping and changing with the name. In the seventies it became Moulin des Carruades, but since 1986 it has reverted to Carruades once more. With stricter selection, the quantities of Carruades have greatly increased in recent years.

The Lafite vineyards lie on slopes in a compact group at the northern end of Pauillac. One piece is actually in St Estèphe, adjoining Lafon-Rochet, but is allowed the Pauillac *appellation*. Lafite's neighbour in St Estèphe is Cos d'Estournel, and in Pauillac adjoins Mouton at many points. The château itself is a pleasing compendium of medieval turrets and seventeenth- and eighteenth-century buildings, standing among a group of trees on an eminence above the *route des châteaux*. But most impressive of all are the *chais*. After the first year in the great *chai*, the wine is moved into a deeper, cooler one for slow maturation in cask prior to bottling, which at Lafite until recently invariably occurred in the third spring after the vintage, giving the wine on average some two and a half years in cask. There is also a magnificent underground cellar for the storage of Lafite's unique collection of old wines, going back to the 1797 vintage. As at some other châteaux, the wines here are regularly re-corked, on average approximately every twenty-five years. In 1987 a spectacular and original new cask cellar was constructed by cutting into the hillside behind the old farm buildings. The originality consists in its circular form, rising in tiers from the centre, so that visitors will be able to walk around the circumference, looking down on the casks below, without interfering with the cellar work. The soil and vines were then replaced, so that the whole building is underground.

CHÂTEAU LATOUR

Premier Cru Classé. Owner: Allied-Lyons. Administrator: Christian Le Sommer. 60 hectares. 16,000 cases. CS 80%, CF 15%, Mer 5%. Second label: Les Forts de Latour. 8,000 cases

The history of Latour is a good deal less complex than that of Lafite, but its origins are none the less ancient or aristocratic. In the Middle Ages, during the English period, an important fortress stood on this site, protecting the low-lying part of the river estuary from pirates and marauding Frenchmen alike. One of a number of forts guarding the river banks at this time, this fortress was destroyed by the forces of the King of France during the campaigns leading to the final expulsion of the English in 1453. The present tower is all that now remains to remind us of these martial beginnings, but dates from the first part of the seventeenth century (Louis XIII).

Perhaps the most remarkable fact about the ownership of Latour is that from 1670, when it was acquired by the de Charravas family, until 1963, it remained in the control of connected families, passing by marriage first to the Clauzels in about 1677, then to the Ségurs, then to four families of whom the de Beaumonts remained as the principal one down to 1963. The only occasion when the property was actually put up for sale was in 1841, when an auction was held so that the controlling families could buy out Barton, Guestier, and Johnston, the three leading *négociants*, who between them had a 20 per cent share in Latour. The controlling families felt that there was a conflict of interest, and that the *négociants* tried to keep prices low and then sell high with maximum profit to themselves. In the following year a Société Civile was established, to facilitate a smoother administration in a situation where there were a number of shareholders. The nature of this Société Civile was changed fundamentally in 1963, when interests controlled by Lord Cowdray acquired a majority holding, and Harvey's of Bristol a 25 per cent share. Members of the de Beaumont family have retained a minority interest. In practice, Mr David Pollock, until his retirement in 1978, and then the Hon. Alan Hare representing Lord Cowdray's interest, were the final authority on all policy matters. Then in 1989 Pearsons decided to sell to the minority shareholders Allied-Lyons. Alan Hare continued in charge until handing over to David Orr in 1990. Largely through the experience of Mr Harry Waugh, then of Harvey's, Mr Pollock was fortunate in obtaining the services of Monsieur Henri Martin, proprietor of Château Gloria, and Monsieur Jean-Paul Gardère, *courtier* of Pauillac, to manage and advise him on the new regime. I shall say more of this regime in the appropriate place.

Just as Lafite stands watch over the northern limits of Pauillac, so does Latour over its southern approaches. A small stream also marks the boundary between Latour and Léoville-Las Cases in the same way as does another between Lafite and Cos d'Estournel. In this case, the stream is a good deal smaller and the two vineyards are much closer to each other. But the change of soil and the resulting change in the characters of the wines are just as profound. The main vineyard of Latour lies between the road and the river, as at Léoville-Las Cases, but it is not so easily seen from the road, because in the middle of the nineteenth century one of the de Beaumonts carved a piece out of the estate to permit the building of the château now known as Pichon-Lalande, the Comtesse de Lalande being the mistress of the Comte de Beaumont. Today the finest view of the vineyards of Latour is to be had from the terrace at Pichon-Lalande, which was constructed above the new *chai* in the mid-sixties. Another curiosity is that there is no grand, or old, château. In the eighteenth century the owners had fine houses at Lafite and Calon-Ségur, so clearly felt no need to build another one. So it was not until the mid-nineteenth century that the proprietors decided to build the present château, which was completed in 1864. They had grown restive with the accommodation provided by the *régisseur's* house, finding it damp and filthy. But no one was able to agree on the expenditure required to implement the architect's original plans, and eventually a greatly reduced and almost embarrassingly modest villa was sanctioned, that compares oddly with its neighbour at Pichon-Comtesse, completed a decade earlier. The familiar landmark is, rather, the solitary tower and, near it, the *chai*, *cuvier* and cellars, built unusually and perhaps uniquely around a small courtyard planted with plane trees.

It was part of the *ancien régime* at Latour that nothing ever seemed to change and everything was done as it had always been. But the virtual change of ownership in 1963 heralded substantial innovations. The *cuvier* was completely rebuilt, only the walls of the original building remaining, and the great oak fermenting vats gave way to stainless steel ones, which can be thermostatically cooled by allowing water to run down the outside walls of the vats. The effect is hardly an aesthetic delight, and it has since been shown, notably at Château Margaux, that the traditional oak vats are not irreconcilable with effective temperature control. The space available for cask storage – important in a château where there are sometimes three crops in wood for at least part of the year – has been greatly augmented by a fine underground cellar. In the vineyard itself, some sections contained very old vines and many gaps, apart from an important unplanted area. Much replanting has been undertaken, but none of this wine from young vines has found its way into the *grand vin* until judged sufficiently mature.

Through the kindness of Jean-Paul Gardère, I have been able to obtain a remarkable record of every vintage of Latour since 1918. These provide an interesting commentary on the low yields of the past, and the recovery under the new ownership.

In the twenties the average *rendement* was 21.4 hl/ha. In the thirties this fell to 15.9 and in the forties to 15.2. The fifties brought a marked improvement to 27.45, which rose to 35.10 in the sixties. In the seventies this increased with the new plantations to a remarkable 51.9. By this time, however, only about 57.5 per cent of the total yield of the estate was now bottled as Latour. Between 35 and 40 per cent is now bottled as Les Forts and the rest sold as Pauillac, or declassified.

One of the major innovations since 1963 has been the creation of the new *marque* of Les Forts de Latour. This followed the decision to use only those vineyards which were shown on the plan of the domain of 1759 for the *grand vin* of Latour itself, and to replant certain vineyards owned by Latour and which were lying fallow. Thus the Les Forts de Latour comes from three parcels of vineyard called Les Forts de Latour, Petit Batailley and Comtesse de Lalande. The Les Forts vineyard adjoins the Grand Vignoble to the northwest, well placed near the Gironde, Petit Batailley is west of the village of St Lambert and adjoins Batailley, Léoville-Poyferré and Pichon-Lalande, while, as the name implies, Comtesse de Lalande is a small parcel adjoining Pichon-Lalande. In addition the production of young vines from the Latour vineyard can be used if judged to be of sufficient quality. Thus it is not strictly accurate to call Les Forts de Latour the second wine of Latour, since it is based on different vineyards whose production, however good, would never be included in Latour itself.

Before the first vintages of Les Forts, the 1966 and 1967, were placed on the market in 1972, both were tasted blind against the leading second growths and acquitted themselves with distinction. So they are sold at second-growth prices, at which level they offer excellent value. They have the Latour style but are lighter-textured and so tend to mature more rapidly.

The style of Latour's great wine is famous, and it is easy to see why its frank, outspoken qualities have for so long been particularly popular in England, so that Franck wrote that the greater part was consumed in that country, which bought it in nearly every good vintage. Until 1963 Latour was the most unashamedly traditional of Médocs in its style, that is to say, it always had great colour and took a long time to reach maturity. But this gruff and forbidding exterior, compounded of tannin and extract beyond what is usual today, gave way with time and patience to a marvellously rich and truly velvety texture. The incomparable bouquet, the most classic of Pauillac Cabernet aromas, was always evident from the wine's first year in cask; the flavour was always masculine and immensely characteristic, as recognizable as some familiar symphonic theme, at once noble yet often practically undrinkable it was so masked by hardness. This was the dilemma of Latour in the days of high interest rates and expensive storage; everyone admired the wines of great years but wondered when they would be ready to drink and if they would still be alive to enjoy them. It was therefore hardly surprising that the new proprietors decided that some concessions to the times were necessary, and they aim to produce wines which will be ready to drink rather earlier. These wines are certainly going to develop differently – so much is already clear. They do not bear quite the same unmistakable signature when in cask, but the fine character is evident in the flavour.

The oldest Latour I have ever tasted was the 1874. In 1967 I was fortunate to be present when a bottle from Lord Rosebery's remarkable cellar was opened at Christie's. Its fine, deep colour was only slightly tawny. The bouquet was clean and definite, quite distinctly conveying its Pauillac character across the years. The wine itself was full-flavoured, powerful and still rich in texture; there was only a suggestion of the fragility of great age, and the Latour character was unmistakable. This was a great and remarkable wine that had lived its life in England from the time it was first laid down in its infancy by the famous Liberal politician and racing enthusiast. Yet it was distinctly more vigorous than any of the 1875s I have drunk in Bordeaux. I mention all this in some detail because it shows the amazing longevity of the great clarets when properly stored and looked after. The wine, incidentally, had been re-corked some thirty years before by Berry Brothers.

The Latour 1899 at its greatest was a wine to set beside the Lafite; how fascinating it would have been to have had the opportunity to do so. In 1960 I had a marvellous bottle, fresh and vigorous and such typical Latour that I even guessed the château. But only a year later, another bottle was only a shadow of the first, which shows that wines of this age must always be something of a gamble, and one poor bottle may not mean that any others still left will be the same.

One of Latour's outstanding characteristics has always been that it is magnificent in poor and moderate years. In the great years the palm may go to Lafite, but in lesser ones the list of Latour's successes is formidable, and it is certainly one of the most consistently great wines in the Médoc today. Among these successes can be numbered 1936, 1940 and 1944 – full-flavoured, fruity and delicious wine from light years – 1951, 1954 and especially 1958 and 1960, both of which are outstanding in years where rain during the vintage combined with rot to spoil what might otherwise have been very successful years. The charms of the 1958 lasted certainly until 1986 when I had a delicious bottle, while in 1983 a group of leading Parisian *sommeliers*, when tasting the vintages of Latour from 1958 to 1970 blind, actually placed the 1958 first, ahead of the 1959 and 1961! If ever there was a case of judging on immediate drinkability, this must be it. The 1960 was in my judgement the best wine of the vintage, and it had lasted just as well as the 1958. In 1963 Latour made one of the very rare wines in that year which deserved to see the light of day, light but sound and charming. However, this admirable record for sound wines in lesser years stopped short with the 1965; even Latour's skills could make little of this poor year. The 1968 had always seemed a trifle stalky to me, and the lighter Les Forts preferable, but it has now come round very well; the 1969 is most disappointing, however. In the seventies, the 1972 was better than most, with distinct character, and the 1973 was stylish but solid, with charm; but the 1974 was dull, like most wine of this vintage. Surprisingly, the 1977 was disappointingly slight in a year when Latour might have been expected to do something more interesting, and I prefer the balance of Les Forts. The 1980, on the other hand, has the extra richness and balance to make a charming wine which was still improving in 1987, and 1984 is supple and well balanced, without the austerity and dryness so often found in this vintage.

Of Latour's great years, the 1929 is deservedly legendary. Its great fruit and perfect balance made it drinkable at an early age for Latour. Some sound judges thought it about to decline when I first enjoyed it in 1952, yet thirty-five years later, well-stored bottles were still superb – so much for early-developing vintages! The 1928, over-shadowed by the 1929 for many years, has at last come of age, a great wine which will outlast the magical but mortal 1929. The 1934 is a fine wine – one of the great successes in a vintage when many fine growths, and notably Margaux and Lafite, have disappointed. The 1937 is a man's claret – strong, firm and very much a wine of its year, but nevertheless very fine and long-lived. Of the post-war years, the greatest successes have been the 1945 – a timeless giant of a wine – and the 1961, more agreeable already and perhaps another 1929, only more solid. The 1949 is very fine, rich and intense, much superior to the 1947 – several recent bottles of which have proved distinctly edgy and volatile – but perhaps just beaten in this vintage by Lafite and Mouton. The 1948 is, however, a great success; a really classic Latour. The 1952 is too dominated by dry tannins; 1953 is nice enough – never up with the great 1953s, but it has aged gracefully. The 1955 is, in my view, a really great Latour. It matches the magnificent 1959, surpasses the 1962, and must be one of the best wines of a vintage which, while consistent, has conspicuously failed to reach the heights in most cases. The 1962 is a fine wine, the last of the *ancien régime*, masculine and aggressive and slow to develop, but perhaps not quite the peer of Mouton or Lafite in the long run. Latour's new masters have reason to be pleased with their 1964 as things have turned out, for it is probably the best wine in the Médoc, but the Latour character is not quite so aggressively asserted. On the other hand, the 1966 has turned out to be a classic Latour, of great power and vigour, drinkable at the age of thirteen, yet still improving when it came of age – certainly the outstanding wine of the sixties, after 1961. Since then the classic Latours have been 1970, 1975 (the outstanding wine of the decade) and 1976, 1978, a concentrated and rich-textured 1981. Then comes the great 1982, a worthy successor to the majestic 1961 and a complete contrast to the 1983, which is not very distinguished by Latour standards. The 1985 and 1986 should make a good pair, with 1985 having plenty of power and richness, and 1986 the right balance of opulent fruit and concentrated, ripe tannins; 1988 is cast in a similar mould.

However, 1987 saw the end of an era, when Henri Martin and Jean-Paul Gardère formally resigned from the Conseil d'Administration, after twenty-four years' service together. The newcomer, Christian Le Sommer, took over from Jean-Louis Mandrau in 1986 as administrator and is now firmly in charge.

CHÂTEAU LYNCH-BAGES

Cinquième Cru Classé. Owner: Cazes family. Administrator: Jean-Michel Cazes, 80 hectares. 28,000 cases. CS 70%, Mer 18%, CF 10%, PV 2%. Second label: Chateau Haut-Bages-Averous. 7,000 cases

This is one of several properties formerly belonging to the Lynch family, who left Galway to follow James II into exile. The most celebrated member of the family was Comte Jean-Baptiste Lynch, born in 1749. He was a lawyer who played a prominent part in public life, first of all in the Parlement de Bordeaux, of which he became President in 1783, then as a member of the Council of Five Hundred, during the early days of the Revolution, and finally as Mayor of Bordeaux from 1800 to 1815. Although he was made a Comte of the Empire by Napoleon I in 1811, he opened the city to General Beresford, one of Wellington's commanders, on 12 March 1814, and threw in his lot with the Bourbon restoration, proclaiming Louis XVIII as king. This led to his flight to England during Napoleon's Hundred Days, but ensured his position after Napoleon's defeat at Waterloo. He actually died at another of his properties, Dauzac, in 1835, having sold Lynch-Bages in 1824 to a Swiss *négociant*, Sébastien Jurine.

The Tastet-Lawton archives show that the average prices fetched by Lynch-Bages between 1741 and 1774 were above those of Branaire and Pontet-Canet, but below those of La Tour-de-Mons and Beychevelle. By 1815, Lawton was classifying Lynch-Bages among the leading *quatrièmes crus*, and in Charles Cocks's 1846 list it is mentioned as Jurine à Bages. Its present reputation, however, is largely due to the work of Monsieur J.-C. Cazes who managed the property from 1934 – when he became a tenant, prior to buying the property in 1937 – until his death in 1966. He was one of the great characters of the Médoc, and my memory of him is of a man permanently in gumboots, tramping through the sea of mud, which seemed to surround the château in those days, to his office which apart from his desk and chair was completely bare, save for a broken chair in the corner. His son André, the mayor of Pauillac, carried on the good work, aided increasingly by his son Jean-Michel. Jean-Michel Cazes now lives at the château with his family, and the scene is quite transformed. For years during the late seventies and early eighties it was impossible to visit the property without dodging builders. The château now looks immaculate with its gleaming stonework, almost unrecognizable as the place I first visited nearly thirty years ago. Jean-Michel tells me that in those days there was not even a bath in the château – now they have a swimming-pool as well. The enlargement and reconstruction of both *cuvier* and *chai* have been extensive, so that today the château is as well appointed as any in the Médoc. The vineyard and château are very well situated at Bages, just to the south of Pauillac, on high ground to the west of the *route des châteaux*.

The relatively recent reputation of Lynch-Bages is emphasized by the fact that one seldom hears of, or finds, old vintages. In the fifties when the popularity of Lynch-Bages was soaring, it was often alleged by jealous neighbours that the special Lynch-Bages character, so beloved by wine-lovers, was in some dark and mysterious way a creation of Monsieur Cazes. However, when I tasted a bottle of the 1928 close to its fiftieth birthday – the only pre-Cazes Lynch-Bages ever to come my way – its character was completely consistent with more modern vintages. Furthermore, the wine was in superb condition, vigorous and rich, with no signs of excess tannin.

It is this balance which surely lies at the heart of Lynch-Bages's popular success. It always seems to produce easy-to-drink, fruity, ample wines, even in difficult years. Thus, one of the earliest examples I came across, the 1945 (Bordeaux-bottled by Calvet), was extremely enjoyable to drink long before most 1945s could be approached. Looking at my tasting notes, I find myself frequently resorting to phrases such as "typical

Lynch-Bages", for this is a most individual wine. Its rich, plummy flavour and marked Pauillac bouquet remind one in some ways of Mouton – or rather of a young Mouton – before the youthful obviousness has given way to complexity and the breed has come through. Its great merits are its remarkable consistency and the ability to make its wines enjoyable in years like 1945, 1952 and 1957, at a time when most of its neighbours were still tough and ungrateful. This is almost certainly due to a skilful vinification on the part of Monsieur Cazes, by making very well-balanced wines with a lot of colour, extract and fruit, but never too much tannin.

Although this is deservedly a most successful growth, it would be wrong to suggest that it is quite in the top class. Certainly it lacks the breed and distinction of the best second growths such as the Pichons or the Léovilles, while being decidedly superior to its 1855 classification. The 1945, 1952, 1953, 1957, 1959, 1961, 1962, 1966 and 1967 were all very successful examples of their vintages, with the 1962 being really outstanding – among the best wines of the year. Only in 1964 did Monsieur Cazes's predilection for vintaging late get him into trouble, when Lynch-Bages was seriously affected by rain.

After the death of old Monsieur Cazes and before his grandson Jean-Michel gained experience, things were slightly hit and miss. That unmistakable blackcurrant aroma in cask, and the rich, velvety texture of the wine itself, which were the hallmark of good Lynch-Bages, were too often missing. Of the wines of this period, perhaps only the 1970 truly measured up to what one had come to expect, and vintages such as 1975 and 1978, which should have been great wines, are disappointing. The 1979 was still clumsy and coarse in 1987, when in the old days it would have been delicious. It was only with the 1981 that wines with the concentration and style expected were once more established. The 1982 is an outstanding wine, and 1983 combines real depth and power with a lovely supple richness – one of the best Pauillacs of the vintage. The 1984 is almost pure Cabernet Sauvignon, yet seems very harmonious, with a beautifully frank flavour. The 1985 is classic Lynch-Bages, with a terrific *cassis* flavour, and very flattering in cask, while the 1986 manages to combine the great concentration of the year with that lovely cedar-wood character and harmony which is typical of great Lynch-Bages. So the eighties look like setting new standards for this fine *cru*, and all the investment of recent years really seems to be coming through in the wines.

CHÂTEAU LYNCH-MOUSSAS

Cinquième Cru Classé. Owner: Emile Castéja. 25 hectares. 12,500 cases. CS 70%, Mer 30%

This is another property taking its name from the Lynch family. Moussas is the name of the minute hamlet in which it lies. The growth is not mentioned in any of the pre-1855 classifications. It is now the property of the Castéja family and is administered by Emile Castéja, head of the *négociants* Borie-Manoux (see Batailley p. 141). The Castéjas have the distinction of having owned a classified growth in Pauillac ever since the 1855 classification – they were then owners of Duhart-Milon (see Duhart-Milon, p. 146). Although it had been in the family since 1919, it was not until Emile Castéja took sole control in 1969 that progress was made in rebuilding the fortunes of this *cru*. Production had then fallen to only 2,000 cases, and the whole property was in a very run-down condition. Now the *chai* and *cuvier* have been restored and modernized, and the charming eighteenth-century château has been tastefully restored, and is now the home of Emile's son, Philippe Castéja, and his family. Well away from any main road, and looking out on many noble trees, this, the most westerly of the Pauillac *crus*, seems far away from the vine-intensive landscape of most of the Médoc.

The vineyard actually adjoins that of Batailley. Part of it lies near the hamlet of Moussas, and there is also some near Duhart-Milon and Lafite, to the north, and near Pichon and Latour to the south.

Before the restoration of the vineyard, pleasant but rather light wines of no great distinction were made, and were hardly of *cru classé* status. I have good notes of the 1959 vintage and was told by Emile Castéja that he had once found a bottle of the 1834 in the cellar, as a young man, and being a person of good sense had drunk it and found it to be excellent. Now the vineyard is beginning to mature, and it is possible to have some idea of its real potential. At a blind tasting in 1985, the 1980 vintage showed a pleasingly aromatic, rather minty bouquet, and an attractively fruity and individual flavour, so that I marked it more highly than several more prestigious Pauillacs. The 1981 is supple and fruity, but rather short, in contrast to a very rich and really opulent 1982, where the ripeness of the year really takes over to produce something delicious, if untypical. The 1983 is more overtly tannic and complex, and is taking time, like many 1983s, to find its equilibrium, but the promise is there. The 1984 has the fruit and balance to make a pleasant early-drinking wine. In cask, 1985 – a selection representing only 50 per cent of the production – seemed rich but lacking in depth of flavour, while the 1986 looked very tannic and typical of the year. With its higher proportion of Merlot, compared to its neighbour Batailley, the emphasis of the wines here is clearly different, and the aim is to produce softer, more forward wines. Whether they will consistently deserve their *cru classé* status is something that I would reserve judgement on, but at the very reasonable prices at which they are sold, they are clearly of interest to the consumer.

CHÂTEAU MOUTON-BARONNE-PHILIPPE (FORMERLY MOUTON D'ARMAILHACQ)

Cinquième Cru Classé. Owner: Baron Philippe de Rothschild SA. 50 hectares.
15,000 cases. CS 65%, Mer 20%, CF 15%

Until the eighteenth century, this property formed part of Mouton, but then passed to the d'Armailhacq family. In the very year of the Revolution, Joseph-Arnaud d'Armailhacq was born on the property, and under his direction the vineyard became renowned. In 1850 he published a work, *De la culture des vignes, de la vinification et des vins dans le Médoc avec un état des vignobles d'après leur réputation*. It was regarded as the most authoritative book on the subject at that time and went into a number of editions. Subsequently, the property passed to heirs of the Armailhacqs and was finally bought by Baron Philippe de Rothschild in 1933. Baron Philippe used to paint a charming picture of the old Comte Ferrande living a solitary life of genteel poverty in his half-finished château. One of the terms of the sale was that the Baron allowed the old man to remain there until his death, which occurred during the German Occupation. In 1956 the name of the property was changed to incorporate the name of its then illustrious owner, and was modified again in 1975 to "Baronne Philippe" as a tribute to the memory of the Baron's gifted and greatly missed wife.

The château is something of a curiosity, its classical pediment being only half completed, a monument to the economic problems of the 1840s. This and the *chai* lie between Mouton and Pontet-Canet. Although

Mouton-Baronne-Philippe's vineyards run side by side with those of its cousin and were once the same property, it is scrupulously run as an entirely separate property, but with all the same care as the great Mouton.

In style, the wines of the second Mouton are truly Pauillac, with the authentic blackcurrant aroma and the full-flavoured, assertive character, but softer and less massive than Mouton itself, and quicker to mature. Unfortunately, I have no experience of old vintages, save only a marvellously preserved and harmonious 1934; but after some fine vintages in the sixties, especially a memorable 1962, the wines have been through a disappointing period. The best vintages have been a charming, early-developing 1978, a rich and delicious 1979, a 1981 which has a good flavour but is a shade lean, a 1982 which is surprisingly dominated by tannin, but should have the richness to bring it through, 1983 which is again rather lean, but has a classic Pauillac flavour. In cask, 1985 had the classic blackcurrant aroma, and was powerful and four-square, while 1986 was very dense-textured and tannic, with the middle fruit to suggest a fine future. Somehow there has been a lack of flair in these wines, compared with some older vintages, but there are now signs of improvement.

CHÂTEAU MOUTON-ROTHSCHILD

Premier Cru Classé 1973. Owner: Baron Philippe de Rothschild SA. 72 hectares. 20,000 cases. CS 85%, Mer 8%, CF 7%

Mouton was curiously placed at the top of the second growths in 1855, but was universally regarded – and had been for many years – as a first growth. Baron Philippe de Rothschild's crusade for official recognition finally succeeded in 1973 when Mouton was declared a first growth by governmental decree. It has to be remembered that in the middle of the nineteenth century, there did not exist the enormous difference in price between first and second growths that is found today. Thus Charles Cocks recorded in 1846, a decade before the classification, that when the first growths sold for £96 a tonneau, the seconds sold for between £82 and £84 a tonneau. The other factor was that Mouton's fame was relatively recent, whereas the position of the first growths had been clearly consecrated by time.

Mouton really begins to have a distinct history of its own only in the eighteenth century. Most nineteenth-century books say airily that it had belonged to the Brane family for about a century when it was sold in 1830, and Féret states (*Statistique Gen. Tome III 1er partie Biographie* 1889) that Joseph de Brane, who died in 1749, was Baron de Mouton. But the map showing the lands of the Marquis de Ségur shows clearly that Mouton was numbered among them. Monsieur Butel's researches seem to suggest that by 1747 Mouton had passed to the Marquis de Ségur-Calon, who, as the Marquis de Ségur's son-in-law, was to be his principal heir. However, by the end of the century it was certainly the property of Hector de Branes (or Brane), father of the more famous Jacques-Maxime, the virtual creator first of Mouton, then of Gorce – later called Brane-Cantenac. For whereas frequent mention is to be found among eighteenth-century sources of Lafite, Latour and Margaux, nothing is heard of Mouton.

Maps and plans towards the end of the eighteenth century seem to show that it was only then that much of what is today the vineyard of Mouton was actually planted with vines. It was probably only during the last decade of Baron de Brane's ownership that the fame and reputation of Mouton really spread, since he was born only in 1796 and the property was sold to Monsieur Thuret in 1830. As a result, the price was far superior to anything fetched at that time for any wine not a first growth – at 1,200,000 francs (£240,000).

Thuret did not prosper at Mouton in the way that Baron de Brane had done, and sold the property in 1853 to Baron Nathaniel de Rothschild, surprisingly taking a small loss on the transaction. It was, however, noted at the time that the price paid was well below the estate's real value. This cousin of the Rothschild who was later to buy the neighbouring Lafite had settled in England and adopted one of the national pastimes of his adopted country – fox-hunting. It was as a result of a fall while hunting, which had crippled him, that he decided to retire to France and bought Mouton. At this time the property was usually known as Brane-Mouton, and for many years after the Rothschild purchase it was referred to simply as Mouton. It was only after some forty years of ownership, just before the turn of the century, that it became generally hyphenated with the Rothschild name.

As at Lafite, the presence of the Rothschilds at Mouton was at a rather remote level and they much depended on their *régisseurs*. Indeed, some of the labels of Mouton actually bear the name of the *régisseur*, raised to the even more exalted level of *gérant*, or manager – that is, until the arrival of Baron Philippe. It was in 1923 that, as a very young man, he arrived with full powers from his father to manage the estate; he was not to inherit it until several years later. When he arrived, he found the *gérant* burning the records in the courtyard, a spectacular end indeed to the old regime of absentee proprietors. Since that time, for over sixty years, Baron Philippe and Mouton were synonymous. Only Henri Woltner at La Mission, among the contemporary proprietors of great Bordeaux châteaux, has combined over such a span of years a similar love and dedication to his wines which has, at the same time, been illumined with such civilization. While Baron Philippe was certainly a great connoisseur of wine, it will be as a publicist for Mouton and as a man of letters that he will be remembered. Apart from several volumes of poetry, his literary reputation rests on his translations of the Elizabethan poets and of Christopher Marlowe as well as of the modern poet and dramatist Christopher Fry; and the wonderful museum he has created at Mouton is a permanent memorial to the breadth of his interest and taste. The splendid staging of this collection is mirrored in the whole layout of the great *chais* and in the presentation of Mouton's wines with its labels designed by famous contemporary artists, among whom have been numbered Jean Cocteau, Pablo Picasso, Salvador Dali and Marc Chagall. It was this quality of showmanship pursued with such panache and success that brought Baron Philippe criticism bordering on hostility over the years. One cannot fail to detect in this criticism both the innate conservatism of the Bordelais and an undercurrent of envy at the success such methods have brought. But surely, in an age when most publicity is brash and banal, we should be grateful when a fine product is publicized with a knowledge, taste and grandeur which so aptly suit it.

Perhaps the most important contribution made by Baron Philippe de Rothschild towards the evolution of the marketing of Bordeaux wines was the introduction of château bottling. This happened at the beginning of his long reign at Mouton. He persuaded the owners of the first growths to collaborate with him on insisting on selling their wines only in bottle, a revolutionary move at the time, and in spite of a deepening depression in the market. The 1924 was the first vintage, and the trend then set was to lead eventually, in 1972, to compulsory château bottling for all the *crus classés* – something which everyone today takes for granted. He was also instrumental in founding the Commanderie du Bontemps, after the war, which has done much to publicize the wines of the Médoc. His death in January 1988 marked the end of an era, linking the far-off days of the depression with today's high prosperity, which he exploited so successfully.

It is only in the case of Mouton Cadet that I personally would question the wisdom of Mouton's policy in the Baron Philippe era. It is easy to see how this position has grown up and how difficult it is now to decide on a change. The years 1930, 1931 and 1932 were all adjudged unworthy of Mouton's label and Baron Philippe, encouraged by his English agent, Teddy Hammond, hit upon the idea of blending the wines to be sold as a brand under the name of Mouton Cadet. The wine proved popular beyond their wildest dreams, so that what had begun as off-vintage Mouton, or vats not up to the highest standards from Mouton and Mouton d'Armailhacq, with the full Pauillac *appellation*, is now simply a branded claret with a simple *Bordeaux appellation*. It certainly can and does on occasion contain small quantities of Mouton rejected from the final blend, and the majority of the blend is usually from the Médoc, but wines from the other side of the river are nowadays usually used to assist in making a supple, quick-maturing wine. All this is fine, and as a branded claret Mouton Cadet is a worthy example. The trouble is that a great many wine drinkers, including reasonably knowledgeable ones, believe that they are buying a second wine of Mouton comparable, say, to Les Forts de Latour. This intimate association between a great classified growth and an ordinary commercial brand cannot be regarded in the long run as anything but unfortunate, not least for Mouton itself.

As at Latour, the château at Mouton is hardly its crowning glory. It is a small, ugly and curiously suburban Victorian villa, situated in the centre of the open-sided courtyard formed by the *chais* and administration buildings of the property. The Baron almost completely succeeded in hiding it from view by allowing the surrounding trees and shrubs ample scope for unimpeded growth. The Baron himself, assisted by his wife – a woman of unusual gifts and talents – caused another building to be converted into a most delightful flat where he himself stayed and entertained his guests.

The *chais* and cellars at Mouton are one of the showplaces of the Médoc. The great *chai* for the new wine is severely simple, yet the straight rows of casks with the arms of Mouton discreetly illuminated at the far end achieve a splendidly theatrical effect. The fine underground cellars where the wines mature in their second and third years in tranquil coolness are, on the other hand, classically traditional. The collection and range of bottled wines is also impressive, and is certainly one of the finest and most complete in the Médoc. It does not go back so far as the collection at Lafite, but from the 1850s onwards can have few rivals. Here again, wines are regularly recorked. I have one such treasured example in my possession; it says simply: "Mouton Rothschild – 1926 – rebouché au Château en 1957".

It has always seemed curious to me that two such totally dissimilar wines as Lafite and Mouton could possibly adjoin one another. If Mouton's vineyards adjoined those of Latour, it would seem natural enough. It is perhaps this juxtaposition of the two great wines which has led to this long and at times overplayed rivalry. Cyril Ray (see Bibliography) has clearly shown that this rivalry is not one simply between rival branches of the Rothschild family; it goes back to the period in the 1840s when there were no Rothschilds at either château. Probably its origins lie in the fact that Lafite had, since the beginning of the eighteenth century, been undisputed master in the Pauillac vineyards north of the town; Latour seemed almost as distant, no doubt, as Margaux and was in any case a quite distinct wine. Then, in the early years of the nineteenth century, Baron de Brane had set out to build up Mouton right on Lafite's doorstep. The sight of this newcomer achieving such speedy success, the realization that these fine adjoining slopes could, under expert management, produce a great wine – although a different one – no doubt caused uneasiness, even alarm, at Lafite. The aristocrats, as it were, felt threatened by the parvenu. Mouton in her turn was angry and indignant that her merits should not be given full face value, especially when customers were increasingly prepared to pay as much for their Mouton as for the first growths. Prejudice has certainly played its part; some partisans of Lafite and even of Latour affect to see no merit in Mouton, to urge that the 1855 classification was, indeed, correct and that for all her strivings and pretension, Mouton lacks the breed of a first growth. I must confess that I was not myself brought up to admire Mouton, but now that I have had the opportunity of drinking Moutons both old and new, I cannot but reject such judgements as biased and unobjective – though it is not always easy to be objective about such a subjective thing as wine! It seems to me that the very qualities for which, for example, Latour is often rightly praised, are accounted faults at Mouton.

There is no doubt that in the past, Mouton has often proved as hard and stubborn a wine as Latour. The very high percentage of Cabernet Sauvignon, much more pronounced than at Lafite, has much to do with this, as it has with the character of the wine. But there is no doubt that in recent years, Mouton has proved very successful in producing wines which, while maturing more quickly, seem to retain both their essential character and their keeping properties – a good omen, perhaps, for Latour. Nevertheless, it would be a mistake to suppose that the variations in *cépage* between Lafite and Mouton were the main cause of their differences – these merely serve to accentuate the existing differences in soil. It is these subtle but vital changes in soil throughout the great districts of Bordeaux which are the essential bases of the remarkable individuality of its great wines.

It is difficult to describe in words the difference in character between Mouton and Latour. Both have a very distinct Cabernet nose and flavour. Mouton tends to be rather lighter and softer in lesser years; in fine years it seems to have more vinosity and ripeness, with a distinct *cassis* nose and a beautiful harmony, so that while it is firm, it is not as hard as Latour – but some of these differences are certainly due to vinification. The basic difference is the very subtle difference of flavour in that there is, at the finish of a Mouton, some indefinable quality, almost a *goût de terroir*, which is absolutely characteristic. It is this quality which has led some critics of Mouton to assert that it lacks breed. Certainly it is different from Latour; some may prefer one, some the other, but this is a matter of taste and not basically, I would say, one of quality.

Like the other great Pauillacs, Mouton has great staying power, and those fortunate enough to have the chance to drink an old vintage which has been well kept will seldom be disappointed. The oldest good Mouton I have drunk is the 1869, one of the greatest surviving pre-phylloxera vintages of Mouton, which was still in wonderful form in 1969 – certainly one of the greatest Moutons. The 1889 was one of the first successful years after the double scourge of phylloxera and mildew had subsided. The wine tasted clean and had a good flavour, aged but not infirm, when tasted in 1962. The 1900 was a very great wine – in its way one of the most perfect bottles of old claret that it has ever been my good fortune to drink. In 1960 it still had a most beautiful bouquet, the flavour was delicious, full-bodied and fruity, and the whole effect one of perfect balance and harmony. In the twenties there were some very fine wines. Of those I have tasted, the 1921 was interesting because it had much more delicacy than is usual with this very hot year, when so many wines are burnt and a shade coarse. When I drank it in 1966, I felt it was just beginning to fade. The greatest Mouton of the decade for me is the 1926. In 1966 it seemed bigger than the 1945, but with such a wonderful combination of fruit and richness that it was delightful to drink. This is likely to be the wine which will outlive all its contemporaries. The 1928 was famous for its hardness, the 1929 for its charm, but it is now past its best. The 1933 was a magnificent wine, for many years much more enjoyable than the 1934. This wine was for years a good example of what critics of Mouton most disliked. It was very hard and rich with little style or finesse. But by the mid-sixties it was coming round better than had ever seemed possible – still a shade aggressive, but rich and well-rounded on the palate; an excellent wine.

Since the war, there have been many notable successes. The 1945 is a classic. For years it seemed tannic and a shade dry, but by 1987 the fruit had improved with a terrific bouquet of crushed *cassis*, and a flavour that was amazingly youthful and warm, more like a 1961 than a 1945, and certainly superior to Lafite or Latour, if less subtle than the marvellous Haut-Brion. Both the 1947 and the 1949 are great wines, among the top examples of their respective vintages and superior to the 1945 in my view. They are beautifully balanced wines of great vinosity and attraction, and many claret lovers, I suspect, preferred them until recently to the 1945, which took much longer to evolve. Unlike Lafite, at Mouton the 1960 was much more successful than the 1950. For me, the 1953 has certainly proved to be one of the most delightful examples of this charming year and has kept its freshness longer than most. The 1959 rates as a great success; it again kept its youthfulness for a long time and seems to lack the dryness of many 1959s. The 1961 I rated at the beginning as not outstanding for the year; how wrong I was! At Dr Taams's tasting in May 1978, it was clearly superior to Lafite and Margaux, and at least as fine as Latour, with some good judges just preferring the Mouton. It is a wine of great power and majesty with a long life ahead of it. The 1962 is very fine indeed, one of the best wines of the year along with Lafite. The 1963 was, with Latour, one of the few examples of this very poor vintage which was ever worth drinking. The 1964 was a great disappointment, an example of the late vintaging being caught out by the weather. The 1966 was most successful and is one of the best in the Médoc. As with so many wines of that year, the 1969 is something of a disappointment. However, the 1970 is a classic, although 1971 is no more than a pleasant lightweight; the 1973 is ripe and showy, the 1975 a really top wine and the 1976 has great charm; the 1977 is disappointing, but the 1978 has the makings of a great wine. Then came a slight trough in the otherwise consistent flow of good wines. The 1979 is disappointingly lean and dry, and the 1980 seems too dominated by its new oak, without the body to cope. But the lapse was brief, and 1981 began a marvellous series of wines, with rich, concentrated fruit, and a most attractive flavour that was already well evolved by 1987. The 1982 is all one would hope for from Mouton in such a year, while 1983 has real concentration of flavour and a very Mouton character, probably superior to the 1981. The 1984 looks much more successful than the 1980, with the fat to carry off the new oak, and more breed. The 1985 and 1986 should prove a great pair. While at Lafite it is 1985 that sets off the style of the château, at Mouton it is 1986 that is the most Mouton. Tasting it only a few days after drinking a great bottle of the 1945, the comparison was striking. But the 1985 is also a great wine, with all the beauty of flavour and charm to recall, for instance, the 1953.

CHÂTEAU PÉDESCLAUX
Cinquième Cru Classe. Owner: Jugla family. Administrator: Bernard Jugla. 18 hectares. 8,300 cases. CS 70%, Mer 20%, CF 5%, PV 5%

This is one of the obscurer classified growths. I can find no mention of it in any of the pre-1855 classifications. The name comes from a Bordeaux *courtier* who was proprietor at the time of the classification.

The *chai* is situated in the town of Pauillac. The vineyard lies to the northern extremity of the commune near Pontet-Canet. Since 1950 it has belonged to the Jugla family, and is now administered by Monsieur Bernard Jugla. The reputation of the growth does not stand very high today, and the wine is hardly of classified-growth standing. On the few occasions I have tasted it, I have found the wine lacking in style and personality – rather commonplace. But prices are modest, and a new collaboration with Dourthe produced a much improved 1985. So better things may be on the way. The principal export market is Belgium.

CHÂTEAU PIBRAN

Cru Bourgeois. Owner: La Compagnie Axa. 9 hectares. 4,000 cases. CS and CF 70%, Mer 24%, PV 6%. Second label: La Tour Pibran

This small property lies north-east of Pauillac, adjoining Pontet-Canet. It belonged to the Billa family from 1941, until they sold to Axa at much the same time as they bought Pichon-Baron. Under Jean-Michel Cazes's supervision, attractively fruity assertive wines are now being made.

CHÂTEAU PICHON-LONGUEVILLE-BARON

Deuxième Cru Classé. Owner: Société Civile de Pichon-Longueville (La Compagnie Axa). Administrator: Jean-Michel Cazes. 30 hectares. 14,000 cases. CS 80%, Mer 20%. Second label. Les Tourelles de Longueville

This growth is usually known as Pichon-Longueville-Baron, or simply as Pichon-Baron, to distinguish it from its twin across the road, but it is in fact perfectly correct to describe it simply as Pichon-Longueville. In the seventeenth century, the property belonged to Pierre de Masures de Rauzan, a member of the Bordeaux Parlement who, as we have already seen, was an important accumulator of estates at the end of the seventeenth and early eighteenth centuries. At this time the property was called Batisse and it seems also, at an earlier time, to have gone under the name of Badère.

In 1694, Thérèse de Masures de Rauzan married Jacques-François de Pichon, Baron de Longueville, and her father gave this property as her marriage portion. The Pichon family was ancient, noble and distinguished. It can be traced back to the twelfth century, and from the fourteenth century, members of the family played a conspicuous part in affairs of state; thus Bernard, the father of Jacques-François, was a prominent and consistent supporter of the Crown during the troubled years of Louis XIV's minority, being at one time besieged in his house in Bordeaux and then forced to flee the city. In consideration of the support of Bernard de Pichon and his family, they were granted perpetual pensions by Louis XIV, and the King did Bernard de Pichon the honour of staying with him for some six weeks on his way to St Jean-de-Luz for his marriage in 1659, though he passed only one night there on the return journey. After

Bernard de Pichon, the Pichon inheritance split into two parts which remained separate until the middle of the nineteenth century. The elder son took Parempuyre, the second son, Jacques-François, Longueville. This was the son who acquired this property by marriage and so gave his name to the estate. It is interesting to note that there was a dispute shortly after the marriage as to the right of this branch of the Pichon family to nobility, and the judgement was given in its favour by the Intendant of Bordeaux only in 1698. The only other incident of note at this period was that the son of the King of Poland was received by Jacques-François de Pichon at the Château Longueville (not to be confused with the present château).

At the time of the Revolution, the head of the family was Joseph de Pichon-Longueville. He was arrested and imprisoned, but escaped the guillotine. In 1816 he represented the city in congratulating Louis XVIII on the occasion of the Duc de Berry's marriage, and again, in 1820, at the birth of the Duc de Bordeaux. His son and heir, Raoul, also played a prominent part in the events leading up to the Restoration in 1814 and fought and was decorated for the Royalist cause. Like many others, he refused to play any part under the Orléanist regime after 1830. He showed his attachment to legitimist causes in a rather picturesque form by supporting Don Carlos, the founder of Carlism. He received Don Carlos at his house in Bordeaux in 1834, and conveyed him secretly from Bordeaux to Bayonne in his own carriage. He was afterwards decorated by Don Carlos, who was referred to by his supporters as Charles V.

It was during the administration of Raoul de Pichon-Longueville that the château really acquired a reputation for its wines. As with so many properties in the eighteenth century, its proprietors were a good deal more famous than its wines, but during the first half of the nineteenth century, the wines became at least as distinguished as the noble proprietor. A sign of the growing reputation of the wines of Pichon is that in a classification of the 1820s and again in Charles Cocks's classification, only a decade before the Paris Exhibition, Pichon is placed among the third growths, but in 1855 it was placed among the seconds. This was a distinction which was accorded to only one other Pauillac, namely Mouton.

Raoul de Pichon-Longueville had no children, but before he died in 1864, he adopted his cousin of the Parempuyre branch as his heir, thus reuniting the two branches, and this cousin, together with Raoul de Pichon-Longueville's three sisters, inherited the estate. Curiously, though, the portion belonging to the Comtesse de Lalande, which amounted to three-fifths of the original estate, was separated from the rest of the property, although the other sisters and the new Baron continued together at the original Pichon-Longueville. The property belonged to the Bouteiller family from 1933 until 1987, but the family always lived at their other property, Château Lanessan. The château, one of the most striking in the Médoc, with its elegant, slender corner turrets, presents almost a fairy castle impression, but has been empty since the war. The former *hôtel* of the Pichon-Longuevilles, in the Cours du Chapeau Rouge, in Bordeaux, one of the finest eighteenth-century mansions, is now a bank.

The wines of Pichon-Baron are, at their best, very classic Pauillacs, often rather aggressive at first, but acquiring a rich, velvety texture with maturity. The bouquet is particularly distinctive and fine. The 1928 was memorable as one of those that really repaid waiting; in 1965 it was excellent and had probably reached its plateau of maturity. There have been some fine wines since the war, notably the 1947 and 1949, with the 1948 a very good example of the year. The 1950 was for a long time rather too hard for the year, but the 1953 and 1959 were worthy examples of those vintages. More recently, 1962, 1966 and 1970 produced good and typical examples, but sadly there has been a lack both of consistency and of real quality through the sixties and seventies. In 1987 the property was sold by the Bouteiller family to the Compagnie Axa and Jean-Michel Gazes of Lynch-Bages will be overseeing what should prove to be a renaissance at Pichon-Baron.

During the last years of the Bouteiller management, there were moments when it seemed as though matters were improving. A wine would taste exciting in cask, as did the 1979, but time and again the eventual wine in bottle was a disappointment. In the autumn of 1986 I tasted the vintages of 1983 back to 1978, at the château. In the context of the various vintages, 1981 was the best, with a classic Pauillac Cabernet bouquet, and a solid rich flavour but without real flair. It was better than an aggressive 1982 that lacked the opulent fruit of the year. The 1978 was well balanced and pleasant but lacked real breed. The 1979 was coarse and abrasive, and 1983 very light and forward but attractive. The following year I re-tasted the 1981, and found it beginning to drink well, but still decidedly coarse. The skills which Jean-Michel Cazes has shown at Lynch-Bages have immediately produced impressive results, with classic wines in 1988 and 1989. A major rebuilding programme for the *cuvier* and *chais* began in 1989.

CHÂTEAU PICHON-LONGUEVILLE-COMTESSE-DE-LALANDE

Deuxième Cru Classé. Owner: Madame H. de Lencquesaing. 60 hectares. 25,000 cases. CS 46%, Mer 34%, CF 12%, PV 8%. Second label: Réserve de la Comtesse

This is the full and correct name of this château, although it is sometimes referred to as Pichon-Longueville-Lalande. During the administration of Monsieur W. -A. B. Miailhe (1959–1972), the wine was labelled simply as Pichon-Lalande, which had the dual advantage of cutting through the confusion that the use of the full name invokes, and of making the label much cleaner and crisper. This property, of course, shares with its neighbour the same history until the division. The attractive château, built in the 1840s, harks back to the classical forms of the early days of the century, in contrast to the Gothic romanticism of the Baron, built in 1851. Both were built before the actual division of the property. It stands in a small enclave surrounded by the vineyards of Latour, on land presented to the Comtesse de Lalande by her lover, the Comte de Beaumont, one of the principal owners of Latour at the time. One amusing aspect of this story is that the architect, Dupliot, was the same as was responsible, nearly twenty years later, for the far more modest château at Latour. The *chai* was for many years scattered around the village of St Lambert, but now a fine, submerged cellar has been built behind the château, which has served an ingenious dual purpose. On the one hand, it has given Pichon-Lalande a superb new *chai*, on the other, a terrace from which there is an unrivalled panorama of the vineyards of Latour and the river. This major improvement dates from the late sixties. But since Madame de Lencquesaing took charge in 1978, a fine reception hall has been added, and finally, in 1987, the size of the underground *chai* has been doubled – at some cost to the garden.

In the new underground *chai* there are some fine wrought-iron balustrades copied from those at the Hôtel Chapeau Rouge – a nice touch. Another interesting point for the visitor can be seen in the *chai*, where there are bunches of grapes preserved in glass jars, illustrating the principal red grape varieties used in the Médoc. This was, incidentally, one of the last properties where the *égrappage* was still performed by hand, an interesting spectacle at vintage time. New stainless steel fermentation *cuves* were installed just in time to receive the 1980 vintage.

One of the curiosities of Pichon is that it is the only classified growth whose vineyards straddle two *appellations* in any important way. Several leading growths in St Julien, as we have already seen, have small portions of their vineyards in other communes, and Lafite has a small vineyard in St Estèphe. But at Pichon-Lalande, as much as a third of the vineyard lies in St Julien. There was a period when the authorities insisted that the two parts be kept separate, and one had the confusing spectacle of some labels saying "*Appellation* Pauillac" and others "*Appellation* St Julien". Eventually, the proprietor won his fight for common sense against bureaucracy, insisting that Pichon was classified as a Pauillac and has always been regarded as such. But there is no doubt that this St Julien influence is to be seen in the wine and results in Pichon-Lalande's having a distinctly different style from its neighbour. There is not the frank Pauillac character of the Baron, especially on the nose, but something more subtle, perhaps more feminine. In some vintages, the St Julien side of its personality seems more dominant than in others, but at its best this is always a wine of great breed.

Pichon-Lalande came under its present ownership in 1926 when it was acquired by a Société Civile with Edouard F. Miailhe as administrator. The Miailhe family, who now own Pichon-Lalande, were for generations *courtiers* in Bordeaux and one of the few families to have been in business before the Revolution. Monsieur William Alain Miailhe succeeded his father in 1959, and under his enthusiastic guidance progress was made. By one of those coincidences which are so familiar in Bordeaux, his wife is a direct descendant of the Pichon-Longueville family. His administration ended in 1972, in a family row in which the minority shareholders were also involved. Basically his two elder sisters charged him with maladministration. During what became a six-year interregnum, first Monsieur Lahary of Chasse-Spleen, and then, from 1975 to 1978, Monsieur Michel Delon from neighbouring Léoville-Las Cases, were called in by the shareholders to oversee the management of Pichon-Lalande. This, in retrospect, proved to be the beginning of a great new era for the château. Michel Delon found Jean-Jacques Godin, appointed in 1970 by Alain Miailhe as *chef de culture*, and made him *régisseur*. The foundation he received under Michel Delon during this period has proved invaluable to this very able man, who has since had much to do with the rise in the reputation of Pichon-Lalande.

At last, in 1978, the position was resolved. On the advice of their lawyers, the family agreed to draw lots for the properties so that instead of each being part owners of all, each would henceforth become sole owners of one. In the event Madame May-Hélène de Lencquesaing, the second daughter of the late Edouard F. Miailhe, drew the gem of the inheritance. The wife of General Hervé de Lencquesaing, who had a distinguished war record with the Free French of General de Gaulle, she has, since 1978, displayed outstanding gifts of leadership and administration which have perfectly complemented Monsieur Godin's gifts as a winemaker. She has now taken her place as one of the leading personalities of the Médoc, and is a great and effective publicist for her wines all over the world. The difference between the new administration of Madame de Lencquesaing and that which preceded it needs to be seen in perspective. Some very good wines were made before, but both the quantity and quality of the production were inconsistent. On the positive side important additions were made to the vineyard under Alain Miailhe's administration, nearly 10 hectares situated between Pichon-Baron, Latour, Haut-Bages-Libéral and Batailley. Previously Pichon-Lalande's holdings here had been divided into some seventy different lots, making cultivation extremely difficult. A further 5 hectares immediately adjoining Pichon-Lalande, on excellent unplanted gravel, belonging to Léoville-Poyferré, were acquired during Michel Delon's administration. In conclusion, nothing is perhaps more important than the constant supervision which Madame de Lencquesaing lavishes on the property. It is first and foremost her home, when she is not travelling to promote her wine. Nothing can replace such regular attention to every detail of an estate, and this has had much to do with propelling Pichon-Lalande into the forefront of the super-seconds of the Médoc.

In the search for improved quality, between 10 and 40 per cent of the vintage is usually set aside for sale under the Réserve de la Comtesse label, which has now established an excellent reputation for itself.

I was fortunate in 1968 to have the opportunity of comparing side by side, at the château, the 1926, 1928 and 1929 vintages. It was interesting to find that the 1928 was seeing the 1929 out. It was attractive for a 1928, with much more life and vigour than the 1929. The 1929 itself was soft and fine-flavoured, but beginning to fade. But the 1926 made a wonderful pair with the 1928 and in the end, to my way of thinking, it just had the edge over the 1928. The two wines were very comparable, but the 1926 had just a little more fruit and sweetness and so lasted and improved the better in the glass. In two capricious and uneven vintages, 1934 and 1937, Pichon-Lalande was very successful. Indeed the 1934, which I have been fortunate enough to drink on many occasions, is certainly one of the most successful Médocs of the year, with great fruit and charm allied to a well-defined Pauillac character. This was a year when the Pauillac side was dominant. On the only occasion that I drank the 1937, I thought it nearly as good as the 1934, a high compliment indeed.

The 1950 took much longer than most 1950s to reach its best, but after eleven or twelve years, the original hardness fell away to reveal a very pleasant wine of this vintage. The 1952 was particularly successful here, with more fruit and fullness than many wines of this year, more successful perhaps than the 1953, which is charming but not outstanding for the vintage. The 1955 was also attractive, but the 1959 is not quite so outstanding as the Baron.

In the sixties, Lalande really came into its own. The 1960 was very light and seemed to lack personality in the early years, but was a wine which steadily improved. The 1961 is really an outstanding example of the year, a wine of great fruit and richness, so that it was extraordinarily supple at an early age, but it has got better and better in recent years and should last for many more. The 1962 has taken some time to develop, but seems to be more generous and elegant than the Baron. The 1964 is one of the most successful Pauillacs, or indeed Médocs, of this year of varied fortunes. In a vintage where St Julien in general took the palm, there were few better wines made outside it than here. The 1966 is a good example of the year, and in the more difficult 1967 vintage, the Lalande – one of the front-runners from the start – has aged more attractively than most. In the seventies, the wine went from strength to strength. After a fine 1970 and good 1971, the 1975 is excellent, and the 1976 and 1977 are among the best examples of these years. The 1978 and 1979 are a superb pair, with 1978 showing great complexity in a many-layered flavour, a great example of the year, while 1979 has lots of opulent fruit and is more obvious, nevertheless a delicious and delightful wine. The 1980 is rich and quite solid, and has lasted well. Then comes a series of exceptional wines: 1981 has great breed, length and charm, a wine for medium-term drinking; 1982 has an exotic air of almost oriental spiciness and an aroma of prunes – if this over-ripe character is clearly not classic, I certainly find it irresistible; 1983 on the other hand is a classic, with beautifully balanced tannins and fruit – they began vintaging here eight days later than Latour, and the difference is impressive. In the difficult 1984 vintage the selection was severe, only 60 per cent of the small crop going into the *grand vin*, and there was only one vat of Merlot, compared with six in 1983. And yet the wine seemed remarkably flattering and supple in cask – some achievement in this vintage. Finally comes another remarkable pair, 1985 and 1986. With the 1985 one is seduced by the sheer beauty and richness of the wine, in 1986 it is the power and structure of a classic *vin de garde* allied to exotic spicy fruit that arrests one's admiration. In the 1985 one sees comparisons with 1953 and 1929; in the 1986 it is with 1975 (at its finest) and 1949. What a treat lies in store here! There can be no doubt that Pichon-Lalande has now firmly taken its place beside Léoville-Las Cases, Ducru-Beaucaillou and Cos d'Estournel at the head of the second growths, justifying the gap in price which has now opened up between these and the other seconds.

CHÂTEAU PONTET-CANET

Cinquième Cru Classé. Owner: Guy Tesseron. 75 hectares. 30,000 cases. CS 68%, Mer 20%, CF 12%. Second label: Les Hauts-de-Pontet

The fifth group of the 1855 classification began with a string of five Pauillacs, headed by Pontet-Canet. In the classifications of the 1820s it is referred to simply as Canet, the property of de Pontet, and Charles Cocks called it Canet Pontet.

It was Jean-François Pontet, who served as a deputy in the Médoc to the Intendant of Guyenne, and so was a powerful political figure, who pieced together the property in the second quarter of the eighteenth century. Later its reputation grew steadily under Pierre-Bernard de Pontet, who was born in 1764 and died in 1836. Like so many proprietors of the age, Pontet was in politics, and was deputy for the Gironde as well as a member of the Conseil Général in the years immediately after the Restoration. After his death in 1836 the reputation of the wine declined, so that it was placed only among the fifth growths in 1855. But a new age began when Herman Cruse bought the property in 1865. One of the new proprietor's first acts was to entrust the management of the property to Charles Skawinski, second son of the remarkable Pierre Skawinski of Giscours, although he was only twenty-three at the time. It was at this time that the great *chai* and new *cuvier* were built. The arrangement of the fermentation vats was a classic Skawinski design, with easy access to the top of the vats by means of a wooden gallery. Pontet-Canet also has one of the few large underground cellars in the Médoc. Under his management during Herman Cruse's lifetime and afterwards under his widow, Skawinski built up a great reputation for Pontet-Canet, so that it frequently fetched the price of a third or even a second growth. After Madame Cruse's death, the property was managed by the Cruse firm in Bordeaux, until the great crisis in the firm's affairs led to its sale in 1975 to Monsieur Guy Tesseron, son-in-law of the late Emmanuel Cruse of Château d'Issan and himself already proprietor of Château Lafon-Rochet. Under the enthusiastic management of Alfred Tesseron, Monsieur Guy Tesseron's son, the facilities have been thoroughly modernized. As he has now made his home at the château, Pontet-Canet again has a resident proprietor after a gap of many years.

Unfortunately, the reputation of this château does not stand as high as it once did. There was a feeling in the Bordeaux trade that Pontet-Canet was more of a brand than a classified growth, and the refusal to allow château bottling lay at the heart of this distrust, together with the non-vintage wine sold on the French railways. The wine itself is also of variable and rather ordinary quality. One no longer sees the great vintages of the past which made Pontet-Canet famous. The last was the 1929, a very great example of this beautiful year which will long live in the memory of all who were fortunate enough to drink it. It lasted much better than most wines of this year, and when I last drank it in 1967, it was in superb condition at the height of its form, sweet and remarkably long, its flavour the epitome of great Pauillac, and wonderfully ripe. Even in great years such as 1947, 1959 and 1961, Pontet-Canet managed to make dull, commonplace wines during the declining years of the Cruse stewardship. There is no doubt that with its wonderful position on the plateau of Pauillac, adjoining Mouton and Mouton-Baronne-Philippe, Pontet-Canet has the potential to make fine wines.

In 1972, Pontet-Canet at last came into line with other classifed growths and château-bottled. The change of ownership raised expectations of much better things to come, which unfortunately were not fulfilled, at least in the early years. Good wines were made in small vintages such as 1975 and 1981, but there was a lack of class and a touch of coarseness in their make-up. Then in 1982 a second wine, Les Hauts-de-Pontet, was introduced, to make a stricter selection. The improvement was immediately obvious and when one tasted the second wine, one saw why! The Hauts-de-Pontet, especially in large years, tends to have a rather diluted character and to finish rather dry, in spite of the initial youthful fruit. The 1982 is certainly the best wine produced here for a long time, and I am also enthusiastic about the 1985, which has perhaps more finesse and charm. So it looks as if Alfred Tesseron is beginning to get things right, and that we can expect more rewarding wines in the future.

LA ROSE PAUILLAC (*CAVE COOPÉRATIVE*)

Owner: Groupement des Propriétaires-Viticulteurs de Pauillac. 110 hectares.
52,000 cases. CS and CF 45%, Mer 40%, PV 15%

This *coopérative* was founded in 1933, at the height of the financial and viticultural crisis when the outlook for properties great and small was bleak indeed. It marked the beginning of the co-operative movement in Médoc, and began with just fifty-two members. Today there are 125 cultivating 110 hectares of vineyards. In recent years the *coopérative* has lost some members, as the economic situation has improved and more producers have wanted to make and market their own wines.

Although most of the wine is sold under the La Rose Pauillac label, Château Haut-Milon and Château Haut-Saint-Lambert make their own vintage declarations, while Château Le Fournas-Bernadotte is vinified at the co-op, but the *élevage* is done by the proprietor. These are good, solid, attractive Pauillacs which emphasize the fruit and are not too tannic.

ST ESTÈPHE

This is the most northerly of the great *appellations* of the Haut-Médoc, and produces more wine than any other. But it boasts fewer classified growths than Pauillac, Margaux or St Julien, and a very large number of *bourgeois* growths of widely varying quality. It is the only one of the four great *appellations* of the Médoc where the area of the *crus bourgeois* is greater than that of the classified growths, with only 21 per cent of the vineyards being *crus classés*.

In style, the wines have less body than those of Pauillac; at their best, they are very fruity, full-flavoured and quite rich, but, on the other hand, some lesser growths are tough and rather stringy with a certain *goût de terroir* and a certain dry meanness at the finish. So the range of quality is considerable; there are aristocrats worthy to take their place among the great wines of the Médoc, and plebeians which are on a quality level with the least in the backwoods of the Haut-Médoc.

St Estèphe itself lies near, but not on, the river, and there are other villages of some importance, notably Pez and Cadourne. Most of the vineyards lie on gravelly slopes which run from close to the river to some distance inland.

CHÂTEAU ANDRON-BLANQUET

Cru Grand Bourgeois Exceptionnel. Owner: Madame Cécile Audoy. 15 hectares. 6,000 cases. Mer 35%, CS 30%, CF 30%, PV 5%. Secondary labels: Château St-Roch, Blanquet

Andron is the name of one of the families who can be traced, as proprietors in the village of Blanquet, back to 1662, and it passed over the centuries through the Andron, Coucharrière and Lequad families, until bought in 1971 by the Audoy family of Cos-Labory. The vineyard is in the southern part of St Estèphe and adjoins that of the two Cos.

In my experience the wine has quite a strong *goût de terroir*, especially when young, but this is matched by enough fruit and richness to produce a balanced wine after some ageing. The character of the wine is nevertheless quite strong and assertive in contrast to Cos-Labory. There seems to have been an improvement in the wine-making in recent vintages, which has ironed out some of the irregularities of this very typical St Estèphe.

CHÂTEAU BEAU-SITE

Cru Grand Bourgeois Exceptionnel. Owner: Emile Castéja. 27 hectares. 15,000 cases. CS and CF 60%, Mer 40%

This property stands at the entrance to the village of St Corbian at the northern extremity of the St Estèphe *appellation*. An attractive courtyard in front of the *chai* is partly enclosed by wall and railings, marked by small pavilions at each corner. The vineyard runs from the road towards Calon-Ségur.

The vineyard has been classified since 1966 as a *grand bourgeois exceptionnel*. As with many St Estèphes, the wines here have quite a strong flavour at first, but then soon develop the necessary richness to produce something harmonious and pleasing. Sometimes there can be a touch of toughness at the finish, but this usually rounds off with ageing. The most impressive of the recent vintages have been a rich, powerful 1978, a supple, elegant 1981, ready to drink when four years old, a very full-flavoured and harmonious 1982, and a fruity, supple 1983, again delicious when four years old. The property is owned and run by the Castéja family (see Batailley, p. 141), and distributed exclusively by their family firm of Borie-Manoux.

CHÂTEAU BEAUSITE-HAUT-VIGNOBLE

Cru Bourgeois 1932. Owner: Jean-Louis Braquessac. 20 hectares. 8,000 cases.
CS 60%, Mer 30%, PV 10%

This is the property of Monsieur Jean-Louis Braquessac, whose *chai* is only a few yards down the road in St Corbian from Beau-Site. But the wine, although carefully made and very honourable, is not in the same class as Beau-Site. It has a tendency to be rather tough and unyielding and generally takes some time to come round. The lack of richness combined with a certain toughness is characteristic of many of the lesser growths of St Estèphe.

CHÂTEAU CALON-SÉGUR

Troisième Cru Classé. Owner: Capbern-Gasqueton and Peyrelongue families.
Administrator: Philippe Gasqueton. 48 hectares. 15,000 cases. CS 60%, CF 20%, Mer 20%. Second label: Marquis de Ségur

Of the three leading estates in St Estèphe, this is certainly the most ancient. Its origins can be traced back to the twelfth century when the lords of Lesparre gave it to a bishop of Poitiers – Monseigneur de Calon. But the area was also referred to as de Calones after the boats that used to ferry timber across the Gironde. In the eighteenth century it belonged to the famous Marquis de Ségur, then the proprietor of Lafite and Latour. It was he who was supposed to have said that although he made his wine at

Lafite, his heart was at Calon. This is the origin of the heart-shaped device seen on the label and at many places on the property. At this time the Lawton brokerage records show that the prices obtained by Calon between 1741 and 1774 were not far behind Léoville, above all the other second growths. In 1787 Thomas Jefferson reported that Calon was placed in "the third class", a position also ascribed to it in 1815 by Lawton (though he thought recent vintages were not up to its reputation!). In the last century, it belonged to Pierre-Sévère de Lestapis, one of the most famed financiers of his time in France. Curiously, he received his training with Alexander Baring in London. In 1818, together with his two brothers, he established his own firm of Lestapis Frères in Bordeaux. This firm played a very important part in developing trade with India and South America. The property now belongs to the Gasqueton and Peyrelongue families, and has been administered by Philippe Gasqueton since the death of his uncle, Edouard, in 1962. It was Edouard Gasqueton who was responsible for building the modern reputation of Calon for reliability, between the wars and up to the time of his death.

The vineyard is beautifully situated, just to the north of St Estèphe, and is largely encircled by an old stone wall. It is the most northerly of the great St Estèphes, and indeed of all the classified growths. The château itself is one of the finest in the region, with its distinctive squat towers and cloister-like entrance by the *chai*. It dates from the seventeenth century.

The old classic *cuvier* of free-standing wooden *cuves* is still an imposing sight, but has not in fact been used since 1973. Then a new battery of metal *cuves*, each of only 100 hectolitres, representing half a day's picking, was installed, thus giving more control. In 1983 an impressive new underground cellar was constructed in an ingenious manner. It is L-shaped along two sides of the old *chai*, so could be built without disturbing the work there. It is attractively arched and vaulted, extending for 60 metres on one side, and 50 on the other, and has greatly improved the conditions for cask storage at Calon.

In character the wines of Calon are softer and develop their fruit more quickly than Montrose or indeed Cos. If it is seldom the best of the three, it has a virtue of consistency, and this dependability has much to do with its popularity.

Calon is a wine which nevertheless lasts very well, and this has been brought home in the older vintages I have seen. Certainly one of the finest of all Calons was the bottle of 1916 I drank with Philippe Gasqueton on its seventieth birthday: it was perfectly preserved with no sign of decay on nose or palate – I thought it a great wine of the twenties. It matched the magnum of 1924 that I was fortunate enough to drink with Madame Edouard Gasqueton and Philippe when it was forty years old. It had not faded as had most wines of that year by then, but combined power with finesse, and was full of vitality – a delicious wine. The 1926 was also a fine example of the year. Equally memorable is the 1934, certainly one of the most consistently enjoyable wines of that year that I know. In recent years the 1937 has also been impressive, still vibrant with splendid tannins and richness, but no dryness, when fifty years old. Since the war, the 1945 is very fine, having sufficient richness to cope with the tannin – it has been very enjoyable for a number of years and there is plenty of life in it still; 1947 was still opulent and delightful in 1986; the 1948 and 1950 were both outstandingly successful, the 1948 so much so that I have thought it superior to the 1949. In the next decade, the 1952 was unusually attractive for the year, although meatier than the 1953; the 1953, while fine, was not outstanding in this exceptional year; the 1954 was a most attractive wine which was still excellent when nearly fourteen years old; the 1955 was a good wine for the year; and the 1959 has developed well, being big and vigorous. The next decade did not begin so well: the 1960 was a disappointment – not in the class of the 1950 or even the 1954; the 1962 is a good example of the year, but light – a magnum was beautifully silky and mature in 1987; the 1964 started badly with too much rain-water in it – surprisingly, though, it has picked up and although light and of only average quality, has developed into an acceptable bottle; even more surprising was the 1965 which was one of the few drinkable wines in this very poor year; the 1966 was a return to form and has developed very well, as has the 1967. In the seventies, Calon maintained its reputation for reliability. When a blind tasting of leading growths of the Gironde was held in Nicolas's cellars in 1976 for the French gourmet magazine, *La Nouvelle Guide de Gault-Millau*, Calon came out with the highest average mark. The vintages tasted were 1966, 1970, 1971 and 1973. Good wines were also made in 1975 and though the 1976 is ripe and pleasant, it also tastes diluted and was at its peak at ten years of age. But like most properties in the northern Médoc, Calon did less well in 1977. While the 1978 was a wine of breed and charm, some bottles have started to look prematurely aged, but the 1979 is a different matter: rich, tannic and vigorous, it needed ten years to reach its full maturity. After a soft but light-textured 1980 that was delicious at five years of age, 1981 is well structured and quite tannic, developing slowly. The 1982 is a great Calon, and typical of the best 1982s, with a combination of great richness and tannin, a fine *vin de garde*. Like a number of wines in northern Médoc, the 1983 seems soft, ripe and forward, rather fluid and lacking backbone – a sign of high yields. The 1984 is a pleasant, light wine for early drinking. The 1985 in cask was tannic and powerful, with less charm than is usual for 1985 while 1988 and 1989 looked classic Calons in cask.

CHÂTEAU CAPBERN-GASQUETON

Cru Grand Bourgeois Exceptionnel. Owner: Capbern-Gasqueton family.
Administrator: Philippe Gasqueton. 30 hectares. 10,000 cases. CS 60%, Mer 25%, CF 15%. Second label: Le Grand Village Capbern (exclusively distributed by Dourthe)

This leading *cru bourgeois* is under the same management as Calon-Ségur. The solid mansion, which is the château, is in the centre of St Estèphe, next to the church, and apart from its unmistakably French roof-line has something of a Regency look about it. This is the home of Philippe Gasqueton and his family, and has been theirs since the eighteenth century.

The vineyard is in two parts, one adjoining Calon-Ségur, the other Meyney. The wine is matured entirely in cask but no new wood is used. Good, solid and quite powerful wines are made, but Philippe Gasqueton is successful in emphasizing the fruit and avoiding the leanness and harshness often associated with St Estèphe. The wines are very consistent and easy to drink. The 1983, for instance, is very successful here, with plenty of fat, ripeness and character. The second wine, Le Grand Village Capbern, is an exclusivity of Dourthe.

CHÂTEAU CHAMBERT-MARBUZET

Cru Bourgeois 1932. Owner: Société Civile du Château Chambert-Marbuzet (H. Duboscq & Fils). 8 hectares. 3,800 cases. CS 70%, Mer 30%. Second label: Château MacCarthy

The name Chambert belonged to an old family of *vignerons* who lived in Marbuzet in the last century. It is a very Girondin name, and is also used locally to describe an old vineyard tool, rather like a pickaxe, used to dig trenches in the vineyards. This small outpost of the Duboscq empire (see Haut-Marbuzet) was acquired in 1962. The *encépagement* is fundamentally different from Haut-Marbuzet, with much more Cabernet Sauvignon, and until the 1986 vintage, no new wood was used. But the Duboscq wine-making genius works just as well under these different conditions. Again there is depth of colour, and the wines are scented and packed with fruit, with plenty of ripe tannins in support, but not as opulent or complex as Haut-Marbuzet. Nevertheless, this is good, solid, attractive St Estèphe which is most approachable when young, yet with all the elements to age well. Excellent wines were made in 1981, 1982, 1983, 1985 and 1986.

CHÂTEAU LA COMMANDERIE
Cru Bourgeois 1932. Owner: Gabriel Meffre. 16 hectares. 6,000 cases. CS 60%, Mer 40%

This is the northerly outpost of Gabriel Meffre's (of Côtes du Rhône fame) empire. He also owns du Glana in St Julien, and at one time all the wine was made there; now it is made here. This old property also incorporates Canteloup, which takes its name from the Archbishop of Bordeaux of that name who received it from his predecessor, Bertrand de Goth, when he became Pope in 1305 under the name of Clement V. Commanderie itself takes its name from an outpost of the Knights Templar who were themselves savagely suppressed during Clement's pontificate. The vineyard is in the southern sector of the *appellation* between Marbuzet and Leyssac. The grapes are mechanically harvested and aged in cask. The wines, whose reputation is only moderate, are distributed by Dourthe and Kressmann, depending on the market.

CHÂTEAU COS D'ESTOURNEL
Deuxième Cru Classé. Owner: Domaines Prats. Administrator: Bruno Prats. 54 hectares. 18,000 cases. CS 60%, Mer 40%. Second label: Château de Marbuzet

This strikingly placed property lies across the marshy ground of the Jalle du Breuil on a promontory above Lafite. Its pagoda-like façade is one of the most familiar landmarks in the Médoc, and it is rather a disappointment to discover that this is only a *chai* and not the château (there is none). From the direction of St Estèphe, there is a formal entrance to part of the vineyard which now frames a horrific science-fiction view of the enlarged Shell installation at Pauillac.

The property takes its name from Monsieur Louis-Gaspard Destournel or d'Estournel, under whom the fame of the château was established. After he had bought back the property in 1821 – his family having sold it in 1811 – he enlarged the vineyard to approximately its present size and built the famous *chai*. When he began in 1821 there were only 14 hectares of vines, which he increased to 65. At the time of the classification, the property actually belonged to an Englishman, a Mr Martyn, who owned it from 1853 to 1869. Although a largely absentee landlord, he invested in the property, and made Gérome Chiapella, the owner of La Mission-Haut-Brion, his administrator. He must have found it ironic that La Mission was omitted from the 1855 classification, while his efforts at Cos were so handsomely rewarded. In 1919 it was bought by Monsieur Fernand Ginestet, and then for many years formed part of the domains owned, administered and distributed by the Ginestet family, firstly under Pierre Ginestet and more recently by his son Bernard. In 1971, when some of the Ginestet family holdings were divided up, Cos went to Pierre Ginestet's sister, Madame Prats. Her son, Bruno, has taken charge of the running of the property. At the same time, they decided to remove the distribution of Cos from the Ginestet firm and arrange this for themselves, which seems to have proved beneficial for the château. Owing, no doubt, to the very late development of the property at the beginning of the nineteenth century, Cos made a late appearance in the early classifications. It was placed with the third growths by William Franck in 1824, but by 1840 *Le Producteur* was speaking of it as a *deuxième cru*, so its rise was rapid in those days of an unfixed or "floating" classification. There is no doubt that in the years since 1855 it has consistently held its place as one of the leading second growths.

In my experience, Cos at its best is the finest of the St Estèphes, with more breed, delicacy and fruit than is achieved by other properties in the area. Certainly the finest bottles of St Estèphe that I have drunk came from Cos. Like most of the best Médocs, Cos generally requires some time for its various parts to harmonize. The constituents are a great vigour (which here is more than simple tannin), great fruit and charm which, with maturity, produce a mellow richness which is given life, character and verve by a firm backbone. Some lesser St Estèphes remind me of those drawings of Don Quixote by Gustave Doré, large in scale but very bony, so that one is more aware of the skeleton beneath than the flesh so sparsely stretched upon it. With Cos, the skeleton is there but always in the background.

I have been fortunate in drinking some fine vintages of Cos. Outstanding among these was the 1869 which I had with Pierre and Bernard Ginestet on its ninety-sixth birthday. It was certainly one of the greatest bottles of claret I have ever had, the bouquet still fresh and lovely, the wine sweet and full-flavoured with great length – an apparently age-less beauty. In style it reminded me strongly of a 1900. After this, the 1870 was still rich and powerful in 1988. At the same tasting, the 1911 was fresh and delicate, if fading. Among the great vintages of the twenties, I would single out the 1920, 1926, 1928 and 1929 as very fine examples of these years, which have lasted remarkably well. The 1926 was still at the height of its beauty and power when over sixty years old. After the war, Cos produced a great and apparently ageless 1947, and a delicious 1948, now ageing gracefully. The fifties were an outstanding decade for Cos, but I was less enchanted with the sixties, a period which coincided with a decline in the affairs of the Ginestets. The 1950 was attractive and lasted very well; the 1952 has the charm of a 1953, but with much more power, the 1953 is a real beauty and was still on top form in 1986. The 1955 was fine and with more individuality than many; the 1957 was a success in an uneven year; the 1958 had the charm of the year and lasted well; the 1959 was a slow developer and was very rich; the 1960 was less attractive than the 1950; the 1961 is one of the greatest wines of the year, complex and complete, still marvellously fresh in 1988; the 1962 was very slow to come out and show its paces – but has finally developed great finesse and elegance. The 1964, while having more colour and body than some, lacked grace and breed, but 1966 is a lovely cedary, deep-flavoured classic of the year. The 1967 was still remarkably fine in 1983.

The change of management has certainly seen a revitalization at Cos, which has been reflected in the wines. Fine wines were made in 1975 and 1976, while the 1977 was much better than most St Estèphes in that year. The 1978 has proved rather slow and stubborn in its development, but

1979 is a delightful wine, with concentrated richness and breed. There is quite a full-flavoured 1980. Then come the great vintages of the eighties. The 1981 is unfolding slowly, a wine of compact fruit, length and breed. The 1982 is a massive and splendid *vin de garde*, while 1983 is rich and supple and developing more slowly than many wines of this year. In cask the 1985 and 1986 are an interesting contrast, with the 1985 more tannic and powerful than many wines of this vintage and the 1986, almost black in colour, having a remarkable flavour, concentration and extract combined with great fruit and style. Better at this infantile stage, I thought, than the 1985, good as it is, and one of the outstanding wines of the year.

Rather confusingly, the second wine here, Château de Marbuzet, is also a vineyard in its own right, of 7 hectares. The château, a pleasing neo-classical house, in practice serves as the château that Cos itself lacks. The production of de Marbuzet's vineyards is vinified at Cos, and blended with vats excluded from the *assemblage* for the Cos *grand vin*.

A new departure is Maître d'Estournel. This is a branded wine with only a Bordeaux *appellation*, and is not a second wine of Cos. It seems a pity that such a name, which could cause confusion, should have been chosen.

CHÂTEAU COS-LABORY

Cinquième Cru Classé. Owner: Madame Cécile Audoy. 12 hectares. 6,700 cases.
CS 40%, Mer 35%, CF 20%, PV 5%

The small, turreted château is immediately opposite its more famous neighbour, Cos d'Estournel. At the time of the 1855 classification it was under the same ownership as d'Estournel, and this must have helped. It is today one of the less well-known classified growths, but the wine is well made and attractive, while lacking, until recently, the weight and the character of a classified growth. While the 1981 was a good example of the year, all charm and drinkability, the 1982 simply lacked the concentration and richness looked for from this outstanding vintage, although it is stylish and attractive. But much more impressive concentrated wines were made in 1986 and 1989, so this is now a wine to watch.

CHÂTEAU COUTELIN-MERVILLE

Cru Grand Bourgeois. Owner: Guy Estager. 16 hectares. 6,000 cases. CS and CF 65%, Mer 30%, PV and Mal 5%

The Estager family came to St Estèphe from the Corrèze in 1904, and Guy Estager is now the third generation of his family to have worked here. Until 1972 this property was run jointly with Château Hauteillan in Cissac whose vineyard adjoins that of Coutelin-Merville, but then inheritance problems forced the sale of Hauteillan. The wines are matured in cask, but there is no new wood. The wines are powerful and strong-flavoured, needing time in bottle to round them off.

CHÂTEAU LE CROCK

Cru Grand Bourgeois Exceptionnel. Owner: Cuvelier family. Administrator: Didier Cuvelier. 31 hectares. 15,500 cases. CS 65%, Mer 35%

I remember first coming across the name of Le Crock in the diaries kept at Château Loudenne. In the days before the First World War when the Gilbeys spent a good deal of time at Loudenne, and did much entertaining there, they often visited Le Crock when the Mermans, a leading firm of *courtiers* at the time, were owners. The château is not only beautiful in itself with an unusual Louis XV-style façade, although it was actually built in 1820, but is in a ravishing setting on high ground, looking down to a picturesque stream and lake. There are even swans to complete the idyllic landscape, a distinctly unusual one for the Médoc. In 1903 the Mermans sold the property to the Cuveliers, a firm of *négociants* in northern France, who were subsequently to buy Léoville-Poyferré.

Le Crock now benefits from the same dynamic management that Didier Cuvelier has brought to Léoville-Poyferré, and is assisted by Francis Dourthe, the Poyferré *maître de chai*. I have not tasted any old vintages, but the most recent ones have been most impressive. They are scented, powerful and complex on the nose, and have a decided and agreeable personality, rich, with depth and structure on the palate. In a blind tasting of 1979 *crus bourgeois* in 1984, Le Crock was on the same level of quality as Meyney, and an excellent 1983 was produced, full of rich, supple fruit. The vineyard lies between the two Cos and Marbuzet. Le Crock, which had been a rather forgotten wine on export markets, has now clearly reclaimed its place among the best *crus bourgeois* of St

Estèphe, and is a wine worth looking out for, especially in the vintages of the eighties.

CHÂTEAU HAUT-MARBUZET

Cru Grand Bourgeois Exceptionnel. Owner: Henri Duboscq. 38 hectares. 18,500 cases. Mer 50%, CS 40%, CF 10%. Second wine: Château Tour de Marbuzet

This is one of the great success stories of the Médoc, to set beside that of Henri Martin at Gloria. In 1952 Hervé Duboscq bought 6 hectares near the village of Marbuzet with money borrowed from his business partner. Together with his son Henri, who now runs the property, he built on this slender foundation, gradually acquiring small parcels of vines around the village of Marbuzet. In 1958 they bought Tour de Marbuzet, and this name is now used for the second wine, which comes from vines of less than ten years of age. This is much the same way as the *noblesse de robe* in the eighteenth century, and the bourgeois families of Bordeaux in the eighteenth and early nineteenth centuries, assembled the vineyards which were to become the *crus classés*. There is no time limit to this process, only the need to find good sites and the skill to manage them and make the wine to the limit of its potential. Henri Duboscq certainly possessed all these qualities to a marked degree.

As so often in Bordeaux's history, the Duboscqs came from outside the Gironde itself – although the Gers, best known for its Armagnac, is not far away. Other growers have similar proportions of grapes in their vineyards; it is what Henri Duboscq does in his *cuvier* and *chai* which makes his wines outstanding. In the vinification he believes in living dangerously, and is one of the small but growing band who believe that high-temperature fermentation – up to 35°C – gives the exceptional extraction to make the greatest wines. Until recently this has been a very perilous practice but now, with the latest heat exchangers, this sort of fine tuning has become quite practicable, because a vat can very quickly be brought back from the brink of disaster. This is combined with long maturation and as many as ten to twelve *remontages*. This produces a wine which is then capable of sustaining the ageing in 100 per cent new oak that is the next essential ingredient in Haut-Marbuzet. Here again, Henri Duboscq has made an exhaustive study of what he wants and how to achieve it. He uses two types of oak, and chooses his suppliers carefully. The Allier suits the powerful tannic wines of the best years and brings out the opulence and exotic quality of the wine whereas the Nivernais produces more of a vanilla note and rounds off the wine well. He uses more Nivernais in lighter years. Lastly he bottles only by gravity, so that there is no pumping, and this means the wine recovers much more quickly from the bottling.

The result of all this care and study is a wine with great depth of colour, a spicy, opulent and complex bouquet, and a flavour which combines power and tannin with suppleness and fruit. Henri Duboscq is like a conductor of a great symphony orchestra, drawing together many elements into a remarkable and harmonious whole. You can see all the raw materials and learn about the ground plan, but when you taste what is actually in the glass, you are still lost in admiration at how it has been done.

The oldest vintage I have seen is the 1961 (almost sweet, with the taste of concentrated prunes in 1989). The 1962, which we drank at the château on its twenty-fifth birthday, was deep-coloured, the bouquet still wonderfully opulent, the flavour beautifully rounded off and with a freshness and concentration more akin to a 1961. The 1970 drunk at the same time had a classic rich *cassis* perfume, and a beautiful, long, firm flavour that was just opening out. Just to show what can be done even in problem years, the 1972 was one of the very best I ever tasted. The 1976 was more youthful at eleven years than most wines of this year, a big wine with well-balanced fruit and tannins. The 1979 shows the capacity to produce very concentrated rich wines which are at the same time stylish and balanced. In the 1981 one was still conscious of the new oak in 1987, yet the fat and richness in the wine made it already delicious to drink. The 1982 has marvellous opulent richness, with persistence and beauty of flavour and taste of truffles, while the 1983 is rich, solid and already attractive.

The great years 1985 and 1986 are a fascinating study in Henri Duboscq's particular alchemy. The 1985 was kept in 70 per cent Allier and 30 per cent Nivernais, and bottled in April 1987. Tasted after six months in bottle, it was very deep in colour, the bouquet was spicy with vanilla tones, rich and scented, the flavour had opulent fruit and was rich and supple, with just a little tannin at the finish, but the overall impression was harmonious, and the new wood had been beautifully absorbed. With the 1986 in cask, we were able to see the actual differences between the wine in the two different oaks. The Nivernais had a very pronounced perfume of vanilla and was concentrated, rich and fruity. The flavour showed concentrated, longish fruit, and the finish was marked by the wood. The Allier brought out a richer, more exotic, chocolaty note on the nose, while the flavour was very long and opulent with a firm tannic finish. Clearly a great wine in the making. Then gorgeous wines followed in 1988 and 1989, and a charming 1987 aged entirely in Nivernais oak. On this form not only is Haut-Marbuzet worthy of *cru classé* status, but its position would also be well off the bottom rung.

CHÂTEAU HOUISSANT

Cru Bourgeois Supérieur 1932. Owner: Jean Ardouin. 20 hectares. 10,000 cases. CS 70%, Mer 30%

This small but well-reputed *cru* is well situated on high ground inland from Montrose. It used to be even smaller. As Bernard Ginestet wittily put it when Ardouin bought it in 1973: Jean Ardouin had vines but no label, Château Houissant had a label but few vines. His paternal grandfather had worked at Cos d'Estournel before the First World War, while his maternal grandfather had been *maître de chai* at Lafon-Rochet, and both had a few vines of their own. The name has long been known on the English market as a producer of decent, solid wines. At present, no casks are used for the maturation.

CHÂTEAU LAFFITTE-CARCASSET

Cru Bourgeois 1932. Owner: Vicomte Philippe de Padirac. 20 hectares. 8,000 cases. CS 65%, Mer 35%. Second label: Château la Vicomtesse

The name is not an attempt to ape the *premier cru classé* of Pauillac, but the name of an eighteenth-century owner. The property lies north of St Estèphe, just past the *cave coopérative* going north. In 1950 it was bought by Vicomte Pierre de Padirac, but he died in 1961. Now his son, Vicomte Philippe de Foulhiac de Padirac has taken over, and since his marriage in 1978 he has energetically set about improving standards while his wife has been refurnishing and decorating the château in keeping with its eighteenth-century origin. This carefully made wine seeks to emphasize finesse and fruit, although there is also plenty of body and good St Estèphe character. It is not at present a member of the Syndicat des Crus Bourgeois. Clearly this is a *cru* to watch.

CHÂTEAU LAFON-ROCHET

Quatrième Cru Classé. Owner: Guy Tesseron. 45 hectares. 12,000 cases. CS 80%, Mer 20%

Although classified as a fourth growth in 1855, this was a little-known wine until very recently. The situation of the property is not unfavourable: it lies just past Cos d'Estournel (going towards St Estèphe) on the opposite (or inland) side of the *route des châteaux*.

In 1959, the property was bought by Monsieur Guy Tesseron, a *négociant* in Cognac who is married to Nicole, daughter of the late Emmanuel Cruse, of Château d'Issan. The wine was distributed by the firm of Cruse until the early seventies. The château is in fact completely new, a replica of what might have been, in the traditional *chartreuse* style. The vineyard has also been extensively replanted, with much Merlot replaced by Cabernet Sauvignon, so that there is now 80 per cent of the latter, compared with only 60 per cent at Cos d'Estournel across the road, and 65 per cent at Montrose.

The reputation of this growth seems to have been unremarkable for some time, and *bourgeois* growths such as de Pez and Phélan-Ségur were more widely appreciated. When I first drank the wine, it had a pronounced *goût de terroir* and was rather undistinguished, certainly not of *cru classé* standing. Then much more elegant wines were made in the sixties. The 1964, when drunk in 1986, showed lovely, elegant, mature fruit. But once the new plantations of Cabernet started to dominate, the picture changed. Now looking back over my tasting notes, some made at Pontet-Canet, others at blind tastings, I find descriptions such as "austere", "mean", "lean" and "dry finish" cropping up with monotonous regularity. Sometimes the first tasting in cask shows an attractive fruitiness, but this is then coated in a tough, tannic exterior, which then remains dominant. This happened with the 1982 and 1985.

Alfred Tesseron has now taken over the administration of the property from his father and it will be interesting to see if he finds a solution to this problem. At present, I find the 1978 the most rewarding of recent vintages, but there is no doubt that currently Lafon is not up to the standard of unclassified châteaux such as de Pez and Haut-Marbuzet. It seems to me that the high proportion of Cabernet Sauvignon is the basic problem here. The most successful wines of St Estèphe all use more Merlot; this suits the heavier, colder soils of St Estèphe, with their important elements of chalk and clay, on which the Cabernet Sauvignon does not ripen so well as in Margaux and Pauillac, where the highest proportions of Cabernet Sauvignon are to be found.

CHÂTEAU LAVILLOTTE

Cru Bourgeois. Owner: Jacques Pédro. 12 hectares. 5,500 cases. CS 75%, Mer 25%

I had never heard of Lavillotte until it hit the headlines by coming out above several well-known *crus classés* in one of Gault-Millau's famous blind tastings. I then found that not many people in Bordeaux had heard of it either. A sampling of the 1978 vintage quickly showed that the tasters knew what they were doing. Now having met Jacques Pédro I can fully understand why this is one of the new stars of the Médoc.

Jacques Pédro comes of *"pied noir"* stock, as do a number of the most enterprising proprietors in Bordeaux today. After gaining a natural sciences degree and entering Bordeaux University, he decided to return to his roots. In 1962 he bought this vineyard with the *"lieu dit"* of La Villotte (if you consult your Féret 13th edition of 1982 you will find the *cru* indexed under V, but even then the name is mis-spelt!). The vineyard, lying just behind that of de Pez, was in a poor state and had to be almost entirely replanted. There is no château or *chai*, everything is done at Château Le Meynieu in neighbouring Vertheuil, where Jacques Pédro is also mayor.

Like Henri Duboscq at Haut-Marbuzet, Jacques Pédro holds no great brief for oenologists. He too believes in high-temperature fermentation of around 32°C to 33°C to obtain high extract, combined with two *remontages* per day, very long *"cuvaisons"*, sometimes until November, and second-year casks from Latour (whenever possible). On top of this he does not believe in filtering, either in cask, or when the wines are bottled, so even young vintages can need decanting.

The result of all this is that the wines are deep in colour, extremely scented and have a mouth-filling flavour, whether they are rich and powerful like the 1982, or lighter in body like the 1983. The most mature wine I have tasted, the 1978, was deep in colour, heavily perfumed and rich in extract, with an intense, almost minty note. The flavour had plenty of attack and what the Californians would call "up-front fruit", but combined with real length, complexity and a classic structure. The 1979 is scented, with lovely highlights, a beautiful ripe flavour, which has depth and real breed. The 1981 was delightfully attractive to drink at six years of age, without yet having developed the complexity of the mature vintages. The 1982 is a superb wine, a classic 1982, very concentrated with that distinctive taste of prunes – the complexity and character were already developing at five years of age. In contrast the 1983 is much lighter in body, but had a lovely heady, vivid bouquet and so much flavour, length and charm. It is hard on a wine to taste it only two days after bottling, even so the 1985, with its rich, soft, ripe fruitiness, charm and character, promised well. The 1986 in cask was again very scented, and in bottle quickly confirmed a length and opulence of flavour which promise an outstanding bottle. The 1987 is rich for the year, while 1988, with 90 per cent new oak has powerful spicy tannins and great ripeness. I hope these detailed notes will have conveyed something of the excitement and pleasure I have experienced from these wines, and that they will become known to a wider circle of wine lovers.

CHÂTEAU MACCARTHY

Cru Grand Bourgeois. Owner: Henri Duboscq. 12 hectares, 5,000 cases. CS 65%, Mer 35%

Exiled Irishmen have certainly left their mark on Bordeaux, but only the MacCarthys seem to have ventured as far north from Bordeaux as St Estèphe. Denis MacCarthy was the first of the family to leave Ireland and settle in Bordeaux. They were admitted to the nobility in 1756 under the title of de Beauje et Fonvidal. They established this *cru* in the eighteenth century, and their heirs continued to own it until 1854, when the Raymond family bought it.

In January 1988 Henri Duboscq succeeded in acquiring yet another piece in the jigsaw puzzle of Marbuzet vineyards. He had united the vineyard with that of Chambert-Marbuzet and retained the name for the second label.

CHÂTEAU DE MARBUZET

Cru Grand Bourgeois Exceptionnel. Owner: Domaines Prats. 7 hectares. 10,000 cases. Mer 56%, CS 44%

This is one of several properties incorporating the name of Marbuzet and situated around the village of that name, lying between Cos and Montrose. It was classified by the Syndicat des Crus Grands Bourgeois et Crus Bourgeois as a *grand bourgeois exceptionnel* in 1966 and 1978. The property is well situated close to the river and the elegant porticoed château in the style of Louis XVI was built only at the beginning of this century as something of a folly, although not quite in the usual sense of that word. Jules Merman, leading Bordeaux *courtier* and owner of nearby Château Le Crock, built it to house his mistress Régina Badet, a celebrated opera singer. The project was to ruin him, and he lost his prima donna as well, being compelled to sell to Fernand Ginestet in 1918. Since Cos d'Estournel has no château and this is the home of the Prats family, in practice it serves as the château for Cos. The wine is actually made at Cos and is then blended with certain wines of Cos which have been excluded from the *grand vin*. The result is that Marbuzet is neither a straight *cru bourgeois* (in spite of being classified as a *grand bourgeois exceptionnel*) nor a straight second wine for Cos, but is in the same position as Haut-Bages-Averous in relation to Lynch-Bages. The wines are pleasantly harmonious and age more quickly than Cos, and so fulfil a useful commercial purpose.

MARQUIS DE ST ESTÈPHE (*CAVE COOPÉRATIVE*)
Owner: Société de Vinification de St Estèphe. 375 hectares. 100,000 cases. CS 60%, Mer 35%, CF 5%

This important *cave* was founded in 1934, during the years of economic depression, by just forty-two *viticulteurs*. Today there are over 200 *adhérents* and this is one of the best-run and most up-to-date *coopératives* in Médoc. Only grapes from within the St Estèphe *appellation* are received here. There is storage capacity for 56,000 hectares and 1,500 hectolitres are aged in cask.

Apart from sales under the *marque* of Marquis de St Estèphe, a number of the more important properties are kept separate and commercialized under their respective names. They are as follows: de Mignot, Lille-Coutelin, Gireaud, Moutinot, L'Hôpital, Le Roc, Haut-Coteau, La Croix des Trois Soeurs, Palmier, Faget, Les Pradines, La Croix de Pez, La Balangé, Ségur de Cabanac, Graves de Blanquet, Tour de Pez, Haut-Verdon, Ladouys, Les Combes, Violet, Lartigue. Of course the quality varies according to the sector from which the grapes come, but all are well made. They need some bottle age and usually show well when four to six years old.

CHÂTEAU MEYNEY
Cru Grand Bourgeois Exceptionnel. Owner: Domaines Cordier. 50 hectares. 27,000 cases. CS 70%, Mer 24%, CF 4%, PV 2%. Second label: Prieur du Château Meyney

This large property lies between the road and the river south of St Estèphe, and the long, blank wall of the *chai* with its characteristic tower rising from the middle is just visible across undulating vineyards from the *route des châteaux*. Although St Emilion abounds with memorials to its ecclesiastical past, such remains are rare in Médoc, and Meyney certainly provides the best-preserved example. The present buildings are situated on the ridge of gravel which runs up from Marbuzet to St Estèphe, and date from 1662–6. The large courtyard, even today, has a distinctly monastic air about it. At that time, and until the Revolution, it was called the Prieuré des Couleys, and this appeared on the label of Meyney until recently. Now the connection is maintained through the name of the second wine. Since just after the First World War it has belonged to the Cordier family.

The growth has a good reputation for sound, robust and consistent wines. They can, however, be somewhat on the coarse side and lack, for instance, the breed of de Pez. Perhaps because of these characteristics, I have usually found Meyney to be most enjoyable drunk young, when the youthful fruit blends pleasingly into the powerful, rich texture. Because of its weight, one feels that it should age well, but in fact it tends to become dull, the wine dries up and the *goût de terroir* dominates. This has happened, for instance, to the 1961 and 1962 vintages. More recently the 1970 was still mellow and rich when fifteen years old, and the 1975, while strong-flavoured and powerful, is softer than one might expect. The 1978 and 1979 are both rich and attractive, with the 1979 having more fruit. The 1980 was a full-flavoured, attractive wine for drinking by 1987–8. The 1981 again is strong-flavoured but ready to drink when six years old. I find the 1982 rather surprisingly too tannic and tough, but while the 1983 has a strong, earthy after-taste, it was already well advanced when four years old. The 1984 is pleasantly fruity and well balanced. There was a strong contrast between 1985 and 1986 in cask, with the 1985 having only medium weight, good fruit, and looking like an early developer while 1986 had rich, opulent fruit and lots of strong, earthy tannins behind.

CHÂTEAU MONTROSE

Deuxième Cru Classé. Owner: Jean-Louis Charmolüe. 67 hectares. 23,000 cases. CS 65%, Mer 25%. CF 10%. Second wine: La Dame de Montrose

This is the most modern of all the leading Médoc growths, although in most other respects it is the most traditional. The vineyard was created out of woodlands on the Calon estate only at the beginning of the nineteenth century. On the Belleyme map, at the end of the eighteenth century, the future vineyard is identified as the "Bois des Escargots or Escargons". But once under vine, Montrose was not slow to make its mark. Already, by 1840, *Le Producteur* placed it among the second growths, although in 1846 Charles Cocks put it only with the third growths.

The large vineyard with its chalet-like château and *chai* lies on slopes bordering the Gironde near the town of St Estèphe, but well away from the main *route des châteaux*. This very well-run estate has belonged to the Charmolüe family since 1896; Madame Charmolüe, who was widowed in 1944, was for many years a well-loved and respected figure in the Médoc, both before and after she handed over the administration to the present owner, her son Jean-Louis, in 1960. The *chai* is well ordered but traditional, with beautifully kept, wooden fermentation vats. Now that Latour has gone modern, this is probably the most traditionally made wine among the classified growths – not that things have stood still. Recently a new *chai* of a distinctly modern aspect has been built, and the proportion of Merlot has been increased, although it still lags well behind that at Cos d'Estournel. The wine is usually hard and tannic to start with and takes a long time to come round. Its qualities are usually very obvious at an early stage, then a dull period sets in. Off-vintages are sometimes very good, if they are not unbalanced, but in the past good vintages did not always fulfil their early promise. Tasting the wine each year against other leading St Estèphes, I found Montrose was always impressive to begin with, but often failed to develop well, owing to an imbalance of tannin, but when I did a retrospective tasting in 1985, the results were impressive.

The oldest vintages I have seen were the 1893 and 1899; both showed charm and breed but were fading. Undoubtedly the best bottle of an old Montrose I have had was the 1920 which was robust, but with great charm and vinosity, closely rivalled by the glorious 1929 which, though fading by the mid-sixties, still had a lovely bouquet and great charm.

In the fifties, the 1953 was easily the best, while the 1952 and 1955 were for years rather tough and dull. But a bottle of the 1952 drunk in 1986 had developed impressively, and had plenty of fruit. If Cos had the best of things in the fifties, Montrose had the edge in the sixties. The 1960 itself was one of the best in the Médoc, with a fine colour and plenty of body and flavour; the 1961 promised to be a classic but was most disappointing at the Taams tasting (see Chapter 12, p. 656); the 1962 developed slowly but is very fine; the 1964 is a shade austere but is probably the best in St Estèphe; the 1966 is a very big wine, marvellously rich and complex, at its best by 1985; 1967 was still generous and full, with no bitterness – very good for the year. In the seventies, 1970 itself is outstanding, the mature tannins and richness were in perfect harmony by 1985 to give a really complete wine, just ahead of the fine 1966. In contrast the 1971, tasted at the same time, was just beginning to decline; it was very soft and losing its definition. The 1975 is a most impressive wine, full of richness and glycerine, but still very tannic and firm at the finish, a wine for the nineties. Unlike some wines of the vintage, the 1976 has been a very slow developer. Not until 1987 did it really fulfil its promise, and even then it was still improving with a distinctive roasted character. The 1978 and 1979 show the contrast between the vintages very well with the 1978 full of subtle complexity and nuances of flavour, the 1979 more opulent and powerful. The 1980 is rather short, lean and sinewy, and has been slow to evolve. The 1981 is exactly the sort of Montrose that is hard to fathom in its early years in bottle. In 1985 it showed delicacy and finesse, a year later it looked austere, tannic and closed. But there can be no doubting the greatness of the 1982. There is the smell of prunes, typical of the over-ripe character of the year, and the wine is dense-textured and many-layered, a wine for the twenty-first century. The 1983 is also a great success here; there is a lovely opulent flavour, and real depth, power and breed. The 1984 ended up with 85 per cent Cabernet Sauvignon because of the *coulure* in the Merlot, but looked well balanced and rather agreeable in cask. Also in cask, the

1985 and 1986 were a formidable pair, with the 1985 more powerful and tannic in emphasis than most 1985s, and the 1986 almost over-poweringly massive and tannic. On past form they will take a very long time to emerge from the chrysalis. The wines of 1988 and 1989 are of outstanding promise.

This is a classic claret drinker's wine, not perhaps for beginners, but with its strong character and full-blooded qualities, a wine to appeal to English and, even more perhaps, to Scottish tastes.

CHÂTEAU MORIN

Cru Grand Bourgeois. Owners: Marguerite and Maxime Sidaine. 10 hectares. 4,750 cases. CS 65%, Mer 35%

Situated at St Corbian in the northern sector of the *appellation*, the vine-yard of Morin lies in a single piece behind the château on the highest ridge in the commune. There are old vines, and indeed everything about the property is highly traditional, including the delightful label, which has a distinctly *belle époque* air about it. This *cru* has been in the same family since 1800. The wines are deep-flavoured with a spicy-minerally character and some finesse.

CHÂTEAU LES ORMES-DE-PEZ

Cru Grand Bourgeois. Owner: Cazes family. Administrator: Jean-Michel Cazes. 30 hectares. 12,500 cases. CS 55%, Mer 35%, CF 10%

This is a well-known and well-regarded wine in England. The property is just outside the village of Pez and belongs to André Cazes and his son Jean-Michel, the proprietors of Lynch-Bages. The family acquired the property in 1930 at the same time as Lynch-Bages, and their gift for wine-making, so evident at Lynch-Bages, has also stood Les Ormes-de-Pez in good stead. Over the years attractively fruity and fleshy wines have been made, even in difficult vintages. I still remember my surprise at the 1957, a delicious wine made at a time when most *bourgeois* St Estèphes were tough and angular, and in a vintage which was not one of the most attrac-tive, with very little Merlot owing to *coulure*.

The château, an austerely simple neo-classical house, and its out-buildings date from 1792, when the property was created at the time of the sale of de Pez as *bien national* (see de Pez). The vineyard is in two main blocks, in the centre and to the north of the village of Pez. For many years the wines were actually made and kept at Lynch-Bages, but the old *cuvier* and *chai* were modernized and extended in time for the 1981 vintage. Stainless steel vats with a temperature control system are used and, after the *assemblage*, the wine is put in cask for twelve to fifteen months prior to bottling. No new oak is used at present. Very good wines were made here in 1978, 1979, 1981, 1982 (especially opulent and promising), 1983, 1985 and 1986, 1988 and 1989, while 1984 is particularly successful for the year. While Ormes-de-Pez seldom disappoints, and is one of the most consistent and enjoyable *crus bourgeois* of St Estèphe, it lacks something of the breed that distinguishes its neighbour de Pez. An unusually supple and attractive wine for a St Estèphe, however, it has a lot of fruit and richness and can usually be drunk with pleasure when fairly young.

CHÂTEAU DE PEZ
Cru Bourgeois Supérieur 1932. Owner: Société Civile du Château de Pez (Robert Dousson). 23.2 hectares. 14,500 cases. CS 70%, CF 15%, Mer 5%

With Haut-Marbuzet, de Pez is today the leading growth in St Estèphe after the big three. The property has ancient origins which can be traced back to the fifteenth century; in 1585 Jean de Pontac, owner of Haut-Brion, acquired de Pez, but it was not for another hundred years that we find references to wine production at de Pez, when mention is made of 100 casks of "*grand vin*" being sent from de Pez to Bordeaux. This makes it one of the earliest substantial wine producers in northern Médoc, together with Calon-Ségur. The de Pontacs remained here until it passed by inheritance to Pierre d'Aulède, owner of Château Margaux, in 1744. By then de Pez is described as a "*maison noble*", and is surrounded by a *clos* of vines of about 23 hectares, out of a total property of some 50 hectares. A new *chai* was built in 1749, capable of holding 400 casks, and at the same time a new *cuvier* holding eight *cuves* and 8 tonneaux was constructed, so the property was clearly being developed at this time. On Pierre d'Aulède's death, de Pez passed to the related Fumels, of whom Comte Joseph de Fumel was Commandant of Guyenne. It was de Pez's fate to be sold off as a result of the Revolution to much less illustrious owners. It is interesting to speculate as to what might have happened had it still had noble owners in 1855.

The vineyard and château with its two massive, squat towers, lie by the village of Pez, just to the west of St Estèphe, on a fine, gravelly plateau which has an ideal exposure. From 1920 it belonged to the Bernard family and the present owner, Robert Dousson, actually took on the management from his aunt in 1955, since when the reputation of this old property has reached new heights.

The estate is very well run and the wine meticulously made. There is a high proportion of Cabernet Sauvignon. It is interesting that the Cabernet vines were largely replanted in 1950 and reached maturity in the seventies. When I first tasted the wine in the 1950s, it seemed an admirable *bourgeois* growth but no more; since the following decade, the wines have taken on an extra dimension, an extra richness, so that they are more and more comparable with the big three. The 1959, the first great vintage produced by Robert Dousson, was still spicy and full of exuberance, tannic and powerful, in 1986; the 1964 was one of the best in St Estèphe with a magnificent colour and great vinosity; while the 1966 has great richness and concentration of flavour. Even in poor years the Cabernet Sauvignon combined with careful selection has produced good results – the 1965 was far better than most wines of that year, and the 1968 was a most attractive wine. The 1970 is a classic for the year, and also witnessed a most interesting experiment. At the suggestion of the late Martin Bamford, the head of Gilbey-Loudenne who buy and distribute the wine, a cask of each of the *cépages* represented in the vineyard was kept separately at the time of the *assemblage*. These were Cabernet Sauvignon, Cabernet Franc, Merlot and Petit Verdot. Owing to the ideal conditions in 1970, even the Petit Verdot reached perfect maturity. To taste these four wines and then the finished product is most instructive, for not only does one see the characteristics of each *cépage*, but the greatest lesson of all is how much better the *assemblage* is than any of its constituent parts. A most stylish 1971 was made, a tremendous 1975 and a fine 1976. More recently, 1978 has real depth of flavour and length while lacking the extra dimension of the top *crus*. The 1979 is a very attractive wine with luscious rich fruit, and more successful for once than the 1978. There is an excellent 1980 with a lovely fullness of flavour, better for instance than the Calon-Ségur. The 1981 is a great favourite of mine, having an impressive intensity of flavour and real breed, without being really full-bodied. The 1982 fully lives up to expectations, ripe and luscious with a marvellous flavour and real concentration. The 1983 is also a great success here, opulent with a ripe, powerful flavour. After a respectable 1984, 1985 in cask was rich and dense-textured, the 1986 even more impressive, a rich sheen covering the tannins, and great fruit. On current form, de Pez can certainly take its place alongside the leading classified growths of the *appellation*.

CHÂTEAU PHÉLAN-SÉGUR

Cru Grand Bourgeois Exceptionnel. Owner: Société Château Phélan-Ségur SA (President, Xavier Gardinier). 70 hectares. 25,000 cases. CS 60%, Mer 30%, CF 10%. Second label: Frank Phélan. 8,330 cases

After the big three (Cos d'Estournel, Montrose and Calon), Phélan is certainly one of the most important properties in St Estèphe today, both in terms of production and potential quality.

The property itself is situated between the road and the river, occupying the northerly part of the gravelly outcrop which it shares with Meyney and Montrose, overlooking the river, and is placed between Meyney and the town of St. Estèphe. There is a château with a comfortable country-house appearance, commanding a good view of the river from its promontory. From 1924 to 1986 it belonged to the Delon family, Roger Delon and his son Guy being the uncle and cousin respectively of Michel Delon at Léoville-Las Cases. In 1986 they sold to Xavier Gardinier, formerly of Pommery, through his Groupe d'Enterprises et de Participations Gardinier (GEPAG), which created the Société Château Phélan-Ségur SA actually to acquire the domain. Then began a *cause célèbre*. There had been complaints from a number of buyers about the quality of the 1983 vintage. I tasted it twice, in October 1984, at a tasting of 1983 *crus bourgeois* when I marked it as out of condition and untastable, and in April 1985 at the château, when it was under finings but nevertheless better, if not exactly good. Then in 1987 Xavier Gardinier announced that he was taking back all the 1983 which had been sold, and would not sell the 1984 or the 1985, stating that the nose and flavour of all the wines were affected by a chemical product which had been used in the vineyard under the Delon régime. A legal action was then begun against the American chemical company which had manufactured the product. The implications of this are obviously far-reaching, especially at a time when there is increasing concern about the ecological results of the use of an increasing variety of chemical products, both in vineyards and in farming in general. The case was settled, but the terms kept secret.

The domain was actually founded at the beginning of the nineteenth century by Monsieur Phélan, partly from land which had belonged to the Marquis de Ségur. Outstanding bottles of 1964 and 1955 are enough to make it plain that Phélan has in the past made really fine wines, as one would expect from the position of the vineyard. In recent vintages the quality has been very variable. The 1978 is quite good, but 1981 most disappointing, and the powerful 1982 lacks breed or finesse. A new *cuvier* had been installed in time for the 1977 vintage, but when I was there in 1985 it was clear that there was still much to do in the *chai*, with too much old wood clearly evident.

The challenge for the new régime is clearly an exciting one, with competition in St Estèphe really keen. Newly established *crus* such as Haut-Marbuzet, and now Lavillotte, are making wines which challenge those of old-established *crus* and no one can rest on his laurels. In the autumn of 1989, I was able to see what had been achieved. The results were a powerful, impressive 1986, an above average 1987, and an exceptional 1988 with opulence, structure and length, while the new second wine was excellent, even in 1987.

CHÂTEAU POMYS

Cru Bourgeois Supérieur 1932. Owner: SARL Arnaud. 6 hectares. 3,000 cases. CS 50%, Mer 30% CF 20%

A wine which is often seen in England. It is a relatively small estate for St Estèphe, the property of the Arnaud family. The wine is attractive, well balanced and reliable. The lovely château is, unfortunately, now in different hands (see Château St Estèphe).

CHÂTEAU ST ESTÈPHE

Cru Bourgeois 1932. Owner: SARL Arnaud. 10 hectares. 4,350 cases. CS 55%, Mer 30%, CF 8%, Mal and PV 7%

Under the same ownership and management as Pomys, this is where the Arnaud family actually live, the lovely château at Pomys now being under different ownership. The property dates only from 1870, and the present house was acquired in 1950. The vineyards adjoin Le Crock and

Houissant, and the wines are sound and typical, but less full-bodied than Pomys.

CHÂTEAU LA TOUR-DES-TERMES
Cru Bourgeois 1932. Owner: Jean Anney. 26.5 hectares. 13,500 cases. CS 55%, Mer 35%, PV 10%

The *cru* is the fruit of three generations' work. The property is in the village of St Corbian, opposite Beau-Site, in the north of the *appellation*. About a third of the vineyard has been recently planted. The examples of the *cru* I have seen are well made, robust with plenty of character, but also supple and quite fine. They are all matured in cask. This is a good *cru* which can only improve as the vineyard matures.

CHÂTEAU TRONQUOY-LALANDE
Cru Grand Bourgeois. Owner: Arlette Castéja. 16.5 hectares. 7,000 cases. Mer 50%, CS and CF 50%

This is an old property, formerly of more importance than it is today. Lalande is the name of the place, Tronquoy of the family who owned it early in the nineteenth century. It opened as a fourth growth in classifications of 1824 and 1827, but has failed to make the grade since. Before I knew of the *cru* or its wines, I was immediately attracted by the château with its two distinctive towers at each end of a *chartreuse*-type building.

The wine has a very marked *goût de terroir*, which may not be to every taste, but it is undeniably a wine of some character and interest. With maturity the wine develops a pleasing harmony. The 1964 was delicious when sixteen years old. More recently it has been noticeable that the wines often seem rather tough and rustic at first, but usually come through this awkward stage. I have found the most rewarding recent vintage to be the 1983, at a time when the 1982 was still sulking in a corner! Madame Arlette Castéja now brings a woman's touch to the running of the property, and receives technical assistance from *négociants* Dourthe, who distribute the wine. At present the maturation of the wines is partly in *cuve* and partly in cask.

6

Moulis and Listrac: Haut-Médoc and Bas-Médoc

MOULIS

In the introduction to the wines of the Haut-Médoc (see Chapter 4), I said that there were really two lines of vineyards, one lying close to the river, the other on a series of ridges and plateaux further inland. All the finest wines are produced from the vineyards near the river, but there are two groups of vineyards which produce wines of a quality superior to those generally made in the second line, and these have been given special recognition by being allowed their own *appellations*. They are Moulis and its neighbour, Listrac.

The vineyards of Moulis lie on a high plateau north-west of Margaux and almost directly west of Arcins. The wines have much more body and richness than those of Margaux, and also a tendency to firmness at first, but they do have more fruit and finesse than those of St Laurent to the north. When the wines are mature, they have a fineness about them which justifies their classification, and a fruitiness which is reminiscent of some Margaux. They also have the ability to age very well, when they develop characteristics which might be compared to some Pauillacs. The best growths cluster about the village of Grand Poujeaux to the east of Moulis itself. A number of them hyphenate their names with that of Grand Poujeaux. Although no wines from Moulis were included in the 1855 classification, Chasse-Spleen is today recognized as of classified-growth standing, and some of the others are certainly well ahead of the old classified growths in St Laurent. Although the area under vine has increased by over 5 per cent in the last decade to 502 hectares in 1987, it is still the smallest *appellation* in the Médoc.

CHÂTEAU ANTHONIC

Cru Bourgeois Supérieur. Owner: Pierre Cordonnier. 18 hectares. 5,000 cases.
Principally CS and Mer

This is a relatively old *cru* for Moulis, but has changed name several times after first appearing in Cocks & Féret in 1850 under the name of Puy de Minjon, until it settled on the present name in 1922. The château and vineyards lie just north of the village of Moulis, and are some of the oldest in the commune. Recently the vineyard has been going through the throes of reconstruction.

The four examples I have tasted from this *cru* have been deep-coloured, tannic and rather rough and rustic, but then I have not seen a mature example.

CHÂTEAU BEL-AIR-LAGRAVE

Cru Bourgeois 1932. Owner: Madame Jeanne Bacquey. 15 hectares. 5,500 cases.
CS 60%, Mer 35%, PV 5%

The vineyards are just to the north of the village of Poujeaux, in what is certainly the best sector of the *appellation*. It has belonged to the same family for 150 years. The policy here is to concentrate on low yields, through hard pruning, in order to achieve the best quality.

The wines are carefully made, and the aim is to emphasize fruit and charm. Certainly the wines are mostly more supple and more refined then some of their neighbours, with individuality and a definite finesse without a hint of anything rustic. I have recently tasted good wines from the 1979 and 1981 vintages. One of several less well-known *crus* which are worth looking for.

CHÂTEAU BISTON-BRILLETTE

Cru Bourgeois 1932. Owner: Michel Barbarin. 18 hectares. 7,000 cases. Mer
50%, CS and CF 50%

The old-fashioned and rather rustic label hardly does justice to the impressive wines now being made here. The property is on the southern edge of the village of Petit Poujeaux. The wines are typically Moulis with their dense texture, and there is a nice hint of complexity in the spicy, concentrated fruit which lifts it above the general run of wines from the *appellation*. The attractive emphasis on fruit and balance makes this a wine which is enjoyable young, without sacrificing its keeping qualities.

CHÂTEAU BRANAS-GRAND-POUJEAUX

Owner: Jacques de Pourquéry. 6 hectares. 4,000 cases. CS 60%, Mer 35%, PV 5%

This small property lies just to the east of the village of Grand Poujeaux, so is very well placed on the best gravelly outcrops of the *appellation*. In the hands of an enthusiastic owner, dedicated to making fine wines, the results are worth discovering. In a blind tasting of 1981 Moulis wines held in 1984, I placed Branas on the same level as some *crus bourgeois exceptionnels*. The wine had both charm at this early stage and a fine middle flavour and richness that had real style and breed. All the wine is aged in casks, of which one-third are new each year. Clearly this is a wine worth searching for.

CHÂTEAU BRILLETTE

Cru Grand Bourgeois. Owner: Société Civile du Château Brillette. Administrator: Madame Berthault. 30 hectares. 11,000 cases. CS 55%, Mer 40%, PV 5%

This property lies east of the village of Petit Poujeaux and south of the road leading from that village to Grand Poujeaux. In 1976 the property was bought by Raymond Berthault, owner of Viniprix and Euromarché, really as a hobby and relaxation. There was much to do to bring the property up to standard, and Bertrand Bouteiller (also manager of Pichon-Baron until 1987) was brought in to act as *régisseur* while Professor Peynaud advised on the improvements. One-third new wood is now used in the cask maturation.

Unfortunately, Raymond Berthault did not enjoy the fruit of his labours for long, dying in 1981, but his widow and son-in-law are continuing along the lines already laid down. This was always a good, solid, if rather rustic, Moulis; now it is better made but still has a strong personality, characteristic of Moulis. In the recent vintages I have noted a 1980 that was very good and solid for the year, a good 1981 and a really concentrated and fine 1982, while the 1983 has a strong, assertive style. Not quite in the very first line Moulis *crus*, but certainly well up among the second-line ones.

CHÂTEAU CHASSE-SPLEEN

Cru Grand Bourgeois Exceptionnel. Owner: Société Civile du Chasse-Spleen. Administrator: Madame Bernadette Villars. 75 hectares. 23,000 cases. CS 60%, Mer 35%, PV 3%, CF 2%. Second label: L'Ermitage de Chasse-Spleen. 5,000 cases

This has for long been regarded as the leading growth of Moulis, and rightly so. In 1932, when an attempt was made to classify the *crus bourgeois*, this was one of six growths in the whole Médoc which was accorded the status of *crus exceptionnel*. Today it is certainly of *cru classé* standard. The vineyard lies between Arcins and Grand Poujeaux.

The name of the property can be roughly translated as "dispels melancholy", and there is an attractive story as to how it was acquired. When Lord Byron visited the property in 1821, he fell in love with the wines and is supposed to have said, "Quel remede pour chasser le spleen!" But another version has it that the name came from Baudelaire's poem "Spleen", which begins with the words: "J'ai plus de souvenirs que si j'avais mille ans." Between 1909 and 1914, it belonged to the Segnitz family from Bremen, one of the best-known wine merchants in northern Germany, and still going strong today. They did much to improve quality and build up the reputation of the wine throughout northern Europe. It was confiscated as enemy property after the outbreak of the First World War, and was eventually bought at auction by the Lahary family in 1922. It is they who have been responsible for the excellent standing and reputation of this *cru*. In 1976 they sold to a consortium controlled by the Merlaut family. Jacques Merlaut, who lives at the château, has wide interests which include the control of the Ginestet *négociant* company and an important shareholding in Mestrezat, as well as ownership of Haut-Bages-Libéral and La Gurgue. The management of Chasse-Spleen is now in the hands of his very talented daughter, Madame Bernadette Villars.

Since the change of ownership much work has been done, including new stainless steel fermentation tanks, an extension to the *chai*, a modern laboratory, and a computer program to determine the optimum order for picking grapes. Madame Villars has also done much work in the different types of oak used in the making of casks. The proportion of new casks used is high, usually 50 per cent, although for 1985 it was 60 per cent. An example of her meticulous approach is that she insists that, in between each racking, the casks are steamed for four minutes, because this enables her to use less sulphur. On a recent visit I mentioned that on a previous visit during the Lahary regime I had pleasant memories of seeing large numbers of eggs being broken here to prepare the fining (*collage*) in the traditional manner. I was assured the same methods are still used. The wine has the marked character of all Moulis wines; but while having a good deal of richness, it lacks the toughness which characterizes most of them, and has markedly more finesse and breed. It is this which sets Chasse-Spleen apart from its neighbours and justifies its special position in the district.

The wine often has an initial toughness amounting almost to coarseness, that can lead to it being misjudged at an early stage, especially in blind tastings. But this brusqueness is soon dispelled and the true character of the wine then emerges. I have seen few old vintages, but I remember particularly the 1938, a wine of great charm still when nearly thirty years old. More recently, the wines have been consistently fine. I must own to being a little disappointed with the 1961 in its early stages – I have not seen it recently. 1962, 1964, 1966, 1967 and 1970 have all produced fine wines worthy of the year, with the 1966 and 1970 the best. Under the new management, the 1976 was ripe, mellow, with good depth of flavour, and at its best by 1987. The 1978, with its rich, dense bouquet, was still surprisingly tannic and powerful but unready when eight years old. In contrast, the 1979 had lovely ripe, opulent fruit, with concentration and charm. The 1980 was a delightful success, at its charming best when five years old. The 1981 is outstanding: a wine of real depth, breed, and great charm. The 1982 is much more tannic and less evolved, but with a fine flavour and great style. The 1983 shows more of the strong-flavoured Moulis style, with a touch of "*terroir*" character and even some coarseness – still young and vibrant, but promising well at four years. The 1984 lacks something of the charm of the 1980, but could yet prove a pleasant surprise. The 1985 is a great success. The lovely ripe fruit, underpinned with power and depth, promises a very stylish, attractive bottle. The 1986 had a more tannic, austere character in cask, but the richness and power promise something outstanding.

A second wine, L'Ermitage de Chasse-Spleen, has now been introduced, and is made in a much softer, fruitier style for early drinking. It is clear that steady progress has been made here in the last decade, consolidating the already excellent standing of this *cru* as an undisputed claimant to *cru classé* status.

CHÂTEAU LA CLOSERIE-GRAND-POUJEAUX

Cru Bourgeois. Owners: GFA du Château La Closerie-Grand-Poujeaux.
Administrator: Jeanne Bacquey. 4 hectares. 3,500 cases. CS 65%, Mer 30%, PV 5%

This vineyard was the creation of Monsieur Segonnes, a former *régisseur* of Chasse-Spleen. Since 1941 it has been in the possession of the Donat family, and for some years now the redoubtable Mademoiselle Marguerite Donat continued her father's work. In 1966 it was classified as a *grand bourgeois exceptionnel* but demoted to simple *bourgeois* in 1978. The property is run on very traditional lines and Mademoiselle Donat was a businesswoman to be reckoned with. Madame Bacquey took over the management in 1984.

The wine is very solid, often very fruity and powerful, and can last very well. I remember especially a remarkable bottle of 1947. The quality and style can be compared with Dutruch.

CHÂTEAU DUPLESSIS (HAUCHECORNE)

Cru Grand Bourgeois. Owner: Société Civile des Grands Crus Réunis.
Administrator: Lucien Lurton. 17.5 hectares. 8,000 cases. CS 65%, Mer 20%, Mal 10%, PV 5%

This property was formerly part of the Richelieu property just to the south (see Duplessis-Fabre). In 1971 it was bought jointly by Mestrezat and Lucien Lurton (see Brane-Cantenac). It was only in 1983 that Lucien Lurton took over the administration of the property, until then in the hands of Mestrezat. Another complication has been the name. First, the rather cumbersome Hauchecorne (the name of a former owner) was dropped for simplicity's sake, from the traditional black and gold label. Then there were protests from the owners of Duplessis-Fabre that the unqualified Duplessis was causing confusion, and talk of changing the name once more. So far nothing has happened. The reputation was for supple, early-drinking wines; but Lucien Lurton's second fine vintage, the 1985, I found impressive and promising in cask, very scented, with marked Moulis character, very fruity and very ripe.

CHÂTEAU DUPLESSIS-FABRE

Cru Bourgeois. Owner: Société Civile du Château Fourcas-Dupré. Administration:
Patrice Pages. 14 hectares. 5,500 cases. Mer 45%, CS 42%, CF 8%, PV 4%, Mal
1%

The property lies just to the west of Moulis and Petit Poujeaux, and across the road from the other Duplessis *cru*. Both take their name from Louis-François-Armand de Vignerod-Duplessis, who is better known as Duc de Richelieu, a great-great-nephew of the even more celebrated Cardinal Richelieu. This extremely colourful figure was born in 1696 but lived until the eve of the Revolution, reaching the age of ninety-two in apparently undiminished vigour. He was a diplomat; as a soldier he distinguished himself at Fontenoy in 1745, became a marshal of France and Governor of Guyenne in 1755; and as a man was famed for his gallantry towards, and success with, women – he married three times, on the last occasion when he was eighty-four. Today the property belongs to the branch of the Pagès family who own Fourcas-Dupré in neighbouring Listrac.

Since the untimely death of Guy Pagès in 1985, Duplessis-Fabre has been run by his son, Patrice. The wines are well made, powerful and assertive with just enough suppleness to make them pleasurable.

CHÂTEAU DUTRUCH-GRAND-POUJEAUX

Cru Grand Bourgeois Exceptionnel. Owner: François Cordonnier. 2,5 hectares.
10,000 cases. CS and CF 60%, Mer 35%, PV 5%

In 1967 the present owner, François Cordonnier, took over from Monsieur Lambert, but as so often, it was a change of name by inheritance. This led to the relinquishing of the house that served as château for a rather similar one outside the village of Grand Poujeaux, while the *cuvier* and *chai* were retained.

Under Monsieur Lambert, the property was run with great dedication and care, and I noted that the wines of this period had more body and richness than Chasse-Spleen or Gressier, but less finesse and breed. The quality was very consistent. In recent years I have had the impression that the wines are a shade rustic and have not kept pace with the improvements made at neighburing properties. Nevertheless, I have notes of good, attractive, solid wines in 1979 and 1981, that compared well with a number of their neighbours, as well as an attractive 1980.

CHÂTEAU GRESSIER-GRAND-POUJEAUX

Cru Bourgeois Supérieur 1932. Owner: Héritiers de Saint-Affrique. Administrator: Bertrand de Marcellus. 18 hectares. 9,000 cases. CS 50%, Mer 40%, CF 10%

This château has the distinction of having been in the hands of the same proprietors, the Saint-Affrique family, since 1724, although since the death of old Monsieur Saint-Affrique, the venerable name has sadly changed. But there was much that needed doing, too much old wood in the *chai*, and a tendency to leave wines in cask too long before château bottling, just in case there should be any further sales in cask! This often meant that Gressier bottled in England could be better than the château-bottled version – 1970 was an example of this. The château and *chai* lie almost in the village of Poujeaux, and the vineyard lies between the village and Chasse-Spleen. This was a homely place, with a pleasantly intimate and traditional appearance about the *cuvier* and *chai*, and Monsieur de Saint-Affrique very much in evidence. Now Bertrand de Marcellus has spruced things up, and long-overdue improvements and modernizations have been undertaken. Some new oak is now used in the cask ageing, as befits the quality of the wine. The château label is very distinctive, with the Saint-Affrique arms with its three negro heads as the main feature.

The wine is sometimes a shade stubborn at first, but with a tendency to be more fruity than some of its neighbours, with a little more finesse and elegance. It is very consistent: 1962, 1964 (with a small crop owing to hail, but of fine quality), 1966 (particularly successful), 1967 and 1970 were all very good examples of their years. More recently, after a good 1980 that combined character with lots of plummy fruit, the 1981 had a lovely smooth-textured flavour and real breed, only just approaching drinkability after six years, while the 1982 was more massive, yet the concentrated, ripe tannins were very harmonious, a fine *vin de garde*. The 1985 was more obviously tannic, with an assertive Moulis character, but plenty of fruit – a wine with a fine future. The improvements in what was always a good wine are clear from the vintages of the eighties and it is good to see the considerable potential of this fine vineyard being more fully realized.

CHÂTEAU LESTAGE-DARQUIER

Cru Bourgeois Supérieur 1932. Owner: François Bernard. 4 hectares. 1,800 cases.
CS 50%, Mer 40%, CF 10%

This very small property lies on the north-eastern side of the village of
Grand Poujeaux, well placed on the best gravelly ridges of the *appellation*.
It has belonged to the Bernard family for several generations. I have
found the wines very deep-coloured with a bouquet rich with dense fruit,
and a very distinctive, assertive flavour, tannic, and with the promise of
something quite fine when mature.

CHÂTEAU MAUCAILLOU

Cru Bourgeois. Owner: Dourthe family. 55 hectares. 19,000 cases. CS 45%, Mer
35%, CF 15%, PV 5%

This grandiose Victorian château lies a little outside the village of
Poujeaux on the Arcins side, and has belonged to the Dourthe family
since 1929. However, at that stage, this was a much smaller vineyard of
only 20 hectares, of much less importance in Moulis than today. It was
only after Roger Dourthe took over in 1961 that the vineyard was
extended to its present size. In those days the château was the centre for
the Dourthe firm as well, but when the company was sold to Dutch
interests in 1983, the Dourthes retained Maucaillou. The present owner,
Philippe Dourthe, has something of his uncle's prodigious energy and
athleticism – they sailed both ways across the Atlantic in a ketch in 1972,
when Roger Dourthe was a sprightly seventy-two. He also has the build
of one of those famous rugby players from "Sud-ouest"! Although the
original Dourthe business has gone to Parempuyre as part of CVGB,
Philippe Dourthe now runs his own Dourthe Père et Fils business from
here, as well as a large bottling company specializing in château bottling
for châteaux (which are legion) which do not have their own facilities.
The name of the château comes from the land on which the vineyard is
situated.

Although three-quarters of the wine here is matured in new oak casks,
an unusually high proportion for a *cru bourgeois*, the wines are consistently precocious, and for this reason often do well in blind tastings of
young vintages, where they show as softer and more mellow than other
Moulis wines. Thus, at a tasting of 1979s held in 1984 I placed
Maucaillou first. In 1986 the 1983 vintage did exceptionally well, as did

the 1985 in 1988. The 1982 is very attractive and has good concentration as well. This is certainly a very good *cru*, but in a different mould from Chasse-Spleen and Poujeaux, without their long ageing potential. It is certainly very good value for earlyish drinking.

The wine has the distinctive Moulis *goût de terroir* and is quite rich. It is never easy to judge the reputation of a growth which is exclusively marketed by a *négociant*, because when one tastes a range of Moulis wines, Maucaillou would tend to be missing as it is not on the general market. But I should say that the quality and style is somewhere near Dutruch and La Closerie.

CHÂTEAU MAUVESIN

Cru Bourgeois Supérieur. Owners: Vicomte and Vicomtesse de Baritault du Carpia. 53 hectares. 21,000 cases. CS 50%, Mer 50%. (In addition, 7 hectares have the Haut-Médoc *appellation contrôlée* and produce 3,780 cases.)

This is the largest property in Moulis, and lies in the south of the *appellation*, south of the hamlet of Bouqueyran. A *maison noble* is recorded here in the fifteenth century belonging to Jean de Foix, whose family also at one time owned d'Issan. The present large Victorian château dates from 1853, and was built by the Le Blanc family who had owned the property since 1647. The founder of the family fortunes, Pierre Le Blanc, was *conseiller du roi* at the Parlement de Bordeaux when he bought it from the de Foix family. From what little I have seen of Mauvesin, the wines seem to be charmingly fruity and quite elegant, but light and soft, designed for early drinking. In strict compliance with the regulations, a small amount of the wine can be found with the Haut-Médoc *appellation*.

CHÂTEAU MOULIN-À-VENT

Cru Bourgeois Supérieur. Owner: Dominique Hessel. 24 hectares. 10,000 cases. CS 65%, Mer 30%, PV 5%. Second label: Moulin-de-St-Vincent. 4,500 cases

The name of Moulis itself is a corruption of Moulin and is witness to the fact that in the Middle Ages a good deal of corn was grown in this part of the Médoc, and the ruins of old windmills are still to be found in many parts of the region. This is one of only two Moulis properties to be found on the western side of the Bordeaux–Lesparre road, just past the hamlet of Bouqueyran, and about one-third of the vineyard is actually in Listrac.

Since Dominique Hessel took over the estate in 1977, great

improvements have been made. He is gradually increasing the percentage of Merlot at the expense of the Cabernet Sauvignon. This will bring it into line with the leading *crus* of Moulis. He is also now ageing all the wines in cask instead of vats. The wines have a fine flavour, and are rich and vigorous, developing a complex bouquet with bottle age. They seem to be improving with every vintage, and the 1985 and 1986 were certainly the most impressive wines so far. Moulin-de-St-Vincent, the second label, used to be an exclusivity of Ginestet under the previous owner. Now a deliciously fruity, early-maturing wine is being made. This is certainly the rising star of the *appellation*, and on recent form is due to take its place among the leading *crus* of Moulis.

CHÂTEAU MOULIS

Cru Bourgeois Supérieur. Owner: Jacques Darricarrère. 12 hectares. 4,500 cases. CS 60%, Mer 40%

In the last century this was a vast estate of about a thousand hectares; now there are only twelve left. The vineyard surrounds the château, just outside the hamlet of Bouqueyran, in the west of the *appellation*. The present owner used to own nearby Moulin-à-Vent. There is a modern, stainless steel installation for the vinification, and all the wine is matured in cask and château-bottled.

CHÂTEAU POMEYS

Cru Bourgeois Supérieur 1932. Owner: Xavier Barennes. 8 hectares. 2,500 cases. CS 67%, Mer 33%

Not to be confused with the *cru* in St Estèphe spelt without an "e", this is the most southerly and westerly *cru* in the *appellation*. It has now belonged to the same family for seven generations, and is traditionally run. The wines are of good repute.

CHÂTEAU POUJEAUX-THEIL

Cru Grand Bourgeois Exceptionnel. Owners: François and Philippe Theil. 50 hectares, 25,000 cases. CS 45%, Mer 35%, PV 11%, CF 9%. Second label: Château la Salle-de-Poujeaux

The actual château is in the village of Poujeaux, and has ancient origins. Known then as La Salle de Poujeaux, it was mentioned in 1544 as a dependency of Château Latour. In the eighteenth century it belonged to

Madame de Montmorin Saint-Herem, sister of the Marquis de Brassier, proprietor of Beychevelle. She sold in 1806 to Monsieur André Castaing, whose family were proprietors until 1920, when it passed into the hands of the present proprietors, who came from the Corrèze, as did the Bories and the Moueixs. When the Theils bought Poujeaux, the property had been divided into three, and one of their first tasks was to reunify it, so that today it covers the same area as it did before 1880. Today two brothers, François and Philippe, grandsons of the purchaser in 1920, run the property with great zeal and ability.

The vineyard is in a single piece on the best *coupes graveleuses* of Moulis, which it shares with Chasse-Spleen. These reach a height of 25 metres, and the drainage is excellent. The *encépagement* is interesting because all four traditional varieties are still used, and the proportion of Petit Verdot is unusually high. The *cuvier* has been temperature-controlled since 1977, but the vinification itself is very traditional, with long fermentations and macerations of six weeks' duration on average. Between 30 and 40 per cent new casks are used, and the Theils do not believe in filtering their wines.

The wines themselves are deep-coloured with an arresting bouquet. Sometimes there are overtones of tobacco, and the flavour is stylish and fine although rich, tannic and powerful. The wines are also long-lived; I have drunk well-preserved and interesting bottles of the 1926 and 1928 vintages. Of the vintages tasted recently, I have noted a particularly fine 1966 with a wonderfully spicy bouquet and a flavour that was complex, rich and quite delicious; an impressive 1976 that had richness and ripeness combined with tannin to make a four-square, strong-flavoured wine of surprising attraction; and a 1979 that was bursting with soft, ripe fruit yet well structured. In the great vintages of the eighties, the 1981 is of only medium weight but had real elegance and finesse and a lovely soft, ripe flavour when five years old. The 1982 has a very opulent bouquet, full of concentrated fruit essences, and really massive. The flavour is extremely harmonious, very rich and complex with massive fruit well underpinned with ripe tannins – a great *vin de garde*.

In this vintage they kept and bottled some examples of the four grape varieties separately, and this made a fascinating comparison (see also under de Pez). I noted that the Merlot was deep and dense in colour, the nose luscious and opulent, but lacking highlights, the flavour very rich and supple with a lot of fruit but lacking in persistence of flavour. The Cabernet Franc was a shade lighter in colour but very vivid and youthful. The nose showed more definition, with nice fruit and structure. The flavour was a little lean but had more length and structure. The Petit Verdot was similar in colour to the Cabernet Franc, but had quite a different character on the nose, raw-boned and full of extract and tannin. The flavour was very concentrated, a clean fresh flavour that seemed to clean the mouth, and a long, hard, tannic finish – hard but not rough or coarse. The Cabernet Sauvignon again had a very similar colour to the Franc, the nose was very Cabernet *cassis*, concentrated and well defined. There was a splendidly powerful flavour: very rich, with length and ripe tannins to match the concentrated fruit – an iron hand in a velvet glove. One could see clearly how important the Merlot fruit and opulence was: the Cabernet Sauvignon gave structure, power and beauty of flavour, which was filled out by the Merlot. The finesse seemed to come from the two Cabernets, and clearly the Petit Verdot adds to the ageing potential. The precise composition of the final *assemblage* was Cabernet Sauvignon 39.5 per cent, Merlot 44.7 per cent, Cabernet Franc 6.3 per cent and Petit Verdot 9.5 per cent.

The 1983 is much more forward, in the pattern of the 1981, with lovely spicy fruit – elegance combined with richness. Lastly, in cask the 1985 was splendidly unctuous and attractive, powerful and fine, with real flair. The 1986 had more tannin, but was accompanied by wonderfully opulent, berry-ish fruit, a great *vin de garde* to follow the 1982. The verdict on Poujeaux must be that it has now taken its place beside Chasse-Spleen as not only one of the leading growths of Moulis, but as being of clear *cru classé* status. There is a contrast in styles between the two wines, with Poujeaux seeming more supple, with just a shade more flesh, but both have great individuality and style. Poujeaux is much less well known than Chasse-Spleen in Bordeaux because the Theils sell direct, both in France and on export markets.

CHÂTEAU RUAT-PETIT-POUJEAUX
Cru Bourgeois 1932. Owner: Pierre Goffre-Viaud. 15 hectares. 5,000 cases. CS and CF 65%, Mer 35%. Second label: Château Ruat

Petit Poujeaux is a small hamlet just outside the village of Moulis and both lie between Grand Poujeaux, the most important centre of the *appellation*, Grand Poujeaux, and the Bordeaux–Lesparre road to the west. Ruat was the name of a property dispersed during the Revolution, but patiently pieced together again following the purchase in 1871 of part of the domain by the present proprietor's great-grandfather. The wines have a tendency to evolve more quickly than many wines of the *appellation*, and have a robust charm and fruit, with a typical Moulis richness and solidity. Sometimes they can be a shade rustic.

LISTRAC

If one drives from Bordeaux to the Pointe de Graves, and speed, rather than vinous scenery, is the order of the day, then one takes the D1 to Lesparre. Very few vines are to be seen from this road, and most of them are around the village of Listrac. This lies to the north and slightly to the west of Moulis.

As with Moulis, there were no classified growths in 1855, but today at least one growth would be in the running. The wines have a certain verve and style which gives them personality and interest. There is also a tendency to be tough and astringent, particularly at first. The wines tend to have less body and less fruit than those of Moulis, and can be compared to the lesser St Estèphes in some respects. Nevertheless, while not reaching the heights, they are very Médoc in style, and as such have many friends. Although the area under vine increased by 45 per cent between 1972 and 1986, this is still the smallest *appellation* in Médoc, after neighbouring Moulis (see Appendix).

CHÂTEAU LA BÉCADE AND LA FLEUR-BÉCADE
Cru Bourgeois. Owner: Jean-Pierre Théron. 23 hectares. 13,000 cases. CS 75%, Mer 25%

This *cru* lies to the north-west of Listrac. The carefully made wines are kept in vat and see no wood during their maturation prior to bottling. It is important to emphasize that there is absolutely no difference between the wines sold under the two different labels. The La Fleur-Bécade bears the *appellation* Haut-Médoc, not Listrac, and is the exclusivity of the CVBG group (since 1966). Apparently the Haut-Médoc *appellation* is considered to be better known on export markets, especially the United States, than that of Listrac. After the fourth racking Jean-Pierre Théron tastes all his vats, and everything deemed worthy of being château-bottled is then put together, so the wines are all the same, whichever label they carry. This is sound, typical Listrac, made for early drinking. I have found a touch of coarseness about them, but they have won a number of medals in recent years.

CHÂTEAU CAP-LÉON-VEYRIN

Cru Bourgeois 1932. Owner: Alain Meyre. 14 hectares. 5,000 cases. Mer 50%, CS 45%, CF 3%, PV 2%

Whether you drive from Bordeaux to Lesparre, or from Lesparre to Bordeaux, you can hardly fail to see the large placards directing you to turn off the D1 to Cap-Léon-Veyrin. Although the vineyards themselves adjoin those of Château Clarke and Château Chasse-Spleen, the actual château is well to the north of Listrac, at Donissan, a village with that forlorn and ruinous appearance that was common enough thirty years ago, but which has happily disappeared in the wake of renewed prosperity. The sad state of this village is due to the neglect of the château bearing the village name, and its numerous dependencies. Fortunately, a happier state of affairs prevails at Cap-Léon-Veyrin, where it is immediately apparent that this is a thriving enterprise. Recently 8 hectares of vineyards have been extended to 14, and there are possibilities for extension by a further 26 hectares. But this is not just a wine estate. Alain Meyre also has a large, although in recent circumstances diminishing, cattle business, one of the rare instances of the mixed farming that formerly dominated the area, and in addition to vineyards and grazing there are also forests. Meanwhile Madame Meyre has organized farm holidays, so that you can actually stay on the domain, enjoy the traditional Médocain cooking and drink the wine.

The property has been in the family since 1810 but, surprisingly, Alain Meyre is only the fifth generation of his family to work the estate. What they acquired by marriage was called Cap-Léon. Much later, in 1908, Guillaume Meyre bought the domain Veyrin, which at that time formed part of Lanessan. Alain Meyre believes in very modern vinification, with stainless steel *cuves* and careful temperature control, but very traditional *élevage* in casks, of which one-third are new. I have found the wines to be deep and vivid in colour, very perfumed and with nuances of new oak at first, and having quite a strong Listrac character on the palate, but with good richness which soon evolves into a nice mellow fruitiness. I have tasted a rich-textured and relatively soft 1982, a rather light 1983 so marked by new oak as to make it look for all the world like a very good Rioja, a fine, rich, clean-flavoured 1985, and a surprisingly supple 1986. These are powerful, well-made wines which evidently keep well, yet can be enjoyed when young.

CHÂTEAU CLARKE

Cru Bourgeois. Owner: Baron Edmond de Rothschild. 144 hectares. 30,000 cases. CS 49%, Mer 37%, CF 10%, PV 4%. Second label: Château Malmaison

This is one of the most remarkable new enterprises seen in the Médoc in recent years. Only Suntory's redevelopment of Lagrange matches it in scope and importance. Baron Edmond de Rothschild wanted to undertake a major viticultural development which was in no way comparable to his family's *crus classés* enterprises. He is himself one of the shareholders of Domaines Rothschild, which comprises Lafite, Duhart-Milon and Rieussec. Apart from this, he is primarily a banker (with wide business interests including the diamond merchants, De Beers) and a noted philanthropist, resident in Switzerland, and is married to Nadine Lhopitalier, formerly a well-known ballet dancer.

Vines were first planted here in the twelfth century by the Cistercian monks from the Abbey of Vertheuil. It was then called Granges, and later passed to the Barons of Blanquefort, who in 1750 sold it to the Clarke family. They were yet another Irish family who had left Ireland in 1692 following the final defeat of James II. One of their descendants, Luc-Tobie Clarke, became a judge of the criminal court of Bordeaux, and in 1810 built a handsome mansion at Granges to which he gave his name. The property remained in the family, via the female side, until 1950. In 1973, together with the adjoining properties of Malmaison and Peyrelebade, it was bought by Baron Edmond de Rothschild.

The development of the property has been all-embracing. Vines are now planted on 144 out of the estate's 173 hectares, representing more than 150 plots. Twenty-three kilometres of ditches have been dug to improve drainage. A large *cuvier* with stainless steel fermentation vats and a spacious *chai* has been created. The fermentation is controlled by a specially developed microcomputer system. After the completion of the fermentation, the wine goes into 150-hectolitre oak vats before being transferred to casks after the first racking. Between 25 and 30 per cent new casks are used, depending on the vintage. The strict selection of *cuves* for the Clarke label, as well as the time of bottling, is determined by Baron Edmond and a strong technical team, which has been headed from the outset by Professor Peynaud. Prominent among them are Gérard Colin, director and oenologist, J.-C. Boniface, director-general (his brother is a noted proprietor in Savoie) and Philippe Bonnin as *maître de chai*. Apart from the second wine, Château Malmaison, an attractively fruity rosé is also made. The publicity machine here is unrivalled in Bordeaux. There is a Cercle Oenologique de Clarke with premises near the church of Moulis. They offer tasting facilities, and the wines can be purchased and dispatched anywhere in France, or exported. In addition there is a restaurant, most welcome in an area poor in gastronomy, offering lunch at moderate prices. There are also facilities for lectures and tastings for groups. There is even a Château Clarke card!

But what of the wines themselves? It has taken time for the vines to mature sufficiently to produce wines with enough fat to match the underlying tannic, assertive style of Listrac. The first wholly successful vintage, for me, was 1982. But this has now developed a rather dry, minerally finish, and seems disappointingly lean. But the 1981, which initially I found too austere and lean, and too marked by wood, has improved significantly, and developed some elegance while not wholly throwing off its toughness. The 1983 also seemed overwhelmed at first by new oak, and then became tough, lacking breed and fruit; however the 1985 is rich and long-flavoured, with real concentration and breed. Nevertheless one notes that the wines are ageing quite quickly – this is especially true of the colours, as one would expect of the produce of young vines. The 1979 I thought too old at eight years. Interestingly, a significant proportion of the wine is now made as kosher wine for sale in the USA.

While Clarke looks like producing elegant if rather austere and assertive wines in the immediate future, their prices more closely reflect the prestige of the Rothschild name and the prodigious investment and effort that has gone into their production rather than their intrinsic merit as wines. The two Fourcases are certainly better wines, and one wonders if, given its location, Clarke will ever approach the quality being achieved by the leading *crus* of Listrac and Moulis. Time alone will tell.

CHÂTEAU DUCLUZEAU

Cru Bourgeois 1932. Owner: Madame Jean-Eugène Borie. 4 hectares. 1,650
cases. Mer 90%, CS 10%

This very small *cru* was larger and more important than it is today. In
1850 Charles Cocks listed it as the second *cru* of Listrac, with a production of 40 tonneaux. It has belonged to the family of Madame Borie, wife
of Jean-Eugène Borie, proprietor of Ducru-Beaucaillou, for over a century,
and is now managed by Jean-Eugène. Until he took it in hand again, the
wine had for some time been vinified at the *cave coopérative*. The present
label was created only in 1976, when château bottling was restored. Most
unusually, the vineyard is planted with 90 per cent Merlot. The wines are
matured in cask for six months, are deliciously perfumed and fruity, and
often quite uncharacteristic of Listrac. The 1979, or the much lighter but
delicious 1984, are perfect for drinking now, while 1982 is splendidly
rich. In contrast, the 1983 is firmer and will take longer to develop. An
ideal luncheon wine!

CHÂTEAU FONRÉAUD

Cru Bourgeois. Owners: Héritiers Chanfreau. Administrators: Madame Léo
Chanfreau and Monsieur Jean Chanfreau. 39 hectares. 20,500 cases. CS 66%,
Mer 31%, PV 3%

The large Victorian château here is a prominent landmark just to the west
of the D1 Bordeaux–Lesparre road, south of Listrac. Part of the large vineyard is actually in Moulis. The management here is the same as at Lestage,
only here part of the crop is aged in cask, and part in vat. The name
derives from Font-Réaux (or Réau) meaning royal fountain, because
according to tradition the King of England once stayed near the lake and
drank its water. This spelling was still employed by Charles Cocks in
1850. In the early nineteenth century it belonged to the Danish Consul in
Bordeaux, and in 1832 was bought by the Le Blanc family of Mauvesin in
neighbouring Moulis. They built the château in 1859.

The present owners acquired the property in 1962, and were among a
number of dispossessed *pieds-noirs* who reinvested in the Médoc at this
time. They are making attractively fruity, well-balanced wines which
seem to be designed for relatively early drinking. A good general standard
is maintained.

CHÂTEAU FOURCAS-DUPRÉ

Cru Grand Bourgeois Exceptionnel. Owner: Société Civile du Château Fourcas-Dupré. Administrator: Patrice Pagès. 42 hectares. 22,000 cases. CS 50%, Mer 38%, CF 10%, PV 2%

Fourcas is the name of a small hamlet, just outside Listrac itself, which also lies on the D1. The *chai* of Dupré can be seen from the road. Dupré was the name of a nineteenth-century owner. In 1970 the property was bought by Guy Pagès, one of the many *pieds-noirs* who moved to Bordeaux, both before and after France left its North African possessions. His brother had acquired La Tour-de-By a few years earlier. Under his management, the reputation of this *cru* rose considerably. After his untimely death in 1985, his capable and enthusiastic son, Patrice, took over.

In 1983, thanks to the kindness of Guy Pagès and Bertrand de Rivoyre and, one must say, their friendship for each other, I was able to taste six vintages of Hosten and Dupré side by side. Generally speaking I found the colours at Dupré lighter and maturing more quickly, the bouquets very perfumed but with less power, the flavours more supple, less tannic and complex, usually more advanced, than Hosten. Interestingly, the only vintage where I thought Dupré better than Hosten was in 1970, Guy Pagès's first vintage, but when Hosten still belonged to the Saint-Affriques. The 1978 I made a dead heat, otherwise Hosten was ahead. Good as the Dupré wines are, the best in Listrac after Hosten, they lack the richness, power, dimension and complexity of that *cru*. There is also a tendency towards dryness in some vintages, which emphasizes the great fruit of Hosten wines. Of the recent vintages at Dupré, I particularly like 1978, 1981, which is forward with very mellow fruit, 1983, with its rich fruit and assertive tannins, and a very scented, ripe and powerful 1986. Given Dupré's careful wine-making (and Patrice Pagès has also assisted Bertrand de Rivoyre at Hosten in recent years), the difference between the two Fourcases serves only to emphasize the role of the soil in determining the quality of Bordeaux wines, and how it can vary from plot to plot in a small area.

CHÂTEAU FOURCAS-HOSTEN

Cru Grand Bourgeois Exceptionnel. Owner: Société Civile du Château Fourcas-Hosten. Administrators: Bertrand de Rivoyre and Patrice Pagès. 46 hectares. 20,000 cases. CS 55%, Mer 40%, CF 5%

Certainly the best-known growth in England and the United States of America, it is also a very old vineyard. It can be located on Claude Masse's map at the beginning of the eighteenth century, which showed very few vineyards by name, as well as on the much more detailed Belleyme one at the end of the century. It also had the distinction of featuring on the earliest pre-classification list, that of Abraham Lawton's hierarchy of thirty-seven *crus* whose prices were recorded between 1741 and 1774. At this time the name was spelt Hostein, but by 1850 Cocks was referring to it as Hosten although the Hostein spelling was to recur in subsequent editions of Cocks & Féret as late as the 1949 edition, while Pijassou uses Hostein throughout his monumental treatise on the Médoc, maintaining that since this is a family name – and the family have always used this spelling – there is no authority for any other usage.

From 1810 to 1971 it was owned by the Saint-Affrique family (see Gressier), and during this time the wine was made and kept at Gressier. Then, in 1971, it was acquired by a syndicate with a number of American members, and with Monsieur Bertrand de Rivoyre of Maison Diprovin & Louis Dubroca as administrator. In 1985 some of the American investors were replaced by Schröder and Schÿler and some Danish investors, so the shareholding is truly international.

The pretty little château has been tastefully renovated and the *chai* and *cuvier* reconstructed and enlarged, with stainless steel fermenting vats. Before the change of ownership, the wine was typical of Listrac in style, with a very strong, firm, frank flavour, but with more fruit than most of its neighbours. From my own experience, even in those days, this was the best of the Listrac growths. Good wines were made in 1959, 1962, 1964 and 1966. However, a serious defect of the Saint-Affrique regime was its cavalier attitude to the time of château bottling. There was an unfortunate tendency to leave any wine not sold in cask, just in case a future purchaser might want to take the wine in bulk for his own bottling. So when the new owners took possession in 1972, they found some of the 1966 crop still in wood and distinctly dried-up, quite unrepresentative of what it had originally been. So pre-1970 vintages have to be treated with some caution.

The transformation from what was quite an acceptable *bourgeois* growth into something to stand comparison with the best that Moulis can do, and challenging for classified-growth status, has been remarkable. First Professor Peynaud's advice was sought, then an experienced *régisseur*, Monsieur de Crèvecoeur, was installed. On his retirement, Bernard Coucharrière took over. He works under the general supervision of Monsieur Bertrand de Rivoyre.

The first vintage for the new owners was 1972, hardly a propitious year to start, but the wine was one of the pleasantest Médocs of the year, far better than that of many more exalted growths. The 1973 was fruity and charming with a nice touch of fullness, but with 1974 the problems of the year were not solved, and the wine was mean; the 1975 was a tremendous wine, very rich and powerful, with considerable weight; the 1976 had more elegance, but again good weight for a Listrac; the 1977 was a success for the year; the 1978 is complex and majestic; the 1979 is strong and assertive in character, but with plenty of richness to temper the Listrac style; a delicious 1980 has lasted well. In the great vintages of the eighties, the 1981 has plenty of fruit, depth and structure; the 1982 has real concentration, great fruit and length; the 1983 is a great success for the year, with real concentration and tannin, a slow developer with the breed coming through; the 1984 is good for the year, with structure and good flavour. The 1985 promises to be an exceptional Fourcas – there are marvellous mellow tannins, great richness and fruit, all adding up to a wonderful flavour – while the 1986 has an exceptional flavour full of overtones of liquorice and tannins, a remarkable concentration of fruit and power. It is hard to tell which will be the greater of these two exceptional vintages. The use of some new wood has certainly helped to lift and embellish the potential of these wines. These are long-maturing wines which always need bottle ageing to show their balance and breed, but then reward the drinker with their considerable character and complexity.

GRAND LISTRAC (*CAVE COOPÉRATIVE*)

Owner: Cave de Listrac. 160 hectares. 66,650 cases. Mer 60%, CS and CF 30%, PV 10%

This *coopérative* gained a well-deserved reputation in France where for many years it represented the best value on the restaurant cars of the French railways. Today there are around seventy members, and their production of Listrac represents about one-third of the volume of the *appellation*. Three properties are marketed under their own names: Château Capdet, Clos du Fourcas and Château Vieux Moulis. The rest is sold under the brand "Grand Listrac". In addition, some fifteen properties in Moulis are also members, of which two are sold under their respective names: Château Guitignan and Château Bouqueyran.

CHÂTEAU LAFON
Cru Grand Bourgeois. Owner: Jean-Pierre Théron. 11.5 hectares. 6,500 cases. CS 75%, Mer 25%

This property is run jointly with La Bécade, another Listrac. When it was bought in the late sixties by Jean-Pierre Théron, it was little better than a ruin. The wine is carefully made and is matured in vat; there is no wood. It is commercialized under two labels, one bearing the Listrac *appellation*, the other the Haut-Médoc one. This latter has been an exclusivity of the CVBG group (Dourthe and Knessmann) since 1970, but the two wines are identical, it being believed that the Haut-Médoc *appellation* is better known, especially in the United States, than the Listrac one. These are soft, light, early-drinking, commercial wines, which are pleasant enough.

CHÂTEAU LESTAGE
Cru Bourgeois Supérieur. Owner: Héritiers Chanfreau. Administrators: Madame Leo Chanfreau and Monsieur Jean Chanfreau. 52 hectares. 25,500 cases. Mer 55%, CS and CF 41%, PV 4%

We know that there was an important vineyard here in the eighteenth century from its inclusion in the Belleyme map. In 1850 Charles Cocks listed it as the first *cru* in Listrac. In 1962 it was acquired at the same time as Château Fonréaud by the Chanfreau family, one of the many *pied-noir* families who bought properties at this time. In contrast to Fonréaud, all the wine here is kept in vat and sees no wood. Again, there is a large and rather ornate Victorian château.

Supple, early-maturing wines are made here. Usually I prefer the wines of Fonréaud to those of Lestage, except for an excellent 1981.

CHÂTEAU SARANSOT-DUPRÉ

Cru Bourgeois Supérieur 1932. Owner: Yves Raymond. 10 hectares. 4,000 cases.
Red: CS 50%, Mer 50%. White: Sém 50%, Sauv 25%, Musc 25%

Yves Raymond is the third generation of his family to own this *cru* and the family has lived in Listrac for 300 years. Apart from the relatively small vineyard, the property has extensive grassland and forests (255 hectares in all) in Listrac and St Laurent. There is a large flock of sheep, which provide all the necessary manure for the vineyards. The wine has a reputation of being rich and supple. In addition, a small quantity of white wine is made, which of course carries only the Bordeaux Blanc *appellation*.

OTHER WINES OF THE HAUT-MÉDOC

We have now dealt with the six major *appellations* of the Haut-Médoc covering, between them, nine communes. But there remain fifteen other wine-growing communes within the area, containing five growths classified in 1855. It is within this area that great changes are to be found. Compared with a hundred years ago, there was a marked decline in the area planted, a movement which gained its greatest impetus in the years between the wars. But from the mid-sixties there has been a dramatic revival in the fortunes of the *appellation*. In 1972 there were 1,740 hectares under vine; but then 2,000 hectares were passed in 1976, and 3,000 hectares in 1985. In 1986 the figure stood at 3,203 hectares, an increase of 84 per cent since 1972.

The view has been expressed, notably by the late Mr Ronald Barton (proprietor of Léoville-Barton and Langoa-Barton), that this decline was largely to be blamed on an *appellation* system which has singled out six areas for special treatment and left the remainder in the limbo of the Haut-Médoc *appellation*. But taking St Laurent as the most notable example, one cannot help feeling that wines of this type do not meet the modern taste, and are unlikely to do so unless methods of vinification are significantly changed. Also, this simple accusation does not explain why La Lagune and Cantemerle are as popular as at any time in their history, while Belgrave and even La Tour-Carnet are rather hazy memories for most claret lovers. The recent revival of Camensac is a good example of what modern vinification can achieve in this area. Most of the back areas of the Médoc also suffer the considerable disability of being more subject to spring frosts, so that over the years, the double penalty of reduced harvests and declining popularity has been too heavy a burden for many proprietors to shoulder.

Of the fifteen communes concerned, eight lie adjacent to the Garonne or the Gironde, the remaining seven are inland. The riverside communes, going north from Bordeaux, are: Blanquefort, Parempuyre, Ludon, Macau, Arcins, Lamarque, Cussac and St Seurin-de-Cadourne. But of these, Blanquefort and Parempuyre in the south have rich alluvial areas, which gave large quantities of wine in the eighteenth century, when soft wines for immediate drinking were required. These were the *vins de l'année* of their day. They only have small outcrops of the fine, gravelly soil on which the best Médocs are to be found.

Between Margaux and St Julien are three communes: Arcins, Lamarque and Cussac. This is a very poor, low-lying area; again there are some good, gravelly outcrops – especially in Cussac – but they are not extensive. Of the remainder, Macau and Ludon in the south do produce some very fine wines, including two very successful growths classified in 1855, La Lagune and Cantemerle. Here there is a significant amount of soil analogous to that found in the communes of the Margaux *appellation*, and the wines have real finesse and breed. Then the most northerly commune of St Seurin-de-Cadourne has some excellent, gravelly ridges which are an extension of St Estèphe, and the wines here are comparable to the lesser St Estèphes; they are often more generous and less tough.

The second line of communes, again going northwards from Bordeaux, consists of: Le Taillan, Le Pian-Médoc, Avensan, St Laurent-de-Médoc, St Sauveur, Cissac and Vertheuil. Of these, the most southerly, Le Taillan and Le Pian, are of little importance today. The few wines produced in Avensan adjoin Moulis and are very similar in character. St Laurent has three growths which were classified in 1855. The best vineyards are all to be found adjoining St Julien, but the strong-flavoured, rather coarse wines do not seem to be attuned to modern tastes. St Sauveur lies immediately behind Pauillac, and its best wines are similar to the lesser Pauillacs, having something of the same body and fullness of flavour. The two most northerly communes, Cissac and Vertheuil, lie immediately behind St Estèphe and, for the most part, their wines are rather light but tough and a shade coarse, like the poorer St Estèphes. Here are some notes on the most important individual growths.

CHÂTEAU D'AGASSAC

Cru Grand Bourgeois Exceptionnel. Owner: Société Civile du Château d'Agassac. Administrator: Philippe Capbern-Gasqueton. 35 hectares. 19,500 cases. CS 60%, Mer 40%

This is the most important growth in Ludon after La Lagune, and since 1966 has been classified as a *grand bourgeois exceptionnel*. It was bought by the Gasqueton family in 1960 and is run by Monsieur Philippe Gasqueton (see Calon-Ségur and Capbern). Philippe Gasqueton, assisted by his son Olivier, has made many improvements to the vineyard and the installations, as well as restoring the château. His *maître de chai*, Madame Chevalier, is one of the few women holding this post in the Médoc. By a strange coincidence, one of the others is at nearby Château La Lagune.

Agassac is one of the very few châteaux in the Médoc which actually has the appearance of a castle. The fortress, one of the few to survive from the Middle Ages in the Médoc, dates from the beginning of the fourteenth century. The origins of the place go back even further, to Gaillard d'Agassac, who was *senéchal* of Guyenne in 1274. From 1580 until the Revolution, it belonged to the Les Pomiès family, members of the Bordeaux *noblesse de robe*. The vineyard itself appears on Belleyme's map at the end of the eighteenth century. In 1755 the vineyard consisted of more than "100 journeaux" of vines (about 32 hectares) and produced 80 tonneaux of wine. It also appeared on Abraham Lawton's list of thirty-seven *crus* quoted between 1741 and 1779, under the name of Pomiès, so may be considered as one of the leading *crus* of the Médoc in this epoch.

The wine is typical of the region, vividly perfumed, with a pronounced fruity character which is most attractive. The reputation of the *cru* is certainly, and deservedly, growing, but much of the crop is still exported to its traditional market, Holland. It is a pity it is not more widely known in the Anglo-Saxon world.

CHÂTEAU D'ARCINS

Cru Bourgeois 1932. Owner: Société Civile du Château d'Arcins. 82 hectares. 45,000 cases. CS 70%, Mer 30%

This is the leading property in this small commune which adjoins Soussans, the most northerly of the Margaux communes. The wine still has some suggestion of Margaux about it, but it lacks the finesse of a Margaux, while having something of the vinosity of the neighbouring growths of Moulis. The château is today the property of a company of whom the chief shareholders are Castel Frères, who have developed it very considerably in the last decade. The wine is mostly sold in northern France.

CHÂTEAU ARNAULD
Owners: Monsieur and Madame Maurice Roggy. 18 hectares. 9,000 cases. Mer 50%, CS 40%, CF 10%

This old property in Arcins was originally a priory, the name coming from Pierre-Jacques Arnauld, *procureur* at the court of the Parlement of Bordeaux in the seventeenth century. The Roggy family, *pieds-noirs* from Algeria, bought the property in 1956 and gradually replanted the vineyard. But then a miracle happened – their two daughters married the two Theil brothers of Poujeaux in nearby Moulis. I have tasted a 1985 with highlighted fruit and charm – an early developer – and a much more powerful 1988. This must be a wine to watch.

CHÂTEAU D'ARSAC
Cru Bourgeois Supérieur 1932. Owner: Philippe Roux. 54 hectares. 5,500 cases. CS 75%, Mer 25%. Secondary labels: Château Ségur-d'Arsac, Château Le Monteil-d'Arsac

This *cru* is something of a curiosity as the only vineyard in Arsac not to have the Margaux *appellation*; instead it is only Haut-Médoc.

When the boundaries of the *appellation* were laid in 1954, no vines were planted on this large old property; the present owner took over only in 1959 and had to reconstruct the vineyard completely. He is understandably hopeful that his vineyards will be included when the *appellation* is next reviewed. There are also 150 hectares of pasture, used for sheep grazing, and extensive woods.

The wines are aged in casks, of which 20 per cent are new. I have found the wines to be big, deep-coloured, and traditional in style, high in extract with plenty of tannin and fruit, quite assertive in character and with a distinctive aromatic bouquet, developing a pleasing suppleness with bottle age. Since the present owner took over in 1986, great progress has been made.

CHÂTEAU BARREYRES

Cru Bourgeois 1932. Owner: Société Civile du Château Barreyres. 100 hectares. 48,000 cases. CS 70%, Mer 30%

This is another property controlled and distributed by Castel Frères since 1973. Again a great deal of work has been undertaken, with a new *cuvier* and *chai* completed in 1981, to cope with the huge production. I have found the wines fruity and quite attractive, if a shade coarse, and slightly less good than d'Arcins.

CHÂTEAU BEAUMONT

Cru Grand Bourgeois. Owner: Garantie Mutuelle des Fonctionnaires. 85 hectares. 30,000 cases. CS 56%, Mer 36%, CF 7%, PV 1%. Secondary labels: Château Moulin-d'Arvigny, Les Tours-de-Beaumont

Old editions of Cocks & Féret show that in the nineteenth century this *cru* vied with Lanessan as the most important in Cussac, yet until recent years it was a forgotten name. When the Bolivars from Venezuela bought it in 1966, there were only two hectares of vines, whereas in its heyday, at the turn of the century, there had been 100 hectares under vine. With only limited resources, they replanted about half the vineyard, and soon one became conscious of large placards on French roadsides, both near and far, advertising the wines of Beaumont for "*vente directe*". But the Bolivar era ended sadly when frost destroyed virtually the whole 1977 crop and Monsieur de Bolivar died. His widow had to sell and in 1989 Bernard Soulas took charge.

He was just what Beaumont needed. A successful farmer with resources behind him, he drained the vineyard, including those parts not yet planted, and planted a further 30 hectares. In addition, he installed stainless steel fermentation vats and insulated the *cuvier*. Then just as the fruits of his labours were beginning to pay off, in December 1986 he sold to the Garantie Mutuelle des Fonctionnaires (the Civil Servants' Pension Fund), which had already taken an interest in Château Beychevelle. They have now completed the renovation of the château, a surprisingly elegant nineteenth-century copy of a Mansart (seventeenth-century) château with some fine mouldings around the windows.

As might be expected from a relatively young vineyard where nothing is much over twenty years old and much of it less than eight years, the wines are at present lighter in style than neighbouring Tour-du-Haut-Moulin. The first vintages I tasted, 1976, 1979 and 1981, were decent but unremarkable, light and without much personality. But the 1982 has the richness and attraction of the year, an early developer, certainly, but more stylish than before. The 1983 is light in body but thoroughly harmonious, fruity and charming, at its best when four years old. The 1984 is also fruity, without any of the dryness sometimes found in this vintage, for early drinking. The 1985 is again only of medium weight, but it has a nice touch of *cassis* on the nose and the flavour has a lot of charm and elegance. The 1986 benefited from 40 per cent new wood, compared with 25 per cent for the 1985. The colour is deeper, the bouquet very scented and rich. It is a much more complete wine than the 1985, rich and tannic, with depth and charm, and has an extra dimension to it, which points to a promising future both for the 1986 and for Beaumont itself.

The situation for the secondary labels is slightly confusing. First of all Bernard Soulas created Château Moulin-d'Arvigny as a second wine, composed of the produce of young vines, for sale through the restaurant trade for early drinking. Thus the 1982 vintage was being sold for drinking in 1984. Then a real second label, Les Tours-de-Beaumont, was introduced in the 1983 vintage, this wine being ready to drink by 1986. The Moulin-d'Arvigny 1986 was already in bottle by October 1987 as a delicious, fruity, simple wine for immediate drinking, the product of the youngest vines only.

So the future for Beaumont, with ample finance and good management, looks excellent, and as the vineyard matures, the depth and breed of the wines are clearly increasing.

CHÂTEAU BEL-AIR

Owner: Henri Martin. 35 hectares. 10,000 cases. CS 60%, Mer 40%

Henri Martin (see Château Gloria) bought this property in Cussac in 1980. At that time seven hectares were planted. The vineyard is in three parcels: one near the church of Cussac, the others near the border with St Julien on either side of the road. The management is in the capable hands of Henri Martin's son-in-law, Jean-Louis Triaud. I have tasted only the

1984 vintage, but that was very perfumed and fruity, dense for the year. On this form, a new *cru* to watch.

CHÂTEAU BEL-ORME-TRONQUOY-DE-LALANDE

Cru Grand Bourgeois. Owners: Madame L. Quié and Jean-Michel Quié. 26 hectares. 10,000 cases. Mer 45%, CS 30%, CF 20%, Mal 3%, PV 2%

Not surprisingly, this is usually known as Bel-Orme for short, and is not to be confused with Tronquoy-Lalande, the growth in neighbouring St Estèphe. At one time the property also belonged to the Tronquoy family. Bel-Orme means beautiful elm.

This is one of the best-known growths of St Seurin-de-Cadourne, and the vineyard is well placed on gravelly slopes between the *route des châteaux* and the river. The château itself is no more than a charming summer pavilion, flanked by a businesslike *cuvier* and *chai*. It is now the property of Monsieur Jean-Michel Quié, son of Paul Quié, of whose kindness and hospitality I have many happy memories. Since there are no châteaux at either Rauzan-Gassies or Croizet-Bages, the Quiés always use Bel-Orme for their visits to the Médoc.

Apart from a serious fall from grace in 1964, Bel-Orme has consistently produced good wines in recent years, and was classified as a *grand bourgeois* in 1966 and 1978. Monsieur Paul Quié kept a remarkable library of old vintages in the cellar here and in the early sixties released some of them to some of his English friends. I myself have pleasant memories of the 1911, 1924, 1926, 1928 and 1929. They were most interesting in showing how wines in this part of the Médoc will develop and age. While they lack the fineness of bouquet of the great growths, they all developed a warmth and richness of texture which made them delicious and attractive wines with a surprising degree of delicacy and style. It is seldom that one sees *bourgeois* growths of this age, and it is a revelation to see how such wines can develop, and emphasizes again the remarkable qualities of Médoc wines. More recently, in 1986, I had the opportunity of tasting a range of vintages from 1971 to 1983. These emphasized that Bel-Orme is still producing strong-flavoured, old-fashioned wines with a lot of extract needing usually eight to ten years to shake off their initial toughness and show at their best. The most impressive vintages were a deliciously rich and well-balanced 1971, a powerful, old-fashioned 1975, a 1979 that was more impressive than the 1978, and a 1981 rich in extract and developing slowly. It was still early to assess the 1982 and 1983: the 1982 will certainly be a slow developer, while the 1983 shows clear signs of dilution, but is a deliciously soft, fruity wine for drinking now.

CHÂTEAU BELGRAVE
Cinquième Cru Classé. Owner: GFA du Château Belgrave. Administrator: Patrick Atteret. 55 hectares. 18,000 cases. CS 60%, Mer 35%, PV 5%
This is one of the more obscure classified growths in spite of its name, which might be thought to be a help in English-speaking markets. It should not be confused with a little-known growth in the St Lambert parish of Pauillac, which is spelt Bellegrave and has an important-looking château near to Pichon-Lalande.

The extensive vineyards immediately adjoin St Julien and lie behind Lagrange. After rather frequent changes of ownership, the château was bought in 1979 by a group in which the Banque Française de l'Agriculture provided the finance and the CVBG (Dourthe and Knessmann) the technical, sales and marketing expertise. Both were badly needed. The vineyard and buildings were woefully neglected and in a literally ruinous condition. The management is now in the capable hands of Patrick Atteret, chief oenologist at CVBG, ably assisted by his wife, daughter of Jean-Paul Jouffret, Director-General of Dourthe. They now live in the restored château. Professor Peynaud advised a reduction in the proportion of Merlot – then standing at 70 per cent – and an increase of Cabernet Sauvignon, as well as more and better wood. Clearly it takes time for all these measures, especially new vines, to show through in the wines.

The wines before the change of ownership are hardly worth speaking of. They were pedestrian and rather common, quite unworthy of a *cru classé*. The wines now being made certainly have some breed and elegance. There is a tendency for them to be rather too marked by new oak for their weight, but the 1981 is now a very pleasing wine. They are sold at modest prices and are now certainly worth watching. There should be steady improvement.

CHÂTEAU LE BOURDIEU

Cru Bourgeois. Owner: Monique Barbe. 30 hectares, 25,000 cases. CS 50%, Mer 30%, CF 20%. Second labels: Châteaux Victoria and Picourneau

The name of this property has both monastic and land-tenure overtones. Vertheuil was the site of a very important Augustinian monastery, and the church there is one of the finest examples of Romanesque architecture to survive in Médoc. Bernard Ginestet traces the derivation of the word *"bourdieu"* from *"pour Dieu"*, in this case the systematic clearance of woodlands for agriculture as part of the monastic work of the monks, done not simply for profit but "for God". This name *"bourdieu"* then came to be applied to small parcels of land which were share-cropped. The name is more widely found in the Libournais and was a much smaller form of *"métayage"*. This property did certainly once belong to the Augustinians of Vertheuil, but its present prosperity began when Ernest Barbe bought it in 1943 in a very run-down condition. He had to reconstruct the vineyard completely. On his death in 1977 his daughter Monique Barbe took over and has continued the good work. Château Victoria, named to commemorate a visit by Queen Victoria, was acquired in 1961.

This is now one of the leading *crus* of Vertheuil, and the vineyards run from the village to the boundary with St Estèphe. The wine is matured in cask and perhaps a woman's hand can be found in the carefully made wines, which are rich and supple with some finesse. The style is that of a good, rather flattering St Estèphe.

CHÂTEAU DU BREUIL

Cru Bourgeois Supérieur. Owner: Vialard family. 20 hectares. 11,600 cases (red). Mer 34%, CS 28%, CF 23%, PV 11%, Mal 4%

Until recently it was not unfair to say that the château here was more interesting than the wine, for it is a genuine medieval fortress, still imposing in its ruined state. It was a place of importance during the English period, and especially in the Hundred Years War. But the barony of Breuil has been traced back to the sixth century, making this the oldest recorded property in the Médoc. Part of the château was still lived in until 1861, when it collapsed. Since then a modest but not unpleasing Victorian villa has served as château.

In 1987 this ancient property was bought by the Vialard family, whose existing vineyards of Cissac and Tour-du-Mirail adjoin those of du Breuil on the plateau of Cissac. The 1987 crop was harvested and made under the new owners' direction. When they took over, the *chai* and *cuvier* were decrepit, filthy and neglected, so there is much to be done. Surprisingly, perhaps, some good wines have been made in recent years but mercifully they were kept in vat. Good wines, rich, full-flavoured and full of character, were made in 1981 and 1982. The potential can be gauged by the fact that the 1988 was already better than Cissac. So the future looks bright under the direction of Louis Vialard and his daughter Danielle, who is now responsible for the wine-making. It would be nice if they could also find the time and resources to save the majestic ruins of the château from further deterioration.

CHÂTEAU CAMBON-LA-PELOUSE

Cru Bourgeois Supérieur 1932. Owner: Indivision Carrère Fils, Frère and Gendre.
60 hectares. 35,000 cases. Mer 50%, CS 30%, CF 20%

This is an old *cru*, as can be seen from nineteenth-century editions of Cocks & Féret, but was completely frosted in 1956, and went out of production for some time. It was then bought by the energetic Carrère family, owners of Château Grand-Barrail-Lamarzelle-Figeac in St Emilion, who have now completed the reconstruction of the vineyard. This occupies a magnificent *croupe* between Cantemerle and Giscours, in a single piece.

The wines here have real breed, and the emphasis is on an elegant fruitiness. They are soft and satiny in texture, developing quickly for early drinking, still reflecting the youth of the vineyard. No casks are used, and the resulting wines are fresh, clean and eminently attractive. At the present stage of the redevelopment of the vineyard, this policy obviously makes sound commercial sense. Very good wines were made in 1981 and 1983, with both 1982 and 1985 producing something extra. I noted a lovely scent of cherries and liquorice with a deliciously rich flavour and also some complexity in the 1982, while the 1985 in vat had an extraordinary aroma of exotic fruits, coupled with a remarkable flavour full of vivid tones of *cassis* and elderberry. This must be a *cru* with an exciting future.

CHÂTEAU DE CAMENSAC

Cinquième Cru Classé. Owner: Forner family. 65 hectares. 29,000 cases. CS 60%, CF 20%, Mer 20%

If there were a contest for the least known of the classified growths, Camensac would, until very recently, have been a very strong contender. It adjoins Belgrave and La Tour-Carnet, lying behind Lagrange and close to St Julien. It appears on the Belleyme map at the end of the eighteenth century, and in Lawton's 1815 classification, under the name of Popp, and is listed among the St Juliens. Charles Cocks also listed it as a *cinquième cru* in 1850, again as Popp, the name of the owners, although elsewhere in his book it is listed as Camensac. Camensac's period of obscurity certainly seems to have been a long one, and I for one do not remember ever seeing a bottle before the new proprietors took over in 1965. Since then Messieurs Forner, father and son, have made considerable efforts both here and at Larose-Trintaudon, which they also bought. Professor Peynaud has also played a large part in the revival. There has certainly been a considerable outlay in modernizing the *cuvier* and *chai*, and the results are promising. In spite of the French-sounding name, the Forners came from Rioja, where they also have vineyards.

The vinification methods now being used here are producing light-textured, fruity, harmonious wines, which are eminently drinkable and thus commercial – a far cry from the old style of St Laurent wines. The earliest vintage I have seen is the 1970, an attractive, forward wine. The 1972 was better than that of many better-known châteaux, and I liked both the 1973 and the 1975. However, more recently, as the vineyard has matured and the wines become more tannic and powerful, I have found a coarseness creeping into the wines, and this is true even of vintages such as 1978 and 1982. Perhaps it is the residual character of the soil reasserting itself as the vines mature, since it is hard to believe the wines are any less carefully made. One will watch with interest as the vintages of the eighties mature. While I do not think the wines are of classified-growth quality, one must remember that they do not sell at classified-growth prices either. But as attractive, easy-to-drink wines sold at a reasonable price, they are finding a ready market and deserve to do so.

CHÂTEAU CANTEMERLE

Cinquième Cru Classé. Owner: Société Assurances Mutuelles du Bâtiment et
Travaux Publics. Administrator: Jean Cordier. 53 hectares. 20,000 cases. CS 40%,
Mer 40%, CF 18%, PV 2%

A very ancient property with a history going back to the Middle Ages,
from 1579 until 1892 it remained in the hands of a single family,
Villeneuve. Then, for over fifty years, it was owned and run by Monsieur
Pierre Dubos, one of the outstanding proprietors of his generation. I shall
always have a strong affection for Cantemerle and for Pierre Dubos, since
this was the first Bordeaux château I ever visited, and Pierre Dubos was
the first proprietor I ever met. I shall also remember being shown the
remarkable weather records he kept, and the notes he made on everything that had to be done during the harvesting and vinification. He
illustrated the difference between vintages by showing me the records for
1920 and 1921: 1920 had been very straightforward, but 1921 had been
full of headaches and the pages were covered in notes in red ink – indicating corrective measures. He remembered having to get up in the
middle of the night to check the temperature in his fermentation vats and
take appropriate action. We had drunk the 1921 at lunch and it was an
eloquent tribute to the care that had accompanied its birth. After Pierre
Dubos's death, his son-in-law, Monsieur Henri Binaud, of the house of
Beyerman, lavished almost as much care on the wine, but with the
ownership divided among a number of heirs, there was a shortage of
funds for investment, and some disappointing wines were made in the
seventies. However, in 1980 it was sold to a syndicate in which the
Cordiers have a small share, but provide the management and marketing,
while their partners provide the finance. As a result, the *cuvier* has been
virtually rebuilt and equipped with stainless steel *cuves* in place of the old
wooden ones. The *chais* have also been extensively repaired and modernized, and a programme of replanting in the vineyards undertaken, where
a significant area was lying fallow.

There is mention of the production at Cantemerle of three tonneaux of
wine in 1575, one of the earliest recorded references to wine production
at a specific property. It appears on the Belleyme map at the end of the
eighteenth century, but not in classifications before Charles Cocks in
1850. The estate is the second of the classified growths to be seen on the
route des châteaux as one leaves Bordeaux. The château itself is hidden in

a heavily timbered park lying immediately to the left of the road. A turreted, nineteenth-century building replaced a medieval fortress, and there are fine and extensive *chais*. The vineyards are on fine, gravelly ridges going towards Ludon.

Holland was the historic market for Cantemerle, and it is said that this is the reason why it was placed only last of the fifth growths in the 1855 classification. Indeed, a look at the manuscript of the famous list shows Cantemerle added in, in small print, as something of an afterthought. It is said that the wine was hardly known in Bordeaux, and that this is the reason it was underrated, as it most certainly was. The general quality is certainly on a par with La Lagune, a third growth, and it often sells at second-growth prices.

In style, Cantemerle has the lightness and elegance of a Margaux, but tends to be fatter, with less verve and sheer breed than a second-growth Margaux. The charming bouquet and supple fruitiness of the wine naturally account for its great popularity, now especially marked in England, and for many years now this has been allied to remarkable consistency, due to the care with which the wine is made. I remember especially the excellence of the 1957 and 1958, but good vintages like 1952, 1953, 1955, 1959, 1961 and 1962 have all been highly successful. The 1964 was one of the outstanding wines in the Médoc in this very mixed year, although, like many 1964s, it has not lived up to its early promise. The seventies were probably the most disappointing decade for Cantemerle since the period before Pierre Dubos took charge. There have been many other decades which lacked the fine vintages of the seventies, but probably none where Cantemerle failed to make the most of them. The decline was due to a slow, but nevertheless systematic, run-down of the property. There were many shareholders and nobody seemed prepared to make the investment necessary to renovate the *cuvier* and *chais* or maintain the rotation in the vineyard. Although it is sad to see an association which has lasted since 1892 finally severed, one can at least be sure that the new owners have the necessary finance and experience to restore Cantemerle to its legitimate position for quality and consistency. They have certainly lost no time. The 1980 and 1981 were made under very difficult conditions of rebuilding and reequipping the *cuvier*. The wines are sound but not special. But then came a splendid 1982 and an exceptional 1983 with an opulence and richness found here only in the greatest vintages. There is a good 1984, attractive and forward but with just a touch of firmness behind it. The 1985 is just what one would have hoped for: intense, ripe fruit on the nose and a lovely long, lingering flavour with breed and elegance. In 1986 they were unlucky enough to catch some hail, and a first sight of the wine was disappointing; it lacked the richness and power of the year. But with vintages such as 1982, 1983 and 1985, the reputation of Cantemerle will soon be re-established. I have only one complaint about the new regime – they have dropped the very distinctive old label and substituted a Lafite look-alike. What a pity. I hope they have second thoughts.

CANTERAYNE

Owner: Cave Coopérative de St Sauveur. 113 hectares. 5,000 hectolitres (of which some 19,000 cases are sold in bottle). CS 60%, Mer 35%, CF, Mal and PV 5%

Founded in 1934, there are now sixty-nine members producing well-made wines with the firmness and solidity typical of this good commune behind Pauillac.

CHÂTEAU CARONNE-STE-GEMME

Cru Grand Bourgeois Exceptionnel. Owners: Jean and François Nony-Borie. 45 hectares. 23,000 cases. CS 65%, Mer 35%

The only growth in St Laurent to be classified as a *grand bourgeois exceptionnel* in 1966 and again in 1978, it deserves to be more widely known. The position of the vineyard is quite unlike that of the other *crus* of St Laurent, since it lies south of the Jalle du Nord, immediately behind or to the west of the vineyard of Lanessan, so that geologically it has more in common with its neighbours in Cissac than with the other *crus* of St Laurent. Indeed, before the Revolution of 1789, Lanessan and Caronne were grouped together in the ancient parish of Ste Gemme, and were separate from those of Cissac and St Laurent, between whom they were then divided. Both the quality of the wine and its dissemination on export markets have much increased since François Nony-Borie became involved in the management in the early eighties. It has belonged to the Nony-Borie family since 1900. The vineyard was previously expanded from a mere 15 hectares to 45 hectares during the period from 1854 to 1885, which Professor René Pijassou has called the "*belle époque*" of the Médoc. François Nony-Borie has improved the equipment in the *cuvier*, especially for controlling the temperature of the fermentation, and the *remontage*. During the exceptional cold of January 1985, nine hectares of vines were lost. Six hectares have so far been replanted, and the opportunity taken to improve drainage and use the best clones. In average years 15 to 20 per cent new casks are used, but 30 per cent were used for the 1985 and 40 per cent for the 1986. Following the introduction of EC legislation which says that only awards for the vintage in the bottle may appear on the label, the old label with its large array of ancient *médailles d'or* has had to go, and a new one showing the design of the château in outline has been introduced.

Overall, the wines here are now very well made, and have more style and breed than most wines from St Laurent, with nothing in the least rustic about them. Certainly they have a strongly assertive character, but this is combined with nicely balanced fruit, and there is a degree of complexity. Good, typical wines were made in 1978, 1979, 1980 and 1981. The 1982 has the concentration of the year; the 1983 is full-bodied and deliciously fruity. The 1985 in cask had lovely, vibrant fruit and real concentration, while the 1986 was perhaps more powerful with lots of extract and once more a very fine flavour. At present this *cru* offers exceptional value for a Médoc at this level of quality.

CHÂTEAU CHARMAIL
Owner: Roger Sèze. 20 hectares. 12,000 cases. Mer 50%, CS 45%, CF 5%

This is a well-placed property in St Seurin-de-Cadourne, lying just west of the village and adjoining Sociando-Mallet, on the gravelly ridges near the river. The vineyard and pleasant nineteenth-century château were bought and restored by a Monsieur Laly, originally from Burgundy, around 1970. He told me that he had always wanted to own a vineyard but could not afford one in the place of his birth! In 1980 Roger Sèze, proprietor of the highly successful Château Mayne-Vieil in Fronsac, bought a share of the property, and in the following year the rest. The wines are supple, rich and charming, and as the vineyard matures can only improve.

CHÂTELLEINE
Owner: Cave Coopérative de Vertheuil. 110 hectares. 7,000 hectolitres (of which some 16,000 cases are sold in bottle). C5 50%, Mer 50%

There are now some seventy members producing good, solid wines. The following are sold under their own labels: Châteaux Miqueu, Ferré Portal, Fondeminjean, Laride, Julian, Tamière.

CHÂTEAU CISSAC

Cru Grand Bourgeois Exceptionnel. Owners: Vialard family. 50 hectares. 25,000 cases. CS 75%, Mer 20%, PV 5%

This is the property of Monsieur Louis Vialard, brother of the notary of Pauillac. It was classified as a *grand bourgeois* in 1966, and an *exceptionnel* in 1978. Monsieur Vialard is an enthusiastic owner, and his wines enjoy a wide reputation. They are typical of the region and have a certain finesse and style, but also a certain asperity. The Vialards are an old family of vinegrowers who count *régisseurs* of both Lafite and Latour among their forebears. They bought Cissac in 1885, and Louis and his family have lived there since 1940. Now he is assisted by his daughter, Danielle, on the wine-making side, and son, Pascal, on the commercial side. In recent years the *cuvier* and *chai* have been extensively modernized and enlarged, with stainless steel now sharing in the vinification with the traditional oak vats.

In April 1983 Louis Vialard gave a tasting of his wines at the Ritz, which provided a unique opportunity to assess the vintages of the sixties and seventies. To give added point to the proceedings, we were told that there had been a deliberate change of styles during the period and were invited to spot the moment of change and say which we preferred. It emerged that 1970 had been the last of the old-style years. The changes had consisted of using only the free-run juice after that time, thus eliminating the *vin de presse* which had been judiciously added before, according to the character of the year. Then Louis Vialard began vintaging later, thus using riper grapes, and finally he increased a proportion of Cabernet Franc at the expense of Cabernet Sauvignon.

For me, the single step which had had the greatest impact on Cissac was the character of the *vin de presse*. It gave the older vintages a background of flavour and a complexity lacking in most of the younger wines. It was significant that the most successful of these was the 1975, a year exceptionally rich in extract and tannin, where the *vin de presse* was less missed. However, in otherwise excellent vintages such as 1976, 1978 and 1979, a certain leanness was noticeable, whereas the 1962 was wonderfully complete and harmonious still, after twenty-one years. Professor Peynaud has shown that *presse* wine is more concentrated in all the elements of acidity, tannin and colour than free-run wine, so it is at its best in ripe years of quality. What the wine-maker has to be careful about is the use of *presse* wine in years without real ripeness, when it can simply make a wine tough, harsh and unbalanced. I remember this happening with some of the 1960s, and more recently some 1980s suffered from the same problem. While it is certainly not always an easy judgement to know precisely how much *vin de presse* to add, depending on the weight of the wine and the quality of the *vin de presse*, to eliminate it entirely does seem to be a mistake, certainly for a wine of Cissac's composition.

Choosing the time to pick is as often as not a question of nerve, and of knowing how long it will take to bring in the harvest. Fortunately the Merlot ripens before the Cabernets, and the Cabernet Sauvignon takes the longest of all to ripen. With refractometers now widely used, it is a simple matter to check on the progress of the ripening of the different grape varieties in different locations of the vineyard. Provided the balance between rising sugar content and falling acidity is carefully matched, waiting for perfect ripeness is certainly the right policy.

The question of the right balance between the different grape varieties depends so much on the soil and exposition of the individual vineyard. There is some evidence that vineyards in Cissac's position in Médoc do better with Cabernet Sauvignon or Merlot than with Cabernet Franc, and Louis Vialard has since eliminated the Cabernet Franc. Although it accounted for only 15 per cent of the total, against 60 per cent Cabernet Sauvignon and 20 per cent Merlot, with a mere 5 per cent Petit Verdot, its wines at Cissac tended to lack body and colour, so giving a slightly diluted quality to the final blend.

A survey of such a range of vintages when all are tasted side by side is obviously of more than academic interest in the contrasts it provides. The 1959 still had great intensity of bouquet and flavour, but with less fruit and balance than the 1961 and a very dry finish. The 1960 was one of the surprises of the tasting, with a fine flavour and generous character, if drying at the finish. The 1961 was, of course, the best wine of the tasting, with a marvellous, mellow richness. The 1962 was an outstanding example of this underrated year, more complete than either the 1964 or

1966 and perfect for drinking. There was no 1965, and the 1966, after a lovely full middle flavour, seemed to be fading slightly at the finish. The 1967 was disappointing: the acidity was now showing through and the wine was fading and drying out. The 1968 bore the sweet smell of death with a bitter finish – well past its best. The 1969 was typical of this disappointing year with a smell of decay and a lack of flavour and character. The 1970 still looked very young and was still improving, as so many Médocs of this year are. It had a depth of flavour, structure and character to be expected in a fine year. The 1971 was attractive but showed signs of beginning to fade at the finish. I was amazed by the 1972: this terrible vintage produced few wines which have given much pleasure, but this wine had charm with none of the awkward acidity of the year, and I would rather have drunk it than either the 1974 or the 1977. The 1973 was at its charming best, ripe and still lively, a good example of the year. The 1974, while having more vinosity than the 1977, was a small wine, light but pleasant. The 1975 was easily the outstanding wine among the younger vintages, less dry than the 1970 and with real depth of flavour and character, together with a harmony that not all wines of this year showed at this age. The 1976 was a charming wine, with soft fruit and length but somehow lacking background, an example of where some *vin de presse* would have improved the overall balance. The 1977 was not a success; light and thin, it seemed to have no future. The 1978 still showed extreme youth and was very tight and closed, but with signs of complexity and depth of flavour to suggest a promising future. I was disappointed with the 1979 at this stage; it seemed one-dimensional and short, still very raw and undeveloped.

In more recent tastings, the 1980 showed charming fruit and a nice, frank Médoc flavour, but was a little dry. The 1981 is a great success, with a classic flavour, taut and vibrant but with no spare flesh. The 1982 is tannic and slow-developing but with plenty of ripeness, a *vin de garde* for the nineties. The fruit so evident in early tastings of the 1983 was rather masked by tannin after two years in bottle, when the wine looked lean and austere, a slow developer. The 1984 is very Médoc in character but lean and short. In cask, the 1985 had great fruit and charm, backed by good tannin, while the 1986 is very tannic and powerful, a really long-term wine.

This will give some idea of the interest and variety to be found in a good *bourgeois* growth in this part of the Médoc, and of how well the successful years can keep.

CHÂTEAU CITRAN

Cru Grand Bourgeois Exceptionnel. Owner: Fujimoto. 92 hectares. 41,500 cases. Mer 60%, CS 35%, PV 5%

This is a property with a long history, and for six hundred years belonged to the noble family of Donissan. In 1832 it was acquired by the Clauzel family, then in 1945 the Miailhe family bought a very run-down property, with scarcely any vineyards left and the château and buildings in a ruinous condition, an all too familiar story in the Médoc at this time. They lovingly restored it and rebuilt the vineyard, the largest parcel of 49 hectares of which lies between the château and Paveil-de-Luze. Jean Miailhe, cousin of Alain Miailhe of Siran and Madame de Lencquesaing of Pichon-Lalande, in particular did much to re-establish the reputation of the wine as a leading *cru* in Avensan. In 1980 his sister and her husband, Jean Cesselin, took over the management, but then sold to the large Japanese property company, Fujimoto, in 1986. Since then, they have added the Relais de Margaux, the Médoc's leading hotel, to their empire.

The vineyards of Citran most closely resemble those of Moulis. The size and early organization of the vineyard are shown by the fact that it appears in Claude Masse's map at the beginning of the eighteenth century, and among Abraham Lawton's list of thirty-seven *crus* between 1741 and 1774. At this time it achieved a higher average price than Lynch-Bages or Pontet-Canet. I have seen no old vintages of Citran, but in recent years its reputation has been good. My own experience of it is mixed. The wines often have a good flavour, and are robust with a rather minerally taste, but there has been a tendency towards dilution and dryness in some years of high production such as 1979 and 1983, and I think there was some falling-off in quality after Jean Miailhe's departure. The first efforts from the new regime in 1988 and 1989 have been impressive.

CHÂTEAU CLÉMENT-PICHON

Owner: Clément Fayat. 23 hectares. 9,000 cases. CS 60%, CF 10%, Mer 30%

In the woods of Parempuyre just outside Bordeaux, the young Louis XIV broke his journey to St Jean-de-Luz to meet his bride in order to enjoy the hunting provided by Bernard de Pichon, President of the Bordeaux Parlement. The property remained in the hands of the Pichons until 1880. The new owners quickly built a château, to replace the old one which had been burnt down, in the most flamboyant, romantic-Gothic revival style of the age. The architect Michel-Louis Garros was also responsible for Lanessan and Fonréaud, but he excelled himself here. In 1970 the last Durand-Dassier died and three years later the château and estate were bought by the *négociants* Delor. When I dined there soon afterwards, it was fascinating to see how everything had been preserved as it was, down to the old proprietor's desk. But Delor were soon caught up in one of those volte-face of policies which afflict large organizations, when Allied Breweries decided to sell both property and Delor in 1976. Now the Fayat family live here in baronial splendour. Clément Fayat made his fortune building autoroutes and was already the proud owner of La Dominique in St Emilion.

Since then, the vineyard has been replanted, and new installations with computer-controlled fermentations have been created, as well as a new system of drainage for the vineyard. But the greatest stir was caused by the change of name from Château Parempuyre to Château Pichon. The two *deuxièmes crus* of Pauillac were most upset and a legal challenge ensued. As the vineyard matures this should be pleasant, easy-drinking claret.

CHÂTEAU COUFRAN

Cru Grand Bourgeois. Owner: Société Civile du Château Coufran. Administrator: Jean Miailhe. 64 hectares. 33,600 cases. Mer 85%, CS 10%, PV 5%. Second label: Château La Rose-Maréchale

This is a château whose configuration is well known to me from my years at Loudenne. The vineyard lies on a large outcrop of gravelly soil close to the Gironde and overlooking Château Loudenne. It is the last vineyard in the Haut-Médoc, with a prominent look-out tower which serves as something of a landmark. The proprietor is Monsieur Jean Miailhe, cousin of the proprietors of Pichon-Lalande and Siran. His father, Louis, had bought the property in 1924. In the eighteenth century it had belonged to the de Verthamon family, who also owned neighbouring Loudenne. Since 1973 the actual wine-making has been in the hands of Jean's son, Eric Miailhe.

The wine is lighter than the neighbouring Bel-Orme, owing to an unusually high proportion of Merlot, and is also classified as a *grand bourgeois*. The style is fruity and attractive, and recent vintages seem distinctly richer and more stylish than in the past, when the wines were sometimes rather fluid. The best recent vintages are 1982, a big wine which was initially a little austere for this *cru*; a most attractive and quite concentrated 1983; an excellent 1985 full of luscious fruit; and a 1986 which in cask looked for once to be suffering from the lack of Cabernet – it seemed gamy and lacking in definition. The fermentation is now in stainless steel and the wine is matured in cask, with 25 per cent new oak. This is an attractive, dependable Médoc, drinkable young and offering good value.

CHÂTEAU DILLON

Cru Bourgeois 1932. Owner: Lycée Agricole de Bordeaux-Blanquefort. 35 hectares. 18,500 cases. Red: Mer 50%, CS44%, CF 6%. White: Sauv 100%. Second label: Château Lucas (Bordeaux Blanc)

This attractive property was bought by the Ecole Régionale d'Agriculture de Blanquefort in 1956. The château dates from the beginning of the eighteenth century and the property was once much more extensive than it is now. The name comes from Robert Dillon, who acquired the estate from the Comte de Marcellus in 1754. At this time it was called Terrefort. Unlike most of the Irish *émigrés* he did not leave Ireland until 1746, and then did well in banking in Bordeaux, as did a number of the Irish. (For this and other information about the Dillon family, I am indebted to *Les Irlandais en Aquitaine*, privately printed in Bordeaux in 1971 by the Miailhe family. See especially Dr Richard Hages's *Les Familles en exil* and Colonel J. Weygand's *Le Régiment de Dillon*.) So unlike many members of this illustrious family from County Mayo, he did not embark on a military career in the Dillon Regiment (a body with a remarkable history of service to the kings of France throughout the eighteenth century). However, several of his children did serve in the regiment, notably Edward Dillon, born in Bordeaux in 1751. As colonel of the regiment he saw distinguished service during the American War of Independence. Later, he accompanied the Comte d'Artois (the future Charles X) into exile and helped to form an Irish Brigade to fight on the English side against the revolutionary armies of France. After the Restoration, he returned to France as a lieutenant-general, and served as ambassador in Dresden and then Florence.

Curiously, for a wine made at what amounts to a wine school, the wines of Dillon have not been noted for their consistency. At its best, Dillon is an elegant, attractive claret, on the light side but with finesse. The 1970 is excellent, as is the 1975, there is a good if light 1976, and an attractive 1979. Then young vines were introduced with little or no selection, and the wines took a step backwards again. But eventually good wines should be made here.

CHÂTEAU FONTESTEAU
Cru Grand Bourgeois. Owner: Jean Renaud and Dominique Fouin. 11 hectares.
5,000 cases. Mer 40%, CS 30%, CF 30%

This old property, with its tower going back to the thirteenth century, really is in the backwoods of St Sauveur. It is "off the map" as far as Hugh Johnson's *World Wine Atlas* is concerned! From 1939 until 1984, the owner was René Eglise. Now Jean Renaud and Dominique Fouin have taken over. The name derives from a number of ancient wells to be found on the property; so *"fontaines d'eau"* has become Fontesteau, and if you know the sound of the Girondin patois, you will understand how it happened.

The new owners hope to increase the size of the vineyard to 20 hectares in time. This is a fairly traditional wine, made in concrete vats, and matured in cask. The reputation of the wine is that it needs long maturing before the strong, tough character mellows to become attractive to drink, but I found the 1979 already attractive when five years old, with a decided *goût de terroir* still, but otherwise rather lacking personality, owing, perhaps, to the high yields of the year. It will be interesting to see what the new management produces.

CHÂTEAU GRANDIS
Cru Bourgeois 1932. Owner: GHF du Château Grandis (François Vergez and Paul Figerou). 7 hectares. 2,000 cases. CS 40%, CF 30%, Mer 30%. Other label:
Maurac-Mayor

This is an old property in St Seurin-de-Cadourne, named after a Dutch family that came to Bordeaux in the seventeenth century. The head of the family at the time of the Revolution had the misfortune to be guillotined.

The property was bought by Armand Figerou in 1857, and has belonged to his heirs ever since. I have tasted only one vintage in recent years, the 1970 in 1982. It had the typical solidity and richness of St Seurin, but was also rather fine. The 1985 also has a lot of character and is ripe and powerful. Clearly a wine that repays keeping and is still very traditionally made.

CHÂTEAU HANTEILLAN

Cru Grand Bourgeois. Owner: SARL du Château Hanteillan. 83 hectares. 35,000 cases. CS 48%, Mer 42%, CF 6%, PV and Mal 4%. Second label: Château Larrivaux-Hanteillan

This large vineyard is right on the boundary of the commune of Cissac with St Estèphe, and also just to the south-east of the communal boundary with Vertheuil. In 1972 Maurice Mathieu, at the head of a group of shareholders connected with France's largest construction company, provided a substantial investment to breathe new life into the property. The ruined buildings were transformed into an ultra-modern *cuvier* and a charming and immaculately kept *chai*. The existing 30 hectares of vineyards were gradually replanted, and a further 30 hectares were bought from the adjoining Château Larrivaux, hence the name of the second wine. There is a high proportion of Merlot to suit the rather heavy soils in parts of the vineyard.

Now Maurice Mathieu's daughter, Catherine Blasco, is the administrator. A graphic designer by training, her impact has been considerable, from designing a new label, supervising the smooth running of the property, organizing the commercialization of the wines, to designing the publicity and actually gracing it with her charming presence. The progress which has been made can be judged from the fact that before 1972 Hanteillan was under the same ownership as Château Coutelin-Merville in St Estèphe, whose vineyard it adjoins. Today, despite Coutelin-Merville's superior *appellation*, I have found that it is Hanteillan which is making the more impressive wine. The rich, well-structured 1979 is a serious wine with real breed, and shows both how well the young vineyard was maturing and the careful selection that must have been exercised in a year of high yields. In contrast, I found the 1981 rather slight yet tannic. But the 1982 is excellent and promises a long evolution. This is clearly a *cru* to follow as the vineyard matures.

CHÂTEAU HAUT-MADRAC

Owner: Emile Castéja. 20 hectares. 5,500 cases. CS 70%, Mer 30%

This Castéja property (see Lynch-Moussas) actually adjoins their property at Lynch-Moussas, but is in St Sauveur and not in Pauillac. It was bought by Emile Castéja's father in 1919. The emphasis now is on well-made, light, fresh, fruity wines for early drinking. The wines certainly have charm and do their job very well. Even the 1984 I found pleasingly supple.

CHÂTEAU LA LAGUNE

Troisième Cru Classé. Owner: Société Civile Agricole du Château La Lagune. Administrator: Jean-Michel Ducellier. 55 hectares. 25,000 cases. CS 55%, CF 20%, Mer 20%, PV 5%. Second label: Château Ludon-Pomies-Agassac

The first classified growth, or indeed château of any real importance, to be found when coming from Bordeaux, the very extensive vineyard – which is in a single piece – can be seen on a ridge above the *route des châteaux* on the side towards the river. The château, a small but elegant pavilion on a single storey, dates from about 1715, the earliest example in Médoc of the classical style of architecture that dominated the eighteenth century. It is situated not far from the road, and adjacent to the vineyard.

La Lagune was originally planted as a vineyard in 1724, but its fame dates from the first part of the nineteenth century, although it appeared on Belleyme's map at the end of the eighteenth century. In 1815 it appeared in Lawton's classification among the *quatrièmes crus*, and by the time Charles Cocks wrote in 1846, its position was assured. Later in the century, special mention was made of the wine's longevity.

From being one of the best-known and most sought-after third growths, the vineyard gradually declined in importance until, by the fifties, only about 20 tonneaux were being made and great tracts of the vineyard lay fallow. In 1954 there were only four hectares of vines left, and these were severely frosted in February 1956. Then, in 1958, the property was acquired by Monsieur Georges Brunet, a man of energy and vision, from the south of France. The vineyard was replanted in the space of only two years, and the *chai* was transformed into one of the show-places of the Médoc. It is also a big farm. One interesting feature is that stainless steel pipes carry the new wine directly from the fermentation vats to the new casks in the *chai*, thus saving a great deal of handling.

Unfortunately, the new proprietor did not stay to reap the benefit of his reconstruction. Like many other proprietors, he was tempted by the market conditions in the summer of 1961 to sell extensively *sur souche* (on the vine, that is, before the harvest), and found himself oversold when the vintage proved smaller than had been hoped for. He sold to Monsieur René Chayoux, from Ayala champagne, whose heirs now own it. Ayala continued the work of restoration and investment begun by Georges Brunet, so that today La Lagune is a model property.

In the last twenty years, the reputation of La Lagune has climbed steadily, in spite of the youth of most of the vines. The wine is undoubtedly very well made and, although still rather light in colour and body, has a charming and most individual bouquet allied to great elegance and breed. I had only limited experience of the wine before its rebirth. The 1920 was unfortunately already well past its best by 1962, when I saw it, but the 1921 was a remarkable wine the following year. In England the 1926 was sometimes seen and was, like the 1921, a big, strong wine. Just before the change, Allan Sichel shipped several vintages. I remember particularly the 1950 and the glorious 1953.

Since the reconstruction, the 1961 was a strange wine, typical neither of the year nor of La Lagune. The 1962 was too much of a lightweight, and the 1964 was the first undisputed success. Naturally the wine matured quickly and is soft and mellow. Nevertheless, there is great individuality, some depth, and a really fine flavour. The 1966 was really fine, the 1967 had great charm, while the 1968 was one of the more successful wines of the vintage. If the sixties were years of steady improvement, then the seventies saw the flowering of La Lagune, the fulfilment of work and investment begun by Georges Brunet in 1958. The decade began propitiously with the 1970 and the 1971, and after a beautifully balanced 1975, the 1976 was one of the outstanding successes of the year. The 1977 was above average for the year, and the 1978 is very fine. The 1979 is lighter, has great charm, but there is just the suspicion of over-oaking and somehow the 1980 has proved disappointing. By La Lagune standards, it is still rather mean in its maturity. In the great vintages of the eighties, there is a classically elegant and compact 1981 which should come on stream around 1989–90, a magnificent 1982 which is dense-textured with a many-layered flavour and a great future, one of the finest of all La Lagunes, while the 1983 has a lovely, opulent flavour, stylish and long-flavoured with real depth and breed, a great success. The 1984 was impressive early on with good fruit (there was only one vat of Merlot instead of the usual five). The 1985 and 1986 are another pair of great vintages: with the 1985 one is seduced by the deliciously opulent fruit with its velvety texture and richness, while the 1986 is more tannic, well balanced with richness, and there is the usual elegance holding out the prospect of a fine *vin de garde*. It is interesting to note that 80 per cent new wood was used in the 1986 instead of the usual 100 per cent, and if I have any reservations about this excellent *cru*, it is that the 100 per cent new wood policy can prove rather severe especially in the lighter vintages.

The vineyard has truly come of age, and La Lagune is now one of the most consistently attractive and enjoyable of the leading classified growths in the Médoc, and with its very reasonable pricing policy, the *rapport qualité-prix* is outstanding. An unusual feature of La Lagune today is that it has a woman *régisseur*. When her husband died some years ago, Madame Jeanne Boyrie succeeded him, and proved a great success; in particular, her approach to cleanliness was rigorous – for instance, she always had a roll of absorbent paper at hand to wipe the glasses whenever one tasted from cask, and any dirty glasses disappeared very rapidly afterwards. It was a shock to everyone when she died in October 1986, but the traditions and standards she set should be maintained by the appointment of her daughter, surely the first time this can have happened in Bordeaux.

CHÂTEAU DE LAMARQUE
Cru Grand Bourgeois. Owner: Société Civile Gromaud-d'Evry. Administrator: Roger Gromaud. 47 hectares. 25,000 cases. CS 50%, Mer 25%, CF 20%, PV 5%.
Second label: Réserve du Marquis d'Evry

The name of Lamarque will probably be most familiar to many visitors to the region, as it is the Médoc end of the Blaye ferry. But the Château de Lamarque is of considerable interest as the best-preserved of the medieval fortresses dating from the English period. Although the main defences and part of the chapel date from the eleventh and twelfth centuries, the main structure is fourteenth-century and was built by Pons de Castillon. Both Henry V and the Duke of Gloucester stayed in the castle, and later it was used as the residence of the governors of Guyenne. In the seventeenth century it belonged to the Duc d'Epernon (see under Beychevelle, p. 110), who carried out extensive alterations. In 1841 the château became the property of the Comte de Fumel and passed, via his daughter, to the Marquis d'Evry in 1901. Now Marie-Louise Brunet-d'Evry has married Roger Gromaud and they own the property today. As so often in Bordeaux, the names have changed but the families have not.

Before the First World War, the wines of Lamarque were sold to northern Germany. By the time that Monsieur Roger Gromaud took over the management of the estate in the early 1960s, the vineyard was much diminished and the wine almost forgotten. Now extensive replanting has been undertaken and under the supervision of Professor Peynaud a serious attempt has been made to re-establish the reputation of the wine. Charles Cocks noted in 1846 that the wines of Lamarque are similar to those of Arcins but are more mellow, light and aromatic. Certainly in the seventies I found the wines light and agreeable in good vintages, but rather lacking in personality. But then the 1981 was soft and delicious with definite breed at five years, and the 1983 has been markedly successful, with rich opulent fruit. In cask the 1985 was powerful and pleasantly fruity, if rather strongly marked by new oak, while the first impression of the 1986 was of a solid, powerful, tannic wine, rather lacking charm. This is good, dependable *bourgeois* claret, which has gained in depth as the vineyard has matured. It may lack the finesse of the top *bourgeois crus*, but one feels that the potential of the *cru* is now being fully realized.

CHÂTEAU LAMOTHE-BERGERON

Cru Bourgeois. Owner: Société Civile Grand-Puy-Ducasse. 60 hectares. 25,000 cases. CS 66%, Mer 30%, CF 4%

This good *cru* at Cussac was bought as yet another addition to the Mestrezat-Merlaut empire in 1978. The word Lamothe – and a number of Bordeaux châteaux use this name – indicates a property on a "*motte*" (a piece of high ground), which in the Médoc can be a very relative term! Bergeron was the name of an owner of the last century. I have noted a well-made, attractive 1979, a 1981 with firmness and structure but good fruit and definite quality, and a deliciously plummy, rich 1982. These are well-made and consistently reliable wines, sold at very reasonable prices.

CHÂTEAU LAMOTHE-CISSAC

Owner: Société Civile du Château Lamothe. Administrator: G. Fabre. 47 hectares. 22,000 cases. CS 70%, Mer 26%, CF 2%, PV 2%

This Lamothe is of course in Cissac. It is an old property, and Roman pottery has been found in the soil. In the seventeenth century, it was a *maison noble*. But by the time the Fabre family came here in 1964, there was not a vine left, and the buildings were in a dilapidated state. The turreted château dates only from 1912. Now there is a modern *cuvier* with stainless steel vats and a new *chai* as well as an underground cellar. Casks are used for the maturation with 20 per cent new oak each year. Eric Fabre, the son of Gabriel Fabre, is now married to Hélène Vialard of Château Cissac and La Tour-Mirail, so local ties are close. The wines are sold direct and not through the Bordeaux trade. Stylish, full-flavoured, fruity wines are being made, especially now the vineyard is maturing. The 1981 is probably the first of a line of steadily improving wines. I was impressed by the style and solidity of the 1983 in the context of the year, while the 1985 in cask was opulent, rich and solid, promising a delicious bottle.

CHÂTEAU LANESSAN

Cru Bourgeois Supérieur. Owner: Bouteiller family. Administrator: Hubert Bouteiller. 40 hectares. 12,000 cases. CS 75%, Mer 20%, CF and PV 5%

This must surely be one of the best growths in the Médoc not to be classified in 1855. And the strange thing is that its excellence is no recent feature. Nineteenth-century editions of Cocks & Féret sing its praises and speak of its wines as above their class, and the old vintages of Lanessan that I have drunk have all been superb. The pedigree of the *cru* may be judged from the fact that it featured on the Belleyme map at the end of the eighteenth century, and was listed as a *quatrième cru* by Lawton in 1815, when under the name Duboscq. But unfortunately, Louis Delbos, the proprietor in 1855, refused to submit samples of his wines for consideration for the famous classification, which he regarded as bureaucratic nonsense, a piece of high-handedness that has cost Lanessan dear.

The property lies close to the border with St Julien and extends back almost to St Laurent. The château itself is an elaborate Victorian pile lying on high ground and is approached by a road going inland from the *route des châteaux*, just before one reaches Beychevelle. More interesting are the fine, extensive *chais* and the old stables which house a comprehensive and impressive collection of carriages and harnesses which may be viewed upon request. Effectively Lanessan has belonged to only two families since 1310, an extraordinary record. From its sale to the widow of Henry de Lanessan in 1310, it passed to her heirs until 1793 when it was acquired by Jean Delbos, a Bordeaux *négociant*. In 1907 a Delbos daughter married Etienne Bouteiller, the grandfather of Hubert and Bertrand Bouteiller, today's owners. Until recently Bertrand managed the family's other principal *cru*, Pichon-Baron, sold in 1987, but he is still administrator of Palmer, where the Bouteillers are shareholders through their Mahler-Besse connections.

Some of the old vintages of Lanessan are remarkable. I have had the 1916, the 1920, which was one of the best-preserved 1920s I have seen, the 1933, which is rather firmer than most wines of that year, and the 1934, which was outstanding and reminded me strongly of a St Julien of the Gruaud-Larose type. Since the war, the 1947 was outstandingly fine for the year, with a bouquet of great power and ripeness; the 1952 was beautifully balanced and has given much more pleasure than most wines of its year; the 1953 was surprisingly big and full for the year; the 1955 I found rather unsympathetic; the 1959 was fine; the 1960 was one of the most attractive and sound wines of the year; the 1961 was worthy of its year; the 1962 was fine and distinctive if a little on the dry side; and the 1964 was rather light and matured quickly, but was most attractive. More recently, the 1981, 1982, 1983, 1986, 1988 and 1989 were all fine examples of these vintages, and in lesser years even the 1977 was good, and an elegant 1980 was made.

This is a wine, then, of strong individuality, having a very marked bouquet, great fruit and richness in some years, a tendency to firmness at first, with rich finesse and breed. When these are allied to considerable consistency, it is easy to see that Lanessan deserves its reputation in Bordeaux and ought, indeed, to be even better known. It was classified as a *grand bourgeois exceptionnel* in 1966, but has since withdrawn from the Syndicat.

CHÂTEAU LAROSE-TRINTAUDON

Cru Grand Bourgeois. Owner: Assurances Générales de France. Administrator: Elisée Forner. 172 hectares. 80,000 cases. CS 60%, CF 20%, Mer 20%

On my early visits to the Médoc I was always intrigued to see, when driving from St Laurent to Pauillac, this vast, nineteenth-century mansion standing in a completely derelict condition amidst ruined *chais* and fallow vineyards. The scene has now been transformed and desolation banished. The large plateau on either side of the road was replanted after the Forner family bought the property, which had lain fallow for forty years, in 1965, and the property incorporates the former vineyards of Larose-Perganson, making it the largest vineyard in Médoc.

All this was the work of the enterprising Forner family, Spaniards who now also own Camensac. Mechanical harvesting is used, an ideal site for this new technology. However, all the wine is matured in casks, of which 30 per cent are new each year – quite a feat. The object has been to produce a very large quantity of quickly maturing, pleasant, easy-to-drink claret, and they certainly seem to be succeeding in this. I have tasted the 1972, unusually acceptable for the year, the 1973, typical of the merits of the vintage, and the 1976. All were well-made, light-textured and attractively fruity. With reasonable prices, it is not surprising that they are finding a ready market in a number of countries. More recently, I have noted an untypically aggressive 1979, but a good, if rather one-dimensional, 1982 and an exceptionally good 1983 with really opulent fruit and tannins.

Just after the 1986 vintage, the property was sold to Assurances Générales de France, one of a number of notable purchases made by financial institutions in recent years. However, Elisée Forner will continue to manage the property, with his nephew, Henri, in charge of sales and marketing.

CHÂTEAU LESTAGE-SIMON

Cru Bourgeois. Owner: Charles Simon. 32 hectares. 16,600 cases. Mer 68%, CS 22%, CF 10%

The Simon family have tended the vines of Lestage for several generations, but it was only in 1972 that the present owner, Charles Simon, added the family name which serves to distinguish it from others of the same name. The château, *cuvier* and *chai* lie just to the west of St Seurin-de-Cadourne. Part of the vineyard adjoins it on chalky/clay soil – hence the high proportion of Merlot – and part is on gravelly soil near the river. A good proportion of new oak is used each year in the maturation.

I was once given a bottle of the 1929 by Charles Simon's father, and it was splendid when over thirty years old. Today the wines enjoy a fine reputation. They are robust and solid with plenty of fruit and suppleness, and are to be found in many of the best restaurants in France. The 1978, 1981, 1982, 1983 and 1985 are all especially successful.

CHÂTEAU LIVERSAN

Cru Grand Bourgeois. Owner: Prince Guy de Polignac. 48 hectares. 20,000 cases. CS 49%, Mer 38%, CF 10%, PV 3%

This very good estate has experienced a complete transformation since it was acquired in 1983 by the de Polignacs, formerly the principal share-holders in Champagne Pommery. They rebuilt the *cuvier* and installed stainless steel vats, as well as modernizing the *chai* and completely restoring and redecorating the charming château. Here the Prince and Princesse Guy de Polignac made their home, together with one of their sons, Henri-Melchior, who actually manages the property. Sadly, the Princesse died in 1987, and will be much missed as a charming and interesting hostess. Professor Pascal Ribereau-Guyon oversees the vinification.

The vineyard lies between the village of St Sauveur, whose leading *cru* this is, and Pauillac. The de Polignacs were fortunate to inherit a vineyard which was mature and in reasonable order, with 50 per cent of the vines over twenty-five years old, "a situation rare enough to be pointed out", as Professor Peynaud remarked. Now all the wine is matured in cask with a proportion of new oak. The previous owners, Louis Labeunie (1955–71) and Asche von Campe (1971–83), a German agricultural engineer, had rebuilt the vineyard and made wines which gave at least a glimpse of the vineyard's potential. I remember especially a good 1962, while under the von Campe regime some *médailles* were awarded.

Although the 1983 was the first vintage for the de Polignacs, it was made under difficult conditions and must be regarded as an interim effort, with good Cabernet Sauvignon characteristics, firm and quite tannic. It is a shade austere and a slow developer. The 1985 has lovely, scented fruit and is opulent and elegant, with a fine flavour combining richness, finesse and considerable charm. In 1986 only 65 per cent of the crop went into the final *assemblage*, and only 26 per cent was Merlot. The result is a wine of concentrated extract, tannin and fruit with fine flavour, length and finesse. These two wines certainly show the potential of this *cru* to produce powerful, long-lasting wines of real style which can bear comparison with some of the best of the *crus* from the inland communes in northern and central Médoc. The change in style which has now taken place at Liversan is eloquently expressed in the new label bearing the de Polignac crest.

CHÂTEAU MAGNOL

Cru Bourgeois. Owners: Barton and Guestier. 17 hectares. 6,250 cases. CS 75%, Mer 25%

The headquarters of Barton and Guestier, the old Anglo-French *négociant* house now a Seagram subsidiary, is now at Château Dehez in Blanquefort close to Bordeaux. In 1979 they bought the vineyard of Magnol, whose name derives from "magnolia". Twelve hectares had been planted and cultivated for the previous thirty years, and the new owners planted a further five hectares, which were first used for the 1985 vintage. Vinification is temperature-controlled at under 30°C in stainless steel vats, and then the wine is matured for twelve months in two-year-old casks. These are rich, full-flavoured, supple wines for enjoying when youthful, and are carefully and consistently well made.

CHÂTEAU MALESCASSE

Cru Bourgeois. Owner: SCI Château Malescasse. Administrator: Alfred Tesseron. 32 hectares. 16,000 cases. CS 70%, Mer 20%, CF 10%

Like so many good *crus* outside the great village *appellations* of the Médoc, this property suffered greatly during the years of recession. When an Anglo-American financial group bought it in 1970, only four hectares of vines were left, whereas at its zenith in the last century, 100 tonneaux was a normal crop. The charming high-roofed château was built in 1824, and the vineyard incorporates the highest gravelly ridges in the commune of Lamarque, which are also some of the best between Margaux and St Julien. In 1978 Guy Tesseron (see Pontet-Canet and Lafon-Rochet) bought the property. The work of replanting was already well in hand, but further work remained to be done on the *chai* and roofing. The replanting of the vineyard is not due to be finished until 1992 by which time there will be 40 hectares under vine.

Casks from Pontet-Canet and Lafon-Rochet are used for the

maturation. The first vintage I tasted was also the first one for which the Tesserons were wholly responsible: 1979. It was an impressive wine at five years of age, with light-textured fruit and tannin, and distinct breed and style. I found the 1981 rather coarse-grained but solid, still needing time after five years. I have not tasted the 1982 or 1983, but the 1985 showed a distinct advance when tasted in cask, with its stylish and harmonious balance of fruit and tannins, while the 1986 promised to be every bit as good: very balanced for the year with clean, rich fruit and a long, firm finish. The quality and style of these wines are already impressive for a vineyard which is still not mature and, at the very modest prices asked, this must be one of the best current buys in the *appellation*.

CHÂTEAU DE MALLERET

Cru Grand Bourgeois. Owner: Société Civile du Château de Malleret (Marquis du Vivier). 59 hectares, 25,000 cases. CS 70%, Mer 15%, CF 10%, PV 5%. Second label: Château Lemoine-Nexon

This is another château near Bordeaux where horses are even more important than the wine (see du Taillan). The total estate covers about 400 hectares in the communes of Pian-Médoc, Ludon and Parempuyre, and both racehorses and hunters are bred here. One of them, La Lagune, won the Oaks in 1968. There is a spacious late eighteenth-century mansion. The estate has belonged to the du Vivier family since 1827, but in 1931, at the height of the slump, the vines were pulled up and the present vineyard was replanted only when the present owner, Comte Bertrand du Vivier, took charge in 1958.

This is a very well-run property. The vinification is meticulously done in stainless steel and the ageing is in cask, with some 20 per cent new wood. The light soils of this part of the southern Médoc suit the Cabernet Sauvignon, so that even in a year such as 1980, when there was less Merlot than usual, the wine seemed fruity, elegant and easy to drink. At one place the vineyard adjoins that of La Lagune. I have found the wines to be scented and elegant, very fruity in flavour, with good length and a seductive charm. Attractive wines are consistently made, not only in the best vintages, but in lesser ones such as 1980 and 1984. This is good early-drinking claret of character sold at very reasonable prices.

CHÂTEAU LE MEYNIEU

Cru Grand Bourgeois. Owner: Jacques Pédro. 14 hectares. 5,000 cases. CS 70%, Mer 30%

In 1962, when Jacques Pédro bought this old property in Vertheuil, there was only one hectare of vineyard left, a situation echoed all over the back-woods of the Médoc, and eloquent testimony to the long hard years of depression and stagnation which first gripped the region at the end of the twenties. At the same time he bought Lavillotte in neighbouring St Estèphe, and developed the *chai* and *cuvier* here to cope with the produc-tion and maturation of both properties, and later for Domaine de Ronceray as well. He is now mayor of Vertheuil and one of the most respected of the new generation of wine-makers. Of *pied-noir* origins, he arrived straight out of Bordeaux University where he gained a degree in natural sciences. The feel you get when you arrive at Le Meynieu is of a large working farm. An underground cellar has been constructed to keep the large bottled stocks that are held here. The wine is vinified in concrete vats and matured in cask. Jacques Pédro has his own ideas about handling wine. He believes in relatively high temperatures for his fer-mentations, around 32° to 33°C, and does not filter his wines before bottling.

If the wine does not rise to the heights of Lavillotte, it is nevertheless very good, and probably the best in Vertheuil today. The 1985 showed light easy fruit on the nose, and was very supple and attractive at this early stage, while the 1986 in cask was rich and scented on the nose and had a rich, unctuous flavour and a solid, distinctive *terroir* character behind – a very promising and harmonious wine. With less power than Lavillotte, it develops quite quickly in bottle, yet keeps well.

LA PAROISSE

130 hectares. 6,000 hectolitres (of which some 16,000 cases are sold in bottle). CS 50%, Mer 50%

There are a number of *caves coopératives* in Haut-Médoc, all in the large northern sector. Of these, the most important, in terms of its reputation, is La Paroisse at St Seurin-de-Cadourne.

This *coopérative* was founded in 1935 and has some sixty members. It is now well equipped with ninety-eight *cuves* – five times as many as in 1946. Its excellent wines, which are fleshy, solid and fruity, lie at the heart of many a good generic blend, while its bottled wines are of the quality of a decent *cru bourgeois*. The following wines are sold under the names of their respective *crus*: Château Quimper, Domaine du Haut et de Brion, Château La Tralle, Domaine de Villa, and Château Maurac.

CHÂTEAU PEYRABON

Cru Grand Bourgeois. Owner: J. Babeau. 53 hectares. Red: 20,500 cases. CS 50%, Mer 27%, CF 23%

This is one of several large properties in St Sauveur, and has come to prominence since the Babeau family bought it in 1958. Prior to that the wine had been sold only privately and not through the Bordeaux trade, so was virtually unknown. The attractive château, with its distinctive twin towers, boasts a music room in which Queen Victoria attended a concert.

Jacques Babeau has run the property since 1976, and in 1978 extended the vineyard by acquiring some unplanted land from Liversan. The wine is fermented in concrete vats and matured in casks of which 25 per cent are new. The wines are supple and quite rich, with that touch of *terroir* at the finish often found in this part of the northern Médoc, and have a good reputation.

CHÂTEAU PONTOISE-CABARRUS

Cru Bourgeois. Owner: SICA de Haut-Médoc. Administrator: F. Tereygeol. 24 hectares. 15,000 cases. CS 60%, Mer 30%, CF 6%, PV 4%

It seems almost bizarre today to connect this modest, sober *cru bourgeois* in St Seurin-de-Cadourne with the high drama of the French Revolution. The Cabarrus family have owned more illustrious châteaux in their time – Lagrange, as well as neighbouring Coufran – but only here is their name preserved. During the fateful days of the Terror in Bordeaux, Thereza Cabarrus, daughter of the Comte de Cabarrus, played a prominent part and saved many lives in her role as mistress of Tallien. Later she was a witness at the marriage of Napoleon and Josephine (see Didier Ters's Haut-Médoc book, quoting Roger Galy, for a lively account of her colourful career). When Emile Tereygeol bought the property in 1960, his was only the third family to own it in the last two hundred years. Then only seven hectares were planted. Since then he, and now his son François, an INAO technical inspector until 1981, have slowly replanted and added to their property. The family are Corrézien in origin, via Morocco.

This is carefully made, sound, solid, strong-flavoured wine that needs time to show its worth.

CHÂTEAU PUY-CASTÉRA

Cru Bourgeois. Owner: Henri Marès. 25 hectares. 10,800 cases. CS 60%, Mer 30%, CF 8%, Mal 2%

This is another story of a property brought back to life. When Henri Marès bought this *cru* in 1973, most of the land had returned to sheep and cattle grazing, and the buildings were in a ruinous condition. By 1974 there were 12 hectares planted, 18 by 1975, and the objective of 25 hectares was reached in 1980. Bertrand de Rozières from Château Sestignan took charge of the wine-making. The name comes from "Puy", the old French word for "*haut*" and "Castéra" from the Latin "*castrum*": thus, a high camp, the site of a Roman military encampment.

The first vintage I tasted was the 1979, made from very young vines. It was light, but with pleasantly balanced fruit and tannins. The 1985 was much fuller, with richness, fruit and good tannins at the finish. This well-sited vineyard, close to St Estèphe and Lafon-Rochet, is making very steady progress and as the vineyard matures can only improve. A wine with a future.

CHÂTEAU LA RAMAGE-LA-BATISSE

Cru Bourgeois. Owner: Société Civile du Château La Ramage-la-Batisse. 52 hectares. 25,000 cases. CS 60%, Mer 40%. Alternative label: Château Tourteran. Second label: Château Dutellier

New *crus* were not only created in the eighteenth century. This is a new *cru* created entirely since 1961. Originally Francis Monnoyeur was advised by his doctor to drink Bordeaux wines for his health and began by buying just four hectares of vines. Once started there was no stopping. Piece by piece, by patient negotiation with many small growers, the present substantial domain was created. The first to be bought was Ramage, then La Batisse, then Tourteran and Dutellier. The same wine is sold under both the Ramage-la-Batisse and Tourteran labels, with Dutellier being the second *marque*.

In recent years this wine has had a great success in England, especially with the 1978 and 1979 vintages. But then 1981 had a disappointingly bitter after-taste. The 1983 was light and aged quickly, but was very fruity and attractive for early drinking. The 1984 is also most attractive with a beguiling smell of violets. This is good commercial *bourgeois* claret, early-maturing and easy to drink.

CHÂTEAU DU RETOUT

Cru Bourgeois 1932. Owner: Gérard Kopp. 25 hectares. 10,800 cases. CS 60%, Mer 20%, CF 10%, PV 7%, Mal 3%. Alternative labels: Châteaux-La Tour-du-Moulin and Lalande-Sourbet (exclusivity of Schröder and Schÿler)

This vineyard in Cussac contains an old mill tower which dates from 1395 and was used as a watchtower against the incursions of British ships up the Gironde during the Seven Years War (1756–63). Gérard Kopp bought the property in 1963 and restored the vineyard and the buildings. Unusually all the five principal grape varieties are planted here. When I tasted the 1984 (under the La Tour-du-Moulin label) blind, I was pleasantly surprised to find it came from this vintage. It was better than a number of 1983s! This is well-made, serious wine sold at very reasonable prices.

CHÂTEAU REYSSON

Cru Bourgeois. Owner: Mercian Corporation. Administrator: Jean-Pierre Angliviel de la Beaumelle. 66 hectares. 24,000 cases. CS 56%, Mer 44%. Second label: Château de l'Abbaye. 12,000 cases

Bought by the Mestrezat Group in 1972 when there was much to do but now the installations have been restored and modernized and the vine-yard enlarged. In 1988 they sold to the Japanese Mercian Corporation, part of the Ajimoto Group, but run the property on their behalf. The 1982 is full and fruity with a pleasing plumpness and a touch of style and breed. It is already suitable for drinking. This is good, commercial, *bourgeois* claret which offers value for money and does not need long ageing before being enjoyable.

CHEVALIERS DU ROI SOLEIL

Owners: SICA des Viticulteurs de Fort-Médoc (President: Demes Fedieu). 45 hectares. 27,500 cases. CS 50%, Mer 40%, CF 10%. Other labels: Fort-Médoc, Château Les Capérans, Château Eglise Vieille, Château les Jacquets, Château Le Neurin

When one drives north from Lamarque towards Cussac, the flat landscape is suddenly interrupted on the left-hand side by a surprisingly ultra-modern and very un-Médocain group of buildings. It is only the legend "SICA Viticulteurs" that assures one that this is indeed a wine establishment.

This is an unusual collaboration between small growers and a *négociant*. In 1966 a group of growers decided to pool their efforts to improve their quality and marketing effectiveness. In 1972 they formed the SICA in collaboration with Ginestet and the present *chai* was constructed. The first vintage of the new enterprise was 1973, and the *marque* Fort-Médoc, exclusively distributed by Ginestet, was created. The new *marque*, Chevaliers du Roi Soleil, came in 1981. Today there are twenty-two members, predominantly from Cussac but including growers from St Laurent, Lamarque and, rather surprisingly, from Blanquefort. The result is something on a smaller, more personal level than a *coopérative*, producing good, sound claret with the personality of its origins.

CHÂTEAU SÉNÉJAC
Cru Bourgeois Supérieur 1932. Owner: Charles de Guigné. 18 hectares. 7,500 cases. CS 40%, Mer 30%, CF 24%, PV 6%

The first time I visited Sénéjac, I made the mistake of going at night. It is not the easiest place to find in daytime; the dark gives a fresh dimension to the navigation problems for a property lost among the woods between Pian and the main Lesparre road. The imposing gateway dates from an earlier epoch than the actual château, and a vaguely "Sleeping Beauty" other-timeliness hangs over the whole place. In fact the de Guigné family have been largely absentee landlords since first acquiring the property in 1860. This perhaps explains why they did not bother to change their entry in Cocks & Féret for over 100 years. But in 1973 Comte Charles de Guigné, born in San Francisco where his family had settled, decided to have a look at the family property in the backwoods of the Médoc, and has made his home there ever since.

If this gives the impression that everything has become super-modern at Sénéjac, nothing could be further from the truth. Rather, Charles de Guigné has become a traditional Médocain. His most radical move has been a recent one: to bring in as *maître de chai* a New Zealander, Jenny

Bailey. Since her arrival in 1983, she has made quite an impression in the area and has certainly helped to improve standards.

The wines themselves could not be more different from those produced at the other important *cru* of Pian, Château de Malleret. They are deep-coloured and perfumed, but classically austere and tannic – Cabernet Sauvignon-styled wines. They last well, as some of the older vintages, such as the 1945, show, and it is easy to see why they have found favour among many traditional English wine merchants. The 1985, tasted in cask, was actually just over one-third Merlot, the rest being the two Cabernets, with a morsel of Petit Verdot for good measure. It was rotated between vat and cask. There was a lovely ripe, full, rich flavour, rather fine-textured and with a lot of finesse. Certainly it captured all the charms of the year, and seemed to show that Jenny Bailey has got the hang of the Médoc. This *cru* is a good example of some of the idiosyncrasies which go to make the Médoc such a fascinating place.

CHÂTEAU SOCIANDO-MALLET

Cru Grand Bourgeois. Owner: Jean Gautreau. 30 hectares. 18,500 cases. CS 60%, Mer 30%, CF 10%. Second label: Château Lartigue-de-Brochon

In 1969 Jean Gautreau, a *négociant* from Lesparre, bought a vineyard with only five hectares in production and dilapidated buildings. Today, twenty years later, this is one of the most reputed and sought-after wines among the *crus bourgeois* of the Médoc – no mean achievement. But this is no new upstart. The first reference to the property goes back to 1633, when a document speaks of the "*nobles terres*" belonging to Sièvre Sociando at St Seurin-de-Cadourne. In about 1850 the estate was bought by Madame Mallet. The second English edition of Cocks & Féret, of 1883, reported that having already been classified as one of the two leading *crus* of St Seurin (the other being Verdignan), it had, since its acquisition by Léon Simon in 1878, improved still further. It was also noted that the vineyard was the best situated in the commune. This seems to have been the high-water mark of the château's fortunes. Then frequent changes of ownership and the years of depression prevented any growth of the reputation of the *cru*, so that by the time Jean Gautreau bought it in 1969 it was a forgotten wine.

Of course, everything has been renewed, and there is a completely new *chai*. Unusually, 50 per cent new oak is used for the maturation, and the aim is to produce uncompromising *vin de garde*. To begin with, this policy led to some rather austere, lean wines when the vineyard was still very young. I found this to be true of the 1971, which after fifteen years was still parched by wood and unattractively austere and one-dimensional. But in the same year, 1986, I tasted a range of recent vintages which told a very different story. The 1978 was scented and elegant, its lovely flavour just had a touch of tannin still at the finish, a harmonious wine with a fine future ahead of it. The 1980 is really a great success here, complex and spicy, surprisingly rich and solid for the year. By 1989 the 1981 was mature, full-flavoured and delicious, although still very youthful and tannic. The 1982 is a classic, its scented, still youthful aromas leading to a lovely concentrated richness, tightly knit and tannic but harmonious – a *vin de garde* of real class. The 1983 is spicy and scented on the nose, with lovely juicy richness; an excellent 1983 without a hint of dilution. The 1984 is impressive for the vintage, with its frank Cabernet Sauvignon aroma and rich, elegant flavour. The 1985 has finely balanced fruit and tannins combining concentration with finesse, needing more time than many 1985s. The 1988 is also marvellously concentrated and dense-flavoured.

The recent record is undeniably impressive. As the vineyard matures, so the wines are filling out and have more depth and dimension. Because of the way it is made and handled, it does not always do well when compared with other *crus bourgeois* at an early stage, but the wines are now maturing impressively. It has certainly overtaken the other *crus* in the commune and can compete with the leading *crus exceptionnels*. But today, even higher claims are being made for it. Certainly no *cru* north of St Estèphe has ever before aspired to *cru classé* status, and I feel that such claims, after such a comparatively short time, may be premature. In another decade, it might be a different story.

CHÂTEAU SOUDARS

Cru Bourgeois. Owner: Eric Miailhe. 15 hectares. 10,000 cases. CS 60%, Mer 40%

You will search the old Cocks & Féret in vain for this *cru*, because it was entirely the creation of Eric Miailhe in 1973. The vineyard lies north of Verdignan near the river and opposite Coufran, properties bought by his father Jean and grandfather Louis. The soil is chalky/clay, and so stony that previous generations have been discouraged from exploiting it. Eric Miailhe cleared 2,500 tons of stones before planting his vineyard!

The wines are made with the same care as at the other Miailhe properties in St Seurin, and matured in cask, including some new oak. The vineyard of course is still very young and the first really fine vintage for me was 1982. The 1983 was attractive but needed drinking by the time it was four years old. The 1985 and 1986 are much better, richer and more solid, with a definite style and breed about them. This is a good new *cru bourgeois* just coming into its own.

CHÂTEAU DU TAILLAN

Cru Grand Bourgeois. Owner: Henri-François Cruse. 20 hectares. 8,000 cases. CS 55%, Mer 40%, CF 5%. White wine: Château La Dame-Blanche. 5 hectares. 2,500 cases. Sauv 66.7%, Colombard 33.3%

Physically this is the first château in the Médoc, only 12 kilometres from Bordeaux. The château itself dates from the early eighteenth century and has an attractive classical façade. It has always amused me that in successive editions of Cocks & Féret, one side of the château was used to illustrate the du Taillan entry, and the other to grace the La Dame-Blanche entry, this being the name for the white wine produced at the property. It is classified as a historic monument, as is the 300-year-old *chai*, the only one in Médoc thus classified. The estate has belonged to the Cruse family since 1806 when it was bought by Henri Cruse; today his grandson, Henri-François Cruse, is the owner. On the large estate of 150 hectares, more land is actually devoted to the breeding of fine horses than to the raising of wine.

The wine is light and supple, easy to drink and without much tannin. Note the presence of one-third Colombard in the white wine, giving it a much more obvious flowery fruit than is usually to be found in a Bordeaux Blanc.

CHÂTEAU LA TOUR-CARNET

Quatrième Cru Classé. Owner: Marie-Claire Pèlegrin. 31 hectares. 14,000 cases. CS 33%, Mer 33%, CF 33%, PV 1%

This growth enjoyed a considerable reputation in the nineteenth century. It is mentioned in Cocks's classification of 1846, the only growth of St Laurent in his list. The property has a long history and takes its name from Jean Caranet, or Carnet, who was one of the heirs of Jean de Foix when he died in 1485. It was Jean de Foix who seems to have built the actual tower which is now part of the name. In 1774 it was acquired by Henri de Luetkens, a Swede, and this family owned it at the time of the classification. It appears in both Claude Masse's map at the beginning of the eighteenth century and Belleyme's at the close of the century. It is on Thomas Jefferson's list in 1787 and Lawton's classification of 1815. It passed through a number of hands, including those of Fernand Ginestet in the twenties, until by the fifties it was an almost forgotten growth and production had fallen to a very low level. In 1962 it was acquired by Louis Lipschitz, who reconstructed the vineyard and lavished much time and effort in re-establishing its reputation. Since his death the property has been run by his daughter and her husband, who have continued the long work of improvements, the most recent being a new *cuvier*.

The wine now being produced is highly coloured and with a rather crude *goût de terroir* flavour. Its vivid, extrovert character requires a certain amount of ageing. In recent vintages I have found a rather tough, minerally flavour and a tendency to dryness at the finish. The 1976 was attractive, but the more recent vintages seem disappointing, certainly in their youth. A number of unclassified growths are producing better results than this.

CHÂTEAU LA TOUR-DU-HAUT-MOULIN
Cru Grand Bourgeois. Owner: Laurent Poitou. 32 hectares. 12,000 cases. CS and CF 50%, Mer 45%, PV 5%

The label of La Tour-du-Haut-Moulin gives the idea of a very simple *cru*, but really the only simple or ordinary thing here is the modest house which it features. The vineyards, which have been steadily extended since 1968, lie beside those of Beaumont on some of the best gravelly ridges of Cussac, close to the river. Laurent Poitou is the fifth generation of his family to make wine in Cussac, and until recently he managed a number of other properties as well. His son has now passed through the viticultural school at La Tour-Blanche, so the succession is assured.

An unusual feature of the vinification here is that the different *cépages* are mixed in the vinification *cuves*, rather than being kept separate, as is normal. Twenty-five per cent new oak is used for the maturation in cask. The wines here are in marked contrast to those of neighbouring

Beaumont; of exceptional colour, rich in extract, they are tannic and powerful but well balanced, wines of real character which with age develop undoubted breed. I remember being very struck by them when I first tasted them in the sixties, and had a particular affection for the 1966. More recently, the 1981 was still rather tough and powerful, with a certain minerally character, when five years old. The 1982 is a massive wine, with great richness and fat covering considerable tannin, yet the breed showed through at an early stage, while the 1983 has real opulence for the year with plenty of structure behind, a wine of decided class which is now drinkable. Both the 1985 and the 1986 in cask promised fine things. Today the wines of La Tour-du-Haut-Moulin are second only to those of Lanessan in Cussac, and as such are exceptional value, with a deservedly growing reputation as they become more widely known.

CHÂTEAU LA TOUR-DU-MIRAIL

Cru Bourgeois 1931. Owners: Hélène and Danielle Vialard. 18 hectares. 9,000 cases. CS 70%, Mer 25%, PV 5%

The vineyard lies on the excellent gravelly plateau to the east of the village of Cissac, and is contiguous with those of Cissac and du Breuil. Since 1970 it has belonged to the daughters of Louis Vialard of neighbouring Château Cissac, but the wines are kept quite separate. Vinification is in stainless steel, and the wines are matured in cask. They have a well-projected and perfumed bouquet and plenty of flavour, and are light in body, with a certain Cabernet Sauvignon "edge" to them, despite the fact that there is slightly less Cabernet in the vineyard than at Cissac. In spite of their firmness, I have found that in light years, such as 1973 and 1980, it is advisable to drink them young, before the fruit fades, while some good vintages, such as 1981, seem too skeletal and tough. The 1985 has more fruit. At present the wines are not as good as those of Cissac and lack style and charm.

CHÂTEAU VERDIGNAN

Cru Grand Bourgeois. Owner: Société Civile du Château Verdignan. Administrator: Jean Miailhe. 47 hectares. 30,000 cases. CS 55%, Mer 40%, CF 5%. Second label: Château Plantey-de-la-Croix

Just as one drives out of St Seurin-de-Cadourne northwards towards the Bas-Médoc, as I did frequently when I was working at nearby Château

Loudenne, the turreted Château Verdignan provides a distinctive landmark. In those days it belonged to a Bordeaux *courtier*, and whenever a sample made its appearance in the tasting-room, I found it tough and rustic in character. Then, in 1972, Jean Miailhe and Jacques Merlaut bought it, and in 1976 Jacques Merlaut sold his share to the Miailhes when he had the chance to buy Chasse-Spleen.

The charming château, dating from the eighteenth and early nineteenth centuries, owes its rather lopsided appearance to a fire in the last century which destroyed nearly half the building. All the nineteenth-century editions of Cocks & Féret listed Verdignan as the leading *cru* of St Seurin and its vineyard is well placed on gravelly ridges overlooking the river, just to the north of those of Bel-Orme and Sociando-Mallet. Jean Miailhe's son Eric has been responsible for the wine-making here since 1973, as he is at the family's two neighbouring properties of Coufran and Soudars. The wine is fermented in stainless steel vats and matured in casks, of which 25 per cent are new oak each year. Unlike Coufran, the *encépagement* is more traditionally Médocain here, with pride of place going to the Cabernet Sauvignon.

The improvement under the Miailhe regime has been very marked. The wines are strong-flavoured and quite tannic but with much more fruit than in the past. I have noted good examples in 1978, 1982, 1985 and 1986. The 1981 is tannic and dry but in the 1983, after an uncertain start, the structure and fruit have become more harmonious. The 1984 is promising and has more fruit than the others. At its best, Verdignan now produces wines with a classic Médoc flavour, and if it has yielded pride of place in St Seurin to Sociando-Mallet, it is certainly much better in the eighties than it was in the sixties, and is more often the best of the three Miailhe *crus* than previously.

CHÂTEAU DE VILLEGEORGE

Cru Bourgeois Supérieur Exceptionnel 1932. Owner: Lucien Lurton. 12 hectares. 2,700 cases. Mer 60%, CS 30%, CF 10%

This growth was classified as one of the six *crus exceptionnels* in 1932, and in 1966 it was placed with the *grands bourgeois exceptionnels*, but when Lucien Lurton bought it in 1973, he took it out of the Syndicat, so it did not feature in the 1978 list. For many years it has been regarded as the leading growth of Avensan. When the soil was analysed at the time the property was bought by Lucien Lurton (see Brane-Cantenac and Durfort-Vivens), it was shown to have deep gravel, almost identical to that in nearby Margaux. For this reason, much of the surrounding countryside has been despoiled by gravel pits. Lucien Lurton is now engaged in a battle to save the countryside from further ravage. I always believed that the wine more closely resembled a Moulis, with its deep colour and forthright character. Certainly, it is quite unlike its closest Margaux neighbour, Paveil-de-Luze. If comparisons are to be made with the Margaux of Soussans, La Tour-de-Mons is a more apt one. The vineyard itself is very prone to frost, so yields are very irregular.

Although, as we shall see, very good wines were made in the sixties, Villegeorge was an expensive property to run because it was frosted so often. The purchase by Lucien Lurton in 1973, therefore, was a welcome fillip for this fine old *cru*. He bought only the vineyards and the *chai*, not the château, which still appears on the very distinctive black and gold label. Fermentation is now in stainless steel, and the wine is matured in cask, with 25 per cent new wood.

In character the wines are deep-coloured, their bouquet is markedly fruity and perfumed, and they have an assertive, powerful flavour. I first made their acquaintance through the marvellous vintages of 1959 and 1961; the latter was still remarkable when twenty-five years old. Good wines were also made in 1962, 1964 – above average for the year – and 1966. Recent successes include an attractive vibrant 1979, while the 1983 has plenty of richness to clothe the aggressive, muscular character of the wine, a definite success. The 1984 is strong-flavoured but well balanced. The 1985 is fruity and flattering but well structured. The 1986 has good ripeness and is very harmonious and attractive – not too tannic. The wines of Villegeorge are certainly as good now as they have ever been, and deserve to be better known.

BAS-MÉDOC

This is the name traditionally given to the northern part of the area. As far as the *appellation* is concerned, it is simply Médoc. But it can be confusing to refer to this region as Médoc without qualification, since the whole of the Haut-Médoc and Médoc together are often loosely referred to as the Médoc. Geographically the area runs from St Yzans and St Germain d'Esteuil in the south all the way up to Soulac, but in practice the vineyards stop at Vensac, between Lesparre and St Vivien. The Belleyme map shows that by the end of the eighteenth century the most extensive vineyards in the region were at St Christoly. Apart from the village names, there are very few property, or "lieux-dits", names which are familiar today, but Landon, Loudenne, St Bonnet, By, La Cardonne, Preuillac and Laujac are all marked.

One has only to turn the pages of an old edition of Cocks & Féret to see how much the picture has changed. Now there are sixteen wine-producing communes; in the 1870s and 1880s there were as many as twenty. The population figures also make interesting reading: a comparison of those published by Cocks & Féret in 1969 with those they published in 1883 shows that in most villages there are hardly more than half the inhabitants that there once were – even the regional centre of Lesparre has 1,200 less. The countryside itself has a very different aspect from that of the Haut-Médoc; generally more low-lying, it is much more remotely rural, with vineyards far less in evidence among the trees and green fields. But the wines themselves are well worth attention. While they generally lack the bouquet and delicacy of the Haut-Médoc, they are robust, full-flavoured wines which keep extremely well and have plenty of character, like the men who make them. This is an area of coopératives today; in the Médoc the coopératives are larger and more important than in the Haut-Médoc, and there is a keen demand from the Bordeaux trade for these sound wines for the generic blends. By far the largest is at Bégadan, which also has members in the neighbouring communes of Valeyrac and Civrac. There are also important coopératives at St Yzans (St Brice), Ordonnac and Potensac (Caves Bellevue) and at Prignac.

Although this has never been a region producing wines of the highest class – so that none of its wines was classified in 1855 – it has always been an area for good bourgeois growths. There is reliable evidence, both from the Gilbey diaries at Loudenne and from contemporary editions of Cocks & Féret, that before the phylloxera, little or no distinction was made between the best Bas-Médoc bourgeois growths and those in the neighbouring communes of the northern Haut-Médoc. I believe that this still accords with the facts. Indeed, the best growths of Bégadan, St Christoly, Ordonnac and Potensac, St Yzans, and St Germain d'Esteuil are often the equal of, and sometimes surpass, the wines from Cissac, Vertheuil and St Seurin-de-Cadourne.

While no properties were classified as *grands bourgeois exceptionnels* in 1966 or 1978, there are nine *grands bourgeois* and twenty *crus bourgeois*. Since then a further eighteen *crus* have joined the Syndicat.

CHÂTEAU DE BY

Cru Bourgeois. Owner: J.-C. Baudon. 10 hectares. 4,500 cases. Mer 40%, CS 30%, PV 20%, CF 10%

This is a modest but interesting *cru*. To start with, the *encépagement* is most unusual, with its high proportion of Petit Verdot. The vineyard is like La Tour-de-By and La Clare, on the ridge of By, between Bégadan and the Gironde. The *cuvier* was changed from the traditional wooden *cuves* to metal lined with enamel in 1972. Monsieur Baudon told me he prefers them to stainless steel because he maintains they are easier to clean. He also believes in the minimum of *chaptalisation*, a refreshingly novel outlook these days. This gives the wines a very clean and deliciously natural character. Normally the wines have no more than 11.5 per cent alcohol by volume although the 1982 had 12 per cent naturally, owing to the exceptional ripeness of the year.

The wines have a very vivid colour, assisted by the Petit Verdot, and there is a charming bouquet reminiscent of geraniums, a characteristic often noted at Loudenne, while the flavour is delicate, light and supple, with definite finesse, full-flavoured sometimes, as in 1982, but never full-bodied. The wines develop fairly quickly. This is a good *cru*, with a real individuality and Médoc breed.

CHÂTEAU LA CARDONNE

Cru Grand Bourgeois. Owner: Guy Charloux. 85 hectares. 35,000 cases. CS 72%, Mer 23%, CF and PV 5%

This is the most important growth of Blaignan. After belonging to the Crédit Foncier de France for over fifty years, it was acquired in 1953 by Monsieur Ludovic Cattan, who in 1973 sold to the Lafite-Rothschilds. They in turn sold in 1990, having greatly improved the property, and wines. The vineyard is well placed on the central gravelly plateau of the Médoc and enjoys a good reputation for its deep-coloured, perfumed, deliciously fruity and frank wines. This is good, straightforward Médoc, easy to enjoy young. The 1985 was already a delight to drink by the beginning of 1988, and these wines are usually at their best when between three and six years of age. Maturation is entirely in vat, with no wood used at all. The wines of the mid-eighties are a little fuller than earlier vintages, as the vineyard, considerably expanded since 1973, matures.

CHÂTEAU CASTÉRA

Cru Bourgeois. Owner: Alexis Lichine & Cie. 45 hectares. 15,000 cases. CS and CF 60%, Mer 40%

One of the more important growths in St Germain d'Esteuil, and indeed in the whole Bas-Médoc, Castéra lies on a series of high, gravelly ridges which are a continuation of the outcrops found in Vertheuil to the south. The property has a very long history, the original château having been besieged by the Black Prince. The de Verthamon family, once proprietors also of Loudenne, owned it for some 200 years until 1901. Since 1973 it has belonged to Alexis Lichine & Cie, the Bordeaux *négociants* (now a subsiduary of Pernod-Ricard) who have enlarged the vineyard and modernized the facilities. I have found the wines scented and rather minerally on the nose, with a pleasantly spicy flavour, but lacking in richness with a tendency to be dry at the finish.

CHÂTEAU LA CLARE

Cru Bourgeois. Owner: Paul de Rozières. 20 hectares. 10,000 cases. CS 57%, Mer 36%, CF 7%. Second wines: Laveline, du Gentilhomme

The Belleyme map at the end of the eighteenth century shows vines planted at Condissas on the ridge of By. This is the modern Château La Clare. This name itself apparently has the same origin as the word "claret". After the property had belonged to the Fontaneau family for generations, the habitual problems of inheritance led to its sale in 1969 to the de Rozières family who came, like so many others, from Tunisia, where they had been vineyard owners. Since 1970 they have been responsible for replanting 50 per cent of the vineyard. At vintage time the old vines – some 15 per cent are around sixty years old – are harvested by hand, the rest mechanically. The vinification is carefully temperature-controlled with frequent *remontages*. Then the ageing takes place in cask, with the final fining in vat.

The wines here are very well made and most attractive. There is a scented spiciness on the nose with luscious, opulent, plummy fruit on the palate, but also an excellent solidity about the wines so that when I drank the 1971 and 1973 in 1986, they were still fresh and vigorous. In more recent years there is a 1982 with depth of flavour, fruit and richness, a well-above-average 1983, with no signs of the dilution affecting many wines of the northern Médoc in this year, a typically attractive 1985, and a 1986 which combines powerful tannins with elegant fruit, producing a long flavour. This is an excellent example of what this area is capable of, and its reputation has deservedly advanced in recent years. Most of the wine is commercialized through Dulong Frères et Fils.

CHÂTEAU GREYSAC

Cru Grand Bourgeois. Owner: Domaines Codem. Administrator: Philippe Dambrine. 60 hectares. 35,000 cases. CS and CF 60%, Mer 38%, PV 2%

Since 1973, when the late Baron François de Gunzburg bought this *cru*, it has increased considerably in importance. There is now fermentation in stainless steel and maturation in cask. Thanks to the Baron's previous experience as managing director of Barton and Guestier, an extensive export market in the United States was soon built up. Since his death the property has been run by Philippe Dambrine. These wines can usually be drunk with great enjoyment when three or four years old. I particularly enjoyed the 1979 with its opulent fruit and rather over-ripe style, but the 1983 showed signs of dilution. The 1986 has a distinctive terroir character and is firm and assertive with a very good finish.

CHÂTEAU LAUJAC

Cru Grand Bourgeois. Owner: Madame H. Cruse. 30 hectares. Red: 12,500 cases

One of several well-known properties in Bégadan, Laujac is situated on the large, central plateau of the Médoc. Since 1852 it has belonged to the Cruse family, and as a result is very widely known and distributed. But the property is nothing like as important as it once was. In the last century, 300 to 400 tonneaux were made and even between the wars 150 were recorded; then at one stage in the sixties it sank to 20 tonneaux, or a mere 1,700 cases. Now there has been some revival. The reputation, objectively speaking, is not quite what it was. Although the wine is pleasant enough, it lacks the individuality and style of several other growths in Bégadan.

CHÂTEAU LIVRAN

Cru Bourgeois. Owner: Robert Godfin. 50 hectares. 20,000 cases. Mer 50%, CS 25%, CF 25%. Second label: Château La Rose-Goromey

I often drove past this property, with its impressive squat towers of feudal appearance, on my way to Loudenne. It once belonged to the de Goth family, whose most famous member became Pope under the name of Clement V in 1305. From 1889 until 1962 it was the proud possession of James I. Denman, a famous firm of London wine merchants who unfortunately did not survive the widespread changes that affected the trade after the Second World War. The present proprietor is Denman's former manager. On the only occasion in recent years when I have tasted this wine, I was delighted to find the 1983 had very pleasing, vivid fruit, and was fresh and clean-flavoured, a well-made and very honourable wine for the vintage in northern Médoc, whose many wines were rather dilute.

CHÂTEAU LOUDENNE

Cru Grand Bourgeois. Owner: W. & A. Gilbey Ltd. 50 hectares. Red: 15,000 cases. CS 53%, Mer 40%, CF 7%. White: 5,000 cases. Sauv 50%, Sém 50%

I hope I shall be forgiven if I wax a shade eloquent on a property I know so intimately. Geologically, Loudenne is a continuation of the gravelly ridges of St Seurin-de-Cadourne, and an illustration of the fact that communal boundaries do not always coincide exactly with natural formations of the soil. A curious feature of the property is that nowhere else in the Médoc or Haut-Médoc do these ridges approach the river so closely, and as a result Loudenne enjoys an unparalleled view over the Gironde, with hardly any intervening *palus*. The "hill" of Loudenne actually rises to 16 metres, which corresponds to some of the best sites in St Estèphe, and is the highest in the Bas-Médoc. In 1815, in his survey of the communes of the Haut-Médoc, Lawton singled out Loudenne as worthy to be classed with the wines of St Seurin-de-Cadourne.

Loudenne is first recorded as belonging to the de Pons family in the fourteenth century, before it had any importance as a wine-growing estate. In 1482 it belonged to Odet Daydie, the seigneur of Lescun and admiral of Guyenne, in 1516 to Vicomtesse Magdelaine de Lescun and eventually, in 1784, to the Verthamon family. In 1875 the owner was the Vicomtesse de Marcellus, who was a Verthamon, and it was from her that Walter and Alfred Gilbey bought the property.

The château itself dates from the early part of the eighteenth century and is of the traditional *chartreuse* type, with a central single storey linking two-storeyed buildings with turrets. It is situated on a narrow ridge of ground between the two main parts of the vineyard, and from the terrace in front commands an unrivalled view of the river, while on the landward side the ground again falls away sharply, offering a fine vista for some miles.

The history of Loudenne since its acquisition by the Gilbeys in 1875 provides a microcosm of the ebb and flow of fortunes in Bordeaux. First of all, the property was adapted to its new role as the centre of Gilbeys' Bordeaux operations. A large *cuvier* and *chai* were built near the river for the assembling of wine from the whole region prior to shipment for England, and a small port was constructed in front of the *chai*, from which wine was taken by barge to Bordeaux. (This port remained in use until after the Second World War.) Plans greatly to increase the production of Loudenne's own vineyards received a setback with the phylloxera, but by the end of the century between 300 and 400 tonneaux were being made, including a certain quantity of white wine.

After the First World War, Loudenne rapidly declined in importance. Claret shipments fell to a fraction of what they had been before the war, and the Gilbeys themselves, much absorbed in building up their business in the Empire and Commonwealth, had less and less time for Loudenne. There was even talk of disposing of the property, and only the dogged persistence of Gordon Gilbey saved it for better days. At this period, the *régisseur*, Monsieur Gombaud, even made a dessert wine, Medullio, as a method of using up the unwanted surplus production. It was sold locally and is still remembered by many of the older generation in the Médoc.

After the Second World War, the property was in a very run-down condition. Under the German occupation, the vineyards in the *palus* had mostly been pulled up and the land turned over to cattle grazing, and production had shrunk to 30 or 40 tonneaux, half of it white wine. When I first visited Loudenne in May 1960, the reconstruction of the vineyard under Monsieur Bouilleau, the new *régisseur*, had recently begun, but the great *chai* was distressingly empty and the château extremely dilapidated, only habitable during the summer months.

Since that time, progress has been steady and at times spectacular. In 1963 the château was completely restored and modernized, and in 1970 a model estate of new houses for the families now living on the property was opened, to replace those originally built nearly one hundred years before. Extensive alterations have been made in the *cuvier* and *chai*, and the *chai* itself now positively bulges with wine in cask and in bottle, for large stocks of château-bottled wines from all the main Bordeaux districts are kept here. A happy renaissance indeed, and one which mirrors many others throughout the Bordeaux *vignoble*.

The white wine has been retained, but the quantity made has been reduced and the quality improved so that it would be hard to find its peer in the Médoc. It is made principally of Sauvignon with a small amount of Sémillon and, after a controlled fermentation in tank, is kept in stainless steel *cuves* until the bottling the following spring.

But while the white wine is a pleasing curiosity, the reputation of Loudenne rightly rests on its red wines. These are distinguished by a fine and individual bouquet, said by some to be reminiscent of chrysanthemums, while the wine soon develops a mellow and expansive flavour and keeps extremely well. It is interesting to compare Loudenne with the neighbouring Coufran, which is in the Haut-Médoc. There is a marked similarity of style, but the Loudenne loses nothing by the comparison. The colour is not as deep as some of its neighbours' at first, but fills out with maturity. Some of the old vintages are remarkable and provide yet another demonstration of the quality attainable by the best-known *bourgeois* growths in this part of the Médoc.

The oldest bottle of Loudenne that I have tasted was the 1896, still wonderfully fresh and pleasant to drink when sixty-seven years old. The 1926 and 1928 were outstanding, the 1934 and 1937 had some of the shortcomings of their vintages, but many of the lesser years are delicious, particularly the 1923 and the 1938. More recently, the 1961 was quite outstanding – the best wine made since the war, remarkably concentrated and generous. Since then, the 1962 was classic and lasted well, the 1964 rather full-blown and an early developer, the 1966 very fine indeed, with more body than the 1964 and more fruit and vinosity than the 1962, while the 1967 was light but charming. The poor years of 1963, 1965 and 1968 were not sold under the château name. During the seventies, excellent wines were made in 1970, 1975, 1976, 1978 and 1979, while the 1971 was charming if rather light. It was perhaps a sign of increasing commercial pressures that the 1972 was bottled under the château label. In the eighties there is a rich, mellow 1982 and a most attractive, stylish, more forward 1983. Both 1985 and 1986 produced fine wines, with the 1986 already very elegant for the vintage after a year in cask.

No mention of this period of renaissance for Loudenne would be complete without a tribute to the work of the late Martin Bamford. Between 1968 and his premature death in 1982, he was the presiding genius. At the beginning and end of his stewardship, he was based at Loudenne. He supervised numerous improvements, always careful that everything should be in keeping with what was there. Most important of all, perhaps, he created a sound and imaginative commercial base, without which the whole enterprise would not have been viable, so that by the seventies Loudenne had achieved a prosperity not seen since before the First World War. But above all he was one of the great personalities of the Médoc, an incomparable host and friend to visitors from all over the world, whose death has left a void in the place that was most nearly his home.

As the reconstituted vineyard matures, so production increases, and the vineyard now covers most of the area originally planted in the early years of the Gilbey era, save for some of the *palus*. Whereas until recently the wines of Loudenne were to be found almost exclusively in the UK and Ireland, they are now exported to the United States and many other markets.

CHÂTEAU DE MONTHIL

Cru Bourgeois. Owner: Les Domaines CODEM. 20 hectares. 8,000 cases. CS 30%, CF 30%, Mer 30%, Mal 5%, PV 5%

This property is north of Bégadan, in the direction of Valeyrac. A good, traditionally run property, it belonged to the Gabas family, who sold to the present owners in 1986. They also own the well-known property of Greysac, also in Bégadan, as well as Château Les Bertins in the same commune. Until the time of its sale, Monthil was mainly sold to good restaurants in France; now it is intended to place the wine on export markets as well. In 1985 it was placed equal fifth with no less a wine that

Château Sociando-Mallet, in the final of Gault-Millau's tasting of 1982 *crus bourgeois* – no mean achievement. This will certainly be a wine to watch in future, outside France as well as within.

CHÂTEAU LES ORMES-SORBET

Cru Grand Bourgeois. Owner: Jean Boivert. 20 hectares. 10,000 cases. CS 65%, Mer 35%

The small and obscure commune of Couquèques lies inland from the Gironde between St Yzans and St Christoly. The name itself is derived from the fossilized sea-shells which are richly deposited on this particular outcrop of gravelly ridges which provide the soil for this excellent growth. The reputation of the wine has increased of late, and this was recognized when the 1978 classification raised Les Ormes-Sorbet to a *grand bourgeois*. In 1966 it had been given the status of a simple *bourgeois* only.

Jean Boivert, who has run the property since 1969, comes from a long line of wine-growers who have owned land in this commune for over two hundred years. Les Ormes-Sorbet and de Couques actually comprise what was formally the Domaine de Couquèques, an estate first mentioned in 1580, which was divided up in 1827 between five heirs, but was eventually painstakingly reassembled in 1908. Jean Boivert is a *technicien viticulture-oenologie*, and a taster for the Service de la Répression des Fraudes. His wines are an excellent example of what can be achieved in this area with skill and dedication.

The vineyard is very stony and has good natural drainage. The soil is sandy clay and sandy gravel on a chalky subsoil. Vinification is in metal *cuves* of 130 hectolitres and, unusually, the Cabernets are fermented at the rather low temperatures of 22–25°C, and ageing is in cask, with some new oak used since the 1982 vintage.

In style the wines are perfumed, with plenty of flavour but not a lot of body, a characteristic often found in the northern Médoc. Particularly typical and classic examples are the 1978 and 1981, while the 1979 is a bigger, more strongly flavoured wine. The 1982 closed up at first in bottle, but its underlying richness promises a good future, and the 1983 should be rather similar to the 1981. Until the 1985 vintage, about half the crop was sold in bulk to Schröder & Schÿler and bottled in Bordeaux.

CHÂTEAU PATACHE-D'AUX

Cru Grand Bourgeois. Owner: Société Civile du Château Patache-d'Aux.
Administrator: Claude Lapalu. 38 hectares. 21,500 cases. CS 70%, Mer 20%, CF 10%

This growth first made its appearance in the 1886 edition of Cocks & Féret as Cru Patachon, and until quite recently was called a simple *cru* and not a château. But the property has survived and prospered while many others have disappeared, and today it is one of the most important wines of Bégadan. The d'Aux which is now affixed refers to the family d'Aux, descendants of the Comtes d'Armagnac, who owned the property before the Revolution. The family was long associated with the running of the *diligences*, which in those days provided the only alternative to the river as a means of reaching Bordeaux. The connection is attractively commemorated on the label.

The property – now formed into a company – had for many years belonged to the Delon family (see Léoville-Las Cases and Phélan-Ségur) until Claude Lapalu bought it in 1964. The château itself now belongs to the municipality. The fermentation is still partly in the fine, free-standing wooden *cuves* and partly, since 1978, in stainless steel vats. Maturation is in cask.

These are finely perfumed wines, developing attractive overtones of violets, a particularly Cabernet characteristic in this part of the Médoc. They are finely flavoured, fruity and supple when mature, full-flavoured but light in body. In big years such as 1970, 1975, 1982 and 1986 they can be rather tannic and abrasive, with a certain *goût de terroir* at first, but this mellows pleasantly. The 1975 was excellent by 1988. Good examples were also made in 1979, 1981, 1983 and 1985. The wines have been admirably consistent for many years.

CHÂTEAU POTENSAC

Cru Grand Bourgeois. Owner: Madame Paul Delon. Administrator: Michel Delon. 40 hectares. 20,000 cases. CS 55%, Mer 25%, CF 20%. Secondary labels: Château Gallais-Bellevue, Château Lassalle

Several good wines are made on the gravelly outcrop of Potensac which lies between St Yzans and St Germain d'Esteuil, and Château Potensac is the best known of these. For long the property of the Liquard family, it now belongs to the wife of Monsieur Paul Delon of Léoville-Las Cases, who is herself a Liquard, and it is administered by her son, Michel Delon, who is also the administrator of Léoville-Las Cases.

Consistently good wines have been made here for many years, but as elsewhere in Bordeaux, they have taken on a fresh dimension of excellence in recent years, especially since Michel Delon took over in the mid-seventies. As can be seen above, there are actually three properties here, which are run together. Potensac is the largest and best, and all occupy a good gravelly outcrop at Potensac. The *cuvier* has been re-equipped with stainless steel *cuves* and the wine is matured in casks from Léoville-Las Cases, with the addition of 20 per cent new casks each year. Part of the *chai* is a de-consecrated church, whose Gothic arches now rise above serried rows of bottles.

The wines of Potensac have a depth of colour, power and complexity rare in the northern Médoc, together with a bouquet which has the vigour and assertiveness typical of the region, but coupled with spicy and often floral overtones. The flavour is concentrated, powerful, and often rather angular in structure. Their evolution is slower than most of their neighbours – one must expect to wait five or six years before beginning to drink them with pleasure. Outstanding recent vintages are 1976, 1981, 1982, 1985 and 1986. Very good examples are to be found in 1978, 1979 and 1983, while 1980 is particularly good for the year. This is now one of the more expensive wines in the *appellation*, but is certainly better than many *crus bourgeois* in the northern part of the Haut-Médoc, and as such deserves its considerable following. It is clearly one of the top *crus* of its *appellation*, if not the topmost.

CHÂTEAU PLAGNAC

Crus Bourgeois. Owner: Domaines Cordier. 30 hectares. 15,000 cases. CS 60%, Mer 40%

Cordier acquired this Bégadan property in 1972. The vineyard has been reconstructed, and is now adapted to mechanical harvesting. The vineyards enjoy a south-westerly aspect. The fermentation is in stainless steel *cuves*, the maturation in wooden *foudres* and casks. The wines here are steadily becoming more impressive as the vineyard matures. A solid, robust wine, it is now becoming more scented, and the fruit more luscious. Exceptionally good wines were made in 1985 and 1986, while 1984 is remarkably attractive for the year. Good but more pedestrian wines were made in 1981 and 1982. This is one of a number of fast-improving *crus bourgeois* in this *appellation*.

CHÂTEAU PREUILLAC

Cru Bourgeois. Owner: Raymond Bonet. 30 hectares. 16,500 cases. Mer 50%, CS 45%, CF 5%

This old property – it appears on the Belleyme map at the end of the eighteenth century – is the most important *cru* now in the commune of Lesparre, lying to the east of the town near La Cardonne. It is a well-kept and well-managed property where the vinification is still done in a fine battery of the traditional wooden *cuves*. The maturation is in a combination of oak *foudres* and casks. The bottle stocks are kept in underground cellars.

The Merlot gives these wines more body than some of their neighbours. The 1982 was particularly successful, with spicy, pungent fruit on the nose, delicious full-flavoured fruit and real length on the palate. Certainly this is a *cru* worth looking for.

CHÂTEAU ST-BONNET

Cru Bourgeois 1978. Owner: Michel Solivères. 35 hectares. 18,000 cases. CS 50%, Mer 50%

The wines of St Christoly have long enjoyed an excellent reputation, and there was a time when some English wine merchants sold wines under the generic name of this commune, such was its *réclame*. This is one of the best known of its *crus*. It is a very traditional Médoc with a very strong character and a distinctive and minerally *goût de terroir*. The wines are highly coloured with a distinctively spicy bouquet and a robust, powerful flavour in which fruit and tannin are well balanced. Particularly massive wines were made in 1982 and 1986.

CHÂTEAU ST SATURNIN

Cru Bourgeois. Owner: Adrien Tramier. 21 hectares. 10,000 cases. Mer 50%, CS 30%, CF 15%, PV 5%

This property is just outside Bégadan, to the west, on the road to Laujac. The label depicts a greyhound and a lion – an unusual combination. The wines are matured in vat and see no wood. They are pleasantly perfumed, often rather light, and at their best when three to four years old. The

1983 was particularly successful, brimming over with delicious, easy fruit.

CHÂTEAU SESTIGNAN
Cru Bourgeois. Owner: Bertrand de Rozières. 8.5 hectares. 5,000 cases. CS 76%, Mer 22%, Mal 2%

This vineyard really lies on the outer frontiers of the Bas-Médoc. The commune of Jau-Dignac-et-Loirac consists of three small villages lying between St Vivien (with the most northerly vineyards in the Bas-Médoc) and Valeyrac, to the south-east, almost an island surrounded by *palus* and drainage canals. The proprietor here is a member of the same family of *pieds-noirs* as that of Château La Clare in nearby Bégadan. The 1982 here was the most highly placed *cru* from the Médoc *appellation* in Gault-Millau's tasting of 1982 *crus bourgeois* (see Château de Monthil), obtaining a remarkable fourth place, ahead of Sociando-Mallet. I found the 1985 to have quite a pronounced *goût de terroir* at a blind tasting of this vintage in the spring of 1986, but there was also excellent fruit and a good, solid structure. Clearly this is a *cru* to follow.

CHÂTEAU SIGOGNAC
Cru Grand Bourgeois. Owner: Société Civile Fermière du Château Sigognac. Administrator: Madame Colette Bonny-Grasset. 44 hectares. 20,000 cases. CS 33.3%, CF 33.3%, Mer 33.3%

A Roman villa once stood on the site, and one can see some of the pottery found here exhibited at the *Mairie* of St Yzans. When Paul Grasset bought the property in 1964 there were only four hectares of vines left, a familiar situation at that time. The transformation he began has been continued after his death in 1968 by his widow, now married to Monsieur Bonny. The fermentation is in concrete vats, and the wine is matured partly in vat and partly in cask. I have found the wines well coloured, full and soft on the nose, with pleasing fruit and tannin on the palate, elegant rather than powerful. There is not the same finesse as at its more famous neighbour, Loudenne, but this is nevertheless a pleasant and thoroughly honourable Médoc which maintains a good general standard.

CHÂTEAU LE TERTRE-CAUSSAN

Cru Bourgeois. Owner: Guy Caussan. 11 hectares. 6,500 cases. Mer 55%, CS 40%, CF 5%

This is another *cru* in the village of Caussan. The wines are attractive with some finesse. Good wines were made in 1975 and 1978, but more recently they have been richer with more flesh. Good examples are 1982 and 1985.

CHÂTEAU LA TOUR-DE-BY

Cru Grand Bourgeois. Owner: Société Civile du Château La Tour-de-By (Cailloux, Lapalu, Pagès). Administrator: Marc Pagès. 61 hectares. 39,000 cases. CS 65%, Mer 32%, CF 3%. Secondary labels: Château La Roque-de-By, Château Moulin-de-la-Roque

This is probably the most important growth in Bégadan today. It is beautifully situated on a series of gravelly ridges near to the Gironde, which here reach a height of 11 metres, compared to 16 metres at Loudenne, but still one of the highest in this low-lying region. A special feature is the tower, which stands close to the château. It was in fact built as a lighthouse serving the estuary, and carries the date 1825 above its doorway. The attractively colonnaded château was built in the nineteenth century, but some of the farm buildings which incorporate the original château are older.

The wine is most distinctive. It is highly coloured and has a powerful bouquet with a very characteristic perfume, often reminiscent of violets. The wine is full-bodied and has real depth, length of flavour and, overall, a certain style and elegance. The whole character is highly Médocain with its rugged individuality of style.

The property came into the hands of three partners, Messieurs Cailloux, Lapalu and Pagès, in the 1960s, and since then there have been many improvements. The old wooden *cuves* have been retained and are now surrounded by safety nets to prevent injury should someone miss his or her footing on the gangways around the top of the vats. This is now an increasingly common sight wherever the old-style *cuviers* survive. The original *cuvier*, now too small and cramped, has been extended, and the new part has both wooden and stainless steel vats, built in 1973. Marc Pagès, who actually lives in the château and manages the property is yet another of that energetic band of *pieds-noirs* who have made such a contribution to Bordeaux since the last war, and is the brother of the late Guy Pagès who bought Fourcas-Dupré. All the wine is matured in cask, with a proportion of it new. This is today one of the best wines of the Médoc and fetches one of the top prices. The 1962, 1964, 1966 and 1967 were all very successful. More recently, excellent wines were made in 1979, 1982, 1983, 1985, 1986, 1988 and 1989.

CHÂTEAU LA TOUR-HAUT-CAUSSAN

Cru Bourgeois. Owner: Philippe Courrian. 10.5 hectares. 6,000 cases. CS 50%, Mer and Mal 50%

This *cru* is one of several around the village of Caussan in the commune of Blaignan. The vineyard was part of the Château de Caussan, bought in 1877 by the Courrian family, who can trace their residence in Médoc back to 1615. In the centre of the vineyard stands a windmill dating from 1734 – evidence of the mixed farming still practised at that time – which was restored in 1981. No weedkillers are used in the vineyard, which is worked in the traditional way, and the harvesting is still done manually. Philippe Courrian believes in a high-temperature (32–34°C) fermentation for his Merlots and a lower one (27–28°C) for his Cabernets. Maturation is in casks, of which 25 per cent are new. This carefully made wine has won many awards in Paris and Bordeaux in recent years, and is well distributed in France, mainly direct to private customers and to good restaurants, although about 20 per cent is exported.

CHÂTEAU LA TOUR-ST-BONNET

Cru Bourgeois. Owner: Pierre Lafon. 41 hectares. 20,000 cases. Mer 50%, CS 28%, CF 22%. Second label: Château La Fuie-St-Bonnet

This is now the largest property in St Christoly, and has been in the hands of the same family since 1903. It is an amalgamation of three *crus*: La Fuie-St Bonnet, La Croix-St Bonnet and La Tour-St Bonnet itself. The label shows the familiar tower. The vineyard is splendidly placed on the best gravelly outcrop of the commune. This has been an important property since at least the middle of the last century, being mentioned in the 1868 edition of Cocks & Féret. This is the archetypal Médoc, highly coloured, with depth of flavour, and a fresh crispness that can almost be called refreshing. The 1981, 1983 and 1985 vintages all produced excellent examples, while the 1982 has more concentration, and that minerally *goût de terroir* character often found in years of high extract in these parts. Altogether an admirable *cru bourgeois*, normally excellent drinking when around five years of age.

CHÂTEAU LA VALIÈRE

Cru Bourgeois. Owner: Cailloux family. 15 hectares. 7,500 cases. CS 74%, Mer 25%, PV 1%

This is now one of the best *crus* in St Christoly. Formerly known as Château des Châlets, it was given the name of La Valière by its present owners. The vineyard is on the gravelly ridges, for which St Christoly is famed, close to the Gironde. This is solid but also thoroughly attractive wine, with plenty of fruit to charm as well as structure to give it life. I have been impressed by its showing in several blind tastings. The 1979 was especially impressive, and since then their 1984 and 1985 wines have brought them success in the Troisième Coupe des Crus Bourgeois organized by Gault-Millau in 1987.

VIEUX CHÂTEAU LANDON

Cru Bourgeois. Owner: Philippe Gillet. 35 hectares. 16,500 cases. CS 70%, Mer 25%, Mal 5%

This is one of a number of good *crus* in the commune of Bégadan, lying just to the south-east of the village, on the road to Couquèques. It appeared on the Belleyme map at the end of the eighteenth century and has been in the same family for several generations. The present owner had the good fortune to marry the previous owner's daughter. The vinification is in stainless steel, the maturation in cask. This is good, stylish, fruity Médoc, which is both attractive and ages well. This is an important region for *caves coopératives*. They produce the base material for most of the good, generic blends which appear under *négociants'* own *marques*. Here is a guide to them.

BÉGADAN. CAVE ST JEAN

President: René Chaumont. 567 hectares. 300,000 cases. Mer 50%, CS 24%, CF 24%, PV 2%

This is by far the largest *coopérative* within the Médoc *appellation*. It draws its 170 members not only from this commune, but also from the neighbouring ones of Valeyrac and Civrac. The extensive buildings have a capacity of more than 60,000 hectolitres. A number of *crus* are individually vinified at the *cave* and sold under their own labels: Meilhan, Breuil-Renaissance, Le Barrail, Labadie, Pey-de-By, Lassus, Le Bernet, Le Monge, Bégadanet, Vimenay, Rose du Pont, Haut Condisas. The *cave* is also a member of Uni-Médoc, a grouping of four *coopératives* for the stocking and maturing of the wines of the region. This is the heartland of the *appellation*, and produces attractive wines combining fruit and solidity.

ORDONNAC. CAVE DE BELLEVUE
266 hectares. 100,000 cases. Mer 50%, CS 45% CF 5%,
This *coopérative* in the southern part of the *appellation* was founded in 1936 and now has seventy-five members drawn from this commune, as well as the neighbouring one of St Germain d'Esteuil. The following *crus* are individually vinified: de Brie, Belfort, Lagorce, Moulin-de-Buscateau, Moulin de la Rivière, l'Oume de Pey, La Rose-Picot, du Grand Bois and Les Graves. Some of the wine is sold under the *cave's* own *marque* of Pavillon de Bellevue, but as the *cave* is one of the members of Uni-Médoc, much goes in bulk for *négociants'* own brands. These are good dependable wines, that make their own contribution to the high overall standard achieved by generic Médoc in recent years.

QUEYRAC. CAVE ST ROCH
125 hectares. 50,000 cases
This *coopérative* was formed in 1939, and now has 165 members, drawn from the rather scattered vineyards of the northern communes of Queyrac, Gaillan, Jau-Dignac-et-Loirac, Vensac, Valeyrac and Vendays. Three *crus* are individually vinified: Laubespin, Les Trois-Tétous and Pessange. The *cave* is also a member of Uni-Médoc, so that although some of its wines are sold under its *marque* of St Roch, much goes in bulk for *négociants'* own blends.

PRESTIGE-MÉDOC. CAVE COOPÉRATIVE DU VIEUX-CLOCHER
Owner: Uni-Médoc. 1,200 hectares
This, the most recent by far of the Médoc *coopératives*, was established only in 1979. Situated two kilometres north of Lesparre at Gaillan, it is different in kind from the essentially commune-based *coopératives* founded in the years of the great depression in the thirties. No wines are

actually vinified here, it is entirely a centre for storage. This is an extension of the direct selling and marketing collaboration of the five *coopératives* at Bégadan, Gaillan, Ordonnac, Prignac and Queyrac under the umbrella of Uni-Médoc. The aim is to hold a maturing stock of some two million bottles which are commercialized through Sovicop-Producta, the Union des Caves Coopératives Vinicoles, which embraces all the *coopératives* in the Gironde and Dordogne. A good general standard has been established.

PRIGNAC. CAVES LES VIEUX COLOMBIERS
110,000 cases

This *coopérative* was founded in 1950 in order to bring together, and provide more modern facilities for, *vignerons* in the communes of Prignac, Lesparre, and St Germain-d'Esteuil, as well as several other lesser nearby communes. There are now 200 members. The *coopérative* uses the improved and extended *cuviers* and *chais* of the Château de Beusse, and has a capacity of 38,000 hectolitres. Two *crus*, Château de Beusse itself and Château Lafon, are vinified separately. The *cave* belongs to the Uni-Médoc grouping of *coopératives*, so that apart from its own *marque*, Les Vieux Colombiers, an important part of its production is commercialized through Uni-Médoc.

ST YZANS DE MÉDOC. CAVE ST BRICE
200 hectares. 100,000 cases

The *coopérative* at St Yzans was founded in 1934 and now has 120 members, drawn from the neighbouring communes of Blaignan, Couquèques and St Christoly, as well as from St Yzans itself. The wines are sold under the *marque* of St Brice or in bulk. Two châteaux vinify their wines here, Toffard and La Tour St Vincent. The *cave* has a good reputation for making some sound, typical Médocs.

7

Graves: Both Red and White

The Graves is an ancient and singular region: ancient, because its vine-yards are among the oldest in Bordeaux and its wine among the first to be recorded; singular, because it is the only region in Bordeaux where almost every property produces both red and white wines, and they both have an almost equal importance. If one were to mention the name of Graves to the casual wine drinker, it is probable that his first reaction would be to think of a white wine – and, indeed, Graves used to produce much more white than red wine. But in the last two decades red wine has finally over-taken white wine production. The transformation that has taken place in the last two decades is clearly brought home by the figures. In 1970, 40,958 hectolitres of red Graves were produced compared with 55,653 hectolitres of white. By 1989 the production of red had grown to 143,167 hectolitres, overtaking the white which, nevertheless, had risen to 73,842 hectolitres. And the figures for white wines conceal yet another change, from the demi-sec – or the moelleux – style of the past, to the crisp, dry one of today. In 1970 there were only 10,095 hectolitres of Graves Blanc compared with 45,558 hectolitres of Graves Supérieur. By 1989 Graves Blanc had advanced to 56,486 hectolitres, and Graves Supérieur had shrunk to 17,356 hectolitres. The finest wines are the red, grown in a few communes just outside the city of Bordeaux, while more ordinary reds are made throughout the rest of the area. In this same area close to Bordeaux, a much smaller quantity of very fine, dry, white wine is also made.

A glance at the map will show that this is a very large area, stretching some 35 miles (50 kilometres) from the southern limits of the Médoc, round the west and southern outskirts of Bordeaux, past Langon, and almost to the limits of the Bordeaux region along the western bank of the

Garonne to a depth of 10 to 15 miles (15 to 20 kilometres). Inserted in its midst are the districts of Sauternes-Barsac and Cérons, and the white wines produced in the part of Graves adjoining Sauternes are nearer that region in style than Graves. Indeed, many properties in Cérons, Illats and Podensac have the right to call their white wines "Graves" or "Cérons", according to the style of the wine produced. Geographically, the region is a continuation of the Médoc, with the gravelly ridges of the northern part, closest to Bordeaux, most clearly mirroring those of the Médoc. Further south, the soil becomes more varied, with differing amounts of sand and clay, and even some limestone in the communes neighbouring Barsac. Unfortunately, some of the best vineyards are now lost beneath Bordeaux's suburban sprawl. In the four communes of Gradignan, Mérignac, Pessac and Talence there were 119 wine-producing properties in 1908, but by 1981 there were only nine. Old maps of the Bordeaux region show that the name of Graves was used originally to embrace the whole area of the left bank of the Garonne and Gironde, including the Médoc. It was, understandably, those vineyards lying just outside the city limits which first became known, and Haut-Brion is the first growth to be mentioned in English literature, by the indefatigable Pepys in 1663, although his spelling, Ho Bryan, might not be immediately recognizable to today's wine drinkers.

The finest red wines of the Graves are, not surprisingly, nearest in style to those of the Médoc, the gravelly soil and the *encépagement* closely resembling those of its northern neighbour. But, just as there are discernible differences between the various major communes of the Médoc, so the red Graves have their own character – a very marked and powerful bouquet almost with a hint of tobacco, frank and open, but not perhaps as subtle as the Médoc, while the flavour is very clean and almost crisp, pleasantly fruity, but with a firm, often rather tannic background. These are very individual wines, but it should be remembered that there is only a very tiny group of really top-class properties, and that most red Graves are comparable to many of the *crus bourgeois* of the Médoc, although this terminology is not used here. These lesser red wines tend to be light in colour and body, distinctive in bouquet and flavour, usually with a certain *goût de terroir* typical of Graves, and delicious when drunk young.

Today, most of the wine-making is concentrated in eight communes:

Léognan and Martillac in the north, Portets, Illats, Cérons, St Pierre-de-Mons, Langon and Landiras in the south. This shift in emphasis from white to red, the restyling of the whites, the loss of prime sites in the north and the growing importance of the southern area for the production of both red and white wines have created their own tensions within the region. The classified growths are all in the north (six out of thirteen reds and four out of eight whites are in Léognan) and fearful of being lost in a sea of lesser wines, while ever conscious of the threat of further urban encroachments. So they created two new designations in 1984 – Graves-Pessac and Graves-Léognan – which, in 1987, resulted in a new *appellation*, Pessac-Léognan. Meanwhile, improved methods are resulting in much better wines being made in the south.

The thinking behind the new designations is that – the Graves being such a large and disparate region – some such differentiation is necessary and will be commercially beneficial in the long term. They point to the difference between Médoc and Haut-Médoc as an example, and the creation of the communal *appellations* within Haut-Médoc (Margaux *et al.*).

No account of the renaissance taking place in Graves would be complete without mention of some of the people whose dynamism and love of the region have helped create a new image and vitality in recent years. André Lurton and Pierre Coste have made contrasting and complementary contributions. In the sixties, André Lurton bought La Louvière, a well-sited vineyard in Léognan between Haut-Bailly and Carbonnieux, and has steadily raised the quality of its red and white wines until, today, they deserve to take their place among the *crus classés*; indeed, they are better than some. Then, in 1973, he bought two properties where the vineyards had ceased to exist – Rochemorin and Cruzeau – and has transformed them into important vineyards again. Between them, they now have over 100 hectares of vineyards and the wines are improving every year – already providing wines of considerable style and individuality from their gravelly ridges in St Médard-d'Eyrans and Martillac.

Pierre Coste's great contribution has been in the field of wine-making in the southern Graves. Through his *négociant* business in Langon, he has encouraged and assisted many small producers to make exciting wines, and his own generic Graves blends have also helped to raise the

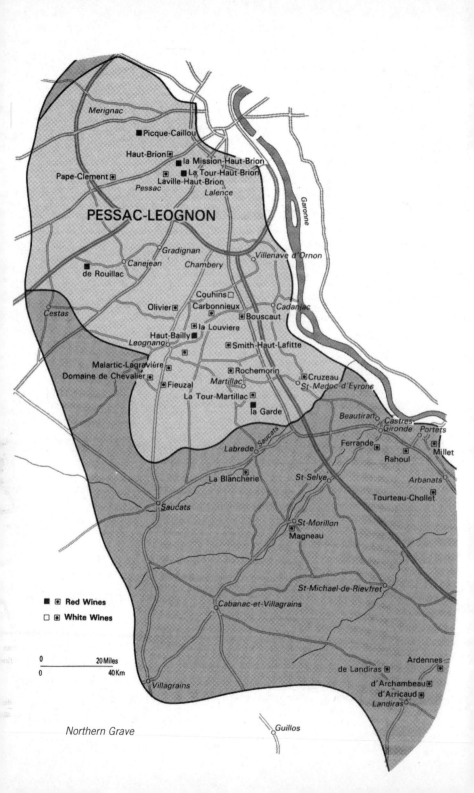

Merignac

■ Picque-Caillou

Haut-Brion ◉
■ la Mission-Haut-Brion
■ La Tour-Haut-Brion
Pape-Clement ◉
Laville-Haut-Brion ■
Pessac
Lalence

PESSAC-LEOGNON

Gradignan
Canejean ○
Chambery
Villenave d'Ornon

■ de Rouillac

Cestas
Couhins □
Olivier ◉
Carbonnieux
◉ Cadaniac
◉ Bouscaut
◉ la Louviere
Haut-Bailly ■
Leognano ○ ◉
◉ Smith-Haut-Lafitte
Malartic-Lagravière ◉
◉ Rochemorin
Domaine de Chevalier ◉
○ Cruzeau
◉ Fieuzal
Martillac
St-Madoc-d'Eyrons
La Tour-Martillac ◉
■ la Garde
Beautiran
◉ Castres
◉ Gironde Porters
Ferrande ◉
◉ Millet
Labrede
Saucats
Rahoul ◉
La Blancherie ◉
St-Selve ○
Arbanats ◉
Tourteau-Chollet ◉
Saucats ○
◉ St-Morillon
Magneau

St-Michael-de-Rievfret ○

■ ◉ **Red Wines**
□ ◉ **White Wines**

Cabanac-et-Villagrains ○

| 0 | 20 Miles |
| 0 | 40 Km |

Ardennes ◉
de Landiras ◉
d'Archambeau ◉
d'Arricaud ◉
Landiras ○
Villagrains ○

Northern Grave

Guillos ○

Garonne

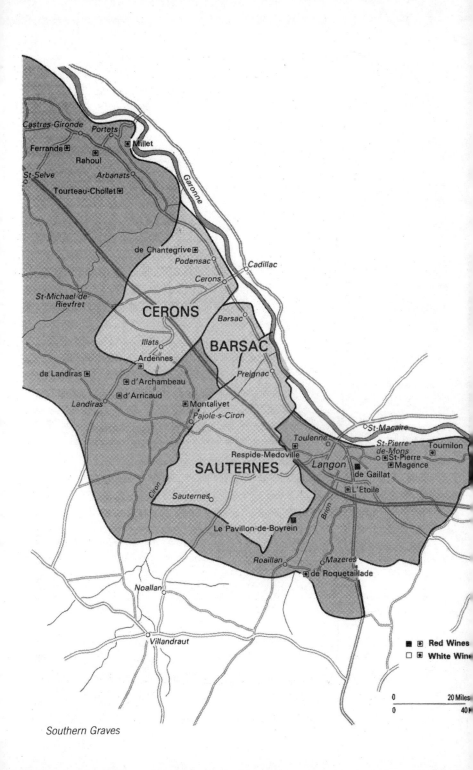

Castres-Gironde
Portets
Ferrande ◉
⊡ Millet
Rahoul ◉
St-Selve ○
Arbanats ◉
Tourteau-Chollet ◉

Garonne

de Chantegrive ◉
Podensac ○
Cadillac ○
Cerons ○

St-Michael-de-
Rievfret

CERONS

Barsac ○

BARSAC

Illats ○
Ardennes ⊡

de Landiras ◉
Preignac

⊡ d'Archambeau
⊡ d'Arricaud
Landiras
◉ Montalivet
Pajole-s-Ciron ○

St-Macaire ○

Toulenne
◉
St-Pierre-
de-Mons
○ ◉ St-Pierre
Toumilon
◉

Respide-Medoville
Langon
◉ Magence

SAUTERNES
■ de Gaillat

Ciron

Sauternes ○
⊡ L'Etoile

Brion

Le Pavillon-de-Boyrein ■

Roaillan ○
○ Mazeres
◉ de Roquetaillade

Noallan ○

Villandraut ○

■ ◉ Red Wines
□ ◉ White Wine

0   20 Miles
0   40 ℍ

Southern Graves

consumers' perception of Graves. As a standard-bearer for the unfashionable and unsung southern parts of Graves, Pierre Coste has been steadily drawing attention to what excellent wines can be made here, and these have now won a considerable following, both in France itself and on export markets.

Another important contribution came from Peter Vinding-Diers when he managed Château Rahoul at Portets. He, too, has shown how modern methods of vinification can transform the wines at what was formerly quite a modest property. In particular, his work on yeasts promises to give food for thought for some time to come.

Turning to the wines themselves, what impresses me most about the new red Graves of the south is their delightful individuality of character. They tend to be lighter in texture than most *crus bourgeois* from the Médoc, but have a piercingly vivid fruitiness which is all their own. Less tannic than Médoc, these wines are usually delicious to drink when young, yet also keep well. I have tasted several 1985s which were already quite mouth-watering when two years old. Cabernet Sauvignon, Cabernet Franc and Merlot all play an important part in the make-up of these wines, although the proportion of Cabernet Sauvignon tends to be lower than among the leading *crus* of the northern Graves.

The use of stainless steel tanks to achieve low-temperature fermentations has transformed the quality of many white wines. Tastings in this category show that some wines still have a rather coarse, earthy character, but a number are achieving a delicacy and finesse comparable to some of the prestigious northern *crus*. Here it has been interesting to note the revival of the fortunes of the Sémillon. There was a time when everyone wanted to produce more or less pure Sauvignon wines, but experience showed that such wines did not age well, and also lacked real Graves style – the all-pervading varietal character proved too dominant. Now, one can see how a judicious blending of the two traditional varieties provides wines which benefit from the immediate charm of the Sauvignon for early drinking, but can then fall back on the slower-developing Sémillon for bottle ageing – when required.

The INAO produced a classification of both red and white Graves in 1953, which was revised in 1959. It lists only thirteen red wines and eight white wines, but without any distinction between them. Haut-Brion was, of course, the only growth of Graves to be included in the 1855 classification, and belongs in the category of the great first growths of the Gironde. La Mission-Haut-Brion now holds a position similar to that of Mouton in the mid-nineteenth century, in between the first and second growths – not quite accepted as a first growth, but nearly there. Then come Domaine de Chevalier, Haut-Bailly and Pape-Clément, which by both price and merit belong with the best second growths of the Médoc. The remainder belong further down the scale, so that the Graves contribution to the great growths of the Gironde is small in number but memorable in quality.

GRAVES: 1959 OFFICIAL CLASSIFICATION

The vineyards of the Graves district were officially classified in 1953 and in 1959. Château Haut-Brion is also officially classified with the great Médocs.

	COMMUNE	CASES
Classified red wines of Graves		
Château Bouscaut	*Cadaujac*	11,500
Château Carbonnieux	*Léognan*	15,000
Domaine de Chevalier	*Léognan*	5,000
Château de Fieuzal	*Léognan*	8,000
Château Haut-Bailly	*Léognan*	11,000
Château Haut-Brion	*Pessac*	12,000
Château Malartic-Lagravière	*Léognan*	7,500
Château La Mission-Haut-Brion	*Pessac*	7,000
Château Olivier	*Léognan*	8,500
Château Pape-Clément	*Pessac*	12,000
Château Smith-Haut-Lafitte	*Martillac*	22,000
Château La Tour-Haut-Brion	*Talence*	1,500
Château La Tour-Martillac (Kressmann-La Tour)	*Martillac*	8,500
Classified white wines of Graves		
Château Bouscaut	*Cadaujac*	2,100
Château Carbonnieux	*Léognan*	15,000
Domaine de Chevalier	*Léognan*	800
Château Couhins	*Villenave-d'Ornon*	1,900
Château Laville-Haut-Brion	*Talence*	2,000
Château Malartic-Lagravière	*Léognan*	900
Château Olivier	*Léognan*	9,000
Château La Tour-Martillac (Kressmann-La Tour)	*Martillac*	1,500

The white wines are equally varied. There is a tiny number of wines which are the best dry white wines of Bordeaux, and also among the best in France, and there is a great quantity of other wines which vary from stylish, dry and fruity, to mawkish, over-sulphured and semi-sweet – the whole gamut of quality. The traditional style of white Graves was full-bodied with a marvellously honeyed bouquet, a wine with a good deal of alcohol and some richness, which required up to ten years' maturation to give of its best, and could live for many years more. But the poor and cheap imitations of this style were detestable, and helped to give Graves the bad name which still hangs over it. Today, the fashion is to make much lighter, crisper wines which can be bottled and drunk young, in line with dry white wines produced in other regions of France. Such wines are excellent and will, I am sure, win back much of Bordeaux's lost white wine trade.

The best Graves, both red and white, are produced in six communes which lie close to Bordeaux, out of the thirty-seven which today make wines with the *appellation* Graves. These six now form the nucleus of the new Pessac-Léognan *appellation* (see below).

Everything points to a promising future for Graves. The whites are beginning to gain new respect and are overcoming old prejudices. Their exceptional value must gain them an even wider market. The great red wines are now starting to carve out a separate place for themselves after being in the shadow of Médoc for so long, while the variety, quality and individuality of the southern reds – coupled with good prices – must benefit from the ever-increasing demand for good, affordable clarets.

PESSAC-LÉOGNAN

This new *appellation* came into force by a decree of 9 September 1987 – the result of a long campaign by the *crus classés* of Graves and the other *crus* of the northern Graves for a separate status for this historic nucleus of the region – and is on a par with the position accorded the leading communes of the Haut-Médoc. In 1984 they won the right to use the terms "Graves-Pessac" and "Graves-Léognan" on their labels. Now the process has been completed. The *appellation* covers the ten communes of Cadaujac, Canéjan, Gradignan, Léognan, Martillac, Mérignac, Médard-d'Eyrans, Pessac, Talence, and Villenave-d'Ornon. The word Graves will, however, continue to feature on the labels of the new *appellation*, and the wines of the 1986 vintage were the first to be permitted to use this *appellation*.

The northern limits of the *appellation* were simple to set: they are those of the Graves region itself. The southern limits were more difficult. The Belleyme map at the end of the eighteenth century gives the impression of a break in the continuity of the vineyards of Graves at the line of the river Saucats in the parish of La Brède, and when Charles de Montesquieu was selling some of his wines in 1696 his production from Rochemorin obtained a higher price than that of La Brède, the property where he resided. More precise still, William Franck in 1824 specified that the "Vins Rouges de Graves" were those produced on gravelly soils, up to about 12 kilometres to the south and 8 kilometres to the west of the city of Bordeaux. He then went on to detail the communes of Mérignac, Gradignan, Pessac, Talence, Léognan and Villenave-d'Ornon, but those of Martillac and St Médard-d'Eyrans were lumped in with La Brède and St Morillon, under the heading of "Petits Vins Rouges de Graves", although the *cru* de Smith (Smith-Haut-Lafitte) is singled out for special mention. The first French edition of Cocks in 1850 followed exactly the same path, except that it is much more dismissive of the wines of Martillac as "*dur et ordinaire*". By 1881 the fourth edition of Cocks & Féret includes Martillac within the fold, but still excludes Cadaujac and St Médard-d'Eyrans, classed as "Petits Graves". This situation continued until the present century. Thus the appeal to history, which is one of the principal planks of the protagonists of the new *appellation*, is something of a double-edged sword. Certainly there is an excellent historical case for separate treatment of the historic Graves, but some of the communes now chosen never formed a part of that nucleus so long as it possessed a separate identity!

In 1937 there were 1,500 hectares of vineyards within the bounds of this new *appellation*. Since then 500 hectares have been lost, presumably permanently, beneath the suburban expansion of Bordeaux, and today there are 900 hectares planted, of which half – 450 hectares – have been replanted in the last fifteen years, an indication of the strength of the revival of the region. These 900 hectares are divided among fifty-five *crus* producing 34,000 hectolitres on a five-year average. But in 1989 they produced 45,500 hectolitres of red and 10,000 hectolitres of dry white wines, or over 6 million bottles. The target is to have 1,500 hectares again planted by the end of the century. It is interesting to note that 75 per cent of the production is at present exported.

CHÂTEAU BARET

Owners: Mme Lucienne Ballande. Red: 7 hectares. 4,000 cases. CS 72%, Mer 25%, CF 3%. White: 6 hectares. 3,000 cases. Sém 65%, Sauv 32%, Musc 3%

This is a property in the part of Villenave d'Ornon adjoining Léognan. The vineyard dates at least from the eighteenth century. Since the death of his father-in-law André Ballande in 1981, Philippe Castéja has looked after the management of the property, and his company, Borie-Manoux, is also responsible for the commercialization of the wines. The wines have long enjoyed a good reputation, especially the white, but in recent years I have had some disappointingly dull and often over-sulphured examples. However, since Philippe Castéja took over, there has been a marked improvement. When I tasted a range of recent vintages in 1988, I found the whites full-flavoured, quite rich, especially in 1985 and 1986, and having a decided character. The 1983 had matured attractively, while the leaner, tauter 1984 was crisp, stylish and still fresh. The attractive 1987 is really long-flavoured and full-bodied, with marked style. These are fine classic wines which can be enjoyed over a number of years. The reds are now excellent examples of fine Graves, with a delicious light-textured 1983, and 1985 which has much more depth and substance while retaining the attractive spicy fruit. The 1986, in cask, was slightly more tannic but remarkably similar, and very harmonious. Château Baret has clearly joined the upward progression of the region.

CHÂTEAU BOUSCAUT

Cru Classé. Owner: SA du Château Bouscaut (Lucien Lurton). Red: 32 hectares. 11,500 cases. Mer 55%, CS 35%, CF 5%, Mal 5%. White: 10 hectares. 2,100 cases. Sém 52%, Sauv 48%

An impressive and beautifully kept property, it lies on the main road from Bordeaux to Sauternes. Its reputation seems to have been firmly established just before and after the First World War, although there was certainly a vineyard here in the eighteenth century, and Bouscaut is marked on the Cassini map at the end of the eighteenth century. The château dates from the same period; although it had to be largely rebuilt after a serious fire in 1962, the restoration has been done with great care and taste. It produced several vintages of note in the period after the First World War, especially the 1928. Then, in 1968, an American syndicate purchased it from Monsieur Victor Place, the proprietor, and Domain Wohlstetter-Sloan became the owners. Although the estate had been well cared for, the new owners spared no effort to ensure that Bouscaut became a model property. In 1980 they sold to Monsieur Lucien Lurton, the proprietor of Brane-Cantenac.

Lucien Lurton was fortunate to take on a property in such good order, where all the hard and expensive work on the vineyards and the château and *chai* had been done. In addition the re-equipment of the *cuvier* and *chai* had been done under the direction of Jean Delmas, *régisseur* of Haut-Brion, who also acted as *régisseur* here during this period.

The vineyard, which can be seen from the Bordeaux–Toulouse road, is on ridges of gravelly soil on a limestone base, with good natural drainage. The red wines are vinified in stainless steel and lined metal vats, the whites in stainless steel at 18–20°C. The reds are then matured in casks, of which a quarter are new, while the whites spend six months in cask prior to bottling.

I was able to get some idea of what Bouscaut used to produce when lunching with Lucien Lurton and his daughter Brigitte at the château during the 1986 vintage. A bottle of 1928 white had a wonderully preserved bouquet, very nutty with lovely full, ample fruit and no oxidation. The taste was extremely dry with some acidity at the finish, but it drank very well with food and was remarkable for a white wine of this age. A red 1949 had thrown a very heavy colour deposit on the bottle. The bouquet developed well in the glass, with fine fruit and power. The flavour was very tannic at the finish, but the fruit evolved well and the wine drank very pleasurably.

Now the red wines tend to be rather light in colour, soft and supple but somehow lacking any flair or real individuality. But the 1985 is much better, spicy and vibrant, with more potential. The white wines have also shown some signs of improvement, beginning with the 1983 vintage, which had more length and breed than previous recent efforts, while the 1985 had more finesse, fullness and style. The 1986 was the most promising so far, very perfumed with excellent fruit and middle fullness, and just that hint of something extra that these wines have been lacking.

Will the reds show sustained improvement? I suspect that Lucien Lurton is producing the best that this vineyard is capable of, with the vineyard now at optimum maturity – thirty-five years' average age – and a perfectly run and equipped estate.

CHÂTEAU BROWN

Owner: Jean-Claude Bonnel. Red: 11 hectares. 3,750 cases. CS 60%, Mer 40%

I first became aware of this *cru* through some delectable bottles of the 1928 which my father bought from Allan Sichel around 1950. I still remember the vivid colour, great vivacity and lovely flavour, sharply contrasting with the toughness and excess tannin of so many 1928s at that time. I had thought the vineyard lost beneath Bordeaux's urban sprawl, since it quite disappeared from Cocks & Féret, but fortunately this was not the case. In 1939 it was bought by André Bonnel. He also then had large vineyards in Morocco. More recently the vineyard has been largely replanted, so that it averaged nineteen years by 1987. The fine old property, which takes its name from the same family who owned Cantenac-Brown in the mid-nineteenth century, lies just north of Olivier in the commune of Léognan with its vineyard on two fine gravelly ridges called "Le Ciel" and "Roux". The 1981 in 1985 had a marked tobacco aroma and a delicious, rich, soft, spicy flavour, while the 1985 was delicious in 1989. This is a wine whose progress I shall watch with special interest.

CHÂTEAU CARBONNIEUX

Cru Classé. Owner: Société des Grandes Graves. Administrator: Antony Perrin. Red: 35 hectares. 15,000 cases. CS 50%, Mer 30%, CF 10%, PV and Mal 10%.
White: 35 hectares. 15,000 cases. Sauv 65%, Sém 30%, Musc 5%

This is an extremely old property, second only to Pape-Clément in its long and continuous history of wine-making. It is the largest producer of white wine – and is the largest vineyard – among the classified Graves. The turreted château dates from the end of the fourteenth century and, after belonging to the Hospices de Bordeaux, who had it as a gift from the du Ferron family – members of the Parlement de Guyenne for over two hundred years – it passed into the hands of the Benedictine monks from the abbey of Ste Croix-de-Bordeaux in 1741. Up until that time, the Graves region around Bordeaux had produced almost exclusively red wines. The monks were the first to produce white wine on a large scale, and so gave rise to the famous story about Carbonnieux. During the eighteenth century, the wines of Carbonnieux were apparently well known in most parts of Europe and were even sent to Constantinople where, to avoid the strictures of the Koran – which forbids Muslims to touch alcohol – the Benedictines labelled their white wine "Eau minérale de Carbonnieux". In 1956 Marc Perrin, yet another *pied-noir*, bought the property, and his son Antony Perrin now runs it.

Recently, great efforts have been made to improve the quality of Carbonnieux. In 1973, stainless steel *cuves* were installed to control the vinification of the white wines, and they are now bottled in the spring following the vintage. A recent experiment has been to give them three months in cask, to impart a little more complexity. With its proportion of Sauvignon, and the early bottling, the white Carbonnieux is usually delicious to drink very young – nine to eighteen months – then goes through a rather dull phase, as the primal Sauvignon fruit fades, and finally re-emerges as the Sémillon begins to assert itself, after two and a half to three years. This is my rule of thumb, but when I recently charted the evolution of some recent vintages, I found some quite wide varia-tions. Thus the excellent 1980 stayed in its Sauvignon phase for about two and a half years, had a dull period of about two years, and did not begin its mature Sémillon period until 1985, when four and a half years old. The 1982 and 1985 both had initial phases lasting for the first two years of their lives, but whereas the dull middle period lasted nearly two years for the 1982, the transition for the glittering 1985 was only six months. Obviously storage and atmospheric conditions can make a difference. A 1983 tasted in Singapore in January 1987 was more advanced in its Sémillon evolution than the same wine tasted in London four months later. At the limits of longevity, the 1967 still had a beautiful bouquet, nutty and enticing, when twenty years old, but although there was still good acidity, the fruit was going. But some of today's wines may last better than that.

The red Carbonnieux, I have often found disappointing. In the past it was rather rustic, and not among the better classified reds, but there have been determined efforts to improve quality – the 1978 had developed depths of flavour and a very Graves character, spicy with quite soft fruit, by seven years of age. A soft but rather indeterminate 1981 also developed quickly. In their different ways, I found both the 1982 and

1983 disappointing, but then Carbonnieux produced a very respectable 1984. The 1985 had more structure than usual and good fruit, while the 1986 with 80 per cent Cabernet Sauvignon had real concentration and marked tannin in cask. The use now of 25 per cent new oak is clearly having an effect, but as with many wines in Léognan, there is a certain leanness and lack of fat, and also a certain lack of real breed. Nevertheless the red Carbonnieux is not an expensive wine, and does make very enjoyable young drinking.

CHÂTEAU LES CARMES-HAUT-BRION

Owners: Chantecaille family. Administrator: Philippe Chantecaille. 3.5 hectares. 1,500 cases. Mer 50%, CF 40%, CS 10%

My memories of this wine, when I drank it several times in the early sixties, were that it was rather light and charming. But this is certainly not the case now. The 1978, tasted in February 1988, was deep-coloured and distinctly tannic and concentrated, but rather lacked breed. The unconventional *encépagement*, with its high proportions of Merlot and Cabernet Franc, but lack of Cabernet Sauvignon, could be to blame for this, since this is a mature vineyard with an average age of thirty years.

DOMAINE DE CHEVALIER

Cru Classé. Owner: Bernard Family. Administrator: Olivier Bernard. Red: 15 hectares. 5,000 cases. CS 65%, Mer 30%, CF 5%. White: 3 hectares. 800 cases. Sauv 70%, Sém 30%

One of the few leading properties in Bordeaux which still does not call itself a château, Chevalier is a small vineyard surrounded by woods; so that when one discovers it by a quiet country road, it seems like a clearing in the woods, with only a few modest farm buildings at the end of the vineyard.

Chevalier has consistently made both one of the finest red and one of the finest white wines in the Graves over a considerable period, but, owing to the small production, has not become as widely known as other leading wines. It was, incidentally, one of André Simon's favourites. Its fame began towards the end of the nineteenth century when it belonged to the grandfather of the late proprietor, Jean Ricard. Then, from 1900 to 1942, it belonged to Gabriel Beaumartin, a relation of the Ricards, who had a deserved reputation as a great wine-maker. Unfortunately the vineyard was badly frosted in 1945 and, following partial replanting, did not begin to return to its old form until the 1953 vintage.

In style, the red Chevalier is rather lighter in both colour and body than the other leading Graves, with the exception now of Haut-Brion, but has great delicacy and breed, a lovely bouquet and a more refined flavour than most Graves – a very individual wine. The white Chevalier is lighter and more steely in character than the Laville-Haut-Brion, but also takes several years to develop fully its fine bouquet and distinguished flavour. It is probably true to say that this and the Laville are in their different ways the best white Graves today in most vintages. The wine is always bottled after the second winter in about March and is fermented entirely in individual barrels.

I have no personal experience of the old vintages of the red Chevalier, but André Simon (see Bibliography) placed the 1899 among the best wines of that famous year, and the 1907 and 1909 as highly successful in rather average years. Edmund Penning-Rowsell (see Bibliography) records that the 1923, 1924, 1928, 1929, 1934 and 1937 were all good, while useful wines were made in the otherwise poor years of 1931 and 1936. Since 1953, good wines have been made in 1955, 1959, 1961, 1962, 1964 and 1966, while the tradition of making good off-vintage wines was maintained in 1963 and 1968. More recently, the 1978 was outstanding, while 1970, 1975, 1976 and 1979 have produced classic examples of these vintages. The eighties began with a classic wine with a pronounced perfume, very good indeed for 1980. The 1981 is full of powerful richness and has great finesse, an outstanding example of the year which even tasted well after the 1982, a stiff task for any 1981. The 1982 has the lovely supple fruit of the year, but the tannin showed earlier than in many 1982s. The 1983 has a fine bouquet, length of flavour and elegance, with a firm core, yet great charm; it is taking time to evolve. The 1984 is about 95 per cent Cabernet Sauvignon, yet has a beautiful fresh fruitiness and a lovely flavour; but it is light, of course. The 1985 in cask was beautifully supple but with plenty of tannin behind, while the 1986 seemed rich and more opulent but with a lot of tannin supporting it. Both have great finesse. I have the impression that in recent years the red wines here have rather more flesh on them than they used to have.

Of the white Chevalier, the 1937 and 1947 both had fine reputations, and I recently tasted the 1942, which was still interesting to taste, and even drink, while I have memories of the 1957 being outstandingly attractive. Later, the 1961, 1962, 1964 and 1966 were all outstanding wines which still showed well in 1988. As at Laville, the 1976 is magnificent, as is the 1979, which has more finesse than the 1978. The 1970 and, interestingly, the 1973 were particularly good. More recently, after good wines in 1980 and 1981, the 1982 was a classic but the 1983 was outstanding, with an almost Burgundy-like opulence and richness more reminiscent of a great Laville than the more taut wines of Chevalier. Then the 1984 is most attractive, a classic Graves reminding us that the white wines fared much better than the reds in this vintage. There is a 1985, which, while full-flavoured, is still fresh and lively, thanks to the new oak. The 1986 is all perfumed delicacy and complex fruit flavours, with a very long, delicate flavour of great finesse.

In 1983 the Ricard family were obliged to sell to the Bernard family, from Cognac, owing to inheritance problems. Happily Claude Ricard was asked to stay on as co-administrator, and has struck up an excellent partnership with the young Olivier Bernard, so continuity has been assured.

After Haut-Brion and La Mission, Chevalier is always among the top two or three red Graves, and in off-vintages sometimes higher up the scale than that. As the white wine is likewise always in the top two or three, this places Chevalier among the outstanding growths of Bordeaux – alongside the best of the second growths of the Médoc, if one is to make that sort of comparison.

CHÂTEAU COUHINS

Cru Classé. Owner: Institut National de la Recherche Agronomique. White: 2.4 hectares. 1,000 cases. Sauv 82%, Sém 18%. Red: 7.5 hectares. 3,300 cases. CS 45%, Mer 34%, CF 18%, PV 3%

This famous old *cru*, for many years the property of the Gasqueton and Hanappier families, is now divided in two, of which this, the larger portion, belongs to the Institut National de la Recherche Agronomique (INRA) and was acquired by them in 1968. Until then this was the sole Graves *cru classé* producing only white wines. Now the INRA produces some red wine, but this is not classified. The attraction of the vineyard for INRA lies in its proximity to Bordeaux and their Centre de Recherches there, and in the variety of the soils to be found here. The *cru* is in the commune of Villenave-d'Ornon, the most northerly of the Graves communes, with vineyards near the Garonne, and the Couhins vineyard is the best-sited. In fact only a part of the vineyard is used to produce *appellation* wines, about 8 hectares out of 14, the rest being entirely experimental, and including fruit trees and plants as well as vines. As will be seen, the production here of *cru classé* Graves Blanc is minuscule, the main production now being confined to Couhins-Lurton. Of course it is meticulously made, with temperature-controlled fermentation, but when I compared the 1984 vintage with that of its neighbour, side by side, I found it rather anonymous in character, with very clean, soft fruit, but lacking the dimensions of André Lurton's wine, which is barrel-fermented.

CHÂTEAU COUHINS-LURTON

Cru Classé. Owner: André Lurton. 6 hectares. 2,000 cases. Sauv 100%

André Lurton began here as *fermier* in 1967, first for the Gasqueton-Hanappier families then, for a time, for INRA. He was fortunate in being able to buy this portion of one of the finest vineyards for white wines in the Graves, thus ensuring the continued availability in something like commercial quantities of this famous old wine. The gravelly soil in this part of the vineyard has traces of clay in the subsoil, and this gives the wine body. André Lurton has abandoned the classic mixture of Sauvignon and Sémillon for his vineyard in favour of 100 per cent Sauvignon, as at Malartic-Lagravière. Since 1982 the wine has been fermented in new casks at a controlled temperature of 16–19°C. The resulting wines are very scented, with considerable finesse and length, probably at their finest for early drinking. André Lurton would like to buy the château itself, which would give him a *chai* and *cuvier* here, as well as more vineyard, but so far nothing has come of this, and the wine is still vinified at La Louvière. In spite of its former reputation and the excellence of its wines today, Couhins is now rather a forgotten *cru*, and La Louvière is certainly better known today.

CHÂTEAU CRUZEAU

Owner: André Lurton. Red: 36 hectares. 15,000 cases. CS 60%, Mer 40%. White: 11 hectares. 3,500 cases. Sauv 90%, Sém 10%

This is now the most important *cru* in the commune of St Médard-d'Eyrans, and the vineyard runs between this commune and the neighbouring one of Martillac. The position of the vineyard is marked on the Belleyme map in the late eighteenth century, and there were 30 hectares under vine here by 1813. By 1841 *Le Producteur* placed it as *premier cru* of the commune for both its red and white wines. So the pedigree here was impressive when André Lurton bought the property in 1973 and replanted it in 1974. The vineyard is on deep gravel. The red grapes are harvested by machine, and the white are hand-picked. The red wine is vinified in lined cement tanks and stainless steel at 28–30°C, and then matured in cask for a year, with one-third new oak. The white is vinified in stainless steel and glass-lined vats at 16–18°C, and sees no wood at all. In the next stage of development, the existing 50 hectares under vine will rise to 75.

When one remembers that the average age of the red vineyard was only ten years in 1987, the quality of the wines already being produced here is impressive. The 1981 was already scented and attractively fruity, the 1982 and 1983 were fuller and more tannic, with the richness and suppleness of the 1983 being especially fine. The whites, understandably, are making even faster progress. The 1983, 1985 and 1986 showed a beauty and length of flavour, delicious fruit, finesse and stylishness, that already place this wine on a par with some of the *crus classés*. The potential of Cruzeau is clear; it should not be long before the red wine is also of *cru classé* standard. Meanwhile these are delicious wines sold at reasonable prices, which are ready to drink young.

CHÂTEAU FERRAN

Owner: Hervé Béraud-Sadreau. Red: 5 hectares. 1,650 cases. Mer 80%, CS 10%, CF10%. White: 5.5 hectares. 2,000 cases. Sém 80%, Sauv 20%

Not to be confused with the much larger property at Castres in the central Graves, called Ferrande, this is an old property in Martillac, adjoining La Tour-Martillac, and takes its name from Robert de Ferrand, a seventeenth-century *avocat* at the Parlement in Bordeaux. In 1715 it passed to the philosopher Montesquieu at nearby La Brède, on his marriage to Jeanne de Castigue. At some time in the eighteenth century the "d" was dropped: Florence Mothe (*Graves de Bordeaux* in the Ginestet series) mentions a case of the name appearing without the "d" in 1764, yet it appears with the "d" in the Cassini map, which is later – another case perhaps of a rather cavalier attitude to spelling at this time. The family of the present owner have been here since before the war. The very Sémillon white wine takes longer to evolve than its more Sauvignon neighbours, and has notably flowery fruit and definite finesse. It should reward keeping. The red wine is very deep-coloured, with very vivid fruit – a wine that needs time. The 1981 was not nearly ready in 1985.

CHÂTEAU DE FIEUZAL

Cru Classé. Owner: SA Château de Fieuzal. Administrator: Gérard Gribelin. 23 hectares. Red: 8,000 cases. CS 60%, Mer 30%, CF 5%, PV 5%. White: 600 cases. Sauv 50%, Sém 50%

This is a small property producing both red and white wines, of which the red is classified but the white is not. The estate is an old one, and once belonged to the family de la Rochefoucauld. The present excellent reputation was acquired under Erik Bocké, Swedish in origin but Bordelais by adoption, who had married a Ricard daughter before the war. In those days he was a theatre manager in Bordeaux. He and his wife spent the war in Morocco, and on their return found that his father-in-law had died, and that the property was in a sorry state. So Erik Bocké turned his hand to wine-making, and lavished both money and love on the estate; and *chai* and *cuvier* are a showplace of cleanliness and order. In 1973, on the death of his wife, Fieuzal was bought by Monsieur Négrevergne, a Bordeaux pharmaceutical manufacturer, who has continued the good work. The new owners have been very fortunate to have the services of Gérard Gribelin as administrator, who has very much continued where Erik Bocké left off. The *chai* is as pristine as ever, and a new *cuvier* was built on the site of the former château in 1977, with stainless steel fermentation vats and the latest electronic temperature control.

I had the opportunity of tasting several vintages a few years ago, and found the red wine extremely well made, on the light side, but very elegant, fruity and pleasing to drink, well balanced without too strong a Graves character – indeed, some vintages were quite Médocain in style. The 1953 was pleasing without being special, the 1960 highly successful for the year, and the 1962 very well balanced. They were the sort of wines which could take a worthy place with the fourth or fifth growths of the

Médoc. The white Fieuzal is a comparatively recent innovation, introduced by Monsieur Bocké.

The red wines have taken on an extra dimension in recent vintages. The lovely 1978 and elegant 1981 were in line with the light-to-medium-weight wines one had come to expect of Fieuzal, both having real breed. Then the 1982 had much more concentration, but the 1983 is lighter, with breed and charm. With the 1985 the wine reached new heights: this is certainly one of the top Graves of the vintage, adding depth and concentration to its existing breed and elegance. The 1986 was more tannic and massive in cask, with considerable potential. The red Fieuzal is definitely on the move; 50 per cent new oak is now used in its maturation.

The small white wine production is now fermented in new oak and bottled in the spring after the vintage. This is a wine with length of flavour, lovely crisp fruit and quite a floral bouquet; it has a markedly Sauvignon character and is delicious for early drinking. I have not come across any examples with more than two to three years in bottle. In 1983 a second wine, clearly much more Sémillon in character, was sold under the name of L'Abeille de Fieuzal. While attractive and full-flavoured, it lacked the elegance of the first wine.

CHÂTEAU DE FRANCE
Owner: Bernard Thomassin. Red: 26 hectares. 13,000 cases. CS 50%, Mer 50%. White: 4 hectares (vineyard only recently replanted). Sauv 50%, Sém 30%, Musc 20%

This vineyard lies between Fieuzal and Malartic-Lagravière, just south of Léognan. It once belonged to Château Olivier and the Montesquieu family. It took on a new lease of life when bought by its present owner in 1971. The red wine vineyard is now mature but the white one is being replanted. I have found the reds to be very perfumed, developing plenty of soft, lively fruit fairly quickly. The 1983 was at its best by early 1987, but the 1985 promised more breed and substance. This is attractive, stylish and carefully made wine. It will be interesting to see how the white turns out.

CHÂTEAU LA GARDE

Owner: Maison Dourthe. Red: 41 hectares. 20,000 cases. CS 70%, Mer 30%.
White: 6 hectares. 3,000 cases. Sauv 100%

This is an old property which appears on Cassini's map at the end of the eighteenth century. It belonged to Louis Eschenauer from 1926 until its sale to Dourthe in 1990, and, as with their other properties (Smith-Haut-Lafitte, Rausan-Ségla), has in recent years undergone considerable expansion and re-equipment. A few years ago only 15 hectares were planted, compared with 47 today, and a small white wine vineyard has been planted. The red wines are surprisingly soft and opulent in spite of the high Cabernet content in the vineyard; easy and pleasing to drink young, if rather one-dimensional and simplistic.

CHÂTEAU HAUT-BAILLY

Cru Classé. Owner: Robert G. Wilmers. Administrator: Veronique Sanders. Red: 25 hectares. 11,000 cases. CS 60%, Mer 30%, CF 10%. Second label: La Parde de Haut-Bailly

The fame of Haut-Bailly dates from its acquisition in 1872 by a famous viticulturist of the period, Bellot des Minières. The vineyard is situated on one of the highest ridges of fine, gravelly soil in the region, and is dedicated solely to the production of red wine. The château is a simple, four-square, nineteenth-century house which stands next to the *cuvier* and *chai*.

The story of Haut-Bailly is that, after a period of fame under Bellot des Minières (the 1878 was judged one of the outstanding wines of that vintage) the property passed through a period of decline. It was even said at one time that the wine was pasteurized, a story repeated in Morton Shand's classic on the wines of France. In 1955 the property was bought by a Belgian wine merchant, Daniel Sanders, and since then he and his son have worked hard to restore its great reputation.

I shall always remember the first occasion that I ever tasted Haut-Bailly. I was looking at samples of the great 1961s at Loudenne when a sample of the Haut-Bailly appeared. We had never been offered the wine before, and I had never even tasted a bottle of it. The sample was so outstanding that, although the price was very high – even for a 1961 – and the château virtually forgotten then in England, I bought what was offered and never regretted it. Since then, I have grown to love and increasingly admire the wines of Haut-Bailly, although some of the vintages of the seventies do not quite live up to the château's potential. In style, it is probably closer to the wines of Pessac than any other wine of Léognan. It is somewhere between La Mission and Pape-Clément, perhaps, having something of the great vinosity and richness of La Mission, but it is slightly lighter in texture and develops more quickly. The bouquet is often strikingly similar to that of Pape-Clément, but tends to have more definition and style. Above all, this is a wonderfully harmonious wine, never too tannic, never too soft-centred.

The only pre-war wine I have seen was the 1937, which I have drunk on a number of occasions. It is certainly one of the most enjoyable wines I know of from that vintage. The 1928 also had a good reputation. Since the Sanders era began, the 1957 was a great success, with much more vinosity and charm than most wines of that year, not far behind La Mission. In 1959 and 1960, frost struck disastrously, only ten tonneaux being produced in 1959 and six hogsheads in 1960. The 1961 was a great wine which has steadily developed its considerable potential, and this has been followed by a succession of wonderfully consistent and fine years: 1962, 1964 (an outstanding wine in this mixed year), 1966, 1967 and 1970. During the seventies, Daniel Sanders was growing old and less and less able to exercise the meticulous control which had been responsible for the revival of Haut-Bailly's fortunes. Nor, unfortunately, would he entrust the task to his son Jean. The result was a series of disappointing wines, judged by the highest standards. Monsieur Jean Sanders took over the running of the château after the death of his father in 1980, and made the 1979. The result is that the 1978 vintage is fine, but lacks the intensity of the best 1978s, while the 1979 has a wonderfully rich, perfumed bouquet and a fine, opulent, supple flavour, very reminiscent of the good vintages of the sixties. To achieve this one-third of the crop was eliminated. As a result this wine has turned out much better than the 1978. Since then, the 1980 was pleasing but light, and is now past its best. The 1981 has immense breed and charm, and has begun to drink very well. The 1982 lacks the concentration expected in this vintage but has great ripeness and finesse, and is very typical of Haut-Bailly. The 1983 is another stylish wine with good balance which is developing quite quickly. The 1984, which is heavily reliant on Cabernet Sauvignon, is nevertheless very scented and has a fine flavour and a lot of style, although it is light. The two great vintages of 1985 and 1986 provided a great contrast in cask, with the 1985 full of typical Haut-Bailly charm, full-flavoured but relatively open-textured, while the 1986, with hardly any Merlot in it, is exceptionally concentrated and tannic for Haut-Bailly, with a beautiful flavour, finesse and great length. This must be the best wine made here since Jean Sanders took over. It is good to see this fine growth restored to its rightful place and once more being enjoyed in Great Britain and the United States.

CHÂTEAU HAUT-BERGEY

Owner: J. Deschamps. Red: 16 hectares. 7,000 cases. CS 70%, Mer 30%

This is a well-placed vineyard, just outside Léognan to the west. You pass it on the way to Chevalier. The name is clearly marked on the Cassini map in the late eighteenth century, although there do not appear to have been many vines planted then. This is a well-run property of some repute. The wines are aged in casks, of which half are new oak. I have found the wines delicately scented and attractively flavoured, inclined to be light.

CHÂTEAU HAUT-BRION

Premier Cru Classé 1855. Owner: Domaine Clarence Dillon. Red: 41 hectares. 12,000 cases, CS 55%, Mer 30%, CF 15%. White: 3 hectares. 1,300 cases. Sém 55%, Sauv 45%. Second label: Bahans-Haut-Brion

This was the only Graves to be included in the 1855 classification, where it was placed as a first growth. It had long been regarded as being on a par with the leading growths of the Médoc. The origin of the name is obscure, but it can safely be said that Maurice Healy's fond wish to find an Irish connection as a corruption of O'Brien has no foundation in fact. It is said that the name comes from the *seigneurie* of Brion, and that over the years it became transformed to D'Obrion or Daubrion, to Hault-Brion, and finally to its present form. The fame of the place seems to date from its acquisition in 1529, when a de Pontac married Jeanne de Bellon, daughter of Pierre de Bellon, then mayor of Libourne and *seigneur* of Hault-Brion. By the end of the seventeenth century, out of a total estate of 264 hectares, some 38 were given over to vines. From then until just before the Revolution, Haut-Brion remained in the hands of the Pontac family, and was often sold under the name of Pontac. Unfortunately, the

Pontacs were such large proprietors of vineyards in the area that it is not always possible to tell if wine sold during their regime actually came from Haut-Brion or from their other properties as well. Before the Revolution, the property passed by marriage to the de Fumel family, at that time also owners of Margaux.

Haut-Brion first broke upon the world, well before any other Bordeaux *cru*, through the vivid pages of Samuel Pepys. On 10 April 1663 he records: "To the Royall Oake Taverne in Lumbard-Street . . . and here drank a sort of French wine, called *Ho Bryan*, that hath a good and most particular taste that I never met with." And Pepys was not the only Englishman to appreciate the special charms of Haut-Brion. Arnaud de Pontac was also a man of business, and after the Great Fire of 1666, he sent his son François-Auguste to promote his wines further on his best market. The result was Pontack's Head, the first fashionable eating-house in London, according to André Simon. In 1683 that other great diarist of the period, John Evelyn, recorded a conversation with the same François-Auguste. In 1677 the most famous English philosopher of the period, John Locke, actually visited Haut-Brion, and his detached observations are the first we have on the factors which make great wines. He cites four things as necessary to produce good wines: poor soil, good slopes, little manuring and old vines. All remain true today, and only the selection of *cépages* is missing; it was too early for this.

The Revolution began a confused period in Haut-Brion's history. The Comte de Fumel was an *émigré*, and so the property was seized by the state. From then onwards it passed through many hands; for three years it belonged to Talleyrand, and at another time to one of the Beyermans from the old firm of Dutch *négociants*. Eventually, it was bought in 1836 by Joseph-Eugène Larrieu, whose family owned it until 1923. Then there was an unhappy period of decline in the château's fortunes until Mr Clarence Dillon, the American banker, bought the property in 1935. Since then it has gone from strength to strength under the supervision of the devoted Seymour Weller and of the *régisseur*, Jean Delmas, who succeeded his father in 1961 and is now the much-respected doyen among first-growth *régisseurs*. Since Seymour Weller's death, and the succession of a member of the family who actually lives in France, the position of *régisseur* has, if anything, grown in importance. It was, perhaps, appropriate that a wine which had been much loved and praised by

Thomas Jefferson during his stay in France, should later become the property of another distinguished American. Since Clarence Dillon's death in 1979, his granddaughter, the Duchesse de Mouchy, has been head of the company.

The château itself is a charming turreted affair, parts of which go back to the sixteenth century, and it is well depicted on the label. Part of the vineyard adjoins the château and part lies across the road adjoining that of La Mission-Haut-Brion. These two now form an oasis of vineyards surrounded by housing. Haut-Brion went modern in 1960, when stainless steel vats were installed for the vinification. Apart from this, the *chai* is well kept and workmanlike, not as showy as some of the Médoc châteaux.

The wines of Haut-Brion have known their ups and downs. Before Larrieu bought the property in 1836, its reputation lagged behind that of the first growths of the Médoc, but by the late nineteenth century it stood very high indeed. Both the 1899 and the 1900 enjoyed a great reputation, and actually sold at a higher price than either Lafite or Margaux. The 1906 was also one of the successes of that year. The earliest Haut-Brion I have seen was the 1921 which, when I drank it in 1963, was still very dark in colour with a most distinctive "roasted" nose. The wine was still very big, hard and unyielding, and quite without any of the charm of age. This was, I believe, in part the then Haut-Brion style, but also in good part, at least, the character of the 1921 vintage. When tasted again in 1979, sixteen years later, the wine was quite transformed, now elegant with a sweet fruitiness, delicacy and finesse, and a lovely finish. But the finest of the vintages of this decade was probably the 1926. As at Mouton, it has the power of a 1928 but the sweetness of a 1929. In a pre-sale tasting of the late Clarence Dillon's cellar held at Christie's in 1979, the 1926 was comfortably the best of a range of the main vintages between 1921 and 1937. It had a really lovely flavour and was completely harmonious, sweet and rich: altogether a great classic claret in the heroic mould.

The 1928, which I drank against the Latour of the same year in 1957, was a good deal harder than the Latour and very aggressive, with a most distinctive, but not altogether agreeable, character. When I had another bottle of the same wine some years later, it had disintegrated. My impression of the oddness of the 1928 was borne out by the sample from the Dillon private cellar in 1979. I noted that it was still an enormous wine, but quite unbalanced, with a very strange, rather medicinal after-taste. The 1929 had something of the same stamp about it, with an almost port-like character. One classic vintage of the 1920s I have not mentioned is the 1924. This was a wine of considerable breed and elegance, but without the staying power of the 1926 or the 1921, and the sample from the Dillon cellar was clearly past its best.

The thirties produced nothing to match the 1926, nor did they repeat the freaks of 1928 and 1929. The 1934 was still very rich in 1979, with a touch of that port-like style noted in the 1929, but with a very dry finish, yet with more fruit than the 1937. It was clearly the superior wine. When I first tasted the 1937 in 1971, I had quite liked it, noting the distinction of flavour and great richness, and finding it not unduly hard like most 1937s. Yet by 1979, the sample from the Dillon cellar, while retaining the classic flavour, had a very dry, tannic finish which made the wine short and unharmonious.

Since the Second World War, Haut-Brion seems to have undergone a gradual but steady change of style. Gone are the black-strap wines of old, with their very special character; instead, we have much lighter, more elegant wines which develop much more quickly. In some recent vintages, the wines have almost seemed to lack weight and staying power, especially in off-vintages. But in the fine years, wines of great breed and distinction have consistently been made. During the war, the 1940 and 1944 were both delightful, light wines. The 1940 has stayed remarkably well – it still showed well at the Dillon tasting in 1979 – but the 1944 was going downhill rapidly. After this, the 1945 was one of the greatest wines of this remarkable year, complete, complex and powerful, and still free from volatility or dryness, when last tasted in 1985; the 1947 was very concentrated and rich; the 1949 was superbly spicy and rich in fruit, on a par with the great Latour of this year; the 1953 was outstanding, the 1955 a good example of the year, the 1957 stylish and fine, the 1959 again one of the best of the year, the 1961 outstandingly attractive but forward from the start, the 1962 most attractive and fine, and the 1964 again most successful, as was the 1966 and a ripe and richly flavoured 1967. However, years like 1958 and 1960 tended to fade rather quickly and, as with many other châteaux, it was a mistake to offer the 1963 and 1965.

The 1970s have followed a rather similar pattern, with wines of great style and breed in the great years like 1970, 1975, 1976 and 1978, but a terribly light, insubstantial offering in 1977, while in the difficult vintage of 1973 what had seemed a lightweight became – by 1986 – complex and surprisingly rich, with a glorious flavour and real breed. The eighties began with a rather light and lean 1980, but then got into their stride with a solid 1981 of marked Graves character, a 1982 with less fat than many wines of that year, but with elegance, firmness and concentration. In contrast, the 1983 looks exceptional for the year, very ripe and rich with considerable concentration. After a 1984 that is rich and supple for the year came a quite outstanding 1985, one of the top wines of the vintage, and a 1986 which is mostly Cabernet Sauvignon, very tannic, with outstanding power and character. One has the impression that recent vintages have a little more weight than the wines of the seventies; certainly the overall standard is now on a par with the best that is being produced at the other first growths.

There is a second wine, Bahans-Haut-Brion, which at one time was sold without a vintage, but this practice has now changed, and vintage wines are once more appearing. Small quantities of pleasingly elegant wines are made under this *marque*.

Owing to its American connection, Haut-Brion has a great following in the United States and is not, perhaps, seen as often in England as it used to be.

Haut-Brion also makes a very small quantity of white wine. Curiously enough, its very existence has been stolidly denied in both the eleventh (1949) and twelfth (1969) editions of Cocks & Féret, until finally appearing in the thirteenth (1982). Unfortunately the quantity is so small – seldom much more than 1,500 cases – that the demand from the United States means that one seldom finds any in England now. In 1989, Bipin Desai organized a remarkable series of tastings of Haut-Brion Blanc and Laville in the context of skilfully chosen meals in Los Angeles. The outstanding Haut-Brions proved to be an amazing 1916, with a rich Sémillon character; a great 1928, still fresh and elegant with an intensely concentrated flavour; a 1929 with a nose like old Barsac, but now searingly dry. The 1945 was overshadowed by the succulent, luscious 1947. In the fifties, the 1959 was outstanding, very rich with a dry finish, followed by an elegantly dry 1952. The star of the sixties was a classic 1962, full-bodied and intensely flavoured, with more life than the rich, mellow

1961. The seventies produced three outstanding wines, 1970, 1975 and the wonderfully complete 1978. In the eighties, 1980 and 1981 were attractively drinkable wines, but the younger vintages still needed time: 1982, 1984, 1985, 1987, 1988 and, above all, 1989 promise fine things. These are delightful wines if you are lucky enough to be able to obtain a bottle – demand far outstrips supply.

Finally, mention must be made of the important long-term work on clonal selection that has been going on at Haut-Brion under Jean Delmas's direction since 1972. It is in collaboration with INRA and the Chambre d'Agriculture. After preliminary work, it was decided in 1978 to create a collection of clones at Haut-Brion, based on some clones already produced by INRA and some which had been developed at Haut-Brion. As Jean Delmas points out, what may be considered the best clones commercially may not necessarily be the best for a great *cru* such as Haut-Brion, where considerations of yield are less important than those of quality, which is determined by such things as richness in sugar content, acidity, richness in tannin, colour and aroma.

CHÂTEAU LARRIVET-HAUT-BRION

Owners: Gerverson family. Administrator: Philippe Gerverson. Red: 15.4 hectares. 7,600 cases. CS 60%, Mer 35%, Mal and PV 5%. White: 0.76 hectares. 400 cases. Sauv 60%, Sém 40%. Second label: Domaine de Larrivet

This was once a much larger property, and at the time of the French Revolution was called Château de Canolle. After frequent changes of ownership and divisions of the property, the last important one being in 1936, the name Haut-Brion-Larrivet was used. However, the new American owners at Haut-Brion challenged the name, which had to be changed to its present form. From 1941 it belonged to Monsieur Guillemaud, who did much to improve both *chai* and vineyard. Originally only red wine was made on the estate, but a small quantity of white is now also produced. After the death of her husband, the property was run by Madame Guillemaud, assisted by her grandson Francis Bouteney, from 1985, since when there has been an improvement in the wine-making and the selection. Then in 1988 they sold a majority interest to the Gerverson family, owners of Bon Maman, a well-known brand of jams, but with Francis Bouteney staying on to assist. The breed and keeping ability of this *cru* were clearly shown by the 1966, which was still fresh and vivid when over twenty years old. The style is very Graves, with a pronounced tobacco aroma on the nose and a very clean, powerful flavour with vivid fruit and marked character. From 1986 much more serious selection has been made, 40 per cent new oak is now used for the reds, while from 1987 the whites have been fermented in new oak. Larrivet should soon be a candidate for classification; it clearly has the potential.

CHÂTEAU LAVILLE-HAUT-BRION

Cru Classé. Owner: Domaine Clarence Dillon. White: 6 hectares. 2,000 cases. Sém 60%, Sauv 40%

This might almost be called the white La Mission, but in fact it has always been run as a separate property producing only white wines. It was acquired by the Woltner brothers in 1928. It is today the outstanding example of a classic white Graves made in the traditional style. It is full-bodied and takes some time to reach its best. Henri Woltner used to say it could be drunk when five years old, but it is seldom at its best before ten years – in marked contrast to the new style of instant white wines. As with some of the best white Burgundies, the complex flavour and character develop only gradually, until, when mature, it has a marvellous honeyed nose, a pale golden colour and a very complex flavour – dry, yet full in the mouth, with that sort of richness compounded of alcohol and natural glycerine which is found in a fine Montrachet. The production is very small – so that even though white Graves tends to be out of fashion today, there is not too much around for a world demand. Unfortunately, some three hectares of vineyard were lost when the main Bordeaux–Bayonne railway line was re-routed some years ago, a sad hostage to "progress". It is a wine worth searching and saving for.

The soil of the Laville vineyard is richer and less stony than that of La Mission or La Tour. It is interesting to note that this wine is fermented in individual barrels and not in *cuve*, but the temperature of the small *chai* can be controlled. After 1961, the wines were bottled in the late spring to early summer after the vintage, and with only the lightest of filtrations. This was changed by Jean Delmas and the marvellous 1985 was bottled only in March 1987. As with many white wines, the best years are not necessarily the same as for reds, because in the greatest years, the whites are often too alcoholic and lack finesse. Thus I personally prefer the 1962 to the 1961, and the 1971 to the 1970. At the Bipin Desai tastings in Los Angeles in 1989 (see Haut-Brion p. 329), the remarkable longevity of these wines was demonstrated by the extraordinary 1934 and the only 1935 I have ever tasted, while 1945, 1947, 1948, 1950 and 1953 were still in peak condition. The 1952, 1955 and 1959 were showing more age, but were still impressive. In the sixties, if the 1962 was exceptional, 1964, 1966 and 1967 were all superb, with 1965 a delightful surprise. The pick of the seventies is the 1971, closely followed by 1970, 1975 and 1976. Then came several rather austere wines, from 1978 until 1983, which disappoint in the context of Laville, with 1981 the best of these. Under the new management, after a fine 1984 came a lovely, ripe, flattering 1985, followed by very successful wines in 1986, 1987 and 1988, and especially 1989. These recent vintages are richer and more structured than the Haut-Brion Blanc, and more harmonious than those of the Dewavrin epoch.

CHÂTEAU LA LOUVIÈRE

Owner: André Lurton. Red: 37 hectares. 16,500 cases. CS 70%, Mer 20%, CF 10%. White: 18 hectares. 7,500 cases. Sauv 85%, Sém 15%. Secondary labels: Château Cantebeau, Château Coucheray, Château Clos du Roi

This property neatly encapsulates the glories of the past and the new dawn of the revived and reinvigorated Graves. The name reminds us that wolves once roamed the forest, which lay within an easy ride of Bordeaux. The château itself is one of the jewels of the entire region, perhaps the ultimate statement of the Bordelais classical tradition which had begun in 1715 at La Lagune in an austere simplicity and flowered in mid-century in châteaux such as Beychevelle and Langoa and in the urban masterpieces of Victor Louis. Here at La Louvière the embellishments and grandeur of the great buildings of the 1770s and 1780s give way to a stark classicism that reminds us of David's great republican tableaux of the 1790s. The severity of the single-storey building is relieved only by the steep roof-line and the simplest of porticos. In 1965 La Louvière had the good fortune to be bought by André Lurton. It was his first venture into Graves, from his family base at Château Bonnet in the Entre-Deux-Mers. Since then, this dynamic man has acquired Couhins, Rochemorin and Cruzeau, and has spearheaded the campaign for the new Pessac-Léognan *appellation*. He is the first President of the Syndicat Viticole

Pessac-Léognan. The whole region is much in his debt for the tireless energy which he has directed towards the common good in the last twenty years while, at the same time, revitalizing neglected and sometimes completely abandoned vineyards.

We first hear of La Louvière as the home of a poet, Jean de Guilloche, who on his return from the coronation of Charles VIII at Rheims in 1484 wrote a celebrated poem, "La Prophécie du Roy Charles VIII". His descendant, Pierre de Guilloche, who became a member of the *noblesse de robe* in 1533 and Provost in 1543, embraced the Huguenot cause and perished in the infamous St Bartholomew's Day massacre of 1572 at Bazas. But his son Jean was made of less stern stuff and married the heiress of Roquetaillade. La Louvière stayed in his family until 1618 when Armand de Gascq, Abbot of Saint-Ferme, gave the property to the Bordeaux Charterhouse, and it was farmed by the Carthusian monks until the Revolution. In these early days the "v" often becomes a "b"; Pierre de Guilloche was described as Signeur de La Loubière, while on the Cassini map published at the end of the eighteenth century, the name appears as La Loubeyre. With the confiscation of Church property during the Revolution, in 1791 the property was bought for 228,000 *livres* by Jean-Baptiste Mareilhac, a rich businessman who became mayor of Bordeaux in 1796. On 4 Floréal in Year II of the Republic (23 April 1794) he is recorded as having donated 20,000 *livres* for the construction of a warship, so he was a man of substance, a member of precisely that new middle class which threw in its lot with the Revolution. It was he who built the glorious château in 1795. Whether the plans were actually those of Victor Louis or of a pupil named Lhôte is uncertain. This family remained proprietors until 1911, when they sold to Alfred-Bertrand Taquet, the then mayor of Léognan. It is interesting to note that in the first French edition of Cocks (1850), La Louvière and Olivier are the only properties in Léognan to be accorded the name of château, and La Louvière had the highest production in the commune with 80 tonneaux (Carbonnieux was then placed in the commune of Villenave-d'Ornon).

Since La Louvière's renaissance began under André Lurton's direction, progress has been constant. The vineyard is in one of the best sectors of Léognan, between Haut-Bailly and Carbonnieux. It consists of mostly gravelly soils, but there are also limestone and silica. The vineyard had to be reconstituted, and the *cuvier* and *chai* reconstructed. Now the red grapes are mechanically harvested, while the white are hand-picked. The vinification of the white wines is in *cuves* of stainless steel and glass-lined metal at 16–18°C, but part of the production is now fermented in new oak. The cask-fermented wine then goes into *cuve* until bottling, while some of the *cuve*-fermented wine spends some months in these same casks. The red wines are traditionally fermented, and then matured in casks, of which one-third are new. The white wines of La Louvière have shown outstanding qualities of finesse, fruit and delicacy at least since the 1970 vintage. Then 1971,1975,1978,1979,1981,1982,1984 and 1985 all produced wines of real quality, verve and style, while 1986 is exceptional. On this showing it is clear that the white La Louvière more than deserves to take its place with the *crus classés* white Graves.

A red wine vineyard takes longer to mature, so it is not surprising that the progress of the red La Louvière has been more circumspect. Only in 1987 did the average age of the vineyard reach twenty years; at neigh-bouring Haut-Bailly it is forty years. During the seventies the wines were vivid in colour, often quite tannic, but mainly light-textured and with a tendency to be rather one-dimensional, although the 1970 and 1975 are both rich and tannic. But now the wines have acquired an extra dimen-sion of power and complexity. The 1978 showed charm, fullness and style, the 1979 has now developed that lovely scented, spicy fruit with just a hint of tobacco that is one of La Louvière's hallmarks. The 1981 seems even better, with a deliciously mouth-filling flavour, and although very drinkable by 1987, had all the elements to last. With the 1982 the wine really lived up to the vintage; there is great ripeness and power, real depth of flavour, and all the breed of a *cru classé*. The 1983 is lighter in body – but what a glorious flavour it has, with length and great breed. I noted a bouquet full of lingering elegance and with a lovely highlighted tobacco perfume. The beautifully balanced 1985 clearly outshone five *crus classés* Graves when tasted alongside them in 1987, testimony to the quality and breed which this *cru* is now producing. The 1986 in cask was of course much more tannic, but the rich, opulent fruit promised some-thing special. So the red La Louvière has been showing in the last decade a degree of breed, length and finesse which clearly surpasses that found in a number of *crus classés* Graves. To this has now been added just a lit-tle extra weight in recent vintages. Above all I come back to the bouquet, the unmistakable hallmark of every fine wine. Here the complexity and

sheer beauty of many-faceted aromas issue an invitation that is irresistible. The progress made at La Louvière has been the most impressive
to be found anywhere in the Graves.

CHÂTEAU MALARTIC-LAGRAVIÈRE
Cru Classé. Owner: Champagne Vve Laurent-Perrier & Co.14 hectares. Red: 7,500
cases. CS 44%, CF 31%, Mer 25%. White: 900 cases. Sauv 100%

This is another property producing both red and white wines. The vineyard occupies a well-exposed position on quite a high plateau of typically
gravelly soil. It has passed through four interconnected families, all of
whom have made an important contribution. The very Gascon name of
Malartic owes its fame to Comte Hippolite de Maures de Malartic, born in
1730. He saw service under Montcalm in Canada, and had time to have a
tower named after him before General Wolfe drove the French out of
Quebec. The year 1792, found him as Governor of Mauritius, again
defending it against the English. It was his nephew Pierre de Malartic
who, in 1803, bought the Domaine de Lagravière at Léognan. In 1850
Madame Veuve Arnaud Ricard, affectionately known as *"le grand homme
de la famille"*, acquired what was still known as the Domaine Lagravière,
just ten years before she bought Domaine de Chibaley (Chevalier).
Lagravière was to pass to her granddaughter Angèle, who married Lucien
Ridoret in 1876. Their granddaughter Simone Ridoret married Jacques
Marly in 1927, a union blessed by no fewer than ten children. It was
Jacques Marly who, after the bad years of the thirties and the Occupation,
began the job of reconstructing Malartic-Lagravière in 1947. The Marly
family fortune was made in mirrors in the middle of the nineteenth
century. This fact was celebrated in the famous labels which adorned the
1962 and 1964 vintages. It seemed at first sight as if the proprietor had
decided to use the Cyrillic alphabet, until one discovered that if the
bottle was reflected in a mirror all was revealed! More recently, Jacques
Marly's penchant for interesting labels was manifested in the delightful
label for the 1983 vintage, showing the three-masted barque *Marie-
Elisabeth*, built in Bordeaux in 1846 and sailed around the world by his
ancestor, Laurent Ridoret, who was responsible for sealing the alliance
with the Ricard family. It is easy to see from all this why Bordelais
genealogy can become confusing! In 1990 Jacques Marly retired, and
the family sold to the great family champagne house of Laurent-Perrier,

but continuity is assured through Bruno Marly, who now runs the property.

The red wines of Malartic have a very strong and distinct Graves flavour, but tend to lack richness, so that the robust, slightly earthy flavour is not covered with enough fruit or fat in some years, and the wines can be lean. My general criticism of these wines is that they tend to be light, but hard and tannic.

I think the first Malartic that I drank must have been a 1943 which my father had as a concession wine after the war. It was rather tough and not one of my early favourites. Since then, I have had the opportunity of tasting a number of vintages. The 1953 was still surprisingly firm for that year when nine years old, and lacked the usual charm of the year. The 1955 was more successful in the context of that year, a well-balanced wine; the 1957 was all too typical of that year; the 1961 was very big and tough and is a slow developer; the 1962 was light but surprisingly slow to develop, with a hard background; the 1964 was rather lightweight but attractive, and the 1966 was a full, generous wine. More recently, the 1975 was particularly good, with more body and fruit than usual, while both the 1976 and 1978 were very successful, suggesting less lean, more attractive wines than hitherto. This has been followed by a most attractive 1979 with a lot of fruit and character. In the eighties, the 1980 was light but exceptionally attractive for early drinking; the 1981 seemed too marked by new oak for its weight at first but has come through now as an elegant and finely flavoured wine; the 1982 is wonderfully perfumed, rich and supple without having the weight of a Médoc. The 1983 has fine vivid fruit and elegance; the 1985 promised another stylish, charming wine once the new oak had been absorbed. These are wines of character and style, reflecting their owner in many ways. They have more charm and suppleness than was sometimes the case in the past, but I wonder if the 30 per cent new oak now used is not sometimes a bit too much for these slender, elegant wines.

The white Malartic can be one of the most attractive of white Graves, but unfortunately the production is very small. I have not often had the opportunity of seeing this wine, but have always been struck by its outstanding bouquet and charmingly individual character. It is a wine of great breed, very carefully made, in some years rather full and rich like Laville but developing more quickly, in others very dry and delicate with a very grapy and beguiling aroma. Undoubtedly, the reputation and standing of the white Malartic would be much higher than it is, were the production not so small.

This is one of the few exceptions to the general rule that Sauvignon on its own does not age. I enjoyed the 1971 still in 1984 but it was very dry, and without that extra dimension in age which the Sémillon gives to Chevalier. Recently the 1982 was richer than usual, but I particularly liked the 1984 where the Sauvignon character was not too pronounced and the wine had great finesse. Generally speaking, these wines are at their best when two to four years old. After that there can be occasional pleasant surprises, but the wine is more likely to lose fruit and dry out.

CHÂTEAU LA MISSION-HAUT-BRION

Cru Classé. Owner: Domaine Clarence Dillon. Red: 17 hectares. 7,000 cases. CS 60%, Mer 35%, CF 5%

Almost opposite Haut-Brion, a fine pair of wrought-iron gates gives a glimpse of a vineyard as neat as a garden, and a drive leading to a low-built château of modest proportions standing in its midst. This is La Mission-Haut-Brion, the pride of its late owner, Monsieur Henri Woltner, surely the greatest proprietor of his generation who, by his enquiring mind and meticulous attention to detail, raised the reputation of this property so that it can now stand comparison with the finest in Bordeaux. After Henri Woltner's death in 1974, soon to be followed by that of his brother, Fernand, the administration passed into the hands of Monsieur and Madame Francis Dewavrin, Fernand Woltner's daughter and son-in-law. This proved to be a period of steady progress and Henri Woltner's standards were certainly maintained. But, as so often, French inheritance problems and family discord led to the sale of the estate in 1983; very fortunately the Dillon family at Haut-Brion decided to buy, so the future of this great property is now assured.

The lineage of La Mission is long and interesting. Until the seventeenth century it formed a part of the Haut-Brion estate. Then, in 1630, Olive de Lestonnac, widow of Antoine de Gourgue, First President of the Parlement of Guyenne, bequeathed it to a congregation of priests known as the Lazarites, which had been founded by St Vincent de Paul. It was described in the deed as "Ixelle Métaire d'Haubrion, située ez la paroisse de Talence, et une chambre basse à loger des vallets au fond et en suitte un grand chay cuvier garni d'une fauloire en pierre de taille et vingt deux journaux de vignes". In 1698 a chapel was built and consecrated under the name of Notre-Dame de la Mission. Meanwhile, the wine produced by the Lazarites gained a considerable reputation.

With the coming of the Revolution, the estate – like all Church property – was confiscated and sold in 1792 to Martial-Victor Vaillant for 302,000 *livres* in paper money, the equivalent of 100,000 silver *livres*, a great sum for that time. Then, for nearly a hundred years, it belonged to the Chiapelle family. The first member of this family, Célestin Chiapelle, had a great reputation as a viticultural enthusiast, and it is interesting to note that in Cocks's classification of 1846, La Mission is included among the fourth and fifth growths of the Médoc. Evidently, later generations of the family did not continue with his skill and enthusiasm. Henri Woltner's father acquired La Mission in 1918, but in 1921 Henri Woltner assumed the management which, together with his brother Fernand, he retained for fifty years.

The château itself deserves a note. Its charming interior, of comfortably domestic proportions, contained a marvellous collection of *objets d'art*. The staircase displayed a remarkable selection of porcelain: holy water stoups, as well as a fine eighteenth-century altar-piece. Then, in the chapel, there was some attractive sixteenth-century stained glass and some fine church furniture. All this unfortunately was sold by the Woltner heirs, so the new owners have had to refurnish the interior completely, and the delights of the Woltner furnishings will remain only as a memory for those who were fortunate enough to enjoy their hospitality.

The soil of La Mission is remarkable for its stoniness. When an extension had to be made to the cellar, it was found that there was solid gravel to a depth of 18 feet, and Monsieur Woltner estimated that at least two-thirds of the soil was stones. It is noticeable that a high proportion of old vines is maintained. Unfortunately, the size of the vineyard was reduced by the construction of the Bordeaux–Toulouse autoroute. This happened in spite of many representations, proving that even in Bordeaux such things are no longer sacred.

Over the years, Henri Woltner concentrated his attention on perfecting both his vineyard and his wine-making. He used to observe that there comes a moment when the maturation of the grapes ceases, even though in some years they have not attained perfect maturity. When this point has been reached, picking should proceed as speedily as possible, since nothing is to be gained by further waiting. Then, in the most favourable years, the falling acidity must be watched as closely as the rising sugar level, and when they have reached equilibrium, picking should begin if a properly balanced wine is to be made. Henri Woltner believed that some properties today make the mistake of picking too late, thus either endangering their crop without the prospect of making any better wine, or making a wine where there is too much sugar and not enough acidity (essential for a wine to keep well).

Henri Woltner was also a pioneer in vinification techniques. As early as 1926 he installed the first glass-lined steel vat. After years of experiment, when he was confident that better results could be obtained by using this method, he went over completely to this system in 1951. He called his system *fermentation froide*, by which is meant a controlled fermentation at a steady, mean temperature. In 1987 the old *cuvier*, a landmark of its time, was replaced by the latest stainless steel model.

I have seen no wines of the pre-Woltner era. Maxwell Campbell in the *Wayward Tendrils of the Vine* mentions the 1905 La Mission as the outstanding wine of that year, and shows that even at that time, La Mission often rivalled its more famous neighbour. The 1920 was still wonderfully preserved when I saw it on its forty-sixth birthday. At the great retrospective tasting of La Mission vintages held at Christie's in December 1978, it was still a lovely, almost ethereal wine, old but still there. The classic vintages of 1924, 1926, 1928, 1929 and 1934 were all highly successful. A very elegant 1933 is worth noting, but the most surprising item was a delightful 1936, while the delicious and well-preserved 1940 must not be forgotten.

Since the war, the greatest years have been 1945, 1947, 1948, 1949, 1950 (one of the outstanding wines of the vintage), 1952, 1953, 1955 (again one of the most attractive wines of the year), 1957 (a triumph in this usually ungrateful year), 1959, 1961, 1962, 1964 and 1966. The 1958 and 1960, tasted again in October 1978, were both very successful wines and have lasted better than most wines from these vintages. In those two terrible years, 1963 and 1965, surprisingly drinkable wines were made. The 1967 was at its best by the time of the 1978 tasting, with that dry finish that marks so many examples of this year. The 1968 was honourable without achieving the success of 1960, but the 1969 was one of the few wines that I do not care for. In the next decade, 1970 now shows signs of volatility, while 1971, 1975, and 1976 have all produced classic examples of these years, the lighter styles of 1971 and 1976 contrasting with the massive wines made in the other years. The 1973 is a disappointment – the vintage was irreparably damaged by a hailstorm just a few days before the picking. The 1974 deserves mention as above average for the year. The 1977 is certainly one of the very best wines of this modest vintage, and was quite delicious, with a lovely perfume of cedar and truffles, and a frank, full-flavoured character showing real *race* when ten years old. Then came a magnificent 1978, with great richness and power and intensity of flavour, and a less well-bred 1979, still rather tannic and raw when eight years old.

The next decade began with a typically charming and harmonious "off-vintage" in 1980, then a really fine, top-class 1981, complex and concentrated. This will need not less than ten years to approach its best. The 1982 is a worthy example of this great vintage, with an incredible aroma of *cassis*, great concentration and flair, a great wine for the late nineties. The 1983 was the last wine made under Francis Dewavrin's management, and is a fine example of the very best of that vintage, rich, tannic, very concentrated and chewy; this is a real *vin de garde*. The first vintage for which Jean Delmas had responsibility was 1984, and the result was a true La Mission, just in case anyone should have thought anything else! Indeed, it is surprisingly rich for the year, with an excellent flavour and supple fruit, a wine with a good medium-term future. The 1985 is sumptuous, rich and concentrated, and the 1986 has exceptional richness and concentration and is more massive than the 1985. Both wines show their very distinct and different characters in comparison with Haut-Brion.

Thus La Mission is today one of the most consistent of all Bordeaux growths. The wine is distinctly different in style from its neighbour, Haut-Brion, whether one compares it with the old or new style. Always deep in colour, the wine is rich and concentrated in flavour, and although it never seems to be too tannic, it undeniably requires more time to show of its best today than does Haut-Brion. It also lasts very well. Even so, Henri Woltner always considered that even in big years his wines should be capable of being drunk with pleasure at ten years, although they will usually be drinkable well before this. In some ways, the stylistic difference between Haut-Brion and La Mission may be equated to the difference between Lafite on the one hand and Mouton on the other, allowing of course for the difference between Pauillac and Graves. Now that La Mission and Haut-Brion are under the same ownership and management, the old rivalries are a thing of the past. La Mission is now sold at a price only marginally below that of Haut-Brion, and is clearly a first growth in all but name.

There were several other proprietors of Henri Woltner's generation who were every bit as enthusiastic as he, but none who combined this with such a thorough technical knowledge. This is why such progress was made in the quality and consistency of his wines – a legacy much prized by his successors. Certainly it would be a fitting culmination to half a century's work, and a memorial to Henri Woltner as a pioneer in Bordeaux, should La Mission one day be accepted as a first growth by its peers.

CHÂTEAU OLIVIER

Cru Classé. Owner: Madame P. de Bethmann. Administrator: Jean-Jacques de Bethmann. Red: 18 hectares. 8,500 cases. CS 65%, Mer 35%. White: 17 hectares. 9,000 cases. Sém 65%, Sauv 30%, Muse 5%

The château at Olivier must be the most attractive and splendid of the Graves. Classified as a *monument historique*, the oldest parts date from the eleventh century, and the latest additions from the sixteenth century – ranging from a grim medieval fortress to an elegant Renaissance château. At one time it was a hunting lodge of the Black Prince. The property actually belongs to the Bethmann family, once part-owners of Gruaud-Larose, but the estate was for over seventy years run by the Bordeaux *négociants* Eschenauer, who had the monopoly of the production. Then, in November 1981, the Bethmann family decided to repossess themselves of their patrimony, and Jean-Jacques de Bethmann began to run the property himself. The distribution for a part of the crop remained in Eschenauer's hands until 1987, the rest being offered on the Bordeaux market.

The approach to Olivier is discreet in the extreme; as one drives from Bordeaux towards the village of Léognan, the entrance is in what appears to be impenetrable forest, and is easily missed. The vineyard itself is only a small part of the 200-hectare domain, with its marvellous old oaks and pine forest. The château is gloriously situated, in fine condition, and has its original moat. For once the reality lives up to and surpasses the picture on the label. Under Eschenauer's management both red and white wines were fermented in stainless steel and then matured in vat, with no casks at all. Now experiments are being done with barrel fermentation for the white wine. This has great ageing potential because of its high Sémillon content. A bottle of the 1970 tasted in 1987 was in excellent condition, very perfumed, with rich mellow fruit and beautifully balanced. With barrel fermentation and the same care this could be a wine to set beside Laville in years to come. The 1984, which was partly barrel-fermented, had a beautiful and quite individual bouquet, a lovely rich lanolin aroma, and was full-flavoured and most attractive, certainly more stylish than in the past. So the future for white Olivier looks exciting.

In the early to mid-seventies the vineyard was radically reconstructed to increase the size of the red wine production. This means that this part of the vineyard is still very young, with an average age in 1987 of only twelve years. The result is that at present the red wines rather lack body and breed. Although there is an attractive 1982, the 1983 seems too tannic and lean. There was an honourable 1984, and the 1985 has more promise with its vivid fruit and tannin, and there is definite style. One-third of the casks are now new each year. But this is clearly a wine to watch, and as the vineyard matures, the very promising elements already visible must gain in richness and complexity.

CHÂTEAU LE PAPE

Owner: GFA du Château Le Pape. Administrator: Antony Perrin. 5 hectares. 1,600 cases. Red wine: Mer 95%, CS 5%

This is one of the better-known unclassified wines of Léognan, although the vineyard is relatively small. The château itself is particularly pleasing, built on the *chartreuse* plan, but in a very simple and classic First Empire style. Recently Antony Perrin from nearby Carbonnieux has taken over the running of this small property, producing only red wines. The only recent vintage I have tasted was the 1981, which had a very rich, floral, fruity bouquet, and a strong, rather coarse, Graves tobacco flavour. Altogether a fairly typical light-textured Graves in spite of the unusual *encépagement*, with its shortage of Cabernet Sauvignon. It will be interesting to see what changes Antony Perrin makes, and whether he will alter this. The trouble is, the existing vineyard is still relatively youthful, with an average age of only fifteen years.

CHÂTEAU PAPE-CLÉMENT

Cru Classé. Owners: Montagne family. 29 hectares. Red: 12,000 cases. CS 60%, Mer 40%. White: 100 cases. Sém 33.3%, Sauv 33.3%, Musc 33.3%

After Haut-Brion and La Mission, this is the most important vineyard in Pessac-Talence. It has the proud claim of being the oldest clearly identifiable vineyard in the entire region. It was planted in 1300, when it was presented to Bertrand de Goth by his brother, on his appointment as Archbishop of Bordeaux. When, in 1306, he was elected Pope as Clement V, he gave the vineyard to Cardinal Arnaud de Canteloup, the new Archbishop of Bordeaux, for his benefit and that of his successors.

Pape-Clément remained the property of the Church until the Revolution. During the last century it enjoyed a good reputation, and in the twenties some fine wines were made, notably the 1920, 1924 and 1929. Then disaster struck – on 8 June 1937 a hailstorm virtually destroyed the vineyard. This was a bad time commercially for Bordeaux, and the proprietor was in no position to face such a loss. He was compelled to sell, and the property was acquired by developers: it seemed possible that this great vineyard, which had continuously produced wine for over 600 years, might end up as a housing estate.

Fortunately, the property was bought in 1939 by Monsieur Montagne. The vineyard had to be reconstituted from scratch, and it was not until the 1949 vintage that it was to give any hint of its former glory. The château itself rates the 1955 as the first really worthy example – the wine was very fine and typical of the best Graves style, but still distinctly light. The 1959 was really fine, a wine of richness and balance, while the 1961 was truly among the best of this great year. The 1962 was outstandingly successful, the 1964 full and well balanced – very successful, as were most Graves in this year – and the 1966 a very good example of this fine vintage. But in the seventies, standards slipped to a marked degree. In 1987 I was able to taste all the vintages at the château, from 1975 to 1986. The 1975 itself was rich and concentrated, with ripe, harmonious fruit, a very good wine for the year, and more agreeable sooner than most. It was the best wine made here until 1985. The 1976 seemed too fluid and was fading, the 1977 was respectable and pleasant, at its peak; the 1978 had breed and charm, but was light and ready to be drunk; the 1979, after a spicy tobacco nose, lacked charm and was hollow and too diffuse, a sure sign of over-production and a lack of selection; the 1980 had lovely mellow fruit, a charming wine for early drinking; the 1981 was light and soft, and ready to drink, rather lacking in personality; the 1982 lacks the concentration of the year, because it had to be taken off the skins too soon owing to the size of the crop and lack of vat space; the 1983 is a light, early developer with pleasing fruit; the 1984 is elegant and stylish for the year. After all this, the 1985 brought one up with a jolt, with its dense, deep colour, its lovely, rich aroma with complex highlights and its spicy, smoky flavour which was really concentrated and rich. The 1986 had a very powerful crushed-fruit aroma, was very rich in concentrated tannins and fruit, really dense-textured. These two vintages are in the tradition of the greatest Pape-Cléments, and the good work was continued in 1988 and 1989 while 1987 is above average for the year.

The change came when the Montagne family appointed Bernard Pujol as administrator in 1985. He had already worked there for a year, and so knew his way around. The new *chai*, built in 1970, was entirely re-equipped in 1985 – a new *cuvier* with the latest stainless steel *cuves* was ready for the 1985 harvest. A new Amos *égrappoir* and Bucher horizontal press now ensure that the grapes are received and handled in the best possible manner. The future for Pape-Clément now looks set fair once more, and in the next few years it should be vying with Domaine de Chevalier and Haut-Bailly for the honours in Pessac-Léognan, behind the first growths.

A very small quantity of white wine has been made at Pape-Clément for some years, originally simply for the use of the owners. Now the wine is very carefully vinified in small stainless steel *cuves* at 18°C, and the unusual *encépagement*, with its high proportion of Muscadelle, produces a delicious and interesting wine. The 1986, tasted just before its bottling in May 1987, was very scented, with plenty of Sémillon fat, but also with excellent fruit and real style. The 1985 was much richer and more unctuous in style. Much of it is sold in Bordeaux restaurants and, with such a minuscule production, bottles are not easy to find.

So this ancient and famous growth has been successfully resurrected, thanks to the renewed interest of the Montagne family. It is yet another instance of the fact that, were it not for rich enthusiasts being prepared to make investments which cannot yield a return for many years, some great and famous vineyards would not still be delighting wine lovers.

CHÂTEAU PICQUE-CAILLOU

Owner: SCI Château Picque-Caillou. Administrator: Alphonse Denis. 17.5 hectares. 7,500 cases. CS 35%, CF 35%, Mer 30%

In 1899 the third English edition of Cocks & Féret listed over forty *crus* in Mérignac, one of which was said to be on a par with the second growths of the Médoc, two others the equal of fourth or fifth growths. Today this *cru*, together with its subsidiary *cru* Chêne-Vert, are all that remains of this rich viticultural heritage. The rest has disappeared beneath Bordeaux's urban expansion and its airport. The present owners have had a share in the property since 1920 and have been outright owners since 1947. Like most of the *crus* in northern Graves, this is an old property, and is said to have been a favourite of both Napoleon I and of Napoleon III. After this build-up the wine is mildly disappointing, although I have not seen any really mature vintages. It is perfumed, with solid, attractive fruit of some class, but is inclined to be rather one-dimensional, comparable to a middle-range *cru bourgeois* in Médoc.

CHÂTEAU PONTAC-MONPLAISIR

Owner: Jean Maufras. Red: 7.95 hectares. 4,500 cases. CS 60%, Mer 40%. White: 5.68 hectares. 2,700 cases. Sauv 70%, Sém 30%. Second wine: Château Limbourg

This property belonged to the Pontac family during the seventeenth and eighteenth centuries, when the wine was sold as Pontac-Haut-Brion. The name Monplaisir appears on Cassini's map at the end of the eighteenth century. The present proprietor, Jean Maufras, sold the original vineyard, close to Baret, for building. A supermarket now stands on the site. The wine is now made at what used to be Limbourg. Recently there have been determined efforts to restore the fortunes of this fine old *cru*. The red wine is elegantly scented and has a fine Graves character and definite breed. The white is well made and really stylish. The second wine, Château Limbourg, seems to have a more Sauvignon character, while the Sémillon is more obvious in the Pontac-Monplaisir.

CHÂTEAU ROCHEMORIN

Owner: André Lurton. Red: 45 hectares. 18,000 cases. CS 60%, Mer 40%. White: 12 hectares. 2,500 cases. Sauv 85%, Sém 15%

The name comes from Roche-Morine, indicating that this was one of the fortresses which defended Bordeaux from the Moorish incursions during the seventh and eighth centuries, and was probably occupied by them. In 1079 the Lalande family became the proprietors, and they built the château. One of their descendants married the father of Montesquieu, the philosopher, and it was he who reconstructed both vineyard and château. A contract between him and a Bordeaux *négociant*, dated 1696, is the oldest wine contract to survive. The philosopher himself is said to have been born here, although there is no firm proof. The vineyard is clearly marked in both the Belleyme and Cassini maps of the late eighteenth century, which show that this was already a large vineyard at this time. In the 1870s the Montesquieus were still making 100 tonneaux here; but the energy, and perhaps the resources, to overcome the ravages of the phylloxera were plainly lacking since production had slumped to a mere 15 tonneaux by the end of the century. Soon afterwards the Montesquieus finally sold a property which had not changed hands, except through marriage, for over 900 years. In 1919 the property was sold for afforestation; by this time trees had become more profitable than wine.

This was the situation when the dynamic André Lurton (see La Louvière) bought the property in 1973 and began replanting the vineyard in the following year. The vineyard is splendidly placed on the highest ridge in Martillac, between Smith-Haut-Lafitte and the village. When the project is finally completed, this will be André Lurton's largest vineyard in Graves, with 100 hectares. Vintaging, as at the other Lurton properties, is mechanical for the red and manual for the white. Fermentations are controlled at 28–30°C for the red and 16–18°C for the white. The red has a year's maturation in cask with one-third new oak, but the white is kept in vat.

As at Cruzeau, in spite of the youth of the vineyard the red wines are already showing an attractively spicy, aromatic Graves bouquet, and seemed to have slightly more structure than the Cruzeau when I first compared the 1981s. But then, comparing the 1982s and 1983s, the picture was less clear. The most mature wine I have seen is the 1978, which was quite delightful to drink when eight years old, and again two years later, with great breed and the most delectable flavour. The white is markedly different in style from the Cruzeau. It has a less floral bouquet and more body, but is very elegant with a flinty, drier finish than Cruzeau. It will be fascinating to follow these two vineyards over the next few years as they evolve and mature. Clearly the potential here is considerable, and it would not be surprising to see it knocking at the door of the *crus classés* before long.

CHÂTEAU DE ROUILLAC

Owner: P. Sarthou. Red: 5 hectares. 1,650 cases. CS 85%, Mer 15%

This *cru* has two special distinctions: the château itself was built by the famous Baron Haussmann, who changed the face of Paris; and the vineyard is the only one left in the commune of Canéjan. The name is clearly marked on the Cassini map in the late eighteenth century but appears at that time to have been entirely wooded. Baron Haussmann built an attractive mansion, where in 1869 he received Napoleon III, who also served the wine at his table. The Sarthou family bought the property in 1962, but began to replant the vineyard only in 1970. The installations are of the most modern, and some new oak is used in the maturation. The first vintage to be sold under the château label was the 1978. The wine has a pronounced Graves character, is highly flavoured, well made and balanced. This is a wine of character and potential.

CHÂTEAU LE SARTRE

Owner: GFA du Château Le Sartre. Administrator: Antony Perrin. Red: 10 hectares. 2,000 cases. CS 60%, Mer 40%. White: 5 hectares. 2,000 cases. Sauv 70%, Sém 30%

When the Perrin family bought this Léognan property in 1981, the vineyard had been virtually abandoned since 1914. As the vineyard matures the wines should be of real interest.

CHÂTEAU SMITH-HAUT-LAFITTE

Cru Classé. Owner: Cathiard family. Red: 45.4 hectares. 22,000 cases. CS 73%, Mer 16%, CF 11%. White: 5.6 hectares. 3,000 cases. Sauv 100%

The most important vineyard in the commune of Martillac, it belonged to the firm of Louis Eschenauer until 1991. After holding the monopoly for the vineyard for more than forty years, they finally acquired it in 1958.

Since then there has been a considerable investment in both vineyards and buildings, and this *cru*, formerly devoted solely to the production of red wines, now makes a limited quantity of white as well. This has been one of the most important reconstructions of a major *cru* to have taken place in Graves and deserves to be set beside the pioneering work carried out by André Lurton (see La Louvière, Cruzeau and Rochemorin) in its importance in the revival of the region.

The history of the property has been traced back to the seventeenth century when the owners of a *maison noble*, called du Boscq, planted a vineyard on a gravelly plateau with the *lieu-dit* of Lafitte. The soil here has one of the deposits of "gunzien" gravel from the Garonne, rarely found in Graves. This is the type of gravel found in the best vineyards of Margaux, and also especially at Haut-Brion. In 1720 it was bought by one Georges Smith, who added his name to the *lieu-dit* of the best part of the vineyard. By 1824 Wilhelm Franck, while in general dismissive of the wines of Martillac, singled out Smith-Haut-Lafitte for favourable comment.

In 1974 a large new underground cellar was built to hold 2,000 casks, and all the vinification equipment was renewed. However, in spite of all this work and expenditure, the wines remained no more than pleasant and irregular in quality. There was a lack of selection and management commitment to quality. This came only with the arrival of Jacques Théo in the early eighties, and an awareness that the full potential of Eschenauer's properties was not being realized (see also Rausan-Ségla). For the whites, half the harvest was barrel-fermented for the 1984, and the whole crop for the 1985 onwards. The must is first put in *cuve* for the *débourbage*, then transferred to casks in a cellar temperature-controlled to 18°C. The white grapes are all picked by hand. For the reds, the harvesting is by machine, and now 50 per cent new wood is used. Proper selection began with the 1983 vintage.

At a tasting held at the property in October 1985, I was able to see a range of vintages of both red and white wines. The whites began with a rather oily 1979 that had gone flat and flabby. The 1980 was much more elegant with nice Sauvignon character; it was then at its best. The 1981 had a strong, catty Sauvignon smell and a rich, fat Sauvignon flavour. The 1982 was fat and coarse, lacking balance; the 1983 had a pungent Sauvignon aroma, some fat but good acidity, if a shade coarse. The 1984, half barrel-fermented, showed this influence strongly with the oak highlighting the fruit and a very lanolin flavour; very elegant but also distinctly Sauvignon. It had been bottled in May 1985. The 1985 was an even better-integrated wine with marked fruit flavours. It was at the same level of quality as Carbonnieux, indicating that this is now of *cru classé* standard. The improvement in 1984 and 1985 was very marked.

The reds were very mixed, beginning with a stylish 1973 near the end of its life; there was a short, dilute-tasting 1974; a 1975 with a pungent, minerally smell and a strong tarry taste, yet lacking real 1975 concentration; a disappointingly diluted 1976, an astonishingly delicious 1977 which seemed almost overblown, an impressive 1978 which was rich and solid and had an attractive liquorice and tobacco character (but three years later it looked light and diluted in Miami); a soft, ripe, aromatic 1979, quite ready to drink; a delicious, light, soft 1980 for immediate drinking; an aromatic, spicy 1981 with elegant fruit that was quite soft; a 1982 with rich, soft tannins and a powerful minerally aroma. Then came the first wine to undergo selection – the 1983 – and the proof was that it was finer than the 1982! It was elegant and long but also solid with finely balanced fruit and tannin, impressive for wine in bottle for only three months. It has since developed very well. Finally, at this tasting, there was a most successful 1984, with a lovely blackcurrant flavour and some length. Subsequently, an attractive 1985 was rather open-textured and light. The vivid Graves fruit, and a marked individuality, come through very clearly in these wines, also their inherent style and attractiveness. With the consistency now promised, they should win many friends as good-value wines of distinct personality. The quality is in line with a good fifth-growth Médoc.

CHÂTEAU LA TOUR-HAUT-BRION

Cru Classé. Owner: Domaine Clarence Dillon. Red: 4 hectares. 1,500 cases. CS 70%, CF 15%, Mer 15%

This is a small property adjoining La Mission, which was acquired by the Woltner brothers in 1933. It is yet another illustration of the fact that even small differences of soil make for important differences in quality. The wines of La Tour-Haut-Brion are very fine, but they just miss the finesse and breed of La Mission. Henri Woltner's experience over the years was similar to Ronald Barton's with Léoville-Barton and Langoa-Barton. Nevertheless, La Tour-Haut-Brion is a very fine wine and fully justifies its classification as a *cru classé* of Graves. The wine is just as meticulously made as that of La Mission – full-bodied, but perhaps a shade less generous than La Mission. During the Dewavrin administration, the wine was treated as a second wine of La Mission but one of Jean Delmas's first decisions was to treat La Tour-Haut-Brion as a separate *cru* once more.

The vintages of La Tour-Haut-Brion closely followed those of La Mission. Normally the La Tour is more precocious and so the 1975 will be drinkable earlier. But in some years, such as 1976, I detect a lack of La Mission's fat and richness to counterbalance the tannin. The 1971 is particularly attractive, and while the 1966 is noticeably lighter in texture than the La Mission, the 1964 La Tour seems fuller. Excellent wines were made in 1985, 1986, 1987, 1988 and 1989 under the new regime, to mark La Tour's return to a fully independent status.

CHÂTEAU LA TOUR-MARTILLAC

Cru Classé. Owner: Jean Kressmann. Red: 20 hectares. 8,500 cases. CS 60%, Mer 25%, CF 6%, Mal and PV 9%. White: 4.75 hectares, 1,500 cases. Sém 55%, Sauv 30%, other varieties 15%. Second label: Château La Grave-Martillac

This old property once belonged to the Montesquieu family from nearby La Brède. The twelfth-century tower from which the *cru* derives its name was once the staircase of a fort, the ruins of which were used as building materials in the eighteenth century for today's comfortably domestic buildings. In the 1870s Edouard Kressmann began buying the white wines of the property, and to work closely with the owners. At this time nearly all the wines in this part of Graves were red, and this was one of the rare white ones. From these early days there survives a collection of grape varieties selected by Edouard Kressmann and planted in 1884 as first grafts after the phylloxera. This became the basis of Kressmann's famous Graves Monopole Dry, which was introduced in London in 1892. It was a favourite of the great soprano prima donna, Adelina Patti, who is said to have consented to tour in the United States only on condition of being able to obtain Kressmann's "little dry white wine" wherever she went. A Monopole Rouge was launched in 1903.

In 1929 Edouard's son Alfred finally bought the property with which his firm had for so long been associated, and then began to promote the name of the *cru* as well. Up until then no mention had been made of it in successive editions of Cocks & Féret. In 1934 the wine acquired its distinctive, but for me at least curiously unattractive, black and gold striped label. In 1937, the Kressmanns had the satisfaction of having the 1929 vintage red served at Buckingham Palace on the occasion of King George VI's coronation. Jean, the son of Alfred Kressmann, began running the property in 1940 and finally inherited it in 1955. A man of wide culture and literary tastes, he has written a notable novel on his grandfather, *Le Défi d'Edouard*. Now he is assisted by his own sons: Tristan is administrator, while Loïc is *régisseur* and *chef de culture* – note the Celtic names!

This is a meticulously run property. Ten hectares have been preserved for a herd of cattle to provide natural manure for the vineyard. The red grapes are traditionally harvested, and those from the older vines are still fermented in wooden vats at 32–33°C, while the grapes from younger vines go into lined steel vats which are water-cooled. Maturation is in cask with one-third new oak. The second wine, La Grave-Martillac, is made from *vin de presse* and vines which are less than ten years old. This is sold direct from the château, and not through the trade. The white wine is fermented in stainless steel *cuves*.

The red wines have elegant fruit on the nose and a fine flavour with breed and length, and are quite light-textured. Of recent vintages, I have particularly liked the 1981, 1982, 1983 and 1985. The white wines are classic Graves which develop complexity and originality with bottle age and can live and improve for many years with their solid base of Sémillon. But they can also have great charm, freshness and elegance when young, as the 1984 and 1985 have recently proved.

SOUTHERN GRAVES

Originally, forty-four communes were covered by the Graves *appellation*; ten of these have now been hived off into that of Pessac-Léognan. Of the thirty-four remaining communes, much of the wine production is concentrated in six: Portets, Illats, Cérons, St Pierre-de-Mons, Langon and Landiras. If this is the region of what used to be called the *petits Graves*, the quality and production of both its red and white wines have greatly increased in recent years. Cold-controlled fermentations have improved the white wines almost beyond recognition, while the growing rewards for producing good, sound red wines of character, which can be drunk young, have spurred producers to increase the plantings of red varieties, leading to the jump in production mentioned at the beginning of the chapter. INRA has done much to assist in the selection of suitable clones of varieties which are adapted to these varied soils, especially for the Cabernet Sauvignon.

Following the setting-up of the Pessac-Léognan *appellation*, it is already being suggested that Portets should strive to emulate its northern neighbours. It is a move which should be carefully pondered, as it could prove a serious setback for the many other excellent wines which would find themselves excluded from this arrangement. The Haut-Médoc *appellation* proved just this, especially after the large Margaux *appellation* was carved out of it.

Since completing the first edition of this book, I have made a point of making as many visits and tastings in this area as possible, to provide a reasonable guide to some of the excellent things to be found here. These are listed alphabetically and represent a personal selection from sixteen communes, covering the length and breadth of the region. Such a list is inevitably somewhat arbitrary in what is a fast-developing region, but tends to represent wines that are making an effort to be better known.

CHÂTEAU D'ARCHAMBEAU

Commune: Illats. Owner: Jean-Philippe Dubourdieu. 22 hectares. Red: 5,000 cases. Mer 50%, CS 40%, CF 10%. White: 6,000 cases. Sém 70%, Musc 20%, Sauv 10%. Second label: Château Mourlet

The Dubourdieu family have a formidable reputation as wine-makers in Graves and Barsac. Jean-Philippe is the nephew of Pierre Dubourdieu of Doisy-Daëne, while another member of the family is a noted oenologist. The commune of Illats is one of three which make up the old *appellation* of Cérons, adjoining Barsac, but with the declining demand for this type of sweet wine, or indeed of the richer Graves Supérieur, the emphasis at d'Archambeau is on classic dry Graves. Only tiny quantities of Cérons are occasionally made, when conditions favour this. The vineyard is clearly marked as under vine in the Belleyme map in the late eighteenth century, as is that of its second wine, Mourlet. It is very well situated on a commanding ridge of gravelly clay and clay and limestone soils. The white wines are cold-fermented, in lined metal and stainless steel vats, and bottled the following spring. The combination of Sémillon and Sauvignon gives the wines elegance and depth of flavour, while the Muscadelle imparts a pleasing fruitiness, making the wines delicious to drink within months of bottling. But they also keep and mature well. The red wine is a more recent development; the first vintage to be commercialized was 1982. The wines at present are bottled young, in the autumn after the vintage, and have vivid fruit and immediate charm. They are beginning to gain in depth as the vineyards mature.

This *cru* consistently produces very attractive wines which are free from the earthiness which affects many white wines in southern Graves, and are exceptionally well made. It is a good example of the quality of dry white wine that can be made in an area that used to be thought of as one for sweet wines.

CHÂTEAU ARDENNES

Commune: Illats. Owners: François and Bertrand Dubrey. 20 hectares. Red: 7,000 cases. Mer 50%, CS 40%, CF 10%. White: 5,000 cases. Sém 60%, Sauv 40%

This is an old-established *cru*; the names of former owners have been traced back to 1514, and the vineyard is clearly marked on the Belleyme map in the late eighteenth century. The present owners have been here since 1968, since when they have carried out many improvements to the vineyard and installations. The white wines are fruity and well made, but with a certain *goût de terroir*. The red wine is really finer here than the white. I have found a lovely scent of violets and a good depth of flavour, solid and well structured, so that it is capable of some ageing, while many reds in the area need to be drunk young, before their light and rather superficial fruit fades. An excellent example of what this area is capable of.

CHÂTEAU D'ARRICAUD

Commune: Landiras. Owners: Monsieur and Madame Albert Bouyx. 28 hectares. Red: 3,000 cases. CS 65%. Mer 30%, Mal 5%. White: 7,000 cases. Sém 70%, Sauv 25%, Musc 5%

This old property, the most imortant in the commune, lies north-east of the village. Its attractive eighteenth-century château was built by Joachim de Chalup when President of the Bordeaux Parlement. The estate appears as Arricots on the Belleyme map, which shows that the whole area around

Landiras was already given over to vines by the second half of the eighteenth century. The white wines here are well made, scented and elegant on the nose; they are quite full-flavoured with length and some style, quite without the coarseness sometimes found in southern Graves, yet with plenty of character. The red wines are well coloured, very fruity on the nose, with an infectiously attractive sappy fruitiness and charm that simply ask to be drunk young.

CHÂTEAU BELON

Commune: St Morillon. Owner: Jean Depiot. Red: 4 hectares. 3,000 cases. CS 50%, Mer 50%. White: 4 hectares. 2,500 cases. Sauv 45%, Sém 40%, Musc 15%

The Depiot family have owned this *cru* since 1800. St Morillon is one of the most inland communes in the Graves, lying south of La Brède. I have only once come across the white wine, and found it rather coarse and not very well made, so whether I was unlucky or not, I cannot tell. The red is better, with a nice spiciness on the nose and vivid attractive fruit, but also a degree of coarseness.

CHÂTEAU LA BLANCHERIE (CHÂTEAU LA BLANCHERIE-PEYRET FOR RED WINE)

Commune: La Brède. Owner: F.-C. Braud-Coussié. Red: 9 hectares. 4,000 cases. CS 75%, Mer 25%. White: 11 hectares. 6,000 cases. Sém 60%, Sauv 30%, Musc 10%

The name of La Brède is famous for its château, the birthplace and life-long home of one of France's most distinguished philosophers and historians. But today this is the most important wine-producing *cru* in the commune, which lies just outside the new Pessac-Léognan *appellation*, bordering on the communes of St Médard-d'Eyrans and Martillac. La Blancherie also has a history of its own; its proprietors at the time of the Revolution were both guillotined during the Terror. This is a very well-run property today. The red wines which are sold under the La Blancherie-Peyret label are particularly good, receiving a long maceration, and being aged in cask. Their bouquet is particularly arresting, with pronounced tobacco and spice, and there is lots of flavour and character, yet the wines are also supple and rich so that they can be drunk young. There has been a tendency for them to be rather light in colour, but the 1985 showed a marked improvement in this respect. The white wines are fermented at low temperatures. Until recently they were often rather coarse and strong-flavoured, but now the vinification has been modernized and a great improvement has been visible since the 1986 vintage. They are now very scented and deliciously fruity, as well as having quite a lot of body. This is an excellent *cru*.

CHÂTEAU BRONDELLE
Commune: Langon. Owner: Rolland Belloc. 20 hectares. Red: 5,000 cases. CS 60%, Mer 20%, CF 10%, Mal 10%. White: 3,000 cases. Sém 60%, Sauv 30%, Musc 10%. Second label: Château La Croix-Saint-Pey

I do not know if Rolland Belloc can claim any remote relationship with Hilaire Belloc. If he could I am sure the famous author and wine lover would have been delighted with Brondelle as his house claret. Langon, as well as being the focal centre of the southern Graves, is also one of the most important wine-making communes today, and its growers are now benefiting, in terms of the quality of the red wines that are being made, from the work done by INRA. The red wine here has a nice aroma of cherries, and the wine is deliciously fruity and lively, perfect for drinking at about four years of age. If the white is as well vinified it should be well worth looking for.

CHÂTEAU CABANNIEUX
Commune: Portets. Owners: René Barrière, Dudignac family. 20 hectares. Red: 8,000 cases. Mer 55%, CS 35%, CF 10%. White: 4,000 cases. Sém 75%, Sauv 25%

This well-reputed *cru* is situated in the best and highest part of Portets, on well-drained gravelly soil with some traces of clay. The growers of Portets feel that their vineyards are the best in the southern Graves, and certainly the reputation of their wines has much increased in recent years. This *cru* is commercialized by A. & R. Barrière, because of the family connection. The property is very well run. The red wines receive two to three weeks in contact with the skins for maximum extraction. Then part of the crop is put in cask, with a small amount of new wood being used. The result is a wine of deep colour, with a good Graves style and real fullness and depth of fruit, which can be drunk young in most vintages, but which also keeps. It fully deserves its good reputation. The white wine is fermented at below 20°C, and its high Sémillon content produces a wine which develops well, while the Sauvignon gives the initial bouquet. It enjoys the reputation of being one of the best whites in southern Graves.

CHÂTEAU CAZABONNE

Commune: St Pierre-de-Mons. Owner: Marc Bridet. 13 hectares. Red: 2,700 cases. CS 50%, Mer 50%. White: 2,300 cases. Sauv 60%, Sém 40%

This is one of a number of good *crus* in St Pierre-de-Mons, the largest wine-producing commune to the east of Langon. The red wine has plenty of colour and is very scented, with some finesse. The flavour is fruity, but quite compact and with a tendency to firmness. This is a well-made, attractive wine. The white has a flowery bouquet with a certain fruity elegance. It is a wine of character, but without coarseness, and has a pleasing crisp fruitiness, with some elegance and style.

CHÂTEAU DE CHANTEGRIVE

Commune: Podensac. Owners: Henri and Françoise Levèque. Red: 28 hectares. 15,000 cases. CS 60%, Mer 40%. White: 32 hectares. 17,500 cases. Sém 50%, Sauv 30%, Musc 20%. Secondary labels: Château Bon-Dieu-de-Vignes, Château Mayne-Levèque, Château Mayne-d'Anice

The "château" here hardly conforms to any mental image conjured up by this word – it is in reality an ultra-modern house. The Levèques have steadily built up the property from the most modest beginnings until it is now the most important in Podensac. When I first visited Chantegrive, there were only 15 hectares of vines; today there are 60. Henri Levèque is also one of the most noted *courtiers* in Graves and Sauternes, thus fully abreast of all the latest developments in white wine vinification and clonal selection. The soil is white sand mixed with quartz pebbles and the vinification is carefully controlled at low temperatures for the whites. The reds are aged for six months in oak vats, then for a year in cask, of which 20 per cent is new oak, in an underground cellar.

The white wines are fresh and deliciously fruity, aromatic and easy to drink without being quite top-class, but then this is Podensac and not Léognan or indeed Portets! But the Muscadelle makes the wine especially attractive for early drinking. The reds are fruity and supple but have some depth as well. This is just the sort of easy-to-drink wine at a reasonable price that this part of Graves now produces so well. Both wines have collected numerous awards at the Concours Agricole in Paris in recent years. The label for the red wine is white, that for the white one is gold. I cannot vouch for the accuracy of the name: one is lucky in this part of France to find a thrush that has not been made into pâté!

CHÂTEAU CHÉRET-PITRES
Commune: Portets. Owners: Monsieur and Madame Jean Boulanger. 12 hectares. Red only. 7,000 cases. CS 50%, Mer 50%

This is the only *cru* of any significance in Portets that produces only red wines, for which the Boulangers have built up a fair reputation in the past few years. The wines are fully coloured and have a very distinctive Graves character, often with attractive highlights. They are deliciously fruity in flavour, although light in body. The vibrance of the fruit makes them charming to drink young, but the best vintages can also keep well.

CHÂTEAU CHICANE
Commune: Toulenne. Owners: Coste family. 6 hectares. Red only. 3,000 cases. CS 70%, Mer 20%, CF 10%

This is one of the Coste properties, where Pierre Coste has been able to put his ideas into practice. The commune of Toulenne lies just to the east of Coste's home base of Langon, and is the only property in the commune of any significance which produces just red wine. The wines themselves, vinified very much in the Coste style, are spicy and quite full on the nose, light in body, but full of delicious fruity flavours, and designed to be drunk young, at between two to four years of age.

CHÂTEAU DE COURBON
Commune: Toulenne. Owner: Jean Sanders. 6.5 hectares. White only. 3,000 cases. Sauv 60%, Sém 40%

This modest but comfortable property at Toulenne, near Langon, is where you are likely to find Jean Sanders when he is not visiting his more famous *cru classé*, Haut-Bailly. This vineyard, alone of the main *crus* of Toulenne, produces only white wines. The vineyard is on varied soils of sand and gravel with some gravelly clay. The vinification is maintained at a temperature below 22°C, and bottled early after cold stabilization. This particular soil near Sauternes produces wines which are more full-bodied than white wines further north in the Graves, and Jean Sanders believes that it is important to maintain a certain proportion of Sémillon. The result is that the wines are very fruity when first bottled, thanks to the rich Sauvignon, but also supple and not at all acid, thanks to the Sémillon, which also ensures good keeping properties.

CHÂTEAU COUTET

Commune: Pujols-sur-Ciron. Owners: Marcel and Bertrand Baly. White: 38 hectares. 9,000 cases. Sém 80%, Sauv 15%, Muse 5%

This can only be described as a confusing wine. Everyone knows that the dry wines made in Sauternes and Barsac can only be called Bordeaux Blanc. In 1977 the Baly family bought the famous Barsac *premier cru* of Coutet. They were already proprietors in this commune of Pujols-sur-Ciron, which has as its neighbours on three sides the communes of Barsac, Preignac and Bommes. They are now commercializing their Pujols *cru*, formerly known as Reverdon, as "Vin Sec du Château Coutet" with the coveted Graves *appellation*. The wine itself is a very cold-fermentation-style wine which I find rather disappointing at present. There is a strong aroma of gooseberries and the wine is surprisingly skeletal for one so high in Sémillon.

CHÂTEAU L'ETOILE

Commune: Langon. Owner: Domaines Latrille Bonnin. Red: 10 hectares. 6,000 cases. CS 60%, Mer 30%, CF 10%. White: 5 hectares. 3,000 cases, Sauv 50%, Sém 50%

A Langon property partly in Langon, partly in Mazères, not owned by Pierre Coste, but selected and sold by him. The vineyard is on very varied soil, mainly poor gravel and clay. Vinification is supervised by Coste's oenologist, with high-temperature fermentation and long vatting for the reds, and a short maceration before fermentation for the whites, followed by cold fermentation to enhance the aromatic quality of the bouquet. I have found the white to have a particularly good bouquet with compact and concentrated fruit, while the flavour shows marked character; a charming wine which can be drunk with pleasure within six months of the vintage. The red has a rather rustic style but with lovely spicy fruit on the nose, and some body and tannin to support the rich fruitiness of the flavour, so the wine is delicious when two to three years old, but can also age.

CHÂTEAU FERRANDE
Commune: Castres. Owners: Héritiers H. Delnaud. Administrator: Castel Frères. Red: 34 hectares. 15,000 cases. CS 33.3%, CF 33.3%, Mer 33.3%. White: 9 hectares. 5,000 cases. Sém 60%, Sauv 35%, Musc 5%. Second label: Château Lognac

This is the most important *cru* in Castres, which is a small commune viticulturally, virtually an appendage to its neighbour to the east, Portets. Ferrande is marked on the Belleyme map, so was an established *cru* by the late eighteenth century. Indeed Belleyme shows the whole Castres-Portets area to have been well planted with vines by this time. The Delnaud family had the foresight to buy the property in 1954, before the final exodus from Algeria. From 1955, the management was in the hands of Marc Teisseire, and important improvements were made, a new *cuvier* built and the vineyard expanded. Henri Delnaud died in 1970, since when the property has belonged to his two daughters, and they and their families spend the summer here. The management is now overseen by Castel Frères, but day-to-day running of the property is in the hands of the experienced *régisseur*, Monsieur Bortoletto, who has been here since 1969.

After vinification in lined steel and stainless steel vats, the red wine is fermented in cask, with 10 per cent new oak. I have found the wines to be deep in colour with a bouquet which is lively and spicy, with marked tobacco overtones, and a flavour that is frank and fresh, light-textured but full-flavoured and fruity. This is a wine which can be drunk with pleasure when three or four years old.

The white wine has a pronounced Graves character, and is powerful, fruity, but with a slightly earthy after-taste. It has less charm and breed than the red wine. Ferrande has built up a good reputation in recent years and is one of the few unclassified *crus* in Graves to be a member of the Union des Grands Crus.

DOMAINE DE GAILLAT
Commune: Langon. Owners: Coste family. 8 hectares. Red only: 4,000 cases. CS 60%, Mer 30%, Mal 10%

The property and its production may be small, but the wines are well known wherever Pierre Coste has preached the gospel of modern Graves. The wines are bottled early, in the June after the vintage, to capture the maximum fruit. My note on the 1985, made in April 1987, captures what this philosophy is all about: a very dense, deep colour, an explosion of fruit on the nose, a taste of crushed fruit, and already delicious to drink only eighteen months after the vintage. The 1983, tasted at the same time, was looking more dense, and drinking perfectly. However, the 1982, tasted only months later, had already gone rather vegetal and plummy, and was in need of drinking up, emphasizing that this style of wine needs to be drunk early, and is not for keeping.

CHÂTEAU DU GRAND ABORD

Commune: Portets. Owner: Marc Dugoua. Red: 18 hectares. 4,500 cases. Mer 90%, CS 10%. White: 3 hectares. 2,000 cases. Sém 90%, Sauv 10%

This is one of the old properties of Portets, and appears on the Belleyme map in the late eighteenth century. The name is a reminder that at one time the Garonne was much closer to the property than it is now, and that this was an important stopping place for ships plying the river. Most of the vineyard is on the high plateau of Portets, where the soils are gravelly and stony. The red wines are attractively fruity, supple and full-flavoured, generally delicious when young. I have not tasted the white wine.

DOMAINE LA GRAVE

Commune: Portets. Owner: Peter Vinding-Diers. 7 hectares. Red: 3,000 cases. CS 50%, Mer 50%. White: 500 cases. Sém 100%

This was the first wine produced by Peter Vinding-Diers from his own wines (see under Rahoul and Landiras). He acquired the property, formally Château Le Borderie, in 1980. The soil is sandy gravel and gravelly clay. The red wine is quite taut and tannic when young, the white perfumed and elegant but full-flavoured. There is no château. Until 1988 the wines were made at Rahoul, and since then at Landiras.

CHÂTEAU DE LANDIRAS

Commune: Landiras. Owner: Peter Vinding-Diers. Vineyard: under reconstruction

In the last decade, Peter Vinding-Diers has created quite a name for himself, as one of the leading wine-makers in the Graves district. First of all, he built a reputation for Château Rahoul, the Portets property, first under its Australian owners, when he had the opportunity of working with Brian Croser, then under its subsequent Danish and French owners. He also bought some vines of his own in the same commune, selling the wine as Domaine La Graves. Now he has found a property of his own, this historic château at Landiras.

The Belleyme map, based on work done in the 1760s and 1770s, shows the château in its park and with its vineyard. Peter Vinding-Diers plans to reconstruct the vineyard from its present single hectare, to the 20 hectares for which Appellation planting rights exist. This will closely correspond to the vineyard as it was in the second half of the eighteenth century.

The first mention of the property is in 1173, when its owner, by the name of Rostang, sold some land in Barsac to the Archbishop of Bordeaux. In 1243, another member of the family was summoned by Henry III of England (Rustano de Landiras, as he was addressed by the king) to do homage to him in Bordeaux on Palm Sunday. But perhaps the most famous inhabitant of the château down the ages was Jeanne de Lestonac, who became the founder of the Notre-Dame order of nuns. So this is still something of a place of pilgrimage for members of the Order. In 1793 the château was sacked and its land sold when the last Seigneur de Landiras, Michel de La Roque, Baron de Budos, and his son emigrated as a result of the Revolution. But the moated ruins – with the great gateway and a tower still standing – are an impressive reminder of this great feudal castle. The present château, nearby, is a pleasing early nineteenth-century building, with some nice features. The old stables have already been converted into a new *cuvier*, and the new owner moved in just in time to make the 1988 vintage.

The vineyard is on a good ridge of sandy gravel and the soil is significantly better than that with which Peter Vinding-Diers had to work in Portets. At present, the white wine is 100 per cent Sémillon, very scented, quite rich, and with definite breed. The Cabernet-dominated red wine has very vivid fruit, and is stylish yet solid.

CHÂTEAU MAGENCE

Commune: St Pierre-de-Mons. Owner: Dominique Guillot de Suduiraut. Red: 18 hectares. 5,800 cases. CS 41%, CF 32%, Mer 27%. White: 12 hectares. 10,000 cases. Sauv 64%, Sém 36%

This *cru* was probably the first from the far south of Graves to acquire a wide reputation. It is the leading property of St Pierre-de-Mons, which is in turn the largest wine-producing commune lying south-east of the Sauternes enclave. It is clearly marked on the Belleyme map in the late eighteenth century. In spite of the fact that Magence has been in the hands of the same family since 1800, it has been in the vanguard of the new Graves. Fermentation is in stainless steel with careful temperature control. This was one of the first modern-styled white Graves to go entirely Sauvignon, but this has now been balanced with some Sémillon, producing wines of real finesse and style. The reds are also very well made, stylish and attractively fruity and supple with a remarkably good length.

CHÂTEAU MAGNEAU

Commune: La Brède. Owner: Henri Ardurats. Red: 6 hectares. 1,000 cases. Mer 50%, CS 35%, CF 15%. White: 20 hectares. 10,000 cases. Sauv 50%, Sém 30%, Musc 20%. Second label: Château Guirauton (white only)

Another good *cru* in La Brède (see La Blancherie). The important thing here is the white wine, which is well made, fresh and stylish, and without the coarseness of some southern Graves, although there can be a certain earthiness in some years. The red wine has that very pungent, damp, undergrowth smell, which is nevertheless also attractively flowery and fruity. This is a wine, like its neighbour at La Blancherie, which is full of character and ready to drink young. The 1982 was delicious in May 1986.

CHÂTEAU MILLET

Commune: Portets. Owner: De la Mette family. Red: 45 hectares. 25,000 cases. Mer 60%, CF 40%. White: 20 hectares. 9,000 cases. Sém 40%, Sauv 30%, Musc 30%. Second label: Château des Clos-Rénon

This is today the largest property in Portets. The large, ornate, Victorian gothic château was built in 1882, and has an interior to match, which happily has been preserved. The La Mette family have owned it since

1935. The excellent red wine is matured in cask and vintages considered not up to standard, such as 1977 and 1980, are not bottled with the château name. I have found an attractive and pronounced smell of cherries on the nose, and a deliciously full soft fruitiness of flavour, which makes the wine very attractive to drink when around four years old. The whites have a good reputation, and many awards have been gained by both wines. It was recently pointed out that the legend *"Graves Cru Exceptionnel"*, which appears on the label, contravenes EC regulations since it is entirely self-awarded!

CHÂTEAU MONTALIVET

Commune: Pujols-sur-Ciron. Owners: Pierre Coste, Pierre Dubourdieu, Robert Goffard. 14 hectares. Red: 4,000 cases. CS 70%, Mer 30%. White: 1,500 cases. Sém 80%, Sauv 20%

This is another Coste-Dubourdieu collaboration, and one of the most successful of all Pierre Coste's enterprises. Pujols is a commune which lies inland from Barsac and Sauternes, and in fact almost amounts to an enclave of Graves in Sauternes. The red wines here usually have plenty of substance and last better than many of the other Coste reds, but are also deliciously fruity and stylish. The whites, which are Sémillon-based, show what the grape variety is capable of. The bouquet is scented, usually aromatic and sometimes toasty, with a delightful crisp fruitiness on the palate and plenty of character.

CHÂTEAU LE PAVILLON-DE-BOYREIN

Commune: Roaillan. Owner: Société Pierre Bonnet et Fils. Red: 12 hectares. 11,000 cases. Mer 65%, CS 35%. White: 13 hectares. 12,000 cases. Sém 80%, Sauv 20%. Second label: Domaine des Lauriers

There are now only around 40 hectares of vines in the commune of Roaillan, and this is the leading *cru*. It lies south of Langon and also borders on Fargues, one of the communes of Sauternes. The name of Boyrein is writ large on the Belleyme map in the late eighteenth century and seems to have been one of the few vineyards in the area at this time. Nearby, it is interesting to note the *lieu-dit* of Dubourdieu, so presumably the well-known family of wine-growers and oenologists must originally have come from here. The red wines are pleasantly scented, sometimes with some minerally or irony overtones and a nice light, fruity flavour, for drinking when between three and five years of age. The quality is similar to some northern Médoc *crus bourgeois*.

CHÂTEAU PESSAN-ST-HILAIRE

Commune: Portets. Owner: Dominique Haverlan. Red: 10 hectares. 3,350 cases. Mer 60%, CS 35%, CF 5%. White: 4 hectares. 1,650 cases. Sem 80%, Sauv 20%

This was originally part of the fief de Pessan which once belonged to the de Gascq family. The present owner acquired the property only in 1981, but quickly set about improving it, planting more Cabernet Sauvignon, and enlarging the *chai*. He is one of the new breed of proprietors with a training in oenology, who is succeeding, as is his neighbour down the road at Rahoul, in making excellent wines in spite of having vineyards which are not particularly well placed. The cold-fermented white wine shows real finesse on the nose, with quite a flowery elegance. The flavour has quite a strong, earthy note to it, but there is also attractive fruit, and the wine is clearly very well made. The red wine is now matured for twelve months in cask, and is rapidly improving. This is a *cru* to watch.

CHÂTEAU RAHOUL

Commune: Portets. Owner: Alain Thiénot. Red: 11.5 hectares. 5,000 cases. Mer 60%, CS 40%. White: 2.5 hectares. 1,000 cases. Sém 100%

Rahoul is nothing if not international. Between 1971 and 1978 it belonged to David Robson, an Englishman, who restored the charming eighteenth-century château and replanted most of the vineyard. It was then bought by an Australian consortium headed by Len Evans, Welsh by birth and Australian by adoption, with a flair for enthusing Australians with the joys of wine and persuading entrepreneurs to invest in vineyards. They brought in Peter Vinding-Diers who had been working for Martin Bamford at Château Loudenne. Then, when the Australians wanted to sell, Peter found a Danish wine merchant to buy it, and he has now sold to a Frenchman from Champagne, who also owns Château de Ricaud in Loupiac. The new owner took over the management in 1988, when Peter Vinding-Diers left to run his own property (see Château de Landiras). The property is an old one, named after the Chevalier Guillaume Raoul in 1646. The name is prominently marked on the Belleyme map in the late eighteenth century.

The most interesting and eventful period in Rahoul's history has certainly been in the last decade under Peter Vinding-Diers's stewardship. In spite of having a vineyard that is low-lying on sandy gravel and clay-gravel, with some drainage problems, he produced between 1979 and 1987 some white wines which stand comparison with many grown on much more favourable terrain. There was an investment in stainless steel and oak. Some new wood is used for both red and white wines. The white wine has a low-temperature fermentation. But perhaps his most important contribution has been in making selections of the natural yeasts found on the property, and then finding out which gave the best results. R2 is the name given to a strain of yeast which is now used on its own to ferment the white wine, and gives a particularly clean, elegant and very long-flavoured wine. It has since been used as far afield as Australia. It seems clear from Vinding-Diers's work that one of the reasons why Bordeaux produces such complex wines with so much individuality, even from neighbouring vineyards, is the great variety of natural yeasts to be found, and their continued use, while most New World wines are made from a very small selection of cultured yeasts.

The white wines here are those that have brought fame to this *cru* and its wine-maker. Their elegance and length of flavour have already been mentioned; they lack only something of the depth of flavour of the best wines from Pessac-Léognan. The reds are full of vivid, spicy fruit, sometimes with a touch of earthiness in their make-up, are well structured, and probably at their best when young, as are most red Graves in this area. This *cru* is certainly an object lesson in what can be achieved from these less favoured vineyards of the southern Graves by the intelligent use of modern techniques. It also shows how much more could be done in many of the better vineyards in Pessac-Léognan. It is some recognition of what has been achieved that Rahoul is now a member of the Union des Grands Crus.

CHÂTEAU RESPIDE-MÉDEVILLE

Commune: Toulenne. Owner: Christian Médeville. 7.5 hectares. Red: 1,000 cases. CS and CF 65%, Mer 35%. White: 2,500 cases. Sém 50%, Sauv 45%, Musc 5%

The Médeville family are best known for their Sauternes Château Gilette, but since Christian Médeville bought this small property in Toulenne, which lies between Langon and Sauternes, he has maintained and added to its reputation as the best *cru* in the commune. The château was immortalized by François Mauriac, who lived here for a time. The vineyard lies on a ridge of gravelly clay. The white wines have delicacy and some distinction. They have the ability to age well (the 1978 was still fresh, delicate and vigorous in 1985), yet are also charmingly fruity and stylish, with some body when young, as the 1985 showed when eighteen months old. The red wines have a charming soft, mellow fruitiness, with a little extra fullness, compared to some reds in the area, and a delicious flavour that just asks to be drunk and enjoyed young. Certainly this is one of the best *crus* south of Sauternes.

CHÂTEAU DE ROQUETAILLADE-LA-GRANGE

Commune: Mazères. Owner: Pierre and Jean Guignard. 36 hectares. Red: 12,000 cases. Mer 40%, CS 25%, CF 25%, Mal 5%, PV 5%. White: 2,200 cases. Sém 80%, Sauv 20%. Second label: Château Roquetaillade-Le-Bernet

The name of Roquetaillade is famous for the splendid medieval fortress built by a nephew of Pope Clément V (see Château Pape-Clément) at the beginning of the fourteenth century, and regarded as the finest example of military architecture in the whole of south western France. But this property, which lies to the east of the château, on hillsides dominating the valley of the Brion, is actually unconnected with the historic fortress, which owns only a few vines today. Interestingly, though, not only does the name Roquetaillade itself appear on the Belleyme map, at the end of the eighteenth century, but also those of the *lieux-dits* of La Grange and Le Bernet, although there were no vines here then. Lying in the commune of Mazères, astride the Langon-Bazas road, these are the most southerly vineyards in Graves. Under the present owners (also the owners of Château Rolland in Barsac) the reputation of the wines has risen considerably so that the red wine is deservedly regarded as one of the best in the southern Graves, and has won a number of medals in Paris.

The red wines, matured in cask, have real individuality, with lovely mellow fruit on the nose and palate, and sometimes, in years like 1979, an unmistakable hint of cherries. Even more unusually, the 1983 at first reminded me of gamy young Pinot Noir! The initial crushed-fruit character, however, has more to it than most southern Graves reds; there is also tannin and a concentrated middle richness that means these are not instant wines, but need, normally, a minimum of five years in the best vintages such as 1978, 1979, 1981, 1982, 1983, 1985, 1986, before reaching their full potential, and then last very well after that. The 1978 was still superb when seven years old, the 1981 at the height of its powers when over six years old. The white wines were fruity but rather coarse until the vinification was improved for the 1984 vintage; even then there was some coarseness behind the full flavour, but improvements have continued. However, the white wine seems unlikely to achieve the same distinction as the remarkable red.

CHÂTEAU ST AGRÈVES

Commune: Landiras. Owners: Claude and Marie-Christiane Landry. Red: 7.5 hectares. 3,750 cases. CS and CF 70%, Mer 30%. White: 2.5 hectares. 1,750 cases. Sauv 50%, Sém 50%

The commune of Landiras lies south-west of Illats and west of Pujols, making it one of the vineyards furthest away from the Garonne. But as the Belleyme map shows, this is an old-established wine-producing area. This property produces sound red wines which benefit from cask ageing, by no means common in this area. The wines need longer to mature than some of their neighbours, having well-balanced fruit and tannins, plenty of character and some breed. The white wines I have found too earthy and coarse, and not so well vinified as at the neighbouring Château d'Arricaud.

CHÂTEAU ST PIERRE

Commune: St Pierre-de-Mons. Owner: Henri Dulac. 43 hectares. Red: 6,200 cases. CS 60%, Mer 40%. White: 13,800 cases. Sém 67%, Sauv 33%.
Secondary labels: Clos d'Uza, Château Queyrats

In terms of size, this is now the most important estate in St Pierre-de-Mons, which is the largest wine-producing commune in the Graves, south of Sauternes. Effectively it groups together the *crus* of St Pierre itself with those of Queyrats and d'Uza. The vineyard is on ridges of clay and limestone in the south-east of the commune. The carefully made white wines, like those of Magence, were some of the first new-style cold-fermentation Graves to emerge, and have real finesse and character. The 1982 won a gold medal in Paris. The red wines are not as distinguished, but are vivid and quite generous, ageing well for wines in this area. They have an excellent record for consistency over the years.

CHÂTEAU TOUMILON

Commune: St Pierre-de-Mons. Owner: Jean Sévenet. 12 hectares. Red: 3,000 cases. CS 45%, Mer 35%, CF 20%. White: 2,500 cases. Sém 60%, Sauv 40%. Second label: Château Cabanes

This is one of the best red wines in the important commune of St Pierre-de-Mons, although it is much smaller than either Magence or St Pierre. The property has been in the same family since 1783. On the Belleyme map, which is about this period, it appears as Tomillon. The vineyards are on gravelly ridges overlooking the Garonne. Since the 1983 vintage there has been a notable improvement in the white wines, owing to new vinification facilities. Previously they were distinctly pedestrian, with a soapy finish; now they have finesse and delicacy. The red wines have finesse and a distinct personality, a real Graves character, but without the coarseness sometimes found in the south. In flavour they are compact and quite classic, rather than simplistically fruity.

CHÂTEAU TOURTEAU-CHOLLET

Commune: Arbanats. Owner: Société Civile du Château Tourteau-Chollet. 30 hectares. Red: 8,000 cases. CS 60%, Mer 40%. White: 4,000 cases. Sém 50%, Sauv 50%

The viticulturally small commune of Arbanats is immediately to the south-east of the major commune of Portets. Tourteau-Cholley now forms part of the Mestrezat empire (see Grand-Puy-Ducasse and Rayne-Vigneau). Since they bought the *cru* in 1977, there has been a steady programme of modernization and improvements to both installations and vineyard. Now pleasant, fruity red wines and elegant whites are being made. This is certainly a property with some potential.

CHÂTEAU VIGNOLLES-PEYROULE

Commune: St Pardon-de-Conques. Owner: Pierre Dubroca. 7 hectares. Red: 3,000 cases. CS 70%, Mer 20%, CF 10%

St Pardon-de-Conques is the most easterly commune in Graves, and there are some 40 hectares of vines, but this little vineyard, a Coste exclusivity, is well worth noticing. The vineyard is on sand and clay, giving a good maturation to the grapes, which are always low in acidity. The fermentation is supervised by Coste's oenologist, and he aims for a high-temperature fermentation and long vatting to produce rich, concentrated wines. The 1985 really "sang out" in a blind tasting, when eighteen months old, among some quite superior company from the Médoc, with its rich, vibrant fruit and juicy flavour, which also had depth. The balance, in spite of extreme youth, and sheer deliciousness of flavour was most impressive. A fine example of Pierre Coste's discernment and supervision.

CHÂTEAU DE VIRELADE
Commune: Virelade. Owner: Gérard de Bengy de Puyvallé. 25 hectares. Red only: 11,000 cases. CS and CF 70%, Mer and PV 30%

The commune of Virelade, of which this is the principal *cru*, lies between Arbanats and Podensac. This property, unusually for the area, is dedicated entirely to red wines. These are well made and aged in cask with about one-third new oak. I have found the wine to be very perfumed, sometimes rather marked by the wood, but having a decided style and breed which rewards some ageing. This is a good classic Graves.

8

St Emilion

Although the history of the St Emilion vineyards is an ancient and honourable one, it is only in recent years that they have come to receive their just due. The reasons for the late development of their estates and the prejudice against their wines in the Bordeaux trade are long and complex, and have now received detailed study in the late Professor Henri Enjalbert's monumental volume on the region (*Les Grands Vins de St Emilion, Pomerol et Fronsac*, Editions Bardi, 1983). The range and scope of Enjalbert's scholarship has in many cases supplanted legend and conjecture with a sound basis of fact, without which no account of the history and evolution of the region will in future be adequate.

Although archaeologists have proved that there were important Gallo-Roman settlements in the area around today's town of St Emilion, they have also shown that by the time the hermit Emilian came here in the seventh century, the Gallo-Roman estate had vanished and the countryside had reverted to woodland, with only a sparse population. The St Emilion we know today is the result of a deliberate act of policy, as is Libourne, but for different reasons. The eleventh century saw a rapid rise in population throughout western Europe. The decision to build a town here was made by the Archbishop of Bordeaux and the Comte de Castillon, in about 1080, for the then equally compelling reasons of religious prestige and its ease of fortification on a natural hill site. Before the founding of the city, the presence of the saint's hermitage had simply attracted the founding of the monastery of La Madeleine. Only a small chapel and underground ossuary just outside the south gate (Port Ste Marie-de-Fussignac) have survived. The idea of such a town was to gather people together from the countryside where they could be more easily protected from the marauding bands of armed men that were one of the chief hazards of life throughout the Middle Ages. The new town quickly prospered and immediately its religious character was established, with the building at the end of the eleventh and the beginning of the twelfth century of its two most important and characteristic religious monuments: the Eglise Monolithe – the largest entirely underground church in Europe, with its great bell-tower above, and the superb collegiate church, whose chapter, together with the Jurade, was to govern the town until the French Revolution. Beside the Monolithe stands the little chapel of La Trinité, with the saint's hermitage, and its holy well, beneath.

In the thirteenth century the thriving town attracted the new religious orders, whose vocation was essentially missionary, and therefore urban, in character rather than contemplative: the Franciscans – known here as Cordeliers – and the Dominicans, known as Jacobins, a name which took on a sinister ring during the French Revolution, when the most extreme of the revolutionary factions, who were responsible for the Terror, acquired the name of Jacobins through using the Dominican convent in Paris as their meeting place. In the seventeenth century the Ursulines, an order of teaching nuns, also built their convent here. Their main memorial today is the famous macaroons, said to originate from their recipe.

Lay jurisdiction was exercised by the Jurade, whose charter of 1199 was granted by the Plantagenet King John, and extended over that part of the surrounding countryside which now makes up the St Emilion *appellation*. This comprised eight neighbouring parishes outside the walls of the town itself: St Martin-de-Marzerat, St Sulpice-de-Faleyrens, St Brix-de-Vignonet, St Pey-d'Armens, St Laurent-des-Combes, St Hippolyte, St Etienne-de-Lisse and St Christophe-des-Bardes. St Martin was later absorbed into St Emilion, the rest became today's separate communes. The chapter meanwhile both exercised authority in all religious matters within that same area of jurisdiction, and held seigneurial rights. Since its canons were of course celibates, a close relationship grew up between an increasingly prosperous bourgeoisie and the local clergy, as deceased canons passed on their estates to their families, who thus became more involved in the growth of wine estates.

When I first went to Bordeaux in the early fifties the leading Bordeaux merchants still tended to be rather patronizing when speaking of St

Emilion, and there was surprise amounting almost to indignation if any St Emilion proprietor suggested that his wine should merit the same price as a leading classified-growth Médoc. The attitude of Médoc proprietors themselves was quite simply that since St Emilions could not be compared to Médocs and were certainly never as fine, it was an imposition to be asked to pay high prices for such wines. This attitude has died hard, and while wine drinkers in France, and especially in Belgium, have for many years eagerly sought out and paid high prices for the leading St Emilions, some English merchants have continued to reflect the traditional Bordeaux-Médoc view, and this is still apparent from many wine lists – especially in hotels and restaurants.

The physical aspects of the region are in marked contrast to the Médoc in almost every way. In area it is small and compact, but very intensely cultivated, so that its production often rivals that of the Médoc. It is also hilly and rocky, with many remains from the Gallo-Roman period. Because of the large number of small properties, mostly run by working resident proprietors, it is no easy matter for the uninitiated to find their way about, and I have known more people get lost in St Emilion and Pomerol than in any other part of Bordeaux.

The main square is the best vantage point from which to see the small, cramped medieval town. It boasts both the Plaisance, the principal restaurant, with a fine terrace overlooking the town, and the more modest but more homely Chez Germaine. From the terrace of the Plaisance one can see the entrance to the Monolithe below, as well as the tiny chapel of La Trinité, built above the hermitage of St Emilion. Further off, across steep roofs of ancient, mellowed tiles, is the Château du Roi, a narrow medieval keep, and then the vineyards seem to spring out of the town on every side.

Although the town and port of Libourne are outside the bounds of the St Emilion *appellation*, it is the commercial centre of the whole region called the Libournais, which includes Pomerol and Fronsac as well as St Emilion. Not surprisingly, therefore, its history is very bound up with that of the town of St Emilion. It was founded in 1270, at the confluence of the Dordogne with the much smaller Isle. The decision to found a town here was taken by Henry III, King of England and Duke of Aquitaine, as a counter to the founding of similar fortified towns on the French side. Commercially the new port was firmly established within thirty years as an entrepôt for the collection and shipment of wine from the hinterland of the Dordogne.

During the eighteenth century, when Bordeaux merchants were making the reputation of the emerging Médoc *grands crus* in England, the merchants of Libourne were establishing solid, if less glamorous markets in Holland, Dunkirk and Brittany. The development of the vineyards themselves was equally different. Here the amalgamation of many small holdings to create a large domain did not happen. Most of the vineyards were in the hands of share-croppers, small farmers known as *métayers*. These established the basis of today's equally small *crus*. The largest feudal manor, which was on the same scale as the great Médoc estates, was Figeac, but this was partly dismembered, and Ausone, with a mere seven hectares, emerged as the leading St Emilion *cru*. St Emilion as a region did not overtake Canon Fronsac until the beginning of the nineteenth century; Enjalbert puts the date at 1810.

The French Revolution was even more of a watershed in St Emilion than elsewhere in Bordeaux, for here the Church still held a powerful and primary position. The Revolution, especially during the period from 1790 to 1795, was an onslaught on every manifestation of religion, on its monuments as well as its guardians. All Church property was confiscated in 1791, and religious communities were driven from their convents and cloisters. The result was that virtually all St Emilion's historic monuments lay derelict; the heart had been torn out of what was still in essence a medieval town. The decay and desolation, made worse by years of economic decline, continued unrelieved for half a century. In 1841 Lecoutre de Beauvais gives a description of St Emilion which might be appropriate today for some community devastated by urban warfare: "There is a silence almost of the desert; seeing a few scattered souls, one might take them for Arab nomads, trampling on the debris of Africa's ancient civilization." It was not until the early days of the Second Empire brought a new prosperity, at the same time as a new interest arose in works of art and their preservation, that St Emilion's medieval heritage was secure for posterity. The Paris–Bordeaux railway was opened in 1853, with a station in Libourne. The wine trade was on the threshold of its golden age of prosperity, and for the first time Bordeaux *négociants*, faced with increasing demand coupled with shortages in the Médoc caused by the oidium, turned to Libourne. Many set up branch offices there. Fortunately for St Emilion all this brought prosperity to its vine-yards, but with the town having no railway of its own for some years and then nearly a mile from the town, on the branch line running from Libourne to Bergerac, trade and industry stayed in Libourne. So St Emilion remained in its time-capsule, and as one walks its streets today one can gain a clearer impression of a medieval town than anywhere else in the Gironde.

When examining the reasons for St Emilion's neglect by the Chartronnais, one has to begin by emphasizing the actual physical separation. Until the building of the stone bridge at Libourne in 1824, complementing the new bridge across the Garonne in Bordeaux, a journey from Bordeaux to Libourne necessitated no fewer than three ferry crossings, from Bordeaux across the Garonne to Lormont, from St Pardon across the Dordogne to Perpignan, and from Anguieux across the Isle to Libourne. The region was also far behind the Médoc in rationalizing its grape varieties. As late as 1784, thirty-four different varieties of black grapes, as well as twenty-nine varieties of white, are recorded. So in spite of the beginnings of prosperity in the 1850s no St Emilion appeared among the *crus classés* of the Gironde prepared for the Paris Exhibition of 1855. In 1867 a selection of leading growths, thirty-eight in number, were exhibited at the Paris Exhibition of that year. But interestingly there were no representatives from among the *graves* St Emilion, so no Cheval Blanc or Figeac. By 1868 Edouard Féret dignified only five properties with the description "château", signifying a distinguished residence and a *cru* of some reputation: Cheval Blanc, Belair, Mondot, Figeac and Corbin. Of these only Belair and Troplong-Mondot are on the *côtes* and plateau surrounding St Emilion, the others being in the *graves et sables* area adjoining Pomerol. Ausone was not to be placed above Belair until the end of the century, and it was not until after the First World War that any-one thought of Ausone and Cheval Blanc as first growths to be mentioned in the same breath as those of the Médoc, and only since the fifties have they commanded similar prices.

The size of St Emilion's properties remains small when compared to those of the Médoc. The eleven *premiers grands crus classés* average barely 20 hectares, the *grands crus classés* below 10 hectares. In Médoc the small-est of the *premiers crus*, Latour, covers 60 hectares.

One of the features of the district is the magnificent limestone caves which are frequently used instead of a *chai*. Originally constructed when stone was being quarried for building, some are extremely ancient. Among the finest are those at Clos Fourtet, Ausone and Belair, close to the town, and at Pavie, only a little further off. They are, of course, much cooler than the *chais* of the Médoc, and the damp usually makes it impossible to keep the casks free of mould, so that some extra vigilance is required to ensure that the wine remains untainted. On the other hand, the lower temperature safeguards the wine, especially in hot summers. The limestone is also of prime importance to the vineyards, because in winter it soaks up water like a sponge, providing moisture for the vines during dry summer spells. This is why the best St Emilion growths of the *côtes* do so well in dry years compared to the Médoc.

A most important feature of the district is its distinctive *encépagement*. Whereas in the Médoc and Graves the Cabernet Sauvignon is recognized as the most important variety, here it is the Cabernet Franc (called the Bouchet locally) and the Merlot. The disastrous frost of February 1956 did far more serious damage here than elsewhere, and after this much more Merlot was planted. It now seems to be recognized, however, that this movement has gone far enough, and there is a tendency to balance the Merlot with Cabernet Franc in new plantings. It was also as a result of the rot problems of the Merlot that the INAO actively encouraged growers in the sixties to plant Cabernet Sauvignon. The experiment has not been very successful as this vine has proved less suited to the cooler soils of St Emilion, with its limestone substrata, and even less so to those of Pomerol with its higher clay content. The Merlot's susceptibility to rot in damp weather caused 1963, 1965 and 1968 to be even more disastrous in St Emilion and Pomerol than elsewhere. This problem has now largely been overcome by new sprays. The Malbec (here called the Pressac) is also more widely found than in the Médoc.

The wines of St Emilion are generally characterized by their marked richness and suppleness. They are naturally richer in alcohol than other Bordeaux wines, usually between 12 and 14 per cent, so that although they have less tannin than Médocs, their marked vinosity and balance, combined with their natural alcoholic strength, enables them to develop early and then to live and flourish for thirty or even forty years. Often in the past, when Médocs have been spoiled by excessive tannin, St Emilions have continued to be fresh and delicious when their cousins

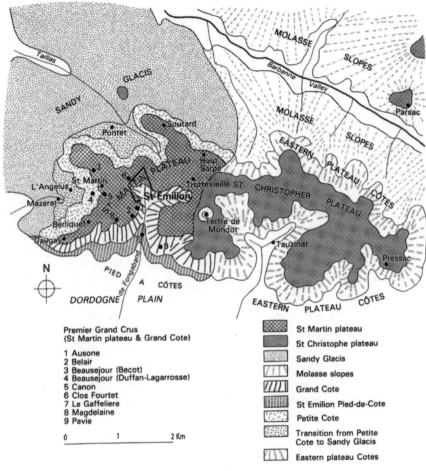

St Emilion: geology

Premier Grand Crus
(St Martin plateau & Grand Cote)

1 Ausone
2 Belair
3 Beausejour (Becot)
4 Beausejour (Duffan-Lagarrosse)
5 Canon
6 Clos Fourtet
7 La Gaffeliere
8 Magdelaine
9 Pavie

0   1   2 Km

St Martin plateau
St Christophe plateau
Sandy Glacis
Molasse slopes
Grand Cote
St Emilion Pied-de-Cote
Petite Cote
Transition from Petite
Cote to Sandy Glacis
Eastern plateau Cotes

have become mean and leathery – 1928 and 1945 were good examples of this.

St Emilion wines are often said to lack finesse, yet their flavour is complex and varied. It is true that they have an immediate appeal which makes them the most readily appreciated among Bordeaux wines. They are sometimes compared to Burgundy and certainly have a similar warmth and vinosity. All these excellent qualities are often quoted to praise and yet disparage. Yet I have often been struck by their consistency compared to Médocs. They seem to stay on form with

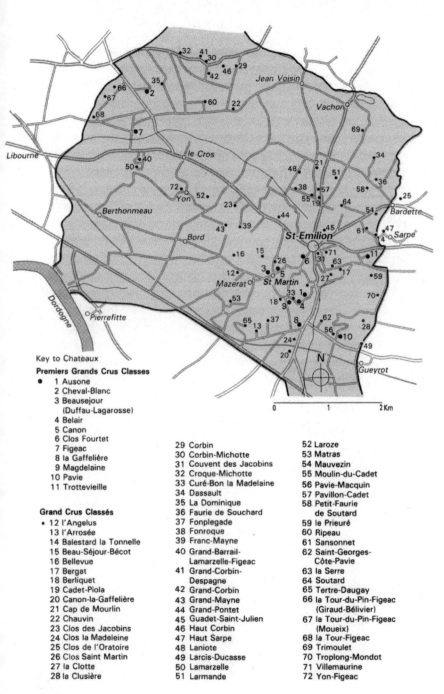

Key to Chateaux

Premiers Grands Crus Classes

- 1 Ausone
- 2 Cheval-Blanc
- 3 Beausejour (Duffau-Lagarosse)
- 4 Belair
- 5 Canon
- 6 Clos Fourtet
- 7 Figeac
- 8 la Gaffelière
- 9 Magdelaine
- 10 Pavie
- 11 Trottevieille

Grand Crus Classés

- 12 l'Angelus
- 13 l'Arrosée
- 14 Balestard la Tonnelle
- 15 Beau-Séjour-Bécot
- 16 Bellevue
- 17 Bergat
- 18 Berliquet
- 19 Cadet-Piola
- 20 Canon-la-Gaffelière
- 21 Cap de Mourlin
- 22 Chauvin
- 23 Clos des Jacobins
- 24 Clos la Madeleine
- 25 Clos de l'Oratoire
- 26 Clos Saint Martin
- 27 la Clotte
- 28 la Clusière

- 29 Corbin
- 30 Corbin-Michotte
- 31 Couvent des Jacobins
- 32 Croque-Michotte
- 33 Curé-Bon la Madelaine
- 34 Dassault
- 35 La Dominique
- 36 Faurie de Souchard
- 37 Fonplegade
- 38 Fonroque
- 39 Franc-Mayne
- 40 Grand-Barrail-Lamarzelle-Figeac
- 41 Grand-Corbin-Despagne
- 42 Grand-Corbin
- 43 Grand-Mayne
- 44 Grand-Pontet
- 45 Guadet-Saint-Julien
- 46 Haut Corbin
- 47 Haut Sarpe
- 48 Laniote
- 49 Larcis-Ducasse
- 50 Lamarzelle
- 51 Larmande

- 52 Laroze
- 53 Matras
- 54 Mauvezin
- 55 Moulin-du-Cadet
- 56 Pavie-Macquin
- 57 Pavillon-Cadet
- 58 Petit-Faurie de Soutard
- 59 le Prieuré
- 60 Ripeau
- 61 Sansonnet
- 62 Saint-Georges-Côte-Pavie
- 63 la Serre
- 64 Soutard
- 65 Tertre-Daugay
- 66 la Tour-du-Pin-Figeac (Giraud-Bélivier)
- 67 la Tour-du-Pin-Figeac (Moueix)
- 68 la Tour-Figeac
- 69 Trimoulet
- 70 Troplong-Mondot
- 71 Villemaurine
- 72 Yon-Figeac

St Emilion

reassuring regularity, while one is often dismayed to find that a fine Médoc growth, which was tasting beautifully six months before, is edgy and disappointing when wheeled out for some important occasion. Such flights of temperament seem foreign to St Emilion.

The most positive qualities of the St Emilion wines, to my way of thinking, are their superb fruit on both nose and palate, that certain hint of the exotic on the nose of many of the finest growths, an outstanding vinosity, sometimes almost approaching unctuousness, and a ripeness and mellowness of flavour which warm the heart on dull days, yet seem fresh and cool on a summer day. How elusive are such flavours to the pedestrian pen; it is easy to see why those who write in praise of wine are often accused of whimsy. It would need a poet's pen to recall such sensations.

A key word in the description of St Emilion, as of all great wines, is balance. The fruit and vinosity are devoid of any hint of the soft-centred or flabby. There is just enough tannin and acidity, yet it is one of the pleasures of St Emilion that one is rarely aware of their presence. It is for this reason that the wines develop more rapidly than Médoc or Graves, usually being ready to drink in anything from two (for a *bourgeois* growth) to four years (for a classified growth) earlier than similar wines across the river. Yet their keeping qualities, as has already been said, are excellent.

St Emilion is subdivided into a number of areas producing differing styles and qualities. Firstly, there is the area of the St Emilion *appellation*. This was defined in 1936 and exactly corresponds to the traditional area administered by the Jurade in the Middle Ages, consisting of eight communes: St Emilion, St Christophe-des-Bardes, St Etienne-de-Lisse, St Hippolyte, St Laurent-des-Combes, St Pey-d'Armens, St Sulpice-de-Faleyrens, and Vignoiret. Then there are the so-called St Emilion satellites, originally six in number: Sables, Lussac, Montagne, St Georges, Puisseguin and Parsac, each of which hyphenates its name with that of St Emilion – thus, for example, St Georges-St Emilion. These six parishes all sold their wines as St Emilion prior to the delineation of the *appellation* in 1936, when they were each granted their own *appellation*, retained their right to use the name of St Emilion, but were obliged to hyphenate it with their own parish names. In 1973 the growers of Parsac were given the option of declaring their wines as Puisseguin. A few loyalists lingered

GRANDS CRUS CLASSÉS DE ST EMILION

Premiers Grands Crus Classés

Ausone	H. Dubois-Challon – H[tiers] Vauthier
Beauséjour	Duffau Lagarrosse
Belair	Pascal Delbeck
Canon	Fournier
Cheval Blanc	Fourcaud-Laussac
Clos Fourtet	Lurton
Figeac	Manoncourt
La Gaffelière	De Malet-Roquefort
Magdelaine	J.-P. Moueix
Pavie	Valette
Trottevieille	Philippe Castéja

Grands Crus Classés

L'Angélus	De Boüard
L'Arrosée	Rodhain
Balestard la Tonnelle	J. Capdemourlin
Beau-Séjour	Bécot
Bellevue	Horeau
Bergat	J. Bertin
Berliquet	de Lesquen
Cadet-Piola	Jabiol
Canon-La-Gaffelière	De Neipperg
Cap de Mourlin	J. Capdemourlin
Chauvin	Ondet
La Clotte	Chailleau
La Clusière	Valette
Corbin	Giraud
Corbin-Michotte	Boidron
Couvent des Jacobins	Joinaud Borde
Croque-Michotte	Géoffrion-Rigal
Curé-Bon	Landé
Dassault	Dassault
La Dominique	Fayat
Faurie-de-Souchard	Jabiol
Fonplégade	A. Moueix
Fonroque	J.-P. Moueix
Franc-Mayne	Theillassoubre
Gd-Barrail-Lamarzelle-Figeac	Carrère

Grand-Corbin	Giraud
Gd-Corbin-Despagne	Despagne
Grand-Mayne	Nony
Grand-Pontet	Bécot and Pourquet
Guadet-St Julien	R. Lignac
Haut-Corbin	Soc. Assurances Mutuelles du Batiment et Travaux Publics
Haut-Sarpe	Janoueix
Clos des Jacobins	Cordier
Lamarzelle	Carrère
Laniote	Freymond-Rouja
Larcis-Ducasse	H. Gratiot
Larmande	Meneret-Capdemourlin
Laroze	Meslin
Clos la Madeleine	H. Pistouley
Matras	Bernard-Lefèbvre
Mauvezin	P. Cassat
Moulin-du-Cadet	J.-P. Moueix
Clos de L'Oratoire	Société Civile
Pavie-Decesse	Valette
Pavie-Macquin	F. Corre
Pavillon-Cadet	Llammas
P^t-Faurie-de-Soutard	Capdemourlin
Le Prieuré	Guichard
Ripeau	M. Janoueix de Wilde
St Georges-Côte-Pavie	Masson
Clos St Martin	Société Civile
Sansonnet	Robin
La Serre	d'Arfeuille
Soutard	Des Ligneris
Tertre-Daugay	De Malet-Roquefort
La Tour-du-Pin-Figeac	Giraud-Bélivier
La Tour-du-Pin-Figeac	A. Moueix
La Tour-Figeac	Société Civile
Trimoulet	M. Jean
Troplong-Mondot	Valette
Villemaurine	Giraud
Yon-Figeac	R. Germain

on, but the declarations in 1973 and 1974 fell to a few hundred hectolitres, and in 1975 the *appellation* disappeared. The even smaller *appellation* of Sables disappeared at a single sweep of the pen, the last declarations being those of the 1973 vintage.

In practice, this division of the region owes more to tradition and parish boundaries than it does to logic and differing qualities and styles. Within the St Emilion *appellation* proper, nearly all the best wines are produced within the commune of St Emilion itself. Thus, when the INAO classification was first drawn up in 1955, only one of the sixty-three *grands crus classés* came from outside the commune of St Emilion itself, namely Château Larcis-Ducasse in St Laurent-des-Combes. For the most part, these other seven communes within the St Emilion *appellation* produce wines which are nearer in quality to the wines produced by the six St Emilion satellites than to those produced in the commune of St Emilion itself. Indeed some of the satellites produce wines which are superior to those from some of the seven communes within the St Emilion *appellation*, but outside the commune of St Emilion itself. The *appellation* thus unduly favours these wines, while placing the satellites at a disadvantage. From a marketing and selling point of view, it is a disadvantage to divide the satellites into four different *appellations* with no opportunity for putting neighbouring wines of similar quality and style together. It would certainly be preferable to group the four together under a general *appellation* such as St Emilion-Villages. Some recognition of this viewpoint was shown when the wines of Parsac were given permission to be grouped with those of Puisseguin. It is interesting to note that in neighbouring Pomerol, since permission was given to sell the wines of Néac as Lalande-de-Pomerol, the latter *appellation* is almost universally used and preferred by the growers of this Pomerol satellite.

In the first edition of this book, I followed the practice, established by successive editions of Cocks & Féret, of dividing the wines of St Emilion into two broad categories; the *côtes* and the *graves*. When they were preparing their thirteenth edition, published in 1982, they had corresponded with Professor Enjalbert who was then preparing his great study of the region for publication the following year. This provided an entirely new classification of soil types, which divides the commune of St Emilion into five zones of production as follows:

1. *Le plateau calcaire* – the limestone plateau.
2. *Côtes et pieds de côtes* – hillsides and foot of the slopes.
3. *Graves et sables anciens* – gravel and old wind-blown (as distinct from alluvial) sand.
4. *Sables anciens* – old wind-blown sand.
5. *Sablo-graveleux* – (recent) alluvial sandy gravel.

It has to be remembered that Professor Enjalbert was first and foremost a distinguished geographer, and for this reason he devoted about 28 per cent of his text to a thorough examination of the soil types of the Libournais and their origins. Most of this is of a highly technical nature and of interest only to specialists. For our purposes the question has to be asked: What impact do the great variety and complexity of the soils of the region have on the character and quality of the wines? He quotes from a study made by three colleagues from the Institut d'Oenologie, and published in 1978: "the most highly regarded wines of the region are produced on soils that are profoundly different and are derived from widely varying parent rocks . . . from the point of view of the high quality of the wines, the role of the parent rock seems to be secondary. The Bordelais has no one geological formation with a prerogative for quality." (*Les Grands Types de sols viticoles de Pomerol et de St-Emilion.*) Enjalbert then goes on to show that it is possible to analyse why certain *terroirs* produce a combination of factors, such as poor soil, shallow soil, permeable soil, and good natural drainage, that makes them more likely to produce great wines than others, and that the great terroirs are those where a combination of favourable qualities occurs.

When it comes down to deciding how to list the wines of St Emilion, I have opted against following the new pattern used by Féret for the thirteenth edition of *Bordeaux et ses Vins* in favour of simply listing all the wines in alphabetical order, indicating for each one the nature of its soil. I found it irritating and inconvenient, for example, to find Ausone and Belair listed in different sections. The problem is also compounded by the fact that two or more soil types are often found in the same property. Both Magdelaine and Belair, placed by Féret among the *plateau* wines, also have important parts of their vineyards on the *côtes*. The complexity of the whole question of using such a soil analysis as a way of classifying vineyards is finally illustrated by the case of Château Petit-Faurie-de-

Soutard. This is listed by Féret, following Enjalbert's advice, among the *sables anciens*, yet in Enjalbert's own book it is described as "*plateau calcaire et côte*", in contrast to "*sables anciens et côtes*" on the manuscript in Claude Féret's possession. Then Couvent-des-Jacobins and Laniote, both described in Féret as *sables anciens*, appear in Enjalbert as being on the "*pied de côte et glacis sableux*". As Claude Féret said, with some feeling, this new division according to the dominant nature of the soil poses great practical problems, because of the diversity of the soils of St Emilion. Then, unfortunately, Enjalbert himself died soon after the publication of his book, and before such questions could be raised and discussed.

My own feeling is that from the purely practical point of view of classifying the *crus* in a way which corresponds with discernible differences in their actual characteristics, it makes more sense to divide the wines of St Emilion into three broader categories.

1. *Plateau et côtes.*
2. *Graves et sables anciens.*
3. *Sables anciens.*

This has the merit of correcting the most glaring anomaly of the old system, by providing a separate category for the *sables anciens*, some of which were previously to be found among the *côtes*, and some among the *graves*, the size of which was misleadingly exaggerated.

Looking back over my tasting notes, and taking simply the *crus classés* into consideration, I have found the most homogeneous group is the small *graves et sables anciens* one. Here the *crus* have a marked family character, with their mixture of tannin and rich fruit, their concentration and complexity, and their ability to be drinkable early yet to develop and last. The wines of the *plateau et côtes* are more varied in style and weight, and there are greater differences of *encépagement*. But most of the wines have a marked firmness which needs time to evolve. Classic examples of *plateau* wines are Canon, La Serre, Haut-Sarpe and Troplong-Mondot. There is more variety of styles on the côtes, where a number of wines are more fleshy and sometimes lighter in body. It is interesting to note that all the *premiers grands crus classés* – save for the two great *graves crus*, Cheval Blanc and Figeac – come from this *plateau et côtes* group clustered around the town of St Emilion. The wines of the *sables anciens*, situated on a *glacis* (a long, gentle slope) which joins the lower slopes of the *côtes* to the *graves et sables anciens* area, close to the borders of Pomerol, have a fleshy softness and sometimes a certain lack of definition to their flavour. A good example of what can be achieved here is Larmande, while Dassault and Laroze are thoroughly characteristic of typical well-made wines from this area. Above all it is the sheer variety and individuality of the wines produced from such a small area, that is so fascinating and remarkable. Nowhere is that subtle alchemy between soil, *cépage* and the hand of man more in evidence than here in St Emilion.

Up until now we have been talking solely of the soils and wines within the commune of St Emilion itself. But the 2,290 hectares of vineyards here make up only 44 per cent of the area under vine covered today by the St Emilion *appellation*. The other 56 per cent, or 2,912 hectares, are to be found in the eight adjoining communes of the old jurisdiction, and these are even more diverse in terms of soil and quality than is St Emilion itself. A brief summary here will give some idea of this diversity.

LIBOURNE

The commune of Libourne comprises 2,056 hectares, but much of this is now covered by the town. Of the vineyards within the commune, those to the north-east are in Pomerol, those to the northwest are only Bordeaux Supérieur or straight Bordeaux rouge, while only those to the south-east are entitled to the St Emilion *appellation*. These vineyards are on terraces of *graves et sables* between the *palus* and the railway. The most important *grand cru* is Château Martinet.

ST CHRISTOPHE-DES-BARDES

Here there are 545 hectares under vine, out of a total of 768 hectares, making this one of the three most important communes among the eight. It lies to the east of St Emilion, with vineyards on *plateau*, on *côtes* and on the *pieds de côtes*, in other words on very good types of soil. There is one *grand cru classé*, Haut-Sarpe, but this belongs geologically to the St Emilion *plateau et côtes*. There are a number of good *grands crus*, among which are Château de Cauze, Château Coudert-Pelletan, Château Fombrauge, Château Laroque, Château Les Baziliques and Château Vieux-Sarpe.

ST ETIENNE-DE-LISSE

This large commune, with 525 of its 709 hectares under vine, is only marginally smaller than St Christophe and is the most easterly of the communes. It extends to the north towards the Barbanne on *sables anciens*, at the centre there is the *plateau calcaire* and its *côtes*, and to the south the plain of the Dordogne, three very different soil types. There are some good *grands crus*, notably Château de Pressac, Château Puy-Blanquet, Château du Rocher and Château Trapaud.

ST HIPPOLYTE

This commune lies east of St Laurent and south of St Christophe, and 235 of its 444 hectares are under vine. These are situated on the *plateau calcaire*, the *côtes* and *pieds de côtes* south of the *plateau*, with some again on the plain, providing a diverse range of qualities. There are several *grands crus*, notably Château Destieux and Château de Ferrand.

ST LAURENT-DES-COMBES

A small commune to the south-east of St Emilion, 235 of its 385 hectares are under vine. The vineyards are mostly on *côtes* and *pieds de côtes*, but there are some on the plain producing less good wines. The leading *cru* is Larcis-Ducasse, a *grand cru classé*, but this is on the Côte de Pavie and immediately adjoins Château Pavie. There are several *grands crus*, among which are Château Bellefont-Belcier, Château La Mondotte, Château Pipeau and Château Rozier.

ST PEY-D'ARMENS

Here 290 out of 420 hectares are under vine. The commune lies on the plain of the Dordogne south of St Hippolyte. The soil here is *sables* with some clay and gravel. Many wines are vinified at the *coopérative*. There are few *grands crus*, the most important being Château de St-Pey.

ST SULPICE-DE-FALEYRENS

This is the largest commune of the eight, with 595 out of 2,000 hectares under vine, in the south-west of the *appellation*. There are two distinct parts of the commune: to the south are low-lying *sables* which do not have the *appellation*, while to the north there are terraces of *graves et sables*. This, of course, is where the best vineyards are. There are a number of *grands crus*, especially Château Haut-Renaissance, Château Lagrange-de-Lescure, Château Le Castelot, Château de Lescours, Château Monbousquet, Château Palais-Cardinal-La-Fuie.

VIGNONET

This, the most southerly of the eight communes, has 275 out of 415 hectares under vine. The vineyards are in the plain bordering the Dordogne on terraces of recent *graves* and *sables*, soils of rather moderate quality. The best known *grand cru* is Château Teyssier.

I have dealt with the St Emilion classification and the 1985 revision in some detail in Chapter 3. While the *premiers grands crus classés* are now much more homogeneous in quality than they were in the seventies, the substantial soil differences discussed earlier in this chapter make for much greater variations among the *grands crus classés* – these will be covered under the individual entries.

Something which helps to give St Emilion its unique character is that this is still, to a large extent, a *vignoble* of resident working proprietors. When they do not actually live on the property, they are usually to be found a few minutes away in St Emilion or Libourne. Only two owners, among the eleven *premières* today, come from outside the Libournais. Everybody knows everybody else. Many *régisseurs* and *maîtres de chai* work on more than one property and for more than one owner. Such small properties, compared with those in the Médoc, are of less interest to the insurance and pension-fund predators that now roam the Médoc. It all adds up to a much closer, tighter sense of community than is possible elsewhere in Bordeaux.

CHÂTEAU L'ANGÉLUS
Grand Cru Classé. Owners: de Boüard de Laforest family. 24 hectares. 12,000 cases. CF 50%, Mer 45%, CS 5%

With its vineyard of 28 hectares, this is one of the most important pro-perties on the *côtes*, only Pavie and Troplong-Mondot being larger. Before they bought L'Angélus in 1924, the de Boüard de Laforest family owned Château Mazerat, which they eventually amalgamated, together with other properties, into the one large estate which is today L'Angélus. This is an old St Emilion family; Georges de Boüard was Jurat in 1564.

The vineyard is situated on the lower slopes of the *côtes*, to the west of St Emilion. There is a large modern *chai*, but maturing in new oak has been practised only since 1980; before this the wine was kept in vat. Note that, unusually, the proportion of Cabernet Franc here is greater than that of Merlot. The two-thirds new oak introduced at this time was interest-ingly cut to 50 per cent for the excellent 1986. The wines are very consistent and clearly well made. They are characterized by a marked perfume and easy, flattering fruit, but on the other hand tend to lack con-centration and depth, even in years like 1982. These were thoroughly pleasant commercial wines; they lacked real excitement but seldom let you down. I have found the best recent vintages to be the 1979, which although forward for the year has more body and extract than usual; the 1982 has style and charm, but it is too full-blown, lacking concentration; the 1983 is better, full of deliciously crunchy fruit, very rich and more solid. This seems to mark the beginning of an important change of gear at L'Angélus, for 1984 produced a remarkably full-flavoured and successful wine; the 1985 is rich and plummy, but also solid and concentrated, while the 1986, in cask, was tannic and powerful with real depth of flavour. Pre-1983 many L'Angélus wines needed drinking young and aged prematurely; from 1983 onwards the picture looks much better. It will be interesting to see how these wines age in future.

CHÂTEAU L'ARROSÉE

Grand Cru Classé. Owner: François Rodhain. 10 hectares. 5,000 cases. Mer 50%, CS 35%, CF 15%

This is an old-established growth, being one of the twenty-nine growths mentioned in the list of 1859 at the St Emilion *mairie*, but it is only recently that its reputation has spread to export markets, especially the United States. The vineyard is well situated on the *côtes*, south-west of the town, above the *coopérative* and below Tertre-Daugay. The name actually means "watered by springs". There are three sections in the vineyard: the *haut de côte*, giving the wine body and power; the *milieu de côte*, giving richness; and the *pied de côte*, providing finesse. It is this that gives L'Arrosée its balance and complexity. Interestingly, an earth-moving exercise to reshape a part of the vineyard a few years ago revealed a large pocket of *sables anciens* in the Molasse formation of the *côtes*. This is a very classic St Emilion, rich, powerful and luscious, with depths of flavour and a marked individuality. Recent vintages have been widely acclaimed in the United States but the wine remains hard to find in the UK, or in Bordeaux for that matter; nor is the proprietor fond of putting it into tastings at the St Emilion syndicate.

CHÂTEAU AUSONE

Premier Grand Cru Classé A. Owners: Pascal Delbeck and Héritiers Vauthier. 7 hectares. 2,150 cases.Mer 50%, CF 50%

This is one of the oldest and most famous properties in Bordeaux, in spite of its very small production. The small steep-roofed château is only nineteenth-century, but according to tradition it stands on the site of the villa of the Roman poet Ausonius, governor of Gaul, who died in AD 395. A number of contemporary writers described a villa called Lucaniacus which belonged to the poet. Gallo-Roman remains have indeed been discovered on the plateau of La Madeleine, near today's Ausone. Elie Vinet of Bordeaux, writing in the eighteenth century, and Vidal, the parish priest of St Martin in 1778, both repeat the story, which no doubt gave Jean Cantenac, cooper and wine grower, the idea of renaming his property Château Ausone. But in 1843 a very fine Gallo-Roman villa was discovered at St André-de-Montagne, and this then became the favourite site for Ausonius's villa. Then in 1881 two mosaic floors were uncovered beside a stream at Le Palat, near Château La Gaffelière below Ausone, and since 1969 a further twelve mosaic floors have been uncovered. This has led to a revision of archaeological opinion in favour of this site. The Latin texts talk of a site on a high place, from which the Dordogne was visible. Enjalbert has suggested that there may have been two villas on the estate, one on the edge of the plateau close to where the present château stands, the other below at Le Palat. Certainly it is likely to have been a large property. Another owned by Ausonius near Bordeaux, of some 264 hectares, was described as only modest, and the average size of Gallo-Roman estates in the third and fourth centuries was about 800 hectares.

The greatness of Ausone is due to a combination of soil and exposure. The soil is a mixture of clay and sand on limestone that is unique in the district, and is planted with old vines. No replanting took place between 1950 and 1976. So the average age of the vines is now about fifty years, with very low yields, ranging from 20 hectolitres per hectare in difficult years to about 36 in abundant years like 1982. Picking can be done at the optimum moment in such a small vineyard, usually in two afternoons. The situation of the vineyard is ideal, with steep slopes arranged like an amphitheatre, facing south-east, and so providing a perfect exposure and the maximum protection from adverse winds. The vines are also protected against frost, so that even in 1956, when many vineyards in the Libournais were virtually destroyed, Ausone's escaped. Similarly, the limestone retains moisture and so protects the vineyard from the effects of drought, even in the hottest years.

The ownership of the property has rested in the same family since the Revolution, from Monsieur Cantenac to Madame Lafargue, and through her nephews to the Dubois-Challon and Vauthier families. Ausone shared its *chai* with Belair until 1976. It is a cave cut into the hillside close by the château, under a cemetery, and reminds one more of Vouvray and Touraine than Bordeaux.

Ausone moved ahead of other St Emilions in general estimation only during the last decade of the nineteenth century, and there is a note in the sixth edition of Cocks & Féret (1898) explaining that Ausone had for the first time been placed above Belair because of the superior prices it had been obtaining, but that this did not indicate that there had been any decline in the quality of Belair. This is an interesting example of a *cru* making its reputation by preserving its old vines during the phylloxera crisis, because the vintages when Ausone's prices overtook those of Belair were 1887 to 1895. This position was well consolidated by the twenties, by which time Ausone's special position had penetrated even the British consciousness with its Médoc bias. Colonel Campbell recalls the excellence of the 1904 and 1905, the earliest Ausones he tasted – he never saw the wine during his stay in Bordeaux in the early 1890s!

I was fortunate indeed to take part in a unique tasting held at the château on 21 and 22 November 1988, the brainchild of Bipin Desai from Los Angeles, and organized in collaboration with previous owner Madame Dubois-Challon and masterminded by Pascal Delbeck. This gave an unrivalled panorama of vintages going back over 150 years to 1831. No fewer than seventeen nineteenth-century vintages were tasted. The 1831 was remarkable; for, in spite of an edgy, cheesy bouquet, it had an amazing volume of flavour, and was still fruity with some richness, an extra-ordinary relic from the age of Louis-Philippe and the young Berlioz. Then came a sweet and charming 1844, better than the 1849 or 1893. The 1850 had great depths of colour, still with amazing structure and power, tannic and four-square; it was even now one of the giants of the century. The 1869 must have been a massive wine; it still had vinosity and power in spite of volatility. The 1877 had a bouquet of ethereal fruit and sweetness that was still fresh and delicious and quite overshadowed the small but nevertheless charming 1879. The 1892 had a lovely opulent scent and a flavour that was still rich and full; even better was the frail but beautifully elegant and long-flavoured 1893; it remained sweet and lovely after half an hour in the glass. On a par with this was the 1894, with its sweet lingering flavour. The 1897 was still freshly scented and fruity, with lovely, gentle, faded fruit, a seamless flavour, an almost age-less beauty. The 1899 was all one could have hoped for from this legendary vintage, a classic and wonderfully ethereal old claret bouquet, all breed and finesse, with a very complete flavour, long and delicate, very dry but quite lovely; it outshone the more opulent 1900. Certainly, the old, damp, chill cellars of Ausone had preserved these nineteenth-century wines in a remarkable way – but more surprising still were some of the wines in what is normally regarded as a dull period, between the great vintages of 1900 and 1920.

After a powerful but untypically aggressive 1904, came three remark-able wines. The 1905 had a bouquet that was really exotic, all concen-trated richness; then came a flavour of great beauty, rich and complex with a wonderful finish – a great wine. The 1906 was only just behind, a more faded beauty, but with a wonderful long flavour, with great fruit and what I can only call gentleness still at the finish. It was in this year that the first grafted vines were planted. Then, challenging the 1905, was the 1908 with its heavenly aromas of an ethereal quality – one of the most sublime bouquets I have experienced – while the flavour had so many highlights and nuances, fruit and lingering elegance. A great wine. After this celestial trio, there was a fine 1912, elegantly scented, imperceptibly echoing away. The lovely ethereal character was there again, but with less power. The 1914 just had the edge on it, exotically scented, very cedary, a wine of ageless charm and elegance, but with less fruit at the finish than the marvellous 1917, which was still deep and dark in colour, with a tactile, opulent quality in the bouquet, lovely complex chewy fruit and just so much life and joie de vivre; it was more tannic and assertive than the 1908, but less beautiful. These forgotten years seem to show that old Ausones do not die, they go to paradise – there to become transfigured into something we dream about, but seldom experience.

The twenties were a great era for Ausone. The 1920 was still extraordinarily powerful, rich and tannic; the 1921 lovely, very concentrated and toasted on the nose, a rich, seamless flavour, but just drying out at the finish; then a curiosity, 1925, with a lovely delicate scent and all the breed of this *cru*, fragile but still beautiful; the 1926, even now a great wine, wonderfully perfumed, with a complex ethereal character, still fresh and sweet on the palate, marvellously harmonious, with its long lingering flavour. The 1928 – a great vintage – was going fast; I have had much finer bottles. But 1929 made up for everything: the bouquet mirrored the 1926, the flavour was majestic, powerful and ripe, with great finesse, long and lingering with incredible nuances. I could only mark it 20/20. In the lean years of the thirties, 1934 had amazing sweetness but was going dry at the finish; it continued to improve in the glass but was less impressive than 1937, which had the rich fruit and body to support some volatility and was sweet, rich and chewy – a wine of great character. The best of the wartime vintages was 1943, very ripe with a smell of liquorice, a supple middle flavour, but rough at the end, while 1940 was light, elegant but fading.

Then began that uneven period between 1945 and 1975. The 1945 had almost entirely surrendered to volatile acidity, the 1947 was very rich and plummy but had a dry finish and yielded pride of place to 1949, the last really great wine before the renaissance ushered in by Pascal Delbeck. The bouquet of the 1949 was exceptionally scented and heady and it had a wonderful sweetness and complexity of flavour – a great wine. In between, 1948 had preserved the Ausone magic on the nose and was powerful and fine, but very dry. The 1953, 1955 and 1959 were more promising on the nose than on the palate, fine but not exceptional wines, with 1959 just the best. The 1960 was surprisingly good and well-preserved for the year; the 1961 was powerful but lacked style; I preferred the 1959. The 1962 was beautifully elegant and stylish, with a lingering flavour; it was fresher and more lively than a 1966 that just missed it, with 1964 the best of the decade, showing very concentrated rich fruit, but lacking the refinement of Ausone's great years.

In the next decade, 1970 had depth of flavour and power, but 1971 was full-blown and beginning to go. Then came the decisive change of management, with the bold decision by Madame Dubois-Challon to appoint the nineteen-year-old Pascal Delbeck, straight out of viticultural school, to take charge. The result was immediate: 1975 is the best wine here since 1949, very concentrated and opulent, rich and tannic; it is still far from ready but immensely impressive. The 1976, although it has the roasted tannic finish typical of the vintage, has far more complexity and a charm and breed that had been lacking for some years, and it is still improving. The lovely 1978 probably has even further to go, while the 1979 is more luscious and extrovert, already a pleasure to drink, but with plenty still to come. After an honourable 1980 that has developed slowly for the year, 1981 is again very fine, elegant but concentrated and firm still. The 1982 is a great wine, with opulent ripeness and concentration and a gorgeous flavour, while 1983 is more open and softer, yet very rich with a roasted exotic quality. The 1985 was in a transitional stage but the quality is there; 1986 had marvellous complex, rich, spicy fruit – a wine of great potential.

I hope that this gives some idea of the extraordinary character and properties of Ausone. Only Lafite among the great Bordeaux can match it for delicacy, dimensions and finesse combined with power, slowly evolving over many decades to give a bouquet unsurpassed for the complexity of its perfume, and a flavour full of multi-layered sensations. The old wines seem to achieve a sort of apotheosis, an ethereal quality that is not quite of this world.

CHÂTEAU BALESTARD-LA-TONNELLE
Grand Cru Classé. Owner: GFA Capdermourlin. Administrator: Jacques Capdemourlin. 10.6 hectares. 5,000 cases. Mer 65%, CF 20%, CS 10%,Mal 5%
This is one of the most venerable growths of St Emilion, owned by one of the oldest families of wine growers. The wine has the unusual distinction of being mentioned in a poem of the fifteenth century by François Villon (1421–85), where the poet speaks of: "ce divin nectar, qui porte nom de

Balestard". The proprietors, the Capdemourlin family, have been wine growers in St Emilion for no less than five centuries – a remarkable record. The curious name owes its origin to a canon of the chapter of St Emilion (Balestard), while Tonnelle refers to an old tower which had always stood on the vineyard.

The vineyard lies just to the east of St Emilion, across the road from Soutard, at the limit of the *plateau calcaire*. Jacques Capdemourlin is the member of the family who has been in charge now for over a decade. He had consistently been making the better wine at Cap de Mourlin itself, when it was divided, so it is not surprising to find a record of consistent and attractive wines here. This is an archetypal St Emilion, big, luscious and full-bodied, but easy to drink early while lasting longer than one might think. The 1947 was still superb when last tasted in 1981. More recently the 1975 smells of prunes and liquorice, is supple, delicious and complex, and by 1988 was one of the most approachable examples of the year. The 1978 was already soft, full and ripe in flavour by 1984. The 1979 had developed complex overtones and was a luscious, attractive wine by 1983. The 1980 was very successful, soft and full-flavoured, ready to drink by 1983. The 1981 is rich and big, but forward; while the 1982 shows real concentration with a rich, meaty structure, and should be delicious to drink relatively early. The 1983 is full of extract and fruit, quite tannic and with some way to go still by 1987. The 1985 is opulent, rich and flattering, an early developer; while the 1986 in cask showed real concentration, with a long, elegant flavour and ripe tannins, a fine harmonious example of this vintage. I find this to be a consistently attractive and enjoyable wine, with charm and breed.

CHÂTEAU LES BAZILIQUES

Owner: Société Civile du Château Le Couvent. 6 hectares. 3,500 cases. Mer 39%, CF 36%, CS 25%

This vineyard is on the lower slopes of the *côte*, north-east of St Christophe, near the Barbanne and in the St Christophe commune. In December 1982 it was bought by François Marret's Bordeaux wine group, an offshoot of Marne et Champagne. It had made good wines before, but now, with the resources of the new owners behind it, the wines have moved up a class. The 1985 had a wonderful bouquet of exotic ripe fruit, with a luscious rich flavour marked by an impressive array of delicious exotic spicy flavours, certainly on a par with some *crus classés*. This is certainly a *cru* to watch.

CHÂTEAU BEAU-SÉJOUR-BÉCOT

Grand Cru Classé. Owners: Michel, Gérard and Dominique Bécot. 18.5 hectares. 7,000 cases. Mer 70%, CS 15%, CF 15%

In 1955 this *cru*, then known as Beauséjour-Dr-Fagouet, and with a vineyard of barely ten hectares, was placed among the twelve *premiers crus* of St Emilion, in the region's first official classification. Thirty years later, amid a welter of controversy, and more publicity than it had ever previously known, it was demoted to the ranks of the *grands crus classés*. In 1970 Michel Bécot, the owner of two neighbouring *crus classés* – La Carte and Trois Moulins – bought Dr Fagouet's portion of Beauséjour, restyling it Beau-Séjour-Bécot. He carried out a thoroughgoing modernization of the *cuvier*, installing stainless steel tanks and going to Professor Peynaud for advice. Then, in 1979, Michel Bécot incorporated his other vineyards with Beau-Séjour, making it the largest of the *premiers* on the plateau of St Martin. Only Pavie on the *côtes* was larger among the *premiers* of the *plateau et côtes*. In Médoc such action would have been perfectly possible and not abnormal. Here, where few vineyards have changed for generations, everyone was up in arms, and the demotion followed when the revision of the classification came up in 1985.

It was pointed out that no application had been made to the INAO, either to upgrade Trois Moulins and La Carte to *premier cru* status, or to incorporate them into Beau-Séjour, and the result was to increase the size of the vineyard by 85 per cent. On his side Michel Bécot countered that his wine had been accepted for the *premier cru* tasting for the *appellation* each year it had been submitted, and claimed that his wines had not suffered in quality, emphasizing the high quality of the soil in the other vineyards. It is possible to see the merits of both sides of the case. It certainly emphasizes the point that St Emilion vineyards are now much more rigidly stratified than those in Médoc, where new estates are still being created. It also suggests a certain indifference to the commercial problems raised by having many small vineyards, yet this has to be reconciled with the need to protect famous names. Clearly there would be no problem, on the other hand, if, for example, it was proposed to reunite the two Beauséjours.

The style of the wines is now in marked contrast to the other Beauséjour, being fuller-bodied, less tannic and almost plummy. They are certainly very attractive and easy to drink, but lack the distinction of most of their neighbours. Of the wines from Dr Fagouet's period, there is a fine 1928 which has lasted well, the 1945 is ripe and powerful, not too tannic, and the 1947 is massive and luscious – a classic 1947 from this region. After these heights the 1959 was mellow but beginning to decay by 1983, while the 1962 was much better, with lovely luscious fruit and balance. In contrast the 1964 was fading and disappointing, the 1966 charming and delicate, but showing its age by 1983. The Bécot era began with a rather overblown and flabby 1971, but the unsung 1973 vintage produced a charming wine that was still fresh and youthful after ten years. The 1975 is rich but lacks backbone. The 1976 is rich and solid, good for this uneven year. The 1978 is perfumed, rich and concentrated; the 1979 is spicy and scented, with velvety-textured fruit and easy charm. The 1980 is dry and short; the 1981 tannic, rich but a shade coarse. The 1982 is big and rich but lacks the style of the best 1982s in the region; I preferred the 1983, with its heady bouquet and luscious sappy fruit and long, lingering finish. It will be interesting eventually to see how the Bécots come to terms with the INAO's decision, and whether they decide that in the end it will be sensible to concede the point, from a purely practical point of view.

CHÂTEAU BEAUSÉJOUR (DUFFAU-LAGARROSSE)

Premier Grand Cru Classé B. Owner: Héritiers Duffau-Lagarrosse. Administrator: Jean-Michel Fernandez. 7 hectares. 3,000 cases. Mer 50%, CF 25%, CS 25%.
Second label: La Croix de Mazerat

Like most of the *premiers grands crus* of the *côtes*, Beauséjour is situated just outside the old ramparts of St Emilion. In the eighteenth century it was known as Puycocu, and passed by marriage in 1722 to the de Carle family, seigneurs of Figeac. It was given its present name in 1787 by Jacques de Carle, who was also a general in the army of Louis XVI. This is one of a number of examples of the judicious renaming of properties at the time. The growth of Beauséjour was a single property until 1869, when the proprietor, Monsieur Ducarpe, a notary, divided it between his two children. His daughter married Docteur Duffau-Lagarrosse, a medical practitioner of St Emilion, and the property now belongs to their heirs. Much of the wine is sold direct to private customers, and with the small production this means that little is seen of these wines in the trade, making it today the least known of the *premiers grands crus*.

The vineyard is on the western edge of the limestone plateau of St Martin, and on the two *côtes*, adjoining Canon on the eastern side, and Beau-Séjour-Bécot to the north. There is a small *cuvier* and *chai* with underground "caves" for bottle stock. About one-third new wood is used for the maturation. Long vatting gives these wines breed and undeniably stylish fruit, but perhaps with rather too much tannin for wines which tend to be light in body, at least prior to the 1979 vintage.

The only old wine I have tasted is the 1955, when it was twenty-five years old. The powerful, rich bouquet was full of character and vigorous, and the wine had developed a really complex, elegant and beautiful flavour; it was full-bodied with good length, mature but in no way too old. This was far better than a tannic but fading 1971, tasted at the same time. There was a disappointing 1964, and a good but unexciting 1966. More recently things have been improving. After a very light 1976, with an over-ripe character that demanded early drinking, the 1978, while scented and fine, seemed to lack the richness for its tannins; then the 1979 was more successful with very concentrated fruit and middle richness to balance the tannin. After a better-than-average 1980, the 1981 was spicy and almost unctuous on the nose, with a lot of fruit and depth of flavour, robust and balanced. The 1982 is very rich and concentrated, with real *race* and style, while the 1985 showed great promise in cask, with real concentration and a rather minerally quality, and the 1986 in cask combined richness and concentration with elegant fruit, another very promising wine. All this adds up to a *cru* which is increasingly making wines which reflect both the fine position of its vineyards and its place among the eleven *premiers crus* of St Emilion. I often suspect that commentators are dismissive about this *cru* because they have seldom seen it. Certainly it is hard to find, and there have been some wines which did not correspond to its potential, but I believe recent vintages, at least, deserve a better reputation.

CHÂTEAU BELAIR

Premier Grand Cru Classé B. Owner: Pascal Delbeck. 13 hectares. 4,000 cases.
Mer 60%, CF 40%

This is a close neighbour of Ausone and hardly less ancient in origin or less famous for the excellence of its wines. Like Ausone, the property is said to have belonged to Ausonius, but its real history begins during the period of English rule. In the fourteenth century it belonged to Robert de Knolles, who was grand seneschal and governor of Guyenne. When the region was finally reconquered by Charles VII, the descendants of Robert de Knolles returned, their name changed to Canolle, but the vineyard was not planted until between 1730 and 1750. When Jacques Canolle died in 1753, we know that the château and vineyard were as we see them today. At that time the family still made a lot of their money from the local quarries, and this was still the case until the Revolution, as the account books of Belair, begun in 1786, show. They also prove that by this time the wines were fetching prices three times those of ordinary St Emilion, thus placing Belair in the forefront of St Emilion *crus*. From 1 January 1786 until 1897 Belair was run by the Goudichau family as *régisseurs*, and it is thanks to the meticulous records they kept that we know so much about Belair in the last days of the *ancien régime*. They faithfully ran the property when it was seized after the Canolles fled during the Terror. As so often happened at this time, the property was bought by a neighbour, acting for the Canolles, who finally returned in 1802. In 1916 it was acquired by the Dubois-Challon family, the owners of Ausone. The wines of Belair are now once more kept in their own ancient caves. The vineyard, unlike Ausone which is wholly on the *côtes*, is half on the *côtes* and half on a plateau above the château, and adjoins Ausone, sharing its fine exposure. It is the latter portion of the vineyard, on the plateau adjoining Canon, which is responsible for the difference in emphasis between Belair and Ausone. Yields have been very low because of the age of the vines. Now a cautious programme of replanting is under way, to restore the rotation.

The reputation of Belair has always been high. For most of the nineteenth century it was regarded as the leading *cru* in St Emilion, and when Cocks & Féret replaced it with Ausone in 1898, they said that this was due to the exceptional prices obtained by Ausone from 1887 onwards, rather than any decline at Belair. This is an interesting example of a *cru* making its reputation by preserving its old vines during the phylloxera crisis. Today, it deserves its place as one of the leading growths of the region. Its wines have a spicy, complex richness of flavour, together with that decided firmness usually found on the plateau of St Martin. Compared to Ausone, the wines tend to be more fleshy, but without the same power and intensity. There is real finesse and great vigour. The most closely comparable growths in style are Canon and Clos-Fourtet. The only pre-war vintage I have tasted is 1920. In 1985 it filled out and became more powerful after half an hour in the glass, developing a surprisingly rich, ripe, sumptuous flavour, still very much alive. The 1945 was a great success, being vigorous and powerful, while the 1947 had a wonderful silky texture and 1955 was rich and powerful still in 1988. The 1961 is enormous and magnificent, the 1962 and 1966 supple and fine. As at Ausone, Pascal Delbeck arrived in 1975, and became fully responsible in 1976. In 2003, Madame Dubois-Challon died and left the property to Pascal Delbeck, a fitting reward for his years of passionately loyal service. Recently the 1975 appears too tannic, the 1976 attractive but soft and forward, the 1978 really fine and concentrated, the 1979 exceptional. There is a decent 1980, then the 1981 is fine, the 1982 rich and much more forward than Ausone; there is a concentrated, spicy 1983, a very concentrated and powerful 1985 and a very rich, tannic 1986. Although Belair is sharing in Ausone's renaissance, there is something a little austere in recent vintages that makes them less appealing than the wines now being made at its neighbour, Canon.

As soon as the 1980 vintage was safely made, the old fermentation vats were removed and a battery of stainless steel vats, of varying sizes to fit into the cramped corners of the caves which house them, were installed. In 1981, in a new departure for Belair, a new *marque*, "Roc-Blanquant", was bottled for the first time. It is a blend of vintages of wines that have been excluded from the *grand vin*. The wine has been bottled only in magnums and will not pass through the normal channels of distribution but rather will be sold direct by the château.

CHÂTEAU BELLEFONT-BELCIER
Grand Cru. Owners: SC BJL. Administrator: Marc Dworkin. 13 hectares. 7,000 cases. Mer 70%, CF 20%, CS 10%

This important and well-known *cru* is in the commune of St Laurent-des-Combes, on the *côte* and its lower slopes. It has belonged to the same family since the end of the nineteenth century. The charming château, covered in creepers, is surrounded by a park containing an arboretum of rare trees, the creation of Professor Jean-Louis Faure, the grandfather of Jean Labusquière, who is equally attached to its conservation. The wines have long enjoyed a good reputation. The 1983 was pleasantly spicy, well structured and harmoniously fruity, very drinkable when four years old. The quality is equivalent to a Médoc *cru bourgeois*.

CHÂTEAU BELLEVUE

Grand Cru Classé. Owner: Société Civile M.-L. Horeau. Administrator: Nicola Thienpoint. 6 hectares. 2,500 cases. Mer 70%, CF 15%, CS 15%

This has the misfortune of bearing one of the commonest names in the Gironde. The twelfth edition of Cocks & Féret reveals no fewer than twenty-three properties at present using this name, and several of these are in the St Emilion region. This property, formerly known as Fief de Bellevue, belonged to the Lacaze family from 1642 to 1938, when it passed to cousins. Gaston Lacaze was well known as a leading Girondin during the French Revolution, and sought refuge here when the Girondins were proscribed by the Jacobins.

The vineyard is well situated on the limestone plateau of St Martin and on the *côtes*, just to the west of Beauséjour. This was one of the thirty-eight *crus* of St Emilion chosen to represent the region at the Paris Exhibition of 1867. I have never succeeded in tasting the wine, but from its position it should be worth trying.

CHÂTEAU BERGAT

Grand Cru Classé. Owner: Madame Clausse Bertin. Administrator: Emile Castéja. 4 hectares. 1,100 cases. Mer 50%, CF 25%, CS 25%

This is one of the smallest and most obscure of the *grands crus classés*. The vineyard is well placed to the east of the town, at the edge of the *plateau and côtes*, overlooking the valley of Fongaband and adjoining La Serre. It is farmed by Emile Castéja from nearby Trottevieille and distributed by his Bordeaux *négociant* firm of Borie-Manoux. On the only occasion I have tasted the wine, in 1984, the 1979 was scented and full on the nose, with a very distinctive spicy character and flavour, quite full-flavoured and still rather tough, but certainly promising. From this evidence, if a bottle of Bergat should cross your path, it should at least be worth a try.

CHÂTEAU BERLIQUET

Grand Cru Classé. Owners: Vicomte and Vicomtesse Patrick de Lesquen. 7.6
hectares. 3,200 cases. Mer 75%, CF and CS 25%

This is an interesting case of a *cru* which, had it not been neglected at
vital periods of St Emilion's development, would probably be a *premier
cru classé* today. This was an important, if small, vineyard in the
eighteenth century, belonging to the notary Jean de Sèze, one of an
important family of lawyers and churchmen. The name is that of a family
of brokers who lived in St Emilion in the eighteenth century. The price of
245 *livres* paid for the wine in 1784 is the highest recorded in Gaston
Jeune's brokers' notebook covering the period from 1778 to 1784. It is
also one of the earliest references to a *cru* by name and with a price in the
Libournais; something which had been happening for some years in
Médoc. A tax roll of 1768 also makes mention of a quarry here, now used
as the *chai*. In 1841 *Le Producteur* placed Berliquet among the *premiers
crus* but no longer in the leading group, and this position is confirmed by
the prices fetched for the 1844 and 1846 vintages, when it was placed on
a level with Beauséjour and Larcis, but below Mondot and Daugay. In
1850 the first edition of Cocks & Féret places Berliquet high among the
premiers crus, immediately after Canon and above Ausone. Until the end
of the nineteenth century Féret always placed it high among the leading
crus, and it was only after 1908 that silence descended – Berliquet's
decline had begun. Having survived the phylloxera crisis, it seems to
have fallen victim to the economic decline which set in before the First
World War and continued in one form or another until the fifties. The
first official St Emilion classification of 1955 found Berliquet's wines
made at the *cave coopérative*, and therefore automatically excluded.

The *coopérative* realized the potential for quality, and with the increasing prosperity of the whole region a new generation of the de Lesquen
family was soon persuaded of the good sense in equipping the *chai* and
cuvier once more for vinifying and maturing the wines of Berliquet.
Stainless steel fermentation vats were installed, the *chai* restored and the
underground caves made ready. The first vintage made here was in 1978.
All the supervision and work are undertaken by the Union des
Producteurs, and one-third new oak is used in the *élevage*.

The position of the vineyard on the Plateau de St Martin and the *côte*
is superb. The immediate neighbours are Canon and Magdelaine. There

is an elegant eighteenth-century château, with pleasing individuality, and a garden which has lovely views of the Dordogne valley. Both are on the edge of the plateau. With everything now being done as it should it came as no surprise when Berliquet was promoted to *grand cru classé* status in the revision of 1985, the sole promotion to be made. When I tasted a range of vintages at the château the same year, the 1978 showed complex aromas, and there were well-matured tannins, still taut but not dry – a wine of breed and style; the 1980 was perfumed with nicely balanced fruit, ready to drink; the 1981 had lovely perfumed highlights, nerve and finesse with a lively flavour and well-balanced fruit and acidity; the 1982 was dense and rich, tannic and powerful, still closed; the 1983 had an intense perfume of roses and tobacco, and a lovely rich, complex, powerful flavour, a fine example of the vintage. One was struck by the authority and obvious breed of these wines, and their clear ageing capacity. It is good to see it taking its rightful place as one of the leading *crus* of the Plateau de St Martin.

CHÂTEAU CADET-BON

Grand Cru. Owner: François Gratadour. 4 hectares. 1,000 cases. Mer 60%, CS 20%, CF 20%

This small *cru* lies north-east of the town, on the *plateau calcaire* and *côtes*, on a promontory and adjoining Soutard. There is an old mill dating from the fifteenth century, which appears on the label. This property lost its *cru classé* status in the 1985 revision. When I tasted two vintages recently, I found the wines distinctly rustic, with a coarse, stalky flavour, suggesting poor vinification.

CHÂTEAU CADET-PIOLA

Grand Cru Classé. Owners: Jabiol family. 6.8 hectares. 3,000 cases. Mer 51%, CS 28%, CF 18%, Mal 3%

This wine is graced by a most unusual and charming label, somewhat à la Watteau. The vineyard is on the *plateau calcaire* and the hillside of the Butte (knoll) de Cadet, due north of St Emilion. The small hill itself is dominated by an eighteenth-century windmill. Note that there is less Merlot here than is normal in St Emilion. This, combined with the soil, no doubt accounts for a wine rather at variance with the label, for fleshy is certainly not one of the adjectives one would use to describe it. On the contrary, this is a wine which needs and rewards some patience, tight-knit and rather austere to start with, but with a structure and style which proclaim it as a wine of class and some distinction.

The property owes its name to a Monsieur Piola, mayor of Libourne, who bought it in 1856 and was the first proprietor in St Emilion to adopt the use of the Guyot pruning method. He was also responsible for favouring the Cabernet Sauvignon, which had been so successful on the great domains of the Médoc. During the first part of this century it belonged to Robert Villepigue, who was also the owner of Figeac. Now, Maurice Jabiol and his son Alain own and run it, in conjunction with another *cru classé*, Faurie-de-Souchard.

The first vintage I ever came across was the 1959, which began as characteristically firm, but unaccountably went to pieces. The 1964 was much better, with concentration, if rather austere. Recently I have found the 1976 exceptionally good for the year with breed and body, still fresh when seven years old; the 1978 a big wine with structure and fruit and a promising future when five years old; the 1979 firm and austere still, with enough fruit but very undeveloped still when four years old; the 1980, at three years old, more open-textured and full-flavoured; the 1981 very tight and austere but with depth of flavour after a year in bottle. There was an attractive scented 1983, firm and tannic still when four years old, but with plenty of fruit; the 1985 has lovely vivid, concentrated fruit and more richness than usual; while the 1986 in cask was very tannic, powerful and rich, but austere, and clearly a *vin de garde*.

CHÂTEAU CANON

Premier Grand Cru Classé. Owner: Eric Fournier. 18 hectares. 8,000 cases. Mer 55%, CF 40%, CS 5%

The château is situated just outside the old town. It has more the appearance and air of a château than most of its neighbours, with an impressive entrance and castellated towers. It was essentially the creation of Jacques Kanon, who in 1760 bought a property of about 12 hectares, most of which was planted with vines, for 40,000 *livres*. The buildings in existence then were small and in poor condition, the proprietor Jean Biés having owned the then more important manor of Pey Blanquet at St Etienne-de-Lisse. The new owner, a lieutenant in the navy, grown rich on prize money, who hailed from Dunkirk, then bought seven small neighbouring vineyards for 6,379 *livres*, increasing the property to 13 hectares. He completed the enclosure of the vineyard with stone walls, a task begun but not finished by his predecessor. A stonemason carved the date of 1767 beside one of the gates when the work was completed. The beautifully proportioned château was built between 1761 and 1764, when Jacques Kanon came to live there. The progress made at this time may be gauged by the fact that when he sold the property to Raymond Fontémoing in 1770, it was for the much higher sum of 80,000 *livres*.

The new owner was the leading *négociant* in the Libournais during the eighteenth century. Since this time only a small addition has been made to the vineyard, and the description given of the château at the time of the 1770 sale closely corresponds to what is there today. At this time it was known as St Martin, the name Canon being adopted only in 1853, much to the fury of the growers of Canon Fronsac. The pretext was that it was in memory of Jacques Kanon. In reality the residual prestige of Canon Fronsac still made this a more attractive name from a promotional point of view.

For many years Madame Fournier was a great figure in the region, and I remember her in the sixties as one of the few St Emilion proprietors to make regular appearances at the dining tables of the Médoc châteaux. She handed over the management to her grandson, Eric Fournier, in 1972, but still welcomed old friends at the château as late as 1980, when she was over ninety.

The wine has long enjoyed a high reputation and deservedly so. The 1929 won great fame as the best wine on the Right Bank, and was still superlative in 1980. When I had the opportunity of trying a bottle of 1933 when it was nearly forty years old, it was still fresh and delicious, although of course light. More recently, the 1947 was magnificent, the 1953 was still superb in 1984, more like a 1955, unctuous and complete; a year later the 1955 itself was less elegant, but still tannic and powerful, in peak condition. The 1959 was big and powerful if a little dry, the 1962 was still wonderfully fresh and perfumed, light-textured and charming in 1985; by 1990 the 1964 was unctuous and rich, still delicious and complex; the 1966 is really fine; the 1967 is now firm and lean, and is beginning to dry out; the 1970 is typical of the year, lacking in flesh but very long-flavoured, elegant and fine; in contrast the 1971 was deliciously soft and forward. The 1975 was typically slow-developing but is harmonious with fine potential; then came a soft, attractive 1976, that was already at its peak in 1984. It was at this point that Eric Fournier's new broom began to be noticeable. The 1978 was deliciously ripe and full-flavoured; it was followed by a compact, long-lasting 1979; a charming, well-structured 1980; a firm, long-flavoured, elegant 1981; a very concentrated and rich 1982; and an above-average 1983 that is rich and fine, with great potential. The compact power and fruit of the 1985 suggests a very fine development, while in cask the 1986 typically had more flesh on it than it would have had a decade ago, the ripe, concentrated fruit aromas leading to a lovely long rich flavour, that was supple in spite of the underlying tannins – a tribute to the balance of power and finesse that Eric Fournier is now achieving. There is no doubt that these wines have acquired a fresh dimension under his hand, which now places Canon in the top echelon of the St Emilion *premiers crus*.

CHÂTEAU CANON-LA-GAFFELIÈRE

Grand Cru Classé. Owner: Comte de Neipperg. 19 hectares. 10,000 cases. Mer 60%, CF 35%, CS 5%

This is one of the easiest of St Emilion properties to find, situated as it is on the small road which runs from the big Libourne–Bergerac road up to St Emilion. Its vineyards lie at the southern foot of the *côtes* and on flat sandy soil, and its relatively large production makes it a well-known and widely distributed wine. This is an old property with a history going back five hundred years, but its reputation really dates from its ownership by the Boitard de la Poterie family, when it was known as Canon-Boitard. Since 1971 it has been owned by the Comte de Neipperg; one of his sons, Comte Stephan, now lives at the château and supervises things. He took over the management from the former *régisseur*, Michel Boutet (see La Tour-Figeac and de l'Oratoire). One-third new oak had been used in the maturation, but this was increased for the 1985, and the 1986 had 60 per cent. This marks a definite change in the style of wines that the property is trying to make.

This has been an attractive, easy-to-drink, quick-maturing wine, relatively lightweight, but if it was not among the leading growths, it was certainly consistently well made and dependable. However, with changes in vinification and *élevage* for the 1985 and 1986 vintages, the wines now seem set to have more depth and richness.

The 1978 was a typical example, already attractive drinking when six years old. The 1979 is a bigger wine with something still in reserve when nearly five years old. The 1980 was already an easy-drinking wine when only three years old. The 1981 is much more forward than most wines of this year, while the 1982 has less concentration than the best wines of the year but is robust and has marked character. The 1983 is supple, fruity and light in body, ready to drink when five years old; the 1985 shows clear evidence of more new oak, but has plenty of rich, elegant fruit; the much bigger 1986 has carried its 60 per cent new oak more comfortably, and is a great success, with a lovely silky texture, fat and body, making a finely balanced wine. It will be interesting to see how these new-style wines develop; they should certainly age better than their predecessors.

CHÂTEAU CAP-DE-MOURLIN

Grand Cru Classé. Owner: Capdemourlin family. Administrator: Jacques Capdemourlin. 14 hectares. 6,000 cases. Mer 60%, CF 25%, CS 12%, Mal 3%

This historic property is the source of a good deal of confusion. During the seventies and until October 1982 the vineyard was not only divided between two parts of the Capdemourlin family, but the wines were made, kept and bottled separately. To make matters more difficult for the consumer, not only was the label the same for both parts of the property, but the sole distinguishing mark, the Christian names of the two branches of the family, began with the same initial, J. Half the property belongs to the widow of Jean Capdemourlin, one of the great figures in St Emilion, largely responsible both for the revival of the Jurade in 1948 and for the official INAO classification in 1955, the other half to his nephew Jacques, who also owns Balestard. Now, since October 1982, the vineyard has been unified under the direction of Jacques Capdemourlin. The two parts of the vineyard are situated north of St Emilion on the lower *côtes* and on sandy soil, adjoining Larmande, so it lies at the northern extremity of the *côtes*, where they join the sandy *glacis*. The association between this property, once called Artugon, and the Capdemourlin family goes back five hundred years, a history of continuity hard to match. If ever a property deserves to be named after its owner, this must be it. As has already been mentioned, since the Second World War the family has played a leading part in the revival and promotion of the wines of St Emilion.

Looking back over my tasting notes, it is clear that, at their best, these are classic St Emilion wines, perfumed and fruity on the nose, and with a generous, sometimes almost unctuous flavour, balanced with a good structure. The oldest vintage I have tasted was the 1955 which was still rich, powerful and fresh when twenty-eight years old, but a bottle of the 1966 was over the top by 1988. In vintages before 1983, I prefer the wines made by Jacques Capdemourlin, which are richer and more generous. So future prospects for the newly reunited property must be bright and should place it once more among the leading *grands crus classés*. A fascinating object-lesson on the influence of soil types in St Emilion was provided when I had the chance to compare the 1975 vintage made here by Jacques Capdemourlin with his Balestard of the same year. The wine from this property was much more tannic and powerful, high in extract, less elegant and fine, but developing the opulence of a very good wine for the year.

In recent years Jacques Capdemourlin produced good and typical wines in 1978 and 1979, a generous and opulent 1981 and a 1982 of real promise, powerful and unctuous. Since the property has been reunited, the 1983 has luscious dense fruit, an archetypical Merlot wine; the 1985 seemed opulent and chocolaty in cask, with more firmness than Balestard; while the 1986 is tannic and concentrated, with firm fruit, a promising *vin de garde*. One-third new oak is now being used with success, as it has at the neighbouring Larmande.

CHÂTEAU CARDINAL-VILLEMAURINE

Grand Cru. Owners: J.-F. and J.-M. Carrille. 18 hectares. 6,000 cases. Mer 75%, CF and CS 25%

This *cru* is on the *plateau calcaire* just outside the town to the east. There are extensive underground cellars. The wines are firm, rather tannic and a shade lean and austere in style. They take time to mature. The 1970 had reached perfect maturity, with a full, firm flavour, by 1984. There was a rich but rather hard 1975; a light and attractive 1976, already fully matured after nine years; a good 1978; a 1979 with more ripeness, more expansive in flavour; a 1981 which was a little lean; and a 1983 with an attractive bouquet of violets, more charm, already quite mellow and ready to drink when three years old. There are signs that the current vintages may prove less uncompromising than those of the past. They have obvious breed and potential, as they should have with the fine position of the vineyard.

CHÂTEAU LE CASTELOT

Grand Cru. Owner: J. Janoueix. 8.5 hectares. 3,000 cases. Mer 60%, CS 20%, CF 20%

This *cru* with its charming château, visible from the Libourne–Bergerac road, lies just below Tertre-Daugay, but on the other side of the road, so in the commune of St Sulpice-de-Faleyrens. The vineyard is on the *pieds de côtes* and sandy plain, so there is a mixture of sand with sandy gravel and traces of iron. It was bought in the late seventies by the Janoueix family, *négociants* of Libourne and owners of Haut-Sarpe, as well as of several Pomerol *crus*. There is an attractive story attached to the name, according to which Henri IV was caught in a thunderstorm when returning from his estate at Puy Normand, and took refuge at the Auberge du Bosquet. He received such a warm welcome that he permitted the building of a *manoir* with a tower – hence Le Castelot, a small château.

The vinification and *élevage*, with 20 per cent new oak, are supervised by the same *maître de chai*, Paul Cazenave, as attends Haut-Sarpe and the other Janoueix properties, as well as Château Canon. These are deep-coloured, rich, plummy wines that sometimes, as in 1982 and 1983, have a rather strong, even coarse, terroir character to begin with, but this strong character quickly mellows to produce wines delicious to drink when four to five years old. The 1985 was especially attractive, with less terroir character in its early stages. This is a good, thoroughly consistent wine, which reflects the high proportion of old vines.

CHÂTEAU CHAUVIN

Grand Cru Classé. Owner: Henri Ondet. 12 hectares. 4,200 cases. Mer 60%, CF and CS 40%

This *cru* is in what used misleadingly to be called the St Emilion *graves*, whereas it is in fact on the sandy *glacis*. It is the most southeasterly of the group of *crus* adjoining Pomerol, east of Ripeau and south of Corbin, of which it once formed a part. One-third new wood is now used in the *élevage*. It is typical of the wines from this sector. At its best, this can be a very fine wine, very unctuous and mellow, but unfortunately the wines are not quite as consistent as could be wished and there is a touch of coarseness in their make-up. The 1966 was excellent, for instance, but the 1967 a disappointment, whereas generally the 1967s in St Emilion were at least as good as the 1966s and sometimes better. There was a delicious 1971, but more recently the 1979 was disappointingly diluted and prematurely aged. These wines seem to give of their best when youthful, and to be suspect when aged.

CHÂTEAU CHEVAL BLANC
Premier Grand Cru Classé A. Owner: Société Civile du Château Cheval Blanc. Administrator: Bernard Grandchamp. 35 hectares. 12,000 cases. CF 66%, Mer 33%, Mal I%

If you were to ask any wine lover what the finest St Emilion is today, he would be most likely to reply, "Cheval Blanc." This was not always the case. Once Ausone had a greater reputation – and perhaps will have again – while Figeac was placed first among the growths of the St Emilion *graves*. Cheval Blanc's reputation in England was certainly made by the 1921 vintage, and from that time onwards it was spoken of in the same terms as the first growths of the 1855 classification, although it did not achieve equality of price until after the Second World War. When the first official classification of St Emilion was made by the INAO in 1955, it was only just that Cheval Blanc, together with Ausone, should be marked out among the *premiers grands crus classés* by means of an "A" category.

Here on the open plateau of the St Emilion *graves*, the properties tend to be larger than those that crowd the cramped hillsides around the ramparts of St Emilion, and Cheval Blanc is no exception. The reason for this is tied up in the history of the neighbouring property of Figeac. The name of Cheval Blanc first appears as a *métairie* of Figeac in 1768, but its history as a separate property begins only in the 1830s. In 1832 President Ducasse bought 16.3 hectares from Figeac, in 1834 he drew up the plans and began building the château, and in 1838 he bought a further 15.4 hectares, virtually doubling the size of the property. At the same time he made three other small purchases to bring the size of the new domain up to 39 or 40 hectares. First, much of the vineyard needed to be drained, because the land was flooded by water coming from land lying to the east (La Dominique, Jean-Faure and Ripeau). This important work, which vitally affected the quality of the wine, was attributed, by the 1868 edition of Cocks & Féret, to Ducasse's son-in-law, Laussac-Fourcaud, who took charge of the estate in 1853, but Enjalbert believes the work probably started before that date. Curiously enough, the wine continued to be sold under the name of Figeac, and was listed as such in the first edition of Cocks & Féret in 1850. The name of Cheval Blanc first appears in print in the 1853 edition of Franck.

Cheval Blanc has never been sold since its creation by President Ducasse in the 1830s, going by marriage to Laussac-Fourcaud in 1853. When he was succeeded by one of his eight children, Albert, in 1893, the latter changed his name to Fourcaud-Laussac. It was one of his children, Jacques, whom I met when first visiting Cheval Blanc, and who ran it until his death in 1972. One of Albert's granddaughters married Jacques Hébrard, who ran the property on behalf of the Fourcaud family heirs until his retirement in 1989. The château itself is a modest but charming house with small turrets and pleasing proportions which, together with its white paint, give the appearance of a summer villa. But this is now completely overshadowed by the palatial new *chai*, which more truly reflects the present prestige of Cheval Blanc. For many years, the wines in their second year in cask had to be moved to a cellar in Libourne where the château bottling was allowed to take place, the *chai* at Cheval Blanc being too small to accommodate all the wine once sales of wine in cask ceased after 1952. Quite a number of English merchants shipped out and bottled the plentiful 1950 vintage, while Christopher's enterprisingly shipped the despised 1951 as "St Emilion", only to find it turned out remarkably well. Now the new *chai* allows ample room for storage and bottling in ideal conditions.

The wine of Cheval Blanc typifies the difference between the *graves* and the *côtes* in St Emilion. It usually has a big colour, a very powerful, enveloping bouquet which is rich and sometimes almost spicy; a very full, mellow, almost unctuous flavour which is very concentrated and takes time to unfurl. In good years, the wine can have as much as 14° of alcohol. It is indeed a stunning wine, not subtle, but winning admiration by its sheer beauty and animal vigour; it assails the palate in the way some of the French Impressionists assail the eye with the brilliance of their colours. It is a quality matched in Bordeaux only by Pétrus, not far away in Pomerol. Yet while Pétrus is mostly Merlot, Cheval Blanc is two-thirds Cabernet Franc, indeed the supreme example in Bordeaux of this grape variety; and the soil is quite different. In 1986 Jacques Hébrard gave a tasting which provided a wonderful panorama of Cheval Blanc from 1908 to 1973. There was some volatile acidity in the 1908, but still plenty of fruit, and one could still see what a beautiful wine it had been. Then came the 1920, with a lovely old sweetness on the nose, and a soft, delicate flavour that had become lacy in texture, a classic old wine. The 1923 went quickly, old and fading, surrendering to volatile acidity. The 1926 was interesting, with plenty of vigour and highlights on the nose, the flavour rich but still tannic and firm, with plenty of life still. The 1934 was in a similar vein to the 1926, lacked its depth but was well preserved. Then came an oddity, the 1936, very pleasant and sound, not of course a great wine, but remarkable for what must always have been a small wine. The 1940 was a disappointment, lively still, but short and tannic; it had seen better days. The great 1947 was as extraordinary as it has ever been, unbelievably rich, concentrated and almost port-like, it grew and grew in the glass, unfurling many layers of richness. I first tasted it in Bordeaux in the early fifties when it was already very drinkable and overwhelming. It is not of course classic claret in any sense of that word, but rather a phenomenon, almost a freak, and one can see why it rapidly became a legend that everyone wanted to own, or at least sample. The 1948 I had not tasted since its extreme youth. It was still powerful and strong in character but oddly coarse and without much style or charm. The 1950, which was delicious in its youth, was now coarse, with an odd damp-earth smell but lots of character still. The 1953, never a great wine here, was most disappointing, dry and fading. The 1958, a difficult year in St Emilion after the 1956 frost, lacked the charm of the Figeac, but was honourable for the year. The 1960 had a bouquet of liquorice, was showing its age but was more stylish, if short. The 1961, which I have always found to be something of an enigma, had the concentrated aroma of prunes, a sure sign of over-ripe fruit; the taste was very tannic and essence-like, developing some opulence in the glass but still to my mind lacking the qualities of a classic Cheval Blanc. In contrast the 1964 is indeed a classic, still with the richness which is missing from the 1966 and 1970. The 1966 itself is a wine of great breed, and an elegance not normally associated with Cheval Blanc. The middle fruit was beginning to fade but the firm structure remains. The 1970 I have found variable over the years, often soft-centred and seeming to lack structure, at other times parched and drying up. This example was delightful, but very forward and soft, lacking power and concentration, showing signs of the high yields of the vintage. A delightful surprise was the 1973, with its lovely spicy bouquet – the old *maître de chai* would have called it bananas – and a remarkably concentrated opulence of flavour, yet still fresh and not overblown like the Figeac, an extraordinary success for the year.

Then, in 1989, Jacques Hébrard gave another tasting to mark his retirement, which filled a number of gaps in the 1986 tasting. To begin with, there was the oldest Cheval Blanc I have tasted, a lovely, long-flavoured, if faded, 1899 that was still remarkably sound. Then there was the legendary 1921, which lived up to its reputation with incredible complex aromas, an aromatic overripe richness, and wonderfully long, harmonious flavour that was still fresh and youthful; it was hard to imagine a better wine. There was a lovely 1924, now drying out, a tannic, densely textured and complex 1928, and a 1929 with a very concentrated bouquet of mocha and prunes, and a remarkable taste of prunes, very rich and sweet. Then came 1943, with a marvellously rich, opulent character, and a lovely sweetness and richness that was remarkable for the year. Even the much less noted 1941 vintage was rich and deep-flavoured. The 1949 was outstanding, very scented and complex, with a marvellous flavour, but with some abrasive tannins at the finish, different in style from the 1947, but superb in a more classic way; a great wine instead of a masterpiece.

After the frankly disappointing vintages of the early and mid-fifties came the disaster of 1956, 1957 and 1958 which produced hardly anything, and 1959, an almost unnaturally plummy wine which turned out better than expected. The 1962 was, frankly, disappointing in a year when most St Emilions were back to their best.

Looking at the wines of the last fifteen years, made with the advantage of the new *cuvier*, and the greatly superior facilities in the great *chai*, the 1975 is very rich, complex and fine, with more structure than the Figeac; the 1978 is a real beauty, all elegant fruit, yet powerful at the finish, suggesting that although it was perfect drinking in 1987–8, yet it will continue to expand and delight for years to come. The 1979 also has a lovely flavour, depth and balance, and makes an interesting comparison with the 1978, a wine to enjoy now and in the next few years. The surprisingly complex and elegant 1980 has lasted well, but should now be drunk. The 1981 is rather open-textured, with a lovely flavour, richness and style, already a joy to drink. The 1982 is probably the best wine made here since 1947 and 1949, undoubtedly a great wine; spicy, opulent and really complex, it started to drink well at an early age, just as those giants of the past did but then clammed up. The 1983 is also a great vintage here. There is a marvellous roasted flavour and it is rich in extract, with lovely fruit but also a fine structure. The contrast with the 1982 should prove fascinating in years to come. The 1984 is pleasantly supple and fruity, a year when Cabernet Franc really came to the rescue. The 1985 was again a bull's-eye for Cheval Blanc; an explosion of flavours fills the mouth, and there is that opulence, amounting almost to sweetness, that marks the greatest years here. In cask the 1986 was very dense-textured, with great body and richness suggesting another remarkable wine.

As can be seen, the performance of Cheval Blanc, especially from 1978 onwards, has really been outstanding, and wines have been produced which will surely rival the greatest from a glorious past. What is more, a standard of consistency has now been established which certainly eclipses anything achieved before. This indeed is the new Golden Age!

CHÂTEAU CLOS-DES-JACOBINS

Grand Cru Classé. Owner: Gérard Frydman. 7.5 hectares. 4,500 cases. Mer 47%, CF 45%, CS 8%

Cocks & Féret (twelfth edition) has the curious suggestion that the origin of this name lies in the revolutionary era. This seems unlikely. The Jacobins of the French Revolution acquired their name solely because they held their meetings in a convent which had belonged to the Jacobin Friars, the name popularly accorded in France to the Dominicans. It seems most likely, therefore, that this vineyard once belonged to the Couvent des Jacobins which was established in St Emilion in the thirteenth century, and part of whose vineyard still goes under this name.

The vineyard lies north-west of the town on the Libourne road, at the point where the last slopes of the *côtes* give way to the sandy *glacis*. Between a quarter and one-third new oak is used in the *élevage*, depending on the constitution of the wine.

These wines have always been notable for their consistency and attractive style but, as elsewhere, I have the firm impression that in the eighties the wines have become more concentrated and impressive. The 1978 had developed into a wine of perfect maturity after ten years; very scented and elegant on the nose, with an intense flavour, fine length but not as much body as one might have expected. In contrast the 1979 was richer and more concentrated, perfect drinking after eight years. Excellent wines were made in 1981, 1982, and 1983, all with real richness and opulence. They managed a light but attractive 1984, then there was a delightful 1985, with a lovely long flavour but only of medium weight, while the 1986 has more extract and tannin, and is full of luscious spicy, ripe fruit. This is one of the finest *crus* in this sector of St Emilion, and shows what can be achieved on these soils.

CHÂTEAU CLOS FOURTET

Premier Grand Cru Classé B. Owner: Lurton Frères. 17 hectares. 5,000 cases. Mer 60%, CS 20%, CF 20%

This famous property is situated immediately opposite the main entrance to the old town of St Emilion, just in front of the collegiate church. The property was modernized and its reputation established by Léon Rulleau in the mid-eighteenth century. His sister Catherine had married Vital de Carle in 1712, and their son was Elie de Carle, later the seigneur of Figeac. Leon Rulleau himself became a Jurat in 1739, and his brother, being a canon of the St Emilion chapter, left his share to his nephew Elie, Léon's son. We know that in 1789 his whole estate was valued at 100,000 *livres*. It was Elie who built the present château, which though simple and modest in appearance has some fine period details. He also worked the quarries under the vineyard, part of which are today's cellars. At this time the property was known as Camfourtet. It was in the following century that the Rulleau family changed it to Clos Fourtet, one of a number of instances of changes of name at this time, as owners became more conscious of the importance of such things. The wine has for some time been one of the best-known St Emilions, perhaps assisted by the fact that it belonged to the Ginestet family until just after the war, so that the wine was more on the general Bordeaux market than many other St Emilions. The Ginestets then sold it to Monsieur François Lurton at the time when they bought control of Château Margaux.

The vineyard, which is on the limestone plateau of St Martin and adjoins that of Canon, also has some sandy soil in its make-up.

For many years the unusually high proportion of Cabernet Sauvignon in the vineyard had an adverse effect on the wines, but during the improvements of the seventies the proportion of Cabernet Sauvignon was reduced, while the Merlot was increased. This, together with improvements in the *cuvier*, with the introduction of stainless steel fermentation vats in 1973, and the enthusiasm and dedication of a new generation of Lurtons, has re-established the reputation of Clos Fourtet as one of the best wines on the plateau of St Martin. Not surprisingly, there are distinct similarities of style with the neighbouring Canon, and also with Belair. All the cask maturation takes place in the splendid underground cellars, with one-third new wood now being used. Traditionally, the wine is much firmer and slower to develop than most St Emilions, but when mature, it has great depth and suppleness, and is very long-lived. I had a bottle of 1917 when it was fifty years old, and the wine was fresh and well-preserved, charming and supple. The 1923 was one of the loveliest examples of this year that I have ever tasted, silky and sweet at the finish, and still fresh when over forty years old and when most 1923s were over the top. But my first memory of Clos Fourtet is of the 1940 which my father had as a "concession wine" after the war. When around ten years old, it was quite delicious and, to my surprise, when another bottle came my way twenty years later, it was still in excellent form and had not faded, although it had lost some punch. In the fifties and early sixties the château went through a disappointing phase; the wines seemed green and mean, lacking fruit and flesh, but the 1961 heralded a return to the old form, and after a stubborn 1962 the 1964 is really fine, and the 1966 followed up the good work.

The results of the improvements to the *cuvier* came through slowly at first. After an unusually attractive 1974, the 1975 was good but not outstanding and the 1976 was too overblown to make old bones; but then the 1978 is outstanding, scented, solid and four-square still, long-flavoured with a finish marked by fruit and still developing when ten years old.

Length of flavour, middle richness and breed also characterize the most successful 1979. The 1981 has more weight than many wines of this vintage, while the 1982 and 1983 are highly successful examples of these outstanding vintages. The 1985 has that extra concentration and richness, allied to a lovely flavour, which promises a great future. Dominique

Lurton and his young family now live at the château, so it is once more a home.

CHÂTEAU LA CLOTTE

Grand Cru Classé. Owners: Héritiers Chailleau. Administrator: Madame Nelly Moulierac. 3.7 hectares. 1,550 cases. Mer 85%, CF 15%

This small property would doubtless be more famous were its production not so limited. But the vineyard is perfectly situated on the best slopes below the ramparts of the town, on the edge of the *plateau calcaire* and the *côtes*. For the last thirty years it has been farmed by Ets J.-P. Moueix, who took three-quarters of the crop in return for running the vineyard and making the wine. The Chailleau family kept the rest, and sold most of it in their small vine-covered restaurant, the Logis de la Cadène, a popular haunt for locals. The Chailleau heirs have now taken over the running of the property. But I have noticed that these wines are not always of the same standard as those bottled by Moueix. Fifty per cent new wood is used in the maturation.

Until 1904 the vineyard was even smaller, but at that time, the Clos Bergat-Bosson-Pegasse was joined to La Clotte to make a single property. The wines are kept in small but very ancient *caves* at the top of the vineyard, which are said to date from the days of English rule.

I have been fortunate in being able to follow the wines supervised by J.-P. Moueix for some years, and they have been marvellously consistent. Normally the wine is among the lighter-styled St Emilions, typical of the finest wines of the *côtes*, with great finesse and delicacy, fresh and very supple, having an exquisite bouquet: the 1959, 1962, 1967, 1969, 1971, 1976 and 1978 were wines like this. But in the best years, the wine can acquire a remarkable body and fleshiness, as was the case in 1964 and 1970 and, to a lesser extent, in 1966. This is a wine which should certainly rank with the best *grands crus*.

CHÂTEAU LA CLUSIÈRE

Grand Cru Classé. Owner: Consorts Valette. Administrator: Jean-Paul Valette. 2.8 hectares. 1,000 cases. Mer 70%, CF 20%, CS 10%

This pocket-handkerchief vineyard forms a small enclave high up among the vines of Château Pavie on the *côtes*. Since 1953 this property has been under the same ownership and management as Pavie, the Valette family, with Jean-Paul Valette in charge. The vinification and *élevage* are carried out in the *chai* and cellars of Pavie.

There is more Merlot here than at either Pavie or Pavie-Decesse, although the percentage has been reduced in recent years in favour of Cabernet Franc; 25 per cent new oak is used in the *élevage*. The resulting wine is solid, full-bodied, four-square and typically St Emilion. It tends to develop more quickly than Pavie-Decesse and is less tannic. The 1970 showed all its virtues at fourteen years of age, being beautifully balanced with only medium weight but with fruit and charm, eminently drinkable. The 1978 and 1979 are both interesting examples of these contrasting years, with the 1978 showing more style in the early stages. The 1981 has fresh, clean fruit and balance, but was initially dry. The 1982 is an early developer, with the most attractive ripe, rich fruit. The 1983 is concentrated with plenty of fruit and tannin. There is a rich if open-textured 1985, while the 1986 is surprisingly light in body with elegant fruit and a firm finish. Accidents of history and inheritance have separated this small property from Pavie, of which it forms a logical part. In the Médoc the owners would probably have incorporated it into the main property. There are parts of Pavie less well sited than La Clusière, yet the ensemble of Pavie is clearly much superior. This is one of the fascinations of Bordeaux.

CHÂTEAU CORBIN

Grand Cru Classé. Owner: Domaines Giraud. 15 hectares. 5,000 cases. Mer 50%, CF 25%, CS 25%

The duplication of names is one of the curses of St Emilion, and this is a bad case. In the sector of St Emilion adjoining Pomerol there are no fewer than five growths, all *grands crus classés*, which incorporate Corbin in their names, to say nothing of lesser growths here and in Montagne-St Emilion. Corbin is especially confusing because it belongs to the Giraud family, another member of which owns Grand-Corbin. The property has interesting origins in that in the Middle Ages it formed part of a much larger domain belonging to the Black Prince. Only traces of the fourteenth-century castle remain, and the present château is a very modest affair.

The wine is best known in northern France, Belgium and Holland, and enjoys a good reputation for being rich and supple, typical of this sector.

The Domaines Giraud, the proprietors, also own Certan-Giraud, a leading growth of Pomerol.

CHÂTEAU CORBIN-MANUEL

Grand Cru. Owner: Pierre Manuel. 12 hectares. 5,500 cases. Mer 45%, CS 40%, CF 15%

This *cru* was once inevitably part of the Grand-Corbin estate, and is on the sandy *glacis* in the section near the Pomerol border, east of Cheval Blanc. The vineyard had to be reconstructed between 1965 and 1970. Note, as at Figeac, the high proportion of Cabernet Sauvignon. The wines are luscious, with real depth of flavour and charm, normally delicious to drink around five years of age, but typically the 1982 had more power and tannins. On current form it is hard to see a difference in class between this *cru* and the Corbin neighbours who are classified.

CHÂTEAU CORBIN-MICHOTTE

Grand Cru Classé. Owner: Jean-Noël Boidron. 6.7 hectares. 3,000 cases. Mer 65%, CF 30%, CS 5%

Another example of the problems of duplicated names in St Emilion: in this case not only the confusion of different Corbins, all adjoining one another because they were all once part of a single property, but of two Michottes. This one lies immediately to the south of Croque-Michotte, and east of La Dominique. We know that when these two properties were sold on 7 January 1852, only 41 ares were fully under vine (100 ares = 1 hectare), clear proof that in these *métairies* on the sandy *glacis*, the vine was still far from being king, and mixed farming was still the norm.

The soil here is basically sandy, with some clay in the subsoil, containing iron traces, and some surface gravel. The proprietor is a qualified oenologist with an old-established family property, Château Calon, straddling the Montagne and St Georges. Since acquiring Corbin-Michotte in 1959, Jean-Nöel Boidron has made many improvements, including entirely rebuilding the *chai* in 1980. Twenty per cent of the wine is matured in new oak, rotated with wine held in stainless steel vats.

This is a wine that has always made a favourable impression whenever I have had the opportunity of tasting it. The rich, plummy texture, very full and mellow in the mouth but not heavy, is typical of the best wines in this corner of St Emilion, near Pomerol. The best recent vintages I have seen are the 1971 and 1979, both excellent in differing ways. Like most of these wines it is generally most enjoyable in its youth, when between four and ten years old.

CHÂTEAU CORMEIL-FIGEAC

Grand Cru. Owners: Héritiers R. and L. Moreaud. 10 hectares. 3,500 cases. Mer 70%, CF 30%

A good *cru* on the sandy *glacis* south-east of Figeac, whose old vines resisted the 1956 frost, preserving the quality better than at many *crus* in the area. No weedkillers are used in the vineyards and they use organic fertilizers. The wines are matured in cask, with 15 per cent new oak used. The wines are very scented, supple and full-flavoured, delicious for early drinking, with plenty of vibrant fruit, yet also age well.

CHÂTEAU CÔTE DE BALEAU

Grand Cru. Owner: Reiffers family. Administrator: Sophie Fourcade. 16 hectares. 8,500 cases. Mer 70%, CF 15%, CS 15%

This is one of the *crus classés* added to the classification in 1969, but it was then demoted in 1985. The vineyard adjoins Laniote, north of St Emilion, and is on the lower slopes of the *côtes* and on the sandy *glacis*. There is an attractive house and park. The owners are the Reiffers family and Baleau was run jointly with two other much smaller properties under the same ownership, Grandes-Murailles and Clos St-Martin, until the decision to relegate this *cru* in 1985. This has led to a reorganization of the three properties so that in future the wines can be made separately. The *régisseur* is the experienced and respected Jean Brun, one of the characters of the district, who also looks after Laniote.

It was during 1983 and 1984 that I had the opportunity of tasting a range of vintages from this property. I found them to be the best from the three properties of the Société des Grandes-Murailles, and in general of a high standard, placing Baleau among the leading wines of the *grands crus classés*. They are wines with plenty of structure and richness of flavour that require some ageing. The 1978 has ripeness and power but was firmer on the palate than expected. The 1979 is characterized by lovely vibrant fruit on the nose and a delicious flavour, full of fruit and very stylish, which should develop well over several years. Even the 1980 was a serious wine, full-flavoured and well structured. The 1981 has depth, and was still *corsé* and closed when three years old. The 1982 is a big strong wine, tannic and forthright, that will need time. The 1985, however, has less fullness and richness than St-Martin, and was soft and attractive. It will be interesting to see whether the 1985 will set the pattern for the future once the reorganization of the cellars is completed, and if, ultimately, this will allow Baleau to return to *cru classé* status.

CHÂTEAU COUDERT

Grand Cru. Owner: Jean-Claude Carles. 6 hectares. 3,000 cases. Mer 50%, CF and CS 50%

A *cru* on the *côtes* and *pieds de côtes* in the west of the commune of St Christophe; the wines are long-flavoured and stylish, with some breed.

CHÂTEAU COUDERT-PELLETAN

Grand Cru. Owner: Jean Lavau et Fils. 10 hectares. 4,000 cases. Mer 60%, CF 30%, CS 10%

A well-placed *cru* on the north *côte* of the commune of St Christophe, near Sarpe. A splendid bottle of the 1970, drunk when over fifteen years old, showed what can be achieved in well-run properties in this position. The wines are stylish and fine.

CHÂTEAU LA COUSPAUDE

Grand Cru. Owner: Vignobles Aubert. 7 hectares. 4,000 cases. Mer 60%, CF and CS 40%

In 1841 *Le Producteur* placed this *cru* among the best in the region, and said the wines were long-lived and could even keep well for twenty years, high praise in those days. But in 1985 La Couspaude lost its place in classification, it seems because it was not bottled at the château. Vignobles Aubert own a number of properties in the Entre-Deux-Mers and the Côtes de Castillon, and apparently it is bottled at one of these. The vineyard is well placed on the *plateau calcaire*, immediately to the east of the town, between Villemaurine and Trottevieille. Presumably the Auberts will re-equip their facilities at the property and reapply for classification.

CHÂTEAU COUTET

Grand Cru. Owner: Jean David-Beaulieu. 11 hectares. 3,600 cases. Mer 45%, CF 45%, CS 5%, Mal 5%

The vineyard lies to the west of the town on the *côtes*, adjoining Grand-Mayne. It lost its *cru classé* status in 1985, and both the vintages I have tasted, 1979 and 1981, were disappointingly light, and lacked charm or depth of flavour. This would seem to be a problem of the hand of man, since the position of the vineyard is good, and of some size in the context of the region.

CHÂTEAU LE COUVENT

Grand Cru. Owner: Société Civile du Château Le Couvent. 0.4 hectares. 100 cases. Mer 55%, CF 25%, CS 20%

This minute vineyard actually lies within the walls of St Emilion, near the Château du Roi. It was a *cru classé*, but after it had been bought by François Marret of Marne et Champagne (see Château des Tours, Montagne-St Emilion) in December 1981, the new owner decided that the vineyard was too small to be commercially viable as a *cru classé*, so did not apply for inclusion in the revised classification of 1985. The vineyard once belonged to the Convent of the Ursulines, now remembered for the famous macaroons; hence the name. The soil is limestone mixed with clay. Maturation is in new casks. The new owner is making really fine wines, with breed and style. There is a delicious 1985, with a long velvety texture, rich and stylish.

CHÂTEAU COUVENT-DES-JACOBINS

Grand Cru Classé. Owner: Madame Joinaud-Borde. 9 hectares. 3,500 cases. Mer 65%, CF 25%, CS 9%, Mal 1%

This growth was added to the classification in 1969. As the name implies, it was a religious foundation belonging to the Frères Prêcheurs Jacobins, or Dominicans. The foundation is an ancient one, resulting from a gift to the Friars confirmed in 1289 by the Duke of Lancaster, son of Henry III and Lieutenant-General of Guyenne at the time. The building itself, situated in the heart of the old town of St Emilion, is of thirteenth-century origin, and the vineyard adjoins the old ramparts. According to tradition, the wines of the Friary not only found favour at the tables of the governors of Guyenne during the fourteenth and fifteenth centuries, but were also shipped to London to be served at coronations and at royal banquets. The Jacobins left their house in the eighteenth century, since when it has belonged to a succession of proprietors. For some time now, the Joinaud family have been owners.

The vineyard is on the edge of the *plateau calcaire* and on sandy soils. This is a traditionally made wine with 20 per cent new wood used in the *élevage*. The label is gold on black, a style much favoured in the past, and still used here and at nearby Trottevieille. The few examples I have tasted have all impressed me as well made, with a distinguished flavour and firm fruit, well-structured serious wines that would doubtless be better known were the production not so small. The 1970 had a rich, concentrated long flavour, still firm and vigorous in 1987. There is a typically backward 1979 and a more charming, forward 1981. The wine is now distributed by Dourthe Frères.

CHÂTEAU CROQUE-MICHOTTE
Grand Cru Classé. Owner: Madame Rigal. 14 hectares. 6,700 cases. Mer 90%, Cab 10%

This estate is on the extreme north-west perimeter of St Emilion, where it adjoins Pomerol. It also marks the most easterly limits of the gravelly outcrops, found in their most concentrated form at Figeac and Cheval Blanc, which then continue through La Dominique to finish at Croque-Michotte. On the Pomerol side L'Evangile lies across the road. However, the main characteristic of the soil here comes from the sandy *glacis*.

Until its sale in 1852, this was a *métairie* of Corbin. Later, great progress was made under the ownership of M. Dubois, who put in a new drainage system and was awarded a silver medal for his pains by the Comice Agricole de Libourne in 1882. In 1890 it was bought by Samuel Geoffrion, father of the present owner.

The high proportion of Merlot is reflected in the rich, robust style of the wines. The first vintage I encountered was the 1950, an enormous dark wine which threw something resembling a port crust in bottle. The 1970 surprisingly faded rather quickly, but more recently the record has been impressive. The 1978 was ripe, forward and attractive, at its best when ten years old, with the 1979 showing as much more massive, with backbone and tannin, holding out real promise for the future. The 1980 is full-flavoured with a soft Merlot style, immediately attractive and accessible when three years old. The 1981 is a serious heavyweight, tannic and robust with a fine finish of much style and richness in 1986. The 1983 is complex and rich, the 1985 has the opulent scent of prunes, matched by the lovely opulent flavour of plums that one finds when there is over-ripe fruit – a luscious and outstanding example of the year. This now seems to be a consistently well-made wine which, while lacking the power of some other wines in this sector, such as La Dominique or La Tour-Figeac, which have more gravel in their soils, is nevertheless above average in quality and consistency.

CHÂTEAU CURÉ-BON

Grand Cru Classé. Owner: Maurice Landé. 5 hectares. 2,500 cases. Mer 95%, Mal 5%

The classification lists this growth as Curé-Bon, but the label says Curé-Bon-la-Madeleine. The property owes its name to a priest, Curé Bon, who planted this vineyard (which had actually been in his family since the seventeenth century) early in the last century. When the vineyard passed to his nephew, Camille Lapelletrie, the latter named it after his uncle and added the suffix "la Madeleine", indicating that the vineyard is situated on the plateau of la Madeleine between Ausone, Belair and Canon. Part of the vineyard lies in the base of an old quarry, now a shallow depression on the surface of the *plateau calcaire* of St Martin. Maturation is in cask, with a small amount of new oak. The wines have a good reputation and tend to be quite firm in spite of the high proportion of Merlot, but are also fleshy and generous, with a distinctive bouquet and breed. This is an honourable *cru classé*, if not in the same class as its illustrious neighbours.

CHÂTEAU DASSAULT

Grand Cru Classé. Owner. S A R L Château Dassault. Administrator: André Vergriette. 23 hectares. 9,000 cases. Mer 70%, CF 20%, CS 10%

This important property is one of the eight growths elevated to *grand cru classé* status in 1969. Much time and trouble have been devoted to the reconstruction of both *cuvier* and vineyard in recent years by the present proprietor, who is the head of Sud-Aviation, makers of Concorde and the Mirage. Monsieur Dassault renamed the château in 1955; prior to that it was called Couperie, and owes its origin to Victor Fourcaud, the elder brother of Laussac Fourcaud who had been proprietor of Cheval Blanc since 1853. He built a château in 1862 at the centre of three *métairies* from which the new estate was formed, and planted 25 hectares of vines. It is interesting to note that this marked an extension of the vineyards, since cereals had been grown here before. The vineyard is on the sandy *glacis*, north of Cadet, and there is some clay in its make-up. The style of the wines is uncomplicated, full-flavoured and supple, with a definite breed and pleasant harmony about them. They are clearly well made, and my recent tastings have shown a commendable degree of consistency. Both the 1978 and 1979 are good here, with the 1979 strong-flavoured and firm, with a distant *goût de terroir*. The 1980 is a light, pleasing wine, the 1981 is full-flavoured and again relatively forward, while 1982 has produced a wine whose beauty of flavour combined with length and moderate concentration promised a highly enjoyable bottle by 1987. The 1983 is very rich and spicy, full of fruit and ripe tannins. The 1985 is dense and powerful, with a minerally flavour, while the 1986 has vivid fruit and a satiny texture, very firm but with a delicious flavour. As one would expect with a proprietor engaged in high technology, the installations at Dassault are thoroughly up to date. Refrigeration is available, and one-third new oak is used in the *élevage*. Nevertheless, much credit must also be due to the energetic and capable André Vergriette who, as resident director, is responsible for the running of the vineyard and the wine-making. The label is an example of an unfortunate tendency to clone certain famous and often long-established labels. This one is "à la Lafite".

CHÂTEAU LA DOMINIQUE

Grand Cru Classé. Owner: Clément Fayat. 18.5 hectares. 6,500 cases. Mer 76%, CF 8%, CS 8%, Mal 8%

The vineyard of La Dominique is beautifully situated immediately to the east of Cheval Blanc on the sandy *glacis* – which includes, however, about one hectare of the same *graves* found in the vineyard of its illustrious neighbour as well as some of the siliceous limestone fragments found only here and at Cheval Blanc.

By St Emilion standards this is an old-established vineyard. The famous maps of Belleyme show that vines were established here by the second half of the eighteenth century when the adjoining Corbins were still producing cereals. The name is traced back to a merchant who made his fortune in the West Indies trade, on the island of Dominica. The system of drainage was organized at the same time as at Cheval Blanc, and La Dominique appears among the list of St Emilion *crus* which collectively took part in the Paris Universal Exhibition of 1867. The 1868 edition of Cocks & Féret placed it at the head of the second *crus*.

In more recent times the reputation of the property has been for making exceptional wines in some vintages, such as 1929 and 1945, but with a lack of consistency. But a new era began when it was purchased in 1969 by Monsieur Clément Fayat, who has made his fortune by building motorways. A modern *cuvier* has been installed, with stainless steel *cuves*, and there are improved conditions for storing bottled stock. One of the most significant investments in quality has been the proportion of new wood used in maturing the wine. The norm is a third, but for the 1982 as much as 50 per cent was used. The result is a blend of fruit, richness and tannin that needs time to mature but then produces impressive wines that place La Dominique among the forefront of the *crus classés* of St Emilion.

Among the vintages of the new regime, the 1970 is a powerful, sinewy wine which has aged impressively, and shows no sign of being finished yet. In contrast the 1971 is a marvellously opulent wine, ripe and full-flavoured with that sort of sheen to it that exceptional wines seem to have. Certainly it is better than several of the *premiers grands crus classés* of the same year. The 1978 was forward and open-textured with robust, solid fruit, and a touch of coarseness, but the 1979 offers a complete contrast, rather closed and tannic but with a lot of fruit and length at four years old. It is full-bodied and rich now, spicy and still improving after nine years. The 1980 is very good for the year, very perfumed, flowery and full of character. The 1981 has a touch of opulence, a fine flavour, with more style and length; it was ready by 1988. The 1982 is a splendid example of the year, with great power, concentration and richness, while the 1983 here is closer to the 1982 than in many other properties, with an exotic quality and a lovely balance of very rich fruit and power. This was one of my favourite 1983 St Emilions in cask. There is a rich, dense-textured 1985, while the 1986 in cask had great concentration of extract and richness, producing outstanding depth and beauty of flavour. This is an outstanding *vin de garde*. This *cru* has made great progress in the last decade and has established a reputation as one of the front-runners among the *grands crus classés*.

CHÂTEAU FAURIE-DE-SOUCHARD

Grand Cru Classé. Owner: Jabiol family. 11 hectares. 4,000 cases. Mer 65%, CF 26%, CS 9%

When there are two châteaux which both bear the name of Faurie, one with the suffix Souchard and the other Soutard, there is likely to be some confusion. This property has recently dropped the prefix "Petit", so at least this is not as confusing as it was. On the Belleyme map Faurie appears along with Soutard as a *lieu-dit* (place name) and both were dependencies of Château de La Salle. Unfortunately Professor Enjalbert gives no information about the Souchards and their doings, although he has plenty to say about Faurie and its detachment from Soutard in 1851. Faurie was the name of a battle fought hereabouts in the Hundred Years War. The present proprietors say that Souchard was the name of an eighteenth-century Jurat and mayor of St Emilion. Yet not until this century did the name Faurie de Souchard feature in Cocks & Féret.

This is a vineyard on the *plateau et côtes*, belonging, since 1933, to the Jabiol family, who also own Cadet-Piola. It lies to the north-east of the town with Souchard and Petit-Faurie-de-Soutard to the south and Dassault just beyond. The fermentation is in concrete vats, and the wine is then rotated between casks, of which one-third are new, and vats. Although the *encépagement* here is noticeably différent from that at Cadet-Piola, with much more Merlot, recent tastings show some similarities of style, a certain lack of flesh and tightness of flavour. I found the most impressive wine was the 1979, which has breed and style but was still undeveloped and rather taut, although with a very harmonious flavour, when four years old. The 1981 was still tough and disappointing after three years in bottle. The 1983 has shown a similar toughness and coarseness, while the 1985 is very disappointing for this glorious vintage; more promising, at least in cask, was the 1986.

CHÂTEAU DE FERRAND

Grand Cru. Owner: Baron Marcel Bich. 28 hectares. 13,500 cases, Mer 66.7%, CF and CS 33.3%

This is cited by Enjalbert as an example of an important seigneurial estate that failed to be developed in the eighteenth century, but was the subject of considerable investment during the prosperous period of the Second Empire, and until just before the phylloxera. Situated on the limestone plateau of St Hippolyte, it is the commune's most important *cru*. But this is the oldest surface rock layer, not the starfish limestone found around St Emilion. It is one of the few vineyards to show traces of siliceous limestone debris, as at Cheval Blanc. Now the new owner, since 1978, is making strenuous efforts to upgrade the wine, and using 100 per cent new oak, the only *grand cru* as distinct from *grand cru classé* to do so, believing the wines have the possibility to equal the *grands crus classés* of St Emilion – a view which, so far as one can judge from his writing, Enjalbert did not share. The aim is to produce rich, tannic wines requiring seven to eight years' bottle age to show their best. It will be interesting to watch developments here. Note that the name is not to be confused with the *cru* in nearby Pomerol, or the well-known one in Graves.

CHÂTEAU FIGEAC

Premier Grand Cru Classé B. Owner: Thierry Manoncourt. 40 hectares. 12,500 cases. CS 35%, CF 35%, Mer 30%

Figeac has one of the finest pedigrees of any property in Bordeaux. The name proclaims its Roman origins, the termination "-ac" coming from the Latin *-acum* or *-acus*. Figeac was the Gallo-Roman owner who gave his name to the estate. It seems to have survived as a large estate from Roman times right through the Middle Ages. In the late fifteenth century the medieval seigneury passed from the Lescours family to the Decazes, who built the château after the Wars of Religion, in about 1595. In 1654 Marie Decazes married François de Carle, to whom it passed in 1661. By the eighteenth century we know that this was a great estate of over 200 hectares, comparable to the finest estates in Graves and Médoc.

It was in the eighteenth century that Vital, and his son Elie de Carle transformed Figeac into one of the first great quality wine-producing estates in the region. Enjalbert has surmised that it was Vital de Carle who replanted the main vineyards on the *graves* on which both Cheval Blanc and Figeac now stand, during the years from 1730 to 1755. In 1731 he bought a property on the Guitres road for use as his *chai*, and renamed it Les Fontaines, indicating that he expected to produce significant quantities of wines from his estates, not only at Figeac but also at Camfourtet (Clos Fourtet) in the Haut-St Emilion. By the 1770s we know that good quantities of the finest-quality wines were being sold at high prices, and that Elie de Carle counted Prince Maréchal de Broglie and the Comte de Calonne as esteemed clients for his wines. Both men played important roles in the fateful reign of Louis XVI. In 1780 Figeac produced 60 tonneaux, excluding white wines, suggesting some 30 hectares of vines. On his death in 1791, Elie de Carle, a bachelor, left Figeac to his uncle Jacques de Carle, a general in Louis XVI's army, whose sense of patriotism made him re-enlist in February 1792, when revolutionary France was threatened by invasion from Austria. At the age of sixty-eight he was a lieutenant-general in charge of the garrisons, first at Dunkirk then at Boulogne. But the ways of his revolutionary masters soon became too much, and in September 1793, now sixty-nine, he asked to retire on account of his age. In February 1794, having settled his pension rights, he returned to Figeac, married, and proceeded to spend 26,000 *livres*, a considerable sum, to renovate the château. The building we see today is substantially his creation, although there is still plenty of evidence of the sixteenth-century château.

At this stage Figeac seemed set fair to take its place beside Haut-Brion and the first growths of Médoc as one of the great wine estates of Bordeaux. Unhappily the general's choice of a distant relative, André de Carle-Trajet, as his heir led to the decline and break-up of this great domain. On succeeding to the estate in 1803, he took up residence and married. The British blockade reduced exports, even to northern France and the Low Countries, to a trickle, and the new owner's expensive lifestyle and enthusiasm for new agricultural ideas to experimentation and speculation. In particular he cut down much of the forest that still occupied an important part of the estate at the end of the eighteenth century, as we know from Belleyme's map, and planted madder. The blockade prevented the importation of Mexican cochineal, used as a dye, and madder was used as a replacement. André de Carle-Trajet not only went into madder production on an industrial scale, he also returned to the system of *joualles*, the planting of crops, in his case clover, between much more widely spaced rows of vines. The vines were then manured in such a way that the yield per hectare was as high as before, from roughly half the number of vines. So quality wine production was seriously impaired. With the fall of Napoleon and the end of the blockade, the market for madder collapsed, and by 1823 de Carle-Trajet was in serious financial trouble; on his death in 1825 his widow inherited a largely ruined estate. The dismemberment of the estate seems to have begun before 1825, but soon accelerated. Land was sold to the owner of La Marzelle, and some good *graves* went to enlarge La Conseillante, but it was the sales of the 1830s which created Cheval Blanc and marked the decisive alienation of a major part of Figeac's patrimony. They effectively divided the finest *graves* soils in the area between the two properties, so that today both have approximately two-thirds *graves* and one-third sandy *glacis* in their make-up. De Carle-Trajet's widow finally sold the estate in 1838, and the period from then until the purchase by André Villepigue in 1892 was a bleak one, with seven changes of ownership and more sales. The prestige of the name lingered on for a while: in 1841 *Le Producteur* shows Ducasse at Cheval Blanc, and Chauvin's and Mlle Largeteau's vineyard at La Marzelle, both still selling these wines under the Figeac name. The new owner was told by the Sous-Préfet in Libourne that "the vines are not very productive at the moment. . . they are French [i.e. ungrafted] vines protected with carbon disulphide, which in my opinion would best be gradually replaced with grafted varieties; but there is no hurry". He added that Albert Macquin, an old school friend of Villepigue, could manage the property for him. Macquin took up his duties in July 1892. When he arrived the domain had 37 hectares planted with old, ungrafted vines. By 1897, out of 36 hectares, 31 were still old vines, 2 were four years old, 2 three years old, and one was two years old. Although these 5 hectares were not yet producing *grand vin*, the yield from the 31 hectares was greater than it had been from 37 hectares. This graphically illustrates the cautious progress from ungrafted old vines to grafted ones in the best vineyards during the phylloxera crisis.

Yet in spite of Macquin's careful restoration of the Figeac vineyard at the turn of the century, Figeac was still overtaken by Cheval Blanc during this period. The absentee owners must have contributed to Figeac's stagnation. Then in 1947 Thierry Manoncourt, a grandson of André Villepigue, took up residence at Figeac to become the first member of the family to manage the property, and under his direction Figeac has blossomed again, and entered its greatest era since the days of Elie de Carle.

Trying to be as objective as possible, I would say that today Figeac often comes close to Cheval Blanc in quality, and even in style, but it seldom achieves the sheer weight of Cheval Blanc. In body it is slightly lighter, with a touch of elegance, yet with that same *graves* power and richness. Certainly, in many vintages it is the second-best wine in the whole St Emilion region, and occasionally it is first. Yet for all its consistency and flair, and in spite of soils that mirror each other, the fact is that side by side, with a few notable exceptions, Cheval Blanc is usually the more outstanding of the two wines. Why? The one crucial difference between the two lies in the *encépagement*. Both have the same proportion of Merlot, planted on the sandy *glacis*, but whereas Cheval Blanc's *graves* are planted entirely with Cabernet Franc, at Figeac the *graves* are planted with Cabernet Franc and Cabernet Sauvignon in equal proportions. Opinion as to the Cabernet Sauvignon's ability to perform satisfactorily in the Libournais is now well known. Admittedly, the *graves* here are a special case. Yet in the great 1982 vintage, a year of exceptional ripeness, it was some of the Cabernet Sauvignon that Thierry Manoncourt excluded from his final *assemblage*, because he believed it would detract from the exceptional quality of the whole.

In December 1989, Bipin Desai organized a retrospective tasting of Figeac at Taillevent in Paris. The finest of the old vintages were a frail but lovely 1906, a faded but charming 1924, a rich and complex 1929, which was the pick of the old vintages, a tannic and rather one-dimensional 1934, which was outshone by the more generous and powerful 1937. The surprise was the only tastable 1939 I have come across, still fresh and sound. The 1943 was actually vinified by Thierry Manoncourt and was strong-flavoured but with a tart finish. The 1945 had great concentration and opulent power, a great bottle, more impressive than a rather subdued but rich 1947. Most enjoyable of all in this section was the 1949, with its lovely rich, sweet flavour and superior finish. The 1950 was exceptional, with great finesse, and 1953 and 1955 confirmed their status as two of the greatest wines Figeac has ever produced, along with 1949; much better than Cheval Blanc, they both had superb richness and depth of fruit, succulent and stylish. Then came the lovely 1961, but the 1964 outshone it, the best wine of the decade, with 1962 attractive but lightweight, and 1966 supple and gorgeous. The 1970 still looks a shade austere and tannic, but 1971 was at its opulent best. A fine 1975 lacks complexity, while 1976 was for drinking, succulent and delicious. Both 1978 and 1979 were very successful, with 1978 having more complexity. The very concentrated 1982 was closed up, but the 1983 was already delicious, with lots of depth for the future. Equally promising was the charming 1985, while 1986 was more powerful and awkward, but very rich: the yield was only 32 hectolitres per hectare, much less than usual for this high-cropping vintage. The 1988 had lovely concentration, a wine of great promise.

CHÂTEAU LA FLEUR

Grand Cru. Owner: Lily Lacoste. 6.5 hectares. 2,500 cases. Mer 75%, CF25%
This is a good vineyard lying north-east of Soutard on the sandy *glacis*. The owner is better known as the co-owner of Pétrus and owner of Latour-à-Pomerol and, like them, La Fleur is distributed exclusively through J.-P. Moueix. These are consistently delicious wines, fleshy and quite rich, full of easy fruit and charm.

CHÂTEAU FLEUR-CARDINALE

Owner: Claude Asséo. 9 hectares. 4,500 cases. Mer 70%, CF 15%, CS 15%
This *cru* is on the *côte* at St Etienne-de-Lisse and is orientated north-south, with calcareous clayey soil on rock. Since taking over in 1982 the present owner has made serious, traditional wines, matured in cask. The result is sinewy, well-structured wine. It needs some time in bottle to mellow.

CHÂTEAU LA FLEUR-POURRET

Grand Cru. Owner: La Compagnie Axa. Administrators: Jean-Michel Cazes, Gilbert Xans. 6.5 hectares, 2,500 cases. Mer 50%, CS 50%
This vineyard is at the foot of the *côte*, just outside the town on the Libourne road. It was formed during the nineteenth century by Fernand Ginestet, grandfather of Bruno Prats, by amalgamating Clos Haut-Pourret with Château La Fleur. In 1989 Bruno Prats sold to Axa (see Píchon-Baron), another victim of Bordeaux's inheritance problems. The unusual feature is the high proportion of Cabernet Sauvignon.

CHÂTEAU FOMBRAUGE

Grand Cru. Owner: Bordeaux Château Invest. 50 hectares. 25,000 cases. Mer 60%, CF 30%, CS 10%
This is one of the leading *crus* of St Christophe, situated on the *plateau calcaire*, the north-facing *côte* and its lower slopes. It was one of St Christophe's two *maisons nobles* identified by the *curé* in the 1770s; it was

mentioned by *Le Producteur* in 1841 and was one of the four *crus* from St Christophe included in the thirty-eight jointly awarded a gold medal in 1867. The wines have a long-established reputation in the UK and are consistently well made, with 25 per cent new oak in the *élevage*. They are solid and full-flavoured and attractively fruity, but usually rather coarse-grained, a feature which distinguishes even the most carefully made wines from the less good soils from those around the town of St Emilion, on its *plateau et côte*. For many years meticulously run by Charles Bygodt, he sold it in 1987 to a Danish consortium.

CHÂTEAU FONPLÉGADE
Grand Cru Classé. Owner: Armand Moueix. 18 hectares. 7,500 cases. Mer 60%, CF 35%, CS 5%

This fine property has a nineteenth-century turreted château more in the style of those found in the Médoc. It belongs to the family of A. Moueix, important proprietors and merchants in both St Emilion and Pomerol, related to – but not to be confused with – their cousins J.-P. Moueix, who are the leading proprietors and merchants in the region. Curiously, the vineyard of Magdelaine, belonging to their cousins' house, overlooks the vineyard and château on three sides, the vineyard forming, as it were, a depression in the *côtes*, and thus being on a lower level. Five hectares of Fonplégade were sold to Magdelaine in 1863. The outlook is towards the *coopérative*. This was an important property by the late nineteenth century and was one of the thirty-eight *crus* representing the region at the 1867 Paris Exhibition. It is interesting to note that this is one of the *crus* where Féret states, in 1893, that some Cabernet Sauvignon was planted when the vineyard was reconstructed, after the ravages of the phylloxera.

The property is carefully managed today by Armand Moueix, and like his other *grand cru classé*, La Tour-du-Pin-Figeac, uses a system of vinification originally perfected in Algeria and also found in Médoc at Branaire. Basically the fermentation takes place in a closed *cuve*; the pressure thus created forces the fermenting must up through a cylindrical column to flood the top of the cap. This provides very good colour extraction.

The wines here are firm and rather tannic to start with, and need time to show the style and finesse that they usually produce with maturity. I remember attractive 1962s and 1964s. More recently the 1978 was still taut but attractive and firm-flavoured in 1987, while the 1979 showed more maturity and charm. The 1980 is stylish and firm, needing more time than many wines of this year. The 1982 promises to be a long-developer, with a powerful flavour and tannic undertones. The 1983 has a luscious Merlot style and was already forward and very drinkable at five years of age. The 1985 is firm, rich, and surprisingly tannic for the year, while the 1986 has firm ripe tannins but is also attractively scented and fruity, promising an exceptional bottle. This is a consistent and reliable wine, if lacking the flair of the top *crus*.

CHÂTEAU FONROQUE

Grand Cru Classé. Owner: GFA Château Fonroque. Administrator: Alain Moueix. 20 hectares. 6,500 cases. Mer 70%, CF 30%

This solid, four-square wine of marked character is now owned by Alain Moueix. Benefiting from the usual Moueix care and attention to detail, it produces very consistent wines. The modest but attractive château, surrounded by quite a substantial park, lies north-north-west of St Emilion and is approached down one of the lesser roads, which makes the task of finding it none too easy. The vineyard is on the *côte* and its lower slopes at about their extremity in this direction. The first vintage I came across was the 1959, which was rich and powerful, and lasted well, and this from a vintage of mixed fortunes in St Emilion because of the 1956 frost and its aftermath. Recently I have much liked the 1978, which was finely perfumed with lots of structure and personality, tannin and fruit. The 1979 was dense and powerful, but also had the length and complexity to make this a wine worth waiting for. It will last at least as long as the 1978. The 1981 has power and depth, with a typically assertive flavour and a certain mineral quality, while the 1982 has a wonderful after-taste, very velvety, rich and delicious. But the 1983 is even better, promising outstanding things with a richness to match the tannin, and a concentration of flavour which gives the wine a marked character and an added complexity, compared to past vintages. This bore witness to some recent improvements in vinification and the use of some new wood to raise the already very honourable standing of this *cru*. The 1985 is solid and strong-flavoured, rich with a minerally character, and rather austere at first, at least for the year. The 1986 shows good fruit but is predictably tannic, a solid *vin de garde*.

CHÂTEAU FRANC-GRÂCE-DIEU

Grand Cru. Owner: Germain Siloret. Administrator: Eric Fournier. 8 hectares.
3,000 cases. Mer 52%, CF 41%, CS 7%

Before 1981 this *cru* was known as Guadet Le Franc-Grâce-Dieu. Then
Eric Fournier of Château Canon took over the direction of the property,
and it was decided to simplify the over-complicated name. The vineyard
lies north-west of St Emilion, on the sandy *glacis*, just off the Libourne
road. The Grâce-Dieu part of the name, shared with several other properties, indicates that this formed part of a Cistercian grange until the
seventeenth century when it was sold off to secular owners. This is a
typically Cistercian name. Since Eric Fournier took charge, the wines
have finesse and style, with intense vibrant fruit, well up to the quality of
a *cru classé*.

CHÂTEAU FRANC-MAYNE

Grand Cru Classé. Owner: La Compagnie Axa. 8 hectares. 2,700 cases. Mer 75%
CF and CS 25%

This *cru* lies just to the south of the D17 St Emilion–Pomerol road, to the
north-west of the town, and adjoins Clos des Jacobins. The vineyard is
well sited on the *côtes*. In recent years the proportion of Cabernet Franc
has been increased at the expense of the Cabernet Sauvignon, in an effort
to produce riper, more elegant wines. In 1987 it was bought by Axa (see
Pichon-Baron) and more interesting wines are already resulting.

CHÂTEAU LA GAFFELIÈRE

Premier Grand Cru Classé B. Owner: Comte Léo de Malet-Roquefort. 22 hectares.
8,000 cases. Mer 65%, CF 25%, CS 10%

The actual château buildings at Gaffelière are older and more interesting
than those of most of its neighbours. The oldest part goes back to the
eleventh century and there is an eighteenth-century wing, the whole
encased in a nineteenth-century copy of the marvellous Logis de Malet-
Roquefort, still to be found in the walls of St Emilion. It has belonged to
the family of the Comtes de Malet-Roquefort for over three centuries, a
record unique in St Emilion. The building stands on the site of a medieval
leper house, and it is from this that the name of Gaffelière derives.
Curiously, however, the growth was entered as Puygenestou-Naudes in
early editions of Cocks & Féret, and it was not until 1898 that it was to

appear under its more familiar name. One point should be cleared up right away. This growth was known as La Gaffelière-Naudes, which name appeared on all its labels until the 1964 vintage, when the Naudes was dropped in the interests of simplicity and clarity.

The château and its *chai*, which is of the conventional type, lie in a small valley a little way outside St Emilion, with the vineyard adjoining those of Ausone and Pavie on the lower hillsides of the *côtes* each side of the valley. After Pavie, it is the largest of the *premiers grands crus* in the *côtes*. As in other St Emilion properties, the experience with Cabernet Sauvignon has not been a happy one, and it is gradually being replaced. It is probably in the last twenty years or so that the wines of Gaffelière have come to be as well known and appreciated in England as they deserve to be. Nevertheless, this was a period of inconsistency for Gaffelière, which the proprietor candidly puts down to the last years of his old *maître de chai*, who was there for over thirty-six years – proof, if one were needed, that men matter more than machines. From 1982 until 1985 Alexandre Thienpont acted as *maître de chai*, until he returned to run Vieux-Château-Certan on the death of his father, when Léo de Malet-Roquefort recruited the present occupant, Ted Garin.

The wines are fuller and more fleshy than most other wines of the *côtes*, without quite the breed of the top growths perhaps, but with a most distinctive savour, a deep colour and a generous bouquet, which quickly develops a flavour of great charm, powerful yet subtle and complex. In 1974 stainless steel vats were installed in the *cuvier*, and this has improved the control of the vinification. Gaffelière made one of the great 1945s, still superb in 1980, but it was the 1953 which was probably the first vintage to win this growth a real reputation among the English trade, and this has been followed by many other fine vintages, among which the 1966, 1970, 1971, an especially impressive 1975, and 1976 are typical. The 1978 is lightweight, and the attractive 1979 is rather diluted. There was a supple 1980, for early drinking, and a decent 1981. Then came a change of gear, with a superb 1982, reminiscent of a 1947 in style, while the 1983 is particularly successful here, being wonderfully rich and complex with real *race* and concentration. At this stage 50 per cent new wood was being used; now they have moved on to 100 per cent new oak. Then a policy of weeding out the less favoured bunches as well as trimming the vines, in early August, was implemented. At the same time a longer maceration and more frequent *remontages* were introduced, together with a second wine, Clos La Gaffelière, to allow for a stricter selection. As a result the 1985 has very vivid, rich, opulent fruit, with plenty of structure, while the 1986 is more tannic and intense. Both wines promise a fine future.

CHÂTEAU LA GRÂCE-DIEU-LES-MENUTS

Grand Cru. Owner: Max Pilotte. 13 hectares. 5,700 cases. Mer 60%, CF 30%, CS 10%

The history of this property is the same as Franc-Grâce-Dieu, and it is on the sandy *glacis*. Recently some new oak has been introduced into the cask maturation, and the quality and reputation of this *cru* are increasing. I have found the examples I have tasted to be light-textured, but elegant and quite fine, suitable for early drinking.

CHÂTEAU GRAND BARRAIL-LAMARZELLE-FIGEAC AND CHÂTEAU LA MARZELLE

Grand Cru Classé. Owner: Association E. Carrère. 34 hectares. 17,000 cases. Mer 75%, CS and CF 25%

These two properties, taken together, form the largest vineyard in St Emilion after Cheval Blanc and Figeac. Lying immediately to the south of Figeac, part of the vineyard occupies the southern extremity of that gravelly outcrop which goes north through Figeac and Cheval Blanc and into Pomerol. In the Middle Ages La Marzelle belonged to the Cistercian monastery at Faize in Les Artigues de Lussac, but was sold in the eighteenth century to three Libourne families. There was an echo of this ecclesiastical past when the wine was served to Pope John XXIII when he visited Lourdes. The estate as it exists today is the creation of a financier from the north of France called Boitard. It is an interesting example of investment occasioned by the phylloxera crisis. He bought several properties, pulled up the vines, carried out drainage work, and then replanted 22 hectares, as well as building a large château in a park (unfortunately on the best *graves* on the estate) and an enormous *chai* beside the Libourne–St Emilion road. The present owners, the Carrère family, bought the properties after the disastrous 1956 frost. Given the position of the vineyard, the real potential for quality has not in the past been realized to the full. In vintages such as the 1979 and 1983 there was a dilution from overproduction, and a lack of selection that made the wines age rapidly. But the 1985 was dense-textured enough to suggest that efforts are now being made to produce better wines. At their best they can be deliciously supple, fruity wines with real appeal.

CHÂTEAU GRAND-CORBIN

Grand Cru Classé. Owner: Alain Giraud. 13 hectares. 6,000 cases. Mer 50%, CF 25%, CS 25%

The history of this property is basically the same as for the other Corbins, and it is under the same ownership and direction as Château Corbin. It lies on the sandy *glacis* between Corbin and Grand-Corbin-Despagne. Maturation is in casks, of which 20 per cent are new. The reputation is for rather blander wines than at Corbin, and they are not of the same quality as Grand-Corbin-Despagne.

CHÂTEAU GRAND-CORBIN-DESPAGNE

Grand Cru Classé. Owners: Despagne family. 25 hectares. 11,000 cases. Mer 70%, CF 25%, CS and Mal 5%

This is the largest portion of what used to be the great Corbin seigneury, second only in importance in the Middle Ages to Figeac, but already in decline by the eighteenth century when this was still an area, with the exception of Figeac, given over to cereals. The property lies on the sandy *glacis* at the northern limits of the *appellation* adjoining Pomerol, and has belonged to the Despagne family for several generations. A new *chai* with stainless steel fermentation vats was built in 1978, and 20 per cent new oak is now used in the *élevage*.

The wines here enjoy a good reputation, which was confirmed by my recent tastings as well deserved. The 1970 was still vigorous and high in extract when tasted in 1988, while the 1976 was perhaps more typical with its heady, exotically scented bouquet and deliciously soft, full, fruity flavour, at its best by 1987. In comparison the 1979, while opulent, was rather minerally and coarse; but then there was a particularly good 1981, with a delicious flavour that was ripe and opulent – with more body than most 1981s in this area. These are good, consistently made wines that are typical of the best *crus* on the sandy *glacis*.

CHÂTEAU GRAND-MAYNE

Grand Cru Classé. Owner: Jean-Pierre Nony. 17 hectares. 11,000 cases. Mer 50%, CF 40%, CS 10%. Secondary labels: Château Beau-Mazerat, Château Cassovert

This is an old domain which was one of the most important properties in St Emilion in the first half of the nineteenth century. It lies to the west of St Emilion, at the limits of the côtes, before the sandy *glacis* takes over. There is a fifteenth-century manor and park. Between 1811 and his death in 1836 it belonged to Jean Laveau, the leading vine grower of the day, who also owned Soutard. Unfortunately he had no direct heirs and his estates were divided up, so we know that by 1836 there were 22.16 hectares of vines here and that, with a production of 80 tonneaux, this was the second largest St Emilion producer, behind Soutard with 100 tonneaux, against an average at that time of only 10–20 tonneaux. The Laveau family had owned the property since 1685, but it was not until now that it was fully exploited, as far as its vineyard was concerned. In 1836 the outbuildings, which would have included the *chai* and *cuvier*, were almost new.

The Nony family have been here since 1934, and Jean-Pierre Nony, who today lives at the property, has been in charge since 1975. Stainless steel vats replaced the wooden ones in that year. Maturation is in cask, with 20 per cent new oak. I have only limited experience of this wine, but enough to suggest that it deserves to be better known than it is. When eleven years old a magnum of the 1976 was quite magnificent; with a lovely lingering, ripe, fruity flavour, stylish and fine, it had a certain originality and was markedly better than many more prestigious *crus* from this region in this vintage. I was also struck by the elegant stylishness and complexity of the 1981. Only the 1979 was somewhat disappointing, with a dry finish and apparent lack of ripeness.

CHÂTEAU GRAND-PONTET

Grand Cru Classé. Owners: Bécot and Pourquet families. 14 hectares. 6,500 cases. Mer 70%, CF 15%, CS 15%

This property is at the foot of the *côtes*, just outside the town on the Libourne road, north-west of St Emilion. From 1965 until 1980 it belonged to Barton and Guestier, the Seagram-owned Bordeaux *négociants*, who completely modernized the property. One of the two new partners also owns nearby Beau-Séjour-Bécot. Under the Barton and

Guestier management sound but unexciting wines were made. I have not tasted the wine since the change, but the quality is said to have improved, and this should be a wine worth looking out for.

CHÂTEAU GRANDES-MURAILLES

Grand Cru. Owner: Reiffers family. Administrator: Sophie Fourcade. 2 hectares. 900 cases. Mer 70%, CF 15%, CS 15%

If you approach St Emilion along the modest D road from Pomerol and arrive at the town in front of the magnificent collegial church, there is an impressive ruin to the right. This is the solitary remaining wall of the church of the Jacobins (Dominicans), still lofty enough to show off the full effect of its slender Gothic tracery. This marks one of the boundaries of the tiny vineyard of Grandes-Murailles, adjoining Clos Fourtet, where the *plateau calcaire* begins to fall away to the *côtes* and sandy *glacis*.

Grandes-Murailles gives its name to the Société Civile which runs the three properties of Côte-Baleau (the largest, where the *chai* is situated), Clos St Martin and this one, for the Reiffers family. Grandes-Murailles lost its *cru classé* status in the 1985 revision, because the wine was made and kept in the same *chai* as Côte-Baleau. The family is now reorganizing its cellars in consultation with the INAO. This is the rich, opulent style of St Emilion which matures relatively quickly. In general I have found it to be not quite as fine or as consistent as Côte-Baleau. The 1978 was rich and concentrated with structure and fruit, which still needed time, when five years old. The 1979 is rich and dense, but will be ready at about the same time as the 1978. The 1981 is Grandes-Murailles at its best – rich, opulent fruit and good structure. The 1982 is finely scented and powerful, with a lovely ripeness and good tannin and structure to support it – a wine for which one will not have to wait too long to enjoy. The 1983 is most attractive, full of fruit and an early developer. The 1985 is luscious, very rich and ripe, likely to develop early. In general then, a highly enjoyable wine, and showing some signs of an improvement in overall standards which should lead to a fuller realization of the potential of this well-placed *cru*. It will be interesting to see if it is reclassified eventually, although with its small size it might be more sensible to seek permission to amalgamate it with nearby Clos St Martin.

CHÂTEAU GUADET-ST JULIEN

Grand Cru Classé. Owner: Robert Lignac. 5.5 hectares. 2,000 cases. Mer 75%, CS and CF 25%

This small vineyard lies immediately to the north of the town on the *plateau calcaire*. There is no château, and the wine is made and kept in cellars dating back to the fifth century in the rue Guadet in the heart of the town, under the house of the owner Robert Lignac. In the eighteenth century the domain of St Julien belonged to the Lacombe Guadet family. The member of the family celebrated on the label is Marie-Elie Guadet, a barrister and deputy for the Gironde, who was guillotined on 19 June 1794, during the Terror. The property was bought by Mathieu Garitey, great-grandfather of the present owner, in 1877.

From the vintages I have seen recently it is clear that this is generally an attractive, supple wine which matures quickly. The 1978 was already most attractive when only five years old, with a firm flavour, fruit balanced by structure: a wine that could be enjoyed already, but with the capacity to keep well. On the other hand, the 1979 was rather tough and astringent after two years in bottle, and not showing the same class as the other vintages. The 1980 was supple and forward after two years in bottle; while the 1981 was rich and powerful, with unusual depth for the year, after three years in bottle. The 1983 is an excellent example of the year, with power, tannins and good fruit, really concentrated. The 1985 has good fruit, but had a rather coarse finish in cask. The 1986 in cask had style and charm in spite of marked tannins and a fair dose of new oak. As with many small *crus*, a large part of this wine is sold direct. It is a pleasant middle-of-the-road wine.

CHÂTEAU HAUT-BADETTE

Owner: J.-F.Janoueix. 4.5 hectares. 2,500 cases. Mer 90%, CS 10%

The vineyard lies below Haut-Sarpe, and benefits from the same management. The soil is silica and clay. It has belonged to the Janoueix family since 1970; the wines are very perfumed, rich and full-bodied with great charm. In most years they seem full of ripe fruit, but the 1983 was lighter and quite elegant. They are ready to drink young yet also last well; the 1978 was splendid in 1986, and had plenty of freshness and vigour still. This wine highlights the anomalies in the St Emilion vineyard system. Le Castelot, under the same management but in St Sulpice, is rated a *grand cru*, which Haut-Badette is not; yet this wine has more breed and none of the *goût de terroir* found at Le Castelot.

CHÂTEAU HAUT-CORBIN
Grand Cru Classé. Owner: A. M. du Batiment et Travaux Publics. Administrator: Domaines Cordier. 7 hectares. 2,500 cases. Mer 67%, CS 33%
This was the only growth in this northern section to be upgraded when the INAO revised the classification in 1969. It lies north and east of the other Corbins, on the sandy *glacis*, and near the border with Montagne-St Emilion. In 1986 the present owners (see Cantemerle) together with their partners Cordier, bought the property, which till then had a very undistinguished record. The 1986 is an impressive wine, rich and meaty, and 1988 and 1989 are set to follow the same path.

CHÂTEAU HAUT-GUEYROT
Owner: Jean-Marcel Gombeau. 7 hectares. 3,500 cases. Mer 85%, CF 15%
A small vineyard on the lower slopes and plain of St Laurent-des-Combes, it is typical of the many attractive, delicious wines that can be found in these outer communes. I have found the wines constantly rich, fruity and quite luscious. They are usually delightful drinking when about three years old.

CHÂTEAU HAUT-PONTET
Grand Cru. Owner: Limouzin Frères. 5.2 hectares. 2,500 cases. Mer 75%, CF and CS 25%
This small vineyard is on the *pieds de côtes* north of St Emilion. It has produced very consistent wines for some years, distributed by J.-P. Moueix. This is solid, distinctive, rich, full-flavoured wine which needs bottle-ageing, not the easy, supple style of St Emilion at all.

CHÂTEAU HAUT-SARPE
Grand Cru Classé. Owner: Jean-François Janoueix. 12.5 hectares. 6,000 cases. Mer 70%, CF 30%
This impressive property straddles the boundary of St Emilion and St Christophe. The park and château are placed on the edge of the *plateau calcaire et côte*, looking across to St Georges. Haut-Sarpe boasts one of the oldest reputations in St Emilion. Already by 1750 Pierre Beylot, then the

leading *négociant* of Libourne, referred to the "cru de Sarpe". This is the first mention of a St Emilion *cru* by name, and with its price. In 1807 Beylot's son Mathieu was buying Sarpe for a very high price for sale to a client in Brussels. In 1867 the two owners of Sarpe had their names inscribed among the thirty-eight *crus* of St Emilion presented at the Universal Exhibition in Paris which were awarded a gold medal. Then, at the end of the century, Sarpe was fortunate to find itself in the hands of a dynamic proprietor – Henri Foussat – to revive its fortunes after the phylloxera. So successful were his efforts that by the turn of the century he was regularly harvesting 100 tonneaux while his two predecessors in the 1860s had made a total of only 20 tonneaux.

To crown this period of achievement Henri Foussat began the construction of a most elegant château, modelled on the Trianon. The central pavilion and the south wing were speedily built, but then in 1906 everything stopped and the final project was never completed, although amusingly the 1908 edition of Cocks & Féret showed the château as finished. Attached to it are an assortment of much older buildings, amounting almost to a hamlet, rather reminiscent of an estate in Tuscany, including a beautifully restored windmill, a reminder that this was still a cereal growing area until the eighteenth century.

The property has belonged to the Janoueix family since 1930; they are also *négociants* in Libourne and own other properties in both St Emilion and Pomerol. As with the Moueixs, the distinctive "eix" ending shows they are Corréziens, people who have made a major contribution to the economy of the Libournais since the turn of the century.

The *cru* was added to the classification in the 1969 revision. Although technically in the commune of St Christophe, it has always been considered as an integral part of St Emilion and adjoins Balestard-La-Tonnelle, Trottevieille and Sansonnet.

Fermentation takes place in a mixture of wooden and enamelled cement vats, with careful control of temperature. The élevage is in cask, with 25 per cent new oak. The *maître de chai*, Paul Cazenave, has been here since 1964 and doubles between here and Canon. My recent tastings have shown this to be a wine of marked character and breed. The older vintages show how well these wines mature. In 1985 I tasted the 1964, still extremely rich and powerful, with great concentration and character, slightly dry and *rôti*; the 1966, lighter than the 1964 but with more breed and finesse, an inner core of firmness still, and very fresh; a flowery, harmonious 1967, with many nuances of flavour, delicious if a little dry, excellent for the year. A year before, the 1970 was already very ripe and mellow in flavour. These are wines that can be misjudged when young, and seem tough and sometimes coarse beside a wine like Balestard, because of their different structure and slower evolution. But they retain their freshness and vigour longer than many other St Emilions. Thus the 1976 was still delicious, lively and fresh when ten years old. The 1978 had lovely fruit and complexity when seven years old, but the 1979 has a big, luscious, chewy style which is attractive and very St Emilion. The wine was perfect when six years old. The 1981 on the other hand was still firm and tannic but definitely stylish and showing breed after three years in bottle. The 1982 promises something special with its rich, attractive fruit, breed on the nose, and marked character, with well-projected tannin and fruit on the palate. The 1983 is a rich, tannic wine which has been going through a tough, irony stage. This is certainly a *cru* to watch in the future. The 1985 is another concentrated wine which firmed up just before bottling. The 1986 seems to have more richness combined with an outstanding flavour, a classic *vin de garde*. Haut-Sarpe has the potential now to move into the top rung of the *grands crus classés*.

CHÂTEAU JEAN-FAURE

Grand Cru. Owner: Michel Amart. 17 hectares. 5,600 cases. CF 60%, Mer 30%, Mal 10%

This property, lying on the sandy *glacis* east of Cheval Blanc and adjoining Ripeau and La Dominique, was for many years run in conjunction with Ripeau, until the present owners bought it in 1976. It was of greater prominence in the last century. In 1841 its production of 80 tonneaux placed it on the same level as Grand-Mayne, second only to Soutard in its production, at a time when much of the Corbins were still under cereals. It lost its *cru classé* status in the 1985 revision. Twenty-five per cent new oak is now used in the *élevage* of this wine, which is distributed by Dourthe Frères. The aim is to produce full-bodied wines which are at the same time elegant. My own limited tastings suggest wines which can be softly fruity but rather lacking personality and style, or, at the other extreme, tough and irony. But neither type was really of *cru classé* standing.

CHÂTEAU LAGRANGE-DE-LESCURE

Grand Cru. Owner: Sociéte Civile du Château Le Couvent. 17 hectares. 8,500 cases. CS 37.5%, CF 37.5%, Mer 25%

This vineyard is on the southern part of the *sablo-graveleux* (recent gravel and sand) terraces which comprise the best vineyard land in the commune of St Sulpice-de-Faleyrens. Since its purchase in September 1982 by François Marret's Bordeaux offshoot of Marne et Champagne, there has been substantial investment in the *chai*, *cuvier* and new casks. The wines are supple and full-flavoured with lots of middle fruit, attractive wines for early drinking. Certainly this is a wine on the upward path.

CHÂTEAU LANIOTE

Grand Cru Classé. Owners: Freymond-Rouja family. 5 hectares. 2,200 cases. Mer 80%, CF 15%, CS 5%

This is a small but well-tended *cru* to the north of the town, at the point where the foot of the *côtes* merges into the sandy *glacis*. It lies between Fonroque and Baleau. This was one of the several *crus* not placed in the original classification of 1955, but added in the first revision of 1969. The label shows not the modest château and its *chai*, but the Chapelle de la Trinité, beneath which lies the famous Grotte de St Emilion, the *raison d'être*, as it were, of the whole place. By an odd quirk of secularization, this most precious of St Emilion's monuments belongs to the proprietors of Laniote.

The experienced Jean Brun, who also looks after the Reiffers family's adjoining property of Côte Baleau, acts as *régisseur* here. Twenty-five per cent new oak is now used in the maturation. The wine is not in the big, beefy tradition of St Emilions, but is notable for its finesse. It is very perfumed, intense, with a long, refined and beautiful flavour, and has real breed. There is an enchanting texture, lush and silky, which lifts the wines above the general run, and makes them really exciting. They develop quite quickly. Of the examples I have tasted, the 1979, 1981, 1982 and 1983 were all excellent in their different ways. Most of the production is exported to Switzerland and Belgium.

CHÂTEAU LARCIS-DUCASSE

Grand Cru Classé. Owner: Jacques Olivier Gratiot. Administrator: Nicolas Thienpoint. 10 hectares. 5,000 cases. Mer 65%, CF and CS 35%

This was the only château outside the commune of St Emilion to be classified in 1955. However, in all but name it is in fact a St Emilion, and has always been regarded as such; its vineyard adjoins and is immediately to the east of Pavie on the Côte de Pavie and its lower slopes. The fact that the boundary of the commune of St Laurent-des-Combes runs through the property says more about the drawing of boundaries than about their relationship to what is on the ground.

The reputation of Larcis-Ducasse is an old one. In 1777 its wines were mentioned as having been bought at a high price by Pierre Beylot. Then in 1841 Lecoutre de Beauvais mentions Larcis as being among the leading *crus* of St Emilion. At this time Monsieur Pigasse of Pavie was also proprietor here. In the middle of the century the property was divided between two owners, one of whom was called Ducasse, and when it was reunited again in the 1890s it was henceforth known as Larcis-Ducasse. In 1867 it was among the thirty-eight *crus* jointly presented at the Universal Exhibition held in Paris, when it gained a gold medal.

The château is a modest farm but is notable for a well of charm and antiquity.

In my experience the *cru* has for some time produced wines of breed and charm, if sometimes on the light side. The delicious 1970 was in perfect balance by 1985. Recent tastings suggest a marked improvement in consistency and quality. Even the humble 1977 has suppleness, breed and charm. The 1978 was most successful here, with concentration, elegance and personality. The 1979 was a little more backward as are so many 1979s. The 1980 was most attractive, if on the light side, while the 1981 had real depth of flavour, length and fine balance. The 1982 was really exceptional here with layers of flavour, complexity allied to real richness and length – just the sort of middle-priced St Emilion which is so exciting in this vintage. The 1983 has a lot of concentration and tannin, but again the breed shines through so this was another very fine year for Larcis. The 1985 had richness and concentration, and lots of finesse, with lovely fruit; the 1986 seemed less concentrated at first, but after the second winter showed lovely ripe tannins and concentrated rich fruit, very well balanced. These two should make a fascinating comparison in years to come. The beneficial influence of more new oak was very clear in these last vintages.

This is a property which increasingly is making wines which reflect the exceptional position of the vineyard. There are few *crus* outside the *premiers grands crus classés* which can match its breed and sheer style, so that sometimes it bears comparison with its neighbour Pavie, a high compliment these days. Certainly this is now among the leading *grands crus classés*.

CHÂTEAU LARMANDE

Grand Cru Classé. Owners: Le Groupe d'Assurances Mondiale. 18.5 hectares. 8,000 cases. Mer 65%, CF 30%, CS 5%. Second Label: Château des Templiers

Among the *grands crus classés* this is one of the most improved wines in the last decade. The property is old: there were vineyards here by the fifteenth century, and in the mid-eighteenth century this was one of the relatively few vineyards directly run by its owner, the Veuve Champagne, rather than by a share-cropper. It has belonged to the Mèneret-Capdemourlin family since the beginning of this century. The vineyard lies north of the town adjoining Cap-de-Mourlin with fine views towards St Georges, and marks the transition from the *côtes* to the sandy *glacis*, so that there is a variety of soils: chalky clay, sandy clay, and *sables anciens* on iron-pan. The improvements began with the building of the new *cuvier*, equipped with stainless steel vats, in 1974. Then the dynamic Jean-François Mèneret, now assisted by his sons Philippe and Dominique, took charge in 1977. They introduced the use of one-third new oak in the maturation in 1978. Work has also been going on in the vineyard which, apart from being enlarged, has seen an increase in the proportion of Merlot at the expense of the Cabernet Franc, but more especially of the Cabernet Sauvignon. The cellars are under the family house in the middle of the town, and are of great antiquity.

The earliest vintage I have tasted was the 1971, which was rich, and also solid and well structured, but the beginning of the present era of excellence really opens with a fine 1979, which is opulent, rich and vibrant. The present style is, typically, perfumed, full and vibrant on the nose, with a flavour that is full and rich, quite spicy, with an excellent harmony and depth. Above all, the wines stand out from many others because they have that indefinable flair which is easy to see but impossible to describe – not only power and structure, but charm as well. The 1981 and 1982 have followed in the same vein, and the 1983 is especially good for the vintage; then the 1985 is typical and the 1986 looked even better in cask, a genuine *vin de garde*. This *cru* shows the excellence that can be achieved on largely sandy soils.

CHÂTEAU LAROQUE
Grand Cru. Owner: SCA du Château Laroque. Administrator: Madame Roger Droin. 44 hectares. 22,000 cases. Mer 60%, CF 20%, CS 20%

This, one of the largest properties in St Emilion, occupies an exceptional site on the *plateau et côtes* in the commune of St Christophe-des-Bardes. The original château, whose massive tower still dominates today, dates from the eleventh century but has an elegantly classical seventeenth-century front, constructed at the time of Louis XIV. The whole impressive building has been carefully restored, and is now one of the showplaces of the region. Enjalbert cites Laroque as an example of a large medieval estate which, in spite of its apparent advantages, played no part in the viticultural revolution of the eighteenth century. We know that Jean-Charles de Lavie had a large estate here in the eighteenth century, and Belleyme's map shows vines over a large area on the plateau, but no proof has so far emerged that quality wines were produced here. Lavie was President of the Bordeaux Parlement, and his was one of the two *maisons nobles* of St Christophe. During the phylloxera crisis this was a scene of bold action. The proprietor, the Marquis de Roquefort-Lavie, put Paul Bissard from Fonplégade in charge when the vineyard was destroyed. He pursued a policy which was possible only on the large estates which still had much unplanted land, unlike the intensively planted small domain of Haut-St Emilion. So the louse was attacked on one front with carbon disulphide, while on the other new vineyards were planted using American root-stocks. By 1897 the reconstruction was complete and 250 tonneaux were produced. By 1908 this had increased to 325 tonneaux.

In 1964 new fermentation *cuves* were installed in the massive *cuvier*, which is 26 metres long and 16 metres high. The wine is rotated between vats and casks, the *chai* having room for 2,000 barrels. The château has a deserved reputation for making sound and consistent wines. I have found them generally light, fruity and charming, designed for early drinking. The supple 1981 was at its best when five years old; sometimes in bigger years, such as 1982, one notices a certain coarseness. This has been an Alexis Lichine exclusivity for some years.

CHÂTEAU LAROZE

Grand Cru Classé. Owner: Georges Meslin. 28 hectares. 11,000 cases. Mer 50%, CF 40%, CS 10%

This is one of the leading properties of the sandy *glacis* which runs between the end of the St Emilion *côtes* and the *graves* soils just before Pomerol, between the two Mayne *crus* and Yon-Figeac. This is an example of the creation of large vineyards by the nineteenth-century amalgamation of several smaller ones. It was created by the Veuve Gurchy by amalgamating Camus-La-Gomerie and de Lafontaine in 1882 and 1883, when it was given its new name. At the same time the solid and substantial château was built in a park, large by St Emilion standards, together with the well-equipped *chai* and *cuvier*.

The present owners are descendants of this creative lady, a family which has been in the Libourne trade for over two centuries. As it now stands, this is one of the five largest *crus classés* in St Emilion.

In recent years the well-laid-out *cuvier* has been improved by the addition of modern vats, and 20 per cent new oak is used in the maturation. The wines are characterized by their very clean, vivid fresh fruitiness. They are perfumed, supple and very easy to drink. They also mature quite quickly – in three to five years, on average – and are at their best when around five to eight years of age. As delicious, flattering, fruity wines, sold at reasonable prices, these are very worthwhile. Recent vintages have been most consistent: the 1978, 1979, 1980, 1981, 1982, 1983, 1985 and 1986 are all good examples of these vintages, and all but the 1985 and 1986 can now be drunk with pleasure.

CLOS LA MADELEINE

Grand Cru Classé. Owner: Hubert Pistouley. 2 hectares. 8,000 cases. Mer 50%, CF 50%

This minute property lies between La Gaffelière and Canon-La-Gaffelière, on the edge of the *plateau* and on the *côtes* at La Madeleine which takes its name from the monastery, now disappeared, just south of today's town. The wines are carefully made and have all the refinement and breed one would hope for from such a site. They are finely perfumed, having charming fruit, and are light-textured and easy to enjoy. The 1979 and 1981 were both ready to drink in 1984, and are good examples of these years. Most of the wine is sold in Belgium, Denmark and California.

CHÂTEAU MAGDELAINE

Premier Grand Cru Classé B. Owner: Ets J.-P.Moueix. II hectares. 4,000 cases.

Mer 80%, CF 20%

For over two hundred years, the property belonged to the Chatonnet family, although it did not reach its present size until they bought five hectares on the *côtes* from the neighbouring Fonplégade in 1863. The château also dates from the Second Empire. It was acquired in 1953 by Monsieur Jean-Pierre Moueix. It is situated close to the town of St Emilion on the edge of the plateau of St Martin and adjoins Belair on one side. Here the hillside gives way to a small plateau above the Dordogne, and five hectares are on the *côtes*, six on the plateau above. Christian Moueix says that the limestone plateau of St Martin, where it adjoins Belair, gives the finesse, while the slopes below, with their element of clay, give the body. Note the unusually high proportion of Merlot, a Moueix hallmark. The average age of the vines is thirty years. Owing to its small production this fine growth is not as well known as it deserves to be. But under the loving care of Monsieur Moueix, who has done so much to spread the fame of St Emilion and Pomerol through England and the United States, the reputation of the wine has spread further afield. It is clear, however, that Magdelaine has long enjoyed a reputation as one of the finest St Emilions. The seventh edition of Cocks & Féret (1898) speaks in glowing terms of the wine, "brilliant and velvety, strong but incomparably delicate, with an exquisite bouquet". It was already famed for its keeping qualities: the 1865 and "even the 1858" were still preserved at the château, still full of freshness and vigour.

Since 1962 I have seen the wine in every vintage, and only in the disastrous years of 1963, 1965 and 1968 or the mediocre ones of 1969, 1972 and 1974 did it fail to produce with wonderful consistency wines of great breed and distinction. The bouquet, which develops quickly, has great finesse and breed and is delicately perfumed. The colour is brilliant, never very deep but not too light, as Ausone and Belair were in the past. The flavour is unfailingly flattering and charming, always the aristocrat, well balanced, with just enough generosity but great delicacy and length on the palate. The years 1962, 1964, 1966, 1967, 1970, 1971, 1973, 1975, 1976, 1977, 1978, 1979, 1981, 1982, 1983, 1985 and 1986 are all worthy examples of their vintages and of the best of St Emilion. Indeed, recently I have placed the 1975, 1978 and 1982 as among the very best wines of their vintages in St Emilion. In the more difficult years of 1969, 1972 and 1974, honourable wines, above the general level of the year, were made, but they lack the personality and breed of a really good Magdelaine. Recent improvements include the use of fifty per cent new oak. Unfortunately production is so small that the circle of friends that Magdelaine has already won must of necessity remain strictly limited.

CHÂTEAU MATRAS

Grand Cru Classé. Owner: Jean Bernard-Lefèbvre. 18 hectares. 6,000 cases. Mer 33%, CF 33%, CS 33%, Mal 1%

This was first classified in 1969. The name has an interesting origin, as Matras means a crossbowman. At the time of the Hundred Years War, it may be remembered, the French had gone over to the crossbow which fired a heavier and more deadly bolt than the arrow from the traditional longbow favoured by the English. But the longbowman could discharge a number of arrows for every bolt fired by the crossbow because of the time it took to wind back the bow. It was this that gave the small English armies under Edward III and Henry V their superiority over the much larger French armies they encountered at Crécy and at Agincourt. Supposedly the property must have belonged to some retired warrior of that time. The device of a crossbow appears on the label.

The vineyard is on the western *côtes* and their lower slopes, below Tertre-Daugay on one side and L'Angélus on the other. For some years its wine was kept in some unsightly tanks standing beside the *cuvier*, but now the proprietor has bought a small redundant chapel facing Vieux Château Mazerat, and this now serves as the *chai*. In spite of its excellent position, and the fact that the proprietor is an oenologist, the only vintages I have tasted, the 1979 and 1981, were most disappointing. They were marked by an unpleasantly obtrusive minerally flavour, and were coarse and charmless. Apparently a cautionary tale for oenologists. Let us hope that the reorganization of the *chai* will usher in a new era.

CHÂTEAU MAUVEZIN

Grand Cru Classé. Owner: Pierre Cassat. 4 hectares. 2,000 cases. CF 50%, Mer 40%, CS 10%

This small vineyard lies to the east of the town, at the limits of the *plateau calcaire*, between Haut-Sarpe and Balestard. The present owner came here in 1968, and has been responsible for much replanting of what was a very old vineyard, thus increasing yields to more normal levels. A high percentage of new oak is used in the *élevage*. In recent years the wines have won many gold medals, attesting to the quality now being achieved. Most of the small production is sold direct to private buyers, and to the French restaurant trade.

CHÂTEAU MONBOUSQUET

Grand Cru. Owners: Querre family. 30 hectares. 12,000 cases. Mer 50%, CF40%, CS 10%

This is the most important property in the commune of St Sulpice-de-Faleyrens. The soil is probably the best in the commune: the recent gravel deposits are deep here and, as elsewhere, mixed with sand and some blue-veined clay. The origins of the property have been traced back to 1590, and the château was reconstructed in 1584. In the early eighteenth century it passed by marriage to the de Carle family, seigneurs of Château Figeac. But the vineyards were not planted on any scale until the nineteenth century, when the Comte de Vassal-Montviel enlarged them to nearly 40 hectares. However, by the time Daniel Querre bought the property in 1945, it had suffered from many years of neglect and had to be completely reconstructed. The success of his work, and that of his son Alain Querre, may be judged by the reputation of the wine, which is now one of the best-known non-classified wines in St Emilion.

The vinification is carefully controlled and maturation is in cask, with 25 per cent new oak used in the *élevage*. These are attractive, rich, solid but supple wines with a distinctive character, sometimes a hint of tobacco on the nose, and a strong, rather earthy flavour. When compared with an equally well-made wine from the *plateau et côtes*, or from the *graves* and sandy *glacis*, there is a lack of real breed and a certain coarseness, which explain why it has failed in its attempts to become the first *cru* from outside the commune of St Emilion to achieve classification. (As has been explained under the respective entries, Haut-Sarpe and Larcis-Ducasse are outside the St Emilion commune only technically and not geologically.) Nevertheless, this is a highly enjoyable and worthwhile wine which gives pleasure when four or five years old, yet also lasts well in the best vintages. A 1964 was still good when twenty years old.

CHÂTEAU MONTLABERT

Grand Cru. Owner: Société Civile du Château Montlabert. Administrator: Jacques Barrière. 13 hectares. 6,000 cases. Mer 50%, CF 40%, CS 10%

This property is on the sandy *glacis* north-west of the town, near Figeac. Since 1967 it has belonged to a company of which Jacques Barrière is a partner, as well as acting as administrator. This is an old property; we know there were vines here by the mid-eighteenth century. The wines here have a good reputation, and are widely exported, thanks to the efforts of the exclusive distributors, A. and R. Barrière.

CHÂTEAU MOULIN-DU-CADET

Grand Cru Classé. Owner: Ets J.-P. Moueix. 5 hectares. 1,800 cases. Mer 90%, CF 10%

This very small property on the *plateau calcaire* takes its name from an ancient windmill, a witness to the cereal farming practised here until the eighteenth century, and the knoll of Cadet, from which several other nearby *crus* derive their names. It also conveniently adjoins the J.-P. Moueix property of Fonroque, since they also farm this vineyard, which bears all the hallmarks of the impeccable care they take of all their properties, both owned and farmed. Recently a small percentage of new wood has been introduced in the *élevage*. The wines are little known, owing to the small production, but I have been impressed by their perfume, breed and elegance. They tend to be finer and more elegant than those at neighbouring Fonroque, but less powerful and robust.

CHÂTEAU MOULIN-ST GEORGES

Grand Cru. Owner: Alain Vauthier. 6.5 hectares. 2,500 cases. Mer 60%, CF 40%

This small vineyard is on the *côtes* and *pieds de côtes*, just south of the town. The proprietor's family is co-owner of Ausone, together with Madame Dubois-Challon. Fine wines are made here, with real breed and style. The 1970 was very perfumed, with finesse, elegance and charm, in perfect condition when fifteen years old, while the 1982 had a lovely ripe, intense fruit, very attractive, perfumed and fine, when only three years old.

CLOS DE L'ORATOIRE

Grand Cru Classé. Owner: Société Civile Peyreau. Administrator: Michel Boutet.
9.45 hectares. 3,700 cases. Mer 70%, CF 30%

This growth entered the classification in the first revision of 1969, and is run in conjunction with the larger Château Peyreau, of which in reality it forms a part. The whole domain was created in the mid-nineteenth century by the Beylot family, an old firm of Libourne *négociants*, still in existence but more important in the eighteenth and nineteenth centuries than today. They built the Château and reconstructed the vineyard. In those days the property name was spelt Peyraud. The Clos de L'Oratoire consists of that part of the vineyard mostly on the sandy *glacis*, situated north-east and just below Soutard and Haut-Sarpe, close to the boundary with St Christophe-des-Bardes. This was reckoned to be the best portion of Peyreau, and was therefore detached from it, and classified in 1969. The wines are kept in the *chai* of Peyreau, and Michel Boutet, the owner, also acts as *régisseur* at La Tour-Figeac. Twenty-five per cent new wood is now used for the *élevage*. The wines are rich and concentrated, very Merlot in style, with a good depth of flavour. Supple and developing quite quickly, they are typically St Emilion of the more uncomplicated sort. On the other hand, I often notice a certain coarseness coming through in the flavour, and a lack of style in comparison with the best *crus classés*. There can be no doubting the care of the wine-making, as is evidenced at the other properties Michel Boutet is involved in, so one must conclude that it is the soil here. This is a rather moderate *cru classé*.

CHÂTEAU PALAIS-CARDINAL-LA-FUIE

Grand Cru. Owner: Gérard Frétier. 16 hectares. 7,500 cases. Mer 50%, CF 35%, CS 15%

This good wine is on the gravelly sandy terraces of St Sulpice-de-Faleyrens. The wines here are very scented, deliciously fruity and supple, for young drinking when three to four years old. However, in some years of high production, such as 1983, a rather rank, coarse flavour can develop quite quickly, in this case by the time the wine was four years old.

CHÂTEAU PATRIS

Grand Cru. Owner: Michel Querre. 11 hectares. 3,000 cases. Mer 70%, CS 20%, CF 10%

This small *cru* is in the little valley of Mazerat, on the sandy *glacis* just below L'Angélus on the southern slope of the St Emilion *côtes*. The property is run in conjunction with Michel Querre's other *cru* in Pomerol, Château Mazeyres. Two-thirds of the wine is matured in casks, of which one-third are new; the rest is kept in vat. The wines are perfumed, with a pleasantly gamy character developing in bottle; they are relatively light-textured with some nice frank, spicy fruit well matched by tannin. This is good, carefully made wine.

CHÂTEAU PAVIE

Premier Grand Cru Classé B. Owners: Consorts Valette. Administrator: Jean-Paul Valette. 37.5 hectares. 12,000 cases. Mer 55%, CF 25%, CS 20%

This property as it now exists owes much to the labours of Monsieur Ferdinand Bouffard, a Bordeaux *négociant*. The family had begun by buying the small vineyard of La Sable, below Pavie. In 1885 Bouffard bought Pavie itself, increasing his holding to 17 hectares. Shortly after this he bought four small adjoining vineyards, La Pimpinelle, Pavie-Dussaut, Pavie-Pigasse, and one of the two Larcis estates, increasing his domain to 35 hectares. Ferdinand Bouffard was one of the pioneers in the fight against phylloxera. The 1881 edition of Cocks & Féret states that he had organized treatments as soon as the aphids appeared in the mid-1870s, and in 1888 he was awarded a medal in recognition of his successful battle against the pest. The treatment itself was on a massive scale. In the plain below Pavie, the Bouffards had bought the *cru* of Simard, which is crossed by the stream called Fongaband. Using a steam pump and a pipeline of 800 metres to bring the water up the hillside of Pavie, he injected carbon disulphide into the 35 hectares of vineyard. By 1886 the phylloxera had been halted, and over 40 tonneaux were harvested from 17 hectares. Then, from the increased vineyard, he was producing 125 tonneaux by 1893, soon rising to 140, and then 150 by 1898. In 1896 he received the gold medal for the best-kept vineyard in the Gironde, and the new, larger Pavie was firmly established as one of the leading *crus* of St Emilion.

It now belongs to the Valette family, and Jean-Paul Valette is the man in charge. Pavie is easily the largest of the *premiers grands crus* as well as being rather larger than any of the *grands crus classés*. It lies a little beyond the other *premiers grands crus* on a long, gently sloping hillside, capped with a rocky outcrop. Into the cliff face of this hilltop are tunnelled out the extensive caves where the wines of Pavie are kept. There are 22 hectares of vines on this *coteau* facing due south, 7 hectares at the foot of the *coteau*, and 8 hectares on the more sandy plain. It is for this reason that Pavie, for all its charm, has, until recently, lacked the concentration of the leading *crus* of the *plateau et côtes*.

Because of its large production, Pavie was in the past frequently shipped to England in bulk for UK bottling, and so the wine was taken out of the Pavie caves to be stored in the *négociants'* cellars for *élevage* prior to shipment. On several occasions I had the opportunity to observe the difference in the development of such wines stored in a normal Bordeaux *chai* as against those kept in the caves of Pavie, and it was interesting to see how the cooler temperature in the caves slowed down the development and seemed to keep the wine fresher. I have also noticed, however, that this advantage was sometimes dissipated by the château's bottling too late – so that when the château-bottled and English-bottled wines of the same vintage were subsequently compared, the château-bottled example seemed parched and lacking fruit compared with the wine bottled in England; which shows that the timing of the bottling can be just as critical as its *élevage*.

In the past the wines were very supple, elegant and charming, at their best. But they were also inconsistent, so that the general reputation of Pavie was below that of the leading *premiers crus*, as was its price. My two favourite vintages during this uneven period were 1961 and 1971; both showed the breed and charm of Pavie, and they have lasted remarkably well for wines which were delicious to drink from an early age. It is since 1978 that matters have really improved and the reputation of Pavie has steadily climbed. The 1978 itself has more depth and richness than in the past, but the 1979 is even more impressive, and is developing more slowly – in 1987 it was still very youthful in appearance, very rich, and quite tannic. After a rather disappointing 1980, the 1981 shows lovely voluptuous fruit on the nose, depth of flavour, richness and tannin – an outstanding example of the vintage. The 1982 was marvellously opulent, and the 1983 outstandingly successful, its concentrated meaty flavour allied with great stylishness and finesse. The small but frank 1984 is largely made from the two Cabernet grape varieties. The beautiful 1985 is a classic, with great richness and style, while the 1986 grew in structure and power throughout its period in cask. It is perfectly harmonious, and the beauty of flavour, opulence and richness, with lots of tannin and structure behind, allied to extremely vivid fruit and a scent of violets, all add up to a great *vin de garde* – one of the giants of the vintage.

Overall, Pavie is the most improved *premier cru* of the eighties, and now stands with Canon at the head of the category B *premiers crus classés*. One-third new wood is now used, and the results of this, and new equipment in the *cuvier*, together with stricter selection, are all being seen in the extra dimension the wines have acquired. The Valette family have every reason to be pleased with Jean-Paul Valette's stewardship, and the extra investment they have made has been amply rewarded by the higher prices the wines have obtained.

CHÂTEAU PAVIE-DECESSE

Grand Cru Classé. Owners: Valette family. Administrator: Jean-Paul Valette. 9 hectares. 4,500 cases. Mer 65%, CF 20%, CS 15%

The name Decesse derives from the Abbé Desèze, who was proprietor here at the beginning of the nineteenth century. In the 1880s it became incorporated into Pavie under the reorganization of Ferdinand Bouffard, but then was detached again at the turn of the century. In 1970 its ownership again became united with Pavie, when it was bought by the Valette family, but they have kept the vineyard and wine production quite separate. The vineyard is actually on the limestone plateau at the top of the Pavie *côte*, south-east of the town. The small building which incorporates the *cuvier* and *chai* was re-equipped with stainless steel fermentation vats in 1973, and one-third new oak is now used in the *élevage*. This is a fine classic *côtes* wine, with both power and breed. As at Pavie one is conscious of improvements in the vintages of the eighties. I have noticed that one tends to be more conscious of tannin here than with Pavie, because the wine has less opulence and fat, so the underlying structure is more in evidence. After an excellent 1975, with fruit balancing the tannins well, the 1976 is harmonious for the year, perfect drinking by 1987; then the 1978 was, unusually, better than the 1979, and the 1980 was delicious and stylish. Then came an excellent 1981, a 1982 that actually had more alcohol even than the Pavie, and a superb 1983. The 1984 is one of the nicest I have seen in St Emilion. The 1985 combines a full, ripe flavour with a lovely after-taste and real finesse, a classic example of the vintage, while the 1986 has much more concentrated tannins and great richness, making a real *vin de garde*. So Pavie-Decesse is certainly coming out from behind the shadow of Pavie, and is now undoubtedly a very fine wine in its own right, a tribute once more to the very able and dedicated team that Jean-Paul Valette has built up at Pavie.

CHÂTEAU PAVIE-MACQUIN

Grand Cru Classé. Owner: Corre family. 10 hectares. 4,000 cases. Mer 80%, CF 10%, CS 10%

This second Pavie "satellite" owes its name to Monsieur Albert Macquin, who was one of the pioneers of grafting European vines on to American root-stocks, and so played an important part in the reconstruction of the Bordeaux vineyards after the phylloxera. He also owned a vineyard in St Georges-St Emilion, which carries his name, and both are now owned by the Corres. Macquin did not come from Bordeaux, but from northern France. In 1875 he spent a year at the Ecole d'Agriculture in Montpellier studying American root-stocks, and grafting techniques. But when he arrived in Bordeaux he found that the new ideas for combating phylloxera were looked on with suspicion by the Faculty of Science there. So Macquin quickly set up in St Emilion, where the phylloxera had just struck, and was soon established as the leading proponent of grafting the European *cépages* on to American root-stocks. As Enjalbert puts it, "for more than 30 years Macquin was a one-man viticultural industry, the mastermind behind the transformation of the St Emilion vineyards." It is an interesting coincidence that while Bouffard was busy fighting a rear-guard action against phylloxera by preserving his ungrafted old vines on the Côte de Pavie, Macquin at the top of the same *côte* was perfecting the ground-plan for the future.

The vineyard here actually adjoins Pavie-Decesse on the plateau above the Côte de Pavie. The wines are elegant, with vivid fruit, charm and finesse. The quality is very consistent, and of dependable quality, sold at reasonable prices.

CHÂTEAU PAVILLON-CADET

Grand Cru Classé. Owner: Anne Llammas. 3.5 hectares. 750 cases. Mer 50%, CF 50%

This is the smallest and most obscure of the several properties around the knoll of Cadet, north of the town, on the *plateau calcaire* and *côtes*. The wines are matured in cask but, apart from this, information is scant and I have never succeeded in tasting the wine.

CHÂTEAU PETIT-FAURIE-DE-SOUTARD

Grand Cru Classé. Owner: Madame Françoise Capdemourlin. Administrator: Jacques Capdemourlin. 8 hectares. 3,500 cases. Mer 60%, CF 30%, CS 10%

It lies on the *plateau calcaire* and the *côte*, north-east of the town, adjoining Soutard, with Balestard the other side of the road. Faurie is the *lieu-dit* and marks the site of battle in the Hundred Years War. The Aberlen family bought it in 1936, and in 1977 Jacques Capdemourlin (see Balestard-La-Tonnelle and Cap-de-Mourlin) took over the management of the property, which had been inherited by his wife. As at Balestard, Jacques Capdemourlin makes stylish wines here, which have been improving. There is real breed and finesse, but because of the higher limestone element in the soil, the wines are less luscious, though they have more structure and nerve. Particularly good wines were made in 1979, 1981, 1982, 1983 and 1985. The 1986 looked rather irony and austere in cask, but should make an interesting bottle.

CHÂTEAU PIPEAU

Grand Cru. Owner: Pierre Mestreguilhem. 30 hectares. 13,000 cases. Mer 75%, CF 20%, CS 5%

Centred on St Laurent-des-Combes, this large estate is on the *pieds de côtes* and the plain, stretching into the neighbouring communes of St Hippolyte and St Emilion. The varied soil includes calcareous clay, siliceous clay, and some gravelly soil in the St Emilion sector of the vineyard. The aim is to produce supple wines with backbone which age well, and the only example I have seen certainly fulfilled this aim. The 1976 had a lovely velvety fullness and excellent finish when nine years old, a good performance in this vintage, not matched by some quite senior *crus* in the district.

CHÂTEAU PONTET-CLAUZURE

Grand Cru. Owner: Société Civile du Château Le Couvent. 9 hectares. 5,000 cases. CF 48%, Mer 46%, CS 6%

This well-placed *cru* on the *plateau calcaire* and the *pieds de côtes*, close to the town and just to the north of it, was the first of François Marret's purchases, in October 1981, for what has become the Bordeaux offshoot of Marne et Champagne. The improvement can be seen in the contrast between the 1981 and 1983 vintages. In a blind tasting the 1983 did better than some *crus classés* in 1987, with its leafy tobaccco-scented bouquet and opulent rich fruit on the palate. This is very much a *cru* to watch – on this form, it must have a fine future.

CHÂTEAU DE PRESSAC

Grand Cru. Owner: Jean-François Quernin. 35 hectares. 14,000 cases. Mer 75%, CF 20%, CS 24%, Pressac 1%

This is one of the historic châteaux of St Emilion. The fine château has a feudal air about it, and is superbly placed on the edge of the *plateau calcaire* in St Etienne-de-Lisse. The vineyard occupies an exceptional site on the *plateau calcaire* and *côte*. Enjalbert identified Pressac as one of only three feudal châteaux in the region which played an important role in the viticultural revolution in the eighteenth century. Between 1737 and 1747 Vassal de Montviel planted a new vineyard here, using a red grape variety he had brought from his native Quercy. It has been identified as the Auxerrois, but as a result of its first introduction to Bordeaux at this estate, was christened the "Noir de Pressac". We know from Léonard Fontémoing, the leading Libournais *négociant* of the age, that in the mid-eighteenth century it was widely planted by the many growers seeking to improve their vineyards and make great wines. Fontémoing himself planted large areas of Noir de Pressac when planting his new vineyards in Pomerol, between 1735 and 1761. When the Belleyme map was being prepared, around 1764, it showed large areas of vine around Pressac. Later, when it was introduced into the Médoc by the Sieur de Malbec, it acquired the name Malbec by which it is now better known, although the term Noir de Pressac is still used in the Libournais.

The property has belonged to the present owners for two generations. They make their own wine traditionally, using oak vats for the vinification. The wines are of good repute.

CHÂTEAU LE PRIEURÉ

Grand Cru Classé. Owners: SCE Baronne Guichard. 5 hectares. 1,500 cases. Mer 70%, CF 30%

This small vineyard was once Church property, being part of the important vineyard of the Cordeliers or Franciscans. It lies between Trottevieille and Troplong-Mondot on one side, and La Serre and Villemaurine on the other. The owners also have the important Château Siaurac in Lalande de Pomerol, as well as Vray Croix de Gay in Pomerol itself. Twenty-five per cent new wood is now used in the maturation. I have found the few examples I have tasted to be attractive, well made, elegant and on the light side. They have breed but lack the power and concentration of their more famed neighbours.

CHÂTEAU RIPEAU

Grand Cru Classé. Owner: Michel Janoueix de Wilde. 20 hectares. 6,000 cases. Mer 40%, CF 40%, CS 20%

We know from the Belleyme map that there were vines here by the second half of the eighteenth century and that they were surrounded by trees. At this time it was a dependency of Corbin, and by the end of that century 36 out of the 40 *journaux* of the Ripeau *métairie* were under vine (a *journal* was roughly the equivalent of one acre). In 1874 the domain had 15 hectares of vines, 2 hectares of woods and 5 hectares of pasture and parkland, much the same situation as the Belleyme map had shown a century before. By this time the vineyard had also followed Cheval Blanc's lead, and had been drained. The vineyard, entirely on the sandy *glacis*, lies east of Cheval Blanc and south-east of La Dominique, just below Jean-Faure. Since the present owners took over in 1976 the *cuvier* and *chai* have been considerably expanded, and the use of casks in the *élevage* has been increased, including some new oak. In style the wines are deep-flavoured, with a perfumed, spicy bouquet, full-bodied and quite fleshy, but also with a touch of firmness and style. They do not develop as quickly as, say, those of Grand-Corbin-Despagne, and have more nerve and complexity. I particularly like the vigorous 1976 and the fine 1981. After La Dominique, this is probably the best wine in this sector, east of Cheval Blanc, now that the wine-making has improved.

CHÂTEAU ROZIER

Grand Cru. Owner: Jean Saby. 17 hectares. 10,000 cases. Mer 65%, CF and CS 35%

This very good *cru* is situated on the *pieds de côtes* in St Laurent-des-Combes. In a limited acquaintance I have been impressed by the deliciously juicy Merlot fruit of its flavour, combined with a vigour which supports some ageing. Thus the excellent 1981 was still at its delicious peak when six years old.

CHÂTEAU ST GEORGES-CÔTE-PAVIE

Grand Cru Classé. Owner: Jacques Masson. 5.5 hectares. 2,000 cases. Mer 60%, CF 40%

This is a small but well-placed *cru* at the western edge of the Côte de Pavie and its lower slope. La Gaffelière is on the other side, and there are views across to Ausone. The property has belonged to the same family for over a century. The fermentation is in stainless steel, with maturation in cask. The wines are notable for their delicious, easy fruit and marked character and breed. They are high-toned in flavour and delicious to drink when four to seven years old. I found the 1979 scented and opulent, the 1981 more spicy, luscious and stylish. This is just the sort of joyous young St Emilion that is irresistible.

CLOS ST-MARTIN

Grand Cru Classé. Owner: Société Civile des Grandes-Murailles. 3.5 hectares. 1,600 cases. Mer 66%, CF 17%, CS 17%

This tiny vineyard lies in the middle of the *plateau calcaire* only a few minutes' walk from St Emilion, and is surrounded by *premiers grands crus classés*, mainly the two Beauséjours and Canon. Nearby stands the church of the same name, one of the oldest in St Emilion, which gives its name to this plateau to the west of the town.

The property belongs to the same owners as Côte-Baleau (where the *chai* is) and Grandes-Murailles. Because all the wines were made together in the same *chai*, the other two properties lost their classification status in the 1985 revision, only this *cru* retaining its position. The Reiffers family have since been reorganizing their facilities, and the result is to be seen in the splendid 1986, which has a bouquet full of vivid scented fruit, and a flavour of real beauty, great breed, elegant fruit, and balanced tannins.

One is reminded that the vineyard is surrounded by *premiers crus*. Before this, the vintages I have tasted have shown a certain unevenness, with the best examples being rich, opulent, and well structured. The most impressive years were the 1979 and 1982. A very good 1970 was made that developed suppleness and fruit earlier than many wines of this year. One may now await the future with eager anticipation.

CHÂTEAU SANSONNET
Grand Cru Classé. Owner: Francis Robin. 7 hectares. 4,000 cases. Mer 60%, CF 20%, CS 20%

We know that this *cru* was in existence by the mid-eighteenth century. It is on the *plateau calcaire*, east of the town, as its culminating point, and immediately to the north of Trottevieille. There is clay mixed with limestone on a rocky subsoil. The wine is matured in oak. These are firm wines which need time to mature, and rather lack lusciousness. Like those of another neighbour, Haut-Sarpe, they need time to unfold and develop. I found the 1979 had a rather irony flavour, but had fat to balance the firmness, while the 1981 was lighter and less concentrated, with pleasing fruit.

CHÂTEAU LA SERRE
Grand Cru Classé. Owner: Bernard d'Arfeuille. Administrator: Luc d'Arfeuille. 7 hectares. 3,000 cases. Mer 80%, CF 20%

The property is actually a very old one. We know it was farmed by a *bordier*, a small share-cropper, in the mid-eighteenth century. The vineyard is only some 200 metres from the western ramparts of the town, by the Porte Brunet, on the *plateau calcaire*, between Villemaurine and Trottevieille. As well as being proprietors in St Emilion, Pomerol and Fronsac, the d'Arfeuilles are also well-respected Libourne *négociants*.

This is a consistent, well-made wine. Thirty per cent new oak is now used in the *élevage*. It is a wine with depth and flavour, well structured, finely perfumed, with the individuality typical of the wines of the plateau around St Emilion. There is a splendid 1982, resembling a 1947 in its opulence and rich, dense texture, an exceptional wine for this *cru*. The 1983 is more elegant and typical, with its spicy flavour, length and decided charm. The fine 1985 has real concentrated opulence, combined with a firm finish. It should prove an interesting comparison with the

1982 in future years. In contrast the 1986 is much more tannic, but this cannot hide the beauty and length of flavour. Exceptionally, 45 per cent new oak was used, and this should prove a fine *vin de garde*. These vintages of the eighties mark a clear advance for La Serre, which is now a classic example of a *plateau* St Emilion. It should be noted that, confusingly, and with the cavalier spirit sometimes found in the French attitude to the use of its definite article, the château appears in lists as Laserre – however, the label says La Serre.

CHÂTEAU SOUTARD

Grand Cru Classé. Owners: Conte François and Comtesse Isabelle des Ligneris. 28 hectares. 8,000 cases. Mer 60%, CF 35%, CS 5%

This is one of the most beautiful châteaux as well as one of the most distinguished wines. The château itself, built around 1770–80, was planned as the centrepiece for a consolidation of a number of properties belonging to Jean Combert de Faurie, Jurat of St Emilion. Enjalbert calls it a symbol of the Libournais' first Golden Age. On Faurie's death in 1809, it was inherited by his nephew, who sold it in 1811 to Jean Laveau, from whom the present owners are descended. Under his dynamic direction (see also under Grand-Mayne) Soutard became the largest vineyard in St Emilion, producing 100 tonneaux by 1841. There were then 19 hectares of vines around the château itself, and 36 hectares in total. Unfortunately the domain was split up in 1850; the other portion is now known as Petit-Faurie de Soutard.

The wines today are very traditionally made. Thirty per cent new oak is used in the *élevage*, and there is rather long ageing in cask before the wines are bottled. The aim is to make long-keeping, classic wines, and the result is rather uncompromising, and needs patience from the consumer. My own feeling is that sometimes the natural charm and fruit of St Emilion are unnecessarily stifled, and that the wines would benefit from earlier bottling and a more delicate touch – but this is of course a matter of taste. In comparative tastings of young wines, Soutard often suffers for the reasons outlined above. The stylishness is there, but the wines too often seem lean and ungrateful. This stricture was certainly true of the 1979, when six years old. On the other hand the 1981 seemed better balanced, if light. Recently I have also enjoyed the 1955, which still had lots of flavour and life when over thirty years old, although it was thinning a little; and the 1970 has developed and lasted well in its rather lean way. Other past vintages, of which I have good memories are the 1962, 1964 and 1966.

CHÂTEAU TERTRE-DAUGAY
Grand Cru Classé. Owner: Comte Léo de Malet-Roquefort. 16 hectares. 6,000 cases. Mer 60%, CF 30%, CS 10%

The vineyard and château here enjoy a quite exceptional site on the spine of the *plateau calcaire*, south-west of the town. Here, in effect, the *plateau* is extended along a peninsula of land from Magdelaine to the Tertre, on which in the eleventh century once stood a fortress, standing guard over the new town. To the south the hillside falls away sharply from the corniche, with views towards the Dordogne. To the west and north more gentle slopes form the *côte* looking across to L'Angélus. The property was in an appalling state of neglect when Comte Léo de Malet-Roquefort bought it in 1978. From that time until reconstruction of the *cuvier* and *chai* was completed in 1984, the wines were made and kept at La Gaffelière. Tertre-Daugay's vineyard and wines now receive the same care and attention as La Gaffelière, the only difference being that here one-third new wood is used for the *élevage*. The potential for quality is clearly considerable. This should be one of the leading *grands crus classés*. The wines are gloriously perfumed and spicy on the nose, and have a rich, ripe fruitiness and sufficient tannin, a fine, powerful, complex flavour with stylish breed shining through. The 1978 was delicious when young but was really too light and was best drunk several years ago. In contrast the 1979 was much more powerful and vigorous. The 1981 was excellent, while the succulent, luscious 1982 had developed quite complex flavours, and was delicious to drink by 1988. The attractive, vibrant 1986 had less tannin than might have been expected from this vintage, when in cask. The progress being made is clear, and the future for Tertre-Daugay must be exciting.

CHÂTEAU TERTRE-RÔTEBOEUF
Owner: François Mitjavile. 4.5 hectares. 2,000 cases. Mer 80%, CF 20%

This small *cru* is sited on the *côte* of the *plateau calcaire*, above the Côte de Pavie, at its south-eastern point, so that – like Larcis-Ducasse below it – it lies in the commune of St Laurent-des-Combes; but geologically is closely allied to the St Emilion *crus* of the eastern plateau. The Tertre in question is the south-eastern promontory of the plateau, while Rôteboeuf is the *lieu-dit* of the slope beneath the *tertre*. The odd name of Rôteboeuf – roast beef – was acquired in the days when the land was ploughed by oxen, and this steep, south-facing slope was such hot work that they "roasted" while ploughing. Until 1961 the property was simply called Le Tertre, then, following the death of the present owner's father-in-law, the wines were combined with those of neighbouring Bellefont-Belcier until he took charge in 1978. This is a very serious wine, very carefully made, and using 50 per cent new oak since the 1985 vintage. François Mitjavile looks for a touch of over-ripeness in the grapes and uses long vatting to produce rich, long-keeping wines: the 1985 and 1986 show much more dimension as a result of the new oak, which is easily absorbed on account of the richness of the wine. The 1985 has very highlighted glycerol fruitiness and is more tender and flattering than the 1986, and its spiciness is more muted.

The 1986 has 13.6 per cent alcohol and, remarkably, 80 per cent new oak. The unusual feature is the combination of ripeness and high sugars with marked acidity, producing a wine of great character, excellent structure and a marked spiciness. All this goes to show, once more, the immense potential which still exists in the less-known vineyards of the region for producing wines of high quality and individuality.

CHÂTEAU TOINET-FOMBRAUGE
Grand Cru. Owner: Bernard Sierra. 8 hectares. 2,900 cases. Mer 85%, CF 15%
A consistently good *cru* that lies at the base of the north *côte* of St Christophe-des-Bardes, on mostly sandy soils. The wines are rich and full-flavoured, inclined to be soft, but of marked character. They are usually very drinkable after three, or at most four years.

CHÂTEAU LA TOUR-DU-PIN-FIGEAC (BÉLIVIER)
Grand Cru Classé. Owner: GFA Giraud-Bélivier. 10.5 hectares. 4,000 cases. Mer 75%, CF 25%
Until 1882 this *cru* shared a common history with its neighbour of the same name, now belonging to Moueix. But most of the *graves* lie in the Moueix property, and in recent years little has been heard or seen of the Bélivier wines, at a time when the other half of the property has been

improving its already good reputation. The Girauds bought the property from the Béliviers in 1972, but there has been little sign that this change has resulted in better wines. I have found the wines to be robust, but rather coarse and ungainly, in recent tastings.

CHÂTEAU LA TOUR-DU-PIN-FIGEAC (MOUEIX)

Grand Cru Classé. Owners: Héritiers Marcel Moueix. Administrator: Armand Moueix. 9 hectares. 4,000 cases. Mer 60%, CF 30%, Mal and CS 10%

A look at the maps will show that there is a wedge of vineyards bounded on the south side by Figeac and on the east by Cheval Blanc (with the road running between them), and on the north-west by Pomerol. Until 1879 this was still part of Figeac, then in 1882 it was divided into three parts: the two La Tour-du-Pins, and La Tour-Figeac. This, the smallest of the three vineyards, was bought by the A. Moueix family of Château Taillefer, cousins of the better-known J.-P. Moueixs, in 1947. It benefits from a higher proportion of the gravelly outcrop, which is principally found at Figeac and Cheval Blanc, than its two La Tour neighbours, with one-third *graves* and two-thirds sandy *glacis*. Extensive improvements to the *cuvier* and vineyards were made in 1955–6, and one-third new oak is now used in the *elevage*.

These are well-made, consistent wines that are powerful, robust and full-flavoured, yet have style. In recent years I have found that they do consistently well in blind tastings, and in tastings with their neighbours. With La Tour-Figeac and La Dominique, this is now one of the outstanding *crus* in this area adjoining Pomerol. Recently the best vintages here have been the 1978, 1979, 1981; an especially fine 1982, an aromatic but rather tannic 1983; an impressively rich 1985, with great extract and that taste of prunes found in very ripe years; and a 1986 that is scented, solid and powerful, full of ripe tannins, a real *vin de garde*.

CHATEAU LA TOUR-FIGEAC

Grand Cru Classé. Owner: Société Civile du Château La Tour-Figeac. Administrator: Michel Boutet. 13.5 hectares. 6,000 cases. Mer 60%, CF 40%

This is the largest of the three adjoining properties which until 1879 formed part of Figeac. Since 1973 it has been owned by German and French shareholders and managed by Michel Boutet (see Clos de L'Oratoire and Canon-La-Gaffelière). The vineyard has a border with

Pomerol and in addition to the predominant sandy *glacis* (three-quarters) there is a quarter of the precious *graves* which dominate Cheval Blanc and Figeac. One-third new oak is now used in the *élevage*. The wines are scented on the nose, combining power and style, with real length of flavour and surprisingly elegant fruit. I have found recent vintages to be most consistent, performing well in blind tasting and in comparison with their neighbours, placing this property alongside La Tour-du-Pin-Figeac (Moueix) and La Dominique as one of the leading *crus* of the region. Successful recent vintages have been the 1978, 1979, 1980 – the last especially good for the vintage; a 1981 with exceptional depth and power for the vintage; 1982; a very concentrated, tannic 1983, with lovely high-lighted fruit; an unusually strong and tannic 1985; while 1986 seems to have a more distinguished flavour, very tannic certainly, but with fine fruit, a classic *vin de garde*.

CHÂTEAU TRIMOULET

Grand Cru Classé. Owner: Michel Jean. 17 hectares. 8,000–10,000 cases. Mer 60%, CF 20%, CS 15%, Mal 5%

This is one of the relatively large properties on the sandy *glacis*, north-west of the town and near the boundary with St Georges. The soils here are sandy, mixed with clay and traces of iron. In the late eighteenth century it was still being used for growing cereals. It has now belonged to the same family for several generations, and, unusually, 100 per cent new wood is used in the élevage. The wines are principally distributed in France, Belgium and Switzerland.

I have enjoyed mature bottles of this wine in restaurants in France, and always found it attractive and quite stylish. But when young the wines can look rather rustic. Of recent vintages I found the 1979 rather coarse and stalky, but the 1981 was much better, well structured with a pleasantly fruity flavour.

CHÂTEAU TROPLONG-MONDOT

Grand Cru Classé. Owner: Claude Valette. 30 hectares. 15,000 cases. Mer 70%, CF, CS and Mal 30%

This is one of the leading properties in St Emilion and second in size, among the *crus* of the *côtes*, only to its neighbour Pavie. The *lieu-dit* Mondot is one of the oldest in the region, and by the end of the eighteenth century the quality of the wines had achieved a reputation on a level with those from the plateau of St Martin. At this time, and in the early nineteenth century, vineyards at Mondot belonged to the Sèze family, one of St Emilion's leading families of lawyers and clerics. Then Mondot passed to Raymond Troplong, eminent Jurat and son of a Bordeaux magistrate, who became a peer in 1846 and a member of the senate in 1852. He it was who regrouped a number of properties at Mondot to create a domain of 30 hectares, with its château and park placed on the highest point, the knoll of Mondot, which is 107 metres high and commands unrivalled views towards St Emilion and the Dordogne. The name of Troplong was not finally added until the end of the nineteenth century.

It is clear from the situation of the vineyard that it should be one of the leading *crus* of the *plateau et côtes*. It is better sited, for instance, than its neighbour Trottevieille. But the full potential has not been consistently or fully realized. Until the early eighties, although one-third new wood was used, another third of the vintage was kept in vat, with the remainder in old casks. Now the wine is all kept in cask, and the percentage of new wood was increased to 50 per cent for the marvellous 1986 vintage.

Of all the vintages of Troplong-Mondot, I shall always remember the 1928, rich and velvety in texture with a lovely bouquet, a perfectly harmonious wine, unlike so many of that year. It was still marvellous when nearly sixty years old. Another classic is the 1949, with a wonderful spicy, liquorice bouquet, and great concentration and charm, still full of life when nearly forty years old. It easily outshone the Pavie 1961 when they were tasted together in 1982. At a vertical tasting also held that year, the outstanding vintages of Troplong-Mondot were 1970 and 1978. The years between were rather moderate, but after a good 1985 the real breakthrough came with the 1986, surely the most impressive wine made here for many years. It is clear that Troplong-Mondot has the potential to be a *premier cru*; the quality has been there in best vintages over the years, and now that Christine Fabre, Claude Valette's daughter and niece of Jean-Paul Valette at Pavie, is supervising things and seems to be getting the resources to do what is necessary, the future looks bright.

CHÂTEAU TROTTEVIEILLE

Premier Grand Cru Classé B. Owner: Philippe Castéja. 10 hectares. 4,500 cases. Mer 60%, CF 25%, CS 15%

This growth lies on a small hillside on the plateau of St Emilion, below Troplong-Mondot and somewhat away from the other *premiers grands crus*, just to the east of the town. What the wine lacks in delicacy is compensated for in generosity and vigour. Although the situation of the property differs from the other growths, there is no doubting the potential for quality. The property was acquired in 1949 by Monsieur Marcel Borie, then head of the firm Borie-Manoux, and I first came across the wine, as did many Englishmen, I suspect, during the late fifties when Monsieur Borie first began selling his wines in England on a direct basis.

The wine has something of the roundness and body of the wines of the *graves*, but with a bouquet and finesse reminiscent of the *côtes*. It is fleshy in the same way as Gaffelière, yet the style is distinctly different. I once tasted the 1943 in Bordeaux and it was very fine and most distinguished. After that, the 1952, 1955, 1959, 1961, 1962, 1964 and 1966 were all very successful and often outstanding examples of their vintage. Then the wines became disappointingly uneven, too often either coarse and dull, or diluted, a far cry from the great vintages of the fifties. The best wines were a 1970 with a rich, firm after-taste, showing ripeness and balance; a luscious, attractive 1975; a soft, ripe and very supple 1979; a concentrated, powerful 1981, with a firm middle flavour. Then Philippe Castéja took matters in hand, introducing 100 per cent new oak from the 1985 vintage. The difference in breed and concentration between 1982 and 1983, on the one hand, and 1985, 1986 and 1988 on the other is very marked, and Trottevieille is now, once more, a worthy *premier cru*. It is interesting to note that this is the only one of the eleven *premiers cru classés* to be owned by a Bordeaux *négociant*. It is worth mentioning that the label is in the traditional black and gold, once very popular in Bordeaux.

UNION DES PRODUCTEURS DE ST EMILION

Members: 380. Director: Jacques Baugier. 1,150 hectares. Production: 50,000 hectolitres

This is one of the great success stories of the Gironde. It was founded on 4 March 1931, in the dark days of economic depression. In 1932, 6,000 hectolitres were produced; the cellars were enlarged in 1935, and again in 1949, this time to service 34,000 hectolitres. Since then production has risen to some 50,000 hectolitres, or about a quarter of the total production of the St Emilion *appellation*. There are 930 vats for storage and vinification with an average capacity of 250 hectolitres, and 600 new oak casks. Five large refrigeration units were installed just in time to cope with the high temperatures encountered during the 1982 and 1983 harvests. In 1981 a new sterile bottling plant was installed. In 1985 a new underground cellar capable of storing 4 million bottles (333,333 cases) was opened, increasing the total ageing capacity of the cellars to 7 million bottles (583,333 cases).

It is a sign of this *coopérative's* commitment to quality that it should have been founded through the enterprise and dedication of Robert Villepigue, owner at that time of Cadet-Piola, and administrator of Figeac from 1906 to 1929, and that more recently it has been instrumental in raising one of its members, Berliquet, to the status of *grand cru classé* in 1985. At present one-third of its members have *grand cru* status. Many of these are individually made and bottled under their own labels. Such wines are labelled as Mis à la Propriété, not to be confused with Mis au Château.

Among the *grands crus* bottled at the cave are: Château d'Arche (St Emilion), Château du Basque (St Pey-d'Armens), Château Bel-Air Ouÿ (St Etienne-de-Lisse), Château La Boisserie (St Pey-d'Armens), Château La Bonnelle (St Pey-d'Armens), Château Destieux-Berger (St Sulpice-de-Faleyrens), Château Franc-Lartigue (St Sulpice), Château Grangey (St Christophe-des-Bardes), Château Haute-Nauve (St Laurent-des-Combes), Château Haut-Montil (St Sulpice-de-Faleyrens), Château Lamartre (St Etienne-de-Lisse), Château Le Loup (St Christophe-des-Bardes), Château Mauvinon (St Sulpice-de-Faleyrens), Château Paran-Justice (St Etienne-de-Lisse), Château Piney (St Hippolyte), Château Viramière (St Etienne-de-Lisse). Other good *crus* bottled here include: Châteaux Jauma and Yon at St Christophe-des-Bardes, Château Franc-Le-Maine (St Laurent-des-Combes), Châteaux Billerond, Capet-Pailhas and Grand-Bouquey (St Hippolyte), Châteaux Hauts-Moureaux, Le Thibaud and de Lisse (Madame Germaine Nébout) (St Etienne-de-Lisse), Châteaux Gombaud-Méni-chout, Juguet, Lavignère, Le Basque and Pegrouquet (St Pey-d'Armens), Châteaux Labrie, Rouchonne and La Tonnelle (Vignonet), Châteaux Despagnet and Hautes-Versannes (St Sulpice-de-Faleyrens).

Of particular interest are the branded wines sold by the *cooperative*.

These come from properties too small to be sensibly commercialized under their own labels. There are four brands, all entitled to the designation *grand cru*.

Côtes Rocheuses   This again represents the production from 40 hectares of vineyards, producing also around 20,000 cases, but here the vineyards are planted with Merlot 60 per cent, Cabernet Franc 25 per cent and Cabernet Sauvignon 15 per cent. As the name suggests, these vineyards are in the *côtes* areas of the *appellation*. This is a wine which takes longer to develop its richness, and has more power and depth of flavour.

Cuvée Galius   This *marque* was introduced with the 1982 vintage. It represents the production from 9.5 hectares planted with Merlot 60 per cent, Cabernet Franc 30 per cent and Cabernet Sauvignon 10 per cent, and some 5,700 cases are made. The *cuvée* is a special selection of wines aged in cask. The first vintage showed intense, compact fruit, with length of flavour, style and finesse, when three years old. Compared with the Haut Quercus, it tends to be less tannic and to develop more quickly. The first vintage gained the Trophée des Honneurs at the St Emilion Chapitre of 1984, and was the first time a commercial *marque* had gained such an honour; a tribute indeed to the dedication to quality shown at the *coopérative*. The quality and consistency of these branded wines are frequently superior to those of many small *crus* which are château-bottled, and provide an admirable source of sound, typical St Emilion. This is now the oldest and also the largest *coopérative* in the Gironde, and the dynamic management of the *cave* has made a major contribution to the raising of standards in the region in recent years.

Haut Quercus   This is the cream of the *coopérative's* production, other than that which goes out under individual property labels. It represents the yield from only 4.2 hectares at present planted with Merlot 60 per cent and Cabernet Franc/Sauvignon 40 per cent, and only 2,500 cases are being made. *Quercus* is the Latin word for oak, and this wine is matured entirely in new oak. This brand was launched only in 1978, and bears handsome numbered labels designed by local artist Michel Pourteyron, with a different design for each vintage. The examples I have tasted have real intensity of flavour, and are quite tannic, very classic St Emilions which take time to mature. The 1979 vintage won the Prix d'Honneur of the 1985 Chapitre d'Honneur de St Emilion. The quality of this *cuvée* can rival that of many *grands crus classés*.

Royal St Emilion   This represents the production from 40 hectares of vineyards, producing on average 20,000 cases, and planted with Merlot 70 per cent, Cabernet Franc 20 per cent and Cabernet Sauvignon 10 per cent. The properties from which it comes are on the plain. The wines are full-bodied, robust and open-textured, with a certain coarseness typical of their origins, but nevertheless attractive.

VIEUX CHÂTEAU MAZERAT
Grand Cru. Owners: Francis and Christian Gouteyron. II hectares. 6,000 cases.
Mer 60%, CF 30%, CS 10%
This well-placed vineyard is on the *côte* and in the sandy valley of Mazerat, lying just below Berliquet, Canon and Beau-Séjour-Bécot, with Matras on the other side. It is the only unclassified *cru* in this sector just to the west of St Emilion, and doubtless if the wine comes to be put in casks it could easily achieve classification. But at present Monsieur Gouteyron seems perfectly content with things as they are and makes very elegant, delicious wines, full of lively fruit and undoubted *race*. They are entirely matured in vat and drinkable young, but their length and style clearly betray their excellent origins. They have proved very consistent in recent years, very good wines being made in 1979, 1982, 1983, 1985 and 1986. Note that until 1983 part of the production was sold under the name Clos Haut-Mazerat. This has now been discontinued, but the name Château Haut-Mazerat is now used in conjunction with that of Vieux Château Mazerat.

CHÂTEAU VIEUX-SARPE
Grand Cru. Owner: J.-F. Janoueix. 6.5 hectares. 4,000 cases. Mer 70%, CF 20%, CS 10%
This small vineyard lies on the limestone plateau to the east of St Emilion, between Haut-Sarpe and Trottevieille. Since the Janoueix family bought it in 1964, it has been run in tandem with their St Emilion flagship, Haut-Sarpe, receiving the same meticulous attention. Twenty per cent new oak is used in the *élevage*.

The differences in soil between Vieux-Sarpe and Haut-Sarpe are slight, but the vines here are younger and the selection less rigorous. The wines have less body and depth than those of Haut-Sarpe, but have a marked character of their own, with a typical and attractive fruit combined with a structure that enables them to age better than many unclassified St Emilions. Thus the excellent 1981 was still vigorous and fresh when six years old. Excellent examples were also made in 1982, 1985 and 1986.

CHÂTEAU VILLEMAURINE
Grand Cru Classé. Owner: Robert Giraud. 7 hectares. 3,800 cases. Mer 70%, CS 30%

The name is derived from Ville Maure, meaning Moorish city, the name given to the site by local inhabitants in the eighth century, when the Saracens or Moors camped here (see also Rochemorin in Graves). This is now the site of the vineyard, immediately beneath the old ramparts of the town. We know that vines were planted here in the mid-eighteenth century, and that this was one of the vineyards run from Soutard, after Jean Combret de Faurie had regrouped his properties in the 1770s. Later, in the first part of the nineteenth century, it belonged to Jean Laveau (see Soutard and Grand-Mayne). The property was bought in 1970 by the growers and *négociants* Robert Giraud, based at Château Timberlay, but it was not until recently that they undertook the work of restoring what are the largest underground cellars in St Emilion. Apart from housing the *cuvier* and maturing cellar for the wine, these now contain a reception area capable of accommodating 1,500 people. New stainless steel fermentation vats have been installed, and 50 per cent new oak is used for the cask ageing, although this was increased to 100 per cent for the splendid 1983.

In style the wines of Villemaurine tend to be taut and rather firm at first, but with time develop a flavour which has a definite breed and style, though it can be a little lean. Certainly, strenuous efforts are being made to improve quality, as in so many properties, though whether they are helped by the relatively high proportion of Cabernet Sauvignon on this chalky soil, must be open to question. Of the vintages I have tasted, the 1979 was still stylish and firm after five years, the 1978 is fine but a little lean, the 1982 is very perfumed and rich, with a very long, attractive flavour, the 1983 was very tannic and still looked rather tough when four years old, and there is a big, powerful 1986. There is no doubt that Villemaurine can produce fine wines, and if the right balance can be struck, should re-establish its reputation. It is certainly a wine to watch.

CHÂTEAU YON-FIGEAC

Grand Cru Classé. Owners: Vins René Germain. 24 hectares. 7,500 cases. Mer 33.3%, CF 33.3%, CS 33.3%

This is one of the typically large estates of the sandy *glacis*, lying north-west of the town between Laroze and Grand-Barrail-Lamarzelle-Figeac. In spite of the Figeac suffix, the Yon domain touched the old boundaries of Figeac, rather than lay within them. The Lussiez family were owners here for four generations, until selling recently to their distributors Vins René Germain. The wines spend about six months in cask, the rest of the time in vat. The wines are very typical of this sector of the sandy *glacis*, very scented, soft, rich and full-flavoured, with a nice underlying firmness. I have good memories of a delicious 1961; more recently the 1979 had a typically rich middle flavour, with a firm assertive fruit, while the 1981 was lighter in weight, with a clean, refreshing flavour.

THE ST EMILION SATELLITES

To the north and north-east of the St Emilion *appellation*, across the Barbanne, lie the so-called St Emilion satellites. Although some of the *crus* on the plateau have been planted with vines since the eighteenth century, there was a great expansion of vineyards here, just before and during the phylloxera crisis, at which time the St Emilion name became attached to the area, hyphened with the commune names.

The area is typified by its large domains, bigger than those within the St Emilion *appellation* (most of the small *crus* are vinified at the two *coopératives*), and by its distinctive soils. These have been summarized by Enjalbert as having "no sandy *glacis* and no gravel. In the Montagne area the slopes are softened by a covering of calcareous clay, while those of the Lussac and Puisseguin areas have been carved out of the gravelly sand formation known as Sables de Périgord . . . these land types lack the very special vinegrowing qualities of the St Emilion commune's '*terroirs*'." He goes on to observe that: "As far as vines are concerned, the only really good land is on the thin red clayey sand over limestone . . . scattered all over the plateau." Unfortunately, the estates in this area have not in the past rigorously selected these zones for their vineyards; had they done so, much better wines would have resulted. "To the extent that this rule [of selection] has been followed, there are some high quality vineyards fully worthy of inclusion in the St Emilion *appellation*." It should be noted then that these are superior to some of the terroirs of the other communes within the St Emilion *appellation*, especially those on the plain.

Originally there were five *appellations* here, but in 1972 the two small ones of St Georges and Parsac were incorporated in the larger one of Montagne. However, some of the best St Georges domains have continued to exercise their right to use this historic name. The enlarged Montagne *appellation* now covers some 1,500 hectares of vineyards, those of Lussac around 1,000 hectares while Puisseguin has 650 hectares of vines. For simplicity's sake I have listed my personal selection of the best ones, alphabetically, irrespective of *appellation*.

CHÂTEAU BEL-AIR
Lussac-St Emilion. Owners: Roi family. 20 hectares. 10,000 cases. Mer 70%, CF 20%, CS 10%

I have found a lack of consistency in this widely distributed wine. The 1980 was surprisingly vibrant and fruity, lasting well enough to be delicious still when seven years old. The 1981 had good extract, and was still youthful and even a little raw when six years old. But the 1983 was clearly diluted and lacking substance through overproduction, and the 1985 had a coarse, rank flavour.

CHÂTEAU BEL-AIR
Puisseguin-St Emilion. Owner: Robert Adove. 12 hectares. 6,000 cases. Mer 70%, CF 30%

The vineyard is on the *plateau calcaire* north of Puisseguin, at the northern extremity of the *appellation*. The wines are quite dense and concentrated, with good fruit and a firm structure.

CHÂTEAU BELAIR-MONTAIGUILLON
St Georges-St Emilion. Owners: Nadine Pocci and Yannick le Menn. 10 hectares. 4,700 cases. Mer 75%, CF and CS 20%, Mal 5%

This excellent *cru* is situated on one of the highest points in St Georges, facing south towards St Emilion on limestone and clay soils. Really delicious wines are now being made, full of lovely rich, supple fruit and having marked character. This is comparable to a good *grand cru* St Emilion.

CHÂTEAU CALON

Montagne and St Georges-St Emilion. Owner: Jean-Noel Boidron. Montagne vineyard: 35 hectares; 15,000 cases; Mer 70%, CF 15%, CS 13%, Mal 2%. St Georges vineyard: 5 hectares; 2,600 cases; Mer 80%, CF 10% CS 10%

It is possible to find this wine under either of its two *appellations*. Although theoretically it could all now be sold as Montagne, the proprietor has elected to continue to keep the small St Georges vineyard separate. The vineyard is on one of the highest points of the district. The remains of a Gallo-Roman grain silo have been found on the site of the present *chai*. There was once a Greek colony in the region, and the suggestion has been made that as Kalon is the Greek word for beauty, and as the *côte* here is of great natural beauty, this might account for the name. Such a delightful and ingenious solution certainly deserves to be right! The well-made wines have an excellent reputation, and keep well. The ownership is the same as at Corbin-Michotte.

CHÂTEAU CORBIN

Montagne-St Emilion. Owner: Francois Rambaud. 20 hectares. 10,000 cases. Mer 75%, CS 25%

This is now the largest remaining portion of the medieval seigneury of Corbin, although less well known than the Corbin *crus* to the east of Cheval Blanc, the other side of the St Emilion border. I once had a customer who bought large quantities of this wine, because he shared the same name! The wines today are fruity and robust but inclined to be rustic.

CHÂTEAU GUIBEAU

Puisseguin-St Emilion. Owner: Bourbin family. Administrator: Henri-François Bourbin. 41 hectares. 25,000 cases. Mer 66%, CF 17%, CS 17%. Secondary labels: Château Guibeau-la-Fourvieille, Le Vieux Château Guibeau, Château La Fourvieille, Château Les Barrails

This is one of the largest properties in the district, lying on the limestone plateau north-east of Puisseguin. Recently the new generation of the Bourbin family have restored the château and modernized the *cuvier*. The *élevage* is accomplished in cask. These are attractively robust, fruity wines, widely exported and also to be found in many leading restaurants in France. They are comparable to a St Emilion *grand cru*.

CHÂTEAU LAROZE-BAYARD

Montagne-St Emilion. Owners: Laporte family. 30 hectares. 15,000 cases. Mer 70%, CF 15%, CS 15%. Second label: Château Les Tuileries-de-Bayard

This old *cru* lies between Montagne and Puisseguin, and has belonged to the same family since 1700. Bayard is the name of the hamlet here. The wines are matured in *cuve*, and are deep-coloured with vivid, rich fruit allied to plenty of substance and body.

CHÂTEAU DES LAURETS

Montagne-St Emilion. Owner: GFA du Domaine des Laurets et de Malengin. 60 hectares. 30,000 cases. Mer 70%, CF 15%, CS 15%. Secondary labels: Château La Rochette, Château Maison-Rose

Enjalbert has pointed out that this was one of only three old seigneurial châteaux in the St Emilion region to be active in the viticultural revolution in the eighteenth century. At that time it belonged to Pierre Combret de la Nauze, a prominent lawyer with a keen scientific interest in agriculture. In 1762 he was urged by the secretary to the Intendant for Guyenne to put down in writing the agricultural experiments he had been carrying out for the past twenty years. His two main interests were in re-afforestation and vines. He pulled up his existing vines and replanted on the poorest soils, which he considered best suited to good *cépages*. We know he made good red and white wines. He has left detailed accounts of rock-clearing on stony land, as well as of cutting trenches in the limestone bedrock. Belleyme's map confirms the existence of large vineyards here by the 1760s. Combret de la Nauze's brother, Combret de Faurie, did similar pioneer work at Soutard.

The vineyard has retained its position as the largest in the district, and lies on the limestone *plateau et côte* south of Puisseguin and north of Pressac. The wines are attractively fruity but on the light side, at their best for early drinking.

CHÂTEAU LYONNAT

Lussac-St Emilion. Owner: GFA des Vignobles Jean Milhade. 50 hectares. 25,000 cases. Mer 50%, CF 50%. Second label: Château La Rose-Péruchon

This *cru* is cited by Enjalbert as the most northerly example of a vineyard on the limestone plateau with the thin red clayey sand covering which provides the finest vine-growing soil in the St Emilion satellites. It is north-west of Lussac. The wines have long enjoyed an excellent reputation for being consistent and reliable. They are fairly light-textured and stylish, yet keep well. I particularly remember the 1964, which was a great standby on many a restaurant wine list for many a long year. This is comparable to a good St Emilion *grand cru*.

CHÂTEAU MACQUIN-ST GEORGES

St Georges-St Emilion. Owner: François Corre. Administrator: Denis Corre. 30 hectares. 15,000 cases. Mer 70%, CF and CS 30%. Second label: Château Bellonne-St-Georges

This domain was created by A. Macquin out of a portion of the St Georges estate. For an account of the pioneer work he did in reconstructing the vineyards of the Libournais, see under Pavie-Macquin. This was the largest of his three *crus*. The vineyard is well placed on the *côteau* near St Georges. These are attractive, luscious wines, consistent and well made, which are bottled and distributed by J.-P. Moueix. They are well up to the standard of a good St Emilion *grand cru*.

CHÂTEAU MAISON-BLANCHE

Montagne-St Emilion. Owners: Gérard and Françoise Despagne. 30 hectares. 15,000 cases. Mer 40%, CF 30%, CS 30%

This large and well-reputed *cru* is on the *côte* at the north-west extremity of the commune, towards Lussac. Rich, pleasing, attractive wines for early drinking are made here. They should obviously be a "hit" in the United States!

LES PRODUCTIONS RÉUNIES DE PUISSEGUIN ET LUSSAC-ST EMILION

Members: 150. 600 hectares (75% Lussac, 25% Puisseguin). 300,000 cases. Mer 70%, CF and CS 30%

Most of the wine is sold under the *marques* Roc de Lussac and Roc de Puisseguin, but in addition six *crus* in Puisseguin and fifteen in Lussac are separately vinified by the *coopérative* and sold under their own labels. These are supple, attractively fruity wines.

CHÂTEAU DE ROQUES

Puisseguin-St Emilion. Owner: Michel Sublett. 25 hectares. 12,000 cases. Mer 60%, CF and CS 40%. Secondary labels: Château Vieux-Moulin, Château des Aubarèdes, Château Roc du Creuzelat

Jean de Roques, seigneur of Roques, was a friend and companion-in-arms of Henri IV, whose letter to Jean de Roques of 2 February 1590 is a precious witness to the ancient lineage of the domain. The vineyard is on the limestone *plateau et côte*, north of Puisseguin, and beneath the attractive old château there are fine cellars carved out of the limestone. The present proprietor has thoroughly modernized the *cuvier*, and the wines are matured in cask. Robustly fruity, delicious wines are made here. I particularly recall the fine 1975, magnificent by the time it was seven years old. This is wine well up to St Emilion *grand cru* standards.

CHÂTEAU ROUDIER

Montagne-St Emilion. Owner: Jacques Capdemourlin. 30 hectares. 15,000 cases. Mer 60%, CF 25%, CS 15%

This outstanding domain today consistently commands the highest prices of any of the satellite wines on the Bordeaux market. (Château St Georges also sells for high prices, but is sold direct and not on the market.) The vineyard is well placed on the *côte*, facing St Emilion, just to the east of St Georges and south of Montagne. This is under the meticulous management of Jacques Capdemourlin, who also runs Cap-de-Mourlin, Balestard-la-Tonnelle, and Petit-Faurie-de-Soutard; but this is his home. The wines are opulent and scented, with a marvellously rich, luscious, gamy flavour, combining very attractive Merlot fruitiness with a firmness in the background which ensures good maturation. The excellence of the 1979 when six years old was testimony to the serious selection here in a year of big yields, and the outstanding 1982 was better than some *cru classé* St Emilions when five years old. This *cru* is clearly better than many *grands crus* and could certainly aspire to *cru classé* status, were it within the St Emilion *appellation*. This certainly demonstrates the justice of Enjalbert's remarks on soil and selection, quoted in the introduction to this section.

CHÂTEAU ST ANDRÉ-CORBIN

St Georges-St Emilion. Owner: Robert Carré. 25 hectares. 12,000 cases. Mer 75%, CF 20%, CS 5%

For many years now this excellent *cru* has been managed, bottled and distributed by J.-P. Moueix. It lies on the limestone plateau and *côteau*, north-west of St Georges. These are well-balanced wines, with richly spiced fruit on the nose and plenty of charm, full-flavoured and quite rich, developing well in three to four years, but with plenty of substance and character. This is well up to St Emilion *grand cru* standards.

CHÂTEAU ST GEORGES

St Georges-St Emilion. Owner: Monsieur Desbois-Pétrus. 50 hectares. 22,500 cases. Mer 50%, CS 30%, CF 10%, Mal 10%

This is one of the great historic domains of the area, and was cited by Enjalbert as one of the three historic châteaux of the region (des Laurets and Pressac were the others) to play an important role in the viticultural revolution in the eighteenth century. In 1770 Guillaume-Ignace Bouchereau, Trésorier de France (in Aquitaine) took possession of the property – then called Puitinaud, under which name it appears in the Belleyme map – as part of his wife's dowry. He proceeded to invest large sums in his new domain, hoping no doubt to join the ranks of the "*princes des vignes*" of the Médoc. He made a walled enclosure of 50 hectares on the slopes around the château, and the new vineyards were laid out in a geometric pattern, with wide drives converging on the château. It was one of the largest vineyards to be planted in the eighteenth century, as well as one of the most up-to-date in Bordeaux. The final touch came with the château itself. The existing one was an old *manoir*. In 1774 Bouchereau commissioned no less a person than Victor Louis, who was in Bordeaux to build the Grand Théatre, to remodel it. The original building was built round a courtyard, with four corner towers; Louis retained the towers but demolished one side, while rebuilding the eastern side in the classical manner, complete with an imposing flight of steps on the west front and an east front that faces on to the gardens and grounds. It all adds up to one of the most imposing and splendid of Bordeaux's many châteaux, in terms of the building and its site.

During the Revolution the domain was confiscated and sold as a *bien national*. We know that as a result the estate was reduced in size to 85 *journaux*, of which 72 were under vines. (1 *journal* = approximately 1 acre). But the estate recovered well: by 1852 it covered 114 hectares, of which 55 were under vines. The vineyard also made a good recovery from the phylloxera crisis. By 1886 Cabernet Sauvignon on American rootstocks was being planted, and the reconstitution of the vineyard was already in hand, so that production was down to 60 tonneaux. With a change of ownership in 1891, the reconstruction was accelerated, and 250 tonneaux were produced in 1897.

Today this is a very well-run property. Fifty per cent new oak is used in the maturation. The wines are elegant and fine, combining attractive fruit with good structure, giving them a considerable life-span. This is a prime example of a wine that is better than many in the St Emilion *appellation*, and it is hard to imagine that this would not be a *cru classé*, were it within the jurisdiction. As it is, the wines have a great reputation in France, where they are mostly sold by mail order.

CHÂTEAU TOUR-DU-PAS-ST-GEORGES

St Georges-St Emilion Owner: Pascal Delbeck. 15 hectares. 6,500 cases. Mer 50%, CF 35%, CS 15%

This small (by satellite standards) property lies on the south-facing *coteau* of limestone and clay, looking towards St Emilion. As it belonged to Madame Dubois-Challon, it now benefits from the gifted touch of Pascal Delbeck, *régisseur* of Ausone and Belair, who is now making the wines. The only example I have seen, the 1982, was deliciously fruity, but still rather inky and raw when six years old. Clearly this is a wine to watch.

LA TOUR MONT D'OR

Montagne-St Emilion. Members: 60. 160 hectares. 90,000 cases. Mer 80%, CF 10%, CS 10%

This is a good robust wine, typical of the area. Two wines, Château La Picherie and Château Baudron, are sold under their own labels, the rest under the *marque* La Tour Mont d'Or, which won Gold Medals in Paris for the 1981 and 1983 vintages.

CHÂTEAU TOUR-MUSSET

Montagne-St Emilion. Owner: Henri Guiter. Administrator: Maurice Guiter. 25 hectares. 12,000 cases. Mer 50%, CS 50%

This vineyard is on the côteau *north* of Parsac. The unusually high proportion of Cabernet Sauvignon results in wines that are tannic and strong-flavoured for the *appellation*, but they also have attractively projected fruit, so should age well. I have tasted only youthful examples. The family also own a *cru* in St Christophe-des-Bardes – Tour-St Christophe – where they actually live.

The smaller properties are vinified and sold by the two *coopératives* of the area.

CHÂTEAU DES TOURS

Montagne-St Emilion. Owner: Marne et Champagne. 72 hectares. 45,000 cases.
Mer 33.3%, CF 33.3%, CS 33.3%. Second label: Château La Croix-Blanche

This is the largest vineyard in the satellites, and the imposing fourteenth-century château is the largest and most complete medieval château in the Libournais. This is an example of a great feudal domain that played no part in the viticultural revolution of the eighteenth century, but was developed during the great period of prosperity and expansion under the Second Empire (1851–70). At this time it produced 500 tonneaux. During the phylloxera crisis it was managed for a time by A. Macquin (see Pavie-Macquin and Macquin-St Georges).

After the Second World War it was bought by an enterprising *pied-noir*, Louis Yerlès, who re-equipped the *cuvier* with modern concrete fermentation vats. He made large quantities of light-bodied, fruity and pleasant enough wines for early drinking, entirely matured in vat. Then in October 1983 the estate was bought by François Marret for the Marne et Champagne group, and is now the flagship for their Bordeaux group (see Pontet-Clauzure, Le Couvent, Lagrange-de-Lescure, Les Baziliques). The group's head offices are situated here. With well-sited vineyards to the east of Montagne and facing towards St Emilion, it was clear that with investment and selection something better could be produced here. With the 1984 vintage the wines were aged in cask, and the difference was immediately obvious. While the 1983 is soft, ripe and rather flat and one-dimensional, the 1984, although light, has more definition and character, while the 1985 has vivid fruit, structure and fullness. This will certainly be a *cru* to watch in future, and it will be interesting to see whether by using strict selection it is possible to produce wines comparable with the leaders of the *appellation*.

9

Pomerol

In terms of area and of production, Pomerol is, by a fair margin, the smallest of the principal regions of Bordeaux. Its area is rather less than that of Margaux, while its production averages just under 30,000 hecto-litres, roughly comparable with St Julien. But the quality and originality of its wines ensure for Pomerol a place among the great wines of Bordeaux.

Curiously enough, Pomerol did not establish a clear identity and fame for itself until comparatively recently. Early editions of Cocks & Féret treat it as no more than an appendage of St Emilion. The neglect which we noticed of the wines of St Emilion in the nineteenth century extended equally to those of Pomerol. The recognition of the separate personality and excellence of the wines of Pomerol is usually dated from 1878, when Pétrus gained a gold medal at the Paris Exhibition. But even after this, the fame of Pomerol still spread slowly and has continued to be hindered by the small production of the *appellation* in general, as well as by the small yield of many leading growths. In addition, there has never been any classification of Pomerol wines, so that no sort of official guide to the many growths exists.

English writers on Bordeaux tend to have given even less space, pro rata, to Pomerol than to St Emilion, and very few of its growths appear among the many wines they mention and describe. The reputation of Pomerol first seems to have gained a firm footing in Belgium, among the export markets, and it is interesting to note that Georges Thienpont, a Belgian wine merchant, acquired Vieux-Château-Certan in 1924. When I first visited Bordeaux in the early fifties, I was surprised to find that there was considerable interest in and enthusiasm for Pomerol among leading Bordeaux houses such as Calvet and Cruse, but that very few of them were being shipped as yet to England. Certainly most English wine merchants at this time listed hardly any Pomerols, and restaurant wine lists were even more conservative. Among the pioneers during this period who bought and shipped fine Pomerols for their more discerning customers were Ronald Avery of Avery's and Harry Waugh of Harvey's – both firms, of course, based in Bristol. Another curiosity is that Pomerol's leading growth, Pétrus, was virtually unknown in England before the Second World War. Even after that, its reputation was better known than the wine itself, and it was only during the sixties that this great wine was at all widely distributed on the English market.

In fact, the origins of Pomerol are as ancient as any in Bordeaux. It seems certain that it was the Romans who first planted the vine there. After this, the Hospitallers of St John of Jerusalem established a commandery in the Libourne area in the twelfth century. The Church remained an important influence, as can be seen today in many of the names of the various growths. The region suffered considerably from the Hundred Years War, and was slow to recover afterwards.

In the eighteenth century the notables of Libourne were much more interested in developing their Fronsac estates than in Pomerol, whose wines were then known as "Graves de Pomerol". A pioneer was Louis-Léonard Fontémoing at his property at Trochau, in about 1760, and he was followed by Léglise at Fazilleau (L'Evangile), Giraud at Trotanoy, Catherine Conseillan, and then the Fourcauds at La Conseillante and Arnaud at Pétrus. Yet in spite of these tentative beginnings, it was not until after 1850 that Pomerol really even began to establish a definite and separate persona for its wines. Enjalbert explains this in terms of the division of the land into small *métairies*, mainly cereal growing, well into the nineteenth century. The units were mostly in the range of seven to twelve hectares, and paradoxically it was their conversion to vine growing which enabled Pomerol to retain its ancient pattern of landholdings almost intact. While this made early progress slow, when in competition with the much larger estates elsewhere, more recently it has given the most sought-after *crus* a rarity value which has boosted prices to levels above those of comparable wines in St Emilion or Médoc.

Much more recently, Pomerol suffered very severely from the 1956 frost, and many growths had to be largely reconstituted as a result. It was noticeable that many growths had still not sufficiently recovered to give of their best in the 1961 vintage, and usually 1962, and still more 1964, were more generally successful in the region. The grape varieties used and the *encépagement* are similar to those found in St Emilion. The Cabernet Franc (here called "Bouchet") is much more important than the Cabernet Sauvignon, the Malbec (here called Pressac) is more widely used than in the Médoc, while the Merlot now tends to be the most important variety.

It is often conveniently said that the wines of Pomerol are a sort of half-way house between St Emilion and Médoc. But such a description does scant justice to the originality of these wines. In terms of alcohol, they tend to be less powerful than St Emilion but more so than Médoc. The *appellation* requirement is 10.5° as against 11° for simple St Emilion, and 11.5° for the *premiers* and *grands crus classés* and the *grands crus*. In Médoc the minimum is 10° for Médoc and Haut-Médoc, and 10.5° for the communal *appellations* (Margaux, St Julien, etc.). On tasting, one finds Pomerol to have something of the same fullness in the mouth as the St Emilion *graves*, but with less alcohol and more finesse and balance. It is also very noticeable that Pomerol is more tannic than St Emilion; all the best wines tend to have a characteristically firm finish when young, but this tannic mask seems to slide away more rapidly than would be the case in the Médoc. This results in very harmonious wines, enjoyable when comparatively young (say at five years), but nevertheless lasting well. I have often heard it said that Pomerol does not last as long as St Emilion, but I have found no evidence for this assertion. I have drunk good middle-range wines, such as Nenin and L'Enclos, of the 1928 vintage, when thirty to forty years old, and they were still highly enjoyable, while the best growths can certainly do every bit as well. The Pétrus 1895 was as fine when around seventy years old as any of the great Médocs of a similar age.

We have measured the characteristics of Pomerol in familiar terms and compared it to other districts, yet, of course, in the final analysis it is impossible, as with all great wines, to convey in words the essential nuances and subtleties which make this a unique and memorable district. It is impossible to pin down that tantalizing hint of the oriental and exotic about the perfume of a mature Pomerol, or that special savour at once spicy and mellow, yet with a touch of the austere, the power mingled with delicacy, the warmth balanced with an invigorating freshness, which go to make up the flavour. I only hope that those who know and love Pomerol will recognize in these words something of what they too have experienced, and that those who have not will be drawn on to discover these glories for themselves.

Pomerol is the only one of the great red wine districts never to have produced a classification of its wines. This leaves the way clear for the commentator to express his own views and, at the same time of course, to note the various traditions and opinions which exist on the subject.

On one point there is no dispute. Pétrus has for long been recognized as *hors classe* in Pomerol, and in recent years this has been reflected in the price, which is usually similar to, and sometimes higher than that of Cheval Blanc. Thus Pétrus has firmly taken its rightful place among the great first growths of the Gironde. It is after this that the problems begin. Professor Roger (see Bibliography) says that the leading growths after Pétrus are usually accepted as being, in alphabetical order: Certan de May, La Conseillante, L'Evangile, La Fleur-Pétrus, Gazin, Lafleur, Latour à Pomerol, Petit-Village, Trotanoy and Vieux-Château-Certan; with La Conseillante and L'Evangile in a different class from the others. They can, and do, produce wines which on occasion rival the first growths, and the others produce excellent and sometimes great wines, comparable to the second growths of the Médoc. After this there is a larger group, of which the principal examples are Beauregard, Le Bon Pasteur, Certan-Giraud, Clos-René, La Croix, Clos L'Eglise, L'Eglise-Clinet, Le Gay, Lagrange, Nenin and La Pointe, consistently producing wines of good average classified-growth standing. Finally, there is a third group corresponding to the lesser *grands crus classés* in St Emilion and to some of the *grands crus*, or to some lesser-class growths and top *bourgeois* growths of the Médoc.

The real centre of Pomerol lies in a commercial sense in the old town of Libourne. In the Middle Ages this was an important port where wines from the length of the Dordogne were assembled and shipped to England. The town was fortified and frequently changed hands during the Hundred Years War. Today it has the air of a provincial market town, with its grey stone houses and well-laid-out but hardly bustling streets. There is a fine old stone bridge, breached in the last war but well restored, and below the bridge and along the river-front are the *chais* and offices of most of the *négociants* of the region, with the important firm of

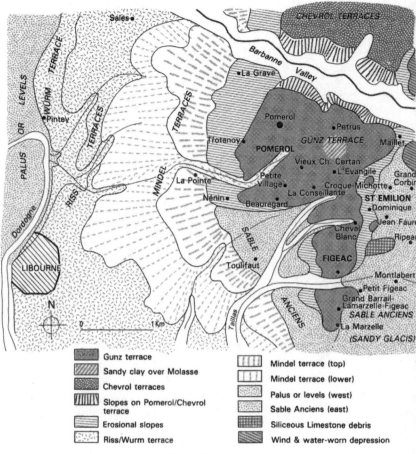

Pomerol: geology

J.-P. Moueix at their head. This is really the only firm of the region which is large and important enough to take its place among the leading Bordeaux merchants. See the introduction to Chapter 8 – St Emilion – for a fuller account of the origins and founding of Libourne.

Pomerol itself is a locality rather than a place. That is to say there is no real village, let alone a town. The church and *mairie* have more vines around them than houses, and one simply finds little groups of houses scattered about, arranged in small hamlets, at Catusseau, Maillet, Cloquet and René. The soils are varied but easily summarized. At the heart of the district is the high plateau or terrace of *graves*. Where the gravel is mixed

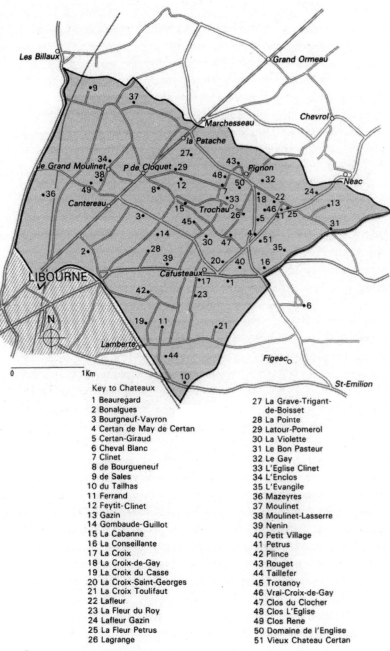

Key to Chateaux

1 Beauregard
2 Bonalgues
3 Bourgneuf-Vayron
4 Certan de May de Certan
5 Certan-Giraud
6 Cheval Blanc
7 Clinet
8 de Bourgueneuf
9 de Sales
10 du Tailhas
11 Ferrand
12 Feytit-Clinet
13 Gazin
14 Gombaude-Guillot
15 La Cabanne
16 La Conseillante
17 La Croix
18 La Croix-de-Gay
19 La Croix du Casse
20 La Croix-Saint-Georges
21 La Croix Toulifaut
22 Lafleur
23 La Fleur du Roy
24 Lafleur Gazin
25 La Fleur Petrus
26 Lagrange

27 La Grave-Trigant-
   de-Boisset
28 La Pointe
29 Latour-Pomerol
30 La Violette
31 Le Bon Pasteur
32 Le Gay
33 L'Eglise Clinet
34 L'Enclos
35 L'Evangile
36 Mazeyres
37 Moulinet
38 Moulinet-Lasserre
39 Nenin
40 Petit Village
41 Petrus
42 Plince
43 Rouget
44 Taillefer
45 Trotanoy
46 Vrai-Croix-de-Gay
47 Clos du Clocher
48 Clos L'Eglise
49 Clos Rene
50 Domaine de l'Englise
51 Vieux Chateau Certan

Pomerol

with clay, it varies in altitude between 40 and 56 metres. It lies south of the Barbanne stream and comprises an area some 1,700 metres square, in the form of a square from which a tongue of similar soil projects southwards into St Emilion, providing an important element in the vineyards of Cheval Blanc and Figeac, as we saw in the last chapter. Surrounding this high terrace and comprising a very narrow strip of land to the north, between the high terrace and the Barbanne, a broader strip to the west, between La Grave and Nenin, and another narrow strip to the south, lie the eroded slopes of the high terrace, consisting of *graves* mixed with blown sand. Then comes the middle terrace consisting again of sandy *graves*, partly sand-covered. This is to the west and south-west of the central plateau. Adjoining this area is the lower part of the middle terrace, which has been considerably eroded, and has a surface smoothed over by sand. Bernard Ginestet refers to this area as "*silico-graveleux*". The above area, with the addition of the "buttonhole" of sandy clay that is Pétrus, an island in the high plateau, comprises the best soils of Pomerol, where all the finest growths are to be found.

In addition, there are three further types of soil, which are of lesser quality. First, a small triangular piece of land to the west of the Tailhas stream is a continuation of the sandy *glacis* which is found in the northwestern sector of St Emilion. Then north of Libourne, along the western boundary of the *appellation*, is the bottom terrace, of sandy soil on recent gravel. The best-known property here is the largest of the *appellation*, Château de Sales. Just north of Libourne this sandy sector is penetrated by a small area of sandy-clayey soil.

I have not mentioned the famous "*crasse de fer*", for so long claimed by so many Pomerol proprietors as present beneath their vineyards, and as the secret weapon which gives their wines a special quality. In over 150 pages (French edition) of exhaustive analysis of the soils and geology of the Libournais, Enjalbert devotes only one paragraph to this topic. He points out that it has regularly been mentioned in successive editions of Cocks & Féret, since the mid-nineteenth century, as present in the sandy areas of St Emilion and Pomerol as well as in the gravelly areas of the terraces of Pomerol. It is a type of iron-pan, that is, a soft ferruginous sandstone, originally formed at the level of the water-table. Usually an iron-pan impedes drainage, but in the sandy *glacis* of St Emilion, and in Pomerol, it is broken up and so discontinuous "forming scattered lens-shaped concretions", thus becoming a positive rather than a negative factor. But as Enjalbert has pointed out, although "there is a fairly constant tradition that sees this *crasse de fer* in a positive light . . . it is not really definitely known how well founded this is". I have certainly observed in some wines a certain character which I have characterized as irony, but whether this can be scientifically proved still seems uncertain. What is clear is that the folklore element remains powerful.

CHÂTEAU BEAUREGARD

Owners: Héritiers Clauzel. 13 hectares. 4,500 cases. Mer 48%, CF 44%, CS 6%, Mal 2%. Second label: Domaine des Douves

This is one of the historic properties of Pomerol, cited by Enjalbert as a prime example of a Pomerol château developed in the first generation of the viticultural revolution. In the eighteenth century it belonged to the Chaussade de Chandos family, friendly rivals of Jacques Kanon in St Emilion (see Château Canon). In 1741 they had one *métairie* with two yokes of oxen and one *bourdieu*, but out of a total of 63 *journaux* (roughly equivalent to 63 acres) only two were under vine. But by 1793 when the property came to be sold there were 6.3 hectares (nearly 18 *journaux*) of vineyard. The buyer was Bonaventure Berthomieu, a wealthy notable of St Emilion. In 1795–7 he built the present château, an imposing edifice on a high terrace, with a moat in front and a courtyard at the back, flanked by the *chai*, all set in grounds of nearly two hectares, quite exceptional for Pomerol. During the nineteenth century it became one of the leading *crus* of the region, and passed into the hands of the Clauzel family in 1920. After the First World War, the château caught the fancy of an American architect, who designed a replica which was built on Long Island, NY, for the Guggenheim family and is known as "Mille-Fleurs".

In style, the wine is rich and full-flavoured; it develops fairly quickly, showing considerable breed and charm. The higher than usual proportion of Cabernet Franc in the vineyard, mirroring that at nearby Figeac and Cheval Blanc, produces a different style of Pomerol from its neighbours. But it is well placed on the high terrace and its southern slope, so there is sand as well as gravel here. Paul Clauzel is the member of the family who now runs the property and lives here. I have good memories of a lovely 1961 that developed relatively quickly to be delicious by 1968. Now a quarter to a third new oak is used in the maturation. The most recent vintage I have tasted was the 1985, which showed great breed with a long, rich flavour and great ripeness in cask.

CHÂTEAU LE BON PASTEUR

Owner: Dupuy-Rolland. Administrator: Michel Rolland. 7 hectares. 3,500 cases. Mer 75%, CF 25%

This has been one of the great success stories of recent years. Since Michel Rolland took over the management in 1978 the wine has been acclaimed in the United States, as well as being found on the wine lists of the greatest Parisian restaurants, such as Maxim's, Robuchon, Taillevent and La Tour d'Argent. The property lies near the village of Maillet, from which most of the neighbouring properties take their name, right on the border with St Emilion in the northeast corner of the *appellation*. It is on the slopes of the high plateau, where the soil is a mixture of gravel, clay and sand. It was bought as a smaller and very modest holding by Michel Rolland's grandparents in 1920, and has gradually been enlarged since, reaching its present size in 1955. Michel Rolland holds the diploma of oenology from Bordeaux University, and now acts as adviser to some of the most prestigious Pomerol *crus*, as well as owning other properties in Lalande de Pomerol, St Emilion, and Fronsac. Small *cuves* of 75 hecto-litres enable him to vinify separately each parcel in his vineyard, using only hand picking. The fermentations are meticulously followed, and the control of temperature is automatic. All this permits the best possible *assemblage*. Unusually, a high percentage of new oak is used, now as much as two-thirds, but on average the wine spends only a year in cask. Michel Rolland is also unusual in bringing his oak direct from the Allier, so that he can then supervise its treatment and conditioning and be sure of its origin.

I have a special fondness for Bon Pasteur, because I can claim to have discovered it well before the days of its fame. I selected the 1970 vintage when at Loudenne and we bottled it in England. Fortunately I kept a few bottles and it is still splendid. My most recent note of September 1988 records a bouquet which was rich but prosaic, but with a dense-textured, rich and powerful flavour that was still youthful, if a shade short, and the fruit was still crisp and clean. The power is now even more underlined by the new oak, and the wine takes time to develop in the big years. Thus the 1982 is concentrated and rich, but also very spicy, exotic and tannic.

But the fruit and charm of the *appellation* is also emphasized. The 1983 is a good example of this, being quite open-textured and already attractive to drink when three years old. But the 1986 was a much bigger wine, and a very good 1987 was also made. This is a very fine *cru* without being quite top-class, but it is now making wines which bring out its potential to the full. The large dose of new oak can be rather dominant at first, but when integrated the overall effect is usually most pleasing.

CHÂTEAU BONALGUE

Owner: Pierre Bourotte. 6.5 hectares. 2,500 cases. Mer 75%, CF and very old Mal 20%, CS 5%. Second label: Château Burgrave

I have never seen this wine in England, but it is now exported to the United States, and I know Pierre Bourotte's excellent Lalande de Pomerol, Château Les-Hautes-Tuileries. The vineyard lies in the extreme south-west of the *appellation*, very near Libourne racecourse, on sandy soils with recent gravel, as distinct from the old gravel of the high plateau. The château was built around 1815 by Antoine Rabioun and it displays the arms of his regiment, for he took part in Napoleon's expedition to Egypt. The Bourotte family bought the property in 1926, and Pierre Bourotte, now assisted by his wife Monique, has had charge since 1961.

The grapes are picked by hand at maximum maturity and fermented in stainless steel *cuves*, installed in 1984. Fifty per cent new oak is now used, with 30 per cent from the previous year, and the rest is kept in vats. The only wines I have tasted were in cask, or just bottled, but the impression is of spicy, scented fruit, with a harmonious, fairly rich, fruity flavour and medium weight. Certainly a wine to watch and likely to make good drinking in five to seven years, since the heavy dose of new oak has to be absorbed.

CHÂTEAU BOURGNEUF-VAYRON

Owners: Charles and Xavier Vayron. 10 hectares. 5,000 cases. Mer 80%, CF 20%

This is a good property on the western slope of the high plateau, beyond Trotanoy. It has belonged to the Vayron family now for six generations, and acquired its present dimensions in 1840 when a vineyard was bought from the Gombault family. The vineyard is in a single piece on gravelly soil with elements of clay. The name of the family has been added to distinguish it from several other *crus* using the name Bourgneuf.

I have found the wines consistently enjoyable over many years. They tend to be light-textured and supple, lacking the concentration of the best *crus* but with a definite breed. There was a delicious 1961 that was already perfect drinking by 1968; the 1966 was very mature but still fresh when sixteen years old. More recently the 1982 was already luscious and delicious when six years old, while the 1983 showed an intense cedary character on the nose and a lovely long, rich, elegant flavour, with succulent fruit and class, when four years old; in cask the 1987 was most impressive, in a higher class than Lafleur-Gazin, and holding its own with Lagrange and Clos l'Eglise. These last two wines suggest to me that there has been an improvement in concentration, and that more power may in future be added to the existing charm and breed.

CHÂTEAU LA CABANNE

Owner: J.-P. Estager. 10 hectares. 5,000 cases. Mer 90%, CF 10%. Second label: Domaine de Compostelle

The curious name derives from the word which has a common root with the English cabin, indicating an extremely simple, indeed lowly, habitation. In the fourteenth century serfs and peasant farmers lived in such isolated dwellings in the countryside, remote from the town. The domain was acquired by the present owner's family in 1951. He was yet another Corrézien (see Moueix and Janoueix) who had made his way to Libourne in the early days of the century. Jean-Pierre Estager took over the property in 1966 and has restored the charming *chartreuse* and modernized the *chai* and *cuvier*. The vineyard itself is on the gravelly western slope of the high terrace and the soil is gravel mixed with clay and a subsoil with a *crasse de fer* (iron-pan).

The vintaging here aims for the maximum maturity of the grapes, with carefully controlled fermentations in stainless steel and lined concrete vats. There is a long vatting for maximum tannic extraction, and selection of *cuves*, with the lighter ones going into the second wine. One-third new oak is used in the maturation. My experience of this wine is really limited to recent vintages in cask, save for the 1964, which was very perfumed, with lovely highlights and depth on the nose, and opulent ripe fruit, still fresh and delicious in 1988. The recent vintages show dense concentrated fruit, which was most attractive in the 1985 and more concentrated and tough in the 1986. The style rather resembles La Croix-de-Gay.

This *cru*, still not well known on export markets, is beginning to make a reputation for itself as a sound, reliable second-tier Pomerol.

CHÂTEAU CERTAN DE MAY

Owner: Madame Odette Barreau-Badar. 5 hectares. 1,750 cases. Mer 65% CF 25%, CS and Mal 10%

Commonly referred to as Certan de May, but its label is more complicated, with the words Château Certan appearing in large script, and below, in a much smaller size, the legend "De May de Certan". And thereby hangs a tale. The family, frequently referred to as Demay, were apparently of Scottish origin, but had lived in France since the Middle Ages and were installed in Pomerol at the end of the sixteenth century, masters of the fief of Certan by royal ordinance. According to local archives, the family were the first to receive royal permission to grow vines in Pomerol, making the original Certan domain, which then encompassed the present Vieux-Château-Certan and Certan-Girau as well as this domain, the oldest *vignoble* in the district. The original domain was broken up during the revolutionary period, finally leaving the de May family with this tiny rump of the original property. The last de May died in 1925, thus finally breaking a connection of over 300 years, and the present proprietors took over.

The vineyard lies between Vieux-Certan, in the direction of the church, and Certan-Giraud, in the very heart of the high plateau, on soil that is predominantly gravel, but with elements of clay. This is the sector around Pétrus, and close to Cheval Blanc, where most of the best Pomerols are to be found. In the past little of the wine was château-bottled, and it had a distinctly rustic character. But new *cuves* were installed in 1976, and Madame Odette Barreau is now assisted by her son Jean-Luc, who attended the viticultural school at Château La Tour-Blanche, and is thus one of the first generation of *vignerons* to have benefited from a technical education. Recent vintages have shown that the wines have an opulent richness and power that are closer in style to Trotanoy than to its more compact neighbour Vieux-Certan. The 1978 was ready to drink by 1988, with a bouquet showing intense and rather minerally fruit, and a flavour which was rich, intense, but supple and thoroughly enjoyable. The 1979 has great character and more opulence, a more massive wine. The 1981 shows more breed than the previous vintages, with lovely scented, highlighted fruit, and a beautiful flavour with a complexity that is really extra for the vintage. The 1982 is altogether more massive, with dense, opulent fruit and strong tannins behind, that suggest a wine that will evolve more slowly than many Pomerols in this year. In contrast the 1983 seems rather coarse, with astringent tannins in the early stages. The 1985 again produced that irony/minerally note on the nose, but the wine is very rich and concentrated with marked individuality, a very positive, assertive style that I find most engaging – but then I adore strong-minded women! The 1986 shows traces of liquorice on the nose and has very rich middle fruit, with liquorice and tannin at the finish: a fascinating contrast with the 1985 for the future. On recent form this famous old château has clearly reclaimed its place among the leading *crus* of Pomerol.

CHÂTEAU CERTAN-GIRAUD
Owner: Domaine Giraud. 6 hectares. 2,000 cases. Mer 70%, CF 30%. Part of crop sold as Certan-Marzelle

The history of this *cru* mirrors that of its neighbours Vieux-Certan and Certan de May, in having been part of the original Certan domain, belonging to the de May family before the Revolution. So the position in the best part of the high plateau, close to Pétrus, is impeccable. It has belonged to the Giraud family, owners of Château Corbin across the border in St Emilion, since 1956. It was at this stage that they added their name to that of Certan. Previously it had been known as Certan-Marzelle, and part of the crop is still sold under this name.

Compared with other leading Pomerols, this *cru* uses very little new oak in the maturation, so that while the wines have the breed and finesse one would expect from the position of the vineyard, there is a certain lack of weight. They are generous and supple in style, finely perfumed, with a tendency to mature relatively quickly. I recall a very attractive 1961. The most recent vintages I have tasted were the 1982, which has a lovely velvety texture and depth of fruit with real *race*, and the 1983, which has lovely opulent ripe fruit, good body and a beguiling flavour, showing real breed. It seemed to mark a real improvement in realizing the true potential of this *cru*. On this form, this is a wine worth following.

CHÂTEAU CLINET

Owner: Georges Audy. 7 hectares. 3,000 cases. Mer 75%, CS 15%, CF 10%

This is an old property. The Belleyme map shows there were vines here in the late eighteenth century. For many years it belonged to the Arnaud family of Pétrus, until it was acquired by the Audys at the beginning of this century. In the 1886 edition of Cocks & Féret, Clinet became one of the very few Pomerols to be dignified with the name of château. The vineyard is situated in a central sector of the high plateau, just north of the church, on deep gravel mixed with some clay. I once had the opportunity of tasting several vintages of the fifties. We actually bought some of them, but I must confess to having been disappointed with them. There was a hardness which did not seem to mellow, and a lack of charm.

This remained the situation until Jean-Michel Arcaute took over the management of the Audy vineyards in the mid-seventies. The rebuilding of Clinet's reputation has been pursued on two fronts. First, the proportion of Merlot in the vineyard has been increased from 60 to 75 per cent, with the Cabernet Sauvignon reduced from 25 to 15 per cent, and the Cabernet Franc from 15 to 10 per cent. Then, in consultation with his oenologist, Michel Rolland, in 1985 Jean-Michel Arcaute introduced a new regime for his wine-making. It is based on four main ideas: harvesting by hand as late as possible to obtain the maximum maturation; a meticulous selection of the berries prior to vinification, long vatting (*cuvaison*) for up to six weeks; and maturation in largely new oak, depending on the characteristics of each year, together with a selection of *cuves* with some being demoted to the second wine, Domaine Ducasse. Just before bottling, I found the 1985 had a fine after-taste, but was rather tough, especially in the context of the year. In contrast the 1986 in cask had a lovely rich middle flavour with real concentration and *race*, and much better-balanced and harmonious tannins. This was easily the best Clinet I have tasted, and on this form Clinet will surely be claiming its rightful place among the leading Pomerols. This was confirmed by the 1987, which had clearly benefited from new oak, and had excellent concentration and a long flavour, together with precisely that charm which was lacking in the past.

CLOS DU CLOCHER

Owner: Ets J.-B. Audy. 6 hectares, 3,000 cases. Mer 80%, CF 20%

This well-known *cru* lies just south of the "new" church of Pomerol, in the centre of the high plateau, on deep gravel mixed with some clay. It was created in 1931 by Jean-Baptiste Audy (Ets J.-B. Audy of Libourne must not be confused with Ets G.A.M. Audy of Château Jonqueyres, owners of Clinet and La Croix-du-Casse), by putting together a number of small plots. There is a long fermentation, and the *assemblage* is done by Michel Rolland (see Château Le Bon Pasteur). Fifty per cent new oak is now used. A bottle of the 1961 tasted in Hong Kong in 1988 had an opulent bouquet with hints of prunes and a certain smokiness; it was very solid and rich with a dry, tannic finish, without much style. The 1980 was attractively spicy, full-flavoured and light-textured, a typical Pomerol, and at its best by 1986, but the 1982 was solid and rather charmless when six years old. More recently there was a promising 1987 in cask, very supple and fruity with a rich middle flavour and good finish. This is well-made, dependable Pomerol, a good second-tier *cru*.

CHÂTEAU LA CONSEILLANTE

Owners: Héritiers Louis Nicolas. Administrator: Bernard Nicolas. 13 hectares. 5,000 cases. Mer 45%, CF 45%, Mal 10%

I shall always remember visiting this chateau for the first time in March 1961, when I was travelling around looking at the very mixed results of 1960. I was deeply impressed by the 1960 here, and noted that this and the Latour were the two best wines I had seen in this vintage. I had not then seen the Pétrus or the La Mission, but time has, I believe, upheld my initial judgement that this was one of the best wines of its year.

The wines of La Conseillante are nearly always among the best three or four wines in Pomerol. They combine concentration and breed on the nose with a flavour of real originality, unctuous and rich yet firm-centred, with marked persistence. With the 1985 vintage they have moved up to 100 per cent new oak, and it is clear that the wines have the richness and power both to absorb and to benefit from it. Bearing in mind the proximity to Cheval Blanc, the high proportion of Cabernet Franc here is worth remarking on; and this is one of the few properties left in the *appellation* with much Malbec left in the vineyard.

La Conseillante was one of a handful of Pomerol properties to establish a reputation in the mid-eighteenth century, at the same time as the leading *crus* of St Emilion were coming to the fore. In 1735 Catherine Conseillan inherited a *métairie* at Belair from her father. She is referred to, rather mysteriously, as a Libourne iron merchant, and apparently had a personality to match. The tax roll of 1741 shows that "la Demoiselle Conseillan" had an estate of 64 *journaux* (23 hectares), but only four *journaux* were under vine. This was a large estate for Pomerol, and in fact resulted from her putting together the *métairie* of La Pipaude with her own Belair. By 1754, like her neighbours at Vieux-Château-Certan and Trotanoy, she was implementing the viticultural revolution. The modest house, for overseeing the harvest, had been built, and, as appears from the Belleyme map, the property was now simply known as La Conseillante. She went to a good deal of trouble to ensure that her carefully assembled estate should not be divided up, and left it to a favourite niece, Marie Despujol, wife of a well-to-do merchant, Jean Fourcaud. They took possession in 1777, and one of their three sons, Pascal, inherited in the early nineteenth century. In the 1830s some high-quality *graves* vineyard was bought from Figeac, then running into difficulties (see under Figeac). Then, in 1871, just before the phylloxera struck, the property was bought by Louis Nicolas. The dreaded aphid arrived here early, in 1875, and the new owner's fight to preserve the old vines at La Conseillante is well documented in the Cocks & Féret of 1897. He began injecting carbon disulphide into the soil in 1878, one of the pioneers of this treatment. He still had 12 hectares in flourishing condition in 1897. At the same time he increased manuring from once in ten years, as had been customary, to once every three years. The results are interesting. In 1874 production was 18 tonneaux, rising to 30 in 1897 and 40 in 1908. The present generation of the family, one a surgeon for many years in Libourne, has maintained and improved its heritage. In 1971 a new *cuvier*, with stainless steel vats, was constructed, and now, since 1985, the final step to 100 per cent new oak has assured La Conseillante's place among the leading Pomerols, at a time of new investment and improvement which is appropriate for Bordeaux's most expensive wines.

The vineyard lies in the best part of the high plateau of Pomerol where it adjoins the St Emilion *graves*, actually opposite Cheval Blanc. Drainage was put in in the mid-nineteenth century, at the same time as at Cheval Blanc. Like several of the best Pomerols, I found it was virtually unknown in England when I first bought it in 1961, although in fact Harry Waugh had bought the 1955 for Harvey's. It is still not as well known or appreciated as its great quality deserves. As with many Pomerols, Belgium has been the first market. The oldest vintage I have tasted was the 1947, rich, powerful and long-lived; this was followed by a good 1955, a 1960 that was one of the best wines of the vintage, and classic examples of the 1961, 1962, 1964 and 1966. In the following decade, the 1970 is rich, assertive and complex, a slow developer, while the 1971 has a full-flavoured spiciness which is complex and many-layered, just coming into its own by 1987. The 1973 was unusually rich for the year. The 1978 has been very slow to develop, still very concentrated, tannic and minerally in 1988. In contrast the 1979 is more opulent, with a marvellously concentrated and complex flavour. The 1980 had exceptional richness for the year, and a lovely flavour, demonstrating again the quality produced here in lesser vintages. This proved a promising prelude to the great vintages of the eighties, with the 1981 showing ripe power on the nose and great breed and lovely fruit allied to power and tannin. The 1982 has great depth and richness of flavour; Dr Nicolas told me it reminded him strongly of the 1947 when just bottled, and it is surely one of the great wines of the vintage. The 1983 has a marked over-ripe character with delicious fruit, but a question mark against its balance and keeping potential. The 1984 maintained the reputation for success in difficult years, with good middle weight and solidity. The 1985 and 1986 are two great years here, the former really massive with beauty of flavour, rich, mellow tannins, and a wonderfully supple, ripe after-taste; the 1986 is more tannic, but also has opulence, and lots of different textures – real complexity. The contrast between the wines should be absorbing in years to come. On this form La Conseillante need not fear comparison with the best in Pomerol – after Pétrus!

CHÂTEAU LA CROIX
Owner: Société Civile J. Janoueix. 14 hectares. 6,100 cases. Mer 60%, CF 20%, CS 20%

This is a very good *cru* in the second tier of Pomerols. It is situated on the southern limits of the high plateau, where the ground begins to fall away. But here in the south, the slope leads not to the middle terrace, as it does to the west, but to the sandy *glacis* and the stream of Toulifaut, with St

Emilion beyond. So the soil here is sandy gravel with an irony subsoil (*machefer*). The vineyard of Nenin lies just to the west, on a slightly lower level, while to the east is Beauregard. The name reflects its history: once the property of the Hospitallers of St John of Jerusalem, it lies on the ancient route to Compostella and the shrine of St James the Apostle, as is witnessed by the stone cross in the vineyard. (Today's "pilgrims" are also sure of a special welcome from the Janoueix family.) In the eighteenth century it belonged to Jean de Sèze, *avocat du Roi*, who was also the proprietor of Berliquet, one of the first great vineyards on the plateau of St Martin at St Emilion.

Since 1960 it has belonged to the Janoueix family (see Haut-Sarpe), noted, like their fellow Corréziens the Moueixs, as both *négociants* and château proprietors. This is their most important Pomerol property, and the centre of their operations here. The remaining 6.5 hectares of their other properties which adjoin La Croix, namely La Croix-St Georges, La Croix-Toulifaut and Clos des Litanies, are dealt with separately. They show how by keeping small parcels of vineyard separate in the mosaic of soils that is Pomerol, wines of contrasting character can be made. It was fortunate that the old vines here, many of them eighty years old, were able to survive the terrible frost of 1956, which devastated so many vineyards in Pomerol. As at their properties in St Emilion, the *maître de chai* here is Paul Cazenave. The meticulously made wines are matured with 25 per cent new oak.

I have found the wines of La Croix to be very well balanced, solid yet attractive, usually enjoyable after four or five years, yet good keepers, acquiring a delicacy and a spicy complexity with age. In 1985 a half-bottle of the 1964 vintage still tasted richly fruity and fresh, while the 1971 had considerable complexity, was spicy with hints of tobacco on the nose, mellow and finely flavoured but with good backbone. The 1978 is exceptional, better than the 1979, with a scent of truffles, gorgeous flavour and extra complexity, while the 1979 was more advanced, ripe, gamy and supple. After a pleasing 1980, the 1981 was attractively perfumed with a hint of prunes, light and rather diffuse in flavour. Here the 1982 and 1983 are surprisingly close in quality. The 1982 has a lovely aroma of bananas (a characteristic often noted in great Cheval Blanc vintages), and is denser in texture but less tannic than the 1983, which has a roasted character on the nose and considerable concentration. Then there is an impressive 1985, with an almost minty character in the bouquet, very rich yet firm-structured, and a very powerful, rich 1986 of considerable potential. These will make a fascinating pair. Once again the superiority of the 1987 on this side of the river comes out in the intense, vivid fruit, and only a hint of weakness at the finish suggests that this is not a top vintage. The consistency over recent years here is impressive, and La Croix has certainly consolidated its position as an excellent middle-of-the-road Pomerol.

CHÂTEAU LA CROIX-DE-GAY

Owner: Noël Raynaud. 11 hectares. 6,000 cases. Mer 80%, CS 15%, CF 5%

The Raynaud family here are truly sons of the soil, being directly descended from the Barraud brothers, who are recorded as having a *métairie* here in 1477. The vineyard is not in a single piece but consists of a mosaic of small parcels, eight in all, on both the high plateau itself and its northern slopes, so there is both gravel mixed with clay and gravel mixed with sand. In the seventies Noël Raynaud bought a parcel of 1.5 hectares near Trotanoy, which significantly improved La Croix-de-Gay. Then, in 1982, it was decided to set aside two parcels of vineyard to make a prestige *cuvée*, La Fleur-de-Gay (see separate entry for details). During the eighties important modifications in both vinification and *élevage* have taken place, under the influence of Professor Pascal Ribéreau-Gayon and Michel Rolland. In 1985 a new horizontal press was installed. The fermentations are carefully controlled, and the *assemblages* done only after a number of tastings. Between 35 and 50 per cent new oak is used now, according to the characteristics of the year, and the cask storage has the advantage of being in an underground cellar – something rather rare in Pomerol.

The changes taking place here are easily followed in the recent vintages. Originally the wines were simply spicy and stylish, but rather lightweight and lacking in concentration. Now the concentration is there, and these are no longer simply supple, fruity, early-drinking wines. Thus the 1981 has a lovely cedary tobacco spiciness on the nose, and a certain raw gaminess about the full, mellow flavour, but was only medium-weight and quite ready to drink when six years old. At the same age the 1982 was firmer at the finish, but the fruit was already mellow, and it lacked the power of the best 1982s. The 1985 is clearly richer and fuller-bodied, without in any way sacrificing the fruit, and the 1986 – with, exceptionally, 80 per cent new oak – combines supple middle fruit with a firm, concentrated tannic finish, promising to be the best La Croix-de-Gay yet. Even the 1987 seems spicy and concentrated. So, the picture of progress here is very positive.

CHÂTEAU LA CROIX-DU-CASSE
Owner: Ets G. A. M. Audy. 9 hectares. 4,500 cases. Mer 60%, CF 40%

I remember being delighted by the sheer beauty and exuberance of the first sample of this *cru* I ever saw, the 1962. The vineyard lies in the south of the *appellation*, north of Taillefer and close to the railway line, on the middle terrace with gravel and *sables anciens* and some *crasse de fer*, or iron-pan, in the subsoil. The management is the same as for Clinet, but the wines are totally different. Here the aim is to preserve and develop the sheer seductive charm of the wine, so the fermentations are shorter and only one-third, instead of 50 per cent, new oak is used. The resulting wines are beautifully perfumed and are rich and long-flavoured, with the new oak giving just the right support and highlighting the delicious fruit. A delightful wine for early to medium-term drinking.

CHÂTEAU LA CROIX-ST GEORGES
Owner: Société Civile J. Janoueix. 4 hectares. 2,500 cases. Mer 60%, CF 20%, CS 20%

This vineyard is run in conjunction with the Janoueixs' largest Pomerol property, La Croix. The main difference is that the vineyard is on the main high plateau of Pomerol, while most of La Croix is on the slope of the plateau, so there is more gravel here. In addition, the wines are younger and there is slightly more Merlot. The wines are quite distinct when tasted side by side, with the St Georges being more supple and less tannic, more immediately flattering than La Croix, and it is more *fin*. I preferred the 1981 and 1979 St Georges, but in 1980 it was the other way round. In 1985 the St Georges had more richness and opulence, but less structure and firmness than La Croix. Another good example of the wisdom of keeping small vineyards separate in the conditions of Pomerol, with its mosaic of shifting soil patterns.

CHÂTEAU LA CROIX-TOULIFAUT

Owner: Société Civile J. Janoueix. 1.5 hectares. 1,000 cases. Mer 100%

Again, exactly the same management as for La Croix, the Janoueixs' major Pomerol property. This tiny vineyard lies south of Beauregard and east of the stream of Toulifaut which mark the boundary with St Emilion, with La Tour-du-Pin-Figeac on the other side. The soil is the same *sables anciens* as is found in St Emilion, with the *crasse de fer* underneath. The wine is kept entirely in new oak for nine months, then in old casks and *cuves*. The resulting wines are deep-coloured and show concentrated fruit and a dense, powerful texture. I found the 1983 much more tannic than La Croix, and austere, but the 1985 seemed richer and more attractive, but still firm. These are the sort of wines that need five or six years to come into harmony.

DOMAINE DE L'EGLISE

Owners: Philippe Castéja and Madame Peter Preben Hansen. 7 hectares. 3,500 cases. Mer 85%, CF 10%, CS 5%

The name and the cross on the label remind us that this was part of the domain of the Knights Hospitallers of St John until the Revolution, when it was sold off as a *bien national*. The vineyard, in three parcels, faces the cemetery at one of the highest points of the high plateau, on deep gravel with strong traces of iron in the subsoil – the famous *crasse de fer*. The vineyard was severely damaged by the 1956 frost, and when Emile Castéja bought the property in 1972 for his son Philippe and daughter (married to a Danish banker) there was still much to do in the vineyard. His Borie-Manoux *négociant* company had for some years distributed the wine on an exclusive basis.

Like those of its neighbour, Clos L'Eglise, the wines here have tended to be rather light and elegant in style, perfumed and fine. A good example was the 1971, still rich and full-flavoured, but soft and elegant when eleven years old. But recently Philippe Castéja has been taking matters in hand. After a fairly typical 1985, supple and charming but lacking in concentration, the 1986 has massively concentrated fruit and richness, most impressive and on quite another level. Then the 1987, with as much as 45 per cent new oak, is very solid and rich, with a lovely flavour and lots of substance, an impressive portent for the future. Clearly the Castéjas have no intention of being left behind in the competition to raise standards and reputations in Pomerol. In deference to the American market, where these things are not always understood, a discreet "Château du" has now been added to the traditional Domaine de L'Eglise, just in case someone should think a *domaine* inferior to a château. Let us hope Chevalier will keep its nerve!

CLOS L'EGLISE

Owners: Moreau family. Administrators: Michel and Francis Moreau. 6 hectares. 1,750 cases. Mer 55%, CF 20%, CS 25%

This property lies just on the other side of the cemetery to L'Eglise-Clinet. Until 1978 there were only four hectares in one piece, surrounding the château, a small eighteenth-century building now transformed into the *chai*. Then two small parcels were added, bringing it up to its present size. So the vineyard is on the high plateau, where the predominantly gravelly soil is mixed with some sand. Stainless steel fermentation vats were introduced in 1983. A small percentage of new oak is now used. At its best, this can be a very fine wine, rather more delicate than some Pomerols, with a lovely bouquet. The 1964 and 1966 were especially good, and more recently the 1978 was opulent, scented and very evolved, with a lovely soft ripe flavour, but absolutely at its best when seven years old. The 1979 seemed to have less breed, but was also soft, ripe and very quick-developing. The 1981 had more firmness, again a fine bouquet, but was a shade dry at the finish, and still needing a little longer by 1988: a good wine but without flair. The 1982 shows some evidence of over-cropping and is rather dry. It was about this time that J.-P. Moueix began to take an interest in the wine – they now sell it exclusively – and the effect of their advice and assistance was certainly clear in the 1987. Again there was the scented fruit on the nose, only now more highlighted, but there was also a depth and substance to the flavour, and firm tannins to support the ample fruit. So this is yet another well-placed Pomerol *cru* which is beginning to develop its real potential, certainly a wine for the nineties.

CHÂTEAU L'EGLISE-CLINET

Owner: Denis Durantou. 4.5 hectares. 1,850 cases. Mer 60%, CF 30%, Mal 10%

No fewer than six Pomerol *crus* incorporate "L'Eglise" in their names. This one overlooks the cemetery, but when the very modest house was built, around 1850, it adjoined the Romanesque church of the Knights Hospitallers of St John, unfortunately demolished as unsafe at the end of the century. Now the new church is a little further away. For a number of years Madame Durantou had the property farmed for her by Pierre Lasserre of Clos-René; now her son Denis Durantou has taken over. The family were certainly fortunate to have found such a dedicated wine-maker to run the property, and under Pierre Lasserre the reputation of L'Eglise-Clinet grew steadily. Now Denis Durantou is following success-fully in his footsteps.

The vineyard here is well placed on the deep gravel of the high plateau. The property was especially fortunate in preserving its old vines in the wake of the terrible 1956 frost. It was decided to leave them to see if they might recover, and not to pull them up prematurely as happened at some properties. Most of them recovered, so that today the vineyard has more old vines than most of its neighbours; this has been an impor-tant factor in the high quality of its wines, and gives them their rich, con-centrated character. One-third new oak is now used. The wines develop a marvellous raw gaminess on the nose and are ample and rich-textured, very harmonious; altogether very classic Pomerol. Fine examples were made in 1978, 1979, 1981, 1982 and 1983. The first vintages made by Denis Durantou seem to have won even greater acclaim. Unfortunately this is not a wine which is easy to find.

CHÂTEAU L'ENCLOS

Owner: Madame Carteau. Administrator: Madame Marc. 10.5 hectares. 3,200 cases. Mer 80%, CF 19.75%, Mal 0.25%

I shall always remember this wine for its wonderful 1929. The examples I saw were bottled by Calvet, and were for some years on the list at the Bell at Aston Clinton. This was just the sort of wine with which Gerry Harris would delight his guests in the fifties when he was building up his reputation. It was velvety and delicious, a real elixir, which remained fresh and charming to the end.

The château and most of the vineyard lie on the far side of the N89 Libourne–Périgueux road. This is the area of that lower part of the middle terrace which has been considerably eroded, and has a surface smoothed over by sand, often referred to as *silico-graveleux*. It has belonged now to the same family for over a century. Its reputation is still good, and it is still a great favourite in Holland, where it is often bought by the Royal Family and used to entertain their guests on state occasions. In style the wines are rather similar to those of its neighbour Clos René, dense-textured, succulent and fruity, enjoyable young, but also with the capacity to age. The fine 1982 is a good example of this, with its lovely exotic over-ripe fruit, already enjoyable and attractive by 1989.

CHÂTEAU L'EVANGILE
Owners: Héritiers P. Ducasse and Domaines Rothschild. 13 hectares. 4,500 cases. Mer 65%, CF 35%

Considering that this is one of the largest and finest *crus* on the high plateau of Pomerol, it is surprising it is not better known on the British market. Perhaps it has something to do with our seeming reluctance to pay the high prices which such wines now command. This was one of the handful of *crus* to establish itself in the eighteenth century. Then called Fazilleau, it was developed by the Léglise family, who had a 13-hectare *métairie* here. In 1741 and 1754 there is also mention of a *bordier* here, in charge of a small area of vines. The Belleyme map, researched between 1764 and 1774, shows vines clustered around the house, and clearly Léglise was gradually extending the vineyard at this time, as were his neighbours at La Conseillante and Vieux-Certan. In the nineteenth century the notary Isabert changed its name to the more flattering one of L'Evangile, following the path set by Arnaud at Pétrus. The Chaperon family became owners during the Second Empire and built the present château and laid out the small park. The house is substantial for this part of Pomerol. The Ducasse family have been owners since 1862.

The vineyard is marvellously placed between Pétrus, La Conseillante, Vieux-Certan and Cheval Blanc. It shares with Vieux-Certan the distinction of having some of the famous "buttonhole" of clay, of which Pétrus has the lion's share. Here there is 30 per cent clay (about four hectares), with the rest being *graves*, or gravel. In spite of this the wines here have always seemed to me to resemble more closely those of La Conseillante than those of Vieux-Certan. But the proportion of Merlot here is higher than at either of its neighbours, and this and the use of the submerged-cap system of vinification give the wine exceptional colour and a rather massive, chewy texture which is quite distinctive. Since the death of her husband in 1984, Madame Louise Ducasse has been in charge. In 1990 the other shareholders sold to Domaines Rothschild.

Cocks & Féret has consistently placed this *cru* high in its own hierarchy, uninhibited by any official classification. It was placed third in the 1908 edition, and then second in the 1982 one. Personally I doubt the usefulness or validity of this sort of approach. There is no doubting the great potential of L'Evangile in terms of its soil, or the fact that it has not been as consistent as some of its neighbours in actually realizing this potential to the full. Vieux-Certan, La Conseillante and L'Evangile are all capable of producing great wines of marked individuality. In some vintages one may rise above another, but generally speaking they are all on the same high scale of excellence. Generally the wines here need time to evolve. The splendid 1964, like Pétrus, has been very slow to develop. There were very fine wines in 1966, 1970 and 1971. When I first compared the 1978 with Trotanoy in 1983, I thought it more powerful, with some firmness at the finish, but when the comparison was done again in 1988 Trotanoy was clearly better, and was taking longer to develop. I also preferred La Conseillante and Vieux-Certan at this stage. The 1979 was very opulent and open-textured, but with great concentration and fat covering the tannin; very much on a level with Trotanoy, although the style of the two wines is very different, with the Trotanoy having a more compact flavour. A delicious 1980 and a fine 1981 were followed by the marvellous 1982 vintage, providing one of the few occasions when I have had the opportunity of comparing this *cru* side by side with La Conseillante, Trotanoy and La Fleur-Pétrus at an early stage. Then it was very exotic, rich and concentrated, really massive and impressive, on the same level as La Fleur-Pétrus and, surprisingly, better than Trotanoy. But La Conseillante was the best of the lot. The 1983 is a great success, rich, chewy, yet complex. Since Madame Ducasse took charge things seem to have improved, if anything, certainly to judge from the sumptuous 1985, although the 1986 lacks concentration. The honourable 1987 was followed by a rich, stylish 1988 and an exceptional 1989.

CHÂTEAU FEYTIT-CLINET
Owners: Successeurs Tane-Domergue. Administrator: Ets J.-P. Moueix. 7 hectares. 3,000 cases. Mer 85%, CF 15%
This property is on the north-western slope of the high plateau, on

gravelly soil mixed with sand. Since 1966 it has been farmed and distributed by J.-P. Moueix, so enjoys all the advantages of their organization, especially as far as the vineyard and the wine-making are concerned. While the wine is all plummy fruit on the nose, the flavour is more elegant than one expects, with length and a firm finish. I was very impressed by the fine 1979, and the 1982 is most attractive, full of ripe fruit and charm, delicious when six years old. More recently the 1986 has lovely vivid fruit and an intense flavour while being light in body, and the combination of fruit, charm and an extrovert personality also comes through in the 1987.

CHÂTEAU LA FLEUR-DE-GAY

Owners: Raynaud family. 1.75 hectares. 800 to 1,000 cases. Mer 100%

In 1982 the Raynaud family, owners of Château La Croix-de-Gay, decided to set aside some vines near Lafleur and Le Gay, in the best part of the high plateau, on deep gravel mixed with clay, to produce a prestige wine made from 100 per cent Merlot. The vinification is quite separate from La Croix-de-Gay, and this *cru* has its own *chai*. Again, the vinification is supervised by Pascal Ribéreau-Gayon and Michel Rolland. Two particularly interesting features are that the fermentation is made at the relatively high temperature of 32°C, and 100 per cent new oak is used. When I tasted the 1986 and 1987 at the end of September 1988, I found the 1986 had very concentrated fruit on the nose, highlighted by new oak, and a marvellous flavour, very rich and concentrated, still marked by the oak but not dried by it, while the 1987 had a concentrated opulent scent, an intense fruit and velvety texture – again a superb wine in the making. I think the style reminds me more of La Fleur-Pétrus than La Fleur, and it is certainly quite different from Le Gay. A good example of the extraordinary richness of the variety to be found within tiny distances in Pomerol, this is likely to become a collector's item in future. With the minute production let us hope that it is drunk with joy and not simply dusted down and looked at!

CHÂTEAU LA FLEUR-PÉTRUS

Owners: J.-P. Moueix. 7.5 hectares. 2,300 cases. Mer 75%, CF 25%

Although this fine *cru* is situated only just the other side of the road from Pétrus, the soil is quite different. The vineyard lies on the northeast edge of the high plateau where the soil is particularly stony, with large gravel but no clay or sand. The resulting wines are less opulent and massive than the leading *crus* of the high plateau, but make up for this with an exceptionally perfumed bouquet and great elegance and power of flavour, which reveal great breed. It has been part of the J.-P. Moueix empire since 1952, and is certainly the finest *cru* on this type of soil, and must be ranked alongside the great wines of the true high plateau. There is an extraordinary label which might suggest it belonged to some private shipping company, but it would be a shame to serve it even on the most luxurious of yachts. One-third new oak is used in the maturation, and the estate benefits from the meticulous care afforded to all the Moueix properties by the team headed by Christian Moueix and his oenologist Jean-Claude Berrouet. The only pre-Moueix vintage I have tasted was 1948: it had that *rôti* and slightly rustic character of the vintage, but was full of vigour and breed when thirty-two years old. The 1964 was very ripe, luscious and delicious when twenty-two years old. The 1970 was spicy and complex with lovely highlights and marvellously fresh, powerful and youthful when fourteen years old. It outlasted the seductive 1971, a wine of extraordinary beauty when five to eight years old. It is noteworthy that the 1970 was already in prime drinking condition when most wines of this vintage were still closed and awkward. The 1979 is finer than the 1978, with richness, complexity and great quality. The 1981 was surprisingly rich and dense for the year, while the 1982 combines great charm and breed with much tannin and more weight than usual. The 1983 has lots of solid, rich fruit but just lacks something – for once I preferred Latour à Pomerol. But the 1985 is outstanding, if less concentrated than some of its neighbours. There is a marvellous fruit and breed, opulence and depth of flavour. The 1986 has an attractively spicy character and is powerful and more tannic than usual, but it seems to lack the special flair of the 1985.

CHÂTEAU LE GAY

Owner: Marie Robin. Administrator: Ets J.-P. Moueix. 8 hectares. 2,000 cases. Mer 50%, CF and CS 50%

This fine *cru* lies at the northern extremity of the high plateau, on deep gravelly soils. In the eighteenth century this was one of the domains owned by Louis Fontémoing, Libourne *négociant* and pioneer of the viticultural revolution in Pomerol. The two Robin sisters, Thérèse and Marie, inherited this property, where they lived in the summer months, and the smaller but even finer Lafleur, from their father in 1946. They ran the properties while the J.-P. Moueix company distributed them, making them famous far beyond France. This partnership lasted nearly forty years, until Thérèse Robin's death. Now the Moueix team have taken over the wine-making of both properties.

I have always had a special affection for Le Gay, ever since I bought it during the sixties, during my Loudenne period. It has long produced big, dense, firm-textured wines, which can seem rather rustic at first, but keep and improve very well. The excellent 1962 was better than the 1961, while the splendid 1964 has kept its form over many years, and was still full of charm and life with its rich, vividly spicy bouquet, and ample gamy, fruity flavour, when last tasted in late 1988. The 1966 was very nearly as good. The 1970 again has great depth and richness, its powerful gamy flavour proving the perfect foil to grouse when last drunk in 1988. When I compared the 1978 and 1979 in 1983, the 1978 was still rather inky, but very rich, tannic and powerful; better than the 1979 which still had an irony rustic character, intense and very tannic. Clear evidence of how Le Gay needs keeping. Going back to my old notes I find that the 1964 looked pretty tannic and a little crude still when five years old. When six years old, the 1982 still had a strong, assertive flavour, with tannin and power matched by great richness and glycerine. More recently the 1986 was true to form, powerful, rich and irony, tough and tannic. These are classic, old-fashioned *vins de garde*, not to be meddled with in youth but making marvellous mature bottles.

CHÂTEAU GAZIN
Owner: Etienne de Bailliencourt. 20 hectares. 8,300 cases. Mer 80%, CF 15%, CS 5%

This is the largest property on the high plateau of Pomerol, in spite of its having sold five precious hectares to Pétrus in the late 1960s, as a result of inheritance problems. It is also a very old one, being originally a farm belonging to the Knights Hospitallers of St John in the Middle Ages, a fact commemorated on the label. In the late eighteenth century it was bought by the Feuilhade family, one of the pioneers of what Enjalbert has called the viticultural revolution, namely the move from cereal farming to producing quality wine. By the 1840s it was counted among Pomerol's leading *crus*. It has belonged to the Bailliencourt family since 1918.

The wines of Gazin had an established reputation in England well before most other Pomerols, so it is unfortunate that at a time when the fame of Pomerol has much increased, the reputation of this famous old château should be at a low ebb. Recently a determined effort has been made to improve matters, and there is a new *régisseur*, but only a small percentage of new oak is used. At its best the wine is certainly opulent and rich, with an extraordinary vivid and forceful character when young, but too often there is also a certain coarseness of flavour. This is a wine which needs more ageing than some Pomerols.

My first memories of Gazin are of the marvellous 1945, bottled by Alan Sichel. The 1947 was also fine but the 1953 was disappointingly light. Good wines were made in 1962 and especially 1964. The 1970 was powerful and exuberant but rather coarse. More recently the 1978 was a great success, very aromatic and spicy on the nose, with a lovely clean, crisp, minty fruitiness: a classic Pomerol without any of the shortcomings I have mentioned. In contrast the 1979 is opulent and rich but has a coarse after-taste. There is an attractively rich and fine 1980, which lasted well and an attractive 1981. The 1982 has a lovely rich, silky texture and is opulent and stylish, a classic Pomerol, while the 1983 has an opulent flavour and easy, attractive fruit. The 1985 is very concentrated and firm, while 1986 is more austerely tannic. The 1988 has a lovely flavour and rich aftertaste, and is more stylish. The 1989 is massively impressive. There is clearly some way to go before Gazin recovers its lost reputation; but more selection and attention to detail are now being applied, so the real potential is now in view.

CHÂTEAU LA GRAVE-TRIGANT-DE-BOISSET

Owner: Christian Moueix. 8 hectares. 2,500 cases. Mer 90%, CF 10%

This vineyard is indeed on gravel, as the name suggests, the large gravel of the middle terrace of Pomerol, just to the west of the high plateau between it and the Libourne-Périgueux road. The complicated name harks back to the eighteenth-century proprietor, but on the label the name La Grave appears in large characters, with Trigant-de-Boisset in much smaller ones underneath. As from the 1986 vintage the name has been simplified to La Grave. In 1971 it was acquired by Christian Moueix

of Ets J.-P. Moueix, who heads the company team which runs all its vineyards, both owned and farmed. Twenty-five per cent new oak is now used
in the maturation. The wines tend to be quite rich, tannic and fine, but
less spectacular than the leading *crus* – a good second-tier Pomerol. The
combination of stylishness and richness but not opulence is well
illustrated in a fine 1978. The 1979 I find more complex, with an intense
rich ripeness on the nose, a rewarding wine full of interest. The consistency comes out in an admirable 1980, deliciously fruity and enjoyable
by the time it was three years old. The 1981 is also a lightweight, but has
curiously kept its original raw gamy character without filling out or
mellowing after seven years. Not surprisingly the 1982 is on a quite
different plane, with its concentrated aroma and its hint of prunes, rich
unctuous flavour and marvellously opulent after-taste. The 1983 is a
good deal less concentrated, and emphasizes the up-front charm and
fruit, but with less behind. The 1985 is scented, ripe and unctuous, its
gorgeous flavour and opulent fruit showing the real breed this *cru* is
capable of, an outstanding wine for La Grave to set beside the 1982. In
cask, the fine 1986, while lacking the sheer flair of the 1985, was finely
perfumed with a very rich, tannic middle flavour.

CHÂTEAU LAFLEUR
Owner: Marie Robin. Administrator: Ets J.-P. Moueix. 4 hectares. 1,500 cases. Mer
50%, CF 50%

This superb little property is one of the gems of Pomerol. Under the same
ownership as Le Gay just across the road, the vineyard is in a single piece,
adjoining La Fleur-Pétrus, and close to Pétrus and the Certans in the best
sector of the high terrace of Pomerol. This is a good example of the
advantages of keeping even very small properties separate. It would have
been perfectly logical to have put Le Gay and Lafleur together and make
one wine, but the difference between the two when under the same
management shows what would have been lost had this been done. The
soil here has more clay mixed with the gravel than at Le Gay. The Moueix
team moved in to run the property for Marie Robin in 1981, having been
responsible for its distribution for many years, and the reputation of this
cru has never been higher, although with so little wine made, one has to
be lucky as well as rich to find a bottle. The style is all opulent charm
with hints of liquorice, a seamless garment all of a piece. The only old

bottle I have had was the 1955; when over thirty years old it was still quite tannic with a powerful and superb flavour and a fascinatingly strong smell of undergrowth, a great wine by any standards. More recently the 1979 has wonderfully spicy highlights on the nose, and is powerful and tannic, closer in style to Le Gay, at least on the palate. The 1981 has a luscious liquorice character on the nose, which is repeated on the palate with lovely opulent frank fruit, a wine to enjoy now. The 1982 and 1983 are well matched: the 1982 is almost sweet, with a very rich, seamless flavour, opulent concentration and glycerine; while the 1983 is also superb, it again having that liquorice character and a sublime flavour, all richness and opulence. The former is a beautiful wine – but overpowered by the latter, which is exceptional.

CHÂTEAU LAFLEUR-GAZIN

Owner: Maurice Borderie. Administrator: Ets J.-P. Moueix. 7.8 hectares. 3500 cases. Mer 70%, CF 30%

This property lies at the north-eastern limits of the high plateau; part of the vineyard is on the gravelly plateau itself and part on the sandy slopes of the terrace. It is across the road from Gazin and to the east of La Fleur-Pétrus. The present owner is the third generation of the family to own the property, which has come into greater prominence since J.-P. Moueix took over as *métayers* in 1976, so that the team of Christian Moueix and his oenologist Jean-Claude Berrouet are now in charge here. The wines are attractive, increasingly rich, often with an underlying firmness, but just lacking the power and presence of the leading *crus*, lying to the west and south-west; no doubt this is partly because of the higher proportion of Cabernet Franc, itself caused by the sandy nature of part of the vineyard. Thus there was a touch of coarseness in the 1979; the 1982, however, was very ripe and full of fruit and ripe tannins, but dense-textured, while the 1983 was much more supple and fine. The 1985 has a touch of tobacco about the bouquet, with a rich velvety flavour with plenty behind. The 1986 is more tannic and powerful, and will be slower to develop. There is an attractive 1987 with scented yet meaty fruit, a medium-weight wine for early drinking. The last few vintages really seem to be exploiting the full potential of this *cru*.

CHÂTEAU LAGRANGE

Owner: Ets J.-P. Moueix. 8 hectares. 2,600 cases. Mer 90%, CF 10%

This has been a Moueix property since 1959, and is situated in the centre of the high plateau, near the church and adjoining Vray-Croix-de-Gay. Again the production is very small, but the reputation is high. One-third new oak is now being used in the maturation, and the wines have an originality of flavour and definite breed allied to structure and charm, which marks them out as very fine wines. They need time to show their true worth. Thus in 1985 I found the 1978 one-dimensional and rather dull, but three years later it had come out of its chrysalis to become marvellously spicy with a firm, dense-textured flavour – a most impressive bottle. When six years old, the 1982 still had a concentrated, firm flavour with notes of liquorice, but the 1983 was already showing great promise with a very clean, crisp flavour, a spicy fullness and firm tannic finish by early 1988. The 1985 has the depth of flavour and power to produce a fine bottle; the 1986, while perfumed and rich on the nose, has the toughness and tannins of a long-distance runner, a real *vin de garde*.

CHÂTEAU LATOUR À POMEROL

Owner: Madame Lily Lacoste. Administrator: Ets J.-P. Moueix. 8 hectares. 2,400 cases. Mer 80%, CF 20%

This famous property has benefited from its close association with Château Pétrus. It belonged to Madame Loubat, who was responsible for establishing the reputation of Pétrus during and after the Second World War, and was then left to her niece in 1961. She is also co-proprietor of Pétrus. J.-P. Moueix are now *en fermage* here. The vineyard is in two parcels: one on the western side of the high plateau, the other, called "Les Grandes Vignes", near the church of Pomerol on the highest point of the plateau. Twenty-five per cent new oak is now used in the maturation and the vineyard and its harvests receive the same meticulous attention from Christian Moueix and his oenologist Jean-Claude Berrouet as do their own properties. This is a wine which has shown very clear improvements, especially in the last decade. Before then, fine bottles were interspersed with disappointments, and sometimes the lovely wines one tasted in cask were not always translated into great bottles. But right through the seventies there were clear improvements as the Moueix team got to grips with the property, and more recently the improvements have been even more noticeable. Now the wines are characterized by their wonderful perfume and delectable beauty of flavour, and by their power and finesse. I have noted a similarity in style to La Fleur-Pétrus, though with the exception of the marvellous 1983, La Fleur-Pétrus usually has the edge on Latour.

The only really old vintage I have drunk was a memorable 1929, still fresh and vigorous when thirty-five years old. The 1964 was an outstanding example of this very successful Pomerol vintage, and good wines were made in 1971 and 1978 – the latter very fine, one of the top wines of the vintage in Pomerol. The 1979 has real class, with depth; rich-textured with a firm finish, it was still improving when tasted in 1987. There is a concentrated yet stylish 1982, and an opulent 1983 with lots of fat and natural glycerine, and a gorgeous flavour – making it an exceptional wine for the vintage and for the *cru*. The richly spiced 1985 is concentrated with a velvety texture and fine potential, while the 1986 is very dense and tannic in style. The 1987 here is promising, with plenty of substance and richness, and tannins to match. On this record there is no doubting Latour's place today among the leading *crus* of Pomerol.

CLOS DES LITANIES
Owner: J. Janoueix. 0.81 hectares. 400 cases. Mer 100%

The name of this tiny vineyard goes back to the days when the Knights Hospitallers were an important power in Pomerol. In 1514 the Commander of the Order nominated Brother Mathieu Bossuet, a native of the parish, to be curé of St Jean de Pomeyrol. This friar was long revered and remembered by the local people for his sanctity and, because he often walked in this *clos* to recite his breviary, the local *vignerons* took to calling it Les Litanies – a charming example of folk memory.

Janoueix (*see* La Croix) have kept this small *clos*, adjoining their other property, La Croix-Toulifaut, separate, and it is interesting to see the justification for this in the wine. Although both vineyards are planted entirely with Merlot, and matured in new oak, this wine is fruitier and more supple than its more powerful neighbour – yet another example of the complex kaleidoscope of soils found in Pomerol.

CHÂTEAU MAZEYRES

Owner: Société Civile du Château Mazeyres (Querre family). 9 hectares. 5,000 cases. Mer 70%, CF 30%

This property lies at the western extremity of the Pomerol *appellation*. Indeed it was only the persistence of the owners during the Second Empire, when rigid boundaries had still to be drawn up, that eventually ensured its inclusion in the *appellation*. This is the soil of the lower terrace, consisting of recent gravel and sand. The comfortable nineteenth-century château stands in a wooded park, the estate covering 17 hectares all told. Recently vestiges of a Gallo-Roman villa, destroyed in the fourth century, have been found, together with some pottery, which is displayed here.

Eighty per cent of the wine is matured in cask, with one-third new oak; the rest is kept in vat. The *chai* was part of a convent built in the sixteenth century. The wines are consistent and well made, but decidedly light-textured; supple with easy, attractive fruit, if rather lacking dimension. But this is a pleasant wine for early drinking. There was a delicious 1980, and even the 1986 is supple and light.

CHÂTEAU MOULINET

Owner: Société Civile du Château Moulinet. Administrator: Armand Moueix. 17.5 hectares. 8,000 cases. Mer 50%, CF 40%, CS 10%

This is one of the largest and oldest properties in Pomerol. It lies beyond the Libourne–Périgueux road near the western boundary of the *appellation*, adjoining Château de Sales, on sandy soil mixed with recent gravel (as distinct from the ancient gravel of the high plateau) at the bottom of Pomerol's three terraces. An ancient boundary stone, at the entrance of the property, bears the cross of the Knights of St John of Jerusalem, a reminder of their presence here until the seventeenth century. In 1971 Moulinet was acquired by Armand Moueix of A. Moueix of Château Taillefer, cousins and fellow Corréziens of the J.-P. Moueixs, and like them *négociants* as well as proprietors. Since then many improvements have been made. In 1975 work was begun to reconstruct the *encépagement* of the vineyard to correspond more precisely with the nature of the soils found here, so the Merlot has been increased. In 1980 a new *cuvier* of stainless steel vats was installed in time for that vintage. There is a long vatting (*cuvaison*) of three weeks, and the wine spends about fifteen months in cask. Owing to the above-average size of the property compared to other Pomerols, and the hard work of the Moueixs, this is a well-known wine on most export markets. It is notable for its elegantly scented bouquet and the supple charm and distinction of its flavour. It develops fairly quickly; the 1978, for instance, was perfect for drinking by 1985, but still fresh and delicious four years later, and the light-textured but fine 1982 was nearly ready to drink when six years old. More recently the 1986 again showed very scented fruit on the nose with a soft, elegant flavour, in spite of the year, very good length and only medium weight. The 1987 was also most attractive. A comparison with de Sales, both in terms of proximity and soil, is unavoidable; generally I have found the wines here to be a little finer, with more length. They are also excellent value for money in these days of expensive Pomerols.

CHÂTEAU NENIN
Owner: François Despujol. 27 hectares, 10,000 cases. Mer 50%, CF 30%, CS 20%

This is one of the largest and best-known properties of Pomerol; indeed it is the largest property to be found on the best soils of the district. It is not on the very best soils, but on the south-western slope of the high plateau, where the deep gravel is mixed with some sand. It is an old property, and we know that the Demay family (see Certan de May) had some vines here in the mid-eighteenth century. But the extensive domain as it now exists was the work of the Paillets in the mid-nineteenth century. The house itself dates from 1848, and during the prosperity of the Second Empire Nenin became one of the leading *crus* of Pomerol. An unusual feature for the district is the park, of no less than ten hectares, which surrounds it, larger than many of the best *crus* on the high plateau, all of which gives Nenin very much the air of a Médoc château.

Given all its advantages and its historic reputation, it is sad to record that Nenin had been passing through a very bad patch. As so often in Bordeaux this had its roots in inheritance problems following the death of Emmanuel Despujol in 1973; these have led to a lack of investment at the time when everyone else has been busy improving their facilities. A visit there in April 1983, to try to pinpoint why a sample of the 1982 had been disappointing, soon highlighted the problem, at least as far as the *chai* was concerned. The smell of mouldy casks and a dirty, damp *chai* are fortunately almost a thing of the past today in Bordeaux, but they are fairly unmistakable, and Nenin had them both. Just in case you may be wondering if Nenin's reputation is something of a myth, I have a note about a wonderful 1929, drunk in September 1964. It had a lovely bouquet – nothing unclean here – belying its age, and the wine was full and generous at a time when most Médocs of the year were beginning to fade. It was a most distinguished wine. There was also a fine 1959, of definite breed, fruity, full-bodied and tannic. But by the 1964 vintage I had become more critical, noting when the wine was four years old that it was clumsy for a top-class Pomerol and lacked the richness and breed of Le Gay, or the attractions of Plince. A bottle of the 1970 was most disappointing in 1983, and on my visit in 1983 both the 1981 and 1982 were not nearly as good as they should have been. The basic elements of the wines, richness, fruit and tannins, were present; these wines were not over-produced, just rustic. However, there are much better reports of the 1985 and 1986, and one gathers that a determined effort is now being made to turn things around. One hopes that this will indeed prove to be the case; it is a pity for such an important producer of fine Pomerol to be operating at anything less than its full potential.

CHÂTEAU PETIT-VILLAGE

Owner: La Compagnie Axa. Administrator: Jean-Michel Cazes. 11 hectares. 3,900 cases. Mer 80%, CF 10%. CS 10%

An important growth formerly belonging to the Ginestet family and then by Domaines Prats, was sold by them in 1989 to Axa (see Pichon-Baron). The vineyard is well placed, one piece on a triangular site at one of the highest points of the high plateau, between the village of Catusseau, Vieux-Certan and La Conseillante. The name appears clearly on the Belleyme map in the second half of the eighteenth century, when the vineyard was already planted. The property rose to prominence under the Dufresne family, whom Enjalbert has characterized as belonging to the second generation of pioneers who established high-quality vineyards in the Libournais. In 1919 Fernand Ginestet caused something of a sensation when he bought the property, as it was the first time one of the leading Bordeaux *négociants* had bought a vineyard in the Libournais.

Unfortunately the vineyard was almost wholly destroyed by the 1956 frost, so had to be replanted, and the mistake, common at the time, was made of planting too much Cabernet Sauvignon. This has now been corrected, and the wines are steadily improving. A minimum of 50 per cent new oak is used in the maturation and sometimes more, according to the characteristics of the year. The style, especially since 1978, is closest to La Conseillante. The wines are characterized by a beautiful aroma and are very rich and deep, firm-centred, with a lovely flavour which shows great breed. The best mature vintage I have tasted was the 1961, which was concentrated and very rich, certainly a very fine wine when nearly twenty years old. The 1970 is rather moderate, and the 1971 is certainly superior if not in the very top class. Then the 1975 is very tannic and seems too dry; the 1976 is better balanced, but with the rather roasted character often found in this vintage; there was a surprisingly good 1977, rich and supple. With the 1978 Petit-Village moved on to a new plane: the bouquet is heady, spicy and opulent, the flavour really complex, ripe and splendidly rich yet crisply defined. The 1979 is, if anything, even better – again the bouquet is very scented and fine, the flavour has real depth and richness with an alluring beauty set off by a lot of extract and glycerine – a very complete wine. The 1981 is sound but not special, while the 1982 is a wine worthy of this great year, with an exotic quality to it. The 1983 has intense tobacco and liquorice notes on the bouquet and an extra dimension of length, tannins and complexity of flavour to suggest an outstanding example of its year. On this form Petit-Village is back in its rightful place among the leading *crus* of Pomerol.

In the mid-sixties, Ginestet introduced a non-vintage wine under the name of "Selection du Maître de Chai", but this had a short life.

CHÂTEAU PÉTRUS
Owners: Madame L. P. Lacoste and Jean-Pierre Moueix. Administrator: Christian Moueix. 13 hectares. 3,700 cases. Mer 95%, CF 5%

"Premier des Premiers Crus"; so ran the motto on an old cork from Pétrus, which I remember seeing once; and indeed, few would quarrel with this confident assertion. While Cheval Blanc has to share its privileged position in St Emilion with Ausone, Pétrus stands proudly alone, not according to any official classification, but by universal consent.

Pétrus's position in the area first became clear when it won a gold medal at the Paris Exhibition of 1878, the first wine from Pomerol to gain this distinction, and in an era when such awards really carried weight. But its modern reputation was the work of Madame Loubat on the one hand and Monsieur Jean-Pierre Moueix on the other. It was Madame Loubat who steadily built up the quality of the wine with meticulous husbandry and impeccable vinification. Like a very great cook, she ensured that attention was paid to every detail: the vineyard was tended with the care of a garden, the *cuvier* and *chai* were so immaculate that it seemed impossible that any work was ever carried on there. While Madame Loubat ensured that the quality of Pétrus matched that of any wine in the Gironde, Jean-Pierre Moueix ensured that, for the first time, it was distributed in such a way that it would acquire the international reputation it deserved. Monsieur Moueix is not only a very successful *négociant*, he is also a great connoisseur of many things that make life noble, and it has been his judgement and discernment, recognized and appreciated by his many customers, which have done much over the last forty years to place Pétrus where it is today. First, he arranged for Pétrus to be regularly distributed in the United States by the Leeds Import Co., then in 1963 he entrusted the UK distribution to International Distillers & Vintners via their Bordeaux subsidiary, Gilbey SA, at Château Loudenne. The present distributors are the old City firm of Corney and Barrow. Now, as auction prices at Christie's and Sotheby's testify, Pétrus is even more keenly sought after than Lafite or Mouton. What has this remarkable success story been built on? The vineyard itself is very small, originally 7 hectares producing on average around 25 tonneaux, now extended to 13 hectares producing up to 40 tonneaux, so that after Ausone it is the smallest of the great wines of the Gironde in terms of quantity. Fortunately, the set-back in 1956 was not as grave as in some vineyards, and a rapid recovery was made, as the quality of the 1959, 1960 and 1961 testifies.

The buildings themselves are minute but beautifully kept. *Cuvier* and *chai* are very small, with scrupulously clean and well-raked gravel on the floor. The *salle de réception* can hold only a very modest-sized party at one time to sign the visitors' book which is kept there. I shall always remember my first visit there in the early sixties, in Madame Loubat's time. She always wore a charming hat, and looked as if she was just going out to tea. After her death, her niece, Madame Lacoste-Loubat, carried on the same tradition for a while, and her hats helped to remind one of the great lady who had gone. Now, Monsieur Jean-Pierre Moueix has become the controlling partner in the property as well as arranging its distribution.

Since the early seventies, Monsieur Christian Moueix has been very much engaged in the actual management of Pétrus, as part of his duties in supervising the Moueix properties in general. In this he is fortunate to have the assistance of one of the leading young oenologists of the region, Monsieur Jean-Claude Berrouet. With the extension of the vineyards, some sceptics thought that Pétrus would no longer be the same, and I asked Christian Moueix how he had maintained the quality. The answer is that each year they taste the different vats blind. Usually there are five vats, three from the original vineyard and two from the new portion. In all their tastings, a wine from the new portion has never actually come last, an interesting commentary on how well the new part fits in with the old. With such a small vineyard, many things are possible which could not be attempted on a larger scale. For instance, in 1976, when the vintage was interrupted by rain, Christian Moueix was able to bring in his workers to pick in the afternoons, when conditions were at the optimum.

It is not always realized that Pétrus is par *excellence* the wine of the Merlot. About 95 per cent of the vineyard is planted with this variety – a monument to what Merlot can achieve when circumstances really suit it. What is so interesting about the wine itself is how distinctly different it is from its neighbours. As one looks out across the modest vineyard, one sees it closely bordered by Vieux-Château-Certan on the one side and by Gazin on another, yet this small parcel of land produces something unique. As usual with vineyards, it is that individual combination of soil and subsoil, isolated by chance, rather than incorporated in some larger parcel, which is responsible. At Pétrus, at the highest point of the high terrace there is an island of clay. The actual size of this "buttonhole" of clay is about 20 hectares, but nearly 11 hectares of this are here at Pétrus, the remaining parts being divided between Vieux-Château-Certan and L'Evangile. The genius, one might say the miracle, of Pétrus is that by the greatest good fortune some 90 per cent of the vineyard lies within this same geological freak. What would have happened had this concentration of clay been diluted in a larger property, can be seen by comparing Pétrus with Vieux-Château-Certan and L'Evangile. There are actually three levels of soil here, sandy loam on the surface, then sandy clay loam at about 20 centimetres and finally, at around 70 to 80 centimetres, clay.

This whole fascinating phenomenon has been brilliantly described and illustrated by Enjalbert, who is well worth reading in full (French edition, pp. 171–4, English edition, pp. 133–4).

In composition, the wine has certain points of similarity with Cheval Blanc. There is an unctuousness and almost a chewy quality of richness and power in common. But Pétrus has in all good years an exceptional depth of colour and a much clearer definition of flavour, that touch of firmness I have mentioned as so characteristic of Pomerol, but which is less marked than in some other growths. The bouquet is also better defined than Cheval Blanc, while just as powerful, and it develops remarkable nuances with age. Curiously, some of the lighter vintages of Pétrus, years like 1954 and 1960, seem to have a character more reminiscent of Ausone than of Cheval Blanc. One of the marvels of Pétrus seems to be its ability to begin life with all the exuberance of a great St Emilion, yet to mature with all the finesse of a great Médoc. It is this balance and finesse, the combination of so many qualities in a single wine, that make Pétrus so great.

I have been fortunate in having been able to taste a number of old vintages of Pétrus, and these confirm that great wines were being made here at a time when its glories were still unsung, and comfortable, bourgeois Bordeaux still thought of Pomerol as an untutored peasant not fit to mix with the nobility of the Médoc. The 1895 vintage was interesting because it was successful in St Emilion and Pomerol but not in the Médoc. The Pétrus of that year was still a great wine, deep in colour, rich and vigorous when over seventy years old. The next landmark was the 1917, which I found superior in almost every way to the 1928 when they were drunk together in 1963 at a dinner organized by Mr David Wolfe at the restaurant he owned at the time. The 1917 was deep in colour, still full of fruit and vigour, while the 1928 was very pale in colour and was drying up.

But the great age of Pétrus really began after the Second World War. The 1943 was the prologue; post-war visitors to Bordeaux were surprised and interested to be told by many fine judges in the trade that the almost unknown Pétrus was the outstanding wine of this war-time vintage. As a footnote, many years later I came across a bottle of the 1940, which was still delicate and delicious although nearly thirty years old. The 1945 was still deep in colour, rich and powerful but with some volatility, and less complex than the marvellous 1947. This would no doubt have become as famous as the Cheval Blanc had it had the same exposure to trade and public alike. On the last occasion when I had the chance of comparing the two in 1986, the Pétrus seemed less fat and more tannic than Cheval Blanc, yet was still very unctuous and shared with its neighbour that same incredible density of texture. But basically they are contrasting wines, endlessly fascinating to compare; would that the chance could arise more often than it does, because the Pétrus is now a very rare wine. The 1949 was only a little behind the 1947. The vintages of the fifties were on form, with an outstanding 1950 that has lasted better than any wine of the vintage I know, except Latour. In 1984 it was still deep in colour, rich and spicy on the nose, and amazingly youthful and assertive on the palate. The 1953 is a real beauty; it still had amazing highlights of mint and violets on the nose, while the flavour was marvellously ripe and full when last tasted in 1986, but the 1955 proved rather a lightweight for the vintage, while the 1954 was a very successful off-vintage. The 1960 was of a similar style, and then came a succession of great wines, 1961, 1962, 1964, 1966, 1967 (perhaps the wine of the vintage), 1968 (one of the few successes of this vintage outside the Médoc), 1969 (probably the wine of the vintage again). Of these my favourites are the 1962 and 1967 for their opulence and charm, and the remarkable 1964, which is the long-distance runner, a mouthful of opulent richness, with more and more layers of flavour opening out in the glass, and a long future ahead of it still when last tasted in 1990. The seventies produced a string of out-standing vintages. In recent tastings the 1971 has come through as the most rewarding wine for drinking in the next few years, a wine of remark-able beauty which almost overwhelms one with its sheer volume of flavour. In contrast the 1970 seems prosaic and reserved. The 1975, 1978 and even 1979 still seem massive and adolescent, some way from reach-ing anything approaching maturity.

This tendency to produce increasingly massive and slow-developing wines, established in the seventies, has continued. The 1980 is tannic and a slow developer for the year. But the 1981 seems closer in style to the 1971, if not so concentrated. It is relatively open-textured, with an opulent taste of prunes, and is ready to drink. The 1982 has all the exotic character of the top 1982s, allied to the remarkable denseness of texture of a great Pétrus, with incredible richness and length: an extraordinary wine with 13.5 per cent alcohol. The 1983 is not far behind, with 13.2 per cent, opulent and heady, very dense-textured and rich, probably a slower developer. The 1984 was declassified, then the 1985 has a beautiful flavour, with a supple, ripe character, but without the concentration of years such as 1982 and 1983. The contrast of the 1986 could not be more complete: this is enormously concentrated and tannic, rich in glycerine, dark and dense in texture, a great *vin de garde*. Thus Pétrus now tends to develop more slowly than other Pomerols, in the way Ausone develops more slowly than the other St Emilions. Speaking purely personally, while I admire and enjoy a wine such as the 1964 is now, or the 1978, I get the greatest pleasure from a wine like the 1971 is now, and perhaps the 1981 and 1985 will follow in this path.

LE PIN

Owner: Thienpont family. 1.2 hectares. 1,500 cases. Mer 88%, CF 12%

This pocket-handkerchief of a vineyard lies on the high plateau of Pomerol, near the hamlet of Catusseau. It appeared from nowhere, as it were, when it was bought in 1979 by the Thienpont family of Vieux-Château-Certan. Since then it has become something of a cult wine, sold at prices which seem unconnected with its real worth, compared to the great wines of Pomerol. The wines are undeniably attractive and flattering, in a rather Californian and simplistic way. The 1982 made delicious drinking when six years old. Le Pin is a good example of the way a small production can be sold at a price which a larger *cru* would find hard to achieve.

CHÂTEAU PLINCE

Owners: Moreau family. 8.3 hectares. 3,400 cases. Mer 70%, CF 20%, CS 10%

This is the sort of growth which used to be sold by English wine merchants in the early fifties for about eight shillings a bottle. I well remember Plince with its Calvet label – my father had bought the 1947 and then the 1953. We drank them young and found them delicious, but never thought of them as anything more than charming small growths, the equivalent of small *bourgeois* from the Médoc. When it was over thirty years old, we unearthed a bottle of the 1947 and found it fresh, rich and full-bodied, with a wonderful bouquet and a long silky elegance worthy of any aristocratic classified growth. Admittedly, it was a 1947, and this was one of the greatest years for Pomerol. If the price reaction of 1971–3 went too far too quickly, so the old prices of the fifties did not reflect the true value of wines like Plince.

The vineyard of Plince is on the *sables anciens*, where the land falls away sharply towards Libourne, south-west of Nenin. Probably because of its proximity of the town, some vines were already planted here by the mid-eighteenth century. The property is under the same ownership as Clos L'Eglise, and is also sold through Ets. J.-P. Moueix. After the 1947 I have notes on particularly successful wines in 1953 and 1964. More recently Plince seems to have followed the improvements at the Moreaus' other property. The 1982 is a delightfully opulent, extrovert wine, already delicious drinking when five years old. There is an attractive but surprisingly solid 1986, and a luscious, attractive 1987 for early drinking.

CHÂTEAU LA POINTE
Owner: Bernard d'Arfeuille. 25 hectares. 9,000 cases. Mer 80%, CF 15%, Mal 5%

This important growth with its distinctive label has long been a favourite in England. The vineyard lies on the gravel and sand of the middle terrace, the other side of the road from Nenin, and is the first important property one sees driving into Pomerol from Libourne on the D244. The situation is lower than Nenin, and La Pointe, like its neighbour, has a fine château but of classical simplicity, and a park, if a less ambitious one. After Nenin it is the largest property on the better soils of Pomerol. La Pointe rose to prominence during the Second Empire, when it was one of only a handful of *crus* to be given the prefix "château" by Cocks & Féret. The d'Arfeuille family are *négociants* in Libourne as well as owners of Château La Serre, *grand cru classé* of St Emilion.

My first acquaintance with the wine was a 1943 shipped as a concession wine by my father. It was one of the most agreeable examples of that uneven year. In style, La Pointe is on the light side, but with a typical Pomerol flavour, and fine bouquet and a finesse and delicacy which show real breed. A retrospective tasting in 1985 confirmed my suspicion that the wines here were not as good as they used to be. The splendid 1970 cast a long shadow over the rest of the decade, making the 1975 seem too tannic and lacking in fruit, and the 1978 and 1979 seem only moderate, if charming, lightweights. Before that the 1955 had for me been a benchmark for La Pointe, and in 1988 it was still in perfect condition, full-flavoured and mellow, light-textured yet remaining fresh and lively. Then there was a fine 1961, massive and complex in flavour still in 1983, and a very solid, tannic 1964, that was less attractive than a delightful 1966 – all tasted at the same time. Since then the 1982 seemed over-produced and lacking concentration, pleasant for early drinking, but no more. But the 1986 showed a marked improvement, with a lovely ripe richness and a fine finish, much more in the old mould. Thirty-five per cent new oak is now being used in the maturation. Let us hope this marks the beginning of a new era, when the wines will recall the delight of the fifties and sixties, rather than the mediocrity of the seventies.

CHÂTEAU PRIEURS DE LA COMMANDERIE

Owner: Clément Fayat. 3.5 hectares. 1,200 cases. Mer 80%, CF and CS 20%

This is an entirely new creation of Clément Fayat, proprietor of La Dominique, *cru classé* of St Emilion. In 1984 he was able to put together a patchwork of about a dozen plots. They are all to be found on the lower part of the middle terrace, where the soil is *silico-graveleux*. An entirely new *chai* and *cuvier*, equipped with stainless steel *cuves* with automatic temperature control, have been built, and 50–60 per cent new wood is used, depending on the vintage.

At present I find it difficult to judge just how good this wine is going to be. The 1985, tasted in late 1988, was suffering from reduction so did not taste well. It was rich and powerful and still marked by oak. The 1986, closed on the nose, had lots of substance and power, but was rather dried by the new oak, while the 1987 had a strong irony aroma and was light-textured, with charm and breed. Both were tasted in the autumn of 1988. Given the dynamic Clément Fayat's record at La Dominique, and with Michel Rolland advising, this must be a wine to watch – let us hope, with the small yield, that it does not become a hype!

CLOS RENÉ

Owner: Pierre Lasserre. 11 hectares. 5,500 cases. Mer 60%, CF 30%, Mal 10%.
Second label: Château Moulinet-Lasserre

This wine was for many years offered by Calvet to its English customers and bought by them with great regularity. The vineyard lies on the far side of the Libourne–Périgueux road, and takes its name from the hamlet of René. The soil here is the gravel and sand of the middle terrace. Pierre Lasserre is the fourth member of his family to own Clos René, and has maintained and improved a marvellous reputation for consistency. He is now assisted by his grandson, Jean-Marie Garde. The wines are very carefully made in the discreet but well-equipped *cuvier* behind the comfortable house. One passes through the garden to get to it. Twenty per cent new wood is now used in the maturation.

In style, this is a wonderfully perfumed, dense, rich and plummy Pomerol, that will seldom disappoint and is usually ready to drink when about five or six years old. The powerful 1975 had just the right balance of richness with tannins to make enjoyable drinking when it was nine years old. The 1976 was an easy wine for early drinking; the 1978 was better than the 1979, although both have taken longer to evolve than at first seemed likely. The 1978 is mature and spicy, powerful with depth and length, still developing when it was ten years old; the 1979 has lots of glycerine and gamy richness, delicious when seven years old. After a delicious and slightly roasted 1981, the 1982 has that smell of prunes characteristic of the year, and an incredibly dense, rich flavour, while the 1983 is more alcoholic and tannic. The 1985 is finely balanced with a lovely frank, rich, long flavour, velvety in texture yet also tannic, while the 1986 has more ripeness, and is extremely tannic with intense fruit and a smell of damsons, an exceptional wine for this *cru*.

CHÂTEAU ROUGET

Owner: François-Jean Brochet. 18 hectares. 6,000 cases. Mer 90%, CF 10%

This growth is chiefly memorable for me as one which had a string of old vintages to offer at one time. Unfortunately, they never came my way. But a fifteen-year-old bottle of 1964 confirmed the frank character and solid virtues of this wine. The vineyard is on the gravelly-clay soils of the northern slopes of the high plateau, adjoining La Croix-de-Gay, and is large for this area. It is also long-established, having belonged to the mayor of Pomerol in 1804. In early editions of Cocks & Féret, it was placed among the leading growths. It was bought by Marcel Bertrand in 1925, and he passed on the management to his nephew François-Jean Brochet in 1974. This is still a very traditionally run property with the old wooden *cuves* still in place, although supplemented by cement ones, and one-third new oak is now used. As a result of its position and the methods employed, this is really powerful, tannic, old-fashioned Pomerol, that demands keeping for its true merits to be appreciated. Thus the 1971 was still very gamy and spicy on the nose, rich, full-flavoured and firm when fifteen years old, at a time when many wines of this vintage were beginning to fade. The 1979 was full-bodied, tannic but unmistakably fine when three years old; the 1982 has a rich, earthy flavour with a scent of truffles, but rather lacking in concentration; while the 1985, when in cask, had lovely perfumed highlights on the nose, and a delightfully opulent, rich flavour, promising an earlier development. This is a property whose reputation probably lags behind its real worth, because its product is not well distributed, and because it is not an immediate charmer, but requires patience.

CHÂTEAU DE SALES

Owner: GFA du Château de Sales (les Héritiers de Laage). Administrators: Henri and Bruno de Lambert. 47.5 hectares. 22,500 cases. Mer 66%, CF 17%, CS 17%. Second label: Château Chantalouette

This is much the largest property in Pomerol. A fine château of the seventeenth and eighteenth centuries is surrounded by a domain of around 100 hectares, including extensive woods, which encircle it. This is the most important example in the Libournais of a great feudal estate to have survived largely intact and in the same hands. Before the Revolution the domain extended for 350 hectares but the vineyard was of small importance, only about two hectares being planted with vines in the 1760s. It was not until the Second Empire, a century later, that de Sales emerged as an important wine estate. It has belonged to the de Laage family since 1550.

As might be expected from such a production, the wine is widely distributed and is well known in England. When I first tasted it, the quality was only average, and I found a certain coarseness of character and lack of true Pomerol breed and distinction. But from 1970 onwards there has been a marked improvement, reinforced since 1982 by Bruno de Lambert, a qualified oenologist, who then took over the management from his father. The wines alternate between vats and used casks for the maturation. In style they are scented, rich, plummy and fairly powerful. There is a pleasing stylishness and they develop quite quickly. Thus by 1988 both the 1978 and 1979 needed drinking, with the deliciously opulent 1978 holding up the better of the two. This is good, uncompli-cated Pomerol sold at a reasonable price.

CHÂTEAU DU TAILHAS

Owner: Société Civile Pierre Nébout & Fils. 10.5 hectares. 5,000 cases. Mer 70%, CF 15%, CS 15%

This is the most southerly of all the Pomerol *crus*. It is on sandy soils, looking across the stream bearing the same name, which is the border between Pomerol and St Emilion, to Figeac. The *chai* is now equipped with the latest in stainless steel *cuves*, and 50 per cent new oak is used in the maturation. The wines are really less reminiscent of Pomerol than of some of the neighbouring St Emilions on the *sables anciens* They are deep-coloured, often with attractive highlights on the nose, plenty of vivid fruit and that slightly earthy taste which often occurs in parts of Pomerol and St Emilion where sand and "iron-pan" are combined. With the modernization that has taken place, these are now more consistent wines than they were; the 1980, for example, was excellent, and the 1982 is compact, firm yet juicy, still needing time when six years old.

CHÂTEAU TAILLEFER

Owners: Héritiers Marcel Moueix. Administrators: Bernard and Jean-Michel Moueix. 18 hectares. 7,500 cases. Mer 50%, CF 30%, CS 15%, Mal 5%

This is the principal property in Pomerol of the important firm A. Moueix & Fils, who make their headquarters here. This energetic family of Corréziens, who like their more famous cousins at J.-P. Moueix are both *négociants* and proprietors, acquired the property in 1923. It is one of the largest properties in Pomerol, with a pleasing nineteenth-century château surrounded by a park. The situation is in the extreme south of the *appellation*, very near Libourne, on mainly sandy soil, with some gravel and the famous *crasse de fer* featuring prominently in the subsoil. There is a very modern installation, which includes a system for automatic *remontage*, three-week *cuvaison*. The wines spend fifteen months in cask, including some new oak.

I remember rather firm, austere wines when I first tasted them in the sixties but now they are scented; and emphasize the fruit and charm, and being light in body can be drunk young with great pleasure. There is a good 1982 with fruit and ripe tannins, which was stylish and still improving when six years old, while the 1986 is a wine of much charm which should be just about ready to drink. An excellent 1987 was also made.

CHÂTEAU TROTANOY
Owner: Ets J.-P. Moueix. 7.5 hectares. 2,300 cases. Mer 85%, CF 15%

This leading growth is now enjoying the acclaim it so rightly deserves. It is in fact one of the old pioneering *crus* of Pomerol. In the eighteenth century it rejoiced in the name of Trop Ennuie, indicating that the soil was hard to work, and its owners, the Giraud family – royal *courtiers* from Libourne – were among the pioneers of the viticultural revolution. It was they who built the simple but stylish house, now the home of Jean-Jacques Moueix, nephew of the legendary Jean-Pierre Moueix, and his wife; and who in the early nineteenth century changed the name to Trotanoy. The soil here is a mixture of gravel and clay on the high plateau, with more clay on the western slope from the high plateau to the middle terrace. This is one of the most lustrous jewels in the Moueix empire, and Jean-Jacques can count on the highest priority from the team working under the direction of his cousin Christian and their oenologist Jean-Claude Berrouet. Fifty per cent new oak is now used for maturation.

In style, the wine is more reminiscent of Pétrus than the other leading growths, with its dense colour, rich, enveloping bouquet, and mellow, fleshy body which develops a flavour of great charm and breed. This is another example of how a predominantly Merlot wine can look remarkably like a Médoc at times, in spite of the difference in grape varieties. The 1949 was a marvellous wine, the 1961 a great, slow-developing one, and the 1962 one of the most attractive and successful in the region. Then, after a fine 1966, came an exceptional 1967 and a long-lasting 1970 which combines richness, tannin, but also plenty of glycerine, and which is outlasting a more opulent and complex 1971, with an exceptional after-taste, a real thoroughbred. The 1973 had a depth of colour and flavour unusual for the year, when thirteen years old; the fine 1975s and 1976s were typical of these years. The 1978 had been slow to develop and in 1988 was still very concentrated with a minerally edge to the flavour, powerful and compact, and of outstanding quality. In contrast the 1979 is all opulent ripeness and richness. After a powerful and fine 1981, the 1982 is a wine of enormous power, majestic enough to sit beside the Pétrus. The 1983 is impressively complex and tannic, with the fat and structure to make a long-term developer. The 1985 is again of the highest class but more flattering in style, closer to the lovely 1979. In its early stages the 1986 looks a very complete wine, with a lovely flavour, real concentration and lots of glycerine. The reputation of Trotanoy is now higher than ever before, as can readily be seen from the prices collectors are prepared to pay for its mature vintages in the auction room. Of course these prices are aggravated by the sheer scarcity of the wine, but there is no gainsaying its real worth.

VIEUX-CHÂTEAU-CERTAN
Owners: Héritiers Georges Thienpont. 13.6 hectares. 5,500 cases. Mer 50%, CF 25%, CS 20%, Mal 5%

This, together with Beauregard, is the most impressive and substantial château on the high plateau of Pomerol. Enjalbert dates it around 1770, when it belonged to the Demay family. The whole building is very pleasing, with its two squat towers of differing ages and proportions at either end. It is beautifully kept by the Thienpont family, Belgian wine merchants who bought the property in 1924. Its position as one of the leading Pomerols at the end of the eighteenth century was further enhanced when the region as a whole gained in reputation during the Second Empire, until it finally yielded pride of place to Pétrus in 1875. After Pétrus, which it adjoins, Vieux-Château-Certan has the largest proportion of the "buttonhole" of clay on the high terrace of Pomerol. Here it comprises 40 per cent of the vineyard, rather more than five hectares, the rest being gravel, or *graves*. The difference between the two wines only serves to underline how important the high concentration of clay at Pétrus has been to the success of that *cru*. Georges Thienpont himself ran the property from 1924 to 1962, then his son Léon was the brother in charge until his death in 1985. Now Léon's son Alexandre has taken over, after serving a very useful apprenticeship at La Gaffelière from 1982 to 1985.

The wines of Vieux-Château-Certan have a very individual style. In colour they are lighter than Pétrus or La Conseillante, but are of a beautifully clear and ruby hue which retains its youthfulness longer than that of many Pomerols. The bouquet is especially marked, and on the palate the wines have a delicacy and breed unsurpassed by any Pomerol, although often markedly firm at the beginning. As with the bouquet, the flavour is very individual, penetrating and fine. Although lacking the flesh and richness of Pétrus, they always seem to have sufficient fruit and body for the tannin, and usually, indeed, the wines are remarkably long on the palate.

In 1987 I had the opportunity of tasting two flights of vintages within a few months of one another, which gave an excellent panorama of most of the best vintages between 1952 and 1983. The deep-coloured 1952 still had power and depth on the nose, with a rather tough, firm, irony flavour, dry at the finish, and much tougher than the 1959. The charming 1953 was missing, but the 1955 easily made up for it, with a lovely spicy, aromatic bouquet and a marvellous flavour; complex, long-flavoured and subtle, it had more fruit than the other wines of the decade, and a touch of the exotic. The 1959, after promising lovely ripe, mature fruit on the nose, had more tannin than expected, but developed richness and subtlety – a fine example of the year, especially after the frost of 1956. In the next decade the outstanding wine was the lovely 1964, still fresh, vigorous and beautiful, with elegance and great style. I was pleased to find the 1967 so good, having noted it at the time as a great success for the year (Pétrus having been the outstanding wine of the vintage). The nose was better than the taste, which was a little tired, but even so I preferred it to the 1970. Unfortunately neither the 1961 nor 1962, both fine wines, was available. In the next decade the 1970 was disappointingly lean and dry at both tastings. In contrast the 1971, tasted two years earlier, was still really luscious and powerful, fresh and in peak condition. I thought the 1975 too dry, and still awkward and tough, but the 1978 has all the breed of the year, being very scented with lovely mature, mellow fruit, beautifully balanced and perfectly delicious. I have not tasted the 1979 since it was a youthful three years old, but at that stage it was most impressive, with a very long compact flavour of real individuality and complexity – so the decade certainly finished on a better note than it had begun. The eighties began with a respectable and pleasing 1980; then the 1981 was beautifully scented and elegant, but has now firmed up and was more tannic then expected, needing time. The 1982 is a classic, with enormous richness and opulence, full of concentrated ripe tannins and fruit, while the contrasting 1983 is also most successful, with vibrant fruit leaping from the glass and a flavour rich in extract and tannins: a great Vieux-Certan in the making. So Léon Thienpont's stewardship finished on a high note of excellence. His son Alexandre had the good fortune to begin with two wonderful years, 1985 and 1986. He introduced the practice of pruning bunches to prevent over-production, used at La Gaffelière when he was there, with great success. The 1985 had the seductive charm of this *cru* in this sort of year, while the 1986 is exceptional, with great power and concentrated tannins and fruit – a true classic in the making. So the outlook for this great *cru* is excellent, as a new generation seizes the tiller with great assurance.

CHÂTEAU VRAY-CROIX-DE-GAY
Owner: Baronne Guichard. 3.7 hectares. 1,200 cases. Mer 55%, CF 40%, CS 5%
A very well-placed vineyard, in the best part of the high plateau, between Lagrange, Le Gay and Lafleur, this is a good example of the cavalier attitude to spelling proper names which is still rife in France. The label has "Vray", but the old notice in the vineyard says "Vraye"! Presumably this was the old and original spelling, but since they were changing it, it seems odd not to have gone the whole way and adopted the more normal form, Vrai. The Guichard family also own Siaurac, one of the best properties in nearby Lalande de Pomerol. In the past there have been inconsistencies here, but recently fine wines have been made. In style they are closest to Le Gay, very dense in texture, rich and tannic, needing time to realize their potential. The 1986 showed great promise in cask, and the 1987 also had a very concentrated flavour with well-matured fruit and tannin. Certainly this is a *cru* to watch.

There are over 140 properties in Pomerol, all selling their wines under their own labels, many of them with less than five hectares. The selection above is based on a combination of availability on at least one export market, and excellence, since within the scope of this book one cannot hope to be truly comprehensive.

LALANDE DE POMEROL

Attached to Pomerol, across the Barbanne, lie the two communes of Lalande de Pomerol and Néac. Like the satellites of St Emilion, they represent a compromise between the desire of these growers to use the name Pomerol, and of those of Pomerol to exclude them. At first there were two separate *appellations*, but some years ago the growers of Néac were permitted use of the more commercially attractive Lalande de Pomerol *appellation*.

This is now an area of increasing importance. As prices in Pomerol have risen, so growers here have been able to obtain the sort of prices which allow for investment in better equipment, and so produce better and more consistent wines. The 900 hectares of vineyard are divided roughly 60:40 between Lalande and Néac. But there are significant differences between the communes. In Lalande the vineyards are on recent gravel and sand terraces, which are relatively low-lying. But in Néac there is a high plateau, with those *crus* facing south towards Pomerol being on very good gravel, corresponding exactly to what is found in Pomerol. The best wines are close in quality to the third tier of Pomerols, and sometimes are better. They normally have less power and tannin, but are unusually seductive, with finesse and style, and develop more quickly.

Professeur Enjalbert singled out five *crus* as the most favourably placed, and capable of producing wines which at their best can approach those in the second tier of the Pomerols.

Château Belle-Graves. Owner: Madame J. Théallet. 10 hectares. 5,000 cases.

Château Moncets. Owner: Baron L.-G. et E. de Jerphanion. 16 hectares. 7,000 cases.

Château Moulin à Vent. Owner: Vignobles Pierre Couffin. 10 hectares. 5,000 cases.

Château Siaurac. Owner: Baronne Guichard. 25 hectares. 10,000 cases.

Château Tournefeuille. Owner: GFA Sautarel. 10 hectares. 5,000 cases.

All these wines have good to excellent reputations. I have known the wines of Siaurac for the longest, and remember a marvellous 1964. Recently, powerful wines were made in 1983 and 1986, and the delicious 1987 had no difficulty in holding its own with Château Plince, Pomerol. The Château Moncets 1981 made a delicious bottle when four years old, opulent and easy, but also with good backbone.

After these Enjalbert lists a further twenty-six *crus* in Néac and forty-two in Lalande, while Bernard Ginestet simply picks out twenty-one *crus* in each commune, including those already mentioned. Of the wines I have tasted recently, the most impressive and enjoyable have been the following.

First, in Néac:

Château Bertineau St Vincent. Owner: Michel Rolland. 4 hectares. 1,800 cases.

Domaine de Grand Ormeau. Owner: Garde et Fils. 15 hectares. 7,000 cases.

Château Haut-Chaigneau. Owner: André Chatonnet. 20 hectares. 10,000 cases.

Château Les Hauts-Conseillants (also sold on export markets as Château Les Hauts-Tuileries). Owners: L. Figeac and P. Barotte. 8 hectares. 3,000 cases.

Château des Tournelles (associated with Château Bertineau). Owner: François-Bernard Janoueix. 12 hectares. 6,000 cases.

Second, in Lalande:

Château des Annereaux. Owner: M. M. Hesset-Milhade. 22 hectares. 11,000 cases.

Château Bel-Air. Owner: L. and J.-P. Musset. 12 hectares. 5,000 cases.

Clos de Moines. Owners: Etienne and Gérard Marten. 14 hectares. 6,500 cases.

10

Fronsac, Bourg and Blaye, and Other Red Wines of Bordeaux

Because Bordeaux is such a vast producer of *appellation* wines, it is almost inevitable that many of its less well-known wines suffer by exclusion from the limelight in which Médoc, Graves, St Emilion and Pomerol bask. I have often thought that if these wines had been situated elsewhere in France, they would have been hailed as great finds. So often when, in recent years, the hunt has been on for "lesser-known wines", these lesser Bordeaux have been forgotten, and wines of less intrinsic merit and interest have been successfully "discovered" and promoted, simply because they lay outside the Gironde. Yet the best of these wines deserve recognition in their own right as wines of charm and character, which have the advantage of reaching maturity earlier than the great growths of the leading *appellations*. It is not surprising that wines like Bourg and Fronsac were preferred to those of the Médoc in the eighteenth century, when wines were not aged in bottle, but drunk young after cask maturation.

I firmly believe that the wines that follow have a very definite place in the cellar of anyone who loves Bordeaux red wines. I, for one, would much prefer to drink a mature Fronsac, a young Bourg or Blaye, even a young Premières Côtes, than an immature Médoc. It is true that a young, voluptuous St Emilion has great appeal, but only for certain occasions and with certain food. The more modest charms of these often delightful wines can sometimes prove more versatile.

FRONSAC

This relatively small district of hilly, partly wooded country lies just to the west of Libourne. In effect, it consists of a giant bluff overlooking the Dordogne, and this special geographical feature is of much importance for the district. In 1956, for instance, the great February frost caused less damage here than anywhere else in the Gironde, because of the elevation of the vineyards. The centre is the small medieval town of Fronsac, a mere two and a half kilometres from Libourne, which lies at the junction of the Isle and the Dordogne. The River Isle forms the western boundary of the district. There are actually two separate *appellations*, Fronsac and Côtes de Canon-Fronsac, which is less confusing than it used to be when Fronsac was known as Côtes de Fronsac. There are just under 700 hectares of Fronsac vineyards, averaging some 30,000 hectolitres a year, while the Côtes de Canon-Fronsac has just under 300 hectares of vineyards producing, on average, just over 12,000 hectolitres a year. So the whole district is about the same size as Pauillac.

The distinction between Fronsac and Côtes de Canon is not always a helpful one for the consumer, at least at present. As Fronsac emerges from its long years of stagnation, the greatest differences today are often between the properties that make their wines well and can afford at least some element of new wood, and those where indifferent wine-making and old casks predominate. The two *appellations* cover six small communes: Fronsac itself, La Rivière, Saillans, St Aignan, St Germain-de-la-Rivière and St Michel-de-Fronsac. In Fronsac itself both *appellations* are to be found, in St Michel only Canon-Fronsac, while the remainder are entirely Fronsac. Canon-Fronsac is the historic heart of the district, where the first properties to produce wines of note in the eighteenth century are to be found. This was around 1730, some twenty years prior to the Haut-St Emilion, when the new vineyards on the *tertre*, *côte* and *pieds-de-côte* were first developed. Here the limestone resembles that of the plateau of St Martin in St Emilion, but is much thinner and is more fertile; the main reason, as Enjalbert has pointed out, that the Fronsac vineyards are less good than those of the best of St Emilion. Further north is the larger plateau area, which is divided into two distinct parts: the southern one, on a thin stratum of limestone; the northern one, which has the much thicker limestone, from Vincent to Jeandeman. The higher plateau most closely resembles those in Montagne, Lussac and Puisseguin, and is richer and more suitable for other crops than vines, unlike the poorer soils of the Canon-Fronsac. Finally, there are the areas of sandstone slopes, so that the total picture, within a small area, is quite mixed and complex.

When I first began to taste young Fronsacs in cask regularly, in the early sixties, I was soon attracted by their very individual character. It is that early aroma of the new wine which develops in bottle into a charmingly distinctive, perfumed bouquet that is the characteristic which singles out Fronsac as certainly the finest wine outside the great districts. Although the Merlot is now generally the principal grape variety in most vineyards, once again its character is subtly transposed on these soils. These wines have a breed and distinction of flavour which sets them apart from the best of Bourg or Blaye. In the past they were noted for their body and firmness, but less rustic vinification has produced wines of finer texture, emphasizing their distinctive fruit. Some years ago, when a most interesting tasting of Fronsacs was held at Christie's, it was noticeable that many wines were parched, because kept too long in cask. In those days, most properties kept their wines in cask as long as possible, hoping for bulk sales to *négociants*, and only château-bottled what was left when sales ceased. This was often too late for the good of the wine. Recently, there has been a noticeable improvement in standards in the district, so that more properties are now bottling wines which really show the full potential of the area. So it is high time that these wines received the recognition they deserve.

In recent years I have done several large tastings of Fronsac wines, some with the help of the two syndicates, some through the kindness of the individual producers. The result is the following personal selection of properties which have impressed, or are at least making sound wines. At present, of the wines where I have tasted several vintages, I would place the following as the leading *crus*. But this selection can only be regarded as personal and provisional, since the whole area is going through a period of advance and evolution.

Château Canon (Christian Moueix)
Château Canon-de-Brem

Château La Fleur-Cailleau
Château Mazeris
Château Mazeris-Bellevue
Château Vray-Canon-Boyer

As elsewhere in this book, the wines are in alphabetical order within the *appellations*.

Canon-Fronsac

CHÂTEAU BARRABAQUE

Owner: Achille Noël-Vincent. 9 hectares. 4,500 cases. Mer 60%, CF 30%, CS 10%

This property is in the commune of Fronsac, north-west of Fronsac with a good site on mid-*côte*. When I first tasted the wines in 1986, the 1983 was much better than the 1982, perfumed with earthy undertones, and had a good flavour with harmonious fruit and tannins. Then the 1987 showed the benefit of new oak, being concentrated and rich in cask, with lovely taut, firm fruit. In contrast, the 1986, just after bottling, was showing less well, with signs of high yields, but with plummy fruit and originality of flavour. This is a good second-rung wine which seems to be improving.

CHÂTEAU CANON

Owner: Christian Moueix. Administrator: J.-P. Moueix. 1.1 hectares. 500 cases. Mer 80%, CF 20%

This minute vineyard on the Côte de Canon marked the Moueixs' first tentative step into Fronsac. The first vintage I tasted was the 1982, which was full of soft, enveloping fruit, and had a lovely lingering flavour. The 1985 was more concentrated, rich, tannic and powerful, an impressive *vin de garde*. This is a wine of clear breed, showing its origins from one of the best parts of the *appellation*, and of course beautifully made, thus realizing its potential.

CHÂTEAU CANON

Owner: Mademoiselle Henriette Horeau. 10 hectares. 4,000 cases. Mer 95%, CF 5%

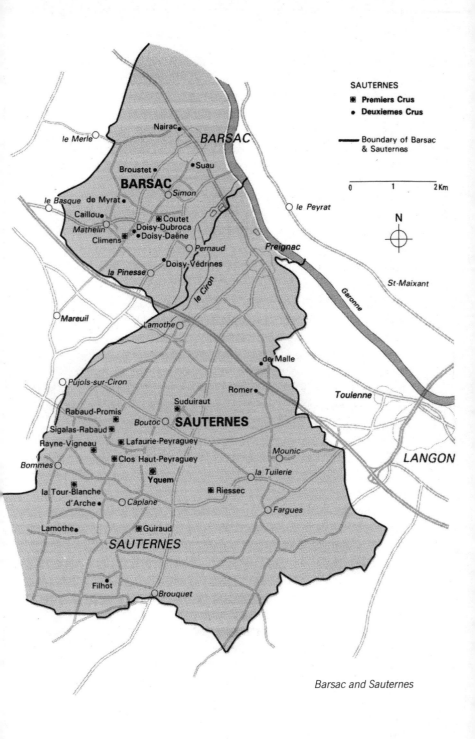

Barsac and Sauternes

The vineyard is in two parts, on the north and south sides of the Côte de Canon, either side of Vray-Canon-Boyer. There is a substantial but classically restrained Second Empire château. This is one of the historic properties of the region, with origins going back to the early eighteenth century; part of the vineyard belonged to the Fontémoing family. The wine is sold exclusively by the oldest Libourne *négociants*, Horeau-Beylot, and its reputation is that of one of the leading *crus* in the *appellation*.

CHÂTEAU CANON-DE-BREM

Owner: J.-P. Moueix. 20 hectares. 8,000 cases. Mer 66.7%, CF 33.3%

This is both one of the largest vineyards in a prime site, and one of the best-known and consistent wines of the entire region. It is in the commune of Fronsac, on the *côtes* above La Dauphine. For many years the property of the de Brem family, its purchase by the Moueixs in 1985 marked that company's major move into Fronsac (La Dauphine and Pichelèbre, both de Brem *crus*, were bought at the same time).

No property underlines more clearly than de Brem the capacity of the best Fronsacs to age elegantly. The 1962 had developed a gloriously complete character, somewhere between Pomerol and Médoc, when tasted in 1985. It had depth and power of flavour, and was richer and fuller than most 1962s at this age. There was lovely ripe middle fruit, complexity and length of flavour, and a firm, dryish finish. In peak condition, this was a stunning wine. More recently the luscious 1979 was delightful drinking when six years old; the 1981 was more spicy with less body but more tannin, a slower developer; the 1982 is very rich and deep-flavoured, a fine *vin de garde*; the 1983 has opulent richness and good concentration – it was enjoyable by 1988 but with plenty of development still to come. The 1985 showed great promise in cask, with concentration and fat balancing the powerful tannins. As will have been seen from this account, de Brem is a wine seldom at its best before five or six years of age, needing more ageing in many vintages, and capable of producing exceptional bottles when between ten and twenty years of age.

CHÂTEAU CANON-MOUEIX (FORMERLY PICHELÈBRE)

Owner: J.-P. Moueix. 5 hectares. 2,000 cases. Mer 70%, CF 30%

As if there were not enough Canons already, the Moueixs have now added another. The habit of changing awkward names for more commercial ones has a long history in the Libournais (Clos Fourtet, Canon (St Emilion), Pétrus, L'Evangile – to mention but a few) so this is nothing new. The vineyard faces south-west and is on clayey limestone, to the west of Fronsac. The wines made under the de Brems were robust and fine, lacking the distinction of Canon-de-Brem but nevertheless deep-coloured, powerful and full of character. At a pre-auction tasting at Sotheby's in 1982 the 1967 was still complex and interesting, there was a typical 1975, tannic but with plenty of fruit, a tannic, powerful 1978 needing time, and an impressive 1979 with lots of character and flavour. In the first Moueix vintage, 1985, the wine was softer and fuller than the Canon-de-Brem, rich and deep with plenty of flavour. This *cru* must now be set fair to claim its place among the *appellation's* leading *crus*.

CHÂTEAU CASSAGNE-HAUT-CANON

Owner: Jean-Jacques Dubris. 10.5 hectares. 4,250 cases. Mer 70% CF 25%, CS 5%

This fine property is on the limestone plateau and *côte*, north-east of St Michel. When I first tasted this wine in the 1982 and 1983 vintages, there seemed to be an *élevage* problem, and they were coarse with a strong, rank flavour behind the fruit. But a tasting of the 1986 and 1987 vintages told quite a different story. Now there is a special selection sold under the name La Truffière (there are truffle oaks on the property – and the name Cassagne derives from the Gallic word cassanus, meaning an oak). Both wines were impressive, with a good deal of new oak, lovely spicy fruit and plenty of middle richness and fat.

CHÂTEAU COPET-BÉGAUD

Owner: Alain Roux. 4 hectares. Mer 80%, CS and CF 20%

This property is under the same ownership as Coustolle. I was impressed by its 1982, with its lovely ripe, rich fruit, depth of flavour and tannic background. The 1985 was softer and mellower.

CHÂTEAU COUSTOLLE

Owner: Alain Roux. 20 hectares. 10,000 cases. Mer 60%, CF 30%, Mal 10%

This *cru*, large by Fronsac standards, is on the *côte*, north of Fronsac. I first came across the wine at the Sotheby's tasting in 1982, when the 1971 was rich and supple, at its peak. When tasted in 1986, however, the 1982 and 1983 were distinctly disappointing, with clear *élevage* problems. Unfortunately, both the 1986 and 1987 (in cask) also showed vinification or *élevage* problems, so clearly the potential of this important *cru* is not as yet being realized.

CHÂTEAU LA FLEUR-CAILLEAU

Owner: Paul Barre. 3 hectares. 1,500 cases. Mer 90%, CF 10%

Certainly a case of small is beautiful: after a firm and rather austere 1982, the 1983 had a really original flavour – spicy, rich and tannic. The 1986 has more new oak, and there are lovely highlights on the nose and a rich tannic flavour which promises well. The 1987 has exceptional finesse and a lovely texture, with an extremely elegant, fruity bouquet, reminiscent of wild cherries. On this form, this is certainly one of the gems of Fronsac worth searching for.

CHÂTEAU LA FLEUR-CANON

Owner: A. de Coninck. 7 hectares. 3,500 cases. Mer 90%, CF and CS 10%

This small property in St Michel on the *tertre* of Canon, belonging to a member of a well-known Libournais family, makes fine wines of character, developing more quickly than some of its neighbours. The 1982 had a bouquet of prunes and a distinctly over-ripe character with concentrated fruit; the 1983 was also good with rich middle fruit and character.

CHÂTEAU DE GABY

Owners: de Kermoal family. Administrator: Henri de Kermoal. 9 hectares. 5,000 cases. Mer 85%, CS and CF 15%

This historic property on the limestone plateau and *côte*, north-west of Fronsac, has a charming château and grounds. The well-managed property produces long-lived wines of breed and style. The 1962 was still delicious in 1982, while the 1979, tasted at the same time, was rich and purple, promising good development.

CHÂTEAU DU GAZIN

Owner: Henri Robert. 30 hectares. 15,000 cases. Mer 50%, CF 50%

This is the largest property in the Canon-Fronsac, in the commune of St Michel, on the limestone plateau and *côte*. There is a château standing in a park. In spite of its size, I never came across the wine until Cordier bought the 1985 vintage. When just bottled it had a lovely scent of violets, obvious breed, a firm, rather austere finish, but elegance and persistence of flavour, all promising a good future. On this form we should hear much more of this Gazin.

CHÂTEAU GRAND-RENOUIL
Owners: J.-F. and M. Ponty. 5 hectares. 2,500 cases. Mer 70%, CF 30%

A small but good *cru* on the *côte* north-east of St Michel, whose wines are scented and quite rich, with marked character and fruit. There was a rich, concentrated 1982 and a powerful, opulent and tannic 1986. From what I have seen, this is certainly a wine worth looking for, in the second rung of Canon-Fronsac *crus*.

CHÂTEAU HAUT-MAZERIS
Owner: Madame Bleynie (*en fermage* M.-C. Ubald-Bocquet). 20 hectares. 4,000 cases. Mer 70%, CF and CS 30%

This property in St Michel is on the *plateau calcaire* north-east of the village. In a tasting organized by the Syndicat in 1986 this *cru* was notable for its consistency in the 1982 and 1983 vintages, which was not a feature of the tasting as a whole. Both vintages were strong-flavoured and assertive in character, tannic and well structured, but also pleasantly balanced with nice fruit.

CHÂTEAU JUNAYME
Owner: René de Coninck. 18 hectares. 8,500 cases. Mer 80%, CF 14%, CS 6%

This is one of the best-known *crus* of Fronsac, sited on the Côte de Canon. There is an imposing nineteenth-century château, and the Coninck-Horeau family are the heirs of Pierre Beylot, who began business as a *négociant* in Libourne in 1740, making Horeau-Beylot the oldest firm on this side of the river. Their archives, thoroughly examined by Enjalbert, are one of the richest sources of information on developments in the Libournais in the second half of the eighteenth century. The wines combine stylish fruit, vigour and a fair measure of finesse, without perhaps quite the concentration of the top *crus* such as Canon-de-Brem. The 1975 and 1982 are particularly successful, but I have also liked the 1979 and 1983.

CHÂTEAU MAUSSE

Owner: Guy Janoueix. 10 hectares. 4,500 cases. Mer 50%, CS 25%, CF 25%

This is a good *cru* on the limestone plateau north-west of St Michel. Note that there is rather more of the two Cabernets than is usual in the *appellation*. The most successful wine I have tasted here was the 1983, with its smell of damp undergrowth and very attractive fruity flavour, with plenty behind it, solid yet with definite *race*.

CHÂTEAU MAZERIS

Owner: Christian de Cournuaud. 14 hectares. 5,000 cases. Mer 80%, CF 10%, CS 10%

This very fine *cru* is on the limestone plateau and *côte* in the commune of St Michel. At present only 14 hectares are planted, but there are plans to increase it gradually to 20 hectares. The present vineyard incorporates a proportion of very old vines, and yields are rigorously controlled. Christian Moueix was so impressed with the 1985 that J.-P. Moueix bought the entire crop, and sent in their own casks for the *élevage*. The wine showed a remarkable originality of flavour, great richness and concentration of tannins and fruit. Before this the 1983 was finer than the 1982, and was again very perfumed with marked character, and vivid delicious fruit. This *cru* is now one of the rising stars of the *appellation* and has the potential to be counted among the best.

CHÂTEAU MAZERIS-BELLEVUE

Owner: Jacques Bussier. 11.5 hectares. 5,000 cases. CS 50%, Mer 40%, Mal 10%

This vineyard is in St Michel, on the edge of the limestone plateau, combining the plateau and the *côte*. The vineyard was reconstituted after the phylloxera crisis by the present owner's grandfather, who was awarded the Grande Médaille d'Or by the Ministry of Agriculture in 1896 for the best-kept property in the Libournais. It is remarkable for having by far the largest proportion of Cabernet Sauvignon of any vineyard in the *appellation*, yet the wines are anything but austere. They are marked by a very distinctive fruity character. After a good 1979, I found the 1981 at its delicious best, soft and rich but still vibrant and fresh, when six years old. There is a massive, concentrated 1986, and the 1987 is full of marvellously rich, vivid fruit. This is an impressive *cru* whose

wines have that real flair that places them among the top wines of
Fronsac.

CHÂTEAU TOUMALIN

Owners: d'Arfeuille family. 8 hectares. 3,500 cases. Mer 80%, CF 20%

This well-known *cru* is on the *côte* above the valley of the Isle, on the road
from Fronsac to Villegouge. This family *négociant* also owns La Pointe in
Pomerol and La Serre in St Emilion. The wines are soft and charming but
develop very quickly compared to the best *crus* of Fronsac, so that the
1983 was ready to drink when less than three years old. However, the
1985 showed a little more concentration.

CHÂTEAU VRAY-CANON-BOYER

Owners: Coninck family. 10 hectares. 3,500 cases. Mer 90%, CS 5%, CF5%

The vineyard occupies an exceptional site on the Côte de Canon, facing
due south, and is one of the most prized possessions of the Coninck
family of Horeau-Beylot, the oldest *négociants* in Libourne (see also
Junayme and Canon). The wines combine beauty of flavour and considerable finesse and elegance, with the power to age well. There is a
lovely 1982, and the 1983 is also fine with more obvious tannin. This is
certainly one of the leading *crus* of Fronsac.

Fronsac

The *cave coopérative* at Lugon, Les Grandes Versannes, apart from producing some 35,000 hectolitres of Bordeaux Supérieur or Bordeaux red
wine, and a smaller quantity of white Bordeaux, also makes some 4,000
hectolitres of excellent Fronsac (approximately 44,000 cases). This
includes Château La Fontaine (6,000 cases) in the commune of Fronsac.
The wines are well made, soft and fruity, excellent for early drinking. My
personal selection of the best Fronsac *crus* at present, from among those
where I have tasted a number of vintages, is as follows (the same reservations that I expressed for the Canon-Fronsac selection apply equally
here):

Château Dalem
Château Mayne-Vieil
Château Moulin-Haut-Laroque

Château La Rivière
Château La Valade
Château Villars

CHÂTEAU CARDENEAU
Owner: Jean-Noël Hervé. 14 hectares. 6,000 cases. Mer 65%, CF 20%, CS 10%, Mal 5%

Situated in the commune of Saillans, this property is marked in the 1986 edition of Féret as being reconstructed. The proprietor also owns the excellent Moulin-Haut-Laroque in the same commune. I first tasted the wine in 1988 and found the 1986 light-textured but with rather harsh tannins, but the 1987 showed raw tannic fruit on the nose and a long, rich, tannic flavour of considerable promise. As the product of young vines this is most impressive, a *cru* for the future!

CHÂTEAU DE CARLES
Owner: Antoine Chastenet de Castaing. 18 hectares. 8,000 cases. Mer 65%, CF and CS 35%

The property is situated on the *côte* north-east of Saillans, overlooking the valley of the Isle. There is an impressive château, built at the end of the fifteenth century, but the name is attributed to Charlemagne, who is said to have camped here on his way to Spain. The only vintage I have tasted was the 1987, which I found tannic but hollow. However, J.-P. Moueix are now taking an interest in the wines, so this fine old *cru* could be worth watching.

CHÂTEAU DALEM
Owner: Michel Rullier. 13 hectares. 6,500 cases. Mer 70%, CF 20%, CS 10%

Michel Rullier has been in the vanguard of the Fronsac revival. The 1945 was still remarkable and suggesting much grander origins, in 1989. The oldest great Fronsac I have tasted. When I first tasted his wines at Sotheby's in 1982 I was impressed by the array of vintages from Dalem, and their high standard of excellence, beginning with a 1964 that was still full-bodied, ripe and fine. The 1967 was surprisingly soft and attractive for the year, then came a delicious 1970; the 1975 was still tannic and closed, but the 1976 was complex, ripe and delightful – at its peak at six years old. Even the 1977 was delicious and ready. The 1978 was impressive, with length, character and balance. More recently there is a fine 1982 with a great depth of flavour and a rich, assertive character, while the 1983 has a powerful tannic character and very good concentration. The 1985 and 1986 are another impressive pair; the 1985 smells of *cassis* and combines length of flavour, finesse and structure, while the 1986 has a sumptuous flavour full of rich, velvety-textured fruit and tannins. The 1987 has fruit and charm well supported by the new oak. This is certainly one of the best and most consistent *crus* in Fronsac today. The vineyard is on the *côte*, south-east of Saillans. There is a comfortable early nineteenth-century house in the classical manner.

CHÂTEAU DE LA DAUPHINE
Owner: Ets J.-P. Moueix. 10 hectares. 4,500 cases. Mer 66%, CF 40%

This was one of the three de Brem *crus* bought by Moueix in 1985 (see Canon-de-Brem and Canon-Moueix). It is situated on the *pieds-de-côte*, west of Fronsac. The fine château is referred to in Féret as the work of Victor Louis, the great architect of the Grand Théâtre in Bordeaux, but according to the latest information (see Robert Coustet, "Histoire de l'architecture viticole" in *Châteaux de Bordeaux*, Editions du Centre Pompidou, 1988) there is no evidence that he was responsible for any Bordeaux château other than the unfinished du Bouilh. The wine was one of the best-known Fronsacs before the Moueix purchase, and can only climb in reputation now. Even before the change the wines had begun to fill out. While the 1976 and 1981 had seemed firm but promising when young, they became lean, dry and rather stringy when six to seven years of age; the 1982 and 1983 seem to have more concentration but were still inclined to be tough. But the first Moueix vintage, 1985, seemed to get the balance right, and there was more middle fruit to balance the tannins. The future here should be bright, but on present form this is no longer a quick developer.

CHÂTEAU FONTENIL
Owner: Michel Rolland. 7 hectares. 3,500 cases. Mer 86%, CS 14%

This small *cru* occupies a south-facing slope at Saillans, next to La Vieille Cure. The *cru* was created by Michel Rolland (see Le Bon Pasteur) in 1986, by purchasing several small plots from different growers. The name Fontenil is the *lieu-dit* of one of these. The 1986 shows a lot of new oak and tannin with good fruit coming through, while the 1987 had a dense purple colour in cask, lots of new oak and concentrated fruit, and looked even more impressive than the 1986. Michel Rolland has a great reputation as an oenologist and consultant, and so this *cru* should certainly be worth watching in future.

CHÂTEAU GAGNARD

Owner: Madame Bouyge-Barthe. 18 hectares. 8,000 cases. Mer 50%, CS 25%, CF 25%

The vineyard lies on the *côte* and sandstone bench north of Fronsac. Some of the production is sold under the name of La Croix-Bertrand, and the proprietor also owns Clos Toumalin in Canon-Fronsac. I found the 1983 showed better than the 1982 when both were tasted at the end of 1985; it had lovely perfumed fruit, good structure and breed. This all adds up to very good Fronsac.

CHÂTEAU JEANDEMAN

Owner: Monsieur Roy-Trocard. 30 hectares. 15,000 cases. Mer 80%, CF and CS 20%

This is one of the largest vineyards in Fronsac, and one of the best known. It is on the limestone plateau, at its highest point – 83 metres – where it is covered with red soil, similar to that found in St Christophe-des-Bardes. It is in the commune of St Aignan. The wines are pleasantly and distinctly perfumed, with a delicious fruitiness of flavour, so they are usually very drinkable when three or four years old. The 1978 and 1979 followed this pattern. The 1983 was more tannic and needed more time, but the 1985 has returned to the old pattern. The wines perhaps lack a little solidity when compared to the best wines of the *appellation*.

CHÂTEAU MAYNE-VIEIL

Owner: Roger Seze. 24 hectares. 12,500 cases. Mer 80%, CF 20%

This well-known vineyard is at the boundary of the communes of Saillans and Galgon. Only a third of the property is within the Fronsac *appellation*; the rest, some 50 hectares, makes Bordeaux Supérieur, and even a small amount of white wine. The soil is sandy, mixed with clay. This is an ancient property with records going back to the fifteenth century, and the Sèze family have been owners since 1918. This is one of the most consistently well-made wines of the region, and has been in the vanguard of those properties which have helped to re-establish the reputation of Fronsac in recent years. The wines are most attractive with a rich middle flavour, structure and character, fairly light in body and usually delicious when three to four years old.

CHÂTEAU MOULIN-HAUT-LAROQUE
Owner: Jean-Noël Hervé. 14 hectares. 6,000 cases. Mer 65%, CF 20%, CS 10%, Mal 5%

This fine *cru* is on the *plateau calcaire* and *côte*, south-west of Saillans. The wines are finely perfumed, and combine power and structure, tannins and fruit, with complexity and breed. New oak is clearly evident in the most recent vintages, which will obviously require longer ageing than in the past. The 1978, 1979 and 1982 were all fine examples, while the 1985 has considerable concentration. This must now be counted as one of the leading *crus* of Fronsac.

CHÂTEAU MOULIN-HAUT-VILLARS
Owner: Madame Brigitte Gaudrie. 4 hectares. 2,000 cases. Mer 70%, CF 30%

This small *cru* on the *plateau calcaire*, west of Saillans, and adjoining parts of Château Villars, has become quite well known in England and Belgium. In the early seventies, when I first tasted these wines while working at Loudenne, they were light-textured, perfumed, and attractive for young drinking. Recently the 1986 was disappointingly stringy and marred by harsh tannins, and the 1987 too dry and tannic for the fruit. The use of some new oak has obviously altered the development cycle.

CHÂTEAU PLAIN-POINT
Owner: Denis Ardon. 32 hectares (out of an estate of 52 hectares). 8,000 cases. Mer 75%, CF and CS 25%

This important *cru* lies on the *plateau calcaire* at the northern limits of the commune of St Aignan. The château, parts of which date back to the fifteenth century, stands on one of the highest points of the hills of Fronsac, and was an important stronghold in the Middle Ages. The production here is rising, because the vineyard has recently been doubled in size. My experiences here have been rather mixed. The 1978 and 1979 were very undistinguished, but the 1982 and especially the 1983 were more impressive, firm and solid with breed and style. But then the 1985 was brittle and disappointingly one-dimensional. This is a *cru* of some potential which is still searching for consistency.

CHÂTEAU PUY-GUILHEM

Owner: Janine Mothes. 10 hectares. 4,000 cases. Mer 60%, CF 20%, Mal 20%

This vineyard is on the limestone plateau and *côte* in Saillans, overlooking the valley of the Isle. I found the 1982 rather tough and tannic after a year in bottle, yet it gained a silver medal in Paris. But the 1983 was very perfumed, with plenty of soft Merlot fruit, attractive, with structure behind. This is a good, improving *cru*.

CHÂTEAU LA RIVIÈRE

Owner: Jacques Borie. 40 hectares. 20,000 cases. Mer 60%, CS 30%, CF 5%, Mal 5%

This is certainly the most spectacular of all Fronsac properties, in terms of its chateau and its site. The actual château dates from the thirteenth century and has been restored a number of times, especially in the last century, and most recently by its present owner in 1962. It is sited on a shelf below the limestone plateau, with 15 hectares of woods providing a magnificent backdrop. The vineyard, the largest in Fronsac, is on the *côte*, below and to the left as one surveys the marvellous view from the terrace. The limestone at this point is an exceptional 30 metres thick, providing perhaps the most remarkable *chai* in the Libournais – there are no less than nine hectares of old quarry workings, so that a thousand casks can be stored in a single gallery, and there is storage for a million bottles.

As with all the best wines, one cannot speak of those of La Rivière without speaking of Jacques Borie. He is an intense and passionate man, and this is clearly reflected in his wines. He believes fervently that he is creating a *cru* which can take its place beside the best in the Gironde, and in the process has certainly been one of the pioneers in the renaissance of Fronsac. The wines themselves are powerful, concentrated and assertive in flavour. When young they have that firm, austere character often found in the wines of the St Emilion *côtes* and plateau, but with ageing they can acquire complexity and finesse (as with the 1978 when ten years old). Two factors contribute to this character, and the slow ageing: the limestone cellars, of course, and the practice of not chaptalizing the wines, but using concentrated must instead, when necessary. This concentrates not only the sugar content but also the acidity, so it produces a quite different emphasis from that given by chaptalization. The 1962 and 1966 were still fine and very stylish in 1986. More recently, apart from the fine 1978 already mentioned, the 1983 is most impressive, with more power and concentration than the 1982. The 1979 was a shade lean, showing traces of the high yields of that year, yet was still inky, tannic and firm though short of fruit when nine years old. There was a charming but very solid 1980, at its best when eight years old, and a 1981 full of character, finesse and breed. The 1985 is spicy and concentrated, and will take time to show its class – an object lesson in the fact that the big years here can often seem rather awkward in the early years in bottle. So just how good are these wines? It is not an easy question to answer. On their own terms they are uncompromising, like their owner, and certainly impressive. But it takes time and trouble really to get to know them, and I think I am still learning.

CHÂTEAU ROUET
Owner: Patrick Danglade. 10 hectares. 5,000 cases. Mer 65%, CF 35%

This well-known *cru* is on the limestone plateau in St Germain-la-Rivière, with its château and grounds on the edge of the plateau commanding fine views. When I first came across this wine, its English agent was Bob de Rouet of Brown Gore & Welch, and the bottle was a curious affair with the label embossed on it in gold. The proprietor, Patrick Danglade, is also a *négociant* and has worked hard for the promotion of the region. The reputation of this *cru* is for producing soft, medium-to-light-bodied wines which are attractive to drink when four to five years old. But I have to say that I seem to have been unlucky with most of the vintages that have come my way. An acceptable but rather ordinary 1978 was very forward when four years old; the 1981 was rustic and disappointing when three years old. The 1987 had a good bouquet in cask, but seemed rather acid and mean. However, the 1985 is reported to be fruity and attractive.

CHÂTEAU LA VALADE

Owner: Bernard Roux. 15 hectares. 7,500 cases. Mer 70%, CF and CS 30%

A *cru* on the *plateau calcaire* and *côte*, in the commune of Fronsac, whose wines I have found consistently attractive and fine, perfumed and vigorous, with plenty of character and richness, and undeniable breed. The 1978 was excellent when four years old, and the 1983 is finer than the 1982.

CHÂTEAU LA VIEILLE CURE

Owner: The Old Parsonage (Colin Levenbach, Peter Sachs, Bernard Soulan). 16 hectares (in production – 5 hectares newly planted). 7,000 cases. Mer 80%, CF 15%, CS 5% (after new vineyard comes into production – Mer 75%, CF 20%, CS 5%). Second label: Château Coutreau

This *cru* is on the *plateau calcaire* and *côte*, above the valley of the Isle, in the commune of Saillans. Following its purchase by an American syndicate in 1986 there has been considerable investment here, including a new *cuvier*, just completed. The 1986 and subsequent vintages have been put into cask for the first time, with one-third new oak. Michel Rolland (see Château Le Bon Pasteur, Pomerol) now acts as both consultant and as administrator, so the future looks bright. I have found the wines generally rich and luscious, very Merlot in character, and usually eminently drinkable soon after bottling, but without any great depth or character. The 1983 and 1985 were especially attractive. It will be interesting to watch developments.

CHÂTEAU VILLARS

Owner: Jean-Claude Gaudrie. 16 hectares planted, out of 25 hectares. 11,000 cases. Mer 60%, CF 30%, CS 10%

This *cru*, on the *plateau calcaire* and *côte* of Saillans, has made consistently impressive wines since the first vintage I tasted, the 1979. These attractively rich, fruity wines are full-flavoured and quite solid. Recently a proportion of new wood has been used in the *élevage* and the wines have become more chunky and spicy, and have real flair. I particularly liked the 1983 and 1986.

BOURG AND BLAYE

These two adjoining areas are of roughly similar standing, although the best growths of Bourg are certainly superior to those of Blaye. Geographically they are opposite the Médoc, with Bourg being partly on the Dordogne and partly on the Gironde. But the countryside, with its picturesquely rolling hillsides and mixed agriculture is quite different from the Médoc. The two old ports of Bourg and Blaye were once important for the control of the river, especially in the days when the kings of England held sway in Aquitaine, and a medieval fortress at Bourg forms the foundation for Vauban's seventeenth-century fortress, which complements his other one at Lamarque in the Médoc. Today a ferry operates between the two, as a reminder of how much more important the river used to be.

While a glance at the map will show that the district of Blaye is far larger than Bourg, the vineyards of Bourg are the more extensive, especially as far as the production of red wines is concerned. In Blaye there are some 2,500 hectares of red wine vineyards and 600 hectares for white wine, while in Bourg over 3,000 hectares are devoted to red wine varieties. Although some white wines are made in both districts, with some of the Côtes de Blaye being quite good, it is the red wines that give them their importance.

The best growths of Bourg are on slopes near the Gironde and are noticeably rich and fleshy in texture, with a good colour and pleasantly fruity bouquet. These are attractive, straightforward wines which develop quickly and are usually delicious to drink when three or four years old, but will hold well for another three or four years in good vintages. As an indication of the intrinsic quality of these wines, I have frequently found that a good Bourg will often be superior to many wines from the St Emilion satellites.

The wines of Blaye have less body and often used to be rather astringent. Now, with improved vinification, they are lighter but with an engagingly vivid fruitiness. However, it must, unfortunately, be emphasized that in both districts there are still poor wines to be found owing to careless vinification. Few of the wines now use any wood in their *élevage* and this has actually helped to improve quality and reliability, producing cleaner wines, ready to drink soon after bottling, by eliminating old casks which often, in the past, tainted the wines.

Bourg

There are many châteaux, some of them with very large productions. Among the best known are:

de Barbe (a large property of 65 hectares, has long had a reputation as one of the best growths, consistent and fine)

Beaulieu

du Bousquet (a large property of 72 hectares)

Brulesécaille

Cana (the proprietor is the first Chinese to own a vineyard in Bordeaux!)

Caruel

Castella-La Rose

La Croix-Davids

La Croix-de-Millorit

Croûte-Courpon

Eyquem

Falfas (there is a fine seventeenth-century Louis XIII-style château)

Grande-Maison

Gros-Moulin

Guerry (since it was acquired by Bertrand de Rivoyre in the early seventies – see Fourcas-Hosten, Médoc – it has risen to become one of the best *crus* of the region, and one of the few to be matured in cask; the château has been restored and is now Monsieur de Rivoyre's home)

Guionne

Haut-Launay

Haut-Maco

Haut-Mousseau

Les Heaumes

Laurensanne

Mendoce

Mercier

Le Nègre

Nodot

Clos du Notaire

Les Rocques

Rousselle
Rousset
Sauman
Tayac
Thau
La Tour-Séguy
Tour-de-Tourteau

Note that the very large *cru* of Mille-Secousses, with 48 hectares and a production of around 30,000 cases, is sold entirely as Bordeaux Supérieur.

Blaye

Again, there are many châteaux, only a few of which are yet much known on export markets. Among these may be noted:

Barbé
Bourdieu
Chante-Alouette
Charron
Les Chaumes
Crusquet-Sabourin
L'Escadre
Grand-Barrail
des Graves
Les Gruppes-de-Pivert
Haut-Sociondo
Loumède
Le Menaudat
Pardaillan
Perdoulle
Perenne
Puy-Benet-Boffort
La Rivalerie
Segonzac
Trinité-Valrose
Videau

PREMIÈRES CÔTES DE BORDEAUX

This district extends south along the right bank of the Garonne from just above Bordeaux itself for nearly 50 kilometres, but is never more than two or three kilometres in depth. It is an extremely attractive, hilly area, in sharp contrast to the flat countryside of Graves, Sauternes and Barsac on the opposite bank.

The white wines are covered in the following chapter on Sauternes and other white wines. Whereas the best white wines are to be found in the southern part of the district towards Loupiac and Ste-Croix-du-Mont, more and more red wines are to be found as one goes north. It is also a district where the balance between red and white has been changing in the last decade. In the early seventies the average yield for whites was 66,267 hectolitres against 36,957 of red wines. By the early eighties the proportion of red and white vineyards seems to have reached a new equilibrium, with the reds showing very little change, although some decline in the whites is still evident. The rise in red production may be gauged from the following figures. In 1979 just over 76,000 hectolitres were produced, just about twice as much as in 1970, while by 1986, 110,703 hectolitres were being produced. The wines themselves have, like many of the lesser reds, much improved in the last few years. The best are very perfumed and attractively fruity, of light to medium body and usually delicious drinking when three to seven years old. The wines sold under château names are sharply divided between those who sell in bulk to *négociants* for bottling in their cellars, and those who château-bottle because the price difference to the producer often represents the difference between improvements at the property and stagnation. Unfortunately, château bottling in this context usually means contract bottling, and is still very variable compared with that carried out in *négociant* cellars. In recent tastings, the following were the wines that impressed me most (because it is often not a simple matter to identify a property from its name alone, I have added that of the commune and the proprietor):

Château Bessan at Tabanac. Owner: SARL du Château Bessan.
Château Brethous at Camblanes. Owner: Denise Verdier.
Château Cayla of Rions. Owner: Patrick Doche (see also under dry and
    sweet whites).

Domaine de Chastelet at Quinsac. Owner: Jean Estansan.

Château de la Closiere at Cadillac. Owner: Pierre Dupleich.

Château Fayau at Cadillac. Owners: Jean Medeville et Fils (see also under sweet white wines).

Château La Gorce at Haux. Owner: Marcel Baudier.

Château Gourran at Langouran. Owners: Pierre and Charles Dutreilh.

Château Grimont at Quinsac. Owner: Pierre Yung.

Château Haux at Haux. Owner: Peter Jorgensen.

Château du Juge at Cadillac. Owners: Pierre Dupleich and Denis Dubourdieu.

Château Lagarosse at Tabanac. Owner: Gerard Pierre Laurencin.

Château Lamothe at Haux. Owners: J. Perriquet and Fabrice Neel.

Château Laroche-Bel-Air at Baurech. Owner: Julian Palau (the suffix Bel-Air is a very recent addition, not mentioned in Féret's 1986 edition).

Château Léon at Carignan. Owner: Société du Château Léon (also sold as Domaine de Camélon).

Château Lezongars at Langoiran. Owner: Madame Reine Loncau.

Domaine de la Meulière at Cénac. Owner: Jacques Fourès.

Château Montjouan at Boulac. Owners: Patrick and Anne-Marie Le Barazer.

Château Nenine at Baurech. Owner: Francis Fouquet.

Château de Paillet-Quancard at Paillet. Owners: Marcel and Christian Quancard.

Château Péconnet at Quinsac. Owners: Cave de Quinsac (this is the only *coopérative* specializing in the production of red Premières Côtes).

Château du Peyrat at Caprian. Owners: Lambert Frères (this wine is also sold as Château de Lucat).

Château Plaisance at Capian. Owner: Patrick Bayle.

Château de Plassan at Tabanac. Owner: Jean Brianceau.

Château Reynon at Béguey. Owners: Denis and Florence Dubourdieu (also produces a well-known dry white wine, which is Bordeaux *appellation contrôlée*).

Château Tanesse at Langoiran. Owners: Domaines Cordier (a smaller quantity of dry white wine is sold as Bordeaux *appellation contrôlée*).

CÔTES DE CASTILLON

This is the only other area of importance not completely hidden behind the anonymity of a Bordeaux Supérieur or Bordeaux *appellation*. There are actually two *appellations* – plain Bordeaux Côtes de Castillon, and Bordeaux Supérieur Côtes de Castillon – depending on the alcoholic degree – but almost all the wine of the district is now declared as Bordeaux Supérieur. This hilly, pleasantly rustic area lies behind the ancient market town of Castillon-la-Bataille, and used to be called St Emilionnais until it was excluded from the name by the *appellation*. In truth, when well vinified, the style of these wines is very close to that of the St Emilion satellites and not far behind in quality. There is a touch of roughness and coarseness at first, but this very soon gives way to a pleasantly robust fruitiness.

Production is tending to increase, and the average for the five years from 1982 to 1986 was 112,135 hectolitres, an increase of over 43 per cent from 1975–9. There are a great many properties now selling under their own label, but none has really established a reputation yet. The great problem has been to find properties which are consistent. The best advice is to try any Château wine you come across; often those selected and bottled by a good *négociant* can be more reliable than a château bottling, although this has improved, especially in the eighties. In recent tastings I have found the following wines offered good value and were well made:

Château de Belcier
Château Castegens (also sold as Fontenay)
Château Chante-Grive
Château La Clarière-Laithwaite (a new enterprise of Tony Laithwaite,
    founder of the British mail-order concern, The *Sunday Times* Wine
    Club, and initially declared simply as Bordeaux Supérieur)
Château de Clotte
Château L'Estang
Château Haut-Tuquet
Château Lardit
Château Moulin-Rouge
Château Pitray (the outstanding wine of the *appellation* and as good as
    many a St Emilion)

Château Puycarpin (now under the same management as Château Guerry in Bourg; unusually for the district, cask maturation has been used here since 1984)

Château Rocher-Bellevue

Château Ste Colombe

Château Thibaud-Bellevue

Château La Treille-des-Girondiers

BORDEAUX CÔTES DE FRANCS

As Féret has pointed out, this *appellation* is really something of an anomaly. It lies immediately to the north of the Côtes de Castillon – at the eastern extremity of the Gironde, and to the east of Puisseguin and Lussac. As in Castillon, the production here has admittedly increased, from an average of 4,700 hectolitres in the seventies to over 20,000 hectolitres by 1989, but this is still minuscule compared with its southern neighbour. Is a separate *appellation* really justified? Certainly the Thienponts at Château Puygueraud have shown that fine wines can be made here, but the same thing can be said of the Côtes de Castillon. The *côtes* have the same clayey limestone in both Castillon and the Francs. But the Côtes de Francs does benefit from a special micro-climate: it has the lowest rainfall in the *département* and the most hours of sunshine. Another factor is that the hillsides are predominantly east-facing, with the vines either running south-east (the Ledone valley) or westwards (Isle valley).

CHÂTEAU PUYGUERAUD

Owner: Nicolas Thienpont. 20 hectares. Mer 40%, CF 30%, CS 30%

Château Puygueraud's history is instructive of the economic ups and downs which have affected Bordeaux in the last hundred years. There was great prosperity in the late nineteenth century and at the beginning of the twentieth. During this period the sweet wines of the region were sought after in Russia. But general economic decline, coupled with the loss of the Russian market, and the 1921 legal decision that the St Emilion name could no longer be used, devastated the area. When Georges Thienpont (see under Vieux-Château-Certan, Pomerol) bought the property in 1946 he pulled up the vineyard and put the property to mixed farming. It was only in the late seventies that the decision to replant the vineyards was taken, although the Côtes de Francs *appellation* had been created in 1967. This was a clear response to the new prosperity of the seventies. Twenty hectares have been planted with 40 per cent Merlot and 30 per cent each of Cabernet Franc and Cabernet Sauvignon. The first vintage to be commercialized was the 1983: it has developed an interestingly gamy/spicy bouquet and a flavour that shows concentration and power, remarkable in young vines, and very spicy, almost oriental overtones. I noted that it was certainly not classic Bordeaux. The 1985, with older vines, has more depth of colour, a similar character on the nose, but was more taut and compact on the palate, with spicy liquorice overtones, and again marked individuality.

The *élevage* is divided between vats and casks with 25 per cent new oak each year, and high-temperature fermentations at 32–34°C are used to obtain maximum extraction.

Georges Thienpont had also reconstructed another vineyard, Château Laclaverie, which he left to his son Nicolas in 1984. The vineyard is only 7.5 hectares and the first vintage was the 1985.

Perhaps the most important publicity for the Côtes de Francs has been the creation, by the Thienponts' new *négociant* business, of the Lauriol brand. This is a selection by Dominique and François Thienpont of the best *cuves* from neighbouring properties. Here the Merlot element tends to be more dominant than at Puygueraud, comprising 50 to 60 per cent. A high standard has been set, and is certainly making the name of the Côtes de Francs more widely known.

It is interesting to note that other leading Libournais owners are also beginning to take an interest in the Côtes de Francs. Jacques Hébrard's son Dominique (see Cheval Blanc, St Emilion) and Hubert de Bonard (see L'Angélus, St Emilion) are now busy reconstructing Château de Francs.

OTHER BORDEAUX AND BORDEAUX SUPÉRIEUR

Because a wine does not bear the name of one of the districts with its own *appellation*, it does not mean to say that it will be ordinary or without interest. More and more such wines are appearing on the market, and if well made and carefully selected, can prove excellent as early-drinking, everyday claret. The main source is now the Entre-deux-Mers, where more red wines are now being made, and sold as Bordeaux or Bordeaux Supérieur, since the Entre-deux-Mers *appellation* applies only to white wines. Several individual properties have now begun to make a reputation for themselves, showing once again that quite humble corners of Bordeaux can produce wines of charm and individuality. Among these can be numbered Château Bonnet at Grézillac, home of André Lurton, who has worked so hard to revive the fortunes of Graves (see La Louvière); Château Charles de Montesquieu (actually Château Raymond at Baron, marketed by Janoueix of Libourne – see Haut-Sarpe, St Emilion) – the proprietor is a descendant of the great philosopher; Château Pierrail at Margueron, an outstanding newcomer with dedicated new owners and a lovely château; and Château Thieuley at La Sauve, which has achieved a wide reputation for both its red and dry white wines. The red wine of Château La Gardéra, Cordier's property at Langoiran, which could be sold as a Premières Côtes, like Tanesse, is instead sold as Bordeaux Supérieur. Château Launay at Saussac and Château de Tourtigeac at Targon both have large productions of good red wines.

Another area without its own *appellation* should also be mentioned – the Cubzaguais. This is a corridor of land astride the Paris road, centred on St André-de-Cubzac, and lying between Bourg and Blaye to the north, the Dordogne on the west and south, and Fronsac to the east. The *appellation* is Bordeaux or Bordeaux Supérieur. There are three important properties with very big productions. Château de Terrefort-Quancard belongs to Les Fils de Marcel Quancard, the well-known *négociants* at St André-de-Cubzac. It makes an attractive wine which can age very well in good vintages. There is the even larger Château Timberlay, which often produces over 42,000 cases of sound, straightforward wine. Then, more for its architecture than for its wine, there is Château du Bouilh, the magnificent mansion designed by Victor Louis, architect of the Grand Théâtre in Bordeaux, for the La Tour du Pin family. Only a fragment of this grand design was completed when the Revolution interrupted the work, which was never to be resumed.

The area also has two properties which are best known for bearing the same names as two classified growths of the Médoc: the Domaine de Beychevelle, close to Timberlay and Bouilh, and the Cru Cantemerle at neighbouring St Gervais. They are both decent enough wines, but their names have obviously been useful in selling their wines, especially on export markets.

If, instead of taking the Paris road from St André-de-Cubzac, you turn eastwards, there is another forgotten corner of the Bordeaux *vignoble*, which Féret calls the Region of Guîtres and Coutras. It is north of Lalande de Pomerol and Lussac-St Emilion. Here an adventurous Englishman, Alan Johnson-Hill, settled in 1980, forsaking the business world of Hong Kong. (Amusingly, his Christian name has been Frenchified by Féret as Alain!) Château Meaume has established a reputation for itself in the UK in quite a short time. Using 80 per cent Merlot on the heavy clay and sandy soil, and advised by Michel Rolland (see Le Bon Pasteur, Pomerol), Alan Johnson-Hill has produced wines which have attractive con-centrated fruit and mature quite quickly; the 1985 was delicious after three years. But the revelation that he has invested about £1 million in re-equipping the *cuvier* and *chai* – there are stainless steel vats – and in replanting parts of the vineyard, gives an idea of how hard it is for the ordinary proprietor to justify such investment when an ordinary bottle of Bordeaux *rouge* fetches only about ten francs a bottle, in spite of a benevolent tax system which permits such investment to be written off against tax.

For the sake of completeness, mention must also be made of several *appellations* which have little commercial importance on export markets:

Sainte-Foy-Bordeaux lies in the extreme north-east corner of the Entre-deux-Mers, with the Dordogne river running between it and the *département* and wines of Dordogne. Twice as much white as red wine is produced.

Graves de Vayres is a small enclave in Entre-deux-Mers opposite Libourne. The commercial advantage of being confused with the Graves district south of Bordeaux does not seem to have brought the area any notable *réclame*. About twice as much white as red wine is produced.

In conclusion, it must be emphasized again that many pleasant, useful wines are to be found under the simple Bordeaux and Bordeaux Supérieur *appellations*. For the minute différence in price, it is usually worth going for Bordeaux Supérieur. These are excellent wines for drink-ing when two or three years old, when their youthful fruit still shows to advantage. There has been a great improvement in recent years in *négociants'* generic blends, and many of the wines sold under individual château names are also excellent value. At this price, one can afford to experiment.

11

Sauternes, Barsac and Other White Wines, Both Sweet and Dry

If one were to ask the most occasional wine drinker to describe Sauternes, the chances are strongly in favour of a reply that it is a sweet white wine. Such is the fame of this *appellation* that it is probably more widely known than any other district name in Bordeaux, and it is certainly one of the most famous of all French wines.

Yet the area producing Sauternes is very small, confined to the five communes of Sauternes itself, Barsac, Bommes, Fargues and Preignac. The district forms an enclave in the Graves, with the Garonne as its north-eastern boundary, some 40 kilometres south-east of Bordeaux. The production is also small, accentuated by the much lower yield resulting from the method of production from shrivelled grapes infected with *botrytis cinerea* or noble rot (*pourriture noble*). (For a description of the vinification of Sauternes, see Chapter 2.) The *appellation* permits only 25 hectolitres per hectare, compared with 40 hectolitres for other Bordeaux white wines, such as Graves or Loupiac.

Unfortunately, the fame of Sauternes has led to widespread fraud, and to the unhappy practice of many producers of sweet wines from countries such as Spain, Australia and the United States adopting this name for their own products. This practice of using a geographical name which has gained worldwide fame for the excellence of its product and then trying to give it a generic significance for the benefit of lesser-known wines – usually inferior in quality and always cheaper in price – is to be deplored. Happily, international agreements, and especially the EC, have banished such malpractices from Europe now, but they are still to be found in the United States and Australia, and have also spread to new wine-drinking countries such as Japan.

Until as recently as the first edition of this book, the generally received wisdom was that it was only in the nineteenth century that "botrytized" wines were made in Sauternes, and that in the eighteenth century dry wines, or at best semi-sweet ones, had been made. Now, as in other parts of Bordeaux, modern research in neglected archives and long-forgotten works is producing a different picture. Richard Olney, in his book on Yquem, mentions a document of 4 October 1666, in which the then owner of Yquem reminded his tenants that it was not customary in Bommes and Sauternes to begin the picking before "about 15 October". This is remarkably late, especially when one remembers that in the last century the vintaging of red grapes was habitually earlier than now, at least partly because high sugar contents in the must often led to stopped fermentations and wines turning to vinegar. So grapes harvested at such a time would usually have been affected by noble rot. Then Bidet's *Traité sur la nature et sur la culture de la vigne*, published in 1759, makes it clear that in the mid-eighteenth century sweet, luscious wines were being produced in Sauternes and, furthermore, were especially notable for their ability to age for twenty or thirty years, again in marked contrast to most wines at that time. It shows that there was an understanding of how to vinify such rich musts, and that the residual sugar helped to preserve such wines at a time when most red wine had to be drunk young because of its technical shortcomings. Finally, several eighteenth-century bottles of Yquem, notably from the 1784 and 1787 vintages, discovered in undisclosed circumstances by the German collector Hardy Rodenstock and believed from their engraved bottles to have belonged to Thomas Jefferson, have been found to be of a liquorous character, as well as being remarkably well preserved. (But one wonders if an archaeologist would be satisfied by the evidence for authenticity so far produced!) At least as interesting is the record in the Yquem cellar book that fifty half-bottles of Yquem 1753 were sold in 1821 to Monsieur Guestier of Barton and Guestier, evidence that a sixty-eight-year-old wine was believed to be in good condition still, although in half-bottles.

As has been explained earlier, the selection of grapes with an unusually high concentration of sugar gives a must which even the vigorous yeast of the Gironde cannot fully ferment, resulting in a naturally sweet wine. The *appellation* insists on an alcoholic strength of not less than 13° in the finished wine. Although no minimum is laid down for the sweetness of the wine, in practice it has to pass a tasting test, and one could say that 2.5°–3° Baumé was the practical minimum, with the fine growths producing 5° Baumé or more in good years.

The wines of Sauternes have often been compared with those rarities produced so much further north in the German vineyards. Although the basic principle of the selection of grapes infected by *botrytis* is similar, all the other conditions are so different as to make comparison of doubtful validity. Without going into great detail, it is worth pinpointing two factors of importance. The Beeren- and Trockenbeeren-auslese are essentially the products of special circumstances, prized rarities produced at admittedly uneconomic cost, as prestige wines – the apotheosis of the German vintners' art. In Sauternes, on the other hand, the conditions for making such wines on a large scale are the norm, and not the exception. Sauternes is unlucky if its ratio of failure is significantly higher than for the red wines of the Gironde, though the record for the sixties was below average, with four bad or poor years, one more than for other areas in the Gironde, and the seventies have been no better. The eighties, however, have produced a remarkable string of good and great vintages. Two or three poor years in a decade is more typical. Whereas a large German estate of, say, 30 hectares will in a very favourable year make perhaps 5 per cent, or at most 10 per cent of its production as Beeren- or Trockenbeeren-auslese, in Sauternes a property will in a normal year be able to declare nearly all its production as good enough to sell under its château label. On the debit side, though, is the sad spectacle of musts of insufficient weight being enriched through chaptalization. Such practices are surely the negation of all that Sauternes stands for, and would be unthinkable in Germany for Beeren- and Trockenbeeren-auslese.

The second point which is worth stressing is the tolerance of yeast to sugar. In the conditions under which German wines are fermented, which are very much cooler than those usual in the Gironde, the alcoholic fermentation usually stops somewhere between 9° and 10° Gay-Lussac. In Sauternes, the fermentation continues until at least 13° and often up to 14° or 15°, if the conditions are favourable. This still leaves 4° or 5° Baumé, that is, of unfermented sugar. In other words, the original musts in Sauternes are richer than in Germany and more sugar is converted into alcohol. If the must of a potential Trockenbeeren-auslese were to be transported down to the Gironde and placed in a Sauternes *chai*, its appearance would be quite transformed and one would end up, I suspect, with a much drier wine with more alcohol, but lacking much of that wonderful elegance and harmony which characterizes such wines. So it is not only soil and climate which shape a wine, but the whole milieu in which it is afterwards reared.

The essential point about the Sauternes region is that nowhere else in the world do conditions exist to produce natural, sweet white wines on such a scale or with such consistency, though recent developments suggest that such wines may be produced with some regularity and in some quantity – but from the Rhine Riesling – in parts of northern California. The grape varieties used are exactly the same as for the other white wines produced in the Gironde – the Sémillon, Sauvignon and Muscadelle – but here they reach perfect ripeness by late September, and then the warm, slightly humid climate, typical of this area, encourages the growth of the *botrytis cinerea*. This rather unattractive, furry mould rapidly dehydrates the grapes, thus greatly enhancing the concentration of sugar. The transformation of the grapes progresses from the *grains verts*, fully ripe golden-coloured grapes which are ready for the spread of the *botrytis cinerea, to grains pourris pleins*, which are grapes affected by the *botrytis* spores but still full of juice and smooth-skinned, with brown skins but not yet dehydrated, to the final stage of *grains rôtis* when the grapes are completely desiccated. *Botrytis* is to be found in other parts of Bordeaux – at its best in Ste-Croix-du-Mont and Loupiac, in parts of the Premières Côtes, in neighbouring Cérons, and down the Dordogne at Monbazillac – as well as up to the Loire and, of course, in Germany. But nowhere else is its growth so uniform and extensive, year in and year out, or the resulting wines so unctuous and vigorous. It is the unique balance of alcohol and sweetness which gives Sauternes its special quality, combined with that unique aroma, texture and savour which the *botrytis* alone can bequeath. Other wines may be more elegant or delicate, but Sauternes has an overwhelming bouquet of ripe fruit and a richness of savour and mellow perfection of sweetness not to be found in any other. Yet at its best it should not, and does not, cloy. The acidity and the alcohol are sufficient to balance the great sweetness.

It is not surprising that poets have been inspired by such a wine. One of the happiest and aptest sentiments is "*l'extravagance du parfait*". But, by the same token, Sauternes has found itself an unfashionable wine in recent years. It is not surprising, perhaps, that the great days of Sauternes were in the nineteenth century with its extravagant and flamboyant way of life, or that the Russian Grand Dukes were among its greatest devotees. Then Yquem was the most expensive wine in Bordeaux, surpassing the great red wines of the Médoc. In recent years, the price of the great Sauternes (apart from Yquem itself) has been no more than that of a good *bourgeois* Médoc or St Emilion. Such is the whim of fashion.

One is possibly tempted to think of Sauternes as a wine made for a more leisured age. Although the great châteaux have often demonstrated that different Sauternes can be served throughout a meal, this is not to the taste of most of us. It has to be confessed that Sauternes is really too rich, both in alcohol and sugar, to drink in this way. Yet, served at the end of the meal as an accompaniment to fresh fruit, especially strawberries, raspberries or peaches, or with any sweet dessert which does not incorporate chocolate, it is incomparable. Indeed, it is the only wine which can be drunk with such sweet dishes with complete pleasure. Many of the finest German wines are better drunk on their own, and seem too delicate beside really sweet and strongly flavoured dishes.

In Bordeaux, there are many advocates of drinking Sauternes at the beginning of a meal with *pâte de foie gras*. The combination is certainly a very rich one and, although undoubtedly successful, it does pose the problem of what to do next. Ideally, a consommé is needed to clean and refresh the palate before going on to a red wine. A glass of Sauternes can also be magnificent with Roquefort cheese, the combination of lusciousness and saltiness being unusually delicious and satisfying.

But even if one has to admit that this is a luxury wine, the total quantity produced for the whole world is not, after all, large in an age of rapidly rising living standards. It would indeed be a sad day if there was not a place for such an exquisite luxury. The most recent signs have been encouraging after a long period in the wilderness. In the early fifties the leading growths of Sauternes commanded a rather better price than the second growths of the Médoc. But when prices for red wines improved in 1955, and again in 1959, the Sauternes were left behind. Right through the sixties the price of Sauternes remained static, with the leading classified growths well below the level of the second growths of the Médoc. It was not until the great price explosion of 1971 that Sauternes at last reaped some reward for its labours, and it began to look as if the lean years were past. The 1976 first growths opened at similar prices to the second and third growths of the Médoc. But it was with the 1983 vintage that the area as a whole really took a step forward with an important increase in prices. It was noticeable that, as a result, there were subsequently more serious, well-made wines in the 1986 vintage than there had been in 1983. More growers had enough faith in the commercial rewards to do things as they should be done. But it still needs to be stressed that even at today's prices the leading growths of Sauternes still represent the finest value of any of the great wines of France.

No survey of Sauternes would be complete without a word on the keeping qualities of the wine. One hears very conflicting views expressed on this. It is sometimes said that this is a wine which must be drunk young, that it is at its best when, say, five to seven years old, and generally begins to decline after ten years. In my view, this is both misleading and mistaken.

The chief enemies of Sauternes are oxidization and volatile acidity. Sauternes is prey to both, even more than other white wines, because the tradition of ageing up to three years in cask before bottling is still followed by some producers. With all we know now about the treatment and clarification of wines, and with the lack of real cellars which command a constant low temperature in summer, this long ageing in wood is almost certainly a mistake. In the last few years, we have seen many of the leading châteaux abandon this tradition in favour of much earlier bottling, early during the second winter – if not before – with a corresponding benefit to the wines. What happens at the moment is that, in years when the concentration of sugar is exceptional, the resulting wines may be slightly unbalanced and will darken in colour rather rapidly, as indeed Trockenbeeren-auslese often does. The sugar caramelizes. The deep mahogany colour which results is, in fact, pleasing to the eye and is quite unlike the horrid browning of a normal oxidized white wine. The wine is still deliciously rich and mellow on the palate in such a state, because the sugar and alcohol have allayed the usual effect of oxidization.

Volatile acidity, on the other hand, is more insidious. Because of present methods, most Sauternes tend to have a rather high volatile acidity, but this is not readily detectable on the palate because of the sweetness of the wine which effectively masks it. However, after some years of maturing, one can begin to discern a hard, astringent taste at the finish of the wine in place of the mellow, velvety texture which usually gives Sauternes such a long, lingering flavour. This is the volatile acidity asserting itself, and after this the flavour will shorten and the wine will appear to lose fruit as well as sweetness. I remember a good example of this in the 1959 Yquem. At a banquet in Bordeaux in 1965, Edouard Cruse said he thought the Yquem 1959 being served had an excessive volatile acidity. It was not readily noticeable, but I remembered what he had said and when, about a year later, a customer returned a bottle of the same wine with some trivial complaint, I asked our laboratory to test the volatile acidity. It showed up well above the level that could be expected. The sequel came at a dinner at Loudenne in 1972. We compared the 1959 Yquem against the Suduiraut of the same year. The flavour of the Yquem was shortened by a hard, tarry taste, while the Suduiraut finished long and honeyed.

When discussing this problem with Monsieur Pierre Meslier, the then *régisseur* at Yquem, I was interested to learn that Yquem has been collaborating with the University of Bordeaux on the whole problem of volatile acidity in sweet wines, and one of the results had been the discovery that two differing types of volatile acidity are found in sweet wines. One comes from yeasts and does not normally damage the taste of the finished wine. The second type comes from bacteria, and this is the sort that gradually masks and eventually spoils the flavour of the wine. To prevent this, great care is needed in the actual picking of the grapes, and there is a real hope that the problem can now be prevented.

I think it is this apparent drying-up of a wine, due to high volatile acidity, which the advocates of early drinking have in mind when they say that a wine should be drunk before it is ten years old. There is also the problem of wines which are really too luscious. The concentration of residual sugar causes such wines to colour rapidly and maderize prematurely. This is happening to some 1975s – notably the Rieussec. In fact, a well-balanced wine of a good year can be extremely long-lived. I have drunk wines of the famous 1893 vintage when they were around seventy years old, and they were still of good colour – deep golden, but not mahogany, and sweet and delicious. More recently, it was interesting to find that the 1890 Yquem – a rather light wine, never really luscious – was perfectly preserved when over seventy years old, while examples of the great years of 1867 and 1868 were well past their best and only interesting ruins. Generally speaking, though, I would say that a good vintage from a good growth could be expected to last for thirty to forty years without disappointment – provided always, of course, the wine is well stored. Such wines will usually become drinkable when five to six years old. The sugar in the wine is not usually sufficiently in balance to make for enjoyable drinking much before this, and sometimes sulphur can spoil the nose initially.

The most interesting recent experiments connected with the production of Sauternes centre around what is curiously called "cryo-extraction". "Cryo" comes from a Greek word meaning chill or frost, and the principle is a simple one. The water content of the grapes is turned into ice, so that when the grapes are pressed the ice particles remain in the press while the grape juice, with its high concentration of sugar, is collected. The machine can now be found in several châteaux. I saw the one at Rayne-Vigneau in action in 1987, and others exist at Yquem, Rieussec and Rabaud-Promis. The work is still in the experimental stage, and is under the control of the Institut d'Oenologie de Bordeaux with the full cognizance of the INAO.

To the uninitiated this may seem like a short-cut to making Sauternes. In fact nothing could be further from the truth. The object is precisely to salvage *botrytis*-affected grapes when the moisture, either from a heavy mist or light rain, threatens to dilute the highly concentrated essence which results when grapes reach the *grains rôtis* stage that we have already mentioned. The grapes enter the machine which reduces them over a twelve-hour span to $-7°C$. Then in the morning they are put into the press, and quickly rise in temperature to $-5°C$ which is sufficient to separate the unwanted moisture, in the form of ice crystals, from the juice, with around 350 grams of sugar per litre, which represents a potential alcohol level of $20°$. But if normal grape juice, unconcentrated by the action of the *botrytis*, were to be treated in this manner, a far higher percentage of the volume of the grape would be frozen and the resulting juice would be both unacceptably high in acidity and far too wasteful to be economically viable. It would also certainly be unsuitable for the production of Sauternes.

So what this process promises to provide is a safety net which will encourage the producer to run the risk of waiting for the *botrytis* to develop in the knowledge that should the weather turn at the crucial moment, all is not lost. Indeed high-quality musts can be produced, purged, as it were, of the last-minute dilution which threatened their quality. It in no way diminishes the necessity of harvesting in the traditional way, using a number of *tres* or *passages* through the vineyard to select only grapes suitably affected by the *botrytis*; rather, it will reward the dedication of the traditional producer, and this will perhaps persuade more to follow the same path. The result can only increase the overall quality of Sauternes and certainly should mean that a larger percentage of the crop can be transformed into Sauternes in certain difficult years, improving quality, rather than actually increasing quantity. It is early days yet to judge results, and of course the final judgement can be made only in the glass.

One point in the naming of Sauternes often causes confusion. I said at the beginning of this chapter that Sauternes is produced in five communes, one of which is Barsac. When the *appellation* system was introduced, a separate *appellation* was given to Barsac, because for generations its wines had been sold under their own name. But, at the same time, they were given the right to use the name of Sauternes, so that a Barsac can always be a Sauternes, but a Sauternes need not be a Barsac. More recently, the habit has grown up in Barsac of labelling their wines Sauternes-Barsac, thus making clear the double allegiance. While dealing with names, it is worth pointing out that the terms Haut-Barsac and Haut-Sauternes have no official validity whatsoever. They were often used by growers in the best-situated vineyards before the introduction of the *appellation*, and by merchants both before and after the *appellation* to indicate a superior brand. Some châteaux still preserve the anachronism on their label blocks, as in pre-*appellation* days.

During the lean years for Sauternes, there was much heart-searching as to how the wine could be more successfully promoted, and as to how fraud on the French and German markets could be stamped out. It was pointed out that many wines were of poor quality and many growers were chaptalizing their wines (concentration of the must is forbidden by the *appellation* regulations), resulting in heavy, dull wines unworthy of Sauternes. It seemed obvious that better prices could come only from a better control of quality. The result of several years' deliberation was a Groupement de Producteurs, officially recognized by government law in 1967. This established that the Union des Syndicats, which formed the

Groupement, would sell only in bottle, and that all bottles should carry the numbered vignettes of the Groupement, guaranteeing that this was the true Sauternes which had passed the surveillance of the Commission de Dégustation. Like nearly every such Bordeaux scheme, it was only partly successful, but did a certain amount of good for the standard of generic wines at the time. The entry of the UK into the EC effectively ended the abuse of the Sauternes name on the British market.

Another development of these lean years was the so-called dry Sauternes. The attraction of the idea was that by picking a part of the crop early, the danger of damage from bad weather was alleviated, and a larger yield ensured. The resulting wine, however, could only be called Bordeaux Blanc and not Sauternes. Some growers aimed to produce a full-bodied, drier wine, preserving some Sauternes characteristics; Ygrec (from Yquem) and the dry Filhot were examples of this style. But over the years the experiment enjoyed a very limited success, the results being really neither one thing nor the other – disappointment to those wanting a sweet wine, but not dry enough for those seeking dry wines. On the other hand, some growers have concentrated simply on producing a really dry wine as well as possible. The dry Doisy-Daëne is an excellent example of this, and has proved successful over a number of years. But of course the real solution to this problem is to allow growers to use the Graves *appellation* for their dry wines. This would enable them to obtain a decent price for their dry wines, and so help to prevent the production of ersatz Sauternes through chaptalization. It is already allowed in Cérons, and it is hard to think of any logical reason why such dry wines should not be allowed the name of Graves.

The wines of Sauternes were classified in 1855, along with those of the Médoc. It is a commentary, perhaps, on the comparative neglect of the region that, whereas there has been much speculation for years on a reclassification of the Médoc, there has been none at all in Sauternes. Yquem clearly deserves its special position as the sole *premier grand cru classé* of the region, and few would quarrel with the eleven *premiers crus*. Of the fourteen *deuxièmes crus classés*, however, while one or two may be thought to deserve elevation, there is little now to distinguish most of them from a number of excellent *crus bourgeois* which today command prices which are just as favourable and sometimes superior.

The total production of the classified vineyards represents

approximately 25 per cent of the total Sauternes production, amounting roughly to 350,000 cases per year.

The following figures of production are approximate, and indicate average annual output, as given by the communes and taken from their Déclarations de Récoltes records.

THE OFFICIAL CLASSIFICATION OF THE GREAT WHITE WINES OF SAUTERNES-BARSAC: CLASSIFICATION OF 1855

	CASES
Premier Grand Cru (First Great Growth)	
Château d'Yquem	5,500
Premiers Crus (First Growths)	
Château Guiraud	7,000
Château La Tour-Blanche	5,600
Château Lafaurie-Peyraguey	3,500
Château de Rayne-Vigneau	12,500
Château Sigalas-Rabaud	2,000
Château Rabaud-Promis	4,000
Clos Haut-Peyraguey	3,000
Château Coutet	7,000
Château Climens	4,500
Château Suduiraut	11,000
Château Rieussec	6,000
Deuxièmes Crus (Second Growths)	
Château d'Arche	4,500
Château Filhot	9,500
Château Lamothe (Despujols)	2,000
Château Lamothe-Guignard	2,000
Château Myrat	replanting
Château Doisy-Védrines	2,200
Château Doisy-Daëne	4,000
Château Doisy-Dubroca	425
Château Suau	1,500
Château Broustet	1,700
Château Caillou	4,000
Château Nairac	2,000
Château de Malle	2,700
Château Romer-du-Hayot	4,000

As in other parts of this book, the châteaux, both classified and unclassified, are arranged in alphabetical order, and since the differences between the wines of the five communes are certainly no greater than those between different *crus*, I have not listed them separately.

CHÂTEAU D'ARCHE
Deuxième Cru Classé. Owner: Bastit-St-Martin family. Administrator: Pierre
Perromat. 35.5 hectares. 4,500 cases. Sém 80%, Sauv 15%, Musc 5%

One of the three growths in the commune of Sauternes which were classified as *deuxièmes crus* in 1855, the property takes its name from the Comte d'Arche, who was owner from 1733 to 1789, and who was responsible for establishing the reputation of the wine. The fact that d'Arche was placed among only the *deuxièmes crus classés* in 1855 was due to the divisions in the property which occurred as a result of the Revolution, so that in 1855 it was of much less importance than it had been in the 1780s. The vineyard is magnificently placed on one of the best ridges in the commune.

Pierre Perromat, for thirty years the President of the INAO and a proprietor in the Entre-deux-Mers, leased the property in 1981, and has set out to make a classic Sauternes again. The traditional *trie* is now made in the vineyard, the musts are also carefully selected and, after fermentation in vat, the wine is matured in cask, with some element of new wood. Immediately the 1981 was a big improvement on the 1980; there is a good 1982, then the 1983 is a really botrytized wine, rich, powerful and fine. The 1984 is very commendable, botrytized, stylish and rich. The 1986 is the best yet: combining opulent lusciousness with *race* and elegance, it was clearly better than a number of *premiers crus*, and comparable in class with the better ones. It should be noted that the formerly well-known second label, d'Arche-Lafaurie, has not been used since Pierre Perromat took charge.

The only fine mature pre-Perromat vintage I have tasted recently was the 1971, which was luscious and fine in 1985, and showed the potential of the vineyard.

CHÂTEAU BASTOR-LAMONTAGNE
Cru Bourgeois. Owner: Crédit Foncier de France. 36 hectares. 7,500 cases. Sém
70%, Sauv 20%, Musc 10%

This excellent *cru*, adjoining Suduiraut in the commune of Preignac, would have been classified in 1855 but for the whim of its proprietor. Today the wines are carefully made and are on the level of the *crus classés*, and better than some of them. The wines are traditionally made and aged for up to three years in cask, of which some are new. The resulting wines are rich and luscious with an aroma and flavour of apricots, and the style and savour of fine classic Sauternes. In recent years the 1975, 1976, 1980, 1982 and 1983 have all been excellent examples of these vintages. In addition to all this, the wines are wonderful value for money.

CHÂTEAU BROUSTET

Deuxième Cru Classé. Owners: Fournier family. Administrator: Eric Fournier. 16 hectares. 1,700 cases. Sém 63%, Sauv 25%, Musc 12%

This good Barsac *cru* is gradually re-establishing its reputation under the careful management of Eric Fournier (see Château Canon, St Emilion). The property has actually been in the family since 1885, although they did not replant it until 1900. At that time it was better known for having the largest *tonnellerie* (cooperage) in the Gironde, and it was the great-great-grandfather of today's owners who established the dimensions of the *barrique bordelaise*, which was then registered by the Chambre de Commerce as the norm for all Bordeaux casks.

The wines are fermented in small stainless steel vats and matured for two years in cask with 50 per cent new oak. They are finely perfumed, generous and quite rich but not very liquorous, with real individuality and breed. The 1947 still had great vinosity and sweetness when tasted in 1985, showing the power and breed of this *cru* in a great vintage. More recently the successes have been a ripe and richly fruity 1979, a delicately lemony 1981, an elegant 1983, a light but pleasing 1985, while 1986, 1988 and 1989 move on to a new level of excellence, with richer, more concentrated wines of real breed. This is now certainly a wine to watch.

CHÂTEAU CAILLOU

Deuxième Cru Classé. Owner: Bravo GFA. 15 hectares. 4,000 cases. Sém 90%, Sauv 10%

This fine old *cru* lies in the extreme south-west of Barsac near Climens. The wines are not very well known on export markets, because 30 per cent of them are sold by *vente directe* in France. The property has been in the same family since 1909, and the present owner has run it since 1969. The wines are traditionally made, with cask maturation for three or four years after vinification in vat. For this reason the wines often taste awkward when young and sometimes seem to have too much sulphur. But I have memories of a marvellous bottle of the 1920, and the present owner maintains stocks of old vintages for sale, which show what this *cru* can achieve with bottle age. There is a stylish 1988, and 1989 promises to be a great wine.

CHÂTEAU CLIMENS
Premier Cru Classé. Owner: Lucien Lurton. 30 hectares. 4,500 cases. Sèm 98%, Sauv 2%

One of the two great wines of Barsac, this is always among the finest wines of Sauternes, and one of the few that can rival Yquem for the perfection of its flavour and breed, if not for its power. It has long enjoyed an outstanding reputation on the English market, where a small but consistent following for these fine wines has been maintained, even in the bleakest years for this district.

It is interesting to note that almost the entire vineyard is planted with Sémillon, which is said to suit the chalky soil. From 1885 until 1971 Climens was the property of the Gounouilhou family, who then sold it to Monsieur Lucien Lurton of Brane-Cantenac. Continuity has been provided by Madame Janin, the *gérante* and *maître de chai*, who has been there for over thirty-five years, and whose family have been here for over a century. The simple but charming single-storey seventeenth-century château was tastefully restored in 1987.

It is amusing to note that early references to Climens in the nineteenth century still used the form Climenz, and anyone familiar with the Girondin patois can readily imagine that this was how the name would have been pronounced until very recently. The name has been traced back to Jehan Climenz, who in the fifteenth century collected a tax on ships navigating the Garonne, and gave to the captains, as a receipt, a branch of blue cypress which became known as the "*cypressat*". This is the origin for the new secondary *marque* used for the 1984 vintage, Les Cyprès de Climens.

The soil here is red sand and gravel over limestone. After pressing and settling for twenty-four hours in vat, the juice is fermented in casks, of which 25 per cent are new, and matured for about two years prior to bottling. There is a tendency to say that Lucien Lurton is a good farmer, but that his wines leave something to be desired. Looking at the wines since 1971, the first decade certainly made the most of the two great vintages, 1975 and 1976, while the successes of the eighties must surely reduce the critics to silence. One problem, of course, is that when the *crus classés* of the region were compared in cask, Climens, like Yquem, was always absent, since until the 1988 vintage it was never offered for tasting before bottling. But as interest in the great sweet wines of Bordeaux revives, and more comparative tastings of bottled wines are held, Climens's true worth is becoming more apparent to its admirers and critics alike.

Looking back over my notes, I am struck by the consistently high quality achieved at Climens over many years, even during the most difficult periods for the region. These are very long-lived wines, combining freshness, elegance and breed without the weight of the very best Sauternes, as distinct from Barsac, but with a lusciousness which slowly opens up with age. The balance, which is one of the greatest charms of the wines, means that it keeps its colour and hardly ever goes dark, so maderization is a stranger here. The oldest wines I have tasted are the 1928 and 1929, an interesting contrast in styles. Thus the 1928 could have been twenty years younger, when tasted in 1988, such were its freshness and balance. There was a beautifully elegant aroma of caramel and apricots; the wine had only medium richness, but had a lovely flavour and was powerful in terms of alcohol and glycerine, all set off by its wonderful freshness. The 1929 was a deep mahogany colour and more like a Sauternes than is usual with Climens. With its magnificent barley-sugar nose and its enormously rich sweet flavour without a trace of volatility to cut the lingering finish, it was certainly one of the giants among all the great sweet wines I have drunk, and worthy to take its place among the great Yquems. After a particularly fine 1943, the best of the wartime vintages, the 1947 is one of the legendary Climens. It was wonderful when ten to fifteen years old, it is still beautiful today. In 1988 I noted its full golden colour in contrast to the mahogany of most wines of this year now, the marvellously exotic highlighted fruit on the nose, the superb flavour with its concentrated sweetness yet with balance and elegance which allow the fruit to sing through, as perfect a wine as one can wish for in an imperfect world. In contrast the 1948 is the only vintage where I have recorded some volatile acidity; it was powerful in flavour but lacking the usual Climens elegance. Then came a classic 1952, serving only to underline the tragedy at Yquem, where the crop was destroyed by hail, followed by the magnificent 1955 – a shade deeper in colour and more liquorous than the 1928 when tasted alongside it in 1988; it was very complete with great power and went magnificently with food. I have always found the 1961 too much of a good thing in Sauternes, too alcoholic and clumsy, but the story is a very different one in Barsac, where both Climens and Coutet are superb. The colour in 1986 was full gold with caramelized sweetness and great richness on the nose, and a flavour which was opulent and concentrated, very sweet, without a hint of volatility. In wonderful condition, it seemed set to follow the path of the 1928. In contrast the 1962 is classic Climens, lighter and only moderately sweet, with typical finesse and freshness. Although 1969 was only a moderate year, the Climens, in spite of a hint of tar on the nose, was still fresh with nice fruit and moderate sweetness, good for the year and fully mature in 1987. The last pre-Lurton vintage, the 1970, is a beautifully balanced wine with its aroma of apricots and long, lingering finish; it was still at its peak in 1989 and is, with Yquem and Suduiraut, one of the best wines of the vintage.

In the same year I had the opportunity of tasting a complete range of the Lurton years, together with Michael Broadbent and my wife, Serena Sutcliffe, prior to a Christie's sale. The first vintage in the range had noticeably the deepest colour, and all agreed the 1971 was a great bottle. The nose was powerful yet not as open as one would have expected, the flavour was very rich and sweet with caramel notes and a marked *botrytis* character, probably near to its best. The 1972 was certainly a surprise for the year, with its light, well-balanced fruit and even a touch of elegance. The 1973 had a pleasing smell of peaches but was not as elegant as usual, being rather short; but it was balanced and pleasant to drink. The 1974 was the least good wine in the range, with less style and sweetness than the 1977, and looked rather coarse and old. Then came the great pair of 1975 and 1976 with their complete contrast in styles. The 1975 is a much more botrytized and concentrated wine with some tarriness, rare in Climens, in the line of the 1961 and 1929, while the 1976 is luscious with great beauty of flavour, but more complex with highlighted fruit, freshness and finesse, more in the style of the 1947, a really great Climens. After the giants, the 1977 is a small wine with light fruit and a touch of acidity, yet the class of the *cru* comes through, and it is eminently enjoyable. The 1978, with no *botrytis*, has luscious sweetness but very scented fruit and attractive vinosity, making it drinkable now yet also, I suspect, a keeper. The 1979 has fresh, elegant fruit on the nose but is a little coarse-grained for Climens, with a pronounced flavour; not top-class but a nice aperitif Barsac. The 1980 has more colour than the 1979 or 1981, with lovely soft, delicious, silky fruit and more typical Climens *race* than the 1979. One can enjoy it now. The 1981 is the best of the vintages between the two peaks of 1976 and 1983. It is very elegant and long on the palate with quite rich fruit and more weight than the 1982, and there is a delightful flavour of barley sugar, oranges and apricots. The 1982 is an early developer with light fruit and medium weight and pleasing barley-sugar touches, a good wine in this uneven year for Sauternes. The 1983 is one of the stars of this great vintage, the nose rich and sumptuous, full of concentrated fruit essences; the flavour has typical Climens balance with rich, complex fruit, promising a great future, along the lines of the 1976. The 1984 marked a departure for Climens: by the time the wine came to be bottled (like Yquem, Climens was never offered for tasting or sale while in barrel at this time) it was known that not only had an outstanding wine been made in 1985, but that the 1986 would rival the 1983. So for purely marketing and commercial reasons, the wine which had been intended for sale as Climens 1984 was instead sold as Les Cyprès de Climens at about one-third of the 1983 price, and about half the price of the 1985. The wine is beautifully scented, light and very elegantly fruity, with typical Climens *race*, and certainly better than several wines sold as Climens in the seventies. Immediately after bottling in October 1987, the 1985 showed lovely complex fruit flavours, a long lingering finish and great style. It has less weight and power than the 1983 or 1986, but is nevertheless a fine wine of real potential for medium-term keeping. The 1986, bottled in September 1988, immediately showed exceptional quality, and was quickly hailed as the outstanding wine of the vintage – prior to the appearance of Yquem. There is a marvellously elevated bouquet of great ripeness and freshness, a lovely botrytized concentration combined with Climens's typical elegance, and great persistence of flavour. With 1988 and 1989 both exceptional vintages this is a remarkable decade for Climens.

CHÂTEAU COUTET
Premier Cru Classé. Owner: Marcel Baly. 36 hectares. 7,000 cases. Sém 80%, Sauv 20%

This is the inseparable twin of Climens, as the other great wine of Barsac. It has been a favourite in England for many years. The relative merits of the two wines have often been debated. In general, it can be said that Coutet has rather more delicacy than Climens, but that Climens is the more powerful. But when I was last able to compare the two side by side, the 1975 Climens had more finesse than the Coutet, and when compared in 1989, the same was true for the 1976, so no generalization is sacrosanct. Curiously, the great years of Coutet often do not coincide with the great years of Climens. Thus Coutet was renowned for its 1949, while the 1947 was the great vintage at Climens.

For thirty years the proprietors of Coutet were the Rolland-Guy family, who tended it with the greatest care. They sold it in 1977 to Monsieur Baly. At the time of the 1855 classification, it belonged to the Lur-Saluces family. The château dates in part from the end of the thirteenth century; another part is fourteenth century, the rest more recent, but harmonizing well with the older parts.

Under the management of the Rolland-Guy family, Coutet had a fine record for excellence and consistency. The only example of the famous 1947 vintage I have tasted was Belgian-bottled, had a very tarry finish by 1986, and was drying up owing to high volatile acidity. This wine never had the reputation of the Climens. Here the great year was 1949, still superb when last tasted in 1972. The 1950 was probably the outstanding wine of the vintage, preferable to the Yquem. The 1955 and 1959 were both excellent, and the 1961 had an elegance and delicacy not normally associated with this vintage, with less weight than the marvellous Climens, but a lovely balance which made it still fresh and on peak form in 1985. After an excellent 1962, the 1966 was rather light, but perfumed and elegant, but the 1967 was disappointing in the context of the year. The 1970, with its perfumed, supple, delicate fruit, is pleasing but understated, while the 1971 was a great success with lovely flowery, elegant fruit and a delicious flavour, fresh and at its peak in 1987, but with no great *botrytis*, simply gorgeous fruit and breed. The 1975 is a classic in a year when many wines were clumsy and unbalanced; the 1976 is perfumed and luscious – it has broadened out considerably since I first tasted it, and by 1989 was more botrytized in appearance than Climens and not as stylish, as it had at first seemed.

Since Marcel Baly took over, the intention has been to continue in the traditional path. But the 1979, although elegant, is rather dry; the 1980 has more finesse, is rather understated, and is light-textured. The 1981 is light and fruity, but a shade skeletal and not really distinguished. The 1983 is much more interesting, very deep in colour for the year, heavily botrytized on the nose, with lots of apricots and *botrytis* character about the flavour, a delightful wine and easily the best since 1976. Both 1988 and 1989 produced wines in a more classic Coutet mould. The emphasis is noticeably different from Climens now in the big years, and the wines promise to develop more quickly.

CHÂTEAU DOISY-DAËNE

Deuxieme Cru Classé. Owner: Pierre Dubourdieu. 14 hectares. 4,000 cases. Sém 100%

This growth, with the charming name, belongs to one of the most avant-garde vinificators in the region. Monsieur Pierre Dubourdieu is a tremendous enthusiast who is always trying to improve his wine. He believes that the consumer today wants wines which are fruity, but light and fresh. He is also a great advocate of drinking wines young. His son, Denis, took over the management in 2000.

One of the most successful dry wines is made here. It is intended for early drinking, and bottling taking place when the wine is about nine months old. But a few bottles of the 1964, which I kept to observe their development, have lasted very well, taking on some body but remaining fresh and acquiring a delicate flavour, not unlike a good Graves. It is made from the unusual combination of 50 per cent Sémillon, 20 per cent Sauvignon, and with the balance comprising Muscadelle, Riesling and Chardonnay. The Sauternes is also bottled earlier than at most properties and has a delicious fresh fruitiness and a really distinguished flavour, always beautifully balanced. Its quality is certainly on a par with the *premiers crus* today, and it enjoys an excellent reputation. It is well known on the English market.

The vineyard lies in the best part of Barsac, between Climens and Coutet. Originally this formed part of Château Doisy, the single property of the 1855 classification. The owner of the undivided property at that time was an Englishman called Deane, whose name, by some extraordinary transmutation, was corrupted into Daëne.

The special methods of vinification and élevage developed and used by Pierre Dubourdieu are certainly worthy of particular note. The sweet wine is made entirely from Sémillon. Modern horizontal presses are used, and the juice from each pressing is fermented in stainless steel vats at a controlled temperature of not more than 18°C. After fifteen to twenty-one days, when the balance between alcohol and residual sugar is judged to be correct, the temperature is lowered to 4°C, which stops the fermentation. The wine is then filtered and racked into new casks, where it remains for only two or three months; in other words, only during the coldest part of the winter. Then the final *assemblage* is made, not later than March, and after another sterile filtration, the wine goes into stainless steel vats and is bottled about a year later. Before bottling, the temperature is again lowered to 4°C and the wine is bottled with a sterile filtration. All this enables Doisy-Daëne to be bottled with far less sulphur than any other Sauternes, and results in a light, fresh style which is a revelation. It also makes the young wines seem easier to drink and much fresher than other Sauternes, besides enhancing their finesse. But it would be a mistake to think that because of this precociousness, they will not keep. The superb balance often ensures a longer life than for many heavier, less balanced wines.

The only old vintage of Doisy-Daëne I have seen is the 1934, a lovely wine which has lasted very well. More recently, the 1953, which has also lasted well, was a great success as were the 1959, 1961 and 1962, followed by the 1967, 1970, 1971, 1975 and 1976 – the 1975 being one of the best-balanced wines from this difficult, because very botrytized, vintage. The 1978 (very late-picked in November) has no *botrytis* but is very elegant, and the 1979, 1980, 1981 and 1982 were all worthy examples. The 1983 is typically elegant and taut, the 1986 was finer, with a wonderfully flowery, delicate bouquet, and complexity, with many nuances of flavour. It has the finesse of a premier *cru*, without quite the weight of the best *crus*.

CHÂTEAU DOISY-DUBROCA

Deuxième Cru Classé. Owner: Lucien Lurton. 3.3 hectares. 425 cases. Sém 90%, Sauv 10%

This is the smallest part of the original Doisy property. It was purchased in 1880 by the Dubroca family, and became connected with Climens when one of the family married a Gounouilhou daughter. Then, just after the First World War, it was bought by Monsieur Gounouilhou. Since then it has effectively been used as the second wine of Climens. When Monsieur Lucien Lurton bought Climens in 1971, Doisy-Dubroca was included in the sale.

The vineyard lies between Climens and Coutet. The wine is now exclusively and appropriately distributed by Louis Dubroca, an excellent firm of *négociants* owned by one of the most respected members of the Bordeaux trade, Monsieur Bertrand de Rivoyre. The wine is liquorous and fine. After a beautiful 1971, a remarkably good 1972 was produced – a surprise indeed from that meagre year – followed by an elegant 1973. The 1974 is full-blown and forward, but remarkable for the year, while the 1975 is elegant and classic yet powerful. Then, after a really fine 1976, the 1979 was very successful for the year, followed by good wines in 1980 and, 1981, a quick-developing 1982, a 1983 with all the character of the year, and an elegant 1985, full of lovely scented fruit, and a richer, more concentrated, 1986.

CHÂTEAU DOISY-VÉDRINES

Deuxième Cru Classé. Owner: Pierre-Antoine Castéja. 20 hectares. 2,200 cases. Sém 80%, Sauv 20%

This is the parent trunk of the original Château Doisy of the 1855 classification. The Védrines comes from the Chevaliers de Védrines, who owned the property for several centuries until 1840. The present administrator, Monsieur Pierre-Antoine Castéja of *négociants* Maison Joanne, comes from a very old Bordeaux family of proprietors, and is connected with the families through which the property has passed by marriage since 1840. This property contains the original Doisy château and *chai*.

The vineyard lies between Coutet and Climens, and the wines are traditionally made with fermentation and maturation in casks, of which 25 per cent are new. The fermentation, carried out under temperature-controlled conditions, is stopped by dropping the temperature to −4°C. The wine enjoys a good reputation and is well known and appreciated in England. There is a marked contrast between Védrines and the other two Doisys, both of which concentrate, in slightly different ways, on elegance and delicacy. Védrines is fuller-bodied and richer, but often at the expense, in my view, of finesse and style. Curiously though, I found the 1975 better balanced than the 1976, whereas at many properties it is often the other way round. Of more recent vintages, the 1982 shows no *botrytis* and is rather dry with a certain coarseness; the 1983 is very botrytized and barley-sugar, very rich and sweet, still ungainly and not quite in balance by 1988. The 1986 will probably be better: also botrytized and slightly tarry in character, it has more style and balance than any wine here since 1975. Then came 1989, the best Védrines I have ever tasted in cask.

It should be noted that whereas the red wine sold as La Tour-Védrines comes from the property, Chevalier Védrines is a Joanne brand quite unconnected with this vineyard.

CHÂTEAU DE FARGUES

Cru Bourgeois. Owner: Comte Alexandre de Lur-Saluces. 10 hectares. 1,000 cases. Sém 80%, Sauv 20%

This *cru* is not as small as its scarcity might suggest. But the owner, Comte Alexandre de Lur-Saluces, sets out to make the best possible Sauternes, with the same team and the same uncompromising standards as at Yquem. Not only are the yields therefore small, but the vineyard is also prone to frost damage, so that there is an unfortunately high failure rate on this account. Wine-making here follows the classic Yquem pattern, with fermentation and maturation in new oak casks. The resulting wines combine lusciousness and elegance with considerable breed and finesse, while being distinctly less liquorous than Yquem itself. Wonderful wines were made in 1947, 1967, 1971, 1975, 1976 – which is better balanced and more elegant than the 1975, 1980, 1981, 1983 and 1985. The wines here achieve the standard of a top *premier cru classé*, but the price reflects this, and this is indeed the most expensive Sauternes after Yquem itself.

CHÂTEAU FILHOT

Deuxième Cru Classé. Owner: Comte Henri de Vaucelles. 60 hectares. 9,500 cases. Sém 60%, Sauv 37%, Musc 3%

This beautiful property of 330 hectares, the largest estate in the district, with a magnificent eighteenth-century mansion, is set among fields and woods. In fact only the *corps de logis* is from this period; the massive scheme in which it is now set is a neo-Louis XVI extravaganza designed in 1850 by Pierre-Alexandre Poitevin for Romain-Bertrand de Lur-Saluces. The English-style landscaped park was laid out at the same time by the celebrated landscape gardener Louis-Bernard Fischer, who was also responsible for the Jardin Public in Bordeaux. The estate belonged to the Lur-Saluces family for many generations until the owner, the Comtesse Durieu de Lacarelle, herself a Lur-Saluces and sister of Marquis Bertrand de Lur-Saluces at Yquem, died, and it passed by inheritance to the Vaucelles family.

Situated in the commune of Sauternes, the vineyard is the most southerly in the commune. The wine is distinctly drier than the other *crus classés* and for a time enjoyed a great following in England. One has the impression that this following is now less strong than it used to be. I remember a glorious bottle of the 1928 I had with Sir John Plumb (Emeritus Professor and past Master of Christ's College, Cambridge) but in recent years I have been unable to be enthusiastic about this growth. It should be noted that, like Guiraud, there is a higher than usual proportion of Sauvignon in the vineyard, so that the wines are not usually very liquorous, except in the great years. One of the greatest vintages here is the 1947, a superbly balanced wine, with honeyed fruit and a gorgeous flavour, but the 1945 is now very caramelized, and lacks the same balance, finesse and charm. The 1969 is a good example of what can be achieved here in a light vintage; there is a delicate, honeyed bouquet and a well-balanced and charming flavour. This was all before the present management took over in 1974. Then it is interesting to note that both the 1975 and 1976 are decidedly more liquorous and fat than older vintages used to be. The 1979 shows combined SO_2, too much in solution giving a soapy taste, in contrast with "free" SO_2, which affects the bouquet. This vintage quite lacks finesse and fruit. The 1981 was sweet and raw, but without much sign of *botrytis* or real style by 1987. The 1982 also has no *botrytis* but is much more stylish and harmonious. The

1983 was much better, with real *botrytis* character and a lovely flavour, although a very raisin-like finish. The 1986 again seemed to underline that very botrytized years are not always the most successful here at the moment. It has a very tarry character and is a bit spiky and coarse, although quite impressive in its way. But it is not so good, for instance, as d'Arche.

To summarize, one feels that the full potential is not at present being realized at an estate where past experience shows that exceptional wines can be made.

Sichel originally pioneered the marketing of a dry wine which was of the Ygrec type but, I thought, more successful. However, its appeal proved limited, and it has been discontinued.

CHÂTEAU GILETTE
Owner: Christian Médeville. 3.5 hectares. 400–900 cases. Sém 83%, Sauv 15%, Musc 2%

This tiny vineyard is one of the marvels and curiosities of Sauternes. It is to be found just outside the village of Preignac, where the soil is sandy with a subsoil of rock and clay. The Médeville family also own the important Graves property of Respide-Médeville, but they were first to be found in the parish of Preignac around 1710.

The particularity of this *cru* lies in the fact that its wines are not "assembled", or bottled at the usual time. Usually between three and seven *tries* are made, with the earliest being of single berries affected by *botrytis*. Then each picking is separately vinified, with the temperature controlled at 24–25°C during the first days of fermentation, and then reduced to 20°C for the remainder of the fermentation. This results in several different *cuves* with differing characteristics, which at most properties would simply be assembled to make the *grand vin*. But here two separate wines are usually made. Christian Médeville believes in allowing the fermentations to finish naturally, and when they have, they are then kept in small concrete vats for at least twenty years. The theory is that the large volume allows a mature bouquet and flavour to develop, while preserving the wines' fruit and freshness, so that the maturation process is slower than in a bottle; the resulting wines are sold mostly to leading French restaurants and to connoisseurs.

In 1985 I had the opportunity to taste and compare a number of vintages prepared and aged in this way. There was an interesting comparison between the 1955 and 1959, which had both been bottled in 1981, twenty-six and twenty-two years respectively after these vintages, and the 1949 and 1950, bottled earlier, in 1955 and 1957 respectively. In both cases I thought the earlier bottlings were clearly superior to the later ones. In particular the 1959 and 1955 lacked the bouquet and wonderful harmony of the 1950 and 1949. Certainly the 1955 and 1959 had great sweetness and concentration, but they seemed lacking in complexity. The 1949 was the finest of the quartet, the 1955 was better than the 1959, and the 1950 a beautifully elegant example of this fine Sauternes vintage. All of these except the 1950 were labelled as Crème de Tête, as was the oldest wine on display, the marvellous 1937, bottled in 1945, which still had a wonderfully honeyed flavour and was fresh and superb.

The conclusion seems to be that while this unique system means you can find an old vintage more readily, it is far from clear that the resulting wines are as good as they would have been had they been bottled earlier, and if you are contemplating buying a vintage of Gilette, it is clearly important to know the date of bottling. You may even prefer more conventionally prepared wine from their other property, Les Justices.

CHÂTEAU GUIRAUD

Premier Cru Classé. Owner: SCA du Château Giraud. Administrator: Frank Narbey. 118 hectares. Main wine: 7,000 cases. Sém 54%, Sauv 45%, Musc 1% Dry white: 4,000 cases. Sauv 100%. Red: 8,000 cases. CS 50%, Mer 50%

This is the only *premier cru*, apart from Yquem, wholly in the commune of Sauternes itself. Curiously, this is the only one of the *premiers crus* to have changed its name completely since the 1855 classification, when it was known as Château Bayle. The last years of Paul Rival's ownership saw a losing battle against falling demand and an enormous property lacking the resources to maintain itself, let alone modernize or improve. When the young Canadian Hamilton Narbey arrived in 1981 the property was badly run down. Fortunately, the Narbey family has had the resources to carry out the extensive repairs needed in the château and *chai*, as well as to improve the vineyard. The aim has been to make classic Sauternes once more, and to generate a regular business with the Bordeaux Sec "G" and La Dauphine du Château Guiraud, which is red Bordeaux Supérieur. This is one of the largest vineyards in the region, and is unusual in the high proportion of Sauvignon. This has led historically to light, elegant wines which are less luscious than those of most of Guiraud's neighbours, but produced very fine wines in vintages such as 1953, 1955, 1957 and 1962. The last fine vintage of this period I have tasted is the 1967, rich in alcohol and *fin* but not really luscious, with the Sauvignon influence coming through, when tasted in 1988. But then, in the last years of Paul Rival's stewardship, the quality greatly suffered. There was no longer the money to mature the wines in cask, and they were kept in vat. Thus the 1975 was heavy and clumsy, and the 1979 dry and disappointing. The 1980 was made by the old regime, but the *élevage* and bottling were the work of Hamilton Narbey and his new team. It is a lightweight, but elegant with nice fruit. Frank Narbey, Hamilton's father, has now taken over.

Now the policy has returned to a more classic path, and cask maturation with 50 per cent new wood is used. The first vintage, the 1981, is not altogether a success in my opinion, with alcohol rather than sweetness at the finish, but there is some pleasing fruit. The 1982 is drier still, and again one is conscious of the alcohol. The real successes begin with the arrival of Xavier Planie as *régisseur* in 1983, so the departure of Hamilton Narbey in 1988 did not interrupt the progress already made. The 1983 itself has a lovely flavour, length and fine fruit, elegance and real *race*. This is the best Guiraud for many a long day and puts this famous old *cru* back where it belongs among the leading wines of the region. The 1984 is rather dry and light; one is conscious of the alcohol because of the lack of sugar. The 1985 is a beauty, classically luscious and honeyed with gorgeous fruit, elegance and breed. The 1986 has an exotic quality, a beautiful flavour, complexity, length and richness, with great *race* – even better than the 1983 in my judgement.

So with these three marvellous wines, the 1983, 1985 and 1986, Guiraud has clearly re-established its position, and can now be regarded as among the leading *premiers crus*. I think back to the greatest old Guiraud I have ever tasted, the 1893, still fresh and sweet when seventy years old, and I am glad to see worthy successors being made today.

The dry "G" however, has not been an unqualified success. It is now cask-fermented, but the right formula does not yet seem to have been found. The wines often look quite attractive to start with, but then the evolution disappoints.

CHÂTEAU GUITERONDE

Owner: GFA du Hayot. 30 hectares. 7,500 cases. Sém 65%, Sauv 25%, Musc 10%

This large and well-known Barsac *cru* lies at the western extremity of the *appellation*, beyond Climens and south of Caillou. André du Hayot makes elegant, stylish wines, as he does at Romer-du-Hayot. A half-bottle of the 1923 drunk in 1985 was so beautifully balanced that I thought it a 1947! It was still in superb condition, with no maderization. More recently there was a good 1982, quite rich with fruit and charm, and an excellent 1985, delicately perfumed, with a beautifully textured flavour showing real finesse and breed. This is good Barsac and good value for money.

CLOS HAUT-PEYRAGUEY

Premier Cru Classé. Owner: Jacques Pauly. 15 hectares. 3,000 cases. Sém 83%, Sauv 15%, Musc 2%

In 1855 there was one *domaine*, Château Peyraguey, belonging to Monsieur Lafaurie, which is now divided between this property and Château Lafaurie-Peyraguey. The division occurred in 1879, and the Pauly family have been proprietors now since 1914. There is a tower in imitation of the one at Lafaurie-Peyraguey, just to remind one of the common origin of the two *crus*. It is run together with Haut-Bommes which they already owned, but is not classified. Today Haut-Bommes is in reality the second wine. The vineyard is very well placed, looking across to Yquem from a hillside of about the same altitude, between 50 and 72 metres. Their fermentation is in vat after *débourbage* at controlled temperature, and the new wine is filtered before going into cask, with 20 per cent new oak, for about eighteen months. The wines have tended to be light with some finesse, but not really as good as the situation of the vineyard would suggest – decent rather than fine. This was true of the 1983, but the 1986 was certainly an improvement, while the 1988 has the makings of a great wine, so the sights have clearly been raised here. There was an honourable 1984.

CHÂTEAU LES JUSTICES

Owner: Christian Médeville. 14 hectares. White: 8 hectares; 1,800 cases; Sém 85%, Sauv 10%,Musc 5%. Red: 6 hectares; 3,000 cases; Mer 50%, CS and CF 50%

You pass this property if you take the road from Barsac to Preignac, just to the north of Preignac, between the road and river. The ownership and management is exactly the same as at Château Gilette, and this is where the Médeville family have been since 1710. But although the harvesting and vinification are the same as at Gilette, the wines here are bottled after four years in small vats.

When tasted in 1985 the 1971 was superb, very perfumed with a lovely ripe fruitiness and concentration of sweetness, fit to bear comparison with a good *deuxième cru classé*, and better than some. Then there is a well-balanced 1975, with a lovely aroma of oranges and lemons, an elegant and charming 1980, and a 1981 with concentration and richness. This is certainly among the best and most reasonably priced of the unclassified wines, and shows what can be achieved from a vineyard not in the best position, when the vintaging and vinification are impeccable.

CHÂTEAU LAFAURIE-PEYRAGUEY

Premier Cru Classé. Owner: Domaines Cordier. 20 hectares. 3,500 cases. Sém 90%, Sauv 5%, Musc 5%

This is the other portion of the former Château Peyraguey of the 1855 classification. Situated in the commune of Bommes, Lafaurie-Peyraguey is notable for a particularly impressive château. The gatehouse and towers date from the thirteenth century and are in a style described as Hispano-Byzantine. The main living quarters date from the seventeenth century. Since 1913 the domain has belonged to the Cordiers, who are also considerable vineyard proprietors in the Médoc and St Emilion. The property is as carefully run as all their other ones. Recently there has been an important change of policy. In 1967 a new system was introduced whereby the wines were kept in glass-lined vats under nitrogen after fermentation in cask. This resulted in light, emasculated wines quite lacking in the distinction of the old vintages, such as the wonderful 1921 I remember from the days it was on the list at The Bell at Aston Clinton, or the 1937, a wine fit to be mentioned beside the Yquem, or the 1947, a great example of that outstanding vintage. Fortunately it was at last decided to reverse this disastrous policy. The proportion of Sauvignon was dropped from 30 per cent to the present 5 per cent and the Sémillon correspondingly increased. The *chai* has been made air-conditioned, and the wines are now both fermented and matured in casks, of which one-third are new.

The result has been much more interesting and altogether finer wines. The change is most clearly noticeable from the 1981 vintage onwards. The 1981 has traces of *botrytis*, but is most elegant, with great finesse and race, very long-flavoured and harmonious. The 1982 is a little tarry and obvious, a good early developer. The 1983 is worthy of the year, combining a lovely concentrated richness with great beauty of flavour. The 1984 is my favourite wine from this vintage; there is a lovely fruity aroma and a beguiling rich after-taste with gorgeous fruit, yet the wine has great finesse and elegance. There is a fine, concentrated 1985, just a little overshadowed, not surprisingly, by the 1983 and still more by the remarkable 1986, which is one of the top wines of the year, with beautifully balanced fruit, power and elegance. It has a great future; 1988 and 1989 promise to follow the same path. How rewarding it is to see the return of the prodigal to its rightful position as one of the very best of all Sauternes.

CHÂTEAU LAMOTHE
Deuxième Cru Classé. Owner: Jean Despujols. 8 hectares. 2,000 cases. Sém 70%, Sauv 20%, Musc 10%

This is part of a divided property. In 1855 there was a single Lamothe, now divided between this *cru* and the adjoining Lamothe-Guignard. Until 1961 it belonged to the same owners as d'Arche, who then sold half the property, including the château and half the cellars, to the Despujols family. The property is just outside the village of Sauternes, and is, with d'Arche, one of the highest vineyards in the commune.

The wines are fermented in vat, and then matured partly in vat and partly in cask. I was never much impressed by the wines here until I tasted the 1986, which is finely perfumed, with middle weight and real *race*, elegant and notably stylish. On this form it will be worth watching.

CHÂTEAU LAMOTHE-GUIGNARD
Deuxième Cru Classé. Owners: Philippe and Jacques Guignard. 11 hectares. 2,000 cases. Sém 85%, Musc 10%, Sauv 5%

Between 1961, when they sold half the property to the Despujols family, and 1981, this property belonged to the owners of d'Arche, the Bastet-St-Martin family, and was known as Lamothe-Bergey. Then they sold the rest of the property to the Guignards, owners of Château Rolland in Barsac, who substituted their name for Bergey.

The new owners favour long, slow fermentation in small *cuves*, followed by cask maturation and early bottling. From their first vintage, the 1981, the wines have shown style and elegance, with delectable fruit, moderate sweetness, length and finesse. The 1982 has a lovely lemony flavour, with lots of fruit and finesse, while 1983 and 1986 both produced fine classic Sauternes, with the new owners realizing the true potential of this well-placed vineyard.

CHÂTEAU LIOT
Owner: J. David. 21 hectares. 5,500 cases (only 4,000 cases château-bottled).
Sém 80%, Sauv 15%, Musc 5%

A well-known Barsac *cru* adjoining Climens, for many years it was a great standby, bottled by Harveys of Bristol. The wine is well made, light and elegant. Normally only the best vintages and *cuves* are château-bottled now, the rest being sold in bulk. After a disappointingly ordinary 1983, the 1988 is back to top form.

CHÂTEAU DE MALLE
Deuxième Cru Classé. Owner: Comte Pierre de Bournazel. 26 hectares. 2,700 cases. Sém 75%, Sauv 22%, Musc 3%

The Château de Malle is one of the delights of the region, built at the beginning of the seventeenth century for Jacques de Malle, President of the Bordeaux Parlement. Unfortunately it was allowed to sink into a sorry state of disrepair, but has now been meticulously restored. The formal garden is also famous, but is of the sort likely to disappoint an English visitor. Apart from some fine statuary, little remains apart from indications of the original layout, but the layout and setting are fine, and both château and garden are classified as *monuments historiques*. The property is in the commune of Preignac.

Comte Pierre de Bournazel, who ran and restored the property from 1956 until his untimely death, was a direct descendant of the Lur-Saluces. Now the property is managed by his widow.

In the past, I have seen some rather disappointing vintages from de Malle, but in the last twenty-five years there has been an improvement; the 1966, for instance, was most attractive, elegant and fruity, with a very marked character of its own. There is a particularly attractive 1975, with delicious rich ripe fruit, balanced and elegant. The 1989 promises to be exceptional, with great breed and more *botrytis* than usual. De Malle can often be drunk young in the lighter years, but also repays keeping as the fruit develops and expands with bottle age. Indeed, its wines are marked by a very definite personality and savour, elegant, but only moderately liquorous. It enjoys a good reputation today, and is certainly worthy of its classification.

CHÂTEAU DU MAYNE
Owner: Jean Sanders. 8 hectares. 1,700 cases. Sém 80%, Sauv 20%
This small Barsac *cru* has belonged to the Sanders family of Haut-Bailly since 1937. It is south-west of Barsac, near Château Suau. Jean Sanders aims for quality in the classic style, and the wine is full-coloured, perfumed, with body and breed, and without a lot of sweetness – an ideal wine to accompany *foie gras*. There is a delicious 1983.

CHÂTEAU MENOTA
Owners: Monsieur and Madame Noël Labat. 29 hectares. 6,600 cases. Sém 50%, Sauv 50%
The impressive fortified château, dating back to the sixteenth century, is in itself worth a visit. The property lies just beyond Broustet, coming from Barsac. There is much more Sauvignon here than is usual, and this is reflected in the wines, which are very perfumed, light and elegant, stylish and always carefully made. Whenever I have come across this wine, I have never been disappointed.

CHÂTEAU MYRAT
Deuxième Cru Classé. Owner: Comte de Pontac. Vineyard in reconstruction
When the last remaining vines here were pulled up after the 1975 vintage, it seemed as if the last chapter in the history of this *cru* might have been written. The proprietor still lived in the château, but decided he could no longer afford the luxury of running a Barsac vineyard. The old Comte died in the summer of 1988, just before the planting rights for the vineyard were due to expire, and his successor managed to exercise these rights just one month before they would have expired. So the Sauternes recovery of the eighties seems to have saved this *cru classé* by

the skin of its teeth. We must await the next decade to see what a Château Myrat can be like.

CHÂTEAU NAIRAC

Deuxième Cru Classé. Owner: Nicole Heeter-Tari. 15 hectares. 1,400 cases. Sém 90%, Sauv 6%, Musc 4%

The name Nairac is that of an important family of eighteenth-century Bordeaux *négociants*, one of those Protestant families who have long played an important role in the commercial life of Bordeaux. The family connections included Balguérie (see Gruaud-Larose), Brown (see Cantenac-Brown), Exshaw, of Cognac fame, and Guestier (see Léoville-Barton). The family was a casualty of the Revolution, so that by the time of the 1855 classification the property was joined to Broustet. Today the most important legacy of the Nairacs is the magnificent château, built just before the Revolution – in 1786 – by Jean Mollié in the prevailing neo-classical idiom. But the style, with its arched ground-floor windows and balustrade along the central roof line, is highly individual, setting it apart from the majority of other châteaux built around this time.

When Tom Heeter, an American from Ohio, newly married to Nicole Tari from Giscours, bought the property in 1972 it was in a very run-down and neglected state. By 1974 they had managed to move in, and the renaissance of Nairac was under way. Under Professor Peynaud's guidance, Tom Heeter set out to make a thoroughly traditional Barsac. The must was fermented entirely in cask, using 65 per cent new oak. However, like Pierre Dubourdieu at Doisy-Daëne, he was concerned to reduce the amount of sulphur traditionally used in the production of Bordeaux's sweet wines. He has not gone as far as Dubourdieu, but by adding phosphate of ammonia and thiamin (Vitamin B_1) as an anti-oxidant, has reduced its use. Following their divorce, Tom Heeter's last vintage was 1986, and Nicole Tari and her children are now sole owners.

The dedicated wine-making here has quickly won admirers for a *cru* previously all but forgotten. The wines are not normally very liquorous, but have power and richness well projected by new oak, and a definite elegance and finesse. Not as modernist as Doisy-Daëne, it is more elegant than Doisy-Védrines. The successes here have been the 1975, 1976, 1980, 1981, 1983 and 1986. It is sad that the dedicated Tom Heeter has now had to leave the scene of his endeavours, but Nicole Tari has excellent advice and is determined to carry on where he left off.

CHÂTEAU RABAUD-PROMIS

Premier Cru Classé. Owner: GFA Rabaud-Promis. Administrator: Philippe Dejean. 32 hectares. 3,750 cases. Sém 80%, Sauv 18%, Musc 2%

The history of this property is described under Sigalas-Rabaud, up until the sale in 1903 to Monsieur Adrien Promis. When he acquired the property, Monsieur Promis built a château for himself on the dominant hilltop of the estate, and this commands a magnificent, unrivalled view over the whole region. The vineyard of Château Peixotto, classified in 1855 as a *deuxième cru classé*, is now also incorporated in Rabaud-Promis. In 1950 the Ginestets of Château Margaux sold the property to Raymond-Louis Lanneluc, and it is now managed by his grandson. It consists of two-thirds of the original property. The two Rabauds were reunited in 1929, but divided again in 1950.

Some of the old vintages were very fine. There was a marvellous 1918 and a fine 1924. At the end of the period of the united property, the 1950 Rabaud was outstanding in this vintage, a wine to set beside the Coutet. Then under the Lanneluc regime the wines were kept in cement vats and saw no wood at all. Most of the wine was sold by mail order in France, and was hardly seen in the Bordeaux commerce. Now Philippe Dejean has improved matters, bringing back some casks, and the wine passes between *cuve* and cask. So the 1975 is merely heavy and dull, over-botrytized and lacking in real distinction, but there is a fine 1983, with real *race*, some *botrytis*, and the style one should expect. The 1986 was more botrytized and rather tarry in cask, but with more distinction than in the past, while 1988 promises to be the best yet.

On this form Rabaud-Promis seems to be returning to the fold.

CHÂTEAU RAYMOND-LAFON

Cru Bourgeois. Owners: Pierre and Francine Meslier. 20 hectares. 2,000 cases. Sém 80%, Sauv 20%

This *cru* has won more accolades in the last decade than any other non-classified growth. But the success is hardly surprising, the owner since 1972 being none other than Pierre Meslier, *régisseur* of Yquem from 1963 until 1989, and his vineyard has Yquem and Sigalas-Rabaud as neighbours. The château is a very pleasant creeper-covered country house with peacocks serving as watch-dogs in the garden. Not surprisingly Pierre Meslier is as meticulous in his wine-making here as he is at Yquem, and is ably assisted by his wife and son. The wine is matured in cask, with as much as a third in new oak. The resulting wines are now well up to *cru classé* standards, both in terms of quality and price, with finely perfumed, luscious wines. The only pre-Meslier wines I have tasted are the 1949, still superb in 1986, balanced, rich and still fresh, in contrast to the 1971, which was overbotrytized and tarry, lacking the same complexity and richness. Pierre Meslier soon got into his stride with fine wines in 1975 and 1976, and in the difficult 1978 vintage, with little or no *botrytis*, a particularly successful wine was made here. The 1979 is very unctuous and smooth, with a lovely finish, while the 1980 has a lot of *botrytis* character, with a rich, full-bodied, high-alcohol flavour, but only moderate sweetness. The 1981 is more elegant, with *botrytis* and a fine rich finish. The 1982 is especially successful for the year, with complexity and a very unctuous, powerful finish. The 1983 has a lovely honeyed sweetness and great richness – a real *vin de garde* of classic dimensions. The 1984 is very successful, with delicious long-flavoured, silky, honeyed fruit. The 1985 has lovely *botrytis* character, really concentrated fruit and richness. Pierre Meslier himself modestly, or diplomatically, eschews comparison with the *premiers crus*, but others are more forthright. Judged by the very highest standards Raymond-Lafon certainly has the concentration and power of the very best Sauternes, but lacks something in the way of finesse and complexity. But then Sauternes these days is so often a question of personal taste, as the very different quality judgements in Bernard Ginestet's book devoted to the region testify.

CHÂTEAU RAYNE-VIGNEAU

Premier Cru Classé. Owner: Société Civile du Château Rayne-Vigneau.
Administrator: Jean-Pierre Angliviel de la Beaumelle. 78 hectares. 16,500 cases (including 4,000 cases of dry). Sém 75%, Sauv 25%

The fourth of the *premiers crus* of Bommes, in 1855 it was known simply as Château Vigneau, the Veuve de Rayne (née de Pontac) being the proprietor. Even the few bottles of the 1893 in the Château Loudenne cellar were marked only as Vigneau on the bin card. It remained in the hands of the de Pontac family until 1961, and since 1971 has belonged to a syndicate of local merchants, which includes Mestrezat, and Merlaut of Chasse-Spleen, whose son Jean has recently taken an active hand in the management of the property. But the château still belongs to and is lived in by the Viscomte de Roton, a de Pontac. Rayne-Vigneau is famous for the semi-precious stones which have been found in its vineyard. These include onyx, agates, quartz and white sapphires.

In the past, some magnificent wines were produced here. I especially remember the 1893 and 1911, and the 1923 which my father bought on his first visit to Bordeaux. We had some half-bottles of the 1923 which continued to keep its colour – a pale golden – and was marvellously perfumed, with a glorious, honeyed flavour of great breed and delicacy, when nearly forty years old. More recently in 1986 the 1928 was still marvellous with its bouquet of honeyed apricots and its rich, complex fruit; it was still in perfect harmony, its delicate sweetness untouched by any sign of volatile acidity. In the early years of the present regime disappointingly dull commercial wines were made, yields were high and the wines light and sweet, rather than luscious and fruity. The best of these wines was the 1976. Things began to improve with the 1983, which is scented and elegant with real finesse and a nice kernel of concentration. Then after a very honourable 1984, the 1985 has a lovely long, supple, rich fruitiness, excellent balance, and great charm and finesse. The 1986 has more concentration and richness and great beauty of flavour, a wine which really holds its own among the *premiers crus* better than any vintage for many a year. The 1988 is just as impressive. How encouraging to see another famous *cru* again fulfilling its potential.

A dry wine is sold under the name Raynesec.

CHÂTEAU RIEUSSEC

Premier Cru Classé. Owner: Domaines Rothschild. 66 hectares. 6,000 cases. Sém 80%, Sauv 18%, Musc 2%. Second labels: Clos Labère, Château Mayne des Carmes

This is the only *premier cru* in the commune of Fargues. The vineyard is actually partly in the commune of Sauternes and partly in Fargues, but the château and *chai* are in Fargues, so the property is usually credited to this commune, although in the 1855 classification it was ascribed to Sauternes. The name was also spelt with only one "s". The vineyard is superbly placed on the highest hill of Sauternes after Yquem. The wine has long enjoyed a very good reputation on the English market, where it is a firm favourite. During the very good post-war period, Monsieur Balaresque was the proprietor, but in 1971 it was sold to Monsieur Albert Vuillier. In spite of, or perhaps, because of being the owner of a super-market chain, Monsieur Vuillier believed in traditional methods when it came to Sauternes. He was the first owner for many years to live in the château, and casks rather than vats are still used here. Then in 1984 he sold to Domaines Rothschild of Lafite, a move much welcomed in Sauternes as confirming the renaissance of the region.

In style, the wine is quite distinct. The bouquet is very marked, and the wine used to be rather less liquorous than some, with a most individual flavour, concentrated and powerful, but elegant. There was a notable consistency for many years, certainly in Monsieur Balaresque's time. But the style of the wines changed sharply under Albert Vuillier. After an absolutely classic 1971, both the 1975 and 1976 took on a lot of colour very quickly. When I first tasted the 1975 in November 1978, it already had a fair amount of colour, but the flavour was complex and distinguished. By October 1979 the wine was dark in colour and smelt distinctly maderized. On the palate it was hard, with a tarry taste. In short, it shows all the signs of excessive *pourriture noble*. The 1976, on the other hand, was really dark in colour, the bouquet had opened out but showed far more age than one would have expected, while the flavour was really raisin-like, reminiscent of an old Trockenbeeren-auslese – very rich and liquorous, but somehow unbalanced. In March 1988 a most interesting tasting was held at Lafite to compare the Rieussec of three successive owners: the last three Balaresque vintages, 1967, 1969 and 1970; the Vuillier years from 1971 to 1983; and the first three Rothschild years, 1984 to 1986. Just before this, in Singapore, I had tasted the 1961. It was very powerful, botrytized and tarry on the nose, very rich in flavour with good middle sweetness, but acidity now cut the finish, shortening the persistence of flavour on the palate. Nevertheless it was an impressive wine. At Lafite the 1967 was concentrated but beginning to dry at the finish. It lacked the class of the top 1967s. The 1969 was slightly maderized and very tarry, on the way down, while the 1970 was a disappointment for the year, rather coarse and dull. In contrast the first Vuillier vintage, the 1971, was outstanding, with great fruit and complexity. Then those two controversial wines: the 1975 was extraordinary, concentrated to the point of being almost syrupy, but it began oxidizing in the glass – my earlier fears for it had been justified, yet for all its faults there was still something impressive about it. The 1976 was very liquorous with a concentrated botrytized character, but it lacked complexity and seemed to have reached its limits. Then there was a very disappointing 1978, volatile and coarse, yet only months before I had a delicious magnum, intense yet delicate and fresh, so there is some inconsistency here. The 1979 had concentrated fruit and balanced sweetness without much finesse and was beginning to dry out at the end. The 1980 had a very tarry character, but was one-dimensional and too sweet. The 1981 was concentrated and rich, with more balance, an early developer. The 1982 was less good, a little flat on the nose, rather sweet but superficial, an early developer. The Vuillier years ended, as they had begun, with a classic. The 1983 has honeyed, scented fruit, is very concentrated, with similar weight to the 1986, and has the sheer breed and finesse one had missed in the intervening years. The first Rothschild vintage, the 1984, is tarry and very sweet, distinctly botrytized, but without the style of Lafaurie-Peyraguey. At this stage Charles Chevallier took over as *regisseur*. But then come two great successes, the 1985 with lovely fresh ripe fruit, less concentrated than the 1986 but with real breed and finesse. The 1986 is a great wine because it has a marvellous honeyed *botrytis* character yet is elegant. There is great weight and richness, and the balance, present in the 1983, which had been absent in the 1975 and 1976. The 1988 and 1989 promise to be even better. On this form the future here looks brilliant indeed, another jewel in the Rothschild diadem, and one of the glories of the region returned to its marvellous best. There is a dry wine, "R" the Rieussec, rather in the style of Ygrec.

CHÂTEAU DE ROLLAND

Cru Bourgeois. Owners: Jean and Pierre Guignard. 20 hectares. 4,000 cases. Sém 60%, Sauv 20%, Musc 20%

This good Barsac *cru* is just off the N113 Bordeaux–Toulouse road, the last property in Barsac before you cross the Ciron into Preignac. It belongs to the same family that now own Lamothe-Guignard in Sauternes and Roquetaillade-La Grange in Graves. They also run a restaurant and hotel here, which is the only place to stay, if you wish to be in the middle of the Sauternes vineyards. The vinification and *élevage* here are traditional, with some new casks and the rest purchased from Yquem. When I tasted the 1981 and 1982 in 1985, I found the 1981 had more finesse and delicacy, with very harmonious fruit and sweetness, and was light in body with a dryish finish, while the 1982 had classic Sémillon botrytized fruit and was attractively fruity, again with a dryish finish: just the characteristics in fact that you would look for in a good Barsac. This is a thoroughly good, seriously made *cru bourgeois*.

CHÂTEAU ROMER-DU-HAYOT

Deuxième Cru Classé. Owner: André du Hayot. 15 hectares. 4,000 cases. Sém 70%, Sauv 25%, Musc 5%

This vineyard adjoins de Malle, on the edge of the commune of Fargues, where it adjoins Preignac. Unhappily it is also now somewhat overshadowed by the Bordeaux–Toulouse autoroute. For some years the ownership of this *cru* has been divided between the du Hayot and Fargues families, but since 1977 the Fargues portion has been leased to the du Hayots, so that the property is now again run as a single entity, in spite of there being two owners.

The wine is both fermented and matured in vat, with early bottling. This is good modern-style Sauternes, with the emphasis on fruit and freshness. The yields are high for the *appellation*, but the wine is well made, and is good value for money, if not of classic style. In the 1976 there was a lot of sweetness, but the wine was balanced, fresh and attractive. Then came a full, rich 1979 and an elegant 1980, and fruity, stylish wines in 1988 and 1989. The proprietor also owns Château Guiteronde in Barsac, where this wine is actually made.

CHÂTEAU ST-AMAND

Owner: Louis Ricard. 22 hectares. 4,500 cases. Sém 85%, Sauv 15%. Second label: Château La Chartreuse

This good *cru* is in the sector of Preignac near the village, across the road from Les Justices as one enters the commune from Barsac. It is very well known under both its names, and in England La Chartreuse is probably even more familiar than St-Amand. This is a thoroughly reliable *cru bourgeois* made in a fairly traditional style, perfumed, full-flavoured, quite rich, yet with elegance and definite breed. The 1980 and 1981 under the

La Chartreuse label were particularly good, while there is a really fine 1983 St-Amand with lovely flowery fruit and a beautiful flavour.

CHÂTEAU SIGALAS-RABAUD

Premier Cru Classé. Owners: Héritiers de la Marquise de Lambert des Granges. 14 hectares. 2,000 cases. Sém 90%, Sauv 10%

This is another story of a divided *domaine*, also in the commune of Bommes. The domaine of Rabaud (or Rabeaud, as it appears in the 1855 classification), has a long history. It takes its name from the de Rabaud family, who owned it until 1660, when Madame Peyronne de Rabeau married Arnaud de Cazeau, a member of the *noblesse de robe*. It remained in this family until 1819, when it was sold to Monsieur Deymès, the proprietor at the time of the 1855 classification. But it was under Henri Drouilhet de Sigalas, who acquired it in 1864, that the great reputation of the wine was really built. It was his son, Gaston Drouilhet de Sigalas who, in 1903, sold about half of the property to Monsieur Adrien Promis. Since then, the remaining portion has been known as Sigalas-Rabaud and ownership has stayed with the same family. The present owner, the Marquis Emmanuel de Lambert des Granges, is a descendant of Monsieur Drouilhet de Sigalas. There was a brief period, from 1929 to 1950, when the property was again reunited, but the Promis part was then again sold, this time to Monsieur Lanneluc. In this short period, I particularly remember the Rabaud 1950 as a delightful wine, perfumed and elegant.

The reputation of this *cru* has been high in the last twenty years, and certainly well ahead of Rabaud-Promis. The yields here are low, and the traditional *trie* is made through the vineyard four or five times on average. The vinification is in stainless steel *cuves*, and the *élevage* is also largely in *cuve*, with only very few casks used. In spite of this departure from tradition, the wines are undeniably impressive. They have a particularly fine bouquet, are liquorous and have great breed. The oldest vintage I have tasted is the 1962, which was still wonderful in 1986, with a honeyed, perfumed bouquet and a fabulous flavour, sweet and ripe, in peak condition. The 1967, an old favourite of mine from this vintage, has a fine *botrytis* character, and still showed complex character with barley sugar and supple rich fruit in 1988. More recently the 1979 has more finesse and freshness than most wines of this year; then, after a balanced and attractive 1982, the 1983 has a long, lingering flavour, some *botrytis*, and the usual breed, while the 1986 is extremely perfumed with a very fine flavour, richness, and again that lovely lingering finish. There is probably a little more weight than in the 1983. One of the charms of Sigalas is that it is usually enjoyable when five or six years old, yet lasts very well and retains its freshness and balance. I rate it highly.

CHÂTEAU SUAU

Deuxieme Cru Classé. Owner: Roger Biarnès. 6.5 hectares. 1,500 cases. Sém 80%, Sauv 10%, Musc 10%

This is certainly the least known of the *crus classés*, excepting only Myrat, which has not produced since 1975. The property is an old one, and in the eighteenth century belonged to the Lur-Saluces family. Since 1967 it has belonged to the present proprietors, who actually make the wine at their principal property, Château Navarro, in vats. Suau is situated in Barsac, just south of the village. The wine is fermented in vat, and then matured in used casks. The first vintage I tasted was the 1988, which was delicate and quite fine. Its general reputation is uninspiring, but Bernard Ginestet speaks well of it as a decent modern-style Barsac. If you can find a bottle you can make up your own mind!

CHÂTEAU SUDUIRAUT

Premier Cru Classé. Owner: Héritiers Fonquernie. 70 hectares. 11,000 cases. Sém 80%, Sauv 20%

This is the most important *premier cru* domain in Sauternes, surpassing even Yquem in the size of its magnificent estate. Of the 200-hectare estate, 75 hectares are at present under vine. The vineyard adjoins that of Yquem, lying partly in the commune of Sauternes and partly in that of Preignac, whose only *premier cru* this is.

This ancient *domaine* takes its name from the family of Suduiraut, who were proprietors until the Revolution. One of the Suduiraut daughters married a Monsieur du Roy, and the property briefly bore his name before reverting to its original one. Hence the rather misleading motto "ancien cru du Roy" which appears on the label, and which I had always supposed meant that the château had once been royal property! The lovely château and its delightful gardens were laid out by Le Nôtre, the famous architect of many such splendours in the age of Louis XIV, and are among the finest to be seen in the region. The *chai* is massive and cavernous.

This famous property had reached a stage of sad decline and neglect when it was acquired in 1940 by Monsieur Fonquernie, who was responsible for reconstructing the vineyard and restoring the name of the wine until it today enjoys the reputation of one of the finest of all the great Sauternes. Monsieur Fonquernie insisted on the most meticulous standards, and has been fortunate in several able and dedicated *maîtres de chai*. I remember visiting the château during the gathering of the 1966 vintage. There had been some rain the previous day, which had caused the must readings to fall to 15°, whereas they had been obtaining around 20°. Monsieur Fonquernie had immediately given instructions for picking to stop until conditions improved. At Yquem, which I visited on the same day, exactly the same thing had occurred, but picking continued.

When I first entered the wine trade, Suduiraut was unknown on the English market. The 1955 which I bought must have been some of the first Suduiraut to be shipped to England after the reconstruction of the vineyard. Since then its reputation has climbed steadily, until today it enjoys a wide following. In tastings of the *premiers crus* over a period of years, I usually found that Suduiraut came first, and it consistently fetched a higher price on the Bordeaux market than the other *premiers crus* for a number of years.

I must preface my remarks on modern vintages by recalling the 1899 vintage. I owe this to the late Martin Bamford's generosity. The bottle had come from an impeccable cellar in Paris. We were all astonished by the wine's fine golden colour, the absence of maderization, and the velvety sweetness which still pervaded it. The wine was just eighty years old, but one could not have placed it further back than the twenties: a very great bottle of Sauternes. Almost as remarkable was the 1928, tasted twice in 1988 in its sixtieth year. Two bottles from the château varied, but the best was superlative, with great concentration, very complex fruit flavours and a lovely honey finish. A few months later in Stockholm I enjoyed a bottle that was fresher and more perfect. These old vintages demonstrate Suduiraut's ability to age without losing sweetness, because of its wonderful balance and the absence of volatile acidity, the enemy of mature Sauternes. The first vintage produced under Monsieur Fonquernie's regime that I saw was the 1943. It was good, but had not lasted so well as the Château Climens, and was not outstanding. Then came the 1955, certainly one of the best wines of the year; the 1957 was elegant and fine; the 1958 quite exceptional in its balance, fruit and sweetness. The 1959 was a great and classic wine. The 1961 was almost too overpowering – I have always preferred the more elegant 1962, which is in the mould of the 1959. The 1965 was a charming off-vintage, light but fine; the 1966 was good for the year but not special; the 1967 was again outstanding. The 1969, like most Sauternes of that year, was not of any special note. Then came the 1970, an outstanding example of the year, with more elegance and balance than many examples. In contrast, the 1971 was not so good, probably because at this time the château started economizing and cutting corners. The wine was kept in vat instead of cask and, perhaps more serious, the *deuxième vin* was added to the *grand vin*, increasing the quantity by damaging the quality. This led to a final breach between Monsieur Fonquernie and Gilbey's of Loudenne, who were at that time his main distributors.

After an unsettled period following this rupture, when the property was nearly sold, a good but not outstanding 1975 was made, more tarry and botrytized than usual, with the alcohol too dominant. The 1976 is complex and rich, but by 1988 was looking older than it should, with some maderization on the nose, which is most unusual at Suduiraut. The 1978 is very successful for the year, with scented fruit and finesse; it was young and still developing in 1988. At the same time the 1979 was about ready, a shade coarse and with no great future. The 1980 is a charming lightweight with *race*. The 1982 is fine, with an aroma of peaches, elegant and fruity but without the complexity of the great years. But a small *tête de cuvée*, sold as Cuvée Madame, representing the cream of the vintage, made on a single day, has great concentration and is very honeyed and complex. The 1983 is very concentrated with a fine after-taste; the alcohol was showing through a little in 1988, but the wine was very much in evolution. After an honourable but not special 1984, the 1985 seemed to have a slight alcohol burn at the finish, but there is a fine flavour and the wine should settle down. The 1986 has great promise, with wonderful sheeny fruit and something quite exotic in its make-up. But with only 4.2° Baumé, it lacks the unctuousness of the great Suduirauts of the sixties and earlier.

It is clear from these notes that the seventies and eighties have seen some ups and downs compared to the fifties and sixties. Looking at these vintages in the presence of the great 1967 and 1959 at a tasting in 1988, I felt the recent vintages lacked something of the beauty and flair of their predecessors, because, with less sugar, the alcohol is more dominant.

The characteristics of Suduiraut deserve special note. In colour, it is usually golden rather sooner than most Sauternes; the bouquet is exquisite and especially perfumed and penetrating; the flavour is very rich and vigorous with a most distinctive and beautiful savour, honeyed, suave, but of great finesse and breed. The richness of Suduiraut in its best period, was rivalled only by Yquem; even the 1958 had 4.9° Baumé, and in good years it can easily exceed 5° Baumé. Now it seldom exceeds 4° Baumé.

CHÂTEAU LA TOUR-BLANCHE

Premier Cru Classé. Owner: Ministry of Agriculture. Administrator: Jean-Pierre Jausserand. 30 hectares. 5,600 cases. Sém 70%, Sauv 27.5%, Musc 2.5%

The commune of Bommes produced four *premiers crus* in 1855, more than any other commune. La Tour-Blanche was considered the finest of these, and indeed was placed at the head of all the *premiers crus* in the classification. At that time, the name appeared as Latour-Blanche. In 1910 the proprietor, Monsieur Osiris, gave the estate to the French state to be run as an agricultural school. Since then it has been run in a number of different ways but since 1954 has come directly under the Ministry of Agriculture. A good deal of experimental work is carried out, both in viticulture and in the vinification of wines, with the aim of assisting the growers of the region to improve their methods. The school receives many students wishing to do practical work.

One might have thought that, as a result of all this, La Tour-Blanche would produce one of the outstanding wines of the region. Unfortunately this is not so. One can only suspect the dead hand of institutionalism, although the present administrator is clearly very keen to improve matters. The fermentation was in temperature-controlled *cuves*, and the *élevage* in cask, with 40 per cent new oak now used, until the 1988 vintage. Then some cask fermentation was introduced, and the results immediately looked promising. In general, I would describe the wines as decent but uninspired. I have enjoyed only a glimpse of what they used to be like. The 1876, tasted in 1988, had a tremendous aroma of honeycombs, and was quite caramelized, with a lovely flavour which quickly faded; it was like seeing a phantom – one had a spectacular impression, but it was gone almost before one could take it all in. The 1923, on the other hand, was still in lovely condition in the same year, gold in colour without the darkness of the 1928s or 1937s. There was a wonderful *crème brûlée* bouquet and a long, elegant flavour, with the sweetness just gently beginning to tail off, but still lovely to drink. In recent years the best efforts have been a rich but well-balanced 1976, a supple and moderately rich 1981, a rich, sweet, but rather clumsy 1983, and a very botrytized 1986, which has more individuality than usual but is very tarry.

CHÂTEAU D'YQUEM
Premier Grand Cru Classé. Owner: Aymeric de Montault. 102 hectares. 5,500 cases. Sèm 80%, Sauv 20%

The supreme Sauternes, this is one of the most famous wines of the world. Appropriately, Yquem lies in the commune of Sauternes itself, occupying the most superb position, with the great medieval château dominating the splendid slopes below it and commanding an unrivalled view over the surrounding countryside. The château itself is a real castle in the English sense – indeed, one of the finest examples of a medieval fortress in the whole Gironde. While the massive towers remind us of its original purpose, the elegant windows which now adorn even the exterior walls are witnesses of more tranquil times, when civilization was permitted to beautify the fortress. The spacious courtyard of the château is a perfect setting for the concerts given here during the Bordeaux Festival each May.

Since 1593, only two families have owned it. The continuity of ownership lasted for 400 years, as the Lur-Saluces married the last de Sauvage heiress in 1785. Alexandre de Lur-Saluces succeeded his uncle in 1968. In 1999, Alexandre de Lur Saluces lost his long battle to retain his independence, but remained to guide this unique *cru* into the next millennium. He officially retired from his executive duties at the end of 2003 to be succeeded by Aymeric de Montault, who has worked with the team since 2002.

In one sense, Yquem remains a very traditional growth. The wines are still kept for a full three and a half years in cask. But, in another way, they have broken from tradition by introducing a dry wine sold under the name of Ygrec (this is the French for the letter Y), but still using the traditional Yquem label. This bastard was conceived during Sauternes' lean years, the first vintage being 1959. A number of leading growths in the region started to produce dry wines at this time, but there were two schools of thought as to what the style of the wine should be. Some argued that the wine must be full-bodied and fairly rich in alcohol, with even a suspicion of residual sugar to preserve the identity of the wine against other Bordeaux. Others thought that the object should be to produce as good a dry white wine as they could, and that the wine should bear no resemblance to the original Sauternes at all. Ygrec belongs to the first and more traditional school. Here it should be emphasized that there is never, at Yquem, any deliberate intention to make dry wines. What happens is that the normal *assemblage* at Yquem is 80 per cent Sémillon and 20 per cent Sauvignon. Since the Sauvignon is both a more erratic yielder and tends to produce wines with less residual sugar and more alcohol than the Sémillon, there can be years when there is a surplus of dryish Sauvignon casks. This is then blended on a 50–50 basis with some rather low-degree Semillons, which are unsuitable for the Yquem *assemblage*, since high-residual-degree Sémillons are needed to balance the lower-degree Sauvignons. The result then is a wine which is not luscious but has some Sauternes character, especially on the nose. I find Richard Olney's remark about the bouquet carrying "memories of Yquem" a very apt one: perfect as an aperitif, or indeed with some terrines – even *foie gras* – for those who find a Sauternes too much of a good thing. For these reasons 1978, with its small incidence of *botrytis*, but with excellent ripeness, was a classic Ygrec year, with 40 per cent of the crop going in this direction. In 1977 the proportion was 50 per cent, and in 1979, 30 per cent. There was no Ygrec in 1975, 1976, 1981, 1982 or 1983.

There can, I think, be some confusion, with the label so closely resembling that of Yquem and with the similarity of names; it is easy for the unknowledgeable to be deceived. I was once on the receiving end of this when ordering a glass of Yquem at a famous London restaurant offering Yquem by the glass. It was late, and the sommelier had evidently left. I had great difficulty in persuading the young waiter on duty that the bottle of Ygrec from which he had poured my glass was not the Yquem I had ordered.

A good vintage of Yquem is the quintessence of Sauternes. The nose is marvellously perfumed and flowered, the flavour incomparably luscious, yet fresh and invigorating. The harmony seems perfect, very sweet, yet with the concentration of great fruitiness, and without any hint of cloying. In comparison with other leading Sauternes, Yquem is both richer and has their virtues, only to a more marked degree. In some years, it can attain as much as 7° Baumé after an alcoholic fermentation which has produced over 15 per cent alcohol by volume.

Unfortunately, there was a period when Yquem far too often failed to produce wines worthy of its best traditions. But the marvellous 1967 vintage, followed by the arrival of Alexandre de Lur-Saluces and some changes in staff – notably the appointment of Monsieur Pierre Meslier – have ushered in a new era. Once more, Yquem is producing wines which are worthy of its great reputation.

The domain itself is very extensive, comprising 173 hectares; 102 hectares are actually under vine of which 90 produce wine and the rest are young vines or fallow land awaiting replanting. But such is the nature of Sauternes that these 90 hectares yield on average only about 5,500 cases of the precious wine, while a property in the Médoc could expect to produce about 30,000 cases of red wine from a vineyard of similar size. Of course, one of the problems for a property such as Yquem is the great fluctuations, not only in yields but in the proportion of the crop that is suitable for sale under such a prestigious name. In the last twenty-five years no wine was sold as Yquem in the vintages 1964, 1972 and 1974, while in 1968 only 10 per cent was used, in 1973 only 12 per cent and in 1978 only 15 per cent. Years of high success were 1966 (80 per cent), 1967 (90 per cent), 1970, 1971 and 1975 (each 80 per cent), 1976 (90 per cent) and 1980, 1981 and 1983 (each 80 per cent). To meet this situation Yquem has adapted a system of distribution unique to itself. Having established that the twenty-year average is 66,000 bottles, it releases approximately this figure each year. The task is made simpler since, unlike the great red wines of the Gironde, Yquem is never offered for sale until after it has been bottled. Within the next few years this release figure should increase to 72,000 bottles as the area under productive vines is slowly increased, because when old vines are pulled up for replanting, the new systems for disinfecting the soil enable it to be returned to production more rapidly than in the past. This has increased the productive area by about 10 per cent. In addition, Yquem is now negotiating the purchase of 13 hectares in an enclave of the estate, or bordering it, and half of this is land with the same soil as Yquem. This will increase the vineyard to about 109 hectares.

At Yquem, there are no short-cuts. The botrytized grapes are individually picked by the experienced staff drawn largely from the forty-eight full-time workers on the estate. The aim is to pick the grapes when the refractometer shows a reading of not less than 20°, but not more than 22° Baumé, but in fact life is more complicated than that, as I have already indicated when speaking of Ygrec. These figures apply to what is looked for in the *assemblage*, which may contain elements ranging from 15° to 25° Baumé at the time of pressing. Pierre Meslier believes it is most important for quality not to allow the Baumé degree to rise too high, as many producers did in 1975. This leads to unbalanced wines. He finds that by following this rule, the fermentation will stop naturally at between 13.5° and 14°, thus giving the wines all the richness they need in terms of high residual sugar, without making them too rich in alcohol. The 1971 and 1975 are tributes to the success he has achieved by adhering to these yardsticks. Most of the best Sauternes châteaux produced fine, elegant 1971s, but few could claim these qualities for their 1975s. Yquem can; the 1975 is a worthy successor to the great 1971.

Some of the great vintages of Yquem made in the nineteenth century are legendary, and fetched enormous prices. Such a wine was the 1847. A bottle from St Petersburg was still remarkable in 1989. The only other nineteenth-century wines I have tasted are the 1867 and 1868, both a long way past their best; the extraordinary 1869 – a wine in the same mould as the legendary 1921 – which has a liquor-like concentration and seems nearly immortal; and the 1890, a light wine still holding up well and enjoyable. Between the wars, the great vintages were 1921, still a remarkable essence-like elixir when fifty years old, the 1928 and the 1937, one of the finest Yquems I have tasted – it was at its greatest in the fifties but is now past its prime. After the Second World War, 1945, 1947 and 1949 all produced magnificent wines. In recent years I have found the 1945 and 1947 still so, in their differing ways. During this and earlier epochs Yquem also produced some remarkable off-vintages, a careful selection producing a small quantity of wine worthy of being bottled under the famous label. Examples of this were the 1922, 1931 and 1936 between the two wars.

In the fifties and sixties however, the record was far too irregular. The 1955 did not last as it should, and is now disappointing and past its best. The 1959 went the same way, spoiled by too much volatile acidity. The 1960 was a disappointment after the quite acceptable 1954, throwing a heavy deposit in bottle and ageing rapidly, but the 1957 and 1958 were much better-balanced wines, as they were at neighbouring Suduiraut. The 1961 was rather clumsy and heavy like many 1961s, but is probably good wine for the year, if lacking finesse. This is the sort of wine which will probably become more interesting in old age, when the concentrated botrytized character comes into its own. The 1962 was more successful, probably the best wine made for several years. Then came 1963 and the astonishing decision to offer an Yquem from this vintage. The wine was quite frankly a disgrace and totally unworthy, not only of Yquem, but also of Sauternes. Yquem is unusual among Bordeaux châteaux in never offering its wine until it is in bottle, so there could be no excuse that a rash decision was made too soon – they had had three years to think about it! Most English merchants I know who had automatically reserved the wine when it was first offered, cancelled their orders when they saw the sample. It is said at the château that the 1963 was intended only for the French market and not for export, but the *négociants* did not keep to this agreement. One had hoped that Yquem would have learnt something from this, but apparently not, because the 1968 was nearly as bad. Fortunately, the magnificent 1967 has proved in retrospect to be the beginning of better things. The wine itself is luscious, yet with great elegance and panache. The 1966 is powerful and impressive, but lacks the sheer class and flair of the 1967. One has the feeling that like some other great Yquems of the past, its greatest period may lie between ten and twenty-five years of age. The 1970 is a powerful heavyweight, the 1971 all elegance, a worthy successor to the 1967 but lighter in texture. The magnificent 1975, an object lesson in how to overcome the problems of the year, looks like a great Yquem, more powerful than the beautiful 1967, a wine with a very long future. The 1976 is an unusual wine in that it is made entirely from grapes harvested in the second *trie*. It is more forward and more extrovert in character than the 1975. After a good 1979, the 1980 is a special success here, while the 1981 has great finesse and length, and is very luscious. Remarkable is the 1982, where the sacrifice of using only the first two *tries* (picking began on 16 September, the earliest since 1966) has resulted in a very concentrated wine of great promise. The 1983 is a slumbering giant, and the 1984 again shows that Yquem can make marvellous wines in generally moderate years – the high proportion of 75 per cent of the crop was used for Yquem. In contrast only 20 per cent was used in 1985, with 50 per cent for Ygrec, owing to the slow development of *botrytis*, and this in spite of the longest-lasting picking on record, from 1 October to 19 December.

The Yquem archives confirm that what Enjalbert found in the Libournais was also true here, namely that the phylloxera was for many years successfully resisted by the use of carbon disulphide, and the transition to grafted wines was a very measured one. Thus the great 1899 and 1900 vintages were made entirely from ungrafted vines, while the most fabled Yquem of the twentieth century, the 1921, was the first to be made largely from grafted vines.

The eighties have seen several remarkable tastings of Yquems, most notably one in Los Angeles in 1983, and another in Brussels the following year. In this century the following vintages were singled out as the most remarkable: 1900, 1921, 1928, 1929, 1934, 1937, 1945, 1947, 1949, 1953, 1955, 1962, 1967, 1970, 1971, 1975 and 1976. Looking at some of the notes, I was struck by how personal one's judgements of a wine like Yquem are, much more so than for a red wine perhaps. Thus the 1937 won golden opinions, and yet I preferred it thirty years ago in its glorious youth, when it was between fifteen and twenty years old. Perhaps the 1955 was in a dull trough when I last drank it, and has now blossomed again – the cygnet has finally become a swan. Old Yquems also fascinatingly demonstrate the difference between maderization and oxidization. An oxidized wine is quickly spoiled and dull in colour, a maderized one is often a deep mahogany hue but brilliant, and at this stage the wines often seem almost immortal. (Richard Olney's fascinating monograph on Yquem contains a very full summary of these and other tastings.)

STE-CROIX-DU-MONT AND LOUPIAC

It seems sensible to take these two communes together, because they adjoin each other, their wines are very similar, and they are the closest in style and quality to Sauternes and Barsac.

In contrast to the flat, rolling countryside of Sauternes and Barsac on the left bank of the Garonne, the vineyards of Ste-Croix-du-Mont and Loupiac rise high above the river, sometimes steeply sloping, sometimes on vertical ledges on the hillsides, with the best high up, commanding magnificent views over the Sauternes-Barsac and Graves vineyards across the river. These wines have suffered much the same fate as their peers, Sauternes-Barsac, only the rewards offered for producing good wines are even more meagre. Geographically, Ste-Croix-du-Mont and Loupiac form an enclave in the Premières Côtes – that attractive, hilly, wooded district which, rising steeply from the Garonne, forms the south-western border of the Entre-deux-Mers. But although some modest sweet wines are produced in the Premières Côtes, the wines of Ste-Croix-du-Mont and Loupiac have far more in common with their illustrious neighbours across the water than with their more immediate neighbours.

In practice, there is no meaningful distinction to be made between the two districts. They owe their separateness purely to their being in different communes. Indeed, it would be far more logical if all sweet wines made in Sauternes, Barsac, Cérons, Ste-Croix-du-Mont and Loupiac were allowed a single *appellation*, with worthwhile alternatives available for the production of the good, dry white wines which can also be made there. Then we might have better and more genuine sweet wines and more prosperous growers. But this is crying for the moon!

I have on a number of occasions tasted good Ste-Croix-du-Mont and Loupiac in the company of Sauternes, and experienced Bordeaux tasters have agreed with me that it has in practice been impossible to distinguish these wines from Sauternes. While they lack the sheer liquorousness of the top Sauternes, they have a fruitiness and savour very reminiscent of some Barsacs. Unfortunately, relatively few of these wines reach export markets, so few of the property wines are in any way familiar. But there are a handful which deserve to be singled out.

CHÂTEAU LOUBENS
Ste-Croix-du-Mont. Owner: Antoine de Sèze. Red: 6 hectares. 600 cases. Mer 45%, CS 45%, CF 10%. White: 15 hectares. 1,500 cases. Sem 90%, Sauv 10%.
Second label: Château Terfort
This is a property with a deserved reputation. The château stands on the site of a sixteenth-century fort, and has always been one of the leading

growths of the region. The vineyard is finely placed at the top of the *côte*, producing a wine which combines elegant fruit and freshness with well-balanced sweetness. The second label, Terfort, also maintains an excellent standard, and the dry white wine sold under the name of Fleuron Blanc is most attractive. There is also a small quantity of red wine.

CHÂTEAU LOUPIAC-GAUDIET

Loupiac. Owner: Marc Ducau. Red: 15 hectares. 900 cases. White: 30 hectares. 10,000 cases

This is another well-situated vineyard with origins going back to the fifteenth century. The white wines have been consistently well made over a number of years. They are usually aged in vat and have a pleasing delicacy and finesse combined with a fruity sweetness that ages well. The 1970 and 1971 are both delightful and, while giving much pleasure when young, will age well. The 1971 was still fresh and lemony in 1987.

CHÂTEAU RICAUD

Loupiac. Owner: Société Civile Garreau-Ricard. 45 hectares. Red: 5,750 cases. White: 10,000 cases. Administrator: Alain Thienot

I first came across this wine in Monsieur Choyer's cavernous cellars near Tours. The vintages were 1943 and 1947, both marvellous wines of great breed, very fruity, rich but not really liquorous. The 1943 was still an outstanding wine when thirty-five years old. Because of the special balance of these top Loupiacs, they age marvellously well and keep their colour. This discovery sent me in search of the château, and I ended up by buying the 1970. This very compact, stylish wine is still maturing slowly after nineteen years and promises to have many of the qualities, including longevity, of those vintages of the forties that I first found in the Loire.

Unfortunately, in the last years of the Wells family's ownership the property was neglected and run down. But with a change of ownership in 1980 a new era began, and the progress, gradual at first, has now accelerated. The new owner is also a champagne *négociant*, and has brought some excellent wine-making skills with him. Following the installation of stainless steel fermentation *cuves*, some wood for the maturation was introduced, and this has now been extended. Although attractive Loupiacs were made in 1981, 1982 and 1983, the real breakthrough came with the marvellous 1986, which shows *botrytis* and elegance on the bouquet, and a lovely long, silky flavour and fruitiness combined with a complexity not seen before. It could pass for a good Barsac. Ricaud has now clearly reasserted its position as the leading Loupiac.

Apart from the Loupiac, a dry white wine is now made – the 1986 was pure Sémillon – and an attractively fruity red wine, sold with the Premières Côtes *appellation*. The château itself looks so fairytale-like on the label as to be hardly believable, but for once the label does not lie.

CHÂTEAU DE TASTES
Ste-Croix-du-Mont. Owner: Domaines Prats. I hectare. 400 cases. Sauv 100%

I shall always remember drinking a memorable bottle of 1910 de Tastes at Château Margaux, with Pierre Ginestet. This property goes back as far as 1230, and for many years belonged to, and was distributed by, the Ginestets before the management passed into the hands of Bruno Prats, at the same time as he took over Cos d'Estournel on behalf of his family. Sadly, terribly little of this excellent wine is now made.

Other good wines worth watching out for include, in Ste-Croix-du-Mont: Château Les Courtines, Château des Mailles and Château La Raine; and in Loupiac: Château de Barberousse, Château du Cros, Château La Nère, Domaine des Nobles and Château Terrefort.

CÉRONS AND PRÈMIERES CÔTES

There are two other major categories of sweet wines: Cérons, which adjoins Barsac and has already been mentioned in the chapter on Graves, since its dry white wines have the right to the Graves *appellation*; and the Premières Côtes, immediately to the north of Loupiac.

Because of the declining interest in sweet white wines, and because the growers of Cérons have a lucrative alternative at their disposal, there has been a marked decline in the amount of wine declared as Cérons in the last two decades. Thus in 1970 and 1971 respectively, 20,916 and 19,162 hectolitres were declared. But in the abundant harvests of 1978 and 1979 the figures were 5,041 and 5,069, and by 1986 had fallen to a mere 2,660 hectolitres. At the same time, the production of white Graves and Graves Supérieur increased significantly. Most Cérons is sold under *négociants'* generic labels in France. The best-known château is de Cérons. It produces a very fruity wine of real breed. A good Cérons is very like a small Barsac, and ages well – even if it is not quite as fine as the best of Ste-Croix-du-Mont or Loupiac.

In the Premières Côtes, an attempt was made in 1973 to create a superior category of sweet wine by allowing the best communes in the southern part, adjoining Loupiac, the right to a new *appellation* – Cadillac. The name comes from the commune of the same name, where one of the finest châteaux in the whole Gironde is to be found. This ill-conceived proliferation of *appellations* has met with little success. In the first vintage of 1973, as much as 15,482 hectolitres was declared. But the lack of interest shown by the market in yet another *appellation* for sweet wine, when everyone knows that what is really required is a simplification, was soon felt. In 1978 and 1979, the average was just under 2,000 hectolitres, and the situation has hardly improved since.

The wines of the Premières Côtes are markedly lighter than Sauternes and all too often are little more than simple sweet wines, with no *pourriture noble* character and certainly none of the style of the better *appellations*. There are a few honourable exceptions, of which the admirable Château Fayau is a notable example. The 1970 was a wonderful wine still in 1988, a perfect accompaniment to *foie gras*. This is sold with the Cadillac *appellation*. Other well-made wines are Château Birot and Château de Berbec. More and more growers are now turning to the production of red wines as the figures amply demonstrate. The white wines are mostly used for generic blends, and in the UK were generally used to supply the need for cheap "Sauternes" shipped in bulk, before the day of the enforcement of *appellation contrôlée*. Today, these relatively inexpensive blends – now correctly labelled – still have a certain place on the market, though the wines are seldom more than acceptable.

Although strictly speaking outside the scope of this book, mention should also be made of Monbazillac. Being in the neighbouring *département* of Dordogne, it is not in the Gironde at all, but those wines produced on the north-facing hills just south of Bergerac clearly belong to the Sauternes family of botrytized sweet wines. The conditions are similar, as are the grape varieties and methods of production. A good, properly made Monbazillac can certainly hold its own with all but the best of Bordeaux's sweet wines, but unfortunately, because of the meagre financial rewards, more and more wines are simply sweet and characterless, made without the benefit of *pourriture noble*. Again, many growers are turning to the production of dry white wines, as well as reds.

From the very heart of Sauternes itself, right through the lesser areas, we have noted all the signs of decline in production, often in quality, certainly in consumer interest. Yet no one who has enjoyed the delights of drinking fine Sauternes can doubt that this is one of the great wines of the world, or would wish to see it disappear.

In Germany, there is a buoyant market for the great Beeren- and Trockenbeeren-auslesen. The quantities produced are tiny and the price much higher than for all but Yquem. Even in the more favourable conditions of the Gironde, botrytized wines can never be cheap to make. At the same time, wines so rich in both alcohol and residual sugar can hardly be everyday wines. In Germany the producers of the great sweet wines effectively subsidize them from their much larger production of more commercial wines, so that they are in no sense dependent on them in the way that most Sauternes producers are on their sweet wines.

The logical solution seems clear enough, then. What is needed is a smaller production of top-quality wines. But in order to achieve this, producers must be able to make other, more commercial, everyday wines from the same vineyards. Let us hope that the authorities respond to what is a crisis situation with some common-sense solutions. Sauternes and the other great sweet wines of Bordeaux cannot survive much longer on philanthropy.

OTHER WHITE WINES

Entre-deux-Mers

After Bordeaux Blanc, this is by far the most important *appellation* for white wines in terms of quantity. And against the general tendency, it has been gaining ground instead of losing it over the last decade. Between 1970 and 1974, the production of Entre-deux-Mers averaged 74,463 hectolitres, which represented 6.5 per cent of all Bordeaux dry white wines. But between 1982 and 1986 production averaged over 154,000 hectolitres, representing nearly 19 per cent of all Bordeaux dry white wines. To put it another way, production of Entre-deux-Mers increased by just over 40 per cent at a time when white wine production as a whole was falling. A good part of the reason for this increase lies in the fact that it has become gradually more interesting to sell Entre-deux-Mers than Bordeaux Blanc. In the past, much of the production was declared as Bordeaux Blanc only because sales of Entre-deux-Mers were not sufficiently buoyant to utilize all the white wine produced in the area. But in the last few years, sales of this *appellation* have increased considerably.

Geographically, Entre-deux-Mers is a large wedge of land lying between the Garonne and the Dordogne. On the Garonne side, the Premières Côtes, together with Loupiac and Ste-Croix-du-Mont, occupy the whole of the south-western side of the district, while St Macaire forms a further enclave in the south, Ste Foy a large enclave in the north-eastern corner, and Graves de Vayres a small enclave in the north, opposite Libourne. Scenically it makes up for its lack of vinous distinction with hilly, wooded countryside dotted with quietly decaying châteaux, some of the most picturesque in the whole region.

Although the area contains many large properties, this is *par excellence* the district for *coopératives*, and it is improvements in the vinification of white wines at such *coopératives* which are largely responsible for the gradual revival of the fortunes of Entre-deux-Mers. On the British market, Bordeaux white wines for many years had a poor reputation as sulphurous and therefore mawkish. It has taken a long time to overcome this legacy, and the effects of it are indeed still with us. In addition, it used to be the custom to sell medium sweet wines under the Entre-deux-Mers name in Britain. As a result, when the *appellation* laws were at last enforced here, it took a long time before customers would accept the fact that Entre-deux-Mers was a dry wine.

A good Entre-deux-Mers should be light, crisp, fresh and dry. The wines are usually bottled when three or four months old, and are intended to be drunk within the year. As in other parts of France recently, there is a tendency to increase the proportion of Sauvignon, and some properties produce pure Sauvignon wines. This seems to me to be a mistake. In the Gironde, if the Sauvignon becomes fully ripe, it tends to lose its special aromatic character rather quickly. On the other hand, if it is picked too early, the wine has an unpleasant acidity. It is not for nothing that the Sémillon has for so long been the backbone of Bordeaux white wines, and it is interesting to note that in California they are beginning to experiment with the blending of Sémillon with their Sauvignons, and that in Australia distinguished dry wines are now being made from the Sémillon. I feel sure that in the long run, Sémillon-Sauvignon blends made with slow, cold fermentations are likely to give the best results, and the sooner the Sauvignon fad passes, the better for Bordeaux white wines. Other places can do it so much more successfully. An excellent example of the new wave of dry Sémillons is the new brand recently created by Peter Sichel, Sirius. Another good new generic blend, Dourthe's Numéro 1, uses the classic Sauvignon-Sémillon combination.

A new *appellation*, Entre-deux-Mers-Haut-Benauge, applies to nine communes which adjoin the Premières Côtes, but as so often, it is the dedication and skill of individual growers which seem to produce the best wines, and the only *crus* I have tasted in this *appellation* which stand out are Château Toutigeac and Château Fongrave. Apart from this, there are now a number of properties which are, or have already succeeded in, carving out a more than local reputation for themselves.

CHÂTEAU BONNET
Owner: André Lurton. Secondary labels: Château Tour-de-Bonnet, Château Gourmin, Château Peyraud

This is one of the most impressive properties of the region, with its elegant eighteenth-century château which is the family home for numerous Lurtons, and large vineyard producing red as well as white wines. It is at Grézillac, due south of St Emilion. André Lurton is better known for his prodigious work in the Pessac-Léognan region of Graves, but he also takes a keen interest in the reviving fortunes of Entre-deux-Mers. The *chai* and *cuvier* here are as well equipped as those of his Graves properties. The white wine is cold-fermented at 16–18°C, and part of the red wine is matured in cask and sold in numbered bottles. The proportion of *cépages* for the white wine is interesting, with 60 per cent Sémillon and 20 per cent each of Sauvignon and Muscadelle. The result is a very perfumed wine, with elegant fruity flavours and some body.

CHÂTEAU FONDARZAC
Owner: Jean-Claude Barthe

Situated in the commune of Nauzan-et-Postiac, just south of Branne, this has been home for members of the Barthe family since at least the seventeenth century. Half the 56-hectare vineyard is devoted to white wine-making, the rest to red. There is Sauvignon, Sémillon and 10 per cent Muscadelle. Jean-Claude Barthe comes from the first generation of Bordeaux oenologist proprietors, and is a gifted wine-maker. The wines are very scented and fruity.

CHÂTEAU FONGRAVE
Owner: Pierre Perromat

This important property at Gornac, in the Haut-Benauge area near the Premières Côtes, has been in Pierre Perromat's mother's family since the seventeenth century. The red wine of the property is sold as Château de La Sablière-Fongrave. The wine is a classic Sauvignon-Sémillon mix, resulting in very scented, aromatic wines. The proprietor, who was for many years President of the INAO, also farms Château d'Arche, *deuxième cru classé* of Sauternes.

CHÂTEAU LAUNAY
Owner: Rémy Greffier. Secondary labels: Château Dubory, Château Braidoire, Château La Vaillante

This is a very large property at Soussac, on the road between Pellegrue and Sauveterre in the eastern Entre-deux-Mers. All the wines are château-bottled, and are well reputed and widely distributed.

CHÂTEAU MOULIN-DE-LAUNAY
Owners: Claude and Bernard Greffier. Secondary labels: Château Tertre-de-Launay, Château Plessis, Château La Vigerie, Château de Tuilerie

Another large property in Soussac, unlike its neighbour Château Launay it is entirely devoted to the production of white wines. The wines are very fruity, with elegance and length of flavour.

CHÂTEAU DE LA ROSE
Owner: Jean Faure

A small property by Entre-deux-Mers standards, this *cru* is situated at Guillac, just south-west of Branne, in the northern Entre-deux-Mers. The wines are very perfumed with a lovely flowery, fruity flavour.

CHÂTEAU THIEULEY
Owner: Francis Courselle

This well-known property is at La Sauve, near Créon, in western Entre-deux-Mers. It produces 100 per cent Sauvignon wines which emphasize the attractive fruitiness of the grape variety, without exaggerating its characteristics or its acidity – but then the owner is a professor of viticulture.

CHÂTEAU TURCAUD
Owner: Maurice Robert

With Château Thieuley, this is the leading *cru* at La Sauve, near Créon. The wines have a pleasingly flowery, scented, elegant fruitiness, and quite a strong, full flavour. I have already mentioned that the *coopératives* of the region have played an important role in its revitalization. In recent years their facilities have greatly improved, as has their commitment to quality. A good example of this is the branded Entre-deux-Mers, La Gamage, the quality of which has greatly improved over the last few vintages.

Of the other *appellations* adjoining Entre-deux-Mers, the sweetish wines of St Macaire have declined considerably in importance. In 1970 nearly 12,000 hectolitres were made, but by 1986 this had fallen to under 2,000 hectolitres. Graves de Vayres, with its dry wines, having rather more body than Entre-deux-Mers, still has some following in Germany, but even this has declined slightly in recent years, in spite of the name. Ste Foy, on the other hand, with its close affinity to Dordogne wines, has maintained and even marginally improved its position, but production is really very small.

The white wines of Blaye are more important than those of Bourg. It is confusing to find that white wines in Blaye can be declared as Blaye or Blayais, Côtes de Blaye or Premières Côtes de Blaye. In fact, most of the white wine is declared as Blaye or Blayais, a much smaller quantity as Côtes de Blaye, and only a few hundred hectolitres as Premières Côtes Blaye. The production of white Bourg is now commercially unimportant.

This leaves, of course, the enormous production of simple Bordeaux Blanc. Most of it is produced in the Entre-deux-Mers, but it is produced all over the region, including the Médoc and Sauternes. The variation in quality is considerable. Some of it is sweetish, mostly it is dry. Often there is little difference in quality between a good Bordeaux Blanc and an Entre-deux-Mers. Some property wines are certainly worth looking at. The decline in production experienced during the seventies now seems to have been halted, and a new plateau for production has been established.

12

The Evaluation of Bordeaux Vintages

Anyone unfamiliar with Bordeaux and its wine might wonder why so much time is spent discussing the merits of different vintages. In all wine districts situated in temperate climates, vintages are important to a greater or lesser extent, especially when the wine-grower is striving to produce something really fine to mature over a number of years. Like people, wines develop character and individuality with the passage of time. What makes vintages of particular interest in Bordeaux is the very diversity of the regions. We have already seen why it is that a good year for the Médoc may not be a good one in St Emilion, and why a fine year for red wines may not be echoed in Sauternes. When these differences are added to the climatic instability of the region as a whole, it is easy to see why vintages should assume such importance here.

Whenever a new vintage is born, everyone attempts to find some analogy with a previous one. The history of the weather conditions from flowering to picking is examined in much the same way as parents and relatives look at a newly born child, in an attempt to discern its likely character. The process probably works rather better than for human beings, but only up to a certain point. It will usually establish the type of vintage which has been produced, but will give only a hint as to its eventual character. One has only to read the prognostications of experts made at the time to see how wide of the mark they can be on occasion. The only thing that is certain is that every year does develop its own personality, and the better the vintage the stronger this character becomes. This is the reason why many experienced tasters can often work out the vintage of a particular wine when given it blind, but will often be floored by an off-vintage, especially if it has some age.

As far as red wines are concerned, vintages can roughly be divided between those which mature fairly rapidly, and the more tannic slow developers – although with modern techniques for controlling the fermentation, this distinction can become blurred. It is a popular fallacy that hard vintages last and light ones do not. In the past the light vintages have usually been the well-balanced ones, and for this reason have lasted well and often better than the tannic ones. In the end, it is the harmony of fruit, acidity and tannin that matters most. The 1900 was a classic example of this, being considered too attractive too soon, in comparison to the 1899. (See Ian Maxwell Campbell, *Wayward Tendrils of the Vine*, p. 53.) More recently, some 1945s have disappointed, while the 1949 and 1953 have lasted much better than was expected.

I realize that very few will have the opportunity of drinking a bottle of claret from a vintage prior to 1920 as that, after all, is seventy years ago. Nevertheless, a few notes on the historic vintages of the nineteenth century may be of academic interest at least. In the cellars of Bordeaux, or indeed of British stately homes, as some sales at Christie's and Sotheby's have proved, the best examples of these historic vintages are still good. Usually, as at Lafite and Mouton, these wines have been regularly recorked. Even so, a sense of perspective needs to be kept. Most of these very old wines certainly provide what one would call "interesting bottles". That is to say, they are past their best, but are still alive and interesting to connoisseurs. Only the exceptional wine is still in top form, displaying the full character of its vintage and its château. I remember, after drinking one such exceptional wine, the 1869 Mouton, at the château, remarking on its exceptional preservation to Raoul Blondin, the *maître de chai* at Mouton at that time. He told me that of all the great collections of old vintages stored there, the 1869 and 1870 vintages were now much the best preserved and most consistent of the nineteenth-century wines. Many others were still very interesting but had not retained their full vigour and character to the same degree.

13 SEPTEMBER 1798
The first vintage to be matured in bottle to any degree. There is an example in the collection of Lafite. Cocks & Féret noted "very celebrated for 70 years after".

23 SEPTEMBER 1802

A very good year, but inferior to 1798.

14 SEPTEMBER 1811

An exceptional year; they were known as Comet wines.

15 SEPTEMBER 1815

Small quantity, remarkable wines equal to 1798 and 1811.

20 SEPTEMBER 1819

Plentiful harvest, very good wines. Gruaud-Larose still astonishingly vigorous in 1990!

31 AUGUST 1822

White wines especially good; the reds took a long time to mature.

11 SEPTEMBER 1825

A celebrated year which did not quite live up to its early reputation. The white wines were the best.

15 SEPTEMBER 1828

A fine year for the first growths.

14 SEPTEMBER 1831

A great year, both red and white wines of remarkable quality. Yield reduced by hail in August. In 1988 the Ausone of this vintage still showed an amazing volume of flavour, with fruit and some richness, a remarkable relic which had never moved from the château's cellars. It was the final wine in the great retrospective tasting held there by Madame Helyett Dubois-Challon at the instigation of Bipin Desai, the well-known Los Angeles collector and connoisseur.

9 SEPTEMBER 1834

Considered a great year. Frost and hail resulted in a very small crop. Prices very high. Gruaud-Larose still rich and fruity in 1990.

17 SEPTEMBER 1840

Very good white wines, large crop.

18 SEPTEMBER 1841

An excellent year, but white wines not as rich as in 1840.

7 OCTOBER 1844

An outstanding year for the red wines, with very high prices. At the Ausone tasting in 1988 the wine was still sweet and charming, better indeed than the 1893.

14 SEPTEMBER 1846

After a very hot summer, a vintage producing very big wines which just missed greatness, but the white wines were excellent and fetched very high prices.

25 SEPTEMBER 1847

A large crop, classified as a great year. Reds light, but with a fine bouquet and very attractive. Whites very successful. Among the great years. The Yquem is legendary.

20 SEPTEMBER 1848

A good crop but smaller than in 1847. Red wines more full-bodied than in 1847, wines of remarkable quality which developed very well. The 1847 and 1848 are the first examples of a pair of outstanding but complementary vintages which occur from time to time in Bordeaux. The Yquem is legendary.

27 SEPTEMBER 1851

A very hot summer produced hard, slow-developing wines which were appreciated only as they developed. White wines were excellent. At the Ausone tasting in 1988 the sample from this vintage was virtually finished, yet a sample of the 1850 – a vintage with a poor reputation – was astonishing, with amazing structure and power, and more colour than almost any other wine from the nineteenth century. Could this in fact have been the 1851 due to a muddle in the cellars at some stage?

1853–6
The oidium years.

20 SEPTEMBER 1857
Vines still feeble after the oidium of previous years, but good conditions produced red wines that were truly ripe, delicate and fine – a good vintage.

20 SEPTEMBER 1858
A very hot summer produced a celebrated vintage which set historically new high price levels. Red wines were perfectly ripe and lasted very well, though this is not one of the pre-phylloxera vintages which has survived in more than an occasional "interesting" form to the present day. The white wines were considered to rival the 1847s, and Yquem reached unheard-of price levels.

23 SEPTEMBER 1859
Famous only for the white wines which rivalled, and in some cases surpassed, 1858.

22 SEPTEMBER 1861
Another year for white wines which were very luscious. Red wines proved very ordinary.

17 SEPTEMBER 1864
An outstanding year. Very large crop. Red wines noted for their flavour, delicacy and elegance. The white wines were also very successful. Lafite still superb in 1979.

6 SEPTEMBER 1865
1864 and 1865 are another noted Bordeaux "pair". The crop was even larger than in 1864, but prices reached new records; this was the most expensive vintage of the century. While it was certainly a great year, it is interesting to note that, by 1899, Cocks & Féret were saying the wines "have not entirely realized the great hopes founded on them at first". They have lasted well, but not as well as the 1869s or 1870s. The 1865 was a tannic wine that is sometimes compared to the 1870. In 1988 a

bottle of Lafite at the château was still superb, an incomparable bottle, while another bottle died quickly in the glass.

7 SEPTEMBER 1868
A large crop in spite of spring frosts and hail. At first the red wines seemed to have a beautiful colour, body and a fine flavour, and very high prices were paid for the first growths. However, the wines were hard and slow to mature and so lost favour. The Sauternes crop was destroyed by hail.

15 SEPTEMBER 1869
A very good vintage. A very large crop was harvested in superb weather. At first, the trade was uncertain as to the quality, but the wines developed so well that it was later recognized as one of the great years. Both the Cos d'Estournel and the Mouton reached their centenary in superb condition and with all their faculties intact, a remarkable achievement. In 1988 a bottle of the Ausone was volatile, but still had the vinosity and power to suggest what a massive wine it must have been. The white wines were also very fine. The Yquem is one of the greatest wines produced there, on a par with the 1921. A bottle tasted in 1988, brought back from Russia by the German collector Hardy Rodenstock, was still marvellous.

10 SEPTEMBER 1870
Another very great year, so that 1869 and 1870 were certainly the greatest "pair" in the nineteenth century. The red wines were very full-bodied and had great vinosity, but they developed very slowly. As a consequence, this vintage was preserved in many cellars until modern times and often forgotten about. The greatest bottle I have tasted was a magnum of the legendary Lafite from Glamis Castle prior to the sale of the cellar at Christie's. Characteristically, the whites were good but did not match the reds.

8 SEPTEMBER 1871
This was preceded by one of the severest winters of the century. From 1 to 4 January the temperature dropped to − 14°C and the Gironde was frozen to the sixth arch of the Bordeaux bridge. Nearly a third of the vines in the Gironde were frozen, and at the end of March another severe frost

did much damage. Although the ripening was irregular and the vintage took place under unfavourable conditions, so that the wines were written off as a poor year, they developed much better than expected and some of the best Médocs were excellent, but not on the whole long-lived.

14 SEPTEMBER 1874
A very good year, the yield surpassing 1869. The vintage was heralded as a success even before the harvest was completed, and high prices were obtained. The finest 1874 I have seen was the Latour which was beautifully preserved and still completely characteristic of its origins (this was a bottle from the Rosebery cellar, tasted thanks to the kindness of Michael Broadbent prior to the auction in 1967). If this was typical, the 1874s have lasted better than the 1865s. The white wines were also very successful.

22 SEPTEMBER 1875
The largest vintage of the century and a uniformly very successful one. The 1874 and 1875 were the third and last outstanding "pair" of Bordeaux vintages in the great period between the oidium and the onset of the phylloxera and the mildew. Although the red wines were lighter than the 1874s, they possessed great elegance and charm and this was one of the most admired vintages of its day. Most surviving examples are very pale in colour and have faded, but an occasional bottle still conveys the elegance and breed of this year – I particularly remember the Margaux and the Rauzan. The white wines were not in the same class as the 1874s.

20 SEPTEMBER 1877
Some light and very attractive red wines were made, possessed of a charming bouquet, *race* and elegance. In the main they have not lived, although a number of examples were unearthed to present to André Simon on his ninetieth birthday. At the Ausone tasting in 1988 the bottle from this vintage was still quite ethereal with a lovely sweet fruitiness. The white wines were ordinary.

19 SEPTEMBER 1878
The last reasonable vintage before the onset of phylloxera and the mildew scourge. The wines were not highly thought of at first, but developed a

good bouquet. To some extent their reputation as a good year, if nothing more, was enhanced by the poor years which followed.

1879–86
Years mostly of low yields and poor quality. The vines were debilitated by phylloxera and mildew, and *coulure* was also very prevalent. Very occasionally drinkable bottles do appear. I recall a pleasant Palmer 1880, and the 1879 Ausone, tasted at the château in 1988, was a small but charming wine.

28 SEPTEMBER 1887
The first ray of hope after the lean years, but the yield was very small. The wines had the reputation of being rather graceless.

28 SEPTEMBER 1888
The largest crop of the decade. Produced pleasing light red wines, but only ordinary whites.

6 OCTOBER 1889
Red wines of more colour and body than the 1888s. I have drunk the Mouton and the Langoa, which were both well preserved and attractive.

28 SEPTEMBER 1890
A vintage which was welcomed and enjoyed some reputation, but the wines tended to be hard. Some good whites were made and I have a pleasant recollection of the Yquem.

16 SEPTEMBER 1892
Just missed being a really good year, a very hot, dry wind, a sort of sirocco, causing much harm in August. Nevertheless, the Lascombes was a great wine when over seventy years of age, comparable to an 1899, while the Ausone was still opulently scented with a lovely flavour in 1988.

18 AUGUST 1893
The first unqualified success since the lean years of phylloxera and mildew. The crop was almost as large as the prolific 1875. The flowering

finished by 20 May, a good three weeks earlier than usual, and the heat and drought of the summer were the most intense since 1822. The wines provoked enormous interest and, being offered at moderate prices, business was so brisk that by Christmas all the classified growths were sold – a case of early buying if ever there was one! The wines were very ripe, fruity and attractive and lasted well, but in my experience have tended to decay seriously in the last decade. The Lafite, in particular, was a beauty, reminding me of a 1929 in style, but it suddenly faded, though at the Ausone tasting in 1988 this wine, though clearly in decline, still had great elegance and charm. Some of the Sauternes were wonderfully balanced and preserved their fruitiness and sweetness for an unusual period. The Rayne-Vigneau is the finest example I have seen: it was still superb and not maderized when nearly seventy years old.

5 OCTOBER 1894
A year of no very great reputation, but the Ausone was holding up better than the 1893 when tasted in 1988, with a lovely long, lingering flavour. In contrast the Lafite, drunk at the château in the same year, was no more than an interesting old ruin.

19 SEPTEMBER 1895
This might have been a great year if controlled vinification had been understood or had even been possible. As it was, the wines were rich in sugar and many turned volatile or "pricked". However, there were some notable successes; I have drunk a remarkable Pétrus, and I know Maxwell Campbell records that the La Conseillante was also very fine, although he characterized the vintage as a whole as fat and flabby. In the Médoc both Mouton and Lafite were successful.

20 SEPTEMBER 1896
Owing to very mixed weather conditions, the red wines varied considerably in quality. The successful wines were described as light and elegant but they have been faulted as being dry. In spite of this, the Loudenne of this year was still fresh and well preserved when nearly seventy years of age, while the Lafite was a most beautiful wine, only just beaten by the 1899 when they were drunk together in 1954.

20 SEPTEMBER 1897

Generally a disastrous year, with hail, spring frosts, mildew and scorching salty winds resulting in a tiny crop of mostly indifferent wines. However, the Ausone was still elegantly scented and fruity with gently faded fruit, a seamless flavour – an almost ageless beauty in 1988.

24 SEPTEMBER 1899

The old century went out in a blaze of glory as if to prove that phylloxera and oidium were finally beaten. Although the 1893 had been a great success in many ways, some claret lovers still had their reservations about the vintage as a whole. There was no doubt that the 1899 was a vintage fit to take its place beside the great pre-phylloxera years, and time has certainly vindicated this judgement. In their prime they were described as full-bodied, vigorous, sweet and generous. In old age these wines held their colour very well and the best of them, such as the Lafite and Latour, have remained marvellously vigorous and complete. The most recent example I have tasted was the Ausone in 1988. It still had a deep colour with a wonderfully ethereal yet exotic old-claret bouquet; still a very complete wine with a long, delicate, dry after-taste. In general, however, most wines now show signs of going dry and are fading. Also a great year for white wines. The Suduiraut when nearly eighty years old was one of the finest Sauternes I ever tasted.

24 SEPTEMBER 1900

If the old century went out in a blaze of glory, the new century was not to be outdone, so that these two years provided one of the greatest Bordeaux "pairs", long to be compared and discussed. In size this was the largest vintage since 1875, proving the recovered vigour of the Bordeaux vineyards. What is so interesting about 1900 as a year is that, when young, the wines were described as "light, very light in body, but just as sweet as 1899 and soft and gentle, almost too much so to age well" (Ian Maxwell Campbell, *Wayward Tendrils of the Vine*, p. 53). If ever there was a vintage to prove that light wines last, this was it, for today the rare survivals of this year are still magnificent – in fact I have never had a single disappointment. Of the first growths, I have drunk Lafite, Margaux and Mouton, and they were all superb and apparently ageless. But one of the greatest wines of the year must have been the Léoville-Las Cases. When I first drank the wine in 1962, it was superb and was certainly of first-growth standard, and the last time I saw it, in 1970, it was equally fine, and did not seem to have aged at all in the interval. More recently, at the Ausone tasting in 1988, one bottle still had a very deep colour, was rich and luscious on the nose, and had an amazingly complex richness of flavour, more opulent than the 1899. The outstanding character of the year seems to be its mellow fruitiness which has continued into old age, fresh and completely unfaded.

1901–3
A run of poor vintages and a great let-down after 1899 and 1900. After the failure of 1903, the Loudenne diary noted that nothing marketable had been made since 1900.

19 SEPTEMBER 1904
Hopes were high at first for this year, and it was compared to 1887 and 1890; however, the wines tended to be light, firm, but lacking fruit. Until recently the only example I had seen was Batailley. It was mellow but still firm and was decidedly at the end of its life in 1965. Maxwell Campbell recorded that the Ausone was more smooth and supple than most wines of the vintage. When I tasted this same wine in 1988 it had the appearance of a vintage of the twenties, and the best bottle was still rich and tannic. It is interesting to note that the 1922 edition of Cocks & Féret placed this vintage on a par with 1899 and 1900, and above 1906, a rating repeated uncritically in subsequent editions, which place 1904 as the best vintage between 1900 and 1920. This is a judgement which I would suggest few of those competent to pronounce would endorse today.

18 SEPTEMBER 1905
Attractive and useful wines which do not seem to have lasted, and certainly not in the top flight. At least that is the received wisdom, but the Ausone tasted in 1988 was absolutely outstanding: concentrated, opulent and very exotic on the nose, it had great beauty of flavour, with full fruit and complexity, and a wonderful freshness.

17 SEPTEMBER 1906

A hot summer produced a crop of only average size. In style, these were big, beefy wines with a tendency to coarseness at first which later mellowed, to make this one of the best vintages in the period from 1901 to 1919. The Haut-Brion, Cheval Blanc, Brane-Cantenac and La Lagune all enjoyed a good reputation. I found that the Lafite lacked graciousness. Again the Ausone was still wonderful in 1988, with a marvellously long flavour and great fruit still.

23 SEPTEMBER 1907

The largest vintage since 1900. Wines made towards the end of the vintage were adversely affected by rain. At their best, the 1907s were "deliciously delicate and flavoury in youth", but lacked staying power, so that by the early thirties Maxwell Campbell noted that they had become "plain and rather 'vacant' ". All the examples I have tasted were distinctly too old, with the exception of a single bottle of Margaux in 1962 which, while being very light, still drank very well.

15 SEPTEMBER 1908

A year of no reputation as far as the red wines were concerned. They were considered hard and unattractive, but the white wines seem to have been better, and I once enjoyed a bottle of Guiraud which was still sweet and attractive, with no sign of maderization. Yet in spite of the general reputation of the vintage, the Ausone at the 1988 tasting was quite exceptional with an ethereal bouquet, great finesse and a wonderful lingering flavour, while Cheval Blanc was very stylish two years earlier in spite of volatility.

23 SEPTEMBER 1909

A generally successful year, although there was some trouble with rot. The wines were light and pleasing, somewhat in the style of the 1907s, but with rather more substance. During the early sixties there were still a fair number of examples in the Loudenne cellar, and most of them still had great charm, fruit and finesse. The best were Latour, Margaux, the two Laroses, Cos d'Estournel, Rauzan-Gassies and Léoville-Barton. Although mostly just past their best, they were still immensely enjoyable.

1 OCTOBER 1910
A notoriously poor year and not worth mentioning were it not for the Haut-Brion.

15 SEPTEMBER 1911
The vintage was generally regarded as following 1909 as a good if not exceptional year. I tasted several examples just past their fiftieth year which showed that the year possessed charm and plenty of fruit, though none was quite as good as the 1909s. With the exception of a lovely bottle of Batailley which had not stirred from its original bin at the château, and a remarkable bottle of Bel-Orme, all the wines, including Cheval Blanc, were clearly well past their prime. The whites were fine, and I have had a bottle of Doisy-Védrines which was still full of fruit and richness.

20 SEPTEMBER 1912
A large vintage. The red wines seemed attractive at first, but many suffered from the effects of mildew and did not last. The only example I have tasted was the Ausone at the 1988 tasting. It was elegant, ethereal, delicate, dryish, but quite lovely still.

25 SEPTEMBER 1913
Again, contemporary accounts in Cocks & Féret speak favourably of the year, but Maxwell Campbell says "nor have I seen a '13 that did not have fatal resemblance to 1910". But he might have been surprised by the example at the 1988 Ausone tasting. It was elegantly faded, lean and old, but sound and still a joy to taste.

20 SEPTEMBER 1914
A very large crop, the biggest since 1907. Evidently attractive, supple wines at the start. According again to Maxwell Campbell, these wines seemed most attractive by 1920 when serious claret drinking resumed after the war, but they suddenly folded up "and died as it were in the night". Until recently the only bottle I had drunk was the Lafite, which was light but charming when first opened, but then quickly died in the glass, and that had come straight from the Lafite cellars. However, the Ausone, at the 1988 tasting, was wonderfully scented, with an exotic,

cedary quality to its bouquet, and flavour of ageless charm and great finesse.

20 SEPTEMBER 1915
A year affected by *coulure*, oidium and mildew, so that the crop was the smallest since 1886. The year has a poor reputation, though surprisingly the only bottle to come my way – the Léoville-Barton – had survived forty years, although it was somewhat unbalanced.

25 SEPTEMBER 1916
Oidium reduced the vintage to below average in size, but in spite of this, it proved the most successful vintage of the war years, and one of the relative peaks in this lean period between 1900 and 1920. For long it was understandably criticized as being too hard, although Cocks & Féret say that it was considered less hard than the 1906. All the examples I have seen still showed signs of this excess of tannin when already around fifty years old. On the other hand, these were all wines of character and interest. The best bottle I have had was the Calon-Ségur in 1986, a majestic wine I thought belonged to a great vintage of the twenties. Other good examples were Cantemerle, Larose-Sarget and Lanessan. All were very deep in colour.

17 SEPTEMBER 1917
This is cited as a vintage which might have had a greater success had it not been for the war. In the event, it proved uneven. As it happens, the three examples I have seen were all from the other side of the river, so it could be that St Emilion and Pomerol outshone the Médoc. Pétrus, Clos Fourtet and Ausone were big, dark wines full of vigour and life; while the Clos Fourtet was a shade too alcoholic in style, the Pétrus had fruit and great charm, and the Ausone had lovely complex, cherry-like fruit and still so much life and *joie de vivre*.

23 SEPTEMBER 1918
An average crop of very unequal quality. Maxwell Campbell called them leathery. The erratic behaviour of the vintage was typified for me in some Léoville-Las Cases tasted over the years at Loudenne. When first drunk in 1962, it seemed a little tired, but still hard and ungracious. The following

year it seemed equally unsympathetic. However, in 1967 came a bottle with a gloriously perfumed bouquet far more typical of this growth, and with a lovely long, rich, harmonious flavour to match. The change was extraordinary. The Lafite tasted the same year had gone into a graceful decline and was a shade "watery" at the finish.

20 SEPTEMBER 1919
A light year abundant in quantity which did not live long enough to acquire any lasting reputation.

15 SEPTEMBER 1920
With this vintage there began one of those periods of bounty which nature permits from time to time. Different claret lovers will have their own favourites, but it is undeniable that for anyone who has enjoyed drinking fine claret in the last fifty years, the most frequent pleasure will perhaps have derived from clarets of the twenties. The crop was of good average size and good, if not exceptional, things were thought of it from the start. There were good judges who thought the wines would not last and were lacking fruit, but for the most part these judgements have proved erroneous. Like all the best vintages of this decade, the 1920s have a lot of personality. I noted when drinking one of them that it was more robust than a 1929 and had more elegance than a 1926, and that seems not a bad assessment of the character of the year. I have not had the good fortune to drink the Latour, which was always famed as the outstanding wine of the year, but the Cheval Blanc, which was overshadowed by the 1921, was still a classic with lovely soft fruit and a delicate laciness in 1986. Probably the finest example I have tasted was the La Mission-Haut-Brion, which in 1966 was still in full vigour, with a wonderful flavour, rich and powerful. In 1988 it was run close by the Ausone, which still showed remarkable power, richness and tannin. The other outstanding bottles were the Montrose, the Rauzan-Gassies, and that most dependable of wines, the Lanessan.

15 SEPTEMBER 1921
This exceptionally hot summer produced one legendary wine – the Cheval Blanc – and some great Sauternes, but very few other red wines were really successful because of the inability of the *vignerons* of the day

to control adequately a fermentation made in hot weather of a must unusually rich in sugar. As a result, many wines turned acetic – notably the Lafite – while others suffered from the grapes being scorched, which gave the wines a roasted smell and a heavy but tough texture. The Haut-Brion was such a wine, still unyielding and graceless when over forty years old, though when I again tasted it in 1979 it had improved remarkably. The Mouton, on the other hand, was surprisingly attractive when I drank it at the château with Philippe Cottin in 1966. It had more delicacy than the 1926, plenty of fruit and finesse, and a strong assertive nose that was only just beginning to fade. Also enjoyable was the La Lagune, though there was just a little coarseness about it, which was perhaps almost inevitable in this year. The Cheval Blanc was the precursor of the 1947; its remarkable sweetness and almost overpowering flavour placed this wine firmly among the first growths of the Gironde. The Ausone at the 1988 tasting had a very concentrated, roasted, almost nutty bouquet, and a lovely rich, seamless flavour, drying out but powerful and fine. The Yquem is legendary and rightly so. I have had several bottles in recent years and they have all been remarkable: deep in colour, it is more like an essence than a wine, a unique experience. All the great Sauternes *crus* had great richness and have lasted well.

19 SEPTEMBER 1922

The largest vintage in the history of the Gironde. Not surprisingly, the wines were on the light side and proved something of a drug on the market. However, I suspect that today we should have heralded it as a distinctly "useful" vintage. The only two red wines I have seen, Léoville-Barton and Rausan-Ségla, had both lasted forty years and still managed to be well balanced, fruity and pleasantly flavoured, although by then gently faded. On the other hand, I have had several Sauternes which were very well preserved, although curiously the Yquem was the one wine to have gone completely dry.

1 OCTOBER 1923

Another large crop, if not quite so abundant as 1922. The wines were light, with much elegance and breed. With so much good wine about and claret drinking in decline, this was an underrated year. These were certainly wines of a style that would be highly appreciated today, much as the 1950s were. Both the Clos Fourtet and the Larose-Sarget lasted very well, with a lovely flowery bouquet and a pronounced sweetness on the palate. I have also drunk the Loudenne over a period of years and note that we never had a disappointing bottle. Again, the wine was notable for its sweetness at the finish, and freshness and delicacy of flavour.

19 SEPTEMBER 1924
1922 apart, one has to go back to 1900 to find such a prolific year as this. From the beginning, the wines enjoyed a fine reputation and were generally preferred to the 1923s and thus more widely bought by the English trade. This is a vintage I always associate with Château Margaux because, while still at Cambridge, I attended the then famous Lebègue tasting through the good offices of Harry Waugh, then of Harvey's, in the year that they showed a range of Margaux of the century. I was very struck by the excellence of the Margaux 1924 compared to other vintages of that famous decade, but then both the 1928 and 1929 Margaux were disappointing. Both Lafite and Latour were good, but the finest bottle I have enjoyed, after the Margaux, was a magnum of Calon-Ségur which was full of vitality when forty years old. Generally speaking, though, the 1924s have faded markedly in the last twenty years, and bottles tend to be very variable. At their best, these wines had great charm and plenty of fruit, but in the end lacked the staying power of the 1926s, much as the 1929s compared to the 1928s.

3 OCTOBER 1925
Another prolific year, only slightly less wine than in 1924, but the quality was totally unremarkable. The only example to come my way was certainly quite unrepresentative. The Ausone at the 1988 tasting had a lovely delicate scent and great breed, the flavour was very light and dry, but in no way faulty.

4 OCTOBER 1926
Easily the smallest vintage of the decade. At Latour the yield was a mere 7 hectolitres per hectare. I once asked Baron Philippe de Rothschild why it did not enjoy a greater reputation, as I had just enjoyed a really great bottle of the Mouton of that year. He replied that 1926 held unhappy memories for the Bordeaux trade. There had been a very small crop,

difficult to gather, owing to *cochylis*. (At Mouton, they had gone through the vineyard and filled several barrels with maggots before the vintage.) Prices had opened at record levels – and, indeed, 1926 was to remain the most expensive claret vintage until 1961 – and then the market had collapsed, resulting in very serious losses. Baron Philippe actually cancelled all his contracts and then resold to his original buyers at half the opening price, but one *négociant* at least was made bankrupt. Although decried at first as too tannic, the 1926s have developed into wines of great power and balance. Their tannin was matched by more fruit and sugar than was the case with most 1928s. In recent years I have found them to be the most consistently fine of all the great vintages of the twenties, with more weight and power than 1929s and more fruit and charm than most 1928s, as well as being more dependable now than the 1920s. Although these wines are undeniably tannic and robust, they have an outstanding ripeness about them which gives them a richness and finesse denied to most tannic years. I think the Mouton and Haut-Brion were certainly the finest 1926s I have drunk, but the Calon-Ségur, Cos d'Estournel, Lascombes, La Mission, Pichon-Lalande, Cantemerle and Ducru-Beaucaillou were all excellent, while many *bourgeois* growths like Bel-Orme and Loudenne have lasted and developed well. The Ausone at the 1988 tasting was an exceptional example to set beside the Mouton and Haut-Brion.

27 SEPTEMBER 1927
A year which vies with 1925 as the poorest vintage of the decade. The Ausone smelt of mothballs!

25 SEPTEMBER 1928
A large vintage which enjoyed a very great reputation at the beginning, but has somewhat disappointed since. This is not to say that there are not a number of great wines, but the quality is more mixed than had been expected. Maxwell Campbell noted that his first impression of the 1928s was that "they seemed so well-balanced and well-bred, full to the taste and, at the same time, supple . . . but it seemed to me to be counter-balanced by a sufficiency of fruit and sugar". In the event, some wines turned out to be much more tannic than this description suggests, and some, like the Gruaud-Larose, seem to have dried up. In the Médoc the

great wines for me have long been the Léoville-Las Cases and the Léoville-Poyferré, both wines of great depth and intensity of flavour, gloriously balanced and without a discordant note; another St Julien, the Beychevelle, was not far behind. These are rivals even for the great 1900s, and the Latour was beginning by 1989 to overpower the glorious 1929. Outside the Médoc, the Ausone was a great wine (but the sample at the 1988 tasting was breaking up), outshining even the Cheval Blanc, I thought, while the Pétrus clearly foreshadowed the great reputation it now deservedly enjoys. On the whole, the St Emilions and Pomerols have shown more harmony and regularity in their development than many Médocs, but among the Médocs, Brane-Cantenac, Calon-Ségur, Palmer, the two Pichons and Pontet-Canet all reached maturity still possessed of enough fruit to give them balance and life. This was a particularly fine year for the great Sauternes. Yquem produced one of its greatest vintages, which lasted very well. Generally, 1928 Sauternes were better balanced and lasted better than the 1929s.

23 SEPTEMBER 1929

1928 and 1929 were very well-matched years. In terms of size, they were as near identical as nature is likely to allow. At the same time, proprietors and *régisseurs* spoke of them in the same breath as 1899 and 1900. Certainly they proved the most celebrated pair of years since that time. To turn to Maxwell Campbell once more, he records his first impression of the vintage as finding in them "a small taste of over-ripe grapes . . . the wines seemed . . . soft, mellow, and very sweet, sweeter than the '28s". If he, and most of his contemporaries, were over-optimistic about the 1928s, they were broadly right about the 1929s as wines too pretty and ethereal to make old bones, wines to be drunk while they still gave such pleasure. Certainly, many 1929s have been fading in the last decade. Yet no one who has had the pleasure of drinking a 1929 anywhere near its best can doubt that this was a great vintage. Their quality lay in a bouquet of outstanding brilliance and penetration. The Latour was probably the most famous wine and rightly so, although for some years there has been a degree of variation from bottle to bottle.

Although my father has always been most generous to me, I was rather surprised when, in the early fifties, I received at Cambridge several bottles of Latour 1929 in response to a request for more supplies. I rested the wine for a month or two until my parents came to dinner in my rooms. The wine proved magnificent, and my father then confessed he had had a bottle with Allan Sichel which they had judged to be in decline and Allan, in pessimistic mood, had said he felt the wine should be drunk. We never had a bad bottle again for many a long day! The Mouton was also a famous 1929, but was, I thought, in decline when I last drank it in 1965. One of the most famous wines of the year was the Pontet-Canet, a quite exceptional wine for the growth, far above its class. As in 1928, the Léoville-Poyferré was a great wine with more richness and staying power than many 1929s. The finest example I have seen from the right bank was the Ausone at the 1988 tasting, a perfect wine I scored at 20/20, extraordinary in every way from its healthy brilliant colour, still deep and pinkish, through its ethereal perfumed bouquet, with the vigour of a 1926, to a marvellously majestic flavour, all ripeness, power, finesse, and a lingering finish echoing away like the notes of a great bell, full of wonderful nuances. Other outstanding wines were the Cheval Blanc, Canon, Montrose, Nenin, Pichon-Lalande and Siran. Some beautiful Sauternes were made, but they tended to go very dark – to caramelize. The Guiraud and Rayne-Vigneau were particularly good.

29 SEPTEMBER 1930

The first of three dire vintages! The 1930 was small in quantity and I have never heard any exonerating point in its favour. Not since the 1880s had there been such a trio, and not until the sixties was their like to be seen again – and then not in succession.

21 SEPTEMBER 1931

This was a larger crop, spoilt by rain during the vintage. A few tolerable wines were made, notably at Latour, Margaux, Lanessan and Domaine de Chevalier, while the Yquem was surprisingly acceptable. The 1931 was the best of the terrible trio.

14 OCTOBER 1932

A good-size crop, but one of the latest vintages ever recorded; the quality was "execrable". Teddy Hammond of Edward Young always told the story that it was because of these three vintages (1930, 1931 and 1932) that the idea of Mouton Cadet was born, as a method of using the Mouton and Mouton d'Armailhacq of those years.

20 SEPTEMBER 1933
A moderate yield. A year which deserved a better reputation. Certainly these were the sort of wines which would have been very popular today – light, fruity and most attractive; they were what was then described as "luncheon claret". The Latour, Mouton (still fine in 1979), Beychevelle and Canon (St Emilion) are four fine examples which have come my way.

17 SEPTEMBER 1934
The largest recorded good vintage, exceeded only by the rather ordinary 1922s. This is a vintage which enjoyed a great reputation at the start and then went through a dull period. I am inclined to think it has now come good, and those few 1934s that survive tend to have plenty of fruit and depth of flavour, and to be generally reliable, while seldom perhaps scaling the heights of the greatest years. It is certainly the best vintage of the thirties and perhaps more regular than the 1928, but without the flair of the 1929 or 1926. The Ausone was particularly lovely and the example at the 1988 tasting was still opulent and amazingly sweet, but less impressive than the 1937. The Cheval-Blanc was also an outstanding success. With the exception of Latour, the first growths were rather disappointing, the Lafite being one of the few really dull wines from this great growth, and the Margaux also curiously lacking in breed. The Mouton, which was for years hard and uncouth, has now come good. The Pichon-Lalande, Léoville-Barton, Talbot and Calon-Ségur are all examples of leading Médocs which have truly fulfilled their promise. Among *bourgeois* growths, the Lanessan was particularly fine, but one of the best of all 1934s was the La Mission-Haut-Brion, a marvellously balanced wine of great breed and attraction. This was a good year for Sauternes, although the Yquem was not in the same class as the 1928 or the 1937.

25 SEPTEMBER 1935
A big crop suffered from poor weather during the vintage, and this particularly affected the white wines. Another very poor year. But Laville was a remarkable exception.

2 OCTOBER 1936

A medium-sized crop of clean, sound wines which lacked ripeness and therefore style or attraction. Exceptions I have seen were the Latour, which was attractive and vigorous when thirty years old, and clearly superior to the 1931 which we drank at the same meal, and La Mission-Haut-Brion, still very attractive when over forty years old. The Cheval Blanc was still a pleasant if small wine in 1986. The Domaine de Chevalier also had something of a reputation. I have also seen a sound Yquem.

20 SEPTEMBER 1937

This, the first vintage to take place under the new *appellation contrôlée* regulations, was rather modest in size, about the same as the 1933. It was bottled just in time to be shipped before the fall of France in 1940 cut Bordeaux off from its export markets for five years. For the most part, the 1937s have been found to be stubborn and tough, a recognized vintage which has disappointed, yet I would plead several important qualifications to this rather unfavourable verdict. All 1937s have a certain distinction of flavour which marks them out as wines of breed and individuality – in other words, this is decidedly a class vintage. Then, most St Emilions and Pomerols, as well as some Graves, have more harmony than the Médocs, and have developed better. This was borne out at the 1988 Ausone tasting, where the wine showed rich, sweet, chewy fruit and great character in spite of some volatility. Finally, even some of the top Médocs have in the last decade mellowed sufficiently to give real pleasure. A good example of this is the Latour. I first drank it when it was twenty years old and found it hard and ungracious. I wondered if it would get any better. Eight years later I noted that it was now full in flavour, rich and long on the palate – fairly balanced and still developing well. It has continued to do so, and when compared with the 1934 in 1979 was clearly superior. The Lafite has also come through well, and I certainly find it preferable to the 1934. Other good 1937s I have seen in recent years are the Léoville-Poyferré, Pichon-Lalande, Branaire and Siran, while in the Graves the Haut-Bailly is really fine. Only the Montrose proved to be a disappointment. Certainly these are very masculine wines, but I suggest there could be much enjoyment to be had in the next few years for those fortunate enough still to have some salted away. This was a great year for Sauternes, and the Yquem will always be one of my favourites – in the fifties it was at its glorious best at a time when the 1921 had become undependable and the 1928 was showing signs of maderization. Though it is now past its prime, it is still possible to find enjoyable bottles.

26 SEPTEMBER 1938

A vintage of approximately the same size as the 1937, overshadowed by the war. Unlike many of the wartime vintages, most 1938s seemed to have been bottled at the right time. The wines were on the light side, attractively fruity and quite fleshy. Only a very few were subsequently shipped after the war as "concession wines", during the period of limitation of imports to the UK. They are just the sort of wines we should have been glad to have today. I think the first 1938 I drank was a Talbot, which was such a pleasant surprise that I always looked out for 1938s after that. The Latour was still at its best when nearly thirty years old, and smaller growths like Chasse-Spleen and Loudenne made delicious wines which lasted well.

20 SEPTEMBER 1939

A very large crop of light wines which, for the most part, disappeared during the war. The only examples I have ever seen were the Margaux, which was quite finished when less than twenty years old, and the Ausone, very light and faded almost to oblivion in 1988, and best of all, Figeac, charming and sound in 1989.

25 SEPTEMBER 1940

A rather small crop which, but for the war, might have enjoyed some fame. I first came across the Clos Fourtet – bottled, as were many wartime vintages, in Sauternes bottles – when it was around ten years old. It was deliciously fruity and soft. Since then I have noted that Latour, Haut-Brion, La Mission and Pétrus were all excellent. The Ausone was an emaciated old beauty by 1988.

30 SEPTEMBER 1941

A small and poor year of light wines which lacked maturity. Very few can have survived the war, let alone been shipped afterwards.

22 SEPTEMBER 1942

Another small year which did enjoy something of a reputation, at least in Bordeaux. I remember examining the cellar of a member of the diplomatic service who had served in France just after the war and returned with a number of 1942s, bought on the advice of that sound and experienced judge Henri Binaud. Professor Plumb of Christ's College, Cambridge, once gave me a Lafite 1942, but it was very light and faded when little more than ten years old. It seems probable that these light wines suffered from poor handling, and especially late bottling, owing to the war.

15 SEPTEMBER 1943

In size, just a little smaller than the 1937. In quality, it was on the whole reckoned to be the best of the war-time vintages. Generally, the St Emilions and Pomerols were more successful than the Médocs, and Pétrus was universally accounted the wine of the vintage. I have not seen it now for over a decade, but it was then a really memorable wine. The Ausone showed real ripeness and a supple middle flavour, but a rough finish at the 1988 tasting. Also successful was the Cheval Blanc, and I have particularly pleasant memories of the Trottevieille. In the Médoc the Latour was outstanding, but I have tasted several wines which showed clear signs of having been kept too long in cask. Generally, partly owing to their handling, the Médocs tended to be rather tough and lacking in vinosity and style. This was a very good year for Sauternes – the Climens and Suduiraut being especially fine.

24 SEPTEMBER 1944

A fairly large vintage. Rain during the gathering made for variations in quality. A year not unlike 1960. At their best, the wines were light and very attractive. I remember the Cruses being enthusiastic about them, and unlike the rather cruder 1943s they were most enjoyable when young. The Latour was particularly good, the Lafite faded rather early, but the Haut-Brion was again light and delicious. Pontet-Canet was also delicious when young.

10 SEPTEMBER 1945

A tiny crop – only twice in the previous fifty years had there been a smaller yield. This was due to an unusually late and severe May frost, but the coming of peace was heralded by a vintage of outstanding quality. These are majestic wines, inclined, it is true, to be rather too tannic to begin with and very slow to develop but, as with the best 1928s, they have a depth and intensity of flavour found only in exceptional years. Until the coming of the 1961 vintage, the 1945 was generally regarded as the finest post-war vintage, although some would advance the claims of the 1947, 1949 and 1953 to have been, in their different ways, at least as good, and certainly more enjoyable for longer. Of the first growths, only Margaux disappoints. Both Lafite and Latour are outstanding examples of these two very different wines, as is the Mouton. In Graves both Haut-Brion and La Mission are exceptionally fine. In St Emilion half the crop at Cheval Blanc was *piqué* and had to be pasteurized, but generally the St Emilions and Pomerols were superb and could be drunk long before most of the Médocs. I particularly remember La Dominique and Gazin. Of the Médocs, it is only since these wines passed their twenty-year mark that one began to drink them without a feeling of committing infanticide. Two exceptions were Lynch-Bages and Calon-Ségur, both more supple and less tannic than most. There were some fine Sauternes, especially the Yquem, but generally they were outshone by the 1947s.

28 SEPTEMBER 1946

A rather moderate yield, but higher than 1945. Very much an off-vintage, although both Latour and Mouton made good wines. It was so surrounded by successful years that practically none was shipped and the vintage has been forgotten.

15 SEPTEMBER 1947

A plentiful year which produced wines which were immediately attractive. After the small crop of slow-maturing 1945s, this was greeted with much enthusiasm by the trade, heavily bought, and generally drunk too early. It could be, however, that in many cases this proved to be the right thing to do, because many 1947s, especially in the Médoc, have not lived up to their early promise. However, some good judges in Bordeaux at one time considered the 1947s to be superior to the 1945s. The style of the wines was so completely different that this really resolves itself into a question of taste. The peaks of 1947 certainly vie with 1945, but in general the vintage was not so consistent, although more generally attractive when young, and it has not developed so well. The most famous wines of the vintage appeared in St Emilion and Pomerol. Cheval Blanc was early proclaimed as the wine of the vintage, and has held its position as the most expensive of the 1947s, but on the first two occasions I have had the opportunity of comparing the Cheval Blanc against the Pétrus – at Monsieur Jean-Pierre Moueix's table – I thought the Pétrus to be even finer. More recently, in 1986, I found the Cheval Blanc more overwhelming, the Pétrus has less fat, but is exotically unctuous and tannic – just very different styles. But at that time, of course, Pétrus was not nearly so well known as Cheval Blanc, and with its much smaller production there were fewer opportunities of seeing it. The Cheval Blanc itself is a wine of almost overpowering richness, and was probably most generally drunk in this state when between ten and twenty years old. More recently it seems to have come into better balance, but is probably now at its best, if not a shade past it. I found the Pétrus a more balanced wine. The Ausone is not in this class – actually the 1949 was better at the 1988 tasting – but by normal standards it was still a fine wine. In the Médoc my favourite 1947 has long been the Margaux, the finest wine from this château for many years. The Mouton is also very fine, but the Latour disappoints, and the Lafite is less remarkable than its 1949. Many 1947s seem to have lost colour in recent years and to have become rather "edgy" – a sign of a rather high temperature during the fermentation. Among wines which have come through with honours, I would place the Calon-Ségur, Ducru-Beaucaillou, Grand-Puy-Lacoste and Ducasse, Gruaud-Larose and Langoa-Barton, with Lanessan as an outstanding *bourgeois* growth. La Mission is an outstanding Graves. The Sauternes were especially memorable, wines of great richness, yet graceful and possessed of remarkable finesse. Both the Yquem and the Climens were very great wines.

22 SEPTEMBER 1948

This produced a yield of average size. This vintage suffered from coming between two other outstanding years, 1947 and 1949, and at a time when demand for fine claret was nothing like so keen as it is now. As a result, very little 1948 was shipped to the UK for bottling here, and it was only later that château-bottled examples began to find their way to this country. An early torch-bearer for 1948 was Ronald Avery, of the famous Bristol firm. The 1948s have less breed than the 1947s or 1949s, but are more robust, tannic and masculine. After the initial crudeness had mellowed, they proved to have a pleasing depth of flavour, while lacking the fruit of the 1947s or 1949s. However, they have lasted better than some 1947s and are certainly finer wines than the more highly praised 1952s, for example. One of the best initially was Cheval Blanc, but when last tasted in 1986 it was a disappointment, strong-flavoured but lacking style. The Ausone at the 1988 tasting was better, with an intense perfume and a marvellously powerful, rich flavour. The Calon-Ségur was actually better than the 1949 from the same château. The Lafite was notably better than the Latour at first, but the Latour has improved, and is now better than its 1947. St Julien did particularly well, all three Léovilles being especially good.

27 SEPTEMBER 1949

In volume, this was a year almost identical to 1948, another hot year. As with 1947, the wines were very attractive very early and were much in demand in all markets. At the time there was a tendency to think that 1947 would turn out to be the greater year, but most of the examples I have seen in the last few years suggest the opposite. The great Médocs are marvellous examples of all the virtues of these remarkable wines at their best. Lafite and Mouton are generally considered to be the best, with Latour not far behind, and certainly superior to its 1947. On the other hand, I have generally preferred the 1947 Margaux to the 1949, which is a shade top-heavy. The Pétrus and Cheval Blanc are also very fine, only just behind their remarkable 1947s, but at Ausone it is the other way round, with the 1949 superb, their last great vintage for nearly three decades, while the La Mission-Haut-Brion outshone Haut-Brion, though this was a rather disappointing period for Haut-Brion. Once more, the St Juliens were very fine, and generally the 1949s have proved wonderfully consistent; with their fine colour, body and fruit, they are beautifully ripe, attractive wines with plenty of life and vigour in them still. This was certainly one of the great post-war vintages. It was also a fine year for Sauternes but, like some of the 1945s, they tended to have almost too much sugar and gained colour rather rapidly. The Yquem was again very fine, after which the Coutet was generally considered to be the best.

17 SEPTEMBER 1950

This, the largest vintage since 1939, marked the beginning of a steady recovery in the scale of production in the Gironde, which has continued with only the temporary set-back of the 1956 frost. After a rather wet summer, no great hopes were held out for this vintage, but in the event it turned out much better than expected, and the wines, being both plentiful and cheap, were widely bought. The first growths were generally most successful, on the light side, but full of charm and quick to mature. Margaux and Lafite, also the Carruades, were particularly delightful, the Latour took longer to mature but turned out very well indeed, and only the Mouton disappointed. In the Graves, La Mission was one of the successes of the vintage and firmly established the reputation of this fine wine in England, where it had been surprisingly neglected until then. Pétrus and Cheval Blanc were also great successes. Generally, these delightful wines, which gave so much pleasure in the fifties and early sixties, are now past their best and are fading; but a magnum of Margaux I had in 1978 was still marvellous. Some Sauternes were elegant and very well balanced, the Coutet being particularly successful.

4 OCTOBER 1951

The year was average in quantity, but very poor in quality, owing to a very wet summer. This was the first year that chaptalization was permitted in Bordeaux, but even this could do little for the wines. Only one or two drinkable wines were made, notably Cheval Blanc, Latour and Mouton, but they were no more than decent, ordinary wines.

17 SEPTEMBER 1952

This was another vintage of average yield. The trade had high hopes for 1952 at the start, but it has proved a disappointment. The wines are solid and well constituted but dull. Even as they have slowly mellowed with age, this dullness seems to persist. In the Médoc, although both Lafite and Latour have their advocates, I have found both disappointing, while the Margaux is really poor and graceless. Lynch-Bages is one of the few

Médocs I remember with any pleasure; it was surprisingly fruity and well balanced. On the other hand, Cheval Blanc and Pétrus are decidedly better, and Figeac, La Conseillante and Magdelaine all made fine wines. In the Graves La Mission was particularly rich and fine. In the next few years, it is quite possible that a few bottles of some growths will be unearthed which will show that there was something to wait for after all, but I doubt that it will ever prove to be another 1948, less still a 1937. There were some good Sauternes, although Yquem had a blank year owing to frost and hail. Climens was particularly fine.

28 SEPTEMBER 1953

This was a plentiful vintage, on a par with the 1950. It was a great Médoc year, but the top St Emilions and Pomerols were less successful. Perhaps this is why 1953 has always been very highly rated in England, but less highly so in Bordeaux. From the very beginning, these wines were immensely attractive, delicate, elegant and finely bred, with a very pronounced bouquet. It was the bouquet which reminded many claret lovers of the 1929s, but they lacked the sugar and depth of that great year. Still, it is probably true to say that the 1953s gave more continuous pleasure than any other vintage since the war, until the arrival of the 1961. When they first began to be drunk at only four years, it seemed that their life would be brief but beautiful. In fact, they surprised everyone by going through a change, after which they seemed to take on added depth – almost a new dimension. From the beginning, the Lafite was hailed as the wine of the vintage. Then there was a tendency to decry it, to say it was faltering. In 1967 I had a wonderful bottle with Jean-Pierre Moueix and was surprised to learn that he had got up at 7 a.m. to decant it for lunch, because he had been disappointed with the wine the last time he drank it. A few months later I tried the same experiment at home, decanting the wine five hours before it was to be drunk. The result was again magnificent, and several friends who knew it said that they had never had a finer bottle. But the Lafite has been dogged by inconsistency between bottles. For some strange reason, the Latour has always seemed disappointing, less good than the 1955. The Margaux and Mouton are both superb in their contrasting ways, and have lasted well, while in the Graves both Haut-Brion and La Mission were to be seen at their most attractive. The 1953s which have lasted well include Beychevelle (a real beauty), Cantemerle, Ducru-Beaucaillou (one of the very best), Giscours, Gloria, Grand-Puy-Ducasse and Lacoste, Lascombes, Lynch-Bages, Montrose, Palmer (a glorious wine), the two Pichons and Siran. In St Emilion the Cheval Blanc was light and most attractive, as was the Ausone, while in Pomerol the Vieux-Château-Certan developed slowly to produce an outstanding wine. The Sauternes have style and a lovely balance. Yquem came back into its own after two blank years, and I particularly remember the Doisy-Daëne for being a real "peaches and cream" affair.

4 OCTOBER 1954

Average yield. This was a year spoilt by poor weather. In the event, however, a few surprisingly pleasant wines were made, and while it was less good than 1958, it was decidedly superior to 1951 or 1956. I remember 1954 as the first time I had a hand in buying an off-vintage, and the pleasure it gave when the few reasonable wines that had been picked turned out well. Latour and Mouton, Cheval Blanc and Pétrus all produced very pleasing wines which lasted remarkably well, easy, fruity, agreeable wines that they were. Other agreeable wines were Beychevelle and Calon-Ségur. Rather surprisingly, the Yquem also turned out well, although, of course, it was very light. Another good one was the Domaine de Chevalier.

21 SEPTEMBER 1955

A large crop, on a par with 1953 and 1950, producing very consistent wines. At the time, it was heralded as a really top vintage, more solid than 1953 but with plenty of fruit. Generally, they have proved sound and reliable, well balanced, but dull – somehow lacking that indefinable spark which makes a great year – a quality which 1953 had but 1955 missed. Yet when the wines were looked at analytically, they seemed to have all the components which go to make up a fine year. This is perhaps the last mystery of wine which, for all our scientific knowledge, remains beyond our grasp. The Latour is almost certainly the outstanding wine, better than 1953 or 1959, while in the Graves, La Mission was quite outstanding, more reminiscent of 1953 than 1955, and in a different vein the Domaine de Chevalier was also fine. Both Cheval Blanc and Pétrus were good, and Figeac and Belair especially so. Having said this, few of the other wines will let you down, but few will excite. The Sauternes were also good but not outstanding.

9 OCTOBER 1956
Easily the smallest vintage since 1945, owing to the disastrous February frost which froze the sap in many vines, especially in St Emilion and Pomerol, and damaged many more. This was a serious set-back after the promise of a return to real prosperity with 1953 and 1955, something Bordeaux had not known since the mid-twenties. It was not until 1962 that Bordeaux was to enjoy another good vintage in quantity. The wines were green and small, and are best forgotten. One of the few drinkable wines, oddly enough, was the Lafite which, for once in an off-year, was better than Latour.

3 OCTOBER 1957
The yield was just as poor as in 1956, and a poor summer resulted in imperfectly ripened grapes, so that the wines tended to be hard and short of fruit. Nevertheless, they were widely bought after the disastrous 1956s. With a few notable exceptions, the 1957s have been cold, closed wines short of sunshine, although they have always had their champions, among whom was the late Allan Sichel, who used to say they were claret lovers' claret. If by this he meant that only the most devoted of claret drinkers would be able to perceive much merit in them, he was probably right. The successful 1957s had a lot of character, a notable flavour and even a certain charm. One of the finest was Beychevelle, followed by Ducru-Beaucaillou, Brane-Cantenac, Cantemerle, Lynch-Bages, Cos d'Estournel, Léoville-Poyferré, Gloria and Siran. The first growths tended to disappoint, except for Lafite, which was much better than Latour, but Mouton was acceptable. In the Graves both La Mission and Haut-Brion were most attractive and really untypical of the year. There were a few good Sauternes, particularly the Suduiraut.

7 OCTOBER 1958
The third October vintage in a row, and I can see no other instance of this occurring before. It happened again in 1977, 1978 and 1979. The yield was only slightly better than 1956 and 1957, owing to spring frosts and rain during the vintage which caused some rot, but the market was

getting short of wine and the growers were becoming more skilful in handling difficult vintages, with the result that this was the first off-vintage since the war to be widely bought on the English market. Although the wines were light and have not lasted, they were elegant, fruity and charming, if lacking somewhat in substance and personality. As an off-vintage, it was of sufficient quality to be a most acceptable stop-gap. Latour and La Mission were the most successful wines, I thought, but Ducru-Beaucaillou and Cos d'Estournel both made very pleasing wines, as did Cantemerle. There were a few good Sauternes, of which the Suduiraut was outstanding, surprisingly rich and complete in flavour.

21 SEPTEMBER 1959

Another small yield, only slightly more wine being made than in 1958, but the quality was good, and from the beginning the vintage enjoyed a great reputation and was much sought after. It is probably fair to say that the reputation of the 1959 suffered from over-extravagant praise at the start and then from the arrival of the 1961. However, this is a classic vintage; the wines are both attractive and fine, but probably lack a little backbone to make them really great. There is considerable concentration of fruit and richness as would be expected from a very hot year, but most wines were rather soft to start with. Nevertheless, they have generally developed well, but many now seem rather dry. The only disappointments were in St Emilion and Pomerol, where many vineyards had still not recovered from the 1956 frost. But Ausone did well, and this in a lean spell for this property. It has a lovely concentrated roasted flavour, with sweetness at the end. All the first growths were good, with Haut-Brion being one of the best. Lafite and Mouton were very fine, and Latour is a slow developer. The Margaux, while better than the 1955, is not quite in the 1947/1953 category for this château. Cheval Blanc is a strange, rather unbalanced wine, but Pétrus is magnificent. This is such a fine all-round year that it is really invidious to single out individual wines. The 1959s today are either at their peak or beginning to fade, but there should be few disappointments. The Sauternes are rich, luscious and well balanced. I confess, though, to finding the Yquem disappointing, and when I tasted it against the Suduiraut in 1972, the Suduiraut was clearly the winner.

9 SEPTEMBER 1960

The biggest crop since the 1956 frost, but still well below the level of 1950/1953/1955. The vintage was endangered by a wet September, which caused a good deal of rot. As a result, the quality varied considerably. In general, the wines turned out to be very similar to 1958. Although the reputation of the vintage was poor at first, it was quite well bought owing to the increasing shortage of wine, and prices were higher than for the 1958s. In the end, there were probably rather more successful wines in 1960 than there had been in 1958, and again it proved a very useful stop-gap off-vintage, especially after the results of the tiny 1961 vintage were known. I remember looking at the 1960s very closely, because at that stage my company needed more wine, and stocks of the 1959 were very short. The wines which impressed me most in my first journey round Bordeaux in March 1961 were Latour, La Mission-Haut-Brion and La Conseillante, and all have lived up to their early promise. Subsequently I found the Mouton and Margaux to be very good. Both Lafite and Haut-Brion were most attractive, flowery wines, but really too light and ethereal to last. In St Emilion and Pomerol most châteaux still seemed to be suffering from the effects of 1956, and the Cheval Blanc was not as good as the 1954, but the Pétrus did show better form, although I think the La Conseillante was better. Ausone has a plummy, port-like flavour but was on the turn by 1988. In the Médoc Léoville-Las Cases and Palmer were two of the most successful wines. The Sauternes were not very successful, and the Yquem quickly threw a deposit.

19 SEPTEMBER 1961

A very small yield owing to *coulure*, but a perfect summer and autumn resulted in wines with a great concentration of fruit and extract. Because of more carefully controlled fermentation, the growers avoided making another 1928 or 1945, and the wines were very supple from the beginning. I shall always remember the first tastings of 1961s in Bordeaux because of the remarkably characteristic bouquet which nearly all wines had right from the start. They seemed to possess an extra dimension compared to any other vintage I have seen. One result of the elimination of excess tannin during the fermentation is that there has been an understandable tendency to drink many 1961s too early – people found it difficult to believe that such attractive wines could last.

There are some wines which are too soft and lack the characteristic intensity, rather like some 1929s, and these wines were at their best already at the end of their first decade of life. Another point worth making: 1961 was a wonderful year for the small *bourgeois* growths of Bordeaux. There were scores of delightful wines like this, well above their usual class and wonderful drinking after five or six years. All the top wines are marvellous, and at last Cheval Blanc and Pétrus seemed to be back to their pre-frost best. My early notes indicate a bewildering array of wonderful wines. Haut-Brion and Margaux both showed well early, Lafite and Mouton promised to be great, and La Mission, as usual in recent years, was very well up the field. My own favourites among so many wonderful wines were Palmer, Haut-Bailly, Gruaud-Larose, Léoville-Las Cases, Brane-Cantenac and Pape-Clément. Many of what one might call the second-line classified growths are quite outstanding – Batailley and Croizet-Bages are good examples of these, while Gloria, Villegeorge and Loudenne were marvellous *bourgeois* growths. Like Cheval Blanc, many St Emilions and Pomerols were back to their old form, or nearly so. Some had to wait until 1964 to produce of their best again. Figeac, Magdelaine, Trotanoy and Beauregard are among the most successful. At the 1988 tasting, the Ausone was less good than the 1959, with uncomfortably tough minerally tones marring the finish. In May 1978, thanks to the generosity of Dr Taams, I was able to taste nineteen of the leading 1961s blind, and this was a splendid opportunity to reassess the vintage. It clearly confirmed 1961's claim to be the best vintage since the war, and also underlined the extraordinary consistency of the leading growths. In the first group of ten, I placed Léoville-Las Cases and Lynch-Bages top, closely followed by Ducru-Beaucaillou and Beychevelle. Then came Pape-Clément, Léoville-Poyferré and Lascombes, with Calon-Ségur and Léoville-Barton not far behind. Only the Montrose disappointed. The tasting as a whole placed the Ducru first, just ahead of Beychevelle. Unfortunately, one bottle of Las Cases was corked, which put it out of the race, or the result might have been different. So Ducru went into the second tasting. In that final run-off there was little to separate the top wines, but we were nearly unanimous in placing Palmer top. Then came the Latour, surely the 1961 of the future, followed by Mouton, Ducru, Trotanoy and Margaux, with Gruaud-Larose and Haut-Brion close on their heels. The Cheval Blanc was just behind these leaders, and Lafite trailed disappointingly last, another case of inconsistency from bottle to bottle, since we had a much better magnum at lunch. The Yquem 1961, served also at lunch, was almost overwhelmingly luscious and powerful, but rather top-heavy for my taste.

A few months later in Switzerland, with the Palmer not present, I placed Lafite, Latour and Haut-Brion equal top – all very great wines in their differing styles. The Latour was absolutely true to the form shown at the Taams tasting, but the Haut-Brion and Lafite were much finer examples. Mouton and Margaux were again very fine, while the Calon-Ségur was much better than in Holland, with the Ducru not as good and showing a little overgrown. Taken as a whole, it is clear that the top 1961s are still improving and will repay keeping. But many are marvellously rewarding wines to drink and enjoy now, although they will surely live and even improve for many years to come. There can be no doubt that 1961 has taken its place, as it promised to right from the start, among the very greatest Bordeaux vintages, undisputed champion of the post-war years, and worthy to be placed beside the great wines of the twenties, and to be mentioned as a true successor to the legendary wines of an earlier era.

The 1961 is always said to be a great vintage for Sauternes, but I must confess that in nearly every case where I have been able to compare the two vintages, I have preferred the 1962 to the 1961. It is really a question of style: the 1961s have a rather hard, alcoholic finish for the most part, and the 1962s seem more liquorous and better balanced. But Climens and Coutet are magnificent exceptions to this generalization.

1 OCTOBER 1962

A very large crop, larger indeed than any vintage of the fifties, and the largest vintage also of the sixties, although slightly more red wine was to be produced in 1967. The summer of 1962 was not particularly good but then Bordeaux was blessed by an Indian summer and, as a result, the vintage turned out to be far better than anyone had dared hope. From the start the wines had a very good colour, and the quality was remarkably consisent in all districts. In cask, the 1962s were deceptively flattering and fruity; in bottle they have developed much more slowly than had been expected, owing, I suspect, to just a touch of unripeness in the grapes. Again, the smaller wines were excellent. Although the 1962s have had their detractors, I have always been a firm believer in their merits, and each year that passes seems to confirm this. They have developed a very classic flavour and have a very marked personality. They have a wonderful colour, and the acidity in them is ensuring a long life. While having no pretensions to being a 1961 or a 1966, 1962 is a very good vintage indeed, which is so well constructed that I believe it will have a very long life, giving great pleasure over many years. All the first growths were good, only Cheval Blanc and Margaux falling rather below the standard of the rest. Lafite has always been my personal favourite, the Pétrus is a beauty, the Latour the last wine made there under the *ancien régime*, and a worthy example. There are many fine St Emilions and Pomerols; the Ausone was the best for years – I preferred it to the Cheval Blanc – and Magdelaine was deliciously rich and attractive, while Trotanoy was one of the best Pomerols. In Graves La Mission is outstanding, and both Haut-Bailly and Pape-Clément were excellent. It was a fine year for St Julien: Beychevelle, Léoville-Las Cases, Léoville-Barton, Ducru-Beaucaillou and Gruaud-Larose all made excellent wines. There were many other successes, though, especially Palmer, Montrose, Mouton-Baronne-Philippe and Pichon-Lalande. The Sauternes were also extremely fine, rich yet well balanced and with a fine savour. The Yquem was very successful and the Suduiraut especially fine.

3 OCTOBER 1963

A large crop ruined by persistent rain during September, which caused widespread rot. After the comparative success of 1958 and 1960, the growers refused to believe that the 1963s could turn out as badly as they first appeared – but indeed they could. I shall always remember the unpleasant experience of tasting these wines in wood, looking for the good ones which never really came. They had an unhealthy orange tinge to them, and a sickly hint of rottenness on the nose. Far too many wines were château-bottled, and in the end the only drinkable wines were Latour (easily the best), Mouton, La Mission, Domaine de Chevalier (a remarkably sound wine), and Léoville-Las Cases – and that is probably being generous! The only Sauternes to see the light of day was the Yquem, probably the worst wine ever to go out with this great name. Most English merchants refused the sample when the wine was first offered.

21 SEPTEMBER 1964

Another large vintage; almost as much red wine was made as in 1962. Unfortunately, torrential rain fell from 8 to 17 October, and many of the larger properties in the Médoc, especially Pauillac and St Estèphe, had not completed the vintage. The best wines are to be found in St Emilion and Pomerol, Graves and St Julien. At their best, the 1964s are very ripe, fruity, elegant wines, but with a tendency to be soft. Because of the exceptional summer, the then French Minister of Agriculture made the mistake of proclaiming it the "Vintage of the Century" before the picking had started. Inevitably there was a reaction, but there has, I think, been a tendency almost to underrate the 1964s in recent years. Certainly there are many disappointing wines in the Médoc, such famous names as Mouton, Palmer, Calon-Ségur, Lynch-Bages and Pontet-Canet among them. But on the credit side, the Pétrus is a great wine, probably the wine of the vintage, and the Cheval Blanc a worthy successor to the great pre-frost wines and much better than the 1962, while La Gaffelière, Figeac and Magdelaine all made outstanding wines. In Graves the Haut-Brion is very fine and La Mission one of the best wines of the vintage, while Domaine de Chevalier, Haut-Bailly and Pape-Clément are all highly successful. In the Médoc Latour is generally regarded as the best, while Margaux is honourable but no more. There are more good 1964s to be found in St Julien than anywhere else in the Médoc, the outstanding wines being Léoville-Las Cases and Beychevelle, but Léoville-Barton, Ducru-Beaucaillou and Branaire were also successful. Lower down the Médoc, both Cantemerle and La Lagune made good wines, while Brane-Cantenac is good but light and forward. In Pauillac Pichon-Lalande and Batailley are two of the most successful wines. To summarize, 1964 is a very different style of year from 1962, certainly less consistent, yet at its best producing wines of great class. But recently some Médocs have gone very dull and dumb. Because of the October rains, the Sauternes harvest was ruined and many châteaux wisely did not sell their wine under the château name.

2 OCTOBER 1965

A year of average size which produced some of the poorest wine since 1930–2. The year 1963 was one of rot, in 1965 the grapes were simply unripe, and the wines were green and acid, although they had a better colour than the 1963s. Even Latour failed to produce a reasonable wine – indeed the only passable example I have seen was La Mission – while, by some miracle, the Calon-Ségur turned out more drinkable than the 1963. A year to be quickly forgotten, even in these wine-hungry days. It is reassuring, perhaps, to know that for all our technical cleverness, we still cannot make a decent wine in the finest vineyards if grapes are rotten or unripe. But now we know much more about preventing rot in the first place.

26 SEPTEMBER 1966

A good average yield in this decade of high yields. Conditions were almost perfect and resulted in very ripe, full-bodied wines with a splendid colour. Like the 1962, it was a very consistent vintage in all areas, but the wines were richer and had more sugar than the 1962s, resulting in full, powerful and harmonious wines of considerable charm. I have always believed that after 1961 – which was *hors classe* – 1966 will prove the best vintage of the sixties, and so far the development has been everything that could be hoped for. The first growths are really fine, more consistent and more complete than the 1964s. Especially outstanding are Cheval Blanc, Pétrus and La Mission, while in the Médoc, Latour is developing into an outstanding wine. This is one of the better years for Lafite in a very uneven period, and Margaux – little regarded at this time – is also very fine. One of the great wines of the vintage is Léoville-Las Cases, and the Beychevelle is a delight. On the other side of the river, the wines are also most consistent, with La Gaffelière a special favourite of mine.

For the next few years, 1966 should prove the most abundant source of fine bottles of claret at every level, the liveliness and warmth of the bouquet, the clean, fresh flavour leading to a completely harmonious finish of immense charm; all these are the qualities one looks for in classic claret, and of which 1966 provides an abundance. Most of us can drink 1961s only on rare and special occasions, but 1966s are still widely available and are excellent value. It is also a very good year for the smaller growths and the lesser areas like Côtes de Bourg and Fronsac. The Sauternes are fine and elegant, but lack the richness and completeness of the 1967s.

22 SEPTEMBER 1967

A large vintage, similar in total size to 1964, but the largest crop of red wines of the decade, beating 1962. The wines developed slowly to start with, and it took longer than usual to assess the quality of the wines, which were marked by a certain acidity in the early stages. However, they soon showed a pleasing fruitiness, and seemed to have elegance and style. They are lighter than the 1966s and have something of the consistency of the 1964s. This has proved to be a useful standby vintage. The wines have some class, but fall short of being really first-class, being certainly inferior to 1962 and 1964, but better than 1969. The early fruit has tended to pass rather quickly and most wines have a slightly bitter after-taste, which is very typical of the vintage. Though mostly still enjoyable, this is a vintage which needs drinking and most wines will not benefit from further keeping. At a tasting of 1967s in 1979, all the wines showed these characteristics, with the exception of the Léoville-Las Cases, which was *hors classe*, with the Pichon-Lalande, more harmonious than most, as the runner-up.

It should be noted that, in general, Pomerol produced the best wines this year, with the Pétrus outstanding. In St Emilion the wines of the *côtes* were superior to those of the *graves*, and good St Emilion *côtes* are usually superior to most Médocs. It is often also said that the St Emilion 1967s were superior to the 1966s. While it is true that 1966 on this side of the river fell a little short of the success registered in Médoc and Graves, I do not share this view. Most 1967 St Emilions are now showing their age, while the 1966s, for the most part, are much fresher.

The Sauternes are outstandingly successful, easily surpassing the 1966s – the best vintage since 1962. The most successful wines were Yquem – probably the best since 1949 – Suduiraut and Sigalas-Rabaud. The wines combine a rich lusciousness with great style and breed.

23 SEPTEMBER 1968

A very average crop, spoilt by rain. This time, a number of proprietors made a much more severe selection than had been the case in 1963 or 1965, and the grapes were riper than had been the case in 1965. The result was that, although overall the vintage was poor, more drinkable wines were made in 1968 than in 1963 and 1965 put together. They were naturally light, small wines, but had fruit and charm, ideal wines for early drinking. Among the most successful wines were Pétrus, Latour, La Mission-Haut-Brion and Domaine de Chevalier. In the Médoc, Haut-Batailley, Ducru-Beaucaillou and de Pez showed well. This was another blank year for Sauternes, but unfortunately Yquem, unrepentant evidently after their 1963, again marketed a wine which does no credit to their famous name.

22 SEPTEMBER 1969

A small vintage, indeed the smallest of the decade after 1961. A poor flowering ensured that the crop would be small from the beginning, but the summer was indifferent and the autumn brought only sporadic spells of good weather. The growers were optimistic that the vintage would turn out to be good, and the low yield resulted in high prices. But the wines, after a good start, developed disappointingly in cask, suddenly taking a turn for the worse during the second winter, and there was a rush to get them into bottle. Indeed, many châteaux assisted their wines with a touch of the prolific 1970s before bottling. In general, the wines are dry and short with a mean, rather acid after-taste. When the wines were mature in the mid-seventies, one of the most notable characteristics was quite simply a lack of district and château character − a sure sign of a poor year. One trusts that most of these wines are now dead and buried. At a tasting of a wide range of 1969s in 1977, the best wines were Pétrus, Gruaud-Larose and Magdelaine.

21 SEPTEMBER 1970

Unusual for its combination of quantity and quality, this was the year when everything went right. The flowering began on 5 June in ideal conditions and the season proceeded in copy-book fashion, so that a large crop was brought to perfect maturity and the vintage was gathered in perfect weather. Not since 1934 had there been such a prolific vintage of such quality. But 1970 can also be seen as a watershed, ushering in a decade when there was a marked switch from white to red wines, and when the area under vine was to increase (especially in the Médoc), together with the yields. Thus the yield of red *appellation contrôlée* wine achieved in 1970 was to be surpassed in 1973, 1974, 1976, 1978 and 1979, but its yield of white *appellation contrôlée* was to remain the highest of the decade, so that, finally, 1970's total *appellation contrôlée* yield was to be surpassed only in 1973, 1976 and 1979. In early tastings, the 1970s had a fine, deep colour, a powerful aroma, and were rich and velvety on the palate. The fruit and richness masked the tannin and led to the mistaken notion that these wines would develop rapidly. Actually, their evolution has been steady but rather slow, and the best wines have often gone through a dumb stage when their real virtues lay obscured. Many of the lesser growths showed their paces much sooner and have provided robust and delicious wines which have been excellent drinking for several years. But many of the best wines are still rather stubborn when twenty years old.

This is a great all-round vintage of marked consistency as between different districts and different categories of wine, as great a year for the small growths as for the first growths. The wines have the sort of balance and harmony seen in 1966, but are more tannic and have been slower to evolve, while lacking the remarkable power and beauty of 1961. But beneath a rather shy exterior, 1970s at every level have the depth and complexity of flavour found only in the best years. In recent tastings, I have found Mouton and Latour outstanding in the Médoc, with Lafite good but not great. In Graves La Mission is a prodigious wine of great intensity, remarkable for its sheer beauty of flavour and harmony. In St Emilion both Ausone and Cheval Blanc are very fine in totally different ways, but the palm on the right bank must go to Pétrus. La Conseillante and La Fleur-Pétrus are also outstanding. What is certain is that many years of pleasurable drinking lie ahead for this vintage.

This is a good, but not outstanding, vintage for Sauternes. The wines have great power and richness, but in most cases I prefer the 1971s. An exception was Suduiraut. The Yquem is good, if lacking the style of 1967 or 1971.

25 SEPTEMBER 1971

1970 and 1971 are yet another of Bordeaux's famous pairs of vintages, and provide the most interesting contrast since 1961 and 1962. This was a rather small crop, caused by poor flowering, the smallest of the decade in terms of red *appellation contrôlée*, but producing more white wine than the other small vintage, 1977.

The wines provide a complete contrast to those of 1970. They had an immediate charm soon after bottling, rather reminiscent of the 1953s.

They are very fruity, precocious and showy. There is also about them a distinction of bouquet and flavour which marks a fine vintage. Above all, they have a seductive quality which misled many good judges into believing them to be better than the 1970s. But the one flaw in their make-up is a low fixed acidity, which makes the comparison of 1971 against 1970 that of a brilliant 800-metre runner against the long-distance runner. This is why, in many early comparative tastings, the 1971s were preferred to the 1970s.

Another difference is that the red 1971s are far less consistent than the 1970s, especially among the lesser growths. When they were only three or four years old, it was possible to find *petits châteaux* going brown in colour and beginning to oxidize. Perhaps the greatest wine of the vintage is Pétrus, rather reminiscent of some Cheval Blanc of the immediate post-war period, almost overpoweringly fruity and headily perfumed. None of the Médoc first growths reached the same level, with Latour probably the best. Palmer and Ducru-Beaucaillou are outstanding among the other leading growths. Unfortunately many of these wines are now in decline, and one needs to tread warily.

This is a great year for white wines. The Graves have great finesse and breed, the Sauternes enormous elegance and richness – the Yquem is exceptional.

3 OCTOBER 1972

A year of unhappy memories; there was poor weather during the flowering, which was protracted, and not enough sun, so the late harvest resulted in wines lacking fruit and with too much acidity. At the same time, the growers demanded even higher prices than for the 1971s. This affront to common sense led in a few months to the market crisis which many had feared, and a very difficult period for Bordeaux wines which was to continue for nearly three years.

With cold weather during the vintage, more experience of how to prevent rot by spraying, and making more rigorous selections both in the vineyard and the *chai*, the wines were sounder than might have been expected. But in bottle the colour fell away quickly, there was a lack of clear characteristics on the nose, and the wines were short and mean on the palate, with at best a meagre fruitiness. Probably the most successful wine was Cheval Blanc, which had a mellow richness not found elsewhere. Latour and Lafite in their different ways were the most acceptable Médocs. Curiously enough, many lesser growths were more acceptable than most of the big names. But overall, this is certainly a year Bordeaux will be happy to forget. Many top châteaux would have done better not to have bottled under their own label.

20 SEPTEMBER 1973
This year probably deserves a better reputation than it has. The weather was favourable, hot and exceptionally dry, and the crop exceeded in volume that of 1970. Only 1979 in this decade produced more wine.

The characteristics of 1973 are fruit, charm, a low fixed acidity and a certain irregularity due to very high yields where Merlot is heavily planted. Unfortunately, this large crop of attractive, precocious wines came at a bad moment for the Bordeaux trade, and although prices were very low after the rapid rise beginning in 1970, which reached its final absurdity with the 1972s, trade had virtually come to a standstill. But when the wines were in bottle and trade had recovered, the 1973 proved an ideal vintage for early consumption, cheaper than the 1971s, much more attractive than the 1974, and capable of giving much enjoyment while one waited for the 1970s to mature. There may be no great wines in 1973, but there are plenty of good wines, and very few poor ones have seen the light of day because they found their way into generic blends at an earlier stage. La Mission-Haut-Brion had the misfortune to suffer from a hailstorm on the very eve of the vintage, and lacks the charm of the year.

Generally speaking, these are wines which should mostly have been drunk, although I have had the odd pleasant surprise in the last year or so, such as the delicious Cheval Blanc in 1986, and a lovely succulent Latour in 1988 that still had backbone. This was a mixed year for Sauternes, with wines of only moderate quality. Coutet is one of the best.

20 SEPTEMBER 1974
Another large vintage whose quality was adversely affected by a wet, cold September. The vintage as a whole was slightly smaller than 1970, but produced more red *appellation-contrôlée* wine than that year. The red wines tend to have held their colour rather better than the 1973s, owing to better fixed acidity, but totally lack that vintage's charm and vinosity.

Generally, there is something cold, charmless and austere about them, though they are certainly sounder and more balanced than the 1972s. The best results seem to have been obtained in St Julien and St Emilion. Among the few examples to give pleasure that I have noted are Langoa-Barton, Beychevelle and Figeac. Owing to the sheer quantity produced, I suspect that bottles of 1974 will crop up for some years to come, and no doubt there will be the odd pleasant surprise.

22 SEPTEMBER 1975

After the problems of 1972, 1973 and 1974, Bordeaux needed a top-quality vintage to restore morale, and 1975 provided just what was wanted. After a cold spring, the summer arrived suddenly and the flowering passed in excellent conditions, to be followed by a very dry, hot summer. In September there was just the right amount of rain to adjust the situation. Following two exceptionally large vintages, it was only to be expected that 1975 would be smaller, especially after such a dry summer. Actually, the yield was slightly larger than 1972 or 1971 overall, but the yield of red *appellation-contrôlée* wine was significantly higher than in either of those years, again demonstrating the shift in emphasis from white to red which was occurring throughout the decade.

Owing to the dryness of the year, resulting in rather moderate *rendements*, alcoholic degrees were relatively high, and thick skins resulted in tannic, powerful wines. When I first tasted the young wines in the exceptional heat of the summer of 1976, they seemed massive but disappointingly flat. But in better conditions in the autumn, the remarkable aroma – the most striking in a young vintage since 1961 – was again evident. The wines had a lot of fruit, but this was to some extent masked by the tannin. In bottle, they seem to have shaken off what had appeared in cask to be an excessive tannin content, so that the fruit is now showing through to great advantage. As in 1970, this is a year when lesser growths show especially well, and many *petits châteaux* were already becoming enjoyable after two years in bottle.

One of the many things 1975 will be remembered for is the rebirth of Ausone. The 1975 is certainly one of the top wines of the vintage, and when compared with Pétrus and Cheval Blanc in 1979, came out top. In the Médoc, Lafite, Latour and Mouton all promise to develop to great wines. After that, I single out Léoville-Las Cases and Palmer. In Graves the contrast in style between Haut-Brion and La Mission-Haut-Brion is especially striking, with Haut-Brion being much more forward than the other top growths and La Mission needing a lot of time.

Much has been written about the comparison between 1975 and 1961. Several differences of importance must be noted. In 1961 the *rendement* was much smaller, and the wines were characterized by a remarkable and singular aroma when in cask. Occasionally I noted something similar when tasting a few of the 1975s, but this vintage characteristic was not nearly so marked or so uniform. Then the 1961s were far more flattering in cask than the 1975s which, in my opinion, lack the extraordinary harmony of the older vintage. There certainly are some great wines in 1975, but they have been rather forgotten, though being so slow to develop, and perhaps in the excitement over the 1982s. But in a tasting at Latour in 1988, the 1975 looked more impressive than either the 1970 or the 1978. It is surely time for a reappraisal of the vintage as a whole.

In Sauternes, wines of extraordinary sweetness and power were produced, but many lack balance and may oxidize early. Yquem is an exception to this; other successes are Climens, Coutet and Doisy-Daëne.

13 SEPTEMBER 1976

In many ways, this was a most unusual vintage. From April to July the weather was unusually hot and dry. This resulted in an early flowering and *véraison*. August provided two days of heavy rain, but apart from that was again very hot and dry, so that by the end of the month the grapes were extremely small and the conditions resembled 1921, 1947 and 1949. The vintage started very early (13 September), but there was considerable rain in September which has the effect, at this stage, of diluting the quality. The resulting wines had a deep colour, were fairly rich in alcohol, and were very low in fixed acidity, with unusually high pHs. This suggested fragile wines, but the thick skins produced wines higher in tannin than early tastings had suggested, so masked was it by fruit.

In the lesser districts delicious, elegant, fruity reds were produced which provided delicious robust, fruity wines for early drinking. The development of the top growths has been uneven. Some wines seem to have separated, with the fruit and rather parched tannins not really together, but the best wines are powerful and rich, if a little dry. If 1975 was notable for the first offering of a new regime at Ausone, so 1976 will surely be remembered for a similar occurrence at Lafite. Early tastings in bottle showed Pétrus, Cheval Blanc, Haut-Brion, Mouton, Latour, Lafite, Léoville-Las Cases, La Mission, Pichon-Lalande and La Conseillante as front runners. Now that they have matured, Ausone and Lafite stand out as wines of breed and complexity, capable of offering some years of pleasurable drinking ahead. There are some fine white Graves, and this was another good year for Sauternes, which produced much more elegant wines than in 1975, with Yquem especially notable.

3 OCTOBER 1977

Notable as the first of four unusually late vintages. By early September there were dire warnings of an impending disaster, of a degree of unripeness far exceeding anything known in 1972. Then came an exceptional September, with more hours of sunshine (but not the highest temperatures) and the lowest rainfall recorded for a hundred years. Because of serious frost damage at the end of March (especially in Pomerol and St Emilion), the vintage was easily the smallest overall in the Gironde in the decade, although slightly more red *appellation-contrôlée* wine was produced than in 1971. Few of the wines have a great deal to show for themselves after a decade. Two oustanding exceptions were La Mission-Haut-Brion and Pichon-Lalande, while Les Forts de Latour is much better than the *grand vin*.

No good Sauternes were made.

9 OCTOBER 1978

After the "miracle" vintage of 1977, it seemed impossible that another autumn such as that could be hoped for. In fact, the autumn of 1978 was even more remarkable. If March was the wettest since 1870, the months of July, August and September were notable for their lack of rain, and the heat was even greater than in 1977. This time there was a good-sized crop to bring in; the quantity of *appellation-contrôlée* wine was situated between that of 1972 and 1974, but the quantity of red wine was actually slightly more than in 1974.

First impressions were that the 1978s had an excellent colour, and considerable richness and natural glycerine which masked their tannin.

These are sumptuous wines, certainly finer than the 1976 and more harmonious than the 1975 at the same stage.

Tastings in cask suggested that Margaux, Latour, Mouton, Lafite, Palmer, Léoville-Las Cases, Ducru-Beaucaillou, Pichon-Lalande, Lynch-Bages, Cos d'Estournel, Montrose, Gloria and Prieuré-Lichine, in the Médoc, should be among the most successful wines of the vintage. In Graves, Haut-Brion, La Mission and Domaine de Chevalier promised well. In Pomerol, where there were many fine wines, Pétrus, La Conseillante, Trotanoy, Vieux-Château-Certan and Latour à Pomerol were the leading growths. In St Emilion, where there are fewer successes, Cheval Blanc, Ausone and Figeac looked the pick of the bunch. A retrospective tasting in Miami in 1988, hosted by American collector Bob Paul, provided an opportunity to take an overall view of the vintage after a decade. The outstanding wines proved to be Latour, Margaux, Léoville-Las Cases, Pichon-Lalande, Lafite, Mouton, Palmer, Brane-Cantenac, Montrose, Cos d'Estournel, Gruaud-Larose and Léoville-Barton in Médoc; Haut-Brion, La Mission and Domaine de Chevalier in Graves; Pétrus, Trotanoy, La Conseillante, Gazin, Vieux-Château-Certan and L'Evangile in Pomerol; the general level in St Emilion was confirmed as not so high, but Cheval Blanc, Ausone, Figeac and Magdelaine stood out from the rest. The impression was of wines of great breed and harmony, with the best wines having the concentration and complexity to promise some remarkable bottles in a few years' time, when fully mature. This was a freak year in Sauternes because, although the grapes achieved an excellent ripeness, there was no *pourriture noble* owing to the fine weather and lack of humidity. Doisy-Daëne made their final picking in December.

2 OCTOBER 1979

The third in this remarkable quartet of October vintages was also the largest vintage in the Gironde since the war, and the first time that over 3 million hectolitres of red *appellation-contrôlée* wine had been made. The 3,315,124 hectolitres produced was a huge increase on the previous best – 2,479,382 in 1973. After a mild, wet winter, April was unusually cold, and this held back the vegetation. May began with heavy rain which gave way to periods of better weather, so that by the end of the month, vegetation was rapidly making up for lost time. June provided warm, sunny weather for the flowering which began on the twelfth and passed quickly with excellent setting of the fruit. July was equally beneficial, but with August came a set-back. Temperatures were below average and there was much rain. The development of the vegetation was blocked during an important phase. There followed, however, a warm, generally sunny September, and an October mainly favourable for bringing in the vast crop. There were outbreaks of rain and misty mornings, but the weather remained warm. The state of the grapes was generally healthy with very little rot.

In spite of the record harvest, this was not a year of enormous *rendement* as in 1973; rather, yields resembled those of 1970. Most of the classified growths in the Médoc reported producing between 25 and 35 per cent more than in 1978. This was balanced by the careful selection most of them made.

First impressions were that the St Emilions were unquestionably better than the 1978s, confirmation that this is a Merlot year. All the leading growths on both sides of the river had a depth of colour and individuality which are the hallmark of a fine vintage. First tastings in casks showed uniformly high quality from St Estèphe down to Margaux; among the most impressive wines at this stage were Lafite, Mouton, Margaux, Pichon-Lalande, Montrose, Léoville-Las Cases and Ducru-Beaucaillou, while on the other side of the river Pétrus, Ausone and Cheval Blanc were outstanding, with Figeac, Belair, Canon and Magdelaine not far behind. In general the wines have less finesse and breed than the 1978s, but have proved slower to develop than expected. Nonetheless, by 1986–7 most wines made delicious drinking, yet hold out the prospect of keeping their qualities well into the nineties.

6 OCTOBER 1980

We had thought that three late vintages in a row was remarkable, then came 1980. After a typical Bordeaux winter, humid but without extreme cold, the first buds broke on 2 April, which is about normal, and ten days earlier than in 1979. April was dry but cold, May wet and cold, and the cold weather persisted into June, which was the coldest since 1946. As a result, the flowering, which began on 6 June, was very prolonged and widespread *coulure* and *millerandage* followed. July was the coldest since 1954. At this stage, conditions were comparable to those of 1969 and 1971 and a drop of 40–50 per cent in yield compared to 1979 was forecast. Then fortunes changed. The sun shone in August and through September. The *véraison* began on 18 August, three weeks later than normal, and eight days later than in 1979. September was the hottest since 1964. In early September the vintage was still forecast for 15 October. During the heat of September there were also some serious storms and on 20 September 70 mm of rain fell in some places in twenty-four hours. During the vintage the weather was unsettled and rather cold. Some of the best growths delayed their picking and recorded the latest vintage since 1922. At Mouton they did not begin until 18 October, when 700 pickers brought in the whole crop in eight days. At Ausone the picking did not begin until 20 October.

The total yield of *appellation-contrôlée* wines, at 2,928,083 hectolitres, was the smallest since 1969 but the production of red *appellation-contrôlée* wine, at just over 2 million hectolitres, was in fact larger than that recorded in 1977, 1975 or 1971. The shortfall was in white wine, which, at 866,607 hectolitres, was the smallest for many a long day.

This will certainly go down as a vintage saved by modern treatments. Until very recently, rot would have crippled quality. In fact, because of widespread treatments, there was scarcely any rot at all. Then carefully controlled fermentations made the best of the quality that had been harvested.

Selection of vats was very important, as was the time of vintaging. First tastings revealed supple, fruity wines, light and forward in style but with sufficient tannin and good balance. But some wines are clearly too light and insubstantial and the wines are generally short. In the event, the wines turned out to be commercially very useful, providing wines which have given pleasurable drinking and are at the same time typical of their origins. The best wines have come from the Médoc, with Léoville-Las Cases, Pichon-Lalande, Gruaud-Larose and especially Margaux being the most memorable, with plenty of fruit and real *race*. They have largely been drunk up, and what remains should now be enjoyed while still at its best. There are some better-than-average Sauternes, with Yquem a notable success.

28 SEPTEMBER 1981
After the four preceding late harvests, the growing season of 1981 returned to normal. The main problem was rain during the vintaging, but

thanks to treatments there was little in the way of rot. The red wine crop, at just over 2.5 million hectolitres, was a little larger than 1978, but significantly smaller than 1979, or the bountiful harvests of the eighties that were to follow. In style the wines have more breed but less body than the 1979s. Their true merits have been obscured by the understandable acclaim accorded to succeeding years but these are nevertheless classic wines, with length, style and finish. The Médocs lack the power of 1979 or 1983, but are more consistent than the latter. The St Emilions and Pomerols have a full, luscious flavour, although some are light and developing quickly. The Sauternes are generally finely perfumed and moderately luscious, better than the 1982s. Most of the dry whites, which were elegant wines of medium weight and nice fruit, have been drunk.

13 SEPTEMBER 1982

A very early and rapid flowering – the *demi-floraison* was placed on 5 June – immediately placed 1982 among the small elect of early vintages, along with 1959, 1961 and 1966. It was also clear that the crop would be large. The vines benefited from an exceptionally hot July. August was rather cooler than usual. But then the situation was transformed during the week of 6 to 13 September by exceptional heat, at exactly the right moment. In the month as a whole, the heat was comparable to 1966. The alcoholic degrees were exceptional, with *cuvées* of Merlot at 13° and even 13.5°, while the Cabernet Sauvignon reached 12° in many cases. The final quality of maturity achieved in terms of concentration of tannin and sugar was exceptional, superior for instance to 1975. The richness of the musts, combined with the high temperatures experienced during the period of the harvesting, posed problems of vinification. The *cuviers* were certainly better equipped than ever before – the investment at every level in Bordeaux since 1970 was there for all to see. Nevertheless many found it hard to control the fermentation as they would have wished, and improvements, in terms of heat exchangers in particular, were soon seen as a result of these experiences. In terms of size, this was the largest red wine vintage in Bordeaux at this time with over 3.5 million hectolitres, nearly a million more than 1981 and 200,000 more than in 1979. But these increases were the result of the new plantings in Bordeaux Rouge, and for the quality areas, Graves, Médoc and Haut-Médoc. With the rigorous selection now being practised by the great growths, the quantities made by such *crus* hardly changed.

The wines were characterized by the depth and density of their colour, a bouquet of exceptional concentration, which at the same time was marvellously perfumed, and on the palate great length and sheer beauty of flavour, considerable tannin and extract, largely masked at first by concentrated fruit and fat. What was especially notable in cask was the harmony of the wines. This is a great Pomerol year, with St Emilion not far behind. Here there was a similarity to 1947. In Médoc and Graves this seems the most highly individual vintage since 1961, although of course the wines are quite different from that year of tiny yields. In that sense the comparison is more with 1970, but the 1982s clearly have much more fat and concentrated richness and seem unlikely to go in on themselves in the same way.

All the first growths produced memorable wines, then La Mission, Domaine de Chevalier, Figeac, La Conseillante, Trotanoy, l'Evangile, Brane-Cantenac, Cos d'Estournel, Calon-Ségur, Gruaud-Larose, Léoville-Las Cases and Léoville-Barton all produced exceptional wines. But this was also a year when the *crus bourgeois* made some exceptional wines; indeed there were delicious wines at the humblest level.

In February 1989 Robert Paul, the Miami collector, organized a large retrospective tasting of the Pomerols and St Emilions of the vintage. One interesting general point was that the Pomerols had maintained their colour much better than the St Emilions, and were remarkably rich and powerful, with most of the top *crus* not ready to drink. The outstanding wines in Pomerol were Pétrus, Trotanoy, La Fleur, La Conseillante, Certan de May and L'Evangile; in St Emilion, Cheval Blanc, Ausone, Magdelaine, Figeac, Canon and Pavie among the *premiers grands crus classés*, and Haut-Sarpe, La Dominique, Clos-des-Jacobins, Larmande among the *grands crus classés*. But there were great contrasts in evolution, with the Cheval Blanc already deliciously drinkable, as its famous 1947 had been at the same stage, but the Ausone needing many years yet, again typical of this great wine. The only disappointment in this great year was in Sauternes, where the weather broke too soon, and only moderate wines resulted. But the Yquem and Suduiraut Cuvée Madame show what might have been.

26 SEPTEMBER 1983

The flowering was about a week later than in 1982, with the *demi-floraison* put at 13 June, and took place in perfect conditions, promising another large vintage. There was warm weather for the rest of June, which lasted into July, but was succeeded by warm, humid, showery weather, ideal for the spread of disease, especially black-rot, necessitating many treatments in the vineyard. In August the weather changed after the fifteenth to cool and overcast, and again great vigilance was necessary in the vineyards with more rain than usual. In the critical month of September, the first half of the month greatly increased anxiety, with more warm showery weather. Then, on the eighteenth, hot sunny weather accompanied at first by strong drying winds transformed the situation. From then until 16 October not a drop of rain fell, a most remarkable occurrence in Bordeaux during the vintage. At the moment of the vintage the average sugar content of the Merlot and Cabernet Sauvignon was above the average of the last twenty years but below the phenomenal levels of 1982, with lower acidities in the Merlot than in 1982, but higher levels in the Cabernet Sauvignon. Whereas the excellence of 1982 had depended on the vigilance of the wine-maker, the success of 1983 depended on the care of the *vigneron*. This was precisely the sort of year that would have been largely ruined by rot in the sixties or earlier. The quality was ensured only by the phenomenal weather at the end of the season, and this especially benefited the Cabernet Sauvignon, which is picked later than the Merlot, and also the leading *crus*, which tend to pick as late as possible to ensure maximum maturity. This helps to explain the unevenness of the year, and the fact that the leading wines are on a higher plane than the rest, which suffer from too much dilution through over-cropping and lack of selection. Overall yields were only slightly below the record ones of 1982. The disappointment in Sauternes at having lost out on the 1982 vintage was more than compensated for this time, with the greatest year since 1976. The wines have exceptional concentration and fine *botrytis* character.

The quality in Margaux needs to be underlined in the context of Médoc; the Palmer especially is more successful than its 1982, and the Margaux is outstanding among the first growths. The Haut-Brion and La Mission, Ausone and Cheval Blanc, Léoville-Las Cases and Pichon-

Lalande deserve to be singled out. On the right bank Pavie, Belair and Close Fourtet also stand out.

2 OCTOBER 1984

The character and problems of this vintage spring from the exceptionally severe *coulure* and *millerandage* which devastated the Merlot. The extent of the disaster surprised the most experienced and venerable *vignerons*, since after an unusually cold and wet May, the weather changed on 7 June and remained warm and sunny until the end of the month, with the first flowering observed on 12 June. So the usual rules for a successful flowering were overturned, and it seems that a sudden change in temperature just before the flowering is the most probable explanation for failure. After this inauspicious start, July was warm and very dry, August fine and sunny, with localized showers which assisted the development of the grapes. The first part of September was generally fine, but the second half became very unsettled, with cooler weather and heavy showers. This resulted in a rapid swelling of the grapes, and caused concern in St Emilion and Pomerol for the health of what was left of the crop. On the night of 3–4 October hurricane Hortense struck, uprooting trees and causing widespread power failures. The weather changed for the better on 6 October and from then until the end of the month conditions were warm and hot (up to 32°C) with no rain until 19 October. In terms of yield it was a larger vintage than 1977 or 1975, but in St Emilion one has to go back to 1968, the last great year of rot, to find a smaller yield. For white wines yields were normal.

In Médoc the growers were convinced they had made something better than in 1980, but unfortunately they have been proved wrong, with many wines showing a mean streak, which has been slow to soften. Only the few master wine-makers seem to have overcome these problems; Margaux, Latour, Pichon-Lalande and Léoville-Las Cases all performed honourably as did La Mission. In Sauternes some good results were obtained, thanks to the timing of the change in the weather, and there are some elegant, fruity wines to enjoy while waiting for the more massive 1983s.

23 SEPTEMBER 1985

The character of the vintage was formed by the driest September on record. Only 4 mm of rain fell in the whole month, compared with 28 mm in 1961, the previous driest year. The temperatures were not actually as high as in that great year, but it was still hotter than in 1959, 1964, 1966 or indeed 1982. And the temperature exceeded 30°C on seven days of the month, compared with five days in 1982 and 1966. The year had begun with an exceptionally cold January, with temperatures of –15°C recorded, and some other places in the Gironde registering even lower ones. There was little lasting damage, only a few more vines than usual died, but many château gardens were not so lucky. The flowering was very successful, although there was actually more rain during it than there was in 1984, when it was disastrous. The rest of the summer was unexceptional before the arrival of September, again emphasizing the truism that the quality is made in September. The size of the vintage was well above what was forecast, and I never remember a year when all the experts were so wrong in their estimates. The red wine crop was yet another new record, exceeding 1982 by 12 per cent with 3,945,391 hectolitres. For the first time the production of Bordeaux and Bordeaux Supérieur exceeded a million hectolitres. While the Médoc also showed increases on 1982, St Emilion and – even more so – Pomerol made less. The dryness of September actually blocked the maturation, so that the wines do not have the over-ripe character of 1982, although in the reference vineyards of the Station Oenologique the Merlot had more sugar than in 1982, and the Cabernet Sauvignon exactly the same sugar content as 1982. Acidities were identical for each year. The style of the wines is more classic than 1982 and more flattering and supple than 1983. As they have evolved I have more and more been reminded of the 1953.

The outstanding wines seem to be those made by the leading properties in the Médoc and Graves, where careful selection was made, and in St Emilion and Pomerol. But in Pauillac and the northern Médoc in general it is also possible to find signs of dilution due to overproduction, underlining the importance of selection. Sauternes produced wines of great charm and breed, without the richness of 1983, but nevertheless very fine and well-balanced wines with an excellent future.

23 SEPTEMBER 1986

The record yield of red *appellation-contrôlée* wines set in 1985 was to be short-lived, and not only was the total crop larger than in 1985, but the average *rendement* per hectare for all wines was the highest ever at 66 hectolitres, beating the previous highest in 1979. There were some interesting exceptions, with lower yields than 1985 in St Julien, Pauillac and St Estèphe. Dry and warm conditions ensured a rapid flowering although it was later than average, owing to the abnormally cold spring, which had delayed the development of the vines. It was significant that the time between the *demi-floraison* and the *demi-véraison* was only sixty days, instead of the average sixty-seven, because of the ideally warm weather, so that the vine caught up all it had lost in the spring. In September the weather was again hot, but the dry weather was broken by very heavy rain on the fifteenth and twenty-third, which slowed down the build-up of sugar in the grapes while diminishing the acidity. The danger of rot, especially in the heavily laden Merlot, also increased. Had warm, humid conditions continued the danger of rot would have been grave. Fortunately, after the deluge of 23 September, the weather turned warm and dry and, as in 1983 and 1985, the grapes were gathered in perfect conditions, with not a drop of rain. Because of this later harvesting, the Cabernet Sauvignon benefited to the full from the improvement in the weather, and was picked with superb ripeness – almost the same sugar levels were recorded as in 1985 – while the Merlot fell some way short of the 1985 levels.

The great merits of the 1986 vintage were not fully realized as quickly as those of the 1985s had been. They were particularly hard to judge because of the great concentration of tannin in the wines, which made the balance hard to assess. I found the same problem in the 1975. I believe that the 1986 could turn out to be the type of vintage we all hoped the 1975 would be, but is only in certain cases. In other words, patience will be needed but some of the best wines will surely stand beside, if not surpass, the best of 1982, 1983 or 1985. The wines constantly improved and grew more impressive in the cask and their future progress will be watched with the greatest expectations.

21 SEPTEMBER 1987

The main feature of the year was that Bordeaux's good fortune of marvellous autumn weather in so many recent vintages broke, and it rained almost continuously for most of the vintage, with an intensity not seen since 1964. July, August and September had been months of above-average temperatures, with August very dry and the rain in September largely concentrated in a deluge on the first of the month; then the rainfall in October was more than twice the average, with a large part of it concentrated into the first twenty days. The Merlot had shown good maturation and was ripe by the last week of September, when most growers brought it in. But the Cabernet Sauvignon ideally needed a little longer, and most growers waited. With hindsight they would have done better to pick just in advance of optimum ripeness, since the final degrees were indeed lower. As a result there was no great expectation of quality when the wines were first tasted. But the improvement in cask was encouraging, resulting in what seems likely to be good commercial wines for early drinking with more charm than the 1984s and comparable with the 1980s. The quality in the Libournais is clearly superior to that in the Médoc, owing to the ripeness and sanitary condition of the Merlot, and here some very good, supple, attractive wines have resulted. In the Médoc the wines tend to be short on the palate and lack dimension, but have fruit and pleasing style.

19 SEPTEMBER 1988

The year was characterized by above-average rainfall between November 1987 and June 1988, followed by drier-than-average weather for the months of July, August and September. Temperatures were very close to average during the growing season, but October was much warmer than usual, similar to the Indian-summer conditions of 1985. Significant variations in the maturity of the different *cépages* – and of the same *cépage* in different sites – were observed at the time of the *véraison* in mid-August, and these differences persisted through to the vintage. Such variations of maturity were a feature of the year particularly noted by a number of proprietors and *régisseurs*, and are probably the main cause of the wide fluctuations in quality which have occurred. Following several rainy days after the equinox in late September, some nervous proprietors, with memories of 1987 fresh in their minds, began picking Cabernet Sauvignon prior to perfect maturity.

As a result of all these factors, the Médoc presents a more varied picture than usual. The first impression was that the wines were less impressive than the 1986s at the same stage, with less middle richness to balance the considerable tannins. But the evolution in cask was encouraging, with the wines filling out and becoming more harmonious. The red Graves seem more consistent and well balanced.

On the right bank, a very different picture emerges. Here, the comparison with 1986 tends to favour 1988, with the St Emilions being exceptionally rich and concentrated, and the Pomerols showing really opulent fruit and great depth of flavour.

In Sauternes and Barsac, many growers believe their 1988s will prove to be even better than their 1986s and 1983s. The wines have real *botrytis* character, combined with great breed and balance, and a welcome absence of the tarry elements which have, in the past, often spoilt some heavily botrytized wines.

This is another good year for dry white wines, with the best Graves having complexity and elegance, as well as pronounced fruit.

Whatever its eventual place among the exceptional vintages of the 1980s, this will certainly be one of the years requiring long ageing to reach maturity.

28 AUGUST 1989

Not since 1893 has a Bordeaux vintage begun so early. This decade of exceptional vintages finished with the most remarkable of all. To begin with, it was a year of quite spectacular weather conditions. With the exception of April, it was simply warmer, sunnier and drier, right through to October, than the average for the last thirty years. During the vital period, June to September, the sum total of daily temperatures, the hours of sunshine, the number of days at 30°C or above, the rainfall, all place 1989 at the top of the league in comparison with the other early vintages, going back to 1952, with a single exception: there was even less rain in 1961.

The precocity of the vintage was marked from the outset. The flowering began on 20 May, with the *demi-floraison* noted on 29 May, no less than fifteen days earlier than the average of the last thirty years, and three days earlier than in 1976. The *demi-véraison* on 4 August was sixteen days in advance, and by then this was the earliest date for the last forty years. Remarkably, the vines, with rare exceptions, did not suffer from lack of water. Although rainfall, after the downpours of April, was low in total, it was delivered in short, sharp storms, including some very localized hail.

When the Station Oenologique did its tests in its reference vineyards on 11 September, a week earlier than in 1982, the results showed considerably more sugar in the Merlots than in 1982, a potential alcohol of 13 per cent against 12.2 per cent, with 11.8 per cent against 11.4 per cent for the Cabernet Sauvignon. But the acidity of the Merlots was low: 3.8 against 4.3 in 1982. Happily, the acidity in the Cabernet Sauvignons was virtually identical, 4.9 against 5. So the *assemblages* were even more vital than usual.

After it was realized that the vintage would be unusually early, there were differences of opinion as to when to start picking. It was found that in spite of the concentration of sugar in the grapes, they were often still firm, and were not easily separated from the stems, a particular problem for mechanical harvesting. In addition, the tannins in the skins were often not ripe. So the choice of picking dates was not easy, balancing the consideration of high sugar levels with that of falling acidity levels, while watching for maturity in the tannins.

Great care was needed in the vinification, with the grapes arriving at high temperatures with degrees of sugar seldom seen. The lessons learnt in 1982 and 1985 certainly paid off, in terms of well-equipped *cuveries*, well able to cope with the exceptional circumstances. In general, both Cabernet Sauvignon and Cabernet Franc reached a perfect maturation, rarely achieved, with many instances of *cuves* of between 12 per cent and 13 per cent. The Merlots are exceptionally high in alcohol, with levels up to 14.2 per cent, and they are also very tannic. These are certainly outstanding wines which will take their place with the very greatest Bordeaux years. The yields even surpassed 1986.

For the whites, this is a great vintage for the Sémillon and Muscadelle. The Sauvignon did less well. The wines are very aromatic and full-bodied in character, thanks to the latest techniques of vinification.

For the great sweet wines, an exceptional decade, both for quality and the revival in their fortunes, was crowned by a year that could be set beside the legendary 1947 vintage. In spite of the dryness, *botrytis* spread quickly through the vineyards from around 9 October. The grapes were already high in sugar and in perfect health, so the resulting musts were exceptionally rich. Indeed, even the top châteaux were cutting whole bunches, to include some unbotrytized grapes, to obtain balanced musts. Side by side the wines are even finer than in 1988.

Appendices

RED WINES	1981	1982	1983	1984
Groupe Bordeaux	1,234,351	1,693,328	1,523,339	1,044,053
Bordeaux rouge	845,324	1,229,593	1,099,361	779,055
Ste Foy-Bordeaux	2,615	5,745	2,362	1,714
Bordeaux rosé	12,184	16,420	15,982	12,255
Bordeaux Supérieur	374,228	441,570	405,634	251,029
Groupe Côtes	372,620	525,335	459,357	250,704
Bordeaux Côtes-de-Castillon	91,081	124,060	105,175	44,426
Bordeaux Côtes-de-Francs	8,754	9,769	9,295	5,653
Premières Côtes-de-Blaye	87,254	124,015	131,669	66,156
Côtes-de-Bourg	127,585	174,676	139,280	85,040
Premières Côtes-de-Bordeaux	49,419	82,046	65,500	42,965
Graves-de-Vayres	8,527	10,769	8,438	6,464
Groupe Médoc and Graves	497,516	676,400	662,301	415,605
Médoc	123,990	172,866	158,628	94,158
Haut-Médoc	117,730	156,097	144,543	97,932
Listrac	22,534	31,633	29,500	13,328
Moulis	13,307	20,676	21,680	14,262
Margaux	38,569	50,913	58,226	34,046
St Julien	29,209	40,835	45,940	24,574
Pauillac	35,397	44,440	48,505	38,071
Saint Estèphe	50,311	58,071	60,411	39,161
Graves	66,469	100,869	94,868	60,073
of which Pessac and Léognan				16,843
Groupe St-Emilion-Pomerol-Fronsac	423,808	613,302	552,238	220,218
Saint-Emilion	201,151	290,091	261,838	104,944
of which grands crus	112,037	173,546	150,119	56,626
Montagne	53,322	76,522	74,625	26,238
St Georges	5,568	9,054	8,991	2,934
Lussac	42,307	61,237	57,694	22,397
Puisseguin	25,140	35,832	35,054	10,619
Pomerol	23,720	38,626	30,073	14,683
Lalande-de-Pomerol	32,661	45,871	35,642	20,100
Fronsac	30,028	40,514	36,317	13,187
Canon-Fronsac	9,911	15,555	12,004	5,116
Total AOC Rouges	**2,528,295**	**3,508,365**	**3,197,235**	**1,930,580**

1985	1986	1987	1988	1989
,051,896	2,324,019	1,939,748	1,867,879	2,527,098
,493,426	1,782,743	1,479,785	1,348,677	1,881,241
3,226	4,192	4,201	2,900	2,567
15,856	20,705	19,696	28,758	51,161
539,388	516,379	436,066	490,444	594,696
541,443	687,439	534,754	529,655	740,161
135,031	151,984	115,570	124,707	165,172
14,004	13,891	11,271	15,264	20,616
127,910	179,105	150,468	136,884	193,164
171,677	216,456	157,367	150,724	206,347
78,242	110,703	90,917	89,020	137,694
14,579	15,300	9,161	13,056	17,168
752,982	828,929	712,458	735,174	924,204
208,725	220,956	180,990	194,073	244,519
172,376	184,504	168,693	168,316	213,537
23,669	30,601	26,083	25,694	38,700
21,339	24,751	23,785	16,545	28,960
53,375	63,452	56,835	57,325	68,729
42,444	41,851	38,020	47,254	50,431
60,944	59,402	52,542	54,718	64,968
71,525	71,109	53,532	60,675	71,193
98,585	91,352	78,530	76,107	98,624
19,746	40,951	33,448	34,467	44,543
586,280	673,695	468,575	516,963	678,464
278,621	305,137	201,490	231,005	298,173
164,400	174,604	116,052	136,567	182,239
70,802	84,602	63,167	69,076	89,666
8,022	10,350	8,227	9,528	11,105
64,212	70,652	53,064	55,257	78,404
36,540	40,951	30,270	32,587	42,564
35,565	43,201	26,916	30,260	39,885
29,461	51,301	32,548	39,734	53,382
45,759	48,601	38,393	35,714	48,775
17,298	18,900	14,500	13,802	16,510
3,932,601	4,514,082	3,655,535	3,649,671	4,869,927

WHITE WINES	1981	1982	1983	1984
Groupe Blancs Secs	637,218	887,837	760,340	779,676
Bordeaux	460,480	629,593	543,064	566,035
of which Haut-Benauge	2,916	1,775	2,694	5,044
Blayais	27,133	18,329	11,186	18,942
Côtes-de-Blaye	10,898	11,487	11,834	12,166
Côtes-de-Bourg	5,139	5,129	3,989	3,401
Entre-deux-Mers	99,854	150,797	140,452	118,581
of which Haut-Benauge	6,317	8,596	1,746	5,382
Graves-de-Vayres	11,254	8,459	6,613	11,843
Graves	22,469	64,043	43,202	48,708
of which Pessac and Léognan				6,541
Groupe Blancs Doux	130,963	154,082	156,967	128,153
Bordeaux Supérieur	12,989	16,900	17,064	12,889
Ste Foy-Bordeaux	4,424	9,197	6,114	2,848
Côtes de Bordeaux St Macaire	4,625	3,711	2,982	1,336
Premières Côtes-de-Bordeaux	23,456	24,279	25,789	19,934
Cadillac	2,318	2,329	1,772	1,475
Graves Supérieurs	12,356	20,100	25,953	19,434
Cérons	6,271	5,706	4,870	4,121
Loupiac	10,252	10,696	10,597	9,170
Ste-Croix-du-Mont	13,092	16,294	16,059	14,885
Barsac	12,890	14,794	14,461	13,809
Sauternes	28,290	30,076	31,306	28,252
Total AOC Blancs	**768,181**	**1,041,919**	**917,307**	**907,829**

Summary

Total Rouge AOC	2,528,295	3,508,365	3,197,235	1,930,580
Total Rouge C.C.	285,813	430,414	265,730	121,630
Total Rouge	2,814,108	3,938,779	3,462,965	2,052,210
Total Blanc AOC	768,181	1,041,919	917,307	907,829
Total Blanc C.C.	410,596	951,116	730,910	524,299
Total Blanc	1,178,777	1,993,035	1,648,217	1,432,128
Total AOC	3,296,476	4,550,284	4,114,542	2,838,409
Total C.C.	696,409	1,381,530	996,640	645,929
Total Vintage	3,992,885	5,931,814	5,111,182	3,484,388

Source: CIVB

1985	1986	1987	1988	1989
850,973	946,307	923,436	804,140	900,271
636,728	650,884	641,747	565,420	648,486
900	3,326	1,873	9,269	
13,933	10,753	39,703	28,309	25,352
8,557	10,974	15,619	17,741	18,184
3,576	3,104	2,997	2,369	4,004
129,995	195,433	168,860	133,692	137,259
11,255	14,411	12,388	10,500	
9,370	14,744	11,232	8,651	10,500
48,814	50,660	34,556	39,149	46,403
2,815	9,755	8,722	8,809	10,083
127,316	155,447	133,663	132,977	134,400
9,232	6,851	2,486	5,108	5,392
4,082	4,850	2,764	4,564	3,593
2,298	1,663	1,397	2,118	1,743
24,343	32,147	31,536	26,840	26,775
3,279	1,633	1,351	2,123	3,149
14,516	28,822	20,030	16,945	17,356
2,676	2,660	4,551	2,953	2,899
6,320	10,531	10,568	11,506	13,556
16,021	18,180	19,133	15,566	15,758
14,186	15,076	11,986	12,673	13,637
30,363	33,034	27,861	32,581	30,542
978,289	**1,101,754**	**1,057,099**	**937,117**	**1,034,671**

1985	1986	1987	1988	1989
3,932,601	4,514,082	3,655,535	3,649,671	4,869,927
227,595	406,585	171,196	148,956	316,764
4,160,196	4,920,667	3,826,731	3,798,627	5,186,691
978,289	1,101,754	1,057,099	937,117	1,034,673
461,260	711,783	381,509	249,659	283,098
1,439,549	1,813,537	1,438,608	1,186,776	1,317,769
4,910,890	5,615,836	4,712,634	4,586,788	5,904,598
688,855	1,118,368	552,705	398,615	588,862
5,599,745	6,734,204	5,265,339	4,985,403	6,504,460

APPENDIX II   Areas of AOC vines in production (in hectares) and average yields
(in hectolitres per hectare) 1981–88

RED WINES	1981 Area	1981 Yield	1982 Area	1982 Yield	1983 Area	1983 Yield
Groupe Bordeaux	25,448		27,089		28,792	
Bordeaux rouge and Ste Foy	15,886	53.4	18,542	66.6	19,334	57.0
Bordeaux rosé	233	52.3	266	61.7	305	52.4
Bordeaux Supérieur rouge	9,329	40.1	8,211	53.8	9,153	44.3
Groupe Côtes	8,864		9,145		9,522	
Bordeaux Côtes-de-Castillon	2,191	41.6	2,185	56.8	2,268	46.4
Bordeaux Côtes-de-Francs	198	44.2	178	54.9	206	45.1
Premières Côtes-de-Blaye	2,075	42.0	2,168	51.2	2,382	55.3
Côtes-de-Bourg	2,712	47.0	2,806	62.2	2,900	48.0
Premières Côtes de Bordeaux	1,480	33.4	1,618	50.7	1,556	42.1
Graves-de-Vayres	208	41.0	190	56.7	210	40.2
Groupe Médoc and Graves	11,904		12,243		12,707	
Médoc	2,786	44.5	2,849	60.7	2,976	53.3
Haut-Médoc	2,646	44.5	2,749	56.8	2,942	49.1
Listrac	534	42.2	537	58.9	521	56.6
Moulis	341	39.0	365	56.6	395	54.9
Margaux	1,070	36.0	1,115	45.7	1,150	50.6
St Julien	733	39.8	798	51.2	757	60.7
Pauillac	938	37.7	959	46.3	973	49.8
St Estèphe	1,114	45.2	1,062	54.7	1,089	55.5
Graves	1,742	38.1	1,809	55.7	1,904	49.8
of which Pessac and Léognan						
Groupe St Emilion-						
Pomerol-Fronsac	10,598		10,723		10,815	
St Emilion	4,958	40.6	5,032	57.7	5,021	52.2
of which grands crus	2,793		2,948		2,889	
Montagne	1,278	41.7	1,293	59.2	1,339	55.7
St Georges	153	36.4	151	60.0	152	59.1
Lussac	989	42.8	1,016	60.3	1,046	55.1
Puisseguin	598	42.0	602	59.5	609	57.5
Pomerol	724	32.8	734	52.6	729	41.2
Lalande-de-Pomerol	901	36.2	896	51.2	912	39.1
Fronsac	712	42.2	707	57.3	715	50.8
Canon-Fronsac	285	34.8	292	53.3	292	41.1
Total AOC Rouges	**56,814**		**59,200**		**61,836**	

1984 Area	1984 Yield	1985 Area	1985 Yield	1986 Area	1986 Yield	1987 Area	1987 Yield	1988 Area	1988 Yield
9,401		32,339		33,611		36,716		38,281	
9,774	39.9	21,836	68.5	24,710	72.3	26,855	55.4	25,834	52.3
353	35.9	252	62.9	407	50.9	383	51.4	567	50.7
9,274	27.3	10,251	52.6	8,494	60.8	9,551	45.7	11,945	41.1
9,394		9,881		10,555		11,004		11,571	
2,022	22.1	2,343	57.6	2,348	64.7	2,558	45.2	2,637	47.3
241	23.3	234	59.8	204	68.1	254	44.4	308	49.6
2,429	26.9	2,461	52.0	2,886	62.1	2,908	51.7	2,982	45.9
2,872	30.3	3,017	56.9	3,040	71.2	3,146	50.0	3,224	46.8
1,666	27.7	1,562	50.1	1,832	60.4	1,946	46.7	2,130	41.8
164	37.6	264	55.2	245	62.5	192	47.7	290	45.0
2,463		12,914		13,713		14,361		14,907	
2,940	34.8	3,074	67.9	3,293	67.1	3,481	52.0	3,709	52.3
2,754	36.5	3,174	54.3	3,203	57.6	3,347	50.0	3,464	48.6
523	25.9	555	42.6	555	55.1	576	45.3	620	41.4
420	34.0	603	35.4	448	55.3	502	47.4	480	34.5
1,138	35.3	1,001	53.3	1,212	52.4	1,232	46.1	1,242	46.2
685	35.9	773	54.9	744	56.3	820	46.4	844	56.0
999	39.0	990	61.6	1,022	58.1	1,049	50.1	1,080	50.7
1,080	36.5	1,127	63.5	1,172	60.7	1,142	46.9	1,164	52.1
1,924	32.2	1,617	60.9	2,064	64.1	1,579	49.7	1,594	47.8
435		417		624		633	52.8	710	48.6
0,573		11,095		10,939		11,222		11,217	
4,954	21.2	5,128	54.3	5,043	60.5	5,137	39.2	5,132	45.0
2,770		3,090		3,005		3,052		3,200	
1,298	20.2	1,388	51.0	1,313	64.4	1,346	46.9	1,391	49.7
150	19.6	135	59.4	155	66.8	168	49.0	169	56.4
990	22.8	1,113	57.7	1,079	65.5	1,119	47.2	1,167	47.4
565	18.7	636	57.5	631	64.9	640	47.3	642	50.8
734	19.8	751	47.4	732	59.0	821	32.8	730	41.5
917	22.0	910	32.4	872	58.8	905	36.0	954	41.7
685	19.0	735	62.2	825	58.9	782	49.1	785	45.5
280	18.3	299	57.8	289	65.4	304	47.7	301	45.9
1,831		66,229		68,818		73,303		76,030	

WHITE WINES	1981		1982		1983	
	Area	Yield	Area	Yield	Area	Yield
Groupe Vins Blancs Secs	15,854		13,759		13,232	
Bordeaux	11,015	41.8	9,608	65.5	9,053	60.0
of which Haut-Benauge	62		47		55	
Blayais	771	35.2	339	54.1	399	28.0
Côtes-de-Blaye	325	33.5	213	53.9	218	54.3
Côtes-de-Bourg	183	28.1	118	43.5	84	47.5
Entre-deux-Mers	2,494	40.0	2,507	60.1	2,550	55.1
of which Haut-Benauge	144		133		32	
Graves-de-Vayres	303	37.1	153	55.3	160	41.3
Graves	745	30.1	815	78.6	763	56.6
of which Pessac and Léognan						
Côtes-de-Francs	18		6		5	
Groupe Vins Blancs Doux	5,088		4,678		4,873	
Bordeaux Supérieur	380	34.2	236	71.6	410	41.6
Ste Foy Bordeaux	108	41.0	163	56.4	89	68.7
Côtes de Bordeaux St Macaire	166	27.9	72	51.5	66	45.2
Premières Côtes-de-Bordeaux	794	29.5	635	38.2	692	37.3
Cadillac	91	25.5	96	24.3	77	23.0
Graves Supérieures	562	22.0	601	33.4	654	39.7
Cérons	242	25.9	166	34.4	149	32.7
Loupiac	352	29.1	311	34.4	332	31.9
Ste-Croix-du-Mont	433	30.2	430	37.9	425	37.8
Barsac	552	23.3	595	24.9	608	23.8
Sauternes	1,408	20.1	1,373	21.9	1,371	22.8
Total AOC Blancs	**20,942**		**18,437**		**18,105**	

Summary

Total AOC Rouges	56,814		59,200		61,836	
Total AOC Blancs	20,942		18,437		18,105	
Total AOC	77,756		77,637		79,941	

Source: CIVB

1984		1985		1986		1987		1988	
Area	Yield	Area	Yield	Area	Yield	Area	Yield	Area	Yield
3,553		13,373		13,466		15,251		15,094	
9,503	60.2	9,436	67.5	8,830	73.7	10,345	62.0	9,995	56.6
90		15		50					
365	52.9	290	48.0	158	68.1	669	59.4	794	35.7
267	47.0	211	40.6	182	60.3	287	54.4	394	45.0
90	39.0	84	42.6	69	45.0	89	26.6	89	26.6
2,184	54.9	2,338	55.6	3,079	63.5	2,950	57.2	2,591	51.6
99				294					
221	55.5	170	55.1	231	63.8	193	58.2	194	44.6
917	54.6	844	57.8	913	66.2	709	48.2	832	47.1
115		85		145					
6		4		4					
4,298		4,177		4,357		4,319		4,282	
285	46.3	214	43.1	124	55.3	66	37.7	118	43.3
54	53.9	67	60.9	72	67.4	48	57.6	94	48.6
31	43.1	58	39.6	30	55.4	30	46.6	49	43.2
578	42.7	728	33.4	721	44.6	740	45.8	725	40.7
51	32.8	80	41.0	34	48.0		26.5		32.7
513	40.1	440	33.0	602	47.9	575	34.8	472	35.9
119	33.9	125	21.4	71	37.5	133	34.2	90	32.8
262	34.9	215	29.4	278	37.9	295	35.8	336	34.2
422	36.3	446	35.9	415	43.8	401	47.7	417	37.3
590	23.5	560	25.3	595	25.3	587	20.4	564	22.5
1,393	20.3	1,364	22.3	1,415	23.5	1,944	19.3	1,417	23.0
7,851		17,550		17,823		19,570		19,376	

1984		1985		1986		1987		1988	
1,831		66,229		68,818		73,303		76,030	
7,851		17,550		17,823		19,570		19,376	
9,682		83,779		86,641		92,873		95,406	

APPENDIX III Development of the areas under vine and in production in the
Gironde 1950–89

	AOC % of the total	Vin de table % of the total	Total area (thousand hectares)
1989	95	5	106
88	94	6	103
87	92	8	102
86	86	14	102
85	84	16	103
84	85	15	96
83	80	20	98
82	78	22	99
81	80	20	96
80	79	21	96
79	75	25	99
78	81	19	97
77	78	22	98
76	68	32	105
75	68	32	102
74	65	35	103
73	69	31	102
72	68	32	103
71	65	35	102
70	66	34	105
69	73	27	103
68	69	31	108
67	70	30	109
66	69	31	110
65	65	35	110
64	66	34	112
63	63	37	112
62	66	34	114
61	66	34	108
60	62	38	112
59	61	39	110
58	58	42	111
57	60	40	114
56	54	46	126
55	58	42	132
54	57	43	132
53	53	47	134
52	55	45	132
1951	53	47	132

AOC areas (hectares)

	AOC white wine	AOC red wine
1988	19,376	76,030
1987	19,742	73,303
1986	17,823	68,818
1985	17,550	66,229
1984	17,851	61,831
1983	18,105	61,836
1982	18,437	59,200
1981	20,942	56,814

APPENDIX IV   Development of the vintages of the Gironde 1968–1989

RED WINE

	Vins de table % of the total	AOC % of the total	Total volume (thousand hectolitres)
1989	6	94	5,187
88	4	96	3,799
87	4	96	3,827
86	8	92	4,920
85	5	95	4,160
84	6	94	2,052
83	8	92	3,468
82	11	89	3,939
81	10	90	2,814
80	9	91	2,239
79	12	88	3,769
78	10	90	2,502
77	10	90	1,438
76	18	82	2,992
75	19	81	2,165
74	23	77	2,894
73	16	84	2,938
72	19	81	2,009
71	24	76	1,608
70	23	77	2,685
1969	31	69	1,326

Source: CIVB

WHITE WINE

	Vins de table % of the total	AOC % of the total	Total volume (thousand hectolitres)
1989	21	79	1,318
88	21	79	1,187
87	27	73	1,439
86	39	61	1,814
85	32	68	1,440
84	37	63	1,432
83	44	56	1,648
82	48	52	1,993
81	35	65	1,179
80	39	61	1,412
79	51	49	2,437
78	32	68	1,463
77	34	66	1,046
76	58	42	2,511
75	51	49	2,027
74	56	44	2,568
73	53	47	2,712
72	47	53	1,960
71	57	43	2,123
70	54	46	2,811
1969	28	72	1,387

Source: CIVB

APPENDIX V Development of the patterns of production and ownership in the Gironde 1950–89

Year	Total production area (ha)	Of which AOC (ha)	Of which vins de table (ha)	Yield all wines (hl/ha)	Déclarants de récolte tous vins	Average area per déclarant (ha)
1950	138,780	82,669	56,111	39.3	60,327	2.31
1951	131,883	69,587	62,296	27.3	56,601	2.34
1952	132,120	72,077	60,043	26.8	56,929	2.33
1953	133,798	71,537	62,261	41.1	58,024	2.31
1954	131,698	75,263	56,435	30.3	56,202	2.35
1955	132,337	76,290	56,047	40.1	55,969	2.37
1956	126,204	67,845	58,359	17.0	48,701	2.60
1957	114,002	68,867	45,135	18.1	46,278	2.47
1958	111,379	65,057	46,322	26.8	47,890	2.33
1959	110,602	67,557	43,045	26.9	46,883	2.36
1960	112,840	69,676	43,164	35.4	46,550	2.43
1961	108,612	71,592	37,020	25.7	45,685	2.38
1962	114,286	74,964	39,322	48.6	46,512	2.46
1963	112,501	70,750	41,751	44.3	45,870	2.46
1964	111,988	74,419	37,569	44.6	44,884	2.50
1965	110,283	71,644	38,659	37.4	42,433	2.60
1966	110,416	75,676	34,740	41.2	41,856	2.64
1967	109,103	76,760	32,343	45.2	40,137	2.72
1968	108,308	75,171	33,137	45.2	38,437	2.82
1969	103,321	75,176	28,145	30.6	36,125	2.87
1970	104,782	69,628	35,154	52.6	35,263	2.98
1971	102,355	66,104	36,251	36.5	33,084	3.10
1972	102,636	69,471	33,165	38.7	31,810	3.23
1973	102,171	70,736	31,435	55.3	31,078	3.29
1974	102,839	67,364	35,475	53.2	30,029	3.43
1975	102,128	69,028	33,100	41.0	29,180	3.50
1976	104,668	70,844	33,824	52.7	28,630	3.66
1977	97,576	76,001	21,575	25.4	25,372	3.85
1978	97,004	78,439	18,565	40.9	25,703	3.78
1979	98,611	74,290	24,321	62.9	25,561	3.86
1980	96,458	76,271	20,187	37.8	24,346	3.97
1981	96,353	76,744	19,609	41.4	24,983	3.86
1982	98,710	76,978	21,732	60.0	23,137	4.27
1983	97,805	78,049	19,756	52.2	22,210	4.41
1984	95,605	81,032	14,573	36.9	21,071	4.54
1985	102,874	86,389	16,485	54.1	21,173	4.86
1986	101,772	87,058	14,714	66.0	20,905	4.87
1987	102,151	93,090	8,601	51.5	20,216	5.05
1988	102,976	96,431	6,545	48.7	19,393	5.31
1989	105,774	100,211	5,563	61.5	17,826	5.93

Source: CIVB

Bibliography

Maps
De Belleyme – Carte de la Guyenne
Cassini – Carte de la France No. 104, Gironde.

Historic books
Wm Franck, *Vins du Médoc*, 1860
Ch. Cocks, *Bordeaux et ses Vins*, 1st ed.: 1850. 2nd ed.: 1868. 2nd English
    ed.: 1883. Cocks & Féret: 5th ed.: 1886. 3rd English ed.: 1899. 9th
    ed.: 1922. 11th ed.: 1949, 12th ed.: 1969
E. Féret, *Statistique Générale de la Gironde*, vols I–III, 1874–89.
Germain Lafforgue, *Le Vignoble Girondin*, 1947

Current reference books
On individual châteaux
La Collection Ampelographique du Château Haut-Brion, J. B. Delmas, Arbook
    International, 1989
Le Vignoble de Château Latour, 2 vols, 1974
Lafite, Cyril Ray, 3rd ed., Christie's, 1985
A Victorian Vineyard: Château Loudenne and the Gilbeys, Nicholas Faith, Constable,
    1983
Château Margaux, Nicholas Faith, Christie's, 1980
Château Mouton-Rothschild, Cyril Ray, Christie's, 1980
Mouton-Baronne Philippe, Joan Littlewood, with appendix by E. Penning-Rowsell,
    Christie's, 1982
Yquem, Richard Olney, Dorling Kindersley, 1985
On individual districts
Côtes de Bourg, Bernard Ginestet, Jacques Legrand – Nathan, 1984
Haut-Médoc, Didier Ters, Jacques Legrand – Nathan, 1985
Moulis-Listrac, Didier Ters, Jacques Legrand – Nathan, 1987
St-Estèphe, Bernard Ginestet, Jacques Legrand – Nathan, 1985
Pauillac, Bernard Ginestet, Jacques Legrand – Nathan, 1985
St-Julien, Bernard Ginestet, Jacques Legrand – Nathan, 1984

Margaux, Bernard Ginestet, Jacques Legrand – Nathan, 1984

Graves de Bordeaux, Florence Mothe, Jacques Legrand – Nathan, 1985

Barsac Sauternes, Bernard Ginestet, Jacques Legrand – Nathan, 1987

Saint-Emilion, Bernard Ginestet, Jacques Legrand – Nathan, 1986

Pomerol, Bernard Ginestet, Jacques Legrand – Nathan, 1984

Les Grands Vins de Saint-Emilion, Pomerol et Fronsac, Henri Enjalbert, Editions Bardi, 1983 (N.B. The English translation *Great Bordeaux Wines – St-Emilion, Pomerol, Fronsac* ed. Bardi, 1985, is an excellent translation of the above classic, by Harriet Coleman and Richard Maxwell, but, unfortunately, it lacks an index – vital in a book of this complexity.)

Le Médoc, René Pijassou, 2 vols, Tallandier, 1980

Wines of the Graves, Pamela Vandyke-Price, Sotheby's, 1988

On Bordeaux wines

Bordeaux Châteaux, Wine, Architecture and Civilization, ed. Jean Dethier, Mitchell Beazley (original French edition 1988 Centre Pompidou), 1989

Clive Coates, *Claret*, Century, 1982

Pierre Coste, *Les Révolutions du Palais*, J. C. Lattes, 1987

Hubrecht Duijker, *The Great Wine Châteaux of Bordeaux*, Times Books, 1975

Hubrecht Duijker, *The Good Wines of Bordeaux*, Mitchell Beazley, 1980

Nicholas Faith, *The Winemasters*, Hamish Hamilton, 1978

E. Feret, *Bordeaux et ses Vins*, 13th ed., 1982; English ed. 1986

Billy Kay and Carlean Maclean, *Knee Deep in Claret A Celebration of Wine and Scotland*, Mainstream Publishing, 1983 is a rumbustious and fascinating study of (mostly) Claret in Scotland, that deserves to be more widely known

E. Penning-Rowsell, *The Wines of Bordeaux*, Penguin, 1985, 1989

Robert Parker, *Bordeaux*, Simon and Schuster, 1985; Dorling Kindersley, 1986

Index

Note: the alphabetical order ignores Château, Clos, Cru, Domaine, de, de la, des, du, La, Le, Les.

Bel-Air (Cussac) 245–6
Bel-Air-Lagrave 219
Bel-Air (Lalande de Pomerol) 534
Bel-Air (Lussac) 474
Bel-Air-Marquis d'Aligre 57, 67
Bel-Air-Marquis-de-Pomereu 67
Bel-Air Ouÿ 469
Bel-Air (Puisseguin) 474
Bel-Orme-Tronquoy-de-Lalande 103, 246–7, 260, 635, 640
Belair-Montaiguillon 474–5
Belair (St Emilion) 374, 382, 389, 414, 448; alcohol level 24; classification 53, 379; description 396–8; vintages 652, 670, 675
de Belcier 558
Belfort 301
Belgrave 51, 65, 240, 247
Belle-Graves 533
Bellefont-Belcier 385, 398, 464
Bellegarde 99
Bellegrave 247
Bellerive 105
Bellerose 105
Bellevue 53, 107, 379, 399
Bellonne-St-Georges 477
Belon 354
de Berbec 616
Bergat 53, 379, 399
Berliquet 53, 54, 379, 400–1, 469, 499
Le Bernet 301
Bertineau St Vincent 534
Les Bertins 106, 292
Bessan 556
de Beusse 302
Beychevelle 3, 4, 109, 169, 244, 332; classification 51, 65, 137; description 109–113; vintages 641, 643, 651–3, 656, 658–60, 666
Domaine de Beychevelle 561
Domaine de Bigarnon 131, 134
Billerond 469
Birot 616
Biston-Brilette 219
Blaignan 107, 302
La Blancherie 354–5
La Blancherie-Peyret 354–5
Blanquefort 241, 274
Blanquet 192
Blaye 11, 44, 535, 553–5, 621
La Boisserie 469
Bommes 564
Bon-Dieu-de-Vignes 356
Le Bon Pasteur 481, 490–1
Bonalgue 491

Bonneau (Avensan) 107
Bonneau (St-Seurin-de-Cadourne) 105
La Bonnelle 469
Bonnet 332, 561, 619
Bordeaux Blanc 358, 573, 618, 621
Bordeaux Côtes de Francs 559–60
Bordeaux Sec 'G' 588, 589
Bordeaux Supérieur 545, 548, 558, 561, 561–3
Le Borderi 360
Le Boscq 105
botrytis cinerea 28, 564, 566, 567, 571–2
botrytized wines 616–17
bottles and bottling 42–3, 44
'Bouchet' 11, 375, 484
du Bouilh 547, 561
Bouqueyran 239
Bourdieu (Blaye) 555
Le Bourdieu (Vertheuil) 107, 248
Bourg 11, 43, 44, 535, 553–5, 621
Bourgneuf-Vayron 491
Bournac 107
Bouscaut 102, 309, 312–14
de Bousquet 554
Boyd-Cantenac 65, 67–8, 96
Braidoire 620
Branaire 31, 136, 169, 431; description 113–16; vintages 644, 659
Branaire-Ducru 51, 65
Branas-Grand-Poujeaux 220
Brane-Cantenac 68–9, 72, 73, 102, 144, 175; classification 47, 51, 64; vintages 634, 641, 653, 656, 659, 669, 673
Brane Mouton 47
La Brède 311
Brethous 556
du Breuil 105, 248–9
Breuil-Renaissance 301
La Bridane 105, 116
de Brie 301
Brillette 104, 220
Brondelle 355
Broustet 576, 595
Brown 314
Brown-Cantenac 67
Brulesécaille 554
Les Brulières de Beychevelle 112
Burgrave 491
de By 105, 285, 286

C
Cabanes 368
La Cabanne 492–3
Cabannieux 355–6

Domaine de Chevalier 50, 309, 316–18, 344; vintages 642, 644, 652, 658, 659, 662, 669, 673
Chevalier Védrines 585
Chevaliers du Roi Soleil 276–7
Chicane 357
chlorosis 19
Cissac 241, 286
Cissac, Château 104, 248, 255–8, 282
Citran 104, 258
Civrac 285
de Clairefort 96
La Clare 105, 286, 287–8, 297
La Clarière-Laithwaite 558
Clarke 106, 233–4
classifications 45–58
Clément-Pichon 258–9
Clerc-Milon 51, 65, 143–4
Climens 102, 574, 605; description 577–81; vintages 646, 648, 651, 657, 667
Clinet 495, 501
Clos du Clocher 496
des Clos-Rénon 362
La Closerie 105
La Closerie-Grand-Poujeaux 223
de la Closière 557
de Clotte 558
La Clotte 54, 379, 415
La Clusière 54, 379, 415–6
cochylis 18, 640
Colombard grape 280
Colombier-Monpelou 104, 144
Les Combes 208
La Commanderie 107, 197
Commanderie du Bontemps du Médoc 141, 149, 176
Domaine de Compostelle 492
Connétable Talbot 137, 139
de Conques 107
La Conseillante 428, 483; assessment 56, 485, 505, 506; description 496–8; vintages 631, 651, 655, 663, 668, 669, 673
Copet-Bégaud 541
Corbin (Giraud) 436, 494; classification 54, 374, 379; description 416–17
Corbin-Manuel 417
Corbin-Michotte 54, 56, 379, 417–18, 475
Corbin (Montagne) 475
Cordet 91
corks 42, 44
Cormeil-Figeac 418
Cos d'Estournel 140, 156, 204, 208, 615; classification 47, 50, 64; comparisons 189, 194, 210; description 197–200; grape

varieties 205; vintages 628, 634, 640, 653, 654, 669, 673
Cos-Labory 65, 192, 200
de la Coste 95
Côte-Baleau 418–19, 438, 443, 460
Côte d'Or 7
Côtes de Blaye 621
Côtes de Bourg 660
Côtes de Canon-Fronsac 536
Côtes de Castillon 558–9
Côtes de Francs 559–60
Côtes Rocheuses 470
Coucheray 332
Coudert 419
Coudert-Pelletan 384, 419
Coufran 104, 259–60, 279, 283, 291
Couhins 309, 318–19
Couhins-Lurton 319, 332
coulure 11, 12, 19, 21, 212, 675
Couquèques 302
de Couques 293
de Courbon 357–8
La Couronne 57, 75, 144–5, 153
court-noué 17
Les Courtines 615
La Couspaude 419
Coustolle 541–2
Coutelin-Merville 104, 201, 262
Coutet (Barsac) 574, 581–2, 596; vintages 650, 657, 665, 667
Coutet (Pujols) 358
Coutet (St Emilion) 420
Coutreau 552
Le Couvent 379, 420
Couvent-des-Jacobins 54, 56, 379, 383, 412, 420–21
Crème de Tète 588
Le Crock 104, 201–2, 208
Domaine de la Croix 107
La Croix-Blanche 481
La Croix-du-Casse 501
La Croix-Davids 554
La Croix-de-Gay 492, 500–1, 507
La Croix de Mazerat 395
La-Croix-de-Millorit 554
La Croix de Pez 208
La Croix (Pomerol) 485, 498–500
La Croix-St Bonnet 299
La Croix-St Georges 499, 501
la Croix (St Julien) 116
La Croix-Saint-Pey 355
La Croix-Toulifaut 499, 502, 514
La Croix des Trois Sœurs 208
Croizet-Bages 65, 145–6, 656

Clos du Marquis 131, 134
Marquis d'Alesme 65, 72
Marquis d'Alesme-Becker 88–9
Marquis de St Estèphe 208–9
Marquis de Ségur 193
Marquis de Terme 52, 65, 74, 89–90
Marsac-Séguineau 90–1, 107
Martillac 305, 310, 311
Martinens (Cantenac) 107
Martinens (Margaux) 91, 104
Martinet 384
La Marzelle 428, 435–6
Matras 54, 380, 449
maturation 42–4
Maucaillou 107, 226–7
Maucamps 107
Maurac 274
Maurac-Mayor 261
Mausse 544
Mauvesin 227
Mauvezin 54, 380, 449–50
Mauvinon 469
du Mayne 594
Mayne-d'Anice 356
Mayne des Carmes 598
Mayne-Levèque 356
Mayne-Vieil 254, 545, 548–9
Mazerat 387
Mazeris 538, 544
Mazeris-Bellevue 538, 544
Mazeyres 453, 515
Meaume 562
Médard-d'Eyrans 310
Médoc 3, 8, 57, 109, 285, 305; alcohol levels 24, 34, 484; classification 45–52, 57–8; fermentation 31; grape varieties 10–11; maturation 44; phylloxera 14; vintages 25, 26, 521, 629, 640–51, 644, 646–51, 655, 659, 660, 662–6, 669, 671–6, 678, 679; wines 57–139; yeasts 13
Meilhan 301
Le Menaudat 555
Mendoce 554
Menota 594
Mercier 554
Mérignac 304, 310, 311
Merlot grape 11, 17, 19, 22; Cissac 256; Fronsac 537; Graves 308; Moulis 228, 230; Pomerol 484, 520; St Emilion 375; St Estèphe 205, 214; vintages 665, 670, 674–76, 680
Domaine de la Meulière 557
Meyney 48, 104, 201, 209–10
Le Meynieu 104, 206, 273

de Mignot 208
mildew 4, 16
Mille-Secousses 555
millerandage 19–20, 21, 675
Millet 362–63
Miqueu 255
La Mission Haut-Brion 318, 324, 349–50, 496; classification 50, 198, 309; description 337–41; fermentation 30, 36, 39; vintages 637, 640, 643, 644, 645, 647–56, 658–60, 663, 665, 667–9, 673–85
Clos de Moines 534
Monbazillac 567, 616
Monbousquet 386, 450
Monbrison 91, 107
Moncets 553
Mondot 374, 400, 467
La Mondotte 385
Le Monge 301
Montagne 378, 473, 474
Montalivet 363
Montbrun 91–2
Le Monteil-d'Arsac 243
Montgrand-Milon 148
de Monthil 106, 292–3
Montjouan 557
Montlabert 451
Montrose 194; classification 47, 49, 50, 64; description 210–12; grape varieties 205; vintages 637, 642, 644, 652, 656, 658, 669, 670
Morin 104, 212
Moulin 58
Moulin à Vent (Lalande de Pomerol) 533
Moulin-à-Vent (Moulis) 104, 227–8
Moulin-d'Arvigny 244, 245
Moulin-de-Buscateau 301
Moulin-du-Cadet 54, 380, 451
Moulin-de-Castillon 107
Moulin-de Duhart 146, 147
Moulin-Haut-Laroque 545, 546, 549
Moulin-Haut-Villars 549
Moulin-de-Laborde 108
Moulin-de-Launay 620
Moulin-Riche 108, 134
Moulin-de-la-Rivière 301
Moulin-de-la-Roque 108, 298
Moulin-Rouge (Côtes de Castillon) 558
Moulin Rouge (Cussac) 106
Moulin-St Georges 451
Moulin-de-St Vincent 108, 227
Moulinet 515–16
Moulinet-Lasserre 525
Moulis 49, 57, 59, 218–31